Praise from Reviewers of Previous Editions of *Using Information Technology*

"The major difference that I notice between your text and other texts is the informal tone of the writing. This is one of the main reasons we adopted your book—the colloquial feel."

—*Todd McLeod, Fresno City College, California.*

"I would rate the writing style as superior to the book I am currently using and most of the books I have reviewed. . . . I found this book much easier to read than most books on the market."

—*Susan Fry, Boise State University*

[UIT is] "(1) current with today's and future technology, (2) easy to follow and explain to students who are having difficulty, [and] (3) a great self-study book for the more experienced student."

—*Lonnie Hendrick, Hampton University, Hampton, Virginia*

"The easy-to-understand way of speaking to the readers is excellent. You put computer terminology into an easily understandable way to read. It's excellent."

—*Ralph Caputo, Manhattan College, New York*

"[The text] is written in a clear and non-threatening manner, keeping the student's interest through the use of real, colorful anecdotes and interesting observations. The authors' emphasis on the practical in the early chapters gets the students' interest by centering on real-life questions that would face everyone purchasing a new personal computer."

—*Donald Robertson, Florida Community College–Jacksonville*

"Williams-Sawyer . . . is the most readable textbook that deals with computer terminology in a meaningful way without getting into tech jargon. The concepts are clearly presented and the [photos], illustrations, and graphics become part of the reading and enhance the ability of the reader to comprehend the material. . . . I think the level of difficulty is perfect. I find very few students, even international students, who have difficulty comprehending the book."

—*Beverly Bohn, Park University, Parkville, Missouri*

"This text is written at a level that is fine for most of my students. I have many students for whom English is a second language. These students may have difficulty with certain phrasing. . . . As I read this chapter [Chapter 3], however, I found very little that I thought might cause confusion, even for those ESL students. . . . I have selected previous editions of this text in large part because it is very 'readable.'"

—*Valerie Anderson, Marymount College, Palos Verdes, California*

"[UIT is] geared toward a generation that grew up with computers but never thought about how they work. Should appeal to a younger audience."

—*Leleh Kalantari, Western Illinois University, Macomb*

"Supplemental materials are great! . . . Book is very readable—short sections with excellent illustrations. Students especially seem to appreciate the Practical Action tips."

—*Linda Johnsonius, Murray State University, Murray, Kentucky*

"I really liked the fact that you updated the text with items that would be important to students when they are looking to purchase a PC."

—*Stephanie Anderson, Southwestern Community College, Creston, Iowa*

i

"I like the authors' writing style very much. I found it to be almost conversational, which is good, in my opinion. . . . I truly looked for unclear areas and did not find any at all."

—*Laurie Eakins, East Carolina University, Greenville, North Carolina*

"I like how [the writing] is personalized. It seems as if the writer is speaking directly to the student—not the normal textbook emphasis."

—*Tammy Potter, Western Kentucky Community & Technical College, Paducah*

"The author[s] did a good job taking something that could be considered a complex topic and made it easy to understand."

—*Jennifer Merritt, Park University, Parkville, Missouri*

"[The authors'] writing style is clear and concise. [They have] taken some very technical topics and explained them in everyday language while not 'dumbing down' the material. The text flows smoothly. The inclusion of quotes from real people lends a conversational tone to the chapter [Chapter 6], making it easier to read and comprehend."

—*Robert Caruso, Santa Rosa Junior College, California*

"[The writing] flows very well. Touches on most of the important points, but doesn't bog down in too many details."

—*Morgan Shepherd, University of Colorado at Colorado Springs*

"The level of difficulty is perfect for an intro level computer applications course taught at a 2- or 4-year college."

—*Jami Cotler, Siena College, Loudonville, New York*

"Chapter 2 is written in a readable, motivating style. I found it to be concise, and introducing topics in a proper sequence, defining terms accurately and effectively. I found myself thinking of topics to be added, and then THERE THEY WERE!"

—*Mike Michaelson, Palomar College, San Marcos, California*

"Strong writing style. This chapter [Chapter 8] was extremely thorough. And covered many subjects in depth. . . . Writing style has always been quite clear and concise with these two authors."

—*Rebecca Mundy, UCLA and University of Southern California*

"I think the level [of difficulty] is just right. The author[s] did not include a lot of technology lingo, but enough for the typical student who will be reading this book."

—*Anita Whitehill, Foothill College, Los Altos Hills, California*

"Practicality is in the title of the book and is definitely practiced in each chapter. Readability means clear writing, and that is also evident in the text."

—*Nancy Webb, San Francisco City College*

"The practical approach to information technology, along with the book's superior readability, make this a strong text. The book's emphasis on being current and a three-level learning system are great."

—*DeLyse Totten, Portland Community College, Oregon*

"I enjoyed the writing style. It was clear and casual, without trivializing. I think the examples and explanations of Williams and Sawyer are excellent."

—*Martha Tillman, College of San Mateo, California*

"Ethics topics are far superior to many other textbooks."

—*Maryann Dorn, Southern Illinois University*

"[The critical thinking emphasis is important because] the facts will change, the underlying concepts will not. Students need to know what the technology is capable of and what is not possible . . ."

—*Joseph DeLibero, Arizona State University*

USING INFORMATION
Technology

USING INFORMATION Technology

Ninth Edition

A Practical Introduction
to Computers & Communications

Introductory Version

BRIAN K. WILLIAMS | STACEY C. SAWYER

Connect
Learn
Succeed™

USING INFORMATION TECHNOLOGY: A PRACTICAL INTRODUCTION TO COMPUTERS & COMMUNICATIONS: INTRODUCTORY VERSION

Published by McGraw-Hill, a business unit of The McGraw-Hill Companies, Inc., 1221 Avenue of the Americas, New York, NY, 10020. Copyright © 2011 by The McGraw-Hill Companies, Inc. All rights reserved. Previous editions © 1995, 1997, 1999, 2001, 2003, 2005, 2007, and 2010. No part of this publication may be reproduced or distributed in any form or by any means, or stored in a database or retrieval system, without the prior written consent of The McGraw-Hill Companies, Inc., including, but not limited to, in any network or other electronic storage or transmission, or broadcast for distance learning.

Some ancillaries, including electronic and print components, may not be available to customers outside the United States.

This book is printed on acid-free paper.

1 2 3 4 5 6 7 8 9 0 WDQ/WDQ 1 0 9 8 7 6 5 4 3 2 1 0

ISBN 978-0-07-733108-5
MHID 0-07-733108-7

Vice president/Editor in chief: *Elizabeth Haefele*
Vice president/Director of marketing: *John E. Biernat*
Senior sponsoring editor: *Scott Davidson*
Freelance developmental editor: *Craig Leonard*
Editorial coordinator: *Alan Palmer*
Marketing manager: *Tiffany Wendt*
Lead media producer: *Damian Moshak*
Digital development editor: *Kevin White*
Director, Editing/Design/Production: *Jess Ann Kosic*
Project manager: *Jean R. Starr*
Senior production supervisor: *Janean A. Utley*
Senior designer: *Marianna Kinigakis*
Senior photo research coordinator: *Jeremy Cheshareck*
Photo researcher: *Judy Mason*
Digital production coordinator: *Brent dela Cruz*
Cover design: *Daniel Krueger*
Interior design: *Kay Lieberherr*
Typeface: *10/12 Trump Mediaeval*
Compositor: *Laserwords Private Limited*
Printer: *Worldcolor*
Cover credit: © *Don Bishop/Photodisc/Getty Images*
Credits: The credits section for this book begins on page 413 and is considered an extension of the copyright page.

Library of Congress Cataloging-in-Publication Data

Williams, Brian K., 1938-
 Using information technology : a practical introduction to computers & communications : Introductory version / Brian K. Williams, Stacey C. Sawyer. -- 9th ed.
  p. cm.
 Includes index.
 ISBN-13: 978-0-07-733108-5 (alk. paper)
 ISBN-10: 0-07-733108-7 (alk. paper)
  1. Computers. 2. Telecommunication systems. 3. Information technology. I. Sawyer, Stacey C. II. Title.
QA76.5.W5332 2011
004--dc22
                                                2009048458

The Internet addresses listed in the text were accurate at the time of publication. The inclusion of a Web site does not indicate an endorsement by the authors or McGraw-Hill, and McGraw-Hill does not guarantee the accuracy of the information presented at these sites.

www.mhhe.com

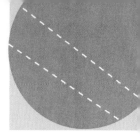

Brief Contents

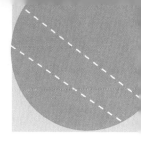

To the Instructor

INTRODUCTION
Teaching the "Always On" Generation

If there is anything we have learned during the 15 years of writing and revising this computer concepts book, it is this: *Not only does the landscape of computer education change, but so do the students.*

USING INFORMATION TECHNOLOGY (abbreviated *UIT)* was written and revised around three important benchmarks:

- **The impact of digital convergence:** The First Edition was the first text to foresee the impact of digital convergence—the fusion of computers and communications—as the new and broader foundation for the computer concepts course.

- **The importance of cyberspace:** The Fourth Edition was the first text to acknowledge the new priorities imposed by the Internet and World Wide Web and bring discussion of them from late in the course to near the beginning (to Chapter 2).

- **The ascendancy of the "Always On" generation:** The Seventh Edition addressed another paradigm change: Because of the mobility and hybridization of digital devices, **an "Always On" generation of students has come of age that's at ease with digital technology but—and it's an important "but"—not always savvy about computer processes, possibilities, and liabilities.**

The appearance of this new generation imposes additional challenges on professors: **Instructors are expected to make the course interesting and challenging to students already at least somewhat familiar with information technology while teaching people of widely varying computer sophistication.**

ADDRESSING INSTRUCTORS' TWO MOST IMPORTANT CHALLENGES

As we embark on our sixteenth year of publication, we are extremely pleased at the continued reception to *USING INFORMATION TECHNOLOGY,* which has been used by well more than a half million students and adopted by instructors in over 800 schools. One reason for this enthusiastic response may be that we've tried hard to address professors' needs. We've often asked instructors—in reviews, surveys, and focus groups—

"What are your most significant challenges in teaching this course?"

Instructors generally have two answers:

The First Most Important Challenge: "Motivating Students & Making the Course Interesting"

One professor at a state university seems to speak for most when she says: "Making the course interesting and challenging." Others echo her with remarks such as "Keeping students interested in the material enough to study" and "Keeping the students engaged who know some, but not all, of the material." Said one professor, "Many students take the course because they must, instead of because the material interests them." Another speaks about the need to address a "variety of skill/knowledge levels while keeping the course challenging and interesting"—which brings us to the second response.

The Second Most Important Challenge: "Trying to Teach to Students with a Variety of Computer Backgrounds"

The most significant challenge in teaching this course "is trying to provide material to the varied levels of students in the class," says an instructor at a large Midwestern university. Another says the course gets students from all backgrounds, ranging from "Which button do you push on the mouse?" to "Already built and maintain a web page with html." Says a third, "mixed-ability classes [make] it difficult to appeal to all students at the same time." And a fourth: "How do you keep the 'techies' interested without losing the beginners?"

Motivating the Unmotivated & Teaching to a Disparity of Backgrounds

As authors, we find information technology tremendously exciting, but we recognize that many students take the course reluctantly. And we also recognize that many students come to the subject with attitudes ranging from complete apathy and unfamiliarity to a high degree of experience and technical understanding.

To address the problem of **motivating the unmotivated and teaching to a disparity of backgrounds,** *UIT* offers unequaled treatment of the following:

1. **Practicality**
2. **Readability**
3. **Currentness**
4. **Three-level critical thinking system.**

We explain these features on the following pages.

FEATURE #1: Emphasis on Practicality

This popular feature received overwhelming acceptance by both students and instructors in past editions. **Practical advice,** of the sort found in computer magazines, newspaper technology sections, and general-interest computer books, is expressed not only in the text but also in the following:

The Experience Box

Appearing at the end of each chapter, the Experience Box is optional material that may be assigned at the instructor's discretion. However, students will find the subjects covered are of immediate value.

Examples: "Web Research, Term Papers, & Plagiarism." "The Mysteries of Tech Support." "How to Buy a Laptop." "Preventing Your Identity from Getting Stolen." "Virtual Meetings: Linking Up Electronically." "The 'Always On' Generation."

EXPERIENCE BOX

Web Research, Term Papers, & Plagiarism

No matter how much students may be able to rationalize cheating in college—for example, trying to pass off someone else's term paper as their own (plagiarism)—ignorance of the consequences is not an excuse. Most instructors announce the penalties for cheating at the beginning of the course—usually a failing grade in the course and possible suspension or expulsion from school.

identical blocks of text. Indeed, some websites favored by instructors build a database of papers over time so that students can't recycle work previously handed in by others. One system, Turnitin's Originality Checking, can lock on to a stolen phrase as short as eight words. It can also identify copied material even if it has been changed slightly from the original. Another pro-

Practical Action Box

This box consists of optional material on practical matters.

Examples: "Serious Web Search Techniques." "Preventing Problems from Too Much or Too Little Power to Your Computer." "When the Internet Isn't Productive: Online Addiction & Other Timewasters." "Evaluating & Sourcing Information Found on the Web." "Tips for Fighting Spam." "Tips for Avoiding Spyware." "Utility Programs." "Help in Building Your Web Page." "Starting Over with Your Hard Drive: Erasing, Reformatting, & Reloading." "Buying a Printer." "Telecommuting & Telework: The Nontraditional Workplace." "Ways to Minimize Virus Attacks." "How to Deal with Passwords." "Online Viewing & Sharing of Digital Photos." "Buying the Right HDTV."

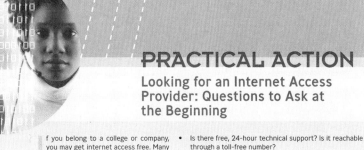

PRACTICAL ACTION

Looking for an Internet Access Provider: Questions to Ask at the Beginning

f you belong to a college or company, you may get internet access free. Many public libraries also offer free net connections. If these options are not available to you, here are some questions to ask in your first

- Is there free, 24-hour technical support? Is it reachable through a toll-free number?
- How long does it take to get tech support? Ask for the tech-support number before you sign up, and then call it to see how long a response takes. Also try connecting

See the list of Experience Boxes and Practical Action Boxes on the inside front cover.

Survival Tips

In the margins throughout we present utilitarian **Survival Tips** to aid students' explorations of the infotech world.

Examples: "Test the Speed of Your Internet Connection." "Some Free ISPs." "Do Home Pages Endure?" "Look for the Padlock Icon." "Keeping Windows Security Features Updated." "New Software & Compatibility." "Where Do I Get a Boot Disk?" "Is Your Password Guessable?" "Update Your Drivers." "Compressing Web & Audio Files." "Try Before You Buy." "Setting Mouse Properties." "Digital Subscriptions." "Cellphone Minutes." "Reformat Your Memory Card to Avoid Losing Your Photos." "Keeping Track of Your Cellphone." "Fraud Baiters." "Alleviating Info-Mania."

Survival Tip

Broadband: Riskier for Security

Unlike dial-up services, broadband services, because they are always switched on, make your computer vulnerable to over-the-internet security breaches. Solution: Install firewall software (Chapter 6).

See the list of Survival Tips on the inside front cover.

How to Understand a Computer Ad

In the hardware chapters (Chapters 4 and 5), we explain important concepts by showing students **how to understand the hardware components in a hypothetical PC ad.**

- 7-Bay Mid-Tower Case
- Intel Pentium Dual-Core Processor 2.80 GHz
- 2 GB DDR2 SDRAM
- 3 MB L2 Cache
- 6 USB 2.0 Ports
- 256 MB DDR2 Nvidia GeForce PCI Graphics
- Sound Blaster Digital Sound Card
- 56 Kbps Internal Modem
- 320 GB SATA 7200 RPM Hard Drive
- 24X DVD/CD-RW Combo Drive
- Full-Sized Keyboard with Numeric Keypad
- Microsoft IntelliMouse
- 17" Flat Panel Display
- HP Officejet Pro K5400

Details of this ad are explained throughout this chapter and the next. See the little magnifying glass:

QUOTE

About *UIT*'s practicality

"The authors' emphasis on the practical in the early chapters gets the students' interest by centering on real-life questions that would face everyone purchasing a new personal computer."
—Donald Robertson, Florida Community College–Jacksonville

FEATURE #2: Emphasis on Readability & Reinforcement for Learning

We offer the following features for reinforcing student learning:

Interesting Writing—Based on Good Scholarship

Where is it written that textbooks have to be boring? Can't a text have personality?

Actually, studies have found that textbooks **written in an imaginative style** significantly improve students' ability to retain information. Both instructors and students have commented on the distinctiveness of the writing in this book. We employ a number of journalistic devices—colorful anecdotes, short biographical sketches, interesting observations in direct quotes—to make the material as approachable as possible. We also use real anecdotes and examples rather than fictionalized ones.

Finally, **unlike most computer concepts books, we provide references for our sources—see the endnotes in the back of the book. Many of these are from the year preceding publication.** We see no reason why introductory computer books shouldn't practice good scholarship by revealing their information sources. And we see no reason why good scholarship can't go along with good writing—scholarship need not mean stuffiness.

Key Terms AND Definitions Emphasized

To help readers avoid confusion about important terms and what they actually mean, we print each key term in ***bold italic underscore*** and its definition in **boldface**. *Example* (from Chapter 1): "***Data*** **consists of raw facts and figures that are processed into information.**"

Material in Easily Manageable Portions

Major ideas are presented in **bite-size form,** with generous use of advance organizers, bulleted lists, and new paragraphing when a new idea is introduced. Most **sentences have been kept short,** the majority not exceeding 22–25 words in length.

"What's in It for Me?" Questions—to Help Students Read with Purpose

We have **crafted the learning objectives as Key Questions** to help readers focus on essentials. These are expressed as "I" and "me" questions, of the type students ask. These questions follow both first-level and second-level headings throughout the book.

*See Ethics examples on
pp. 37, 90, 102, 239, 280,
444, 459*

Emphasis Throughout on Ethics

Many texts discuss ethics in isolation, usually in one of the final chapters. We believe this topic is too important to be treated last or lightly, and users have agreed. Thus, **we cover ethical matters throughout the book,** as indicated by the special icon shown at right. *Example:* We discuss such all-important questions as online plagiarism, privacy, computer crime, and netiquette.

*See Security icons on
pp. 37, 102, 341, 436, 446,
448, 462, 472, 474*

Emphasis Throughout on Security

In the post 9-11 era, security concerns are of gravest importance. Although we devote several pages (in Chapters 2, 6, and 9) to security matters, we also reinforce student awareness by **highlighting with page-margin Security icons instances of security-related material throughout the book.** *Example:* On p. *102*, we use the special icon shown at right to highlight the advice that one

should pretend that every email message one sends "is a postcard that can be read by anyone."

Eight Timelines to Provide Historical Perspective

Some instructors like to see coverage of the history of computing. Not wishing to add greatly to the length of the book, we decided on **a student-friendly approach: the presentation of eight pictorial timelines showing the most significant historical IT events.** These timelines, which occur in most chapters, appear along the bottom page margin. (See the example at the bottom of this page.) Each timeline repeats certain "benchmark" events to keep students oriented, but **each one is modified to feature the landmark discoveries and inventions appropriate to the different chapter material.** *Examples:* In Chapter 4, "System Software," the timeline features innovations in operating systems. In Chapter 7, "Telecommunications," the timeline highlights innovations in data transmission.

See timelines beginning on pp. 14, 50, 166, 196, 260, 310, 410, 516

FEATURE #3: Currentness

Reviewers have applauded previous editions of UIT for being **more up to date than other texts.** For example, we have traditionally ended many chapters with a forward-looking section that offers a preview of technologies to come—some of which are realized even as students are using the book.

Among the new topics and terms covered in this edition are: *active and passive RFID tags, Android, attention/focusing problems, augmented reality, Bing, cellphone voice searches, Chrome, Conficker, cyberwarfare, the "deep Web," e-books, e-book readers, eight-core processors, FiOS, graphics processing units, Google 3D underwater mapping, hafnium and "high-k" technology, Hulu.com, "instant on" booting software, internet-ready TV, iPhone OS 3.0, laptop "cool trays," MiFi, multiscreen use, online "app stores," OpenID, PCI Express bus, "plug computers," portable media players, sentiment analysis, the Singularity, solid-state memory drives, Ubuntu, use of multiple monitors, wireless access points.* In this edition, we have updated the PC advertisement on page 199 and we have also updated the screen shots of software in Chapter 3. Material has also been updated on the following: *bar codes, battery technology, biometrics, Blu-ray, Bluetooth, Cell chip, cellphone address backup, cloud computing, computer graduate starting salaries, damage to computers, data mining, difficulty disconnecting from work, geolocator tags, gesture-reading technology, Google Print Library Project, government uses of computers, image-recognition technology, injuries caused by computers, input help for disabled, multifunction printers, multitasking, netbooks, online storage, photo printers, privacy matters, Roadrunner supercomputer, speech-recognition systems, telemedicine, texting, three-dimensional output, touch-sensitive computers, Twitter, video-rental kiosks, WiMax 4G networks, Windows 7.*

QUOTE

About *UIT*'s currentness

"Very knowledgeable, very good research."
—Maryann Dorn, Southern Illinois University

1994	2004	2005	2011?	2016?
Apple and IBM introduce PCs with full-motion video built in; wireless data transmission for small portable computers; web browser invented	Wireless monitors available for certain industrial applications	Wireless desktop printers commercially available	TV can output odors; full voice interaction with PCs; digital X-ray glasses	Thought recognition as everyday input means

"More Info!" Icons Help Students Find Their Own Answers to Questions

See inside back cover for pages on which MoreInfo! icons appear.

Finding Wi-Fi Hot Spots

www.wififreespot.com/
www.wifihotspotlist.com/
www.wifinder.com/

In addition, **we have taken the notion of currency to another level through the use of the "MoreInfo!" feature to encourage students to obtain their own updates** about material.

   Examples: "Finding Wi-Fi Hot Spots." "Finding ISPs." "Do Home Pages Endure?" "Do You Need to Know HTML to Build a Website?" "Urban Legends & Lies on the Internet." "Blog Search Engines." "Some Online Communities." "Links to Security Software." "Where to Learn More about Freeware & Shareware." "More about Watermarks." See the pages listed on the inside back cover.

FEATURE #4: Three-Level System to Help Students Think Critically about Information Technology

This feature, which has been in place for the preceding three editions, has been warmly received. More and more instructors seem to have become familiar with **Benjamin Bloom's *Taxonomy of Educational Objectives,*** describing a hierarchy of six critical-thinking skills: (a) two lower-order skills—*memorization* and *comprehension;* and (b) four higher-order skills—*application, analysis, synthesis,* and *evaluation.* Drawing on our experience in writing books to guide students to college success, we have implemented Bloom's ideas in a three-stage pedagogical approach, using the following hierarchical approach in the Chapter Review at the end of every chapter:

Stage 1 Learning—Memorization: "I Can Recognize & Recall Information"

Using self-test questions, multiple-choice questions, and true/false questions, we enable students to test how well they recall basic terms and concepts.

Stage 2 Learning—Comprehension: "I Can Recall Information in My Own Terms & Explain Them to a Friend"

Using open-ended short-answer questions, we enable students to re-express terms and concepts in their own words.

Stage 3 Learning—Applying, Analyzing, Synthesizing, Evaluating: "I Can Apply What I've Learned, Relate These Ideas to Other Concepts, Build on Other Knowledge, & Use All These Thinking Skills to Form a Judgment"

In this part of the Chapter Review, we ask students to put the ideas into effect using the activities described. The purpose is to help students take possession of the ideas, make them their own, and apply them realistically to their own ideas. **Our web exercises are also intended to spur discussion in the classroom and other contexts.**

   Examples: "Using Text Messaging in Emergencies." "What's Wrong with Using Supermarket Loyalty Cards?" "Are You in the Homeland Security Database?"

RESOURCES FOR INSTRUCTORS

Instructor's Manual

The electronic Instructor's Manual, available as part of the Instructor's Resource Kit, helps instructors to create effective lectures. The Instructor's

Manual is easy to navigate and simple to understand. Each chapter contains a chapter overview, lecture outline, teaching tips, additional information, and answers to end-of-chapter questions and exercises.

Testbank

The Testbank format allows instructors to effectively pinpoint areas of content within each chapter on which to test students. The text questions include learning level, answers, and text page numbers.

EZ Test

McGraw-Hill's EZ Test is a flexible and easy-to-use electronic testing program. The program allows instructors to create tests from book-specific items. It accommodates a wide range of question types, and instructors may add their own questions. Multiple versions of the test can be created and any test can be exported for use with course management systems such as WebCT, BlackBoard, or PageOut. EZ Test Online is a new service and gives you a place to easily administer your EZ Test created exams and quizzes online. The program is available for Windows and Macintosh environments.

PowerPoint Presentation

The PowerPoint presentation includes additional material that expands upon important topics from the text, allowing instructors to create interesting and engaging classroom presentations. Each chapter of the presentation includes important illustrations, and animations to enable instructors to emphasize important concepts in memorable ways.

Figures from the Book

All of the photos, illustrations, screenshots, and tables are available electronically for use in presentations, transparencies, or handouts.

Online Learning Center

The Online Learning Center *(www.mhhe.com/uit9e)* is designed to provide students with additional learning opportunities. The website includes PowerPoint presentations for each chapter. For the convenience of instructors, all Instructor's Resource CD material is available for download.

RESOURCES FOR INSTRUCTORS

PageOut

PageOut is our Course Web Site Development Center and offers a syllabus page, URL, McGraw-Hill Online Learning Center content, online exercises and quizzes, gradebook, discussion board, and an area for student Web pages.

PageOut requires no prior knowledge of HTML, no long hours of coding, and a way for course coordinators and professors to provide a full-course website. PageOut offers a series of templates—simply fill them with your course information and click on one of 16 designs. The process takes under an hour and leaves you with a professionally designed website. We'll even get you started with sample websites, or enter your syllabus for you! PageOut is so straightforward and intuitive, it's little wonder why over 12,000 college professors are using it. For more information, visit the PageOut website at *www. pageout.net*

The Online Learning Center can be delivered through any of these platforms:

- **Blackboard.com**
- **WebCT (a product of Universal Learning Technology)**

Web CT & Blackboard Partnerships

McGraw-Hill has partnerships with WebCT and Blackboard to make it even easier to take your course online and have McGraw-Hill content delivered through the leading internet-based learning tools for higher education.

McGraw-Hill has the following service agreements with WebCT and Blackboard:

- **SimNet Concepts:** This is the TOTAL solution for training and assessment in computer concepts. SimNet Concepts offers a unique, graphic-intensive environment for assessing student understanding of computer concepts. It includes interactive labs for 77 different computer concepts and 160 corresponding assessment questions. The content menus parallel the contents of the McGraw-Hill text being used for the class, so that students can cover topics for each chapter of the text you are using.

  SimNet Concepts also offers the only truly integrated learning and assessment program available today. After a student has completed any SimNet Concepts Exam, he or she can simply click on one button to have SimNet assemble a custom menu that covers just those concepts that the student answered incorrectly or did not attempt. These custom lessons can be saved to disk and loaded at any time for review.

  Assessment Remediation records and reports what the student did incorrectly for each question on an exam that was answered incorrectly.

ACKNOWLEDGMENTS

This book has only two names on its title page. but we are extraordinarily grateful for the many others who have been important contributors to its development. First, we wish to thank our sponsoring editor and champion, Scott Davidson, for his support in helping roll out this edition, which, because of the surge in technological change, now compels an updating on a yearly basis. Thanks also go to our marketing champion, Tiffany Wendt, for her enthusiasm and ideas and continuing commitment. We were extremely delighted to once again have Jean Starr as our project manager, who was instrumental in keeping the project on track, and we are grateful to her for her professionalism. We also thank Damian Moshak, Kevin White, and Brent dela Cruz for their media and digital support. Thanks are also due Alan Palmer, Jess Ann Kosic, Janean A. Utley, Marianna Kinigakiss, and Jeremy Cheshareck.

Outside McGraw-Hill, we want to state our appreciation for the contributions of Brian Kaspar, our great friend, for his help in checking all the URLs. We also wish to acknowledge the work of Craig Leonard as our freelance development editor. Judy Mason, our San Francisco Bay Area photo researcher, whose history with us goes back many, many years, did her usual always reliable, always superb job in photo research. Peter deLissovoy copyedited the text, David Shapiro was our able proofreader, and James Minkin, who has been a stalwart and sensitive indexer on many of our projects, did his usual satisfying and predictable outstanding job.

Finally, we are grateful to the following reviewers for helping to make this the most market-driven book possible.

Tahir Azia,
Long Beach City College, California

Don Bailey,
Plymouth State University, New Hampshire

Bidi Bruno,
Portland Community College, Oregon

Anthony Cameron,
Fayetteville Technical Community College, North Carolina

Paulette Comet,
Community College of Baltimore County, Maryland

Ron Conway,
Bowling Green State University, Indiana

Rebecca Cunningham,
Arkansas Technical University, Russellville

Susan Fuschetto,
Cerritos College, Norwalk, California

Saiid Ganjalizadeh,
Catholic University of America, Washington, D.C.

Bish Ghosh,
Metropolitan State College, Denver

Mindy Glander,
North Metro Technical College, Acworth, Georgia

Mary Carole Hollingsworth,
Georgia Perimeter College, Clarkston

Linda Johnsonius,
Murray State University, Murray, Kentucky

Hak Joon Kim,
Southern Connecticut State University, New Haven

Nicholas Lindquist,
Arizona State University

Warren Mack,
Northwest Vista College, San Antonio, Texas

Elizabeth McCarthy,
Kirkwood Community College, Cedar Rapids, Iowa

Jacob McGinnis,
Park University, Parkville, Missouri

Janak Rajani,
Howard Community College, Columbia, Maryland

Greg Saxon,
New Jersey Institute of Technology, Teaneck, New Jersey

Barbara Scantlebury,
Mohawk Valley Community College, Utica, New York

Stephanie Spike,
Tallahassee Community College, Florida

Susan Taylor,
Mount Wachusett Community College, Gardner, Massachusetts

David Trimble,
Park University, Parkville, Missouri

Sue VanBoven,
Paradise Valley Community College, Phoenix

Jennifer Cohen,
Southwest Florida College, Fort Myers

Andrew Levin,
Delaware Valley College, Doylestown, Pennsylvania

John Jansma,
Palo Alto College, San Antonio, Texas

Lonnie Hendrick,
Hampton University, Hampton, Virginia

Leon Amstutz,
Taylor University, Upland, Indiana

Reviewers & Other Participants in Previous Editions

We are grateful for the magnificent help over the past 15 years from all the instructors who have given us the benefit of their opinion, as follows:

Nancy Alderdice,
Murray State University;

Margaret Allison,
University of Texas–Pan American;

Angela Amin,
Great Lakes Junior College;

Sharon Anderson,
Western Iowa Tech

Anderson,
Marymount College;

Hashem Anwari,
Northern Virginia Community College–Loudoun Campus;

Connie Aragon,
Seattle Central Community College;

Bonnie Bailey,
Morehead State University;

Robert L. Barber,
Lane Community College;

Vic Barbow,
Purdue University;

David Brent Bandy,
University of Wisconsin–Oshkosh;

Robert Barrett,
Indiana University and Purdue University at Fort Wayne;

Anthony Baxter,
University of Kentucky;

Gigi Beaton,
Tyler Junior College;

Virginia Bender,
William Rainey Harper College;

Hossein Bidgoli,
California State University–Bakersfield;

Warren Boe,
University of Iowa;

Beverly Bohn,
Park University;

Randall Bower,
Iowa State University;

Russell Breslauer,
Chabot College;

Bob Bretz,
Western Kentucky University;

William C. Brough,
University of Texas–Pan American;

Phyllis Broughton,
Pitt Community College;

Charles Brown,
Plymouth State College;

David Burris,
Sam Houston State University;

Jeff Butterfield,
University of Idaho;

J. Wesley Cain,
City University, Bellevue;

Patrick Callan,
Concordia University;

Judy Cameron,
Spokane Community College;

Ralph Caputo,
Manhattan College;

Robert Caruso,
Santa Rosa Junior College;

Joe Chambers,
Triton College;

Kris Chandler,
Pikes Peak Community College;

William Chandler,
University of Southern Colorado;

John Chenoweth,
East Tennessee State University;

Ashraful Chowdhury,
Dekalb College;

Erline Cocke,
Northwest Mississippi Community College;

Robert Coleman,
Pima County Community College;

Helen Corrigan-McFadyen,
Massachusetts Bay Community College;

Jami Cotler,
Siena College;

Glen Coulthard,
Okanagan University;

Robert Crandall,
Denver Business School;

Hiram Crawford,
Olive Harvey College;

Thad Crews,
Western Kentucky University;

Martin Cronlund,
Anne Arundel Community College;

Jim Dartt,
San Diego Mesa College;

Joseph DeLibro,
Arizona State University;

Edouard Desautels,
University of Wisconsin–Madison;

William Dorin,
Indiana University–Northwest;

Maryan Dorn,
Southern Illinois University;

Patti Dreven,
Community College of Southern Nevada;

John Durham,
Fort Hays State University;

Laura A. Eakins,
East Carolina University;

Bonita Ellis,
Wright City College;

John Enomoto,
East Los Angeles College;

Ray Fanselau,
American River College;

Pat Fenton,
West Valley College;

Eleanor Flanigan,
Montclair State University;

Ken Frizane,
Oakton Community College;

James Frost,
Idaho State University;

Susan Fry,
Boise State University;

Bob Fulkerth,
Golden Gate University;

Janos Fustos,
Metropolitan State College;

Yaping Gao,
College of Mount St. Joseph;

Enrique Garcia,
Laredo Community College;

JoAnn Garver,
University of Akron;

Jill Gebelt,
Salt Lake Community College;

Charles Geigner,
Illinois State University;

David German,
Cerro Coso Community College;

Candace Gerrod,
Red Rocks Community College;

Julie Giles,
DeVry Institute of Technology;

Frank Gillespie,
University of Georgia;

Myron Goldberg,
Pace University;

Dwight Graham,
Prairie State College;

Fillmore Guinn,
Odessa College;

Norman P. Hahn,
*Thomas Nelson Community
College;*

Sallyann Hanson,
Mercer County Community College;

Debra Harper,
*Montgomery County Community
College–North Harris*

Albert Harris,
Appalachian State University;

Jan Harris,
Lewis & Clark Community College;

Michael Hasset,
Fort Hays State University;

Julie Heine,
Southern Oregon State College;

Richard Hewer,
Ferris State University;

Ron Higgins,
Grand Rapids Community College;

Martin Hochhauser,
Dutchess Community College;

Don Hoggan,
Solano Community College;

James D. Holland,
*Okaloosa-Waltoon Community
College;*

Stan Honacki,
Moraine Valley Community College;

Wayne Horn,
Pensacola Junior College;

Tom Hrubec,
Waubonsee Community College;

Jerry Humphrey,
Tulsa Junior College;

Christopher Hundhausen,
University of Oregon;

Alan Iliff,
North Park College;

Washington James,
*Collin County Community College–
Plano;*

Jim Johnson,
Valencia Community College;

Julie Jordahl,
Rock Valley College;

Laleh Kalantari,
Western Illinois University;

Jan Karasz,
Cameron University;

Jorene Kirkland,
Amarillo College;

Victor Lafrenz,
Mohawk Valley Community College;

Sheila Lancaster,
Gadsden State Community College;

Dana Lasher,
North Carolina State University;

Stephen Leach,
Florida State University;

Paul Leidig,
Grand Valley State University;

Mary Levesque,
University of Nebraska–Omaha;

Chang-Yang Lin,
Eastern Kentucky University;

Gina Long,
Southwestern Community College;

John Longstreet,
Harold Washington College;

Paul Lou,
Diablo Valley College;

Pamela Luckett,
Barry University;

Deborah Ludford,
Glendale Community College;

Evelyn Lulis,
DePaul University;

Peter MacGregor,
Estrella Mountain Community College;

Donna Madsen,
Kirkwood Community College; Ed Mannion,
California State University–Chico;

Alan Maples,
Cedar Valley College;

Kenneth E. Martin,
University of North Florida;

Thomas Martin,
Shasta College;

Jerry Matejka,
Adelphi University;

Diane Mayne-Stafford,
Grossmont College;

Todd McLeod,
Fresno City College;

Curtis Meadow,
University of Maine;

Jennifer Merritt,
Park University;

Timothy Meyer,
Edinboro University;

Michael Michaelson,
Palomar College;

Cindy Minor,
John A. Logan College;

Norman Muller,
Greenfield Community College;

Rebecca Mundy,
University of California, Los Angeles, and University of Southern California;

Paul Murphy,
Massachusetts Bay Community College;

Kathleen Murray,
Drexel University;

Marry Murray,
Portland Community College;

Sonia Nayle,
Los Angeles City College;

Charles Nelson,
Rock Valley College;

Bruce Neubauer,
Pittsburgh State University;

Wanda Nolden,
Delgado Community College;

E. Gladys Norman,
Linn-Benton Community College;

George Novotny,
Ferris State University;

Janet Olpert,
Cameron University;

Pat Ormond,
Utah Valley State College;

John Panzica,
Community College of Rhode Island;

Rajesh Parekh,
Iowa State University;

Bettye Jewel Parham,
Daytona Beach Community College;

Merrill Parker,
Chattanooga State Technical Community College;

Michelle Parker,
Indiana Purdue University;

Marie Planchard,
Massachusetts Bay Community College;

Jim Potter,
California State University–Hayward;

Tammy Potter,
West Kentucky Community & Technical College;

Leonard Presby,
William Patterson State College;

William Pritchard,
Wayne State University;

Delores Pusins,
Hillsborough Community College;

Eugene Rathswohl,
University of San Diego;

Alan Rea,
Western Michigan University;

Jerry Reed,
Valencia Community College;

John Rezac,
Johnson County Community College;

Pattie Riden,
Western Illinois University;

Jane Ritter,
University of Oregon;

Fernando Rivera,
University of Puerto Rico–Mayaguez Campus;

Donald Robertson,
Florida Community College–Jacksonville;

Stan Ross,
Newbury College;

Russell Sabadosa,
Manchester Community College;

Behrooz Saghafi,
Chicago State University;

Judy Scheeren,
Westmoreland County Community College;

Al Schroeder,
Richland College;

Dick Schwartz,
Macomb County Community College;

Earl Schweppe,
University of Kansas;

Susan Sells,
Wichita State University;

Tom Seymour,
Minot State University;

Naj Shaik,
Heartland Community College;

Morgan Shepherd,
University of Colorado–Colorado Springs;

Elaine Shillito,
Clark State Community College;

Jack Shorter,
Texas A&M University;

James Sidbury,
University of Scranton;

Maureen Smith,
Saddleback College;

Esther Steiner,
New Mexico State University;

Randy Stolze,
Marist College;

Charlotte Thunen,
Foothill College;

Denis Tichenell,
Los Angeles City College;

Angela Tilaro,
Butte College;

Martha Tillman,
College of San Mateo;

DeLyse Totten,
Portland Community College;

Jack VanDeventer,
Washington State University;

James Van Tassel,
Mission College;

Jim Vogel,
Sanford Brown College;

Dale Walikainen,
Christopher Newport University;

Reneva Walker,
Valencia Community College;

Ron Wallace,
Blue Mountain Community College;

Nancy Webb,
San Francisco City College;

Steve Wedwick,
Heartland Community College;

Patricia Lynn Wermers,
North Shore Community College;

Cora Lee Whitcomb,
Bentley College;

Doug White,
Western Michigan University;

Anita Whitehill,
Foothill College;

Edward Winter,
Salem State College;

Floyd Winters,
Manatee Community College;

Israel Yost,
University of New Hampshire;

Alfred Zimermann,
Hawai'i Pacific University;

Eileen Zisk,
Community College of Rhode Island.

Contents

3

SOFTWARE: TOOLS FOR PRODUCTIVITY & CREATIVITY 119

INTRODUCTION to INFORMATION TECHNOLOGY Your Digital World

Chapter Topics & Key Questions

1.1 The Practical User: How Becoming Computer Savvy Benefits You What does being *computer savvy* mean, and what are its practical payoffs?

1.2 Information Technology & Your Life: The Future Now What is information technology, and how does it affect education, health, money, leisure, government, and careers?

1.3 Infotech Is All-Pervasive: Cellphones, Email, the Internet, & the E-World How does information technology facilitate email, networks, and the use of the internet and the web; what is the meaning of the term *cyberspace?*

1.4 The "All-Purpose Machine": The Varieties of Computers What are the five sizes of computers, and what are clients and servers?

1.5 Understanding Your Computer: How Can You Customize (or Build) Your Own PC? What four basic operations do all computers use, and what are some of the devices associated with each operation? How does communications affect these operations?

1.6 Where Is Information Technology Headed? What are three directions of computer development and three directions of communications development?

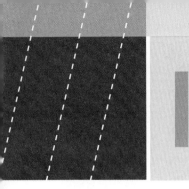

f you are under the age of 30, you live in a world quite different from that of your parents and grandparents.

You are a member of the "Always On" generation, accustomed to spending 8 hours or more a day looking at various screens—on cellphones, on computers, on TVs.[1] You are a "digital native," as one anthropologist put it, constantly busy with text messaging, email, and the internet.[2] If you are an 18-to-24-year-old, you generally watch the smallest amount of live TV (3½ hours a day) compared to any other age group but spend the most time text messaging (29 minutes a day) and watch the most online video (5½ minutes a day).[3]

What are the developments that have encouraged these kinds of behavior? The answer is *information technology*. Of the top 30 innovations of the last 30 years, according to a 2009 panel of judges at the University of Pennsylvania's Wharton School, *most were related to information technology*.[4] The first four items on the list, for example, are the internet, broadband, and the World Wide Web; PC and laptop computers; mobile phones; and email. (● *See Panel 1.1.*) Unlike previous generations, you live in a world of *pervasive computing* or *ubiquitous computing*.

Central to this concept is the internet—the "Net," or "net," that sprawling collection of data residing on computers around the world and accessible by high-speed connections. Everything that presently exists on a personal computer, experts suggest, will move onto the internet, giving us greater mobility and wrapping the internet around our lives.[5] So central is the internet to our existence, in fact, that many writers are now spelling it without the capital

panel 1.1

Top innovations of the last 30 years.
The majority (23 of the 30) are in the field of information technology.*

1. Internet, broadband, World Wide Web	16. Media file compression
2. PC and laptop computers	17. Microfinance
3. Mobile phones	18. Photovoltaic solar energy
4. Email	19. Large-scale wind turbines
5. DNA testing and sequencing	20. Internet social networking
6. Magnetic resonance imaging	21. Graphic user interface
7. Microprocessors	22. Digital photography
8. Fiber optics	23. RFID and applications
9. Office software	24. Genetically modified plants
10. Laser/robotic surgery	25. Bio fuels
11. Open-source software	26. Bar codes and scanners
12. Light-emitting diodes	27. ATMs
13. Liquid crystal display	28. Stents
14. GPS devices	29. SRAM flash memory
15. E-commerce and auctions	30. Anti-retroviral treatment for AIDS

*To be more than just a new invention, an event was defined as an innovation if it created more opportunities for growth and development and if it had problem-solving value.
Source: Adapted from "A World Transformed: What Are the Top 30 Innovations of the Last 30 Years?" *Knowledge@Wharton*, February 18, 2009, *http://knowledge.wharton.upenn.edu/article.cfm?articleid=2163* (accessed May 28, 2009).

"I"—*Internet* becomes *internet*, just as *Telephone* became *telephone*—because both systems belong not to just one owner but to the world. We will follow this convention in this book.

In this chapter, we begin by discussing how becoming computer savvy can benefit you and how computing and the internet affect your life. We then discuss cellphones, the internet, the World Wide Web, and other aspects of the e-world. Next we describe the varieties of computers that exist. We then explain the three key concepts behind how a computer works and what goes into a personal computer, both hardware and software. We conclude by describing three directions of computer development and three directions of communications development.

1.1 THE PRACTICAL USER: How Becoming Computer Savvy Benefits You

What does being computer savvy *mean, and what are its practical payoffs?*

"Just keeping busy." Multiple electronic devices allow people to do multiple tasks simultaneously—multitasking.

There is no doubt now that for most of us information technology is becoming like a second skin—an extension of our intellects and even emotions, creating almost a parallel universe of "digital selves." Perhaps you have been using computers a long time and in a multitude of ways, or perhaps not. In either case, this book aims to deliver important practical rewards by helping you become "computer streetwise"—that is, computer savvy. **Being _computer savvy_ means knowing what computers can do and what they can't, knowing how they can benefit you and how they can harm you, knowing when you can solve computer problems and when you have to call for help.**

Among the practical payoffs are these:

YOU WILL KNOW TO MAKE BETTER BUYING DECISIONS No matter how much computer prices come down, you will always have to make judgments about quality and usefulness when buying equipment and software. In fact, we start you off in this chapter by identifying the parts of a computer system, what they do, and about how much they cost.

Competence. To be able to choose a computer system or the components to build one, you need to be computer savvy.

YOU WILL KNOW HOW TO FIX ORDINARY COMPUTER PROBLEMS Whether it's replacing a printer cartridge, obtaining a software improvement ("patch" or "upgrade"), or pulling photos from your digital camera or camera cellphone, we hope this book gives you the confidence to deal with the continual challenges that arise with computers—and know when and how to call for help.

YOU WILL KNOW HOW TO UPGRADE YOUR EQUIPMENT & INTEGRATE IT WITH NEW PRODUCTS New gadgetry and software are constantly being developed. A knowledgeable user learns under what conditions to upgrade, how to do so, and when to start over by buying a new machine.

YOU WILL KNOW HOW TO USE THE INTERNET MOST EFFECTIVELY The sea of data that exists on the internet and other online sources is so great that finding what's best or what's really needed can be a hugely time-consuming activity. We hope to show you the most workable ways to approach this problem.

YOU WILL KNOW HOW TO PROTECT YOURSELF AGAINST ONLINE VILLAINS The online world poses real risks to your time, your privacy, your finances, and your peace of mind—spammers, hackers, virus senders, identity thieves, and companies and agencies constructing giant databases of personal profiles—as we will explain. This book aims to make you streetwise about these threats.

YOU WILL KNOW WHAT KINDS OF COMPUTER USES CAN ADVANCE YOUR CAREER Even top executives now use computers, as do people in careers ranging from police work to politics, from medicine to music, from retail to recreation. We hope you will come away from this book with ideas about how the technology can benefit you in whatever work you choose.

Along the way—in the Experience Boxes, Practical Action Boxes, Survival Tips, and More Info!s—we offer many kinds of practical advice that we hope will help you become truly computer savvy in a variety of ways, large and small.

From now on, whenever you see the **more info!** icon (above) in the margin, you'll find information about internet sites to visit and how to search for terms related to the topic just discussed.

1.2 INFORMATION TECHNOLOGY & YOUR LIFE: The Future Now

What is information technology, and how does it affect education, health, money, leisure, government, and careers?

This book is about computers, of course. But not just about computers. It is also about the way computers communicate with one another. When computer and communications technologies are combined, the result is *information technology,* or "infotech." **_Information technology (IT)_ is a general term that describes any technology that helps to produce, manipulate, store, communicate, and/or disseminate information.** IT merges computing with high-speed communications links carrying data, sound, and video. Examples of information technology include personal computers but also new forms of telephones, televisions, appliances, and various handheld devices.

The Two Parts of IT: Computers & Communications

How do I distinguish computer technology and communications technology?

Note that there are two important parts to information technology—computers and communications.

COMPUTER TECHNOLOGY You have certainly seen and, we would guess, used a computer. Nevertheless, let's define what it is. **A _computer_ is a programmable, multiuse machine that accepts data—raw facts and figures—and processes, or manipulates, it into information we can use,** such as summaries, totals, or reports. Its purpose is to speed up problem solving and increase productivity.

COMMUNICATIONS TECHNOLOGY Unquestionably you've been using communications technology for years. **_Communications technology,_ also called _telecommunications technology,_ consists of electromagnetic devices and systems for communicating over long distances.** The principal examples are telephone, radio, broadcast television, and cable TV. In more recent times, there has been the addition of communication among computers—which is what happens when people "go online" on the internet. In this context, **_online_**

means using a computer or some other information device, connected through a network, to access information and services from another computer or information device. A _network_ is a communications system connecting two or more computers; the internet is the largest such network.

Information technology is already affecting your life in exciting ways and will do so even more in the future. Let's consider how.

Education: The Promise of More Interactive & Individualized Learning

How is information technology being used in education?

In her physics classes at the Massachusetts Institute of Technology, professor Gabriella Sciolla's high-tech classroom has white boards and huge display screens instead of blackboards. The professor can make brief presentations of general principles, then throw out multiple-choice questions that students "vote" on, using wireless "personal response clickers." These devices transmit the answers to a computer monitored by the professor, helping her gauge the level of understanding in the room. "You know where they are," she says. She can then adjust, slow down, or engage students in guided discussions of their answers.[6] An Indiana University sociology instructor uses similar technology to get students to answer questions about themselves—race, income, political affiliation—showing how, for example, the class is skewed toward wealthier or poorer students, an event that can stir up a half hour of excited class discussion.[7]

Maybe the classrooms at your school haven't reached this level of interactivity yet, but there's no question that information technology is universal on college campuses, and at lower levels the internet has penetrated 99% of schools.[8] Most college students have been exposed to computers since the lower grades. In fact, one-fifth of college students report they were using computers between the ages 5 and 8, and all had begun using computers by the time they were 16–18 years old.

When properly integrated into the curriculum and classroom, information technology can (1) allow students to personalize their education; (2) automate many tedious and rote tasks of teaching and managing classes; and (3) reduce the teacher's workload per student, so that he or she can spend more time on reaching individual students.[9] For instance, **_email_, or "electronic mail," messages transmitted over a computer network, most often the internet,** are used by students to set up appointments (62%) with professors, discuss grades (58%), or get clarification of an assignment (75%).[10]

Besides using the internet to help in teaching, today's college instructors also use _presentation graphics software_ such as PowerPoint to show their lecture outlines and other materials on classroom screens (as we discuss in Chapter 3). In addition, they use Blackboard,

Online Colleges

The following websites provide detailed information about getting college degrees online:

www.classesusa.com/ indexall/?campusType=online

www.guidetoonlineschools.com

www.usdla.org

http://distancelearn.about.com/

http://www.distancelearning.com/

A 6-year-old girl plays a Sesame Street interactive program at Maxwell Memorial Library in Camilluis, New York.

WebCT, and other _**course-management software**_ **for administering online assignments, schedules, examinations, and grades.**[11] One of the most intriguing developments in education at all levels, however, is the rise of _**distance learning**_, **or** _e-learning_, **the name given to online education programs,** which has gone from under 2 million online students in 2003 to an expected nearly 5 million students in 2009.[12] E-learning has had some interesting effects. For example, the availability of the internet has helped to propel the home-schooling movement, in which children are taught at home, usually by parents, to expand from 1.7% of all school-age children in 1999 to 2.9% in 2007.[13] E-learning has also propelled the rise of for-profit institutions, such as DeVry and the University of Phoenix, which 8% of full-time college students now attend.[14] More than a third of institutions of higher education—and 97% of public universities—offer online courses, and many have attracted on-campus students, who say they like the flexibility of not having to attend their classes at a set time.[15]

Avatar. The simulated depictions of humans are a staple not only of videogames but also of computerized training programs. (What culture does "avatar" come from? See _www. answers.com/topic/ avatar?cat=technology.)_

E-learning has been put to such varied uses as bringing career and technical courses to high school students in remote prairie towns, pairing gifted science students with master teachers in other parts of the country, and helping busy professionals obtain further credentials outside business hours. But the reach of information technology into education has only begun. In the future, we will see software called "intelligent tutoring systems" that gives students individualized instruction when personal attention is scarce—such as the software Cognitive Tutor, which not only helps high school students to improve their performance in math but also sparks them to enjoy a subject they might have once hated. In colleges, more students may use interactive simulation games, such as McGraw-Hill's Business Strategy Game, to apply their knowledge to real-world kinds of problems. And employees in company training programs may find themselves engaged in mock conversations with _**avatars**_—**computer depictions of humans,** as are often found in online videogames—that represent imaginary customers and coworkers, combining the best parts of computer-based learning with face-to-face interaction.[16]

Health: High Tech for Wellness

How are computers being used in health and medicine?

Neurologist Bart Demaerschalk of Phoenix, Arizona, was at home tucking into his Thanksgiving dessert when he received a message that a woman 200 miles away had developed drooping facial muscles and slurred speech. Within a few minutes, Demaerschalk was looking at her, asking questions, reviewing her brain scan, and confirming a diagnosis of stroke—all with the help of a two-way video and audio connection set up for just this kind of consultation.[17]

Damaerschalk's story is an example of _**telemedicine**_—**medical care delivered via telecommunications.** For some time, physicians in rural areas lacking local access to radiologists have used "teleradiology" to exchange computerized images such as X rays via telephone-linked networks with expert physicians in metropolitan areas. Now telemedicine is moving to an exciting new level, as the use of digital cameras and sound, in effect, moves patients to doctors rather than the reverse. Already telemedicine is being embraced by administrators in the American prison system, where by law inmates are guaranteed medical treatment—and where the increase in prisoners every year has led to the need to control health care costs.

Computer technology is radically changing the tools of medicine. All medical information, including that generated by X ray, lab test, and pulse monitor,

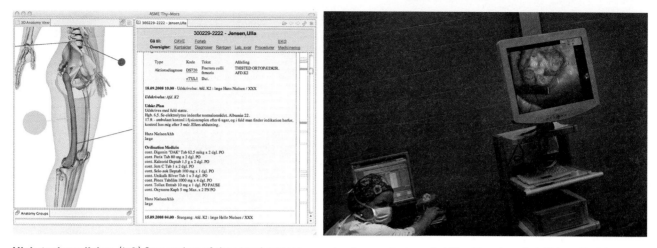

High-tech medicine. (*left*) Screenshot of the visual patient record software pioneered at Thy-Mors hospital. This patient has had a fracture of the femur in the right leg. This computer-based image shows a close-up view of the treated area. A click on the arrow or the highlighted femur would show the pertinent medical information from the record on the right panel. The tool allows doctors to easily zoom in an out on a particular body region or part and choose between many different views, for example, the cardiovascular system, the central nervous system, or the muscular system. (*right*) Open heart surgery is seen on a computer monitor as an Israeli medical team repairs a congenital defect in a boy's heart at the Wolfson Medical Center in Tel Aviv.

can now be transmitted to a doctor in digital format. Image transfer technology allows radiologic images such as CT scans and MRIs to be immediately transmitted to electronic charts and physicians' offices. Patients in intensive care, who are usually monitored by nurses during off-times, can also be watched over by doctors in remote "control towers" miles away. Electronic medical records and other computerized tools enable heart attack patients to get follow-up drug treatment and diabetics to have their blood sugar measured. Software can compute a woman's breast cancer risk.[18] Patients can use email to query their doctors about their records (although there are still privacy and security issues).[19]

Various **_robots_—automatic devices that perform functions ordinarily performed by human beings,** with names such as ROBO DOC, RoboCart, TUG, and HelpMate—help free medical workers for more critical tasks; the four-armed da Vinci surgical robot, for instance, can do cuts and stitches deep inside the body, so that surgery is less traumatic and recovery time faster.[20] Hydraulics and computers are being used to help artificial limbs get "smarter."[21] And a patient paralyzed by a stroke has received an implant that allows communication between his brain and a computer; as a result, he can move a cursor across a screen by brainpower and convey simple messages—as in *Star Trek*.[22]

Want to calculate how long you will live? Go to *www.livingto100.com,* an online calculator developed by longevity researchers at Harvard Medical School and Boston Medical Center. Want to gather your family health history to see if you're at risk for particular inherited diseases? Go to *www.hhs.gov/familyhistory* to find out how. These are only two examples of health websites available to patients and health consumers. Although online health information can be misleading and even dangerous (for example, be careful about relying on Wikipedia for health advice), many people now tap into health care databases, email health professionals, or communicate with people who have similar conditions.

Often patients are already steeped in information about their conditions when they arrive in the offices of health care professionals. This represents a fundamental shift of knowledge, and therefore power, from physicians to patients. In addition, health care consumers are able to share experiences and information with one another. Young parents, for example, can find an online gathering spot (chat room) at pediatrician Alan Greene's website at *www. drgreene.com.* If you want to put your medical records on an electronic keychain storage device, visit *med-infochip.com.*

Health Websites

Some reliable sources:
www.medlineplus.gov
www.nimh.nih.gov
www.4woman.gov
www.mayoclinic.com
www.nationalhealthcouncil.org
www.yourdiseaserisk.wustl.edu/

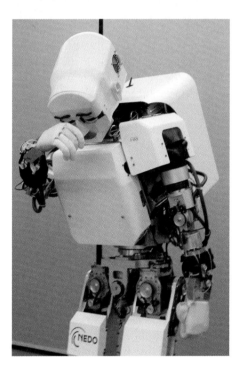

Robots. (*left*) A humanoid robot, HRP-2 Promet, developed by the National Institute of Advanced Industrial Science and Technology and Kawada Industries, Inc. Five feet tall, it performs traditional Japanese dancing. Priced at $365,000, the robot can help workers at construction sites and also drive a car. (*middle*) This sea bream is about 5½ pounds and can swim up to 38 minutes before recharging. The robot fish, created by Mitsubishi, looks and swims exactly like the real thing. (*right*) Humanoid robot KOBIAN displays an emotion of sadness during a demonstration at Waseda University in Tokyo, Japan. KOBIAN, which can express seven programmed emotions by using its entire body, including facial expressions, has been developed by researchers at Waseda's Graduate School of Advanced Science and Engineering.

Money: Toward the Cashless Society

How will computers affect my financial matters?

"The future of money is increasingly digital, likely virtual, and possibly universal," says one writer.[23] ***Virtual* means that something is created, simulated, or carried on by means of a computer or a computer network,** and we certainly have come a long way toward becoming a cashless society. Indeed, the percentage of all financial transactions done electronically, both phone-initiated and computer-initiated, was projected to rise to 18.4% in 2013, up from 0.9% in 1993.[24] Besides currency, paper checks, and credit and debit cards, the things that serve as "money" include cash-value cards (such as subway fare cards), automatic transfers (such as direct-deposit paychecks), and digital money ("electronic wallet" accounts such as PayPal).

Many readers of this book will probably already have engaged in online buying and selling, purchasing DVDs, books, airline tickets, or computers. But what about groceries? After all, you can't exactly squeeze the cantaloupes through your keyboard. Even so, online groceries are expected to reach $7.5 billion in U.S. sales by 2012.[25] To change decades of shopping habits, e-grocers keep their delivery charges low and delivery times convenient, and they take great pains in filling orders, knowing that a single bad piece of fruit will produce a devastating word-of-mouth backlash.

Financial Information

The internet contains lots of financial information. Some of the better sources:

www.finance.yahoo.com

www.fool.com

www.ragingbull.com

www.usatoday.com/money/ default.htm

Only about 46% of U.S. workers have their paychecks electronically deposited into their bank accounts (as opposed to 95% or more in Japan, Norway, and Germany, for example), but this is sure to change as Americans discover that direct deposit is actually safer and faster. Online bill paying is also picking up steam. For more than two decades, it has been possible to pay bills online, such as those from phone and utility companies, with special software and online connections to your bank.

Some banks and other businesses are backing an electronic-payment system that allows internet users to buy goods and services with **_micropayments_, electronic payments of as little as 25 cents in transactions for which it is uneconomical to use a credit card.** The success of Apple Computer's iTunes online music service, which sells songs for 99 cents each, suggests that micro sales are now feasible. All kinds of businesses and organizations, from independent songwriters to comic book writers to the Legal Aid Society of Cleveland, now accept micropayments, using intermediaries such as BitPass and Peppercoin.[26] Thus, you could set up your own small business simply by constructing a website (we show you how later in the book) and accepting micropayments.

Leisure: Infotech in Entertainment & the Arts

How will my leisure activities be affected by information technology?

Information technology is being used for all kinds of entertainment, ranging from videogames to telegambling. It is also being used in the arts, from painting to photography. Let's consider just two examples, music and film.

Computers, the internet, and the World Wide Web are standing the system of music recording and distribution on its head—and in the process are changing the financial underpinnings of the music industry. Because of their high overhead, major record labels typically need a band to sell half a million CDs in order to be profitable, but independent bands, using online marketing, can be reasonably successful selling 20,000 or 30,000 albums. Team Love, a small music label established in 2003, found it could promote its first two bands, Tilly and the Wall and Willy Mason, by offering songs online free for **_downloading_—transferring data from a remote computer to one's own computer**—so that people could listen to them before paying $12 for a CD. It also puts videos online for sharing and uses quirky websites to reach fans. "There's something exponential going on," says one of Team Love's founders. "The more music that's downloaded, the more it sells."[27] Many independent musicians are also using the internet to get their music heard, hoping that giving away songs will help them build audiences.[28]

The web also offers sources for instantly downloadable sheet music (see *www.everynote.com*, *www.musicnotes.com*, *www.sheetmusicdirect.com*, and *www.sunhawk.com*). One research engineer has devised a computerized scoring system for judging musical competitions that overcomes the traditional human-jury approach, which can be swayed by personalities and politics.[29] And a Spanish company, Polyphonic HMI, has created Hit Song Science software, which they say can analyze the hit potential of new songs by, according to one description, "reference to a finely parsed universe of attributes derived from millions of past songs."[30]

As for movies, now that blockbuster movies routinely meld live action and animation, computer artists are in big demand. The 1999 film *Star Wars: Episode I*, for instance, had 1,965 digital shots out of about 2,200 shots. Even when film was used, it was scanned into computers to be tweaked with animated effects, lighting, and the like. Entire beings were created on computers by artists working on designs developed by producer George Lucas and his chief artist.[31]

What is driving the demand for computer artists? One factor is that animation, though not cheap, looks more and more like a bargain, because hiring movie actors costs so much—some make $20 million a film. Moreover, special

Download (reverse the direction of data transmission to **upload**)

Satellite

Upload

Download

Mainframe   Individual PC

Download
(reverse the direction of data transmission to **upload**)

info!

Free Music Online

Places to look for free—and legal—music online:

new.music.yahoo.com

www.epitonic.com

http://memory.loc.gov/ ammem/audio.html

www.archive.org

www.garageband.com

Entertainment. (*left*) Computer-generated special effects shot from the movie *Up*. (*right*) An indoor "winter" sports facility in Japan; the system uses microprocessors to keep lifts running, snow falling, and temperature at 26 degrees.

Online Movie Tickets

Three sites offer movie tickets, as well as reviews and other materials. In some cities you can print out tickets at home.

www.fandango.com
www.moviefone.com
www.movietickets.com

effects are readily understood by audiences in other countries, and major studios increasingly count on revenues from foreign markets to make a film profitable. Digital manipulation also allows a crowd of extras to be multiplied into an army of thousands. It can also be used to create settings: in the film *Sky Captain and the World of Tomorrow*, the actors—Gwyneth Paltrow, Angelina Jolie, and Jude Law—shot all their scenes in front of a blue screen, and computer-generated imagery was then used to transport them into an imaginary world of 1939.[32] Computer techniques have even been used to develop digitally created actors—called "synthespians." (Thespis was the founder of ancient Greek drama; thus, a thespian works in drama as an actor.) Actors ranging from the late James Dean to the late John Wayne, for instance, have been recruited for television commercials. And computerized animation is now so popular that Hollywood studios and movie directors are finding they can make as much money from creating videogames as from making movies.[33]

But animation is not the only area in which computers are revolutionizing movies. Digital editing has radically transformed the way films are assembled. Whereas traditional film editing involved reeling and unreeling spools of film and cutting and gluing pieces of highly scratchable celluloid together, nearly burying the editor in film, today an editor can access 150 miles of film stored on a computer and instantly find any visual or audio moment, allowing hundreds of variations of a scene to be called up for review. Even nonprofessionals can get into movie making as new computer-related products come to market. Now that digital video capture-and-edit systems are available for under $1,000, amateurs can turn home videos into digital data and edit them. Also, digital camcorders, which offer outstanding picture and sound quality, have steadily dropped in price.

Government & Electronic Democracy: Participating in the Civic Realm

In what ways are computers changing government and politics?

The internet and other information technology have helped government deliver better services and have paved the way for making governmental operations more transparent to the public. For instance, during a health crisis involving salmonella-tainted peanut butter, the U.S. Food and Drug Administration sent out information 707 times per minute in response to citizens seeking information about it.[34] The U.S. State Department has a "DipNote" blog read by 2 million readers, and it holds press conferences on YouTube.[35] Congress has a publicly searchable website for all federal contracts and grants over $25,000,

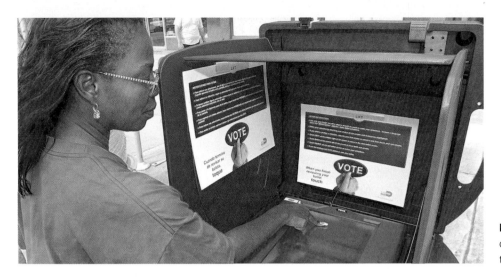

Electronic voting. Voting using computer technology and a touch screen to vote.

and a growing number of states are putting everything from budgets to contracts to travel expenses online for the public to look at.[36] The White House also has its own website (www.whitehouse.gov) with its Open Government Dialogue blog.[37] Many local and state governments also have websites through which citizens can deal with everything from paying taxes and parking tickets, to renewing vehicle registration and driver's licenses, viewing birth and marriage certificates, and applying for public sector jobs.

The internet is also changing the nature of politics, enabling political candidates and political interest groups to connect with voters in new ways, to raise money from multiple small donors instead of just rich fat cats, and (using cellphones and text messaging) to organize street protests.[38] The Barack Obama campaign was said to be particularly adept at exploiting information technology during his run for the presidency in 2008 and afterward for staying in touch with supporters to help him govern.[39] Yet information also has its downside, as computers have allowed incumbent legislators to design (gerrymander) voting districts that make it nearly impossible for them to be dislodged; electronic tools have also made it easier than ever for political parties to skirt or break campaign laws, and computerized voting machines still don't always count votes as they are supposed to. Still, websites and bloggers have become important watchdogs on government. The website E-Democracy (*www.e-democracy.org*), for instance, can help citizens dig up government conflicts of interest, and websites such as Project Vote Smart (*www.votesmart.org*) outline candidates' positions.

Online Government Help

You can gain access to government agencies through the following websites:

www.firstgov.gov
www.govspot.com
www.info.gov

Jobs & Careers

How could I use computers to advance my career?

Today almost every job and profession requires computer skills of some sort. Some are ordinary jobs in which computers are used as ordinary tools. Others are specialized jobs in which advanced computer training combined with professional training gives people dramatically new kinds of careers.

Consider:

- In the hotel business, even front-desk clerks need to know how to deal with computerized reservation systems. Some hotels, however, also have a so-called computer concierge, someone with knowledge of computer systems who can help computer-carrying guests with online and other tech problems.

- In law enforcement, police officers need to know how to use computers while on patrol or at their desks to check out stolen cars, criminal

Careers. Front-desk workers at many hotels use computers to check guests in.

Police work. Syracuse, New York: An Onondaga County sheriff's deputy enters information into a laptop in his squad car as he issues a ticket for an uninspected vehicle. The officer was using the sheriff's department's new computer database system.

records, outstanding arrest warrants, and the like. However, investigators with specialized computer backgrounds are also required to help solve fraud, computer break-ins, accounting illegalities, and other high-tech crimes.

- In entertainment, computers are used for such ordinary purposes as budgets, payroll, and ticketing. However, there are also new careers in virtual set design, combining training in architecture and 3-D computer modeling, and in creating cinematic special effects.

Clearly, information technology is changing old jobs and inventing new ones. To prosper in this environment, you need to combine a traditional education with training in computers and communications. You also need to be savvy about job searching, résumé writing, interviewing, and postings of employment opportunities. Advice about careers, job hunting, occupational trends, and employment laws is available at Yahoo!, Google, and other websites. Some starting annual salaries for recent college graduates are shown below; note that jobs involving degrees in computers and information systems occupy four of the seven top-paying starting salaries (● *See Panel 1.2.*)

Computers can be used both for you to find employers and for employers to find you.[40]

WAYS FOR YOU TO FIND EMPLOYERS As you might expect, the first to use cyberspace as a job bazaar were companies seeking people with technical backgrounds and technical people seeking employment. However, as the public's interest in commercial services and the internet has exploded, the focus of online job exchanges has broadened. Now, interspersed among ads for programmers on the internet are openings for forest rangers in Idaho, physical therapists in Atlanta, models in Florida, and English teachers in China. Most websites are free to job seekers, although many require that you fill out an online registration form. (● *See Panel 1.3.*)

WAYS FOR EMPLOYERS TO FIND YOU Posting your résumé online for prospective employers to view is attractive because of its low (or zero) cost and wide reach. But does it have any disadvantages? Certainly it might if the employer who sees your posting happens to be the one you're already working for. In addition, you have to be aware that you lose control over anything broadcast

Discipline (bachelor's degree)	Current average starting salary
Computer science	$61,280
Computer engineering	$60,280
Electrical/electronics and communications engineering	$57,503
Mechanical engineering	$57,024
Civil engineering	$51,780
Management information systems/Business data processing	$51,489
Economics (business/managerial)	$51,062
Finance	$48,158
Accounting	$48,020
Business administration/Management	$46,171
Marketing/Marketing management	$41,506
Political science/Government	$38,844
History	$38,056
Biological sciences/Life sciences	$35,522
English language and literature/Letters	$35,453
Sociology	$35,434

Source: Adapted from the *NACE Average Starting Salary Offer Survey Results (2008),* Purdue University Calumet, posted February 27, 2009, http://209.85.173.132/search?q=cache:http://webs calumet.purdue.edu/careerservices/files/2008/10/nace-salary-survey.pdf (accessed April 21, 2009). The original survey is by the National Association of Colleges and Employers, copyright holder. © National Association of Colleges and Employers. All rights reserved. 62 Highland Ave., Bethlehem, PA 18017, www.nacewb.org.

panel 1.2

Entering the job market
Average starting salary offers for 2008 college graduates

panel 1.3

Some websites that post job listings

Career One Stop: *www.jobbankinfo.org*
Career Builder: *www.careerbuilder.com*
College Grad Job Hunter: *www.collegegrad.com*
Erecruiting: *www.erecruiting.com*
FedWorld (U.S. Government jobs): *www.fedworld.gov*
NationJob Network: *www.nationjob.com*
Indeed.com: *www.indeed.com*

Yahoo! Hot Jobs: *http://hotjobs.yahoo.com*
Jobs.com: *www.jobs.com*
Jobs on Line: *www.jobsonline.com*
MonsterTrak.com: *www.jobtrak.com*
JobWeb: *www.jobweb.org*
Monster.com: *www.monster.com*
Simply Hired: *www.simplyhired.com*

into cyberspace. You're putting your credentials out there for the whole world to see, and you need to be somewhat concerned about who might gain access to them.

If you have a technical background, it's definitely worth posting your résumé with an electronic jobs registry, since technology companies in particular find this an efficient way of screening and hiring. However, posting may also benefit people with less technical backgrounds. Online recruitment is popular with companies because it prescreens applicants for at least basic computer skills. If you've mastered the internet, you're likely to know something about word processing, spreadsheets, and database searching as well, knowledge required in most good jobs these days.

One wrinkle in job seeking is to prepare a résumé with web links and/or clever graphics and multimedia effects and then put it on a website to entice employers to chase after you. If you don't know how to do this, there are many companies that—for a fee—can convert your résumé and publish it on their own websites. Some of these services can't dress it up with fancy graphics or multimedia, but since complex pages take longer for employers to download anyway, the extra pizzazz is probably not worth the effort. A number of websites allow you to post your résumé for free. Another wrinkle is to pay extra to move your résumé higher in the listings so that it will stand out compared with competing résumés. For example, for an extra $20–$150 apiece, Careerbuilder.com will move your listing toward the top of the search heap, and the company says that employers click on upgraded résumés 200% more often than on regular ones.[41]

panel 1.4

Grandparent and offspring
ENIAC (*left*) is the grandparent of today's smartphones (*right*).

panel 1.5

Timeline
Overview of some of the historical developments in information technology. The timeline is modified in upcoming chapters to show you more about the people and advances contributing to developments in information technology.

1.3 INFOTECH IS ALL-PERVASIVE: Cellphones, Email, the Internet, & the E-World

How does information technology facilitate email, networks, and the use of the internet and the web; what is the meaning of the term cyberspace?

One of the first computers, the outcome of military-related research, was delivered to the U.S. Army in 1946. ENIAC (short for "Electronic Numerical Integrator And Calculator") weighed 30 tons and was 80 feet long and two stories high, but it could multiply a pair of numbers in the then-remarkable time of three-thousandths of a second. (● *See Panel 1.4.*) This was the first general-purpose, programmable electronic computer, the grandparent of today's lightweight handheld machines—including the smart cellphone. Some of the principal historical developments are illustrated in the timeline below. (● *See Panel 1.5.*)

The Phone Grows Up

How has the telephone changed?

Cellphone e-mania has swept the world. All across the globe, people have acquired the portable gift of gab, with some users making 45 or more calls a day. Strategy Analytics has estimated that worldwide mobile phone subscriptions will rise to 3.9 billion in 2013; more than half the world's population will be using mobile phones by 2010.[42] It has taken more than 100 years for the

4000–1200 BCE	3500 BCE–2900 BCE	3000 BCE	1270 BCE	900 BCE	530 BCE	100 CE
Inhabitants of the first known civilization in Sumer keep records of commericial transactions on clay tablets	Phoenicians develop an alphabet; Sumerians develop cuneiform writing; Egyptians develop hierogylphic writing	Abacus is invented in Babylonia	First encyclopedia (Syria)	First postal service (China)	Greeks start the first library	First bound books

Smartphones. (*left*) Motorola Q9c smartphone. (*middle*) Ojo videophone, which allows face-to-face chats long distance. (*right*) Bandai Networks' mobile phone that displays a novel. Bandai offers 150 books on its site for phone owners to download and read on their phones.

telephone to get to this point—getting smaller, acquiring push buttons, losing its cord connection. In 1964, the * and # keys were added to the keypad. In 1973, the first cellphone call was processed.

In its most basic form, the telephone is still so simply designed that even a young child can use it. However, it is now becoming more versatile and complex—a way of connecting to the internet and the World Wide Web. Indeed, internet smartphones—such as the Apple iPhone, the Samsung Instinct, the palm Centro, and the Motorola Q9c—represent another giant step for information technology. Now you no longer need a personal computer to get on the internet. Smartphones in their various forms enable you not only to make voice calls but also to send and receive text messages, browse the World Wide Web, and obtain news, research, music, photos, movies, and TV programs. (And with camera and camcorder cellphones, you can send images, too.)[43] According to one survey, the percentage of people who use nonvoice applications for text messages is 27%; email 11%; internet 9%; and photography 6%—and the numbers of users for these options are growing all the time.[44]

"You've Got Mail!" Email's Mass Impact

What makes email distinctive from earlier technologies?

It took the telephone 40 years to reach 10 million customers, and fax machines 20 years. Personal computers made it into that many American homes 5 years

700–800	1049	1450	1455	1621	1642	1666
Arabic numbers introduced to Europe	First moveable type (clay) invented in China	Newspapers appear in Europe	Printing press (J. Gutenberg, Germany)	Slide rule invented (Edmund Gunther)	First mechanical adding machine (Blaise Pascal)	First mechanical calculator that can add and subtract (Samuel Morland)

October meeting

File Edit View Insert Format Tools Message Help

Send   Cut   Copy   Paste   Undo   Check

🔍 Search ▾ 😊 Smiley Central 🐛 Webfetti »

To: emailassociate@isp.net

Cc:

Subject: October meeting

Bookman Old Style ▾ 10 ▾ ▦, **B** *I* U A, ☰ ☰

Hello Sam--

Please email me the details about the upcoming
October meeting. Please also attach the file with
the agenda items. Thanks-- Kante

after they were introduced. Email, which appeared in 1981, became popular far more quickly, reaching 10 million users in little more than a year.[45] No technology has ever become so universal so fast. Thus, one of the first things new computer and internet users generally learn is how to send and receive email.

Until 1998, hand-delivered mail was still the main means of correspondence. But in that year, the volume of email in the United States surpassed the volume of hand-delivered mail. In 2007, the total number of email messages sent daily has been estimated at 183 billion worldwide.[46] Already, in fact, email is the leading use of PCs. Because of this explosion in usage, suggests a *BusinessWeek* report, "email ranks with such pivotal advances as the printing press, the telephone, and television in mass impact."[47]

Using electronic mail clearly is different from calling on a telephone or writing a conventional letter. As one writer puts it, email "occupies a psychological space all its own. It's almost as immediate as a phone call, but if you need to, you can think about what you're going to say for days and reply when it's convenient."[48] Email has blossomed, points out another writer, not because it gives us more immediacy but because it gives us *less*. "The new appeal of email is the old appeal of print," he says. "It isn't instant; it isn't immediate; it isn't in your face." Email has succeeded for the same reason that the videophone—which allows callers to see each other while talking—has been so slow to catch on: because "what we actually want from our exchanges is the minimum human contact commensurate with the need to connect with other people."[49] It will be interesting to see, however, whether this observation holds up during the next few years if marketers roll out more videophones.

What is interesting, though, is that in these times when images often seem to overwhelm words, email is actually *reactionary*. "The internet is the first new medium to move decisively backward," points out one writer, because it essentially involves writing. Twenty years ago, "even the most literate of us wrote maybe a half a dozen letters a year; the rest of our lives took place on the telephone."[51] Email has changed all that—and has put pressure on businesspeople in particular to sharpen their writing skills. (A countertrend, unfortunately, is that the informal style of electronic messages is showing up in schoolwork.)[52]

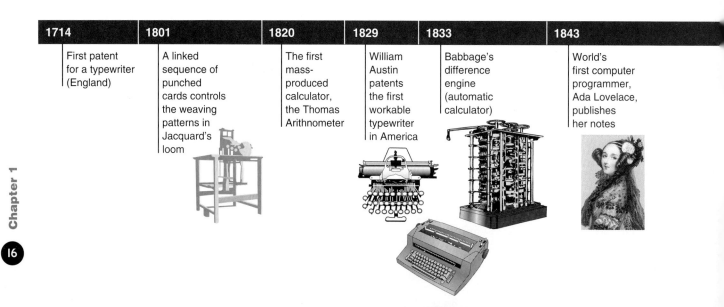

1714	1801	1820	1829	1833	1843
First patent for a typewriter (England)	A linked sequence of punched cards controls the weaving patterns in Jacquard's loom	The first mass-produced calculator, the Thomas Arithnometer	William Austin patents the first workable typewriter in America	Babbage's difference engine (automatic calculator)	World's first computer programmer, Ada Lovelace, publishes her notes

PRACTICAL ACTION

Managing Your Email

For many people, email *is* the online environment, more so than the World Wide Web. According to one study, 60% of people who do emailing at work average 10 or fewer messages a day, 23% receive more than 20, and 6% receive more than 50.[50] But some people receive as many as 300 emails a day—with perhaps 200 being junk email (spam), bad jokes, or irrelevant memos (the "cc," previously "carbon copy," now "courtesy copy").

It's clear, then, that email will increase productivity only if it is used properly. Overuse or misuse just causes more problems and wastes time. The following are some ideas to keep in mind when using email:

- *Do your part to curb the email deluge:* Put short messages in the subject line so that recipients don't have to open the email to read the note. Don't reply to every email message you get. Avoid "cc:ing" (copying to) people unless absolutely necessary. Don't send chain letters or lists of jokes, which just clog mail systems.

- *Be helpful in sending attachments:* Attachments—computer files of long documents or images attached to an email—are supposed to be a convenience, but often they can be an annoyance. Sending a 1-megabyte file to a 500-person mailing list creates 500 copies of that file—and that many megabytes can clog the mail system. (A 1-megabyte file is about the size of a 300-page double-spaced term paper.) Ask your recipients beforehand if they want the attachment.

- *Be careful about opening attachments you don't recognize:* Some dangerous computer viruses—renegade programs that can damage your computer—have been spread by email attachments that automatically activate the virus when they are opened.

- *Use discretion about the emails you send:* Email should not be treated as informally as a phone call. Don't send a message electronically that you don't want some third party to read. Email messages are not written with disappearing ink; they remain in a computer system long after they have been sent. Worse, recipients can easily copy and even alter your messages and forward them to others without your knowledge.

- *Make sure emails to bosses, coworkers, and customers are literate:* It's okay to be informal when emailing friends, but employers and customers expect a higher standard. Pay attention to spelling and grammar.

- *Don't use email to express criticism and sarcasm:* Because email carries no tone or inflection, it's hard to convey emotional nuances. Avoid criticism and sarcasm in electronic messaging. Nevertheless, you can use email to provide quick praise, even though doing it in person will take on greater significance.

- *Be aware that email you receive at work is the property of your employer:* Be careful of what you save, send, and back up.

- *Realize that deleting email messages doesn't totally get rid of them:* "Delete" moves the email from the visible list, but the messages remain on your hard disk and can be retrieved by experts. Special software, such as Spytech Eradicator and Window Washer, will completely erase email from the hard disk.

- *Don't neglect real personal contact:* More companies are asking employees to trade email for more in-person contact with the people they work with, through such practices as banning the use of email on Fridays. This has come about because so many employees complain that they have to leave multiple messages when trying to get answers since coworkers don't respond in timely fashion.

1844	1854	1876	1890	1895	1907	1920–1921
Samuel Morse sends a telegraph message from Washington to Baltimore	George Boole publishes "An Investigation on the Laws of Thought," a system for symbolic and logical reasoning that will become the basis for computer design	Alexander Graham Bell patents the telephone	Electricity used for first time in a data-processing project—Hollerith's automatic census-tabulating machine (used punched cards)	First radio signal transmitted	First regular radio broadcasts, from New York	The word "robot," derived from the Czech word for compulsory labor, is first used to mean a humanlike machine

The Internet, the World Wide Web, & the "Plumbing of Cyberspace"

What's the difference between the net, the web, and cyberspace?

As the success of the cellphone shows, communications has extended into every nook and cranny of civilization (with poorer nations actually the leaders in cellphone growth), a development called the "plumbing of cyberspace." The term *cyberspace* was coined by William Gibson in his novel *Neuromancer* (1984) to describe a futuristic computer network into which users plug their brains. (*Cyber* comes from "cybernetics," a term coined in 1948 to apply to the comparative study of automatic control systems, such as the brain/nervous system and mechanical-electrical communication systems.) In everyday use, this term has a rather different meaning.

Today many people equate cyberspace with the internet. But it is much more than that. Cyberspace includes not only the web, chat rooms, online diaries (blogs), and member-based services such as America Online—all features we explain in this book—"but also such things as conference calls and automatic teller machines," says David Whittler.[53] We may say, then, that **_cyberspace_ encompasses not only the online world and the internet in particular but also the whole wired and wireless world of communications in general**—the nonphysical terrain created by computer and communications systems. Cyberspace is where you go when you go online with your computer.

THE NET & WEB DEFINED The two most important aspects of cyberspace are the internet and that part of the internet known as the World Wide Web. To give them formal definition:

- **The internet—"the mother of all networks":** The internet is at the heart of the Information Age. Called "the mother of all networks," the **_internet_ (the "net") is a worldwide computer network that connects hundreds of thousands of smaller networks. These networks link educational, commercial, nonprofit, and military entities, as well as individuals.**

- **The World Wide Web—the multimedia part of the internet:** The internet has been around for more than 40 years. But what made it popular, apart from email, was the development in the early 1990s of the **_World Wide Web_, often called simply the "Web" or the "web"—an interconnected system of internet computers (called *servers*) that support specially formatted documents in multimedia form.** The word *multimedia*, from "multiple media," refers to technology that presents information in more than one medium, such as text, still images, moving images, and sound. In other words, the web provides information in more than one way.

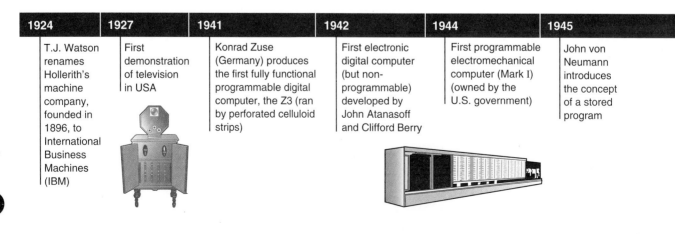

1924	1927	1941	1942	1944	1945
T.J. Watson renames Hollerith's machine company, founded in 1896, to International Business Machines (IBM)	First demonstration of television in USA	Konrad Zuse (Germany) produces the first fully functional programmable digital computer, the Z3 (ran by perforated celluloid strips)	First electronic digital computer (but non-programmable) developed by John Atanasoff and Clifford Berry	First programmable electromechanical computer (Mark I) (owned by the U.S. government)	John von Neumann introduces the concept of a stored program

THE INTERNET'S INFLUENCE There is no doubt that the influence of the net and the web is tremendous. At present, 75% of American adults use the internet, according to the Pew Internet & American Life Project.[54] Seventy-two percent of American adult internet users use the net on an average day, with 60% using it to send or read email.[55] But just how revolutionary is the internet? Is it equivalent to the invention of television, as some technologists say? Or is it even more important—equivalent to the invention of the printing press? "Television turned out to be a powerful force that changed a lot about society," says *USA Today* technology reporter Kevin Maney. "But the printing press changed everything—religion, government, science, global distribution of wealth, and much more. If the internet equals the printing press, no amount of hype could possibly overdo it."[56]

College Students & the E-World

How does my use of information technology compare with that of other students?

One thing we know already is that cyberspace is saturating our lives. The worldwide internet population was 1.59 billion (or nearly 24% of the world's population in 2009). About 251 million of those internet users were in North America, representing a penetration of 74% of the population.[57] While the average age of users is

1946	1947	1951	1952	1958	1962	1969
First programmable electronic computer in United States (ENIAC)	Invention of the transistor (enabled miniaturization of electronic devices)	Computers are first sold commercially	UNIVAC computer correctly predicts election of Eisenhower as U.S. President	Integrated circuit; first modem	The first computer game is invented (Spacewar)	ARPANet established by U.S. Advanced Research Projects Agency; led to internet

rising, there's no doubt that people ages 18–29 love the internet, with 87% of them using it; among all computer users with a college education, 95% use the net.[58]

Teens and young adults (age 18–32) are the most likely of all groups to use the internet for communicating with friends and family; for entertainment—especially online videos, online games, and virtual worlds (such as for multiplayer online role-playing games)—and for obtaining music. They are also considerably more likely than older users to use social networking sites—online communities, such as Facebook and Twitter, that allow members to keep track of their friends and share photos, videos, and the like. In addition, young people are more apt to send instant messages and to do text messaging (texting) with friends—send brief written messages between cellphones.[59] We consider all these technologies later in the book.

1.4 THE "ALL-PURPOSE MACHINE": The Varieties of Computers

What are the five sizes of computers, and what are clients and servers?

When the ★alarm clock blasts you awake, you leap out of bed and head for the kitchen, where you check the ★coffee maker. After using your ★electronic toothbrush and showering and dressing, you stick a bagel in the ★microwave, and then pick up the ★TV remote and click on the ★TV to catch the weather forecast. Later, after putting dishes in the ★dishwasher, you go out and start up the ★car and head toward campus or work. Pausing en route at a ★traffic light, you turn on your ★iPod to listen to some music. And you might use your ★GPS system to get to your destination.

You haven't yet touched a PC, a personal computer, but you've already dealt with at least 11 computers—as you probably guessed from the ★s. All these familiar appliances rely on tiny "computers on chips" called *microprocessors*. Maybe, then, the name "computer" is inadequate. As computer pioneer John von Neumann has said, the device should not be called the computer but rather the "all-purpose machine." It is not, after all, just a machine for doing calculations. The most striking thing about it is that it can be put to *any number of uses*.

What are the various types of computers? Let's take a look.

All Computers, Great & Small: The Categories of Machines

What are the five sizes of computers?

At one time, the idea of having your own computer was almost like having your own personal nuclear reactor. In those days, in the 1950s and 1960s, computers were enormous machines affordable only by large institutions. Now they come in a variety of shapes and sizes, which can be classified according to their processing power: *supercomputers, mainframe computers, workstations, microcomputers,* and *microcontrollers.* We also consider *servers*.

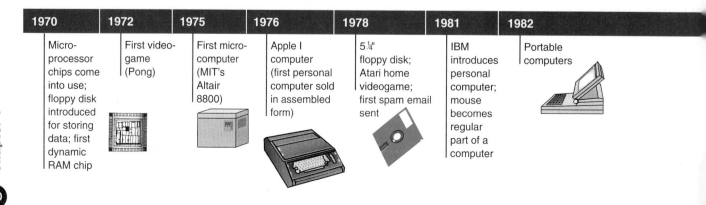

1970	1972	1975	1976	1978	1981	1982
Micro-processor chips come into use; floppy disk introduced for storing data; first dynamic RAM chip	First video-game (Pong)	First micro-computer (MIT's Altair 8800)	Apple I computer (first personal computer sold in assembled form)	5¼" floppy disk; Atari home videogame; first spam email sent	IBM introduces personal computer; mouse becomes regular part of a computer	Portable computers

Supercomputer Maker or Lab	Top Speed, Teraflops	Location
Roadrunner Los Alamos Laboratory and IBM	1,105	U.S.
Blue Gene/L IBM	280.6	U.S.
Molecular Dynamics Machine Riken	78	Japan
Grape-6 U. Tokyo	64	Japan
Columbia SGI	61	U.S.
Earth Simulator NEC	41	Japan

Source: Data from *www.top500.org,* reported in Don Clark, "Los Alamos Computer Keeps Title as the Fastest," *The Wall Street Journal,* November 11, 2008, p. B9; *www.newsfactor. com/story.xhtml?story_id=31771; www.supercomputingonline.com/print.php?sid=8879;* and H. Josef Hebert, "Computer Proves It's World's Fastest," *San Francisco Chronicle,* June 10, 2008, p. 47.

Supercomputers

Is there a chance I might use a supercomputer?

Typically priced from \$1 million to more than \$350 million, **_supercomputers_ are high-capacity machines with thousands of processors that can perform more than several trillion calculations per second.** These are the most expensive and fastest computers available. "Supers," as they are called, have been used for tasks requiring the processing of enormous volumes of data, such as doing the U.S. census count, forecasting weather, designing aircraft, modeling molecules, and breaking encryption codes. More recently they have been employed for business purposes—for instance, sifting demographic marketing information—and for creating film animation. The fastest computer in the world, costing \$100 million and with roughly the computing power of 100,000 of today's most powerful laptops, is the Roadrunner, developed by engineers from the Los Alamos National Laboratory and IBM Corp., primarily for nuclear weapons research, including simulating nuclear explosions. Roadrunner's speed is 1.105 petaflops, or 1,105 trillion operations per second.[60] (● *See Panel 1.6.*) In February 2009, IBM announced its intent to release "Sequoia," a 20 petaflops supercomputer, in 2011. This machine will have the power of approximately 2 million laptops.

Roadrunner supercomputer from Los Alamos National Laboratory and IBM This is the world's fastest supercomputer.

panel 1.6

info!

FLOPS

In computing, FLOPS is an abbreviation of Floating-point Operations Per Second. Flops is used as a measure of a computer's performance, especially in fields of scientific calculations. Using floating-point encoding, extremely long numbers can be handled relatively easily. Computers operate in the trillions of flops; for comparison, any response time below 0.1 second is experienced as instantaneous by a human operator, so a simple pocket calculator could be said to operate at about 10 flops. Humans are even worse floating-point processors. If it takes a person a quarter of an hour to carry out a pencil-and-paper long division with 10 significant digits, that person would be calculating in the milliflops range.

1984	1994	1998	2000	2001	2002	2003
Apple Macintosh; first personal laser printer	Apple and IBM introduce PCs with full-motion video built in; wireless data transmission for small portable computers; first web browser invented	PayPal is founded	The "Y2K" nonproblem; the first U.S. presidential webcast	Dell computers becomes the largest PC maker	Friendster	Facebook MySpace

Supercomputers are still the most powerful computers, but a new generation may be coming that relies on **_nanotechnology,_** **in which molecule-size nano-structures are used to create tiny machines for holding data or performing tasks.** (*Nano* means "one-billionth.") Computers the size of a pencil eraser could become available that work 10 times faster than today's fastest supercomputer.[61] Eventually nanotech could show up in every device and appliance in your life.

Mainframe Computers

What kind of services am I apt to get from a mainframe?

The only type of computer available until the late 1960s, **_mainframes_** **are water- or air-cooled computers that cost $5,000–$5 million and vary in size from small, to medium, to large, depending on their use.** Small main-frames ($5,000–$200,000) are often called *midsize computers;* they used to be called *minicomputers,* although today the term is seldom used. Mainframes are used by large organizations—such as banks, airlines, insurance compa-nies, and colleges—for processing millions of transactions. Often users access a mainframe by means of a **_terminal_**, **which has a display screen and a key-board and can input and output data but cannot by itself process data.** Mainframes process billions of instructions per second.

Mainframe computer

Workstations

What are some uses of workstations?

Introduced in the early 1980s, **_workstations_** **are expensive, powerful personal computers usually used for complex scientific, math-ematical, and engineering calculations and for computer-aided design and computer-aided manufacturing.** Providing many capa-bilities comparable to those of midsize mainframes, workstations are used for such tasks as designing airplane fuselages, developing pre-scription drugs, and creating movie special effects. Workstations have caught the eye of the public mainly for their graphics capabilities, which are used to breathe three-dimensional life into movies such as *WALL • E, Harry Potter,* and *X-Men Origins: Wolverine.* The capabilities of low-end workstations overlap those of high-end desktop microcomputers.

Workstation

Hewlett-Packard Touchsmart
This desktop computer allows users to move items around on the screen with their hands, to open and close files, and to perform other functions manually.

Microcomputers

How does a microcomputer differ from a workstation?

Microcomputers, **also called *personal computers (PCs),* which cost $500 to over $5,000, can fit next to a desk or on a desktop or can be carried around.** They either are stand-alone machines or are connected to a computer network, such as a local area network. **A _local area network (LAN)_ connects, usually by special cable, a group of desktop PCs and other devices, such as printers, in an office or a building.**

Microcomputers are of several types: desktop PCs, tower PCs, notebooks (laptops), netbooks, mobile internet devices (MIDs), and personal digital assistants—handheld computers or palmtops.

2004	2005	2006	2007	2012	2030–2045
IBM PC sold to Lenovo Group Flickr	YouTube Wii	Twitter	Skype	Foldable computers	The Singularity

Small The Mac Mini has the smallest desktop microcomputer case, just 6.5 inches square and 2 inches tall.

DESKTOP PCs _Desktop PCs_ (left) **are older microcomputers whose case or main housing sits on a desk, with keyboard in front and monitor (screen) often on top.**

TOWER PCs _Tower PCs_ **are microcomputers whose case sits as a "tower," often on the floor beside a desk, thus freeing up desk surface space.** Some desktop computers, such as Apple's iMac, no longer have a boxy housing; most of the computer components are built into the back of the flat-panel display screen.

NOTEBOOKS _Notebook computers_, **also called** _laptop computers_, **are lightweight portable computers with built-in monitor, keyboard, hard-disk drive, CD/DVD drive, battery, and AC adapter that can be plugged into an electrical outlet; they weigh anywhere from 1.8 to 9 pounds.**

Notebook computers: Macbooks

NETBOOKS A fairly recent category, _netbooks_ **are low-cost, lightweight, computers with tiny dimensions and functions designed for basic tasks, such as web searching, email, and word processing.** They weigh anywhere from 2.25 to 3.2 pounds, cost generally between $270 and $500, have little processing power, and have screens between 8.9 and 12 inches wide diagonally.[62] Netbooks fill a technological category between notebooks and handheld devices.

Tower PC

Netbook

LG Mobile Internet Device (MID)

MOBILE INTERNET DEVICES (MIDs) **Smaller than notebook computers but larger and more powerful than PDAs** (see below), _mobile internet devices (MIDs)_ **are for consumers and business professionals.** Fully internet integrated, they are highly compatible with desktop microcomputers and laptops. The initial models focus on data communication, not voice communication.

PERSONAL DIGITAL ASSISTANTS _Personal digital assistants (PDAs)_, **also called** _handheld computers_ or _palmtops_, **combine personal organization tools—schedule planners, address books, to-do lists—with the ability in some cases to send email and faxes.** Some PDAs have touch-sensitive screens. Some also connect to desktop computers for sending or receiving information. (For now, we are using the word _digital_ to mean "computer based.") The range of handheld wireless devices, such as multipurpose cellphones, has surged in recent years, and we consider these later in the book (Chapter 7).

Personal digital assistant (PDA)

Microcontrollers

What gadgets do I have that might contain microcontrollers?

Microcontrollers, **also called** _embedded computers_, **are the tiny, specialized microprocessors installed in "smart" appliances and automobiles.** These microcontrollers enable microwave ovens, for example, to store data about how long to cook your potatoes and at what power setting. Microcontrollers have been used to develop a new universe of experimental electronic

Microcontroller The MPXY8020A pressure sensor from Motorola reduces tire blowouts and improves gas mileage. This embedded computer notifies drivers, via a dashboard display, when tire pressure is not optimal.

appliances—e-pliances. For example, they are behind single-function products such as digital cameras, MP3 and MP4 players, and organizers, which have been developed into hybrid forms such as gadgets that store photos and videos as well as music. They also help run tiny web servers embedded in clothing, jewelry, and household appliances such as refrigerators. In addition, microcontrollers are used in blood-pressure monitors, air bag sensors, gas and chemical sensors for water and air, and vibration sensors.

Servers

How do servers work, and what do they do?

The word *server* describes not a size of computer but rather a particular way in which a computer is used. Nevertheless, because servers have become so important to telecommunications, especially with the rise of the internet and the web, they deserve mention here. (Servers are discussed in detail in Chapters 2, 6, and 7.)

A *server*, or *network server*, **is a central computer that holds collections of data (databases) and programs for connecting or supplying services to PCs, workstations, and other devices, which are called *clients*. These clients are linked by a wired or wireless network. The entire network is called a *client/server network*.** In small organizations, servers can store files, provide printing stations, and transmit email. In large organizations, servers may also house enormous libraries of financial, sales, and product information.

You may never lay eyes on a supercomputer or mainframe or even a tiny microcontroller. But most readers of this book will already have laid eyes and hands on a personal computer. We consider this machine next.

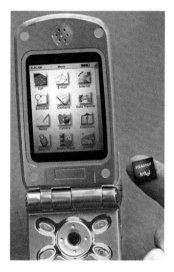

Cellphone microcontroller

Servers A group of networked servers that are housed in one location is called a *server farm* or a *server cluster.*

1.5 UNDERSTANDING YOUR COMPUTER: How Can You Customize (or Build) Your Own PC?

What four basic operations do all computers use, and what are some of the devices associated with each operation? How does communications affect these operations?

Perhaps you know how to drive a car. But do you know what to do when it runs badly? Similarly, you've probably been using a personal computer. But do you know what to do when it doesn't act right—when, for example, it suddenly "crashes" (shuts down)?

Cars are now so complicated that professional mechanics are often required for even the smallest problems. With personal computers, however, there are still many things you can do yourself—and should learn to do, so that, as we've suggested, you can be effective, efficient, and employable. To do so, you first need to know how computers work.

How Computers Work: Three Key Concepts

What are the three fundamental principles everyone should understand about how computers work?

Could you build your own personal computer? Some people do, putting together bare-bones systems for just a few hundred dollars. "If you have a logical mind, are fairly good with your hands, and possess the patience of Job, there's no reason you can't . . . build a PC," says science writer David Einstein. And, if you do it right, "it will probably take only a couple of hours," because industry-standard connections allow components to go together fairly easily.[63]

Actually, probably only techies would consider building their own PCs. But many ordinary users *order* their own custom-built PCs. Let's consider how you might do this.

We're not going to ask you to build or order a PC—just to pretend to do so. The purpose of this exercise is to give you a basic overview of how a computer works. That information will help you when you go shopping for a new system or, especially, if you order a custom-built system. It will also help you understand how your existing system works, if you have one.

Before you begin, you will need to understand three key concepts.

1. PURPOSE OF A COMPUTER: TURNING DATA INTO INFORMATION Very simply, the purpose of a computer is to process data into information.

- **Data:** **_Data_ consists of the raw facts and figures that are processed into information**—for example, the votes for different candidates being elected to student-government office.

- **Information:** **_Information_ is data that has been summarized or otherwise manipulated for use in decision making**—for example, the total votes for each candidate, which are used to decide who won.

2. DIFFERENCE BETWEEN HARDWARE & SOFTWARE You should know the difference between hardware and software.

- **Hardware:** **_Hardware_ consists of all the machinery and equipment in a computer system.** The hardware includes, among other devices, the keyboard, the screen, the printer, and the "box"—the computer or processing device itself. Hardware is useless without software.

- **Software:** **_Software_, or _programs_, consists of all the electronic instructions that tell the computer how to perform a task.** These instructions come from a software developer in a form (such as a CD, or compact disk) that will be accepted by the computer. Examples are Microsoft Windows and Office XP/Vista.

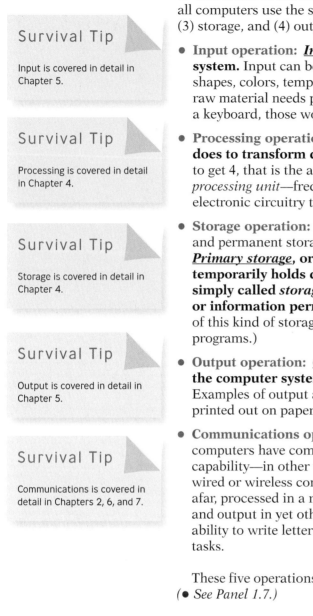

Survival Tip

Input is covered in detail in Chapter 5.

Survival Tip

Processing is covered in detail in Chapter 4.

Survival Tip

Storage is covered in detail in Chapter 4.

Survival Tip

Output is covered in detail in Chapter 5.

Survival Tip

Communications is covered in detail in Chapters 2, 6, and 7.

3. THE BASIC OPERATIONS OF A COMPUTER   Regardless of type and size, all computers use the same four basic operations: (1) input, (2) processing, (3) storage, and (4) output. To this we add (5) communications.

- **Input operation: _Input_ is whatever is put in ("input") to a computer system.** Input can be nearly any kind of data—letters, numbers, symbols, shapes, colors, temperatures, sounds, pressure, light beams, or whatever raw material needs processing. When you type some words or numbers on a keyboard, those words are considered input data.

- **Processing operation: _Processing_ is the manipulation a computer does to transform data into information.** When the computer adds 2 + 2 to get 4, that is the act of processing. The processing is done by the *central processing unit*—frequently just called the *CPU*—a device consisting of electronic circuitry that executes instructions to process data.

- **Storage operation:** Storage is of two types—temporary storage and permanent storage, or primary storage and secondary storage. **_Primary storage_, or *memory*, is the internal computer circuitry that temporarily holds data waiting to be processed. _Secondary storage_, simply called *storage*, refers to the devices and media that store data or information permanently.** A hard disk or CD/DVD is an example of this kind of storage. (Storage also holds the software—the computer programs.)

- **Output operation: _Output_ is whatever is output from ("put out of") the computer system—the results of processing, usually information.** Examples of output are numbers or pictures displayed on a screen, words printed out on paper by a printer, or music piped over some loudspeakers.

- **Communications operation:** These days, most (though not all) computers have communications ability, which offers an extension capability—in other words, it extends the power of the computer. With wired or wireless communications connections, data may be input from afar, processed in a remote area, stored in several different locations, and output in yet other places. However, you don't need communications ability to write letters, do calculations, or perform many other computer tasks.

These five operations are summarized in the illustration on the facing page. (● *See Panel 1.7.*)

Pretending to Order (or Build) a Custom-Built Desktop Computer: Basic Knowledge of How a Computer Works

In what order would components be put together to build a custom desktop computer?

Now let's see how you would order a custom-built desktop PC, or even build one yourself. Remember, the purpose of this is to help you understand the internal workings of a computer so that you'll be knowledgeable about using one and buying one. (If you were going to build it yourself, you would pretend that someone had acquired the PC components for you from a catalog company and that you're now sitting at a table about to begin assembling them. All you would need is a combination Phillips/flathead screwdriver, perhaps a small wrench, and a static-electricity-arresting strap for your wrist, to keep static electricity from adversely affecting some computer components. You would also need the manuals that come with some of the components.) Although prices of components are always subject to change, we have indicated general ranges of prices for basic equipment current as of 2009 so that you can get a sense of the relative importance of the various parts. ("Loaded" components—the most powerful and sophisticated equipment—cost more than the prices given here.)

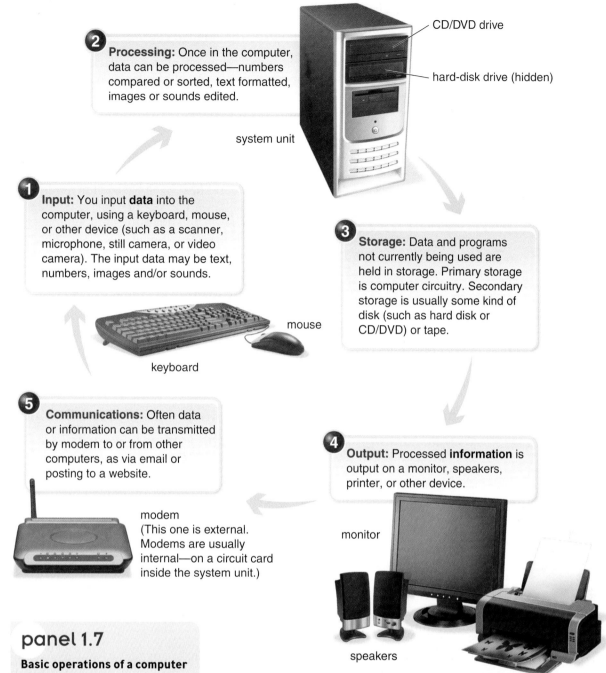

Processing: Once in the computer, data can be processed—numbers compared or sorted, text formatted, images or sounds edited.

CD/DVD drive

hard-disk drive (hidden)

system unit

1 Input: You input **data** into the computer, using a keyboard, mouse, or other device (such as a scanner, microphone, still camera, or video camera). The input data may be text, numbers, images and/or sounds.

keyboard

mouse

3 Storage: Data and programs not currently being used are held in storage. Primary storage is computer circuitry. Secondary storage is usually some kind of disk (such as hard disk or CD/DVD) or tape.

5 Communications: Often data or information can be transmitted by modem to or from other computers, as via email or posting to a website.

modem
(This one is external. Modems are usually internal—on a circuit card inside the system unit.)

4 Output: Processed **information** is output on a monitor, speakers, printer, or other device.

monitor

speakers

printer

panel 1.7

Basic operations of a computer

Note: All the system components you or anyone else chooses *must be compatible*—in other words, each brand must work with other brands. If you work with one company—such as Dell, or Hewlett-Packard—to customize your system, you won't have to worry about compatibility. If you choose all the components yourself—for example, by going to a computer-parts seller such as ComputerGeeks.com (*www.geeks.com*)—you will have to check on compatibility as you choose each component. And you'll have to make sure each component comes with any necessary cables, instructions, and component-specific software (called a *driver*) that makes the component run.

This section of the chapter gives you a brief overview of the components, which are all covered in detail in Chapters 2–6. We describe them in the following order: (1) input hardware—keyboard and mouse; (2) processing and memory hardware; (3) storage hardware—disk drives; (4) output hardware—video and sound cards, monitor, speakers, and printer; (5) communication hardware—the modem; and (6) software—system and application.

Input Hardware: Keyboard & Mouse

What do the two principal input devices, keyboard and mouse, do?

Input hardware consists of devices that allow people to put data into the computer in a form that the computer can use. At minimum, you will need two things: a *keyboard* and a *mouse.*

KEYBOARD (Cost: $5–$100) On a microcomputer, a keyboard is the primary input device. **A _keyboard_ is an input device that converts letters, numbers, and other characters into electrical signals readable by the processor.**

A microcomputer keyboard looks like a typewriter keyboard, but besides having keys for letters and numbers it has several keys (such as *F* keys and *Ctrl, Alt,* and *Del* keys) intended for computer-specific tasks. After other components are assembled, the keyboard will be plugged into the back of the computer in a socket intended for that purpose. (Cordless keyboards work differently.)

Keyboard

MOUSE ($5–$50) **A _mouse_ is a nonkeyboard input device ("pointing device") that is used to manipulate objects viewed on the computer display screen.** The mouse cord is plugged into the back of the computer or into the back of the keyboard after the other components are assembled. (Cordless mice are also available.)

Mouse

Processing & Memory Hardware: Inside the System Cabinet

How do I distinguish the processing and memory devices in a computer? What does the motherboard do?

The brains of the computer are the *processing* and *memory* devices, which are installed in the case or system cabinet.

CASE & POWER SUPPLY (about $10–$200) **Also known as the *system unit*, the _case_ or *system cabinet* is the box that houses the processor chip (CPU), the memory chips, and the motherboard with power supply, as well as some secondary-storage devices**—floppy-disk drive (if any), hard-disk drive, and CD or DVD drive, as we will explain. The case generally comes in desktop or tower models. It includes a power supply unit and a fan to keep the circuitry from overheating.

Case

PROCESSOR CHIP ($20–$1,000 or more) It may be small and not look like much, but it could be the most expensive hardware component of a build-it-yourself PC—and doubtless the most important. **A _processor chip (CPU, for central processing unit)_ is a tiny piece of silicon that contains millions of miniature electronic circuits.** The speed at which a chip processes information is expressed in *megahertz (MHz),* millions of processing cycles per second, or *gigahertz (GHz),* billions of processing cycles per second. The faster the processor, the more expensive it is. For $50, you might get a 2-GHz chip, which is adequate for most student purposes. For $100, you might get a 3-GHz chip, which you would want if you're running software with spectacular graphics and sound, such as those with some new videogames. Only older processors' speed is measured in megahertz now, but if you want a cheap processor—for instance, because you plan to work only with text documents—you could get a 233-MHz processor for about $40.

Processor chip

MEMORY CHIPS ($20–$600) These chips are also small. _**Memory chips,**_ **also known as** _**RAM (random access memory) chips,**_ **represent** _primary_ **storage, or temporary storage; they hold data before processing and information after processing, before it is sent along to an output or storage device.** You'll want enough memory chips to hold at least 1 gigabyte, or roughly 1 billion characters, of data, which is adequate for most student purposes. If you work with large graphics files, you'll need more memory capacity, perhaps 2 gigabytes or more. (We will explain the numbers used to measure storage capacities in a moment.)

Memory chip
(RAM chip)

Memory chips mounted
on module

(Memory chip)

MOTHERBOARD (about $45–$500) **Also called the** _system board,_ **the** _**motherboard**_ **is the main circuit board in the computer.** This is the big green circuit board to which everything else—such as the keyboard, mouse, and printer—attaches through connections (called _ports_) in the back of the computer. The processor chip and memory chips are also installed on the motherboard.

The motherboard has _**expansion slots**_—**for expanding the PC's capabilities—which give you places to plug in additional circuit boards,** such as those for video, sound, and communications (modem). (● _See Panel 1.8._)

panel 1.8

Putting the components together

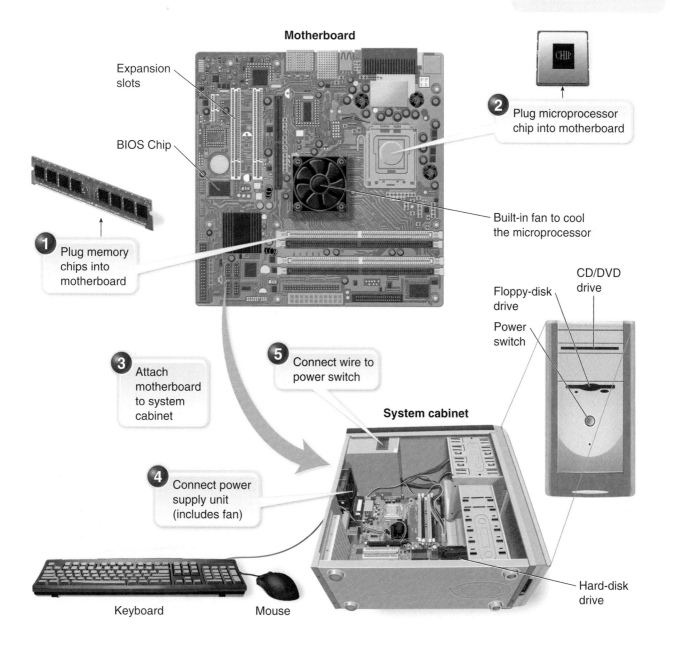

Motherboard

Expansion slots

BIOS Chip

1 Plug memory chips into motherboard

2 Plug microprocessor chip into motherboard

Built-in fan to cool the microprocessor

3 Attach motherboard to system cabinet

5 Connect wire to power switch

4 Connect power supply unit (includes fan)

System cabinet

CD/DVD drive

Floppy-disk drive

Power switch

Hard-disk drive

Keyboard   Mouse

PUTTING THE COMPONENTS TOGETHER Now the components can be put together. As the illustration on the previous page shows, ❶ the memory chips are plugged into the motherboard. Then ❷ the processor chip is plugged into the motherboard. Now ❸ the motherboard is attached to the system cabinet. Then ❹ the power supply unit is connected to the system cabinet. Finally, ❺ the wire for the power switch, which turns the computer on and off, is connected to the motherboard.

Storage Hardware: Hard Drive & CD/DVD Drive

What kind of storage devices would I as a student probably want in my computer?

With the motherboard in the system cabinet, the next step is installation of the storage hardware. Whereas memory chips deal only with temporary storage, *secondary storage,* or *permanent storage,* stores your data for as long as you want.

For today's student purposes, you'll need a hard drive and a CD/DVD drive, and in older systems (called *legacy systems*), you might have a floppy disk drive. These storage devices slide into the system cabinet from the front and are secured with screws. Each drive is attached to the motherboard by a flat cable (called a *ribbon cable*). Also, each drive must be hooked up to a plug extending from the power supply.

A computer system's data/information storage capacity is represented by bytes, kilobytes, megabytes, gigabytes, terabytes, and petabytes, as follows:

1 byte	*= 1 character of data* (A character can be alphabetic—A, B, or C—or numeric—1, 2, or 3—or a special character—!, ?, *, $, %.)
1 kilobyte	*= 1,024 characters*
1 megabyte	*= 1,048,576 characters*
1 gigabyte	*= more than 1 billion characters*
1 terabyte	*= more than 1 trillion characters*
1 petabye	*= about 1 quadrillion characters*

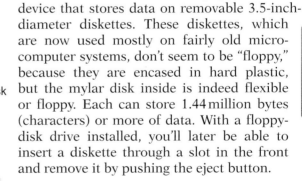

Floppy disk

Floppy disk drive

FLOPPY-DISK DRIVE ($25) A *floppy-disk drive* is a storage device that stores data on removable 3.5-inch-diameter diskettes. These diskettes, which are now used mostly on fairly old micro-computer systems, don't seem to be "floppy," because they are encased in hard plastic, but the mylar disk inside is indeed flexible or floppy. Each can store 1.44 million bytes (characters) or more of data. With a floppy-disk drive installed, you'll later be able to insert a diskette through a slot in the front and remove it by pushing the eject button.

Floppy disk

HARD-DISK DRIVE ($35–$200, depending on storage capacity) A ***hard-disk drive*** **is a storage device that stores billions of characters of data on a nonremovable disk platter.** With 120–200 gigabytes of storage (about $40), you should be able to handle most student needs. (Some hard-disk drives store up to 2 terabytes of data.)

Hard-disk drive (goes inside the computer case)

CD/DVD DRIVE ($30–$180) **A _CD (compact-disk) drive_, or its more recent variant, a _DVD (digital video-disk) drive_, is a storage device that uses laser technology to read data from optical disks.** (Some companies call a DVD a "digital versatile disk.") Today new software is generally supplied on CDs or via the net.

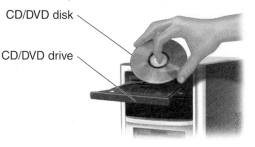

CD/DVD disk

CD/DVD drive

The system cabinet has lights on the front that indicate when these drives are in use. (You must not remove a disk from the drive until its light goes off, or else you risk damage to both disk and drive.) The wires for these lights need to be attached to the motherboard.

Output Hardware: Video & Sound Cards, Monitor, Speakers, & Printer

What kinds of output hardware are standard with a PC?

Output hardware consists of devices that translate information processed by the computer into a form that humans can understand—print, sound, graphics, or video, for example. Now a video card and a sound card need to be installed in the system cabinet. Next the monitor, speakers, and a printer are plugged in.

This is a good place to introduce the term *peripheral device*. **A _peripheral device_ is any component or piece of equipment that expands a computer's input, storage, and output capabilities.** In other words, a peripheral device is not part of the essential computer. Peripheral devices can be inside the computer or connected to it from the outside. Examples include printers and disk drives.

VIDEO CARD ($30–$1,400) You doubtless want your monitor to display color (rather than just black-and-white) images. Your system cabinet will therefore need to have a device to make this possible. **A _video card_ converts the processor's output information into a video signal that can be sent through a cable to the monitor.** Remember the expansion slots we mentioned? Your video card is plugged into one of these on the motherboard. (You can also buy a motherboard with built-in video.)

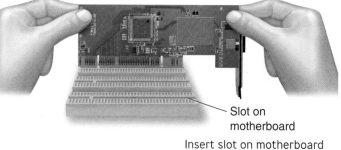

Slot on motherboard

Insert slot on motherboard

SOUND CARD ($15–$300 and higher) You may wish to listen to music on your PC. If so, you'll need a _sound card_, **which enhances the computer's sound-generating capabilities by allowing sound to be output through speakers.** This, too, would be plugged into an expansion slot on the motherboard. (Once again, you can buy a motherboard with built-in sound.) With the CD drive connected to the card, you can listen to music CDs.

MONITOR ($150–$300 or higher for a 17-inch model or a 19-inch model; $300–$1,200 or more for larger displays) As with television sets, the inch dimension on monitors is measured diagonally corner to corner. **The _monitor_ is the display device that takes the electrical signals from the video card and forms an image using points of colored light on the screen.** Later, after the system cabinet has been closed up, the monitor will be connected by means of a cable to the back of the computer, using the clearly marked connector. The power cord for the monitor will be plugged into a wall plug.

Monitor

Speakers

Printer

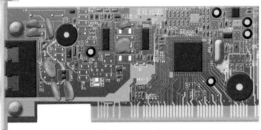

Modem card

System software—a version of Microsoft Vista

System software—a version of Microsoft 7

PAIR OF SPEAKERS ($25–$250) _**Speakers**_ **are the devices that play sounds transmitted as electrical signals from the sound card.** They may not be very sophisticated, but unless you're into high-fidelity recordings they're probably good enough. The two speakers are connected to a single wire that is plugged into the back of the computer once installation is completed.

PRINTER ($50–$1,000) Especially for student work, you certainly need a _**printer**_, **an output device that produces text and graphics on paper.** There are various types of printers, as we discuss later. The printer has two connections. One, which relays signals from the computer, goes to the back of the PC, where it connects with the motherboard. The other is a power cord that goes to a wall plug. Color printers are more expensive than black-and-white printers, and fast printers cost more than slow ones.

Communications Hardware: Modem

How is a modem installed?

Computers can be stand-alone machines, unconnected to anything else. If all you're doing is word processing to write term papers, you can do it with a stand-alone system. As we have seen, however, the communications component of the computer system vastly extends the range of a PC. Thus, while the system cabinet is still open, there is one more piece of hardware to install.

MODEM ($10–$100) **A standard** _**modem**_ **is a device that sends and receives data over telephone lines to and from computers.** The modem is mounted on an expansion card, which is fitted into an expansion slot on the motherboard. Later you can run a telephone line from the telephone wall plug to the back of the PC, where it will connect to the modem.

Other types of communications connections exist, which we cover in Chapters 2 and 6. However, standard modems are still often used.

Now the system cabinet is closed up. The person building the system will plug in all the input and output devices and turn on the power "on" button. Your microcomputer system will look similar to the one opposite. (● *See Panel 1.9.*) Are you now ready to roll? Not quite.

Software

In what order are the two kinds of software installed?

With all the pieces put together, the person assembling the computer (you, if you're building it yourself) needs to check the motherboard manual for instructions on starting the system. One of the most important tasks is to install software, the electronically encoded instructions that tell the computer hardware what to do. Software is what makes the computer worthwhile. There are two types—*system software* and *application software*.

SYSTEM SOFTWARE First, system software must be installed. _**System software**_ **helps the computer perform essential operating tasks and enables the application software to run.** System software consists of several electronically coded programs. The most important is the *operating system,* the master control program that runs the computer. Examples of operating system software for the PC are various Microsoft programs (such as Windows 95, 98, XP, Vista, and 7), Unix, and Linux. The Apple Macintosh microcomputer is another matter altogether. As we explain in Chapter 3, it has its own hardware components and software, which often aren't directly transferable to the PC.

System software comes most often on CDs. The person building your computer system will insert these into your CD drive and follow the on-screen

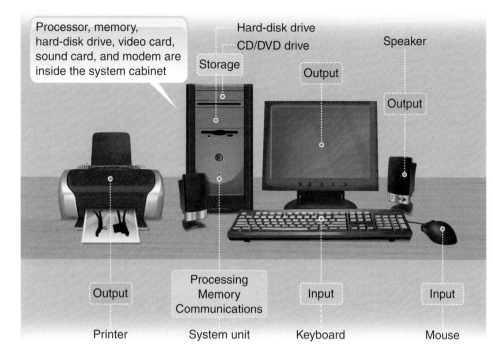

Processor, memory, hard-disk drive, video card, sound card, and modem are inside the system cabinet

Hard-disk drive
CD/DVD drive
Storage

Speaker

Output

Output

Output

Processing
Memory
Communications

Input

Input

Printer

System unit

Keyboard

Mouse

directions for installation. (*Installation* is the process of copying software programs from secondary-storage media—CDs, for example—onto your system's hard disk, so that you can have direct access to your hardware.)

After the system software is installed, setup software for the hard drive, the video and sound cards, and the modem must be installed. These setup programs (*drivers,* discussed in Chapter 3) will probably come on CDs. Once again, the installer inserts these into the appropriate drive and then follows the instructions that appear on the screen.

APPLICATION SOFTWARE Now we're finally getting somewhere! After the application software has been installed, you can start using the PC. ***Application software* enables you to perform specific tasks—solve problems, perform work, or entertain yourself.** For example, when you prepare a term paper on your computer, you will use a word processing program. (Microsoft Word and Corel WordPerfect are two brands.) Application software is specific to the system software you use. If you want to run Microsoft Word, for instance, you'll need to first have Microsoft Windows system software on your system, not Unix or Linux.

Application software comes on CDs packaged in boxes that include instructions. You insert the CDs into your computer and then follow the instructions on the screen for installation. Later on you may obtain entire application programs by getting (downloading) them off the internet, using your modem or another type of communications connection.

We discuss software in more detail in Chapter 3.

Is Getting a Custom-Built PC Worth the Effort?

Why might I want to build a PC myself—and why not?

Does the foregoing description make you want to try putting together a PC yourself? If you add up the costs of all the components (not to mention the value of your time), and then start checking ads for PCs, you might wonder why anyone would bother going to the trouble of building one. And nowadays you would probably be right. "If you think you'd save money by putting together a computer from scratch," says David Einstein, "think again. You'd be lucky to match the price PC-makers are charging these days in their zeal to undercut the competition."[64]

Application software for rendering art

Application software for photo manipulation

But had you done this for real, it would not have been a wasted exercise: by knowing how to build a system yourself, not only would you be able to impress your friends but you'd also know how to upgrade any store-bought system to include components that are better than standard. For instance, as Einstein points out, if you're into videogames, knowing how to construct your own PC would enable you to make a system that's right for games. You could include the latest three-dimensional graphics video card and a state-of-the-art sound card, for example. More important, you'd also know how to order a custom-built system (as from Dell, Hewlett-Packard, Lenovo, or Gateway, some of the online computer makers) that's right for you. In Chapters 4 and 5, we'll expand on this discussion so that you can really know what you're doing when you go shopping for a microcomputer system.

1.6 Where Is Information Technology Headed?

What are three directions of computer development and three directions of communications development?

How far we have come. At the beginning of the 20th century, most people thought they would live the same life their parents did. Today most people aren't surprised by the prediction that the Information Age will probably transform their lives beyond recognition. Let's consider the trends in the development of computers and communications and, most exciting, the area where they intersect.

Three Directions of Computer Development: Miniaturization, Speed, & Affordability

What are the three ways computers have developed?

Since the days of ENIAC, computers have developed in three directions—and are continuing to do so.

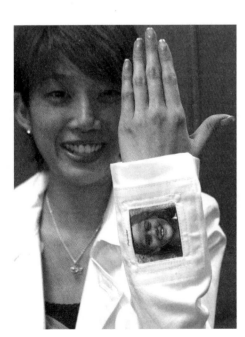

Miniaturization A woman tries on a prototype of a wearable computer, a jacket with a built-in display in its sleeve. This type of computer, from Pioneer, is expected to aid medical workers, firefighters, and farm workers.

MINIATURIZATION Everything has become smaller. ENIAC's old-fashioned radio-style vacuum tubes gave way after 1947 to the smaller, faster, more reliable transistor. A *transistor* is a small device used as a gateway to transfer electrical signals along predetermined paths (circuits).

The next step was the development of tiny *integrated circuits*. Integrated circuits are entire collections of electrical circuits or pathways that are now etched on tiny squares (chips) of silicon half the size of your thumbnail. *Silicon* is a natural element found in sand. In pure form, it is the base material for computer processing devices.

The miniaturized processor, or microprocessor, in a personal desktop computer today can perform calculations that once required a computer filling an entire room.

SPEED Thanks to miniaturization and new material used in making processors, computer makers can cram more hardware components into their machines, providing faster processing speeds and more data storage capacity.

AFFORDABILITY Processor costs today are only a fraction of what they were 15 years ago. A state-of-the-art processor costing less than $1,000 provides the same processing power as a huge 1980s computer costing more than $1 million.

These are the three major trends in computers. What about communications?

Three Directions of Communications Development: Connectivity, Interactivity, & Multimedia

What are three things I do that represent these three features—connectivity, interactivity, and multimedia?

Once upon a time, we had the voice telephone system—a one-to-one medium. You could talk to your Uncle Joe and he could talk to you, and with special arrangements (conference calls) more than two people could talk with one another. We also had radio and television systems—one-to-many media (or mass media). News announcers could talk to you on a single medium such as television, but you couldn't talk to them.

There have been three recent developments in communications:

CONNECTIVITY **_Connectivity_ refers to the connection of computers to one another by a communications line in order to provide online information access and/or the sharing of peripheral devices.** The connectivity resulting from the expansion of computer networks has made possible email and online shopping, for example.

INTERACTIVITY **_Interactivity_ refers to two-way communication; the user can respond to information he or she receives and modify what a computer is doing.** That is, there is an exchange or dialogue between the user and the computer, and the computer responds to user requests. A noninteractive program, once started, continues without requiring human contact, or interaction. The ability to interact means users can be active rather than passive participants in the technological process. On the television networks MSNBC or CNN, for example, you can immediately go on the internet and respond to news from broadcast anchors. Today, most application software is interactive. In the future, cars may respond to voice commands or feature computers built into the dashboard.

MULTIMEDIA Radio is a single-dimensional medium (sound), as is most email (mainly text). As mentioned earlier in this chapter, **_multimedia_ refers to technology that presents information in more than one medium—such as text, pictures, video, sound, and animation—in a single integrated communication.** The development of the World Wide Web expanded the internet to include pictures, sound, music, and so on, as well as text.

Interactivity A dashboard computer allows drivers to request information about the car's operation, location, and nearby services.

Exciting as these developments are, truly mind-boggling possibilities have emerged as computers and communications have cross-pollinated.

When Computers & Communications Combine: Convergence, Portability, Personalization, Collaboration, & Cloud Computing

What are five developments growing out of the fusion of computers and communications?

Sometime in the 1990s, computers and communications started to fuse together, beginning a new era within the Information Age. The result has been five additional developments.

CONVERGENCE *Convergence* describes the combining of several industries through various devices that exchange data in the format used by computers.

According to inventor and futurist Raymond Kuzweil, technological change will become so rapid and so profound that human bodies and brains will merge with machines.

The industries are computers, communications, consumer electronics, entertainment, and mass media. Convergence has led to electronic products that perform multiple functions, such as TVs with internet access, cellphones that are also digital cameras, and a refrigerator that allows you to send email.

PORTABILITY In the 1980s, portability, or mobility, meant trading off computing power and convenience in return for smaller size and weight. Today, however, we are close to the point where we don't have to give up anything. As a result, experts have predicted that small, powerful, wireless personal electronic devices will transform our lives far more than the personal computer has done so far. "The new generation of machines will be truly personal computers, designed for our mobile lives," wrote one journalist back in 1992. "We will read office memos between strokes on the golf course and answer messages from our children in the middle of business meetings."[65] Today such activities are commonplace, and smartphones are taking on other functions. The risk they bring is that, unless we're careful, work will completely invade our personal time.[66]

PERSONALIZATION Personalization is the creation of information tailored to your preferences—for instance, programs that will automatically cull recent news and information from the internet on just those topics you have designated. Companies involved in e-commerce can send you messages about forthcoming products based on your pattern of purchases, usage, and other criteria. Or they will build products (cars, computers, clothing) customized to your heart's desire.

COLLABORATION A more recent trend is mass collaboration. Says *New York Times* technology writer John Markoff, "A remarkable array of software systems makes it simple to share anything instantly, and sometimes enhance it along the way."[67] *BusinessWeek* writer Robert Hof observes that the huge numbers of people "online worldwide—along with their shared knowledge, social contacts, online reputations, computing power, and more—are rapidly becoming a collective force of unprecedented power."[68] Examples are file-sharing, photo-sharing websites, calendar-sharing services, group-edited sites called *wikis,* social networking services, and so-called citizen-journalism sites, in which average people write their own news items on the internet and comment on what other people post—an interactive, democratic form of mass media.[69] Pooled ratings, for instance, enable people to create personalized net music radio stations or Amazon.com's millions of customer-generated product reviews.

CLOUD COMPUTING: THE GLOBAL COMPUTER Not everyone agrees on exactly what "cloud computing" means.[70] Previously called *on-demand computing, grid computing,* or *software as a service,* **cloud computing basically means that, instead of storing your software or data on your own PC or your own company's computers, you store it on servers on the internet.** You don't care where the servers are located; they're out there somewhere—"in the cloud." The idea here is that companies could tap into computers as they are needed, just as they do now with the electric power grid, splitting their computing workload between data centers in different parts of the world. The hope of technology people is that companies will find cloud computing cheaper and more reliable than managing their own PCs, servers, and software.[71] (In a later chapter, we discuss an even more involved concept known as *the singularity.*)

Illuminated plastic balls meant to represent cloud computing go up and down on metal cables at the IBM stand at the CeBIT technology trade fair two days ahead of the fair's opening on March I, 2009, in Hanover, Germany. CeBIT is the world's largest computer and IT trade fair.

"E" Also Stands for Ethics

What are the principal ethical concerns I should be conscious of in the use of information technology?

Every computer user will have to wrestle with ethical issues related to the use of information technology. ___Ethics___ **is defined as a set of moral values or principles that govern the conduct of an individual or a group.** Because ethical questions arise so often in connection with information technology, we will note them, wherever they appear in this book, with the symbol shown at left. Below, for example, are some important ethical concerns pointed out by Tom Forester and Perry Morrison in their book *Computer Ethics*.[72] These considerations are only a few of many; we'll discuss others in subsequent chapters.

SPEED & SCALE Great amounts of information can be stored, retrieved, and transmitted at a speed and on a scale not possible before. Despite the benefits, this has serious implications "for data security and personal privacy," as well as employment, Forester and Morrison say, because information technology can never be considered totally secure against unauthorized access.

UNPREDICTABILITY Computers and communications are pervasive, touching nearly every aspect of our lives. However, at this point, compared to other pervasive technologies—such as electricity, television, and automobiles—information technology seems a lot less predictable and reliable.

COMPLEXITY Computer systems are often incredibly complex—some so complex that they are not always understood even by their creators. "This," say Forester and Morrison, "often makes them completely unmanageable," producing massive foul-ups or spectacularly out-of-control costs.

Ethics and security can often be talked about in the same breath, since secure computer systems obviously go a long way toward keeping people ethical and honest. When we discuss security, you will see this icon:

SECURITY

Survival Tip

Recycling Old PCs

Just got a new computer? Where to donate your old one? Check with schools, after-school programs, churches, and the following websites:
wwwl.us.dell.com/content/ topics/segtopic.aspx/dell_ recycling?c=us&cs=I9& l=en&s=dhs
www.crc.org
www.youthfortechnology.org/ frames.html
http://earth9ll.org/recycling/ computer-recycling-reuse/
www.epa.gov/epaoswer/ hazwaste/recycle/ecycling/ donate.htm
www.recycles.org/
http://wwl.pcdisposal. com/?gclid=COmh6b S75oCFRYiagodNwOFCA
www.computerhope.com/ disposal.htm

EXPERIENCE BOX

Better Organization & Time Management: Dealing with the Information Deluge in College— & in Life

An Experience Box appears at the end of each chapter. Each box offers you the opportunity to acquire useful experience that directly applies to the Digital Age. This first box illustrates skills that will benefit you in college, in this course and others. (Students reading the first eight editions of our book have told us they received substantial benefit from these suggestions.)

"How on earth am I going to be able to keep up with what's required of me?" you may ask yourself. "How am I going to handle the information glut?" The answer is: *by learning how to learn.* By building your skills as a learner, you certainly help yourself do better in college, and you also train yourself to be an information manager in the future.

Using Your "Prime Study Time"

Each of us has a different energy cycle. The trick is to use it effectively. That way, your hours of best performance will coincide with your heaviest academic demands. For example, if your energy level is high during the evenings, you should plan to do your studying then.

To capitalize on your prime study time, take the following steps: (1) Make a study schedule for the entire term, and indicate the times each day during which you plan to study. (2) Find some good places to study—places where you can avoid distractions. (3) Avoid time wasters, but give yourself frequent rewards for studying, such as a TV show, a favorite piece of music, or a conversation with a friend.

Learning to Focus

Multitasking is shifting focus from one task to another in rapid succession. When you read this textbook while listening to music and watching TV, you may think you're simultaneously doing three separate tasks, but you're really not. "It's like playing tennis with three balls," says one expert.[73] Today multitasking is easy and focus is hard because of all the things demanding our attention—phone calls, email, text messages, music, radio, TV, Twitter, MySpace, Facebook, various blogs and websites. "You can drive yourself crazy trying to multitask and answer every email message instantly," says one writer. "Or you can recognize your brain's finite capacity for processing information."[74]

Here are some tips on learning to concentrate:[75]

Choose What to Focus On. "People don't realize that attention is a finite resource, like money," one expert says. "Do you want to invest your cognitive cash on endless Twittering or Net surfing or couch potatoing [watching TV]?" She adds, "Where did the idea come

from that anyone who wants to contact you can do so at any time? You need to take charge of what you pay attention to instead of responding to the latest stimuli."[76] For example, to block out noise, you can wear earplugs while reading.

Devote the First 1½ Hours of Your Day to Your Most Important Task. Writing a paper? Studying a hard subject? Make it your first task of the day, and concentrate on it for 90 minutes. After that, your brain will probably need a rest, and you can answer email, return phone calls, and so on. But until that first break, don't do anything else, because it can take the brain 20 minutes to refocus.

Improving Your Memory Ability

Memorizing is, of course, one of the principal requirements for succeeding in college. And it's a great help for success in life afterward. Some suggestions:

Space Your Studying, Rather than Cramming. Cramming—making a frantic, last-minute attempt to memorize massive amounts of material—is probably the least effective means of absorbing information. Research shows that it's best to space out your studying of a subject over successive days. A series of study sessions over several days is preferable to trying to do it all during the same number of hours on one day. It is *repetition* that helps move information into your long-term memory bank.

Review Information Repeatedly—Even "Overlearn" It. By repeatedly reviewing information—known as "rehearsing"—you can improve both your retention and your understanding of it. Overlearning is continuing to review material even after you appear to have absorbed it.

Use Memorizing Tricks. There are several ways to organize information so that you can retain it better. For example, you can make drawings or diagrams (as of the parts of a computer system). Some methods of establishing associations between items you want to remember are given opposite. (● *See Panel 1.10.*)

How to Improve Your Reading Ability: The SQ3R Method

SQ3R stands for "survey, question, read, recite, and review."[77] The strategy behind the method is to break down a reading assignment into small segments and master each before moving on. The five steps of the SQ3R method are as follows:

- **Mental and physical imagery:** Use your visual and other senses to construct a personal image of what you want to remember. Indeed, it helps to make the image humorous, action-filled, or outrageous in order to establish a personal connection. Example: To remember the name of the 21st president of the United States, Chester Arthur, you might visualize an author writing the number "21" on a wooden chest. This mental image helps you associate chest (Chester), author (Arthur), and 21 (21st president).

- **Acronyms and acrostics:** An acronym is a word created from the first letters of items in a list. For instance, *Roy G. Biv* helps you remember the colors of the rainbow in order: red, orange, yellow, green, blue, indigo, violet. An acrostic is a phrase or sentence created from the first letters of items on a list. For example, *Every Good Boy Does Fine* helps you remember that the order of musical notes on the treble staff is *E-G-B-D-F*.

- **Location:** Location memory occurs when you associate a concept with a place or imaginary place. For example, you could learn the parts of a computer system by imagining a walk across campus. Each building you pass could be associated with a part of the computer system.

- **Word games:** Jingles and rhymes are devices frequently used by advertisers to get people to remember their products. You may recall the spelling rule "I before E except after C or when sounded like A as in *neighbor* or *weigh*." You can also use narrative methods, such as making up a story.

panel 1.10
Some memorizing tricks

1. *Survey the chapter before you read it:* Get an overview of the chapter before you begin reading it. If you have a sense of what the material is about before you begin reading it, you can predict where it is going. In this text, we offer on the first page of every chapter a list of the main heads and accompanying key questions. At the end of each chapter we offer a Summary, which recalls what the chapter's terms and concepts mean and why they are important.

2. *Question the segment in the chapter before you read it:* This step is easy to do, and the point, again, is to get you involved in the material. After surveying the entire chapter, go to the first segment—whether a whole section, a subsection, or even just paragraph, depending on the level of difficulty and density of information. Look at the topic heading of that segment (or first sentence of a very difficult paragraph). In your mind, restate the heading as a question. In this book, to help you do this, following each section head we present a Key Question. An example in this chapter was "What are three directions of computer development and three directions of communications development?"

After you have formulated the question, go to steps 3 and 4 (read and recite). Then proceed to the next segment of the chapter and restate the heading there as a question, and so on.

3. *Read the segment about which you asked the question:* When you read the segment you asked the question about, read with purpose, to answer the question you formulated. Underline or highlight sentences that you think are important, if they help you answer the question. Read this portion of the text more than

once, if necessary, until you can answer the question. In addition, determine whether the segment covers any other significant questions, and formulate answers to these, too. After you have read the segment, proceed to step 4. (Perhaps you can see where this is all leading. If you read in terms of questions and answers, you will be better prepared when you see exam questions about the material later.)

4. *Recite the main points of the segment:* Recite means "say aloud." Thus, you should speak out loud (or softly) the answer to the principal question or questions about the segment and any other main points.

5. *Review the entire chapter by repeating questions:* After you have read the chapter, go back through it and review the main points. Then, without looking at the book, test your memory by repeating the questions and answers you formulated.

Clearly the SQ3R method takes longer than simply reading with a rapidly moving color marker or underlining pencil. However, the technique is far more effective because it requires your involvement and understanding. These are the keys to all effective learning.

Learning from Lectures

Does attending lectures really make a difference? Research shows that students with grades of B or above were more apt to have better class attendance than students with grades of C- or below.[78]

Some tips for getting the most out of lectures:

Take Effective Notes by Listening Actively. Research shows that good test performance is related to good note taking.[79] And good note taking requires that you listen actively—that is, participate in the lecture process. Here are some ways to take good lecture notes:

- *Read ahead and anticipate the lecturer:* Try to anticipate what the instructor is going to say, based on your previous reading. Having background knowledge makes learning more efficient.
- *Listen for signal words:* Instructors use key phrases such as "The most important point is . . . ," "There are four reasons for . . . ," "The chief reason . . . ," "Of special importance . . . ," "Consequently . . ." When you hear such signal phrases, mark your notes with a ! or *.
- *Take notes in your own words:* Instead of just being a stenographer, try to restate the lecturer's thoughts in your own words, which will make you pay attention more.
- *Ask questions:* By asking questions during the lecture, you necessarily participate in it and increase your understanding.

Review Your Notes Regularly. Make it a point to review your notes regularly—perhaps on the afternoon after the lecture, or once or twice a week. We cannot emphasize enough the importance of this kind of reviewing.

application software (p. 33) Software that has been developed to solve a particular problem, perform useful work on general-purpose tasks, or provide entertainment. Why it's important: *Application software such as word processing, spreadsheet, database management, graphics, and communications packages are commonly used tools for increasing people's productivity.*

avatar (p. 6) Computer depiction of a human, often found in online videogames. Why it's important: *Avatars can be helpful in training, such as by representing imaginary customers.*

case (p. 28) Also known as the *system unit* or *system cabinet;* the box that houses the processor chip (CPU), the memory chips, and the motherboard with power supply, as well as storage devices—floppy-disk drive, hard-disk drive, and CD or DVD drive. Why it's important: *The case protects many important processing and storage components.*

CD (compact-disk) drive (p. 31) Storage device that uses laser technology to read data from optical disks. Why it's important: *New software is generally supplied on CDs rather than diskettes. And even if you can get a program on floppies, you'll find it easier to install a new program from one CD than to repeatedly insert and remove many diskettes. The newest version is called DVD (digital video disk). The DVD format stores even more data than the CD format.*

central processing unit (CPU) *See* **processor chip.**

chip *See* **processor chip.**

clients (p. 24) Computers and other devices connected to a server, a central computer. Why it's important: *Client/server networks are used in many organizations for sharing databases, devices, and programs.*

cloud computing (p. 36) Concept of storing your software and/or data not on your own PC or company's computers but rather on servers on the internet. Why it's important: *Users could tap into computers as they are needed, distributing computing workload among data centers in different parts of the world, perhaps making computing cheaper and more reliable.*

communications technology (p. 4) Also called *telecommunications technology;* consists of electromagnetic devices and systems for communicating over long distances. Why it's important: *Communications systems using electronic connections have helped to expand human communication beyond face-to-face meetings.*

computer (p. 4) Programmable, multiuse machine that accepts data—raw facts and figures—and processes (manipulates) it into useful information, such as summaries and totals. Why it's important: *Computers greatly speed up problem solving and other tasks, increasing users' productivity.*

computer savvy (p. 3) Knowing what computers can do and what they can't, knowing how they can benefit you and how they can harm you, and knowing when you can solve computer problems and when you have to call for help. Why it's important: *You will know how to make better buying decisions, how to fix ordinary computer problems, how to upgrade your equipment and integrate it with new products, how to use the internet most effectively, how to protect yourself against online villains, and what kinds of computer uses can advance your career.*

connectivity (p. 35) Ability to connect computers to one another by communications lines, so as to provide online information access and/or the sharing of peripheral devices. Why it's important: *Connectivity is the foundation of the advances in the Information Age. It provides online access to countless types of information and services. The connectivity resulting from the expansion of computer networks has made possible email and online shopping, for example.*

course-management software (p. 6) Software for administering online assignments, schedules, examinations, and grades. Why it's important: *It helps to make administrative "housekeeping" more efficient.*

cyberspace (p. 18) Term used to refer to not only the online world and the internet in particular but also the whole wired and wireless world of communications in general. Why it's important: *More and more human activities take place in cyberspace.*

data (p. 25) Raw facts and figures that are processed into information. Why it's important: *Users need data to create useful information.*

desktop PC (p. 23) Microcomputer unit that sits on a desk, with the keyboard in front and the monitor often on top. Why it's important: *Desktop PCs and tower PCs are the most commonly used types of microcomputer.*

distance learning (p. 6) Also known as *e-learning;* name given to online education programs. Why it's important: *Provides students increased flexibility because they do not have to be in an actual classroom.*

download (p. 9) To transfer data from a remote computer to one's own computer. Why it's important: *Allows text, music, and images to be transferred quickly by telecommunications.*

DVD (digital video-disk) drive *See* **CD drive.**

email (electronic mail) (p. 5) Messages transmitted over a computer network, most often the internet. Why it's important: *Email has become universal; one of the first things new computer users learn is how to send and receive email.*

ethics (p. 37) Set of moral values or principles that govern the conduct of an individual or a group. Why it's important: *Ethical questions arise often in connection with information technology.*

expansion slots (p. 29) Internal "plugs" used to expand the PC's capabilities. Why it's important: *Expansion slots give you places to plug in additional circuit boards, such as those for video, sound, and communications (modem).*

hard-disk drive (p. 30) Storage device that stores billions of characters of data on a nonremovable disk platter usually inside the computer case. Why it's important: *Hard disks hold much more data than diskettes do. Nearly all microcomputers use hard disks as their principal secondary-storage medium.*

hardware (p. 25) All machinery and equipment in a computer system. Why it's important: *Hardware runs under the control of software and is useless without it. However, hardware contains the circuitry that allows processing.*

information (p. 25) Data that has been summarized or otherwise manipulated for use in decision making. Why it's important: *The whole purpose of a computer (and communications) system is to produce (and transmit) usable information.*

information technology (IT) (p. 4) Technology that helps to produce, manipulate, store, communicate, and/or disseminate information. Why it's important: *Information technology is bringing about the fusion of several important industries dealing with computers, telephones, televisions, and various handheld devices.*

input (p. 26) Whatever is put in ("input") to a computer system. Input devices include the keyboard and the mouse. Why it's important: *Useful information cannot be produced without input data.*

interactivity (p. 35) Two-way communication; a user can respond to information he or she receives and modify the process. Why it's important: *Interactive devices allow the user to actively participate in a technological process instead of just reacting to it.*

internet (the "net") (p. 18) Worldwide computer network that connects hundreds of thousands of smaller networks linking computers at academic, scientific, and commercial institutions, as well as individuals. Why it's important: *Thanks to the internet, millions of people around the world can share all types of information and services.*

keyboard (p. 28) Input device that converts letters, numbers, and other characters into electrical signals readable by the processor. Why it's important: *Keyboards are the most common kind of input device.*

local area network (LAN) (p. 22) Network that connects, usually by special cable, a group of desktop PCs and other devices, such as printers, in an office or a building. Why it's important: *LANs have replaced mainframes for many functions and are considerably less expensive.*

mainframe (p. 22) Second-largest computer available, after the supercomputer; capable of great processing speeds and data storage. Costs $5,000–$5 million. Small mainframes are often called *midsize computers.* Why it's important: *Mainframes are used by large organizations (banks, airlines, insurance companies, universities) that need to process millions of transactions.*

memory chip (p. 29) Also known as *RAM* (for "random access memory") *chip;* represents primary storage or temporary storage. Why it's important: *Holds data before processing and information after processing, before it is sent along to an output or storage device.*

microcomputer (p. 22) Also called *personal computer;* small computer that fits on or next to a desk or can be carried around. Costs $500–$5,000. Why it's important: *The microcomputer has lessened the reliance on mainframes and has provided more ordinary users with access to computers. It can be used as a stand-alone machine or connected to a network.*

microcontroller (p. 23) Also called an *embedded computer;* the smallest category of computer. Why it's important: *Microcontrollers are the tiny, specialized microprocessors built into "smart" electronic devices, such as appliances and automobiles.*

micropayments (p. 9) Electronic payments of as little as 25 cents in transactions for which it is uneconomical to use a credit card. Why it's important: *Allows products to be sold that previously weren't worth the effort of merchandising.*

mobile internet device (MID) (p. 23) Fully internet integrated, handheld computer highly compatible with desktop microcomputers and laptops. The initial models focus on data communication, not voice communication. Why it's important: *Some mobile devices are too small to adequately view images on screen, but viewers still want more pocket-size portability than is possible with a laptop.*

modem (p. 32) Device that sends and receives data over telephone lines to and from computers. Why it's important: *A modem enables users to transmit data from one computer to another by using standard telephone lines instead of special communications equipment.*

monitor (p. 31) Display device that takes the electrical signals from the video card and forms an image using points of colored light on the screen. Why it's important: *Monitors enable users to view output without printing it out.*

motherboard (p. 29) Also called the *system board;* main circuit board in the computer. Why it's important: *This is the big green circuit board to which everything else—such as the keyboard, mouse, and printer—is attached. The processor chip and memory chips are also installed on the motherboard.*

mouse (p. 28) Nonkeyboard input device, called a "pointing device," used to manipulate objects viewed on the computer display screen. Why it's important: *For many purposes, a mouse is easier to use than a keyboard for inputting commands. Also, the mouse is used extensively in many graphics programs.*

multimedia (p. 35) From "multiple media"; technology that presents information in more than one medium—including text, graphics, animation, video, and sound—in a single integrated communication. Why it's important: *Multimedia is used increasingly in business, the professions, and education to improve the way information is communicated.*

nanotechnology (p. 22) Technology whereby molecule-size nanostructures are used to create tiny machines for holding data or performing tasks. Why it's important: *Could result in tremendous computer power in molecular-size devices.*

netbook (p. 23) Low-cost, lightweight computer with tiny dimensions and with functions designed for basic tasks, such as web searching, email, and word processing; weighs 2.25–3.2 pounds. Why it's important: *Cheaper computers that fill a technological category between notebooks and handheld devices.*

network (p. 5) Communications system connecting two or more computers. Why it's important: *Networks allow users to share applications and data and to use email. The internet is the largest network.*

notebook computer (p. 23) Also called *laptop computer;* lightweight portable computer with a built-in monitor, keyboard, hard-disk drive, battery, and adapter; weighs 1.8–9 pounds. Why it's important: *Notebook and other small computers have provided users with computing capabilities in the field and on the road.*

online (p. 4) Using a computer or some other information device, connected through a network, to access information and services from another computer or information device. Why it's important: *Online communication is widely used by businesses, services, individuals, and educational institutions.*

output (p. 26) Whatever is output from ("put out of") the computer system; the results of processing. Why it's important: *People use output to help them make decisions. Without output devices, computer users would not be able to view or use the results of processing.*

peripheral device (p. 31) Any component or piece of equipment that expands a computer's input, storage, and output capabilities. Examples include printers and disk drives. Why it's important: *Most computer input and output functions are performed by peripheral devices.*

personal digital assistant (PDA) (p. 23) Also known as *handheld computer* or *palmtop;* used as a schedule planner and address book and to prepare to-do lists and send email and faxes. Why it's important: *PDAs make it easier for people to do business and communicate while traveling.*

primary storage (p. 26) Also called *memory;* internal computer circuitry that temporarily holds data waiting to be processed. Why it's important: *By holding data, primary storage enables the processor to process.*

printer (p. 32) Output device that produces text and graphics on paper. Why it's important: *Printers provide one of the principal forms of computer output.*

processing (p. 26) The manipulation a computer does to transform data into information. Why it's important: *Processing is the essence of the computer, and the processor is the computer's "brain."*

processor chip (p. 28) Also called the *processor,* the *CPU (central processing unit),* or simply *chip;* tiny piece of silicon that contains millions of miniature electronic circuits used to process data. Why it's important: *Chips have made possible the development of small computers.*

robot (p. 7) Automatic device that performs functions ordinarily performed by human beings. Why it's important: *Robots help perform tasks that humans find difficult or impossible to do.*

secondary storage (p. 26) Also called *storage;* devices and media that store data and programs permanently—such as disks and disk drives, tape and tape drives, CDs and CD drives. Why it's important: *Without secondary storage, users would not be able to save their work. Storage also holds the computer's software.*

server (p. 24) Central computer in a network that holds collections of data (databases) and programs for connecting PCs, workstations, and other devices, which are called *clients.* Why it's important: *Servers enable many users to share equipment, programs, and data.*

software (p. 25) Also called *programs;* step-by-step electronically encoded instructions that tell the computer hardware how to perform a task. Why it's important: *Without software, hardware is useless.*

sound card (p. 31) Special circuit board that enhances the computer's sound-generating capabilities by allowing sound to be output through speakers. Why it's important: *Sound is used in multimedia applications. Also, many users like to listen to music CDs and MP3 files on their computers.*

speakers (p. 32) Devices that play sounds transmitted as electrical signals from the sound card. Speakers are connected to a single wire plugged into the back of the computer. Why it's important: *See* **sound card.**

supercomputer (p. 21) High-capacity computer with thousands of processors that is the fastest calculating device ever invented. Costs up to $350 million or more. Why it's important: *Supercomputers are used primarily for research purposes, airplane design, oil exploration, weather forecasting, and other activities that cannot be handled by mainframes and other less powerful machines.*

system software (p. 32) Software that helps the computer perform essential operating tasks. Why it's important: *Application software cannot run without system software. System software consists of several programs. The most important is the operating system, the master control program that runs the computer. Examples of operating system software for the PC are various Microsoft programs (such as Windows 95, 98, NT, Me, XP, and Vista), Unix, Linux, and the Macintosh operating system.*

system unit *See* **case.**

telemedicine (p. 6) Medical care delivered via telecommunications. Why it's important: *Allows physicians in remote areas to consult over a distance.*

terminal (p. 22) Input and output device that uses a keyboard for input and a monitor for output; it cannot process data. Why it's important: *Terminals are generally used to input data to and receive data from a mainframe computer system.*

tower PC (p. 23) Microcomputer unit that sits as a "tower," often on the floor, freeing up desk space. Why it's important: *Tower PCs and desktop PCs are the most commonly used types of microcomputer.*

video card (p. 31) Circuit board that converts the processor's output information into a video signal for transmission through a cable to the monitor. Why it's important: *Virtually all computer users need to be able to view video output on the monitor.*

virtual (p. 8) Something that is created, simulated, or carried on by means of a computer or a computer network. Why it's important: *Allows actual objects to be represented in computer-based form.*

workstation (p. 22) Smaller than a mainframe; expensive, powerful computer generally used for complex scientific, mathematical, and engineering calculations and for computer-aided design and computer-aided manufacturing. Why it's important: *The power of workstations is needed for specialized applications too large and complex to be handled by PCs.*

World Wide Web (the "web") (p. 18) The interconnected system of internet servers that support specially formatted documents in multimedia form—sounds, photos, and video as well as text. Why it's important: *The web is the most widely known part of the internet.*

CHAPTER REVIEW

More and more educators are favoring an approach to learning (presented by Benjamin Bloom and his colleagues in *Taxonomy of Educational Objectives)* that follows a hierarchy of six critical-thinking skills: (a) two lower-order skills—memorization and comprehension; and (b) four higher-order skills—application, analysis, synthesis, and evaluation. While you may be able to get through many introductory college courses by simply memorizing facts and comprehending the basic ideas, to advance further you will probably need to employ the four higher-order thinking skills.

In the Chapter Review at the end of each chapter, we have implemented this hierarchy in a three-stage approach, as follows:

- *Stage I learning—memorization:* "I can recognize and recall information." Self-test questions, multiple-choice questions, and true/false questions enable you to test how well you recall basic terms and concepts.

- *Stage 2 learning—comprehension:* "I can recall information in my own terms and explain it to a friend." Using open-ended short-answer questions, we ask you to reexpress terms and concepts in your own words.

- *Stage 3 learning—applying, analyzing, synthesizing, evaluating:* "I can apply what I've learned, relate these ideas to other concepts, build on other knowledge, and use all these thinking skills to form a judgment." In this part of the Chapter Review, we ask you to put the ideas into effect using the activities described, some of which include internet activities. The purpose is to help you take possession of the ideas, make them your own, and apply them realistically to your life.

 **LEARNING MEMORIZATION**

"I can recognize and recall information."

Self-Test Questions

I. The _____ _____ _____ refers to the part of the internet that presents information in multimedia form.

2. The two main types of microcomputers are the_____ _____, which sits on the desktop, and the _____ _____, which usually is placed on the floor.

3. "_____ technology" merges computing with high-speed communications.

4. A(n) _____ is an electronic machine that accepts data and processes it into information.

5. The _____ is a worldwide network that connects hundreds of thousands of smaller networks.

6. _____ refers to information presented in nontextual forms such as video, sound, and graphics.

7. _____ are high-capacity machines with thousands of processors.

8. Embedded computers, or _____, are installed in "smart" appliances and automobiles.

9. The kind of software that enables users to perform specific tasks is called _____ software.

I0. RAM is an example of _____ storage, and a hard drive is an example of _____ storage.

11. A(n) _____ is a communications system connecting two or more computers.

12. The four basic operations of all computers are _____, _____, _____, and _____.

13. The first programmable computer in the USA, which appeared in 1946, was called the _____.

14. The _____ is the display device that takes the electrical signals from the video card and forms an image using points of colored light on the screen.

15. The base material for computer processing devices is _____, a natural element found in sand.

16. The general term for all the machinery and equipment in a computer system is _____.

17. _____ and _____ are the two most common input devices.

18. The processor chip, commonly called the _____ or a _____, is a tiny piece of silicon that contains millions of miniature electronic circuits.

19. One gigabyte is approximately _____ characters.

Multiple-Choice Questions

1. Which of the following devices converts computer output into displayed images?
   a. printer
   b. monitor
   c. floppy-disk drive
   d. processor
   e. hard-disk drive

2. Which of the following computer types is the smallest?
   a. mainframe
   b. microcomputer
   c. microcontroller
   d. supercomputer
   e. workstation

3. Which of the following is a secondary-storage device?
   a. processor
   b. memory chip
   c. floppy-disk drive
   d. printer
   e. monitor

4. Since the days when computers were first made available, computers have developed in three directions. What are they?
   a. increased expense
   b. miniaturization
   c. increased size
   d. affordability
   e. increased speed

5. Which of the following operations constitute the four basic operations followed by all computers?
   a. input
   b. storage
   c. programming
   d. output
   e. processing

6. Supercomputers are used for
   a. breaking codes.
   b. simulations for explosions of nuclear bombs.
   c. forecasting weather.
   d. keeping planets in orbit.
   e. all of these
   f. only a, b, and c.

7. What is the leading use of computers?
   a. web surfing
   b. email
   c. e-shopping
   d. word processing

8. Which is the main circuit board in the computer?
   a. RAM chip (random access memory)
   b. CPU processor chip (central processing unit)
   c. motherboard (system board)
   d. hard drive

9. A terabyte is approximately
   a. one million characters.
   b. one billion characters.
   c. one trillion characters.
   d. one quadrillion characters.

10. Speakers are an example of
    a. an input device.
    b. an output device.
    c. a processor.
    d. a storage device.

True/False Questions

T F 1. Mainframe computers process faster than microcomputers.

T F 2. Main memory is a software component.

T F 3. The operating system is part of the system software.

T F 4. Processing is the manipulation by which a computer transforms data into information.

T F 5. Primary storage is the area in the computer where data or information is held permanently.

T F 6. The keyboard and the mouse are examples of input devices.

T F 7. Movies are a form of multimedia.

T F 8. Computers are becoming larger, slower, and more expensive.

T F 9. Modems store information.

T F 10. A microcomputer is used to view very small objects.

T F 11. A hard disk is an example of software.

T F 12. Computers continue to get smaller and smaller.

T F 13. Supercomputers are particularly inexpensive.

stage 2 LEARNING COMPREHENSION

"I can recall information in my own terms and explain it to a friend."

Short-Answer Questions

1. What does *online* mean?
2. What is the difference between system software and application software?
3. Briefly define *cyberspace.*
4. What is the difference between software and hardware?
5. What is a local area network?
6. What is multimedia?
7. What is the difference between microcomputers and supercomputers?

8. What is the function of RAM?
9. What does *downloading* mean?
10. What is meant by *connectivity?*
11. Describe some ways that information technology can be used to help people find jobs and to help jobs find people.
12. Compare the use of email to the use of the telephone and of conventional letters sent via the postal system. Which kinds of communications are best suited for which medium?
13. What is the basic meaning of *cloud computing?*

stage 3 LEARNING APPLYING, ANALYZING, SYNTHESIZING, EVALUATING

"I can apply what I've learned, relate these ideas to other concepts, build on other knowledge, and use all these thinking skills to form a judgment."

Knowledge in Action

1. Do you wish there was an invention to make your life easier or better? Describe it. What would it do for you? Come up with ideas on how that device may be constructed.

2. Determine what types of computers are being used where you work or go to school. In which departments are the different types of computer used? Make a list of the input devices, output devices, and storage devices. What are they used for? How are they connected to other computers?

3. Imagine a business you could start or run at home. What type of business is it? What type(s) of computer(s) do you think you'll need? Describe the computer system in as much detail as possible, including hardware components in the areas we have discussed so far. Keep your notes, and then refine your answers after you have completed the course.

4. Has reality become science fiction? Or has science fiction become science fact? First, watch an old futuristic movie, such as *2001—A Space Odyssey,* and take note of the then-futuristic technology displayed. Classify what you see according to input, output, processing, storage, and communications. Then watch a recent science fiction movie, and also list all the futuristic technology used according to the given categories. What was futuristic in the old movie that is now reality? What in the new movie is not yet reality but seems already feasible?

5. From what you've read and what you have experienced and/or observed in your life, do you have a positive, negative, or impartial view of our rapidly converging technological society? Why? Reevaluate your answers at the end of the course.

6. Computer prices are constantly falling. Whatever you pay for a computer today, you can be certain that you will be able to buy a more powerful computer for less money a year from now, and quite possibly even just a month from now. So how can you decide when it's a good time to upgrade to a better computer? Paradoxically, it seems that no matter how you time it, you'll always lose, because prices will go down again soon, and yet you will also always gain, because, since you were going to upgrade sooner or later anyway, you will reap the benefits of having the more powerful equipment that much longer.

    Discuss the benefits and costs, both material and psychological, of "waiting until prices drop." Gather more information on this topic by asking friends and colleagues what choices they have made about upgrading equipment over the years and whether they feel satisfaction or regret about the timing when they finally did upgrade.

7. Computers are almost everywhere, and they affect most walks of life—business, education, government, the military, hobbies, shopping, research, and so on. What aspects of your life can you think of that still seem relatively unaffected by computers and technology? Is this a good thing or a bad thing, and is it likely to last? What aspects of your life have been the most conspicuously affected by technology? Has anything been made worse or harder in your life by the advance of computers? What about things that have been made better or easier?

8. Have you become extremely dependent on some technologies? Some people no longer write down telephone numbers anywhere; instead, they simply program them into their cellphones. Some people feel helpless in a foreign country unless they have a calculator in hand to compute currency conversions. Many people rely on their email archive to hold essential information, such as addresses and appointments. When any of these technologies fails us, we can feel lost.

Make a list of technologies that have become indispensable to your life. Imagine the consequences if any of these technologies should fail you. What can you do to protect yourself against such failure?

9. It has been said that the computer is a "meta medium" because it can simulate (behave as) any other medium. Thus a computer can present text that can be read from virtual "pages" as if it were a book; it can let you compose and print text as if it were a typewriter; it can play music as if it were a boombox; it can display video as if it were a television set; it can make telephone calls as if it were a telephone; it can let you "draw" and "paint"; it can be programmed to serve as an answering machine; and so forth.

Imagine a future in which computers have replaced all the things they can emulate: instead of books and magazines and newspapers, we would have text only on computers. Telephones, PDAs, television sets, VCRs, DVD players, stereo sets, and other electronic devices would all be gone or, rather, subsumed by computers. What benefits to your life can you see in such a future? What things might be worse? What dangers can you see? Do you think this kind of radical convergence is likely? If so, how long do you think it will take?

Web Exercises

If you are not yet familiar with web surfing, wait until you have finished Chapter 2 to do the following web exercises.

1. Are computers, cellphones, and other electronic devices bad for our health? You may have heard the term *electromagnetic radiation* and dismissed it as an obscure scientific term not worth understanding. Visit the links below to become educated on a topic that will be discussed more seriously and frequently when our society becomes completely wireless.

   www.howstuffworks.com/cell-phone-radiation.htm

   www.fda.gov/cellphones/

   www.consumeraffairs.com/news04/2008/03/cells_danger.html

   http://skeptoid.com/episodes/4117

2. List some pros and cons of a "paperless" environment. Do you believe that a paperless environment is something worth striving for in the workplace? In the home? In the classroom? In banking? Run a web search to see what others are doing to implement this idea.

3. Computer pioneer John Von Neumann was one of a group of individuals who conceived the idea of the "stored program." He could also divide two 8-digit numbers in his head. Spend a few hours researching this

remarkable man; at online bookstores, look up some of the books he wrote and read the reviews.

4. Looking for legally free programs? Some great places to start:

   www.download.com

   www.shareware.com

   www.freewarefiles.com/

   www.freedownloadscenter.com/

5. Visit the following websites to become aware of some topics of interest in the computing world. Full comprehension of these topics isn't necessary at this time; this is only to familiarize you with subject matter you may come in contact with.

   www.zdnet.com/eweek

   www.computeruser.com/

   www.computermarket.com/news

   http://slashdot.org

6. "Moore's Law" predicts the rate at which computers will continue to get smaller (and hence faster). The "law" has proved to be astonishingly accurate over many years. Do a web search for Moore's Law, and see if you can find answers to the following questions:

   a. Who is Moore, and when did he make the prediction we know as Moore's Law?

   b. What is the simplest statement of the law's prediction?

   c. How has the law changed over time?

   d. How much longer is the law expected to hold true?

   e. How does the law affect business projections?

7. A Wiki is a website on which authoring and editing can be done very easily by anyone, anywhere, anytime using a web browser such as Internet Explorer or Netscape Navigator, with no need for special software or other special requirements. (*Wiki* is Hawaiian for "quick.") Most web pages are less than perfect. If it is a Wiki-page and you are annoyed by something, you can just hit the Edit button and change it! Over time, the site gets better (people hope)!

   Here are some examples of Wikis that deal with general knowledge:

   http://en.wikipedia.org

   www.wikimedia.org/

   http://wiki.ehow.com/Main-Page

   And here are some specialized Wikis:

   www.rawfoodwiki.org/index.php/Encyclopedia

   http://london-crafts.org/

   www.payrollwiki.com

   www.wikia.com/wiki/Wikia

   http://wikisineducation.wetpaint.com/

   a. Make a small change on a page on one of the listed sites or on some other Wiki site you have identified. Submit your change, and note the results. Anyone navigating to that site will now see your change. Did you know that website authoring could be that easy? Are you surprised that someone would unconditionally open up his or her website for anyone to edit?

b. Since you can make any change you wish, even something totally nonsensical or simply wrong, it's obviously possible for incorrect or misleading content to appear on a Wiki. Given that, why do you think that Wikis have become so popular and so widespread?

c. How significant a problem do you think vandalism and other acts of poor citizenship might be on "open" Wikis? How can you find out?

d. Some Wikis contend with the threat of vandalism by requiring that a password be provided before a user is allowed to make changes. What advantages can you see to this approach? What disadvantages? Do you think the advantages of password protection outweigh the disadvantages? What do the Wikis you browse through have to say about this issue?

e. What measures do you think an online shared space can take to limit the potential damage from vandalism, while not being overly restrictive?

f. If you knew that a particular person was defacing a Wiki, what would you do about it? Report the person? Wait for the vandal to get bored and turn his or her mischief elsewhere? Or try to reform the person? Are the basic ethical considerations here the same as those regarding other forms of vandalism in our society?

g. Do you think that open-access systems such as unrestricted Wikis will become more common over time, or do you think that abuse of such systems will destroy their usefulness and that Wikis will eventually disappear?

2

THE INTERNET &
the WORLD WIDE WEB
Exploring Cyberspace

Chapter Topics & Key Questions

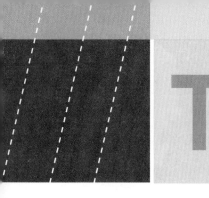

he immensity of the changes wrought—and still to come—cannot be underestimated," says futurist Graham Molitor. "This miraculous information channel—the internet—will touch and alter virtually every facet of humanity, business, and all the rest of civilization's trappings."[1]

Today the world of the internet permits activities hardly imaginable a dozen years ago. (● *See Panel 2.1.*) Indeed, pervasive computing, ubiquitous computing, is already an established fact, with "everything connected to everything," from cellphones to cameras to car navigation systems. Because of its standard interfaces and low rates, the internet has been the great leveler for communications—just as the personal computer was for computing.

The basis for the internet began in 1969 as ARPANET (for ARPA, the Advanced Research Projects Agency of the U.S. Department of Defense), with four linked-together computers at different universities and defense contractors. From there the network expanded to 62 computers in 1974, 500 computers in 1983, and 28,000 in 1987. However, it still remained the domain of researchers and academics, and it was still all text—no graphics, video, or sound. Not until the development of the World Wide Web in the early 1990s, which made multimedia available on the internet, and the first browser (for locating web pages), which opened the web to commercial uses, did the global network really take off. (● *See Panel 2.2 for a brief history of telecommunications.*) Not everyone is interested in the internet—indeed a third of adults says they simply don't want it, 13% can't get access, and 9% find it too difficult.[2] But by 2012, the internet is expected to have 1.9 billion users, or 30% of the world's population.[3]

How does one become a participant in this network of networks? What is the first step? To connect to the internet, you need three things: an *access device,* such as a personal computer with a modem; a *means of connection,* such as a telephone line, cable hookup, or wireless capability; and an *internet access provider,* such as an internet service provider (ISP), a commercial online service provider, or a wireless internet service provider. We cover these subjects in the next section. We then describe how the internet works.

info!

Hobbes's Internet Timeline

For more detailed internet timelines, go to:

www.zakon.org/robert/ internet/timeline

www.computerhistory.org/ internet_history

www.webopedia.com/quick_ref/ timeline.asp

www.factmonster.com/ipka/ A0193167.html

panel 2.2

Timeline: Brief graphical history of telecommunications and the internet

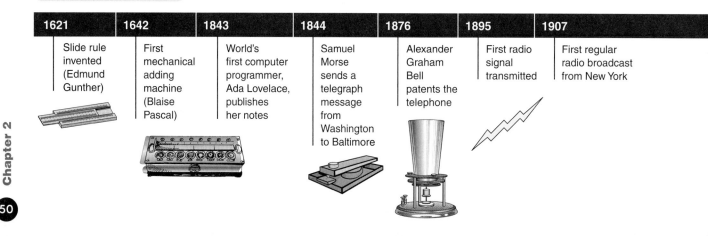

1621	1642	1843	1844	1876	1895	1907
Slide rule invented (Edmund Gunther)	First mechanical adding machine (Blaise Pascal)	World's first computer programmer, Ada Lovelace, publishes her notes	Samuel Morse sends a telegraph message from Washington to Baltimore	Alexander Graham Bell patents the telephone	First radio signal transmitted	First regular radio broadcast from New York

Internet user

Internet access provider

Email & discussion groups
Stay in touch worldwide through email, Facebook, and Twitter.

Research & information
Find information on any subject, using browsers and search tools.

News
Stay current on politics, weather, entertainment, sports, and financial news.

Entertainment
Amuse yourself with internet games, music, videos, and movies.

Download files
Get software, music, and documents such as e-books.

E-shopping
Price anything from plane tickets to cars; order anything from books to sofas.

Financial matters
Do investing, banking, and bill paying online.

Auctions
Sell old stuff, acquire more stuff, with online auctions.

Telephony & conferencing
Make inexpensive phone calls; have online meetings.

Career advancement
Search job listings, post résumés, interview online.

Distance learning
Attend online lectures, have discussions, write research papers, earn degrees.

E-business
Connect with coworkers, buy supplies, support customers, conduct negotiations.

panel 2.1
The world of the internet

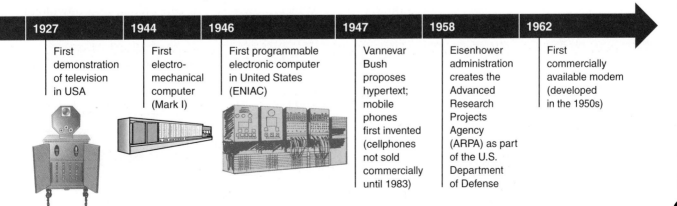

1927	1944	1946	1947	1958	1962
First demonstration of television in USA	First electro-mechanical computer (Mark I)	First programmable electronic computer in United States (ENIAC)	Vannevar Bush proposes hypertext; mobile phones first invented (cellphones not sold commercially until 1983)	Eisenhower administration creates the Advanced Research Projects Agency (ARPA) as part of the U.S. Department of Defense	First commercially available modem (developed in the 1950s)

2.1 CONNECTING TO THE INTERNET: Narrowband, Broadband, & Access Providers

What are the means of connecting to the internet, and how fast are they? What are the three kinds of internet access provider?

In general terms, **_bandwidth,_** or *channel capacity,* **is an expression of how much data—text, voice, video, and so on—can be sent through a communications channel in a given amount of time.** The type of data transmission that allows only one signal at a time is called *baseband transmission.* When several signals can be transmitted at once, it's called *broadband transmission.* **_Broadband_—very high speed—connections** include various kinds of high-speed wired connections (such as coaxial and fiber-optic, described in Chapter 6), as well as DSL, cable, and satellite and other wireless connections, discussed shortly. Today more than half (55%) of all adult Americans have broadband internet connections at home.[4]

THE PHYSICAL CONNECTION: WIRED OR WIRELESS? What are your choices of a *physical connection*—the wired or wireless means of connecting to the internet? A lot depends on where you live. As you might expect, urban and many suburban areas offer more broadband connections than rural areas do. Among the principal means of connection are (1) telephone (dial-up) modem; (2) several high-speed phone lines—ISDN, DSL, and T1; (3) cable modem; and (4) wireless—satellite and other through-the-air links.

DATA TRANSMISSION SPEEDS Data is transmitted in characters or collections of bits. A *bit,* as we will discuss later, is the smallest unit of information used by computers. Today's data transmission speeds are measured in *bits, kilobits, megabits,* and *gigabits* per second:

- **bps:** A computer with an older modem might have a speed of 28,800 bps, which is considered the minimum speed for visiting websites with graphics. The **_bps_ stands for _bits per second._** (Eight bits equals one character, such as A, 3, or #.)

- **Kbps:** This is the most frequently used measure; **_kilobits per second,_ or _Kbps,_ are 1 thousand bits per second.** The speed of a modem that is 28,800 bps might be expressed as 28.8 Kbps.

- **Mbps:** Faster means of connection are measured in **_megabits per second,_ or _Mbps_—1 million bits per second.**

- **Gbps:** At the extreme are **_gigabits per second,_ Gbps—1 billion bits per second.**

UPLOADING & DOWNLOADING Why is it important to know these terms? Because the number of bits affects how fast you can upload and download

1969	1970	1971	1973	1974	1975	1976
ARPANET established at 4 U.S. universities (4 computers linked by leased lines); led to internet (4 hosts)	Microprocessor chips come into use; 15 ARPANET sites established (universities/research), each with own address; 13 hosts on internet	Email invented by computer engineer Ray Tomlinson; 23 hosts on internet	ARPANET becomes international; 35 hosts on internet	TCP (Transmission Control Protocol) specification developed by U.S. Dept. of Defense; 62 hosts on internet	First microcomputer (MITS Altair 8800)	Queen Elizabeth sends the first royal email

information from a remote computer. As we've said (Chapter 1), **_download_ is the transmission of data from a remote computer to a local computer,** as from a website to your own PC. **_Upload_ is the transmission of data from a local computer to a remote computer,** as from your PC to a website you are constructing.

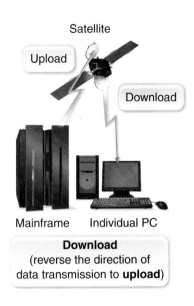

Satellite

Upload

Download

Mainframe   Individual PC

Download
(reverse the direction of
data transmission to **upload**)

Narrowband (Dial-Up Modem): Low Speed but Inexpensive & Widely Available

Why would I want to use dial-up to connect my computer to the internet?

The telephone line that you use for voice calls is still the cheapest means of online connection and is available everywhere. Although the majority of U.S. adults, 55% in 2008, favor broadband internet connections, many home users still use what are called **_narrowband_, or low-bandwith,** connections.[5] This mainly consists of **_dial-up connections_—use of telephone modems to connect computers to the internet.**

CONNECTING THE MODEM As we mentioned in Chapter 1, **a _modem_ is a device that sends and receives data over telephone lines to and from computers.** These days, the modem is generally installed inside your computer, but there are also external modems. The modem is attached to the telephone wall outlet. (● *See Panel 2.3.*) (We discuss modems in a bit more detail in Chapter 6.)

Most standard modems today have a maximum speed of 56 Kbps. That doesn't mean that you'll be sending and receiving data at that rate. The modem in your computer must negotiate with the modems used by your **_internet access provider_, the regional, national, or wireless organization or business that connects you to the internet.** Your provider may have modems operating at slower speeds, such as 28.8 Kbps. In addition, lower-quality phone lines or heavy traffic during peak hours—such as 5 p.m. to 11 p.m. in residential areas—can slow down your rate of transmission.

MODEMS & CALL WAITING One disadvantage of a telephone modem is that while you're online you can't use that phone line to make voice calls unless you've installed special equipment. In addition, people who try to call you while you're using the modem will get a busy signal. (Call waiting may interrupt an online connection, so you need to talk to your phone company about disabling it or purchase a new modem that can handle call waiting. The Windows operating system also has a feature for disabling call waiting.)

You generally won't need to pay long-distance phone rates, since most access providers offer local access numbers. The cost of a dial-up modem connection to the internet is as low as $7.95 a month, plus a possible setup charge of $10–$25.[6]

1976	1978	1979	1981	1984	1986	1987
Apple I computer (first personal computer sold in assembled form)	TCP/IP developed (released in 1983) as standard internet transmission protocol; 111 hosts on internet	First Usenet newsgroups; 188 hosts on internet	IBM introduces Personal Computer; 213 hosts on internet	Apple Macintosh; first personal laser printer; William Gibson coins term "cyberspace"; Domain Name System (DNS) introduced	NSFNET (National Science Foundation Network) backbone established	Digital cellular phones invented; first email message sent from China

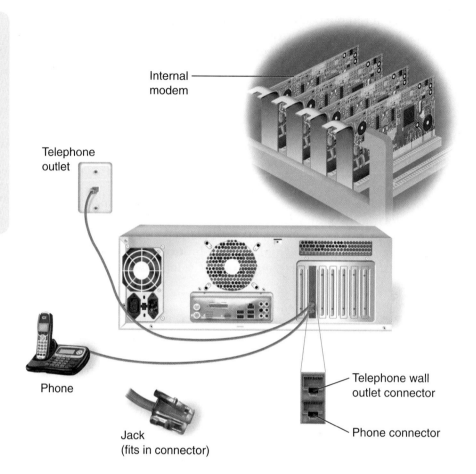

panel 2.3

The modem connection
You connect the modem inside your computer from a port (socket) in the back of your computer to a line that is then connected to a wall jack. Your telephone is also connected to your computer so that you can make voice calls.

Internal modem

Telephone outlet

Phone

Jack
(fits in connector)

Telephone wall outlet connector

Phone connector

High-Speed Phone Lines: More Expensive but Available in Most Cities

What are my choices in high-speed phone lines?

Waiting while your computer's modem takes 25 minutes to transmit a 1-minute low-quality video from a website may have you pummeling the desk in frustration. To get some relief, you could enhance your ***POTS***—**"plain old telephone**

1989	1990	1984	1989–1991	1992	1993	1994
World Wide Web established by Tim Berners-Lee while working at the European Particle Physics Laboratory in Geneva, Switzerland; first home trials of fiber communications network; number of internet hosts breaks 100,000	ARPANET decommissioned; first ISP comes online (dial-up access); Berners-Lee develops first web browser, World Wide Web; 313,000 hosts on internet (9,300 domains)	9.6 K modem	14.4 K modem	"Surfing the internet" coined by Jean Armour Polly; 1,136,000 hosts on internet (18,1000 domains)	Multimedia desktop computers; NAPs replace NSFNET; first graphical web browser, Mosaic, developed by Marc Andreessen; the U.S. White House goes online; internet talk radio begins broadcasting; 2,056,000 hosts on internet (28,000 domains)	Apple and IBM introduce PCs with full-motion video built in; wireless data transmission for small portable computers; Netscape Navigator released; 28.8 K modem; the Japanese Prime Minister goes online; 3,864,000 hosts on internet (56,000 domains)

system"—connection with a high-speed adaptation. Among the choices are ISDN, DSL, and T1, available in most major cities, though not in rural and many suburban areas.

ISDN LINE _**ISDN (Integrated Services Digital Network)**_ **consists of hardware and software that allow voice, video, and data to be communicated over traditional copper-wire telephone lines.** Capable of transmitting 64 to 128 Kbps, ISDN is able to send digital signals over POTS lines. If you were trying to download an approximately 6-minute-long music video from the World Wide Web, it would take you about 4 hours and 45 minutes with a 28.8-Kbps modem. A 128-Kbps ISDN connection would reduce this to an hour.

Basically, ISDN is a viable solution for single users of small business networks when other high-speed options are not available. ISDN is not as fast as DSL, cable, or T1 and is expensive.

DSL LINE _**DSL (digital subscriber line)**_ **uses regular phone lines, a DSL modem, and special technology to transmit data in megabits per second.** Incoming data is significantly faster than outgoing data. That is, your computer can _receive_ data at the rate of 1.5–10 Mbps, but it can _send_ data at only 128 Kbps–1.5 Mbps. This arrangement may be fine, however, if you're principally interested in obtaining very large amounts of data (video, music) rather than in sending such data to others. With DSL, you could download that 6-minute music video perhaps in only 11 minutes (compared to an hour with ISDN). A big advantage of DSL is that it is always on (so you don't have to make a dial-up connection) and, unlike cable (discussed shortly), its transmission rate is relatively consistent. Also, you can talk on the phone and send data at the same time.

There is one big drawback to DSL: You have to live within 3.3 miles of a phone company central switching office, because the access speed and reliability degrade with distance. However, DSL is becoming more popular, and phone companies are building thousands of remote switching facilities to

Check online connections
If you're using Windows XP on your computer, you can check your online connection speed by going to Control Panel, Network Connections; click on your Internet gateway icon, then on View Status of This Connection (on the left side of the screen):

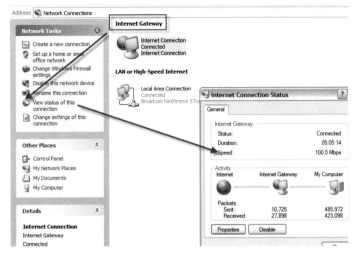

1995	1996	2000	2001	2002	2003	2004
NSFNET reverts to research project; internet now in commercial hands; the Vatican goes online	Microsoft releases Internet Explorer; 56 K modem invented; cable modem introduced; 12,881,000 hosts on internet (488,000 domains)	Web surpasses 1 billion indexable pages; 93,047,785 hosts on internet	AOL membership surpasses 28 million; Napster goes to court	Blogs become popular; Friendster	First official Swiss online election; flash mobs start in New York City; Facebook; MySpace	More than 285,000,000 hosts on internet

enhance service throughout their regions. Another drawback is that you have to choose from a list of internet service providers that are under contract to the phone company you use, although other DSL providers exist.

A new competitor to DSL, available from Verizon, is a service (fiber optic, which we describe later) called FiOS, which is faster than DSL. However, FiOS is not available in all areas (see *www.verizon.com/fios*).[7] Still, the real problem for DSL—or any other kind of broadband—is that it is not available to most rural Americans, who thus lack the sort of high-speed services and opportunities, such as distance learning and web-based commerce, that urban dwellers take for granted.[8]

TI LINE How important is high speed to you? Is it worth $400–$1,500 a month? Then consider getting a ***T1 line***, **essentially a traditional trunk line that carries 24 normal telephone circuits and has a transmission rate of 1.5 to 6 Mbps.** Generally, T1 lines are leased by corporate, government, and academic sites. Another high-speed line, the T3 line, transmits at 6–45 Mbps (the equivalent of about 672 simultaneous voice calls) and costs about $4,000 or more a month. Telephone companies and other types of companies are making even faster connections available: An STS-1 connection runs at 51 Mbps, and an STS-48 connection speeds data along at 2.5 Gbps (2.5 billion bits per second). T1 and T3 lines are commonly used by businesses connecting to the internet, by internet access providers, and in the internet high-speed transmission lines.

Problem for Telephone Internet Connections: The Last Mile

Why does the "last mile" of a wired connection often slow down the data rate?

The distance from your home to your telephone's switching office, the local loop, is often called the "last mile." As we mentioned earlier, if you are using POTS for your initial internet connection—even if you use ISDN or DSL—data must pass back and forth between you and your telephone switching station. (This distance is usually more than a mile; it is shorter than 20 miles and averages about 3 miles in metropolitan areas.) The "last mile" of copper wire is what really slows things down. This problem can be solved by installing newer transmission media, but communications companies are slow to incur this cost. There are about 130 million phone lines in the United States that use 650 million miles of copper wire. Considering that our planet is only about 93 million miles from the sun, 650 million miles of wire represents a huge challenge to replace!

Cable Modem: Close Competitor to DSL

What are the advantages and disadvantages of a cable modem connection?

If DSL's 11 minutes to move a 6-minute video sounds good, 2 minutes sounds even better. That's the rate of transmission for cable modems, which can transmit outgoing data at about 1.4 Mbps and incoming data at up to 30 Mbps. (The common

Cable modem

	2005	2006	2007	2009	2030–2045
	YouTube; Wii	Twitter	Skype	More than 625,226,456 hosts on internet — top 10 are USA, Japan, Germany, Italy, China, France, Australia, Netherlands, Mexico, Brazil	The Singularity

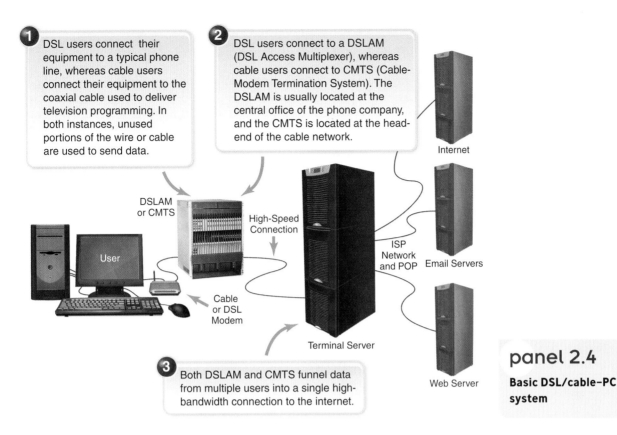

① DSL users connect their equipment to a typical phone line, whereas cable users connect their equipment to the coaxial cable used to deliver television programming. In both instances, unused portions of the wire or cable are used to send data.

② DSL users connect to a DSLAM (DSL Access Multiplexer), whereas cable users connect to CMTS (Cable-Modem Termination System). The DSLAM is usually located at the central office of the phone company, and the CMTS is located at the head-end of the cable network.

DSLAM or CMTS

High-Speed Connection

User

Cable or DSL Modem

ISP Network and POP

Internet

Email Servers

Terminal Server

Web Server

③ Both DSLAM and CMTS funnel data from multiple users into a single high-bandwidth connection to the internet.

panel 2.4

Basic DSL/cable–PC system

residential transmission rate is 3 Mbps.) **A _cable modem_ connects a personal computer to a cable-TV system that offers an internet connection.**

The advantage of a cable modem is that, like a DSL connection, it is always on. However, unlike DSL, you don't need to live near a telephone switching station. (● *See Panel 2.4.*)

A disadvantage, however, is that you and your cable-TV-viewing neighbors are sharing the system and consequently, during peak-load times, your service may be slowed to the speed of a regular dial-up modem. Also, using an internet connection that is always on—and that, in the case of cable, you share with other people—invites outside interference with your computer, a risk that we discuss later in the book.

Cable companies may contract you to use their own internet access provider, but more commonly you may choose your own. (Note that cable modems are for internet connections. They do not by themselves take the place of your voice phone system.)

Satellite Wireless Connections

Why might I consider having a satellite connection?

If you live in a rural area and are tired of the molasses-like speed of your cranky local phone system, you might—if you have an unobstructed view of the southern sky—consider taking to the air. With a pizza-size satellite dish on your roof or on the side of your house, you can send data at the rate of about 512 Kbps and receive data at about 1.5 Mbps from a **_communications satellite_**, **a space station that transmits radio waves called *microwaves* from earth-based stations.**

Satellite internet connections are always on. To surf the internet using this kind of connection, you need an internet access provider that supports two-way satellite transmission. You will also have to lease or purchase satellite-access hardware, such as a dish. (We cover satellites in more detail in Chapter 6.)

Sky connection. Setting up a home satellite dish.

Other Wireless Connections: Wi-Fi & 3G

What are Wi-Fi and 3G wireless connections?

More and more people are using laptop computers, smart cellphones, and personal digital assistants to access the internet through ***wireless networks*, which use radio waves to transmit data.** Indeed, 62% of all Americans are part of a wireless, mobile population.[9] We discuss various types of wireless networks in detail in Chapter 6, but here let us mention just two of the technologies:

WI-FI Short for *Wireless Fidelity*, **_Wi-Fi_ is the name given to any of several standards—so-called 802.11 standards—set by the Institute of Electrical and Electronic Engineers (IEEE) for wireless transmission.** One standard, 802.11b, permits wireless transmission of data at up to 54 Mbps for 300–500 feet from an ***access point*, or *hot spot*, a station that sends and receives data to and from a Wi-Fi network;** 802.11n can transmit up to 140 Mpbs. Many airports, hotels, libraries, convention centers, and fast-food facilities offer so-called ***hotspots*—public access to Wi-Fi networks.** The hotspot can get its internet access from DSL, cable modem, T1 local area network, dial-up phone service, or any other method. (Communications technology is covered in Chapter 6.) Once the hotspot has the internet connection, it can broadcast it wirelessly. Laptops are commonly used for Wi-Fi internet connections; they must be equipped with the necessary Wi-Fi hardware, however.

3G WIRELESS **_3G_, which stands for "third generation," is loosely defined as high-speed wireless technology that does not need access points because it uses the existing cellphone system.** This technology, which is found in many smartphones and PDAs that are capable of delivering downloadable video clips and high-resolution games, is being provided by Cingular, Sprint, Verizon, and T-Mobile.

The table at right shows the transmission rates for various connections, as well as their approximate costs (always subject to change, of course) and their pros and cons. (● *See Panel 2.5.*)

Internet Access Providers: Three Kinds

How do I distinguish among the three types of providers?

As we mentioned, in addition to having an access device and a means of connection, to get on the internet you need to go through an *internet access provider*. There are three types of such providers: *internet service providers, commercial online services,* and *wireless internet service providers*.

INTERNET SERVICE PROVIDERS (ISPs) **An *internet service provider (ISP)* is a company that connects online users through their communications lines to the company's server, which links them to the internet via another company's network access points.** Examples are EarthLink and United Online. There are also some free ISPs.

COMMERCIAL ONLINE SERVICES A *commercial online service* is a members-only company that provides not only internet access but other specialized content as well, such as news, games, and financial data. The two best-known subscriber-only commercial online services are AOL (America Online) and MSN (Microsoft Network).

WIRELESS INTERNET SERVICE PROVIDERS A *wireless internet service provider (WISP)* enables users with computers containing wireless modems—mostly laptops/notebooks—and web-enabled mobile smartphones and personal digital assistants to gain access to the internet. Examples are Cingular, Sprint, T-Mobile, and Verizon.

Service	Cost per Month (plus installation, equipment)	Maximum Speed (download only)	Pluses	Minuses
Telephone (dial-up) modem	$0–$45	56 Kbps	Inexpensive, available everywhere	Slow; connection supports only a single user
ISDN	$40–$110 (+ $350–$700 installation cost)	64–128 Kbps (1.5 Mbps with special wiring)	Faster than dial-up; uses conventional phone lines	More expensive than dial-up; no longer extensively supported by telephone companies for individuals; used mostly by small businesses
DSL	$25–$35, depending on speed	768 kbps–7 Mbps	Fast download, always on, higher security; uploads faster than cable; users can talk and transmit data at the same time	Needs to be close to phone company switching station; limited choice of service providers; supports only a single user
TI line	$350–$1,500 (+ $1,000 installation cost)	1.5 Mbps (T5 = 45 Mbps)	Can support many users: 24 separate circuits of 64 Kbps each; reliable high-speed downloading and uploading; users can talk and transmit data at the same time	Expensive, best for businesses
Cable modem	$40–$100 (+ $5 monthly for leased cable modem)	Up to 30 Mbps (4 Mbps common)	Fast, always on, most popular broadband type of connection; can support many users; downloads faster than DSL; users can talk on phone and transmit cable data at the same time	Slower service during high-traffic times, vulnerability to outside intrusion, limited choice of service providers; not always available to businesses
Satellite	Up to $120 (+ about $300 installation)	512 Kbps–5 Mbps	Wireless, fast, reliable, always on; goes where DSL and cable can't; users can talk on phone and transmit satellite data at the same time	High setup and monthly costs; users must have unobstructed view of the southern sky; because the satellite signals must travel so far (22,000 miles into space and then back again), latency (signal delay) is a problem for users who need real-time interactivity, such as when playing games; bad weather can cause service drop-outs
Wi-Fi	Nothing for users accessing hotspots supplied by others; about $300 for access-point hardware and up to $25 per month for subscription to a Wi-Fi access service	54–140 Mbps	Uses a beefed-up version of the current cellphone network; ultimately should be available everywhere	Range of access is usually only 50–300 feet (to access point)
3G	$250 and up	About 3 Mbps (about 15 seconds to download a 3-minute MP3 song)	Functions like Wi-Fi but without the need for hot spots; uses existing cellphone network	Low battery power on some models; phones are relatively large

f you belong to a college or company, you may get internet access free. Many public libraries also offer free net connections. If these options are not available to you, here are some questions to ask in your first phone call to an internet access provider:

- Is there a contract, and for what length of time? Is there a trial period, or are you obligated to stick with the provider for a while even if you're unhappy with it?

- Is there a setup fee? What kind of help do you get in setting up your connection?

- How much is unlimited access per month? Is there a discount for long-term commitments?

- Is the access number a local phone call so that you don't have long-distance phone tolls?

- Is there an alternative dial-up number if the main number is out of service?

- Is access available when you're traveling, through either local numbers or toll-free 800 numbers?

- Can you gain access to your email through the provider's website?

- Will the provider help you establish your personal website, if you want one, and is there sufficient space for it on the provider's server?

- Is there free, 24-hour technical support? Is it reachable through a toll-free number?

- How long does it take to get tech support? Ask for the tech-support number before you sign up, and then call it to see how long a response takes. Also try connecting through the web.

- Will the provider keep up with technology? For instance, is it planning to offer broadband access? Wireless access?

- Will the provider sell your name to marketers? What kind of service does it offer to block unwanted junk messages (spam)?

Once you have contacted an internet access provider and paid the required fee (charged to your credit card), you will be provided with information about local connections and necessary communications software for setting up your computer and modem to make a connection. For this you use your user name ("user ID") and your **_password,_** **a secret word or string of characters that enables you to _log on,_ or make a connection to the remote computer.** The access provider will also help you establish your email address, which must be unique—that is, not the same as anyone else's.

2.2 HOW DOES THE INTERNET WORK?

What is the basic structure of the internet, and who controls it?

The *inter*national *net*work known as the *internet* consists of hundreds of thousands of smaller networks linking educational, commercial, nonprofit, and military organizations, as well as individuals. Central to this arrangement is the client/server network. **A _client_ computer is a computer requesting data or services. A _server,_ or _host computer,_ is a central computer supplying data or services requested of it.** When the client computer's request—for example, for information on various airline flights and prices—gets to a server computer, that computer sends the information back to the client computer.

Internet Connections: POPs, NAPs, Backbone, & Internet2

How do I distinguish a point of presence from a network access point, and what is the internet backbone? What does Internet2 do?

Your journey onto the internet starts, in the case of dial-up, with your client computer's modem connecting via a local phone call to your internet service provider (ISP). (● *See Panel 2.6.*) This is the slowest part of the internet connection. An ISP's headquarters and network servers may be located almost anywhere.

POINT OF PRESENCE To avoid making its customers pay long-distance phone charges to connect, the ISP provides each customer with a ❶ _point of presence (POP)_—**a local access point to the internet—a collection of modems and other equipment in a local area.** The POP acts as a local gateway to the ISP's network.

NETWORK ACCESS POINT The ISP in turn connects to a ❷ _network access point (NAP),_ **a routing computer at a point on the internet where several connections come together.** NAPs are owned by a _network service provider (NSP),_ a large communications company, such as AGIS or MCI. The four original NAPs in the United States are in San Francisco, Washington, D.C., Chicago, and New Jersey. These NAPs were established in 1993, when the original network that became the internet was privatized.

Much of the internet congestion occurs at NAPs. The four main NAPs quickly became overloaded, so Private/Peer NAPs, called _PNAPs_ ("miniNAPs") were established in the late 1990s. PNAPs facilitate more efficient routing (passing) of data back and forth on the internet by providing more backbone access locations. PNAPs are provided by commercial companies, such as Savvis Communications.

INTERNET BACKBONE Each NAP has at least one computer, whose task is simply to direct internet traffic from one NAP to the next. NAPs are connected by the equivalent of interstate highways, known collectively as the ❸ _internet backbone,_ **high-speed, high-capacity transmission lines that use the newest communications technology to transmit data across the internet.** Backbone connections are supplied by internet backbone providers such as AT&T, Cable & Wireless, GTE, Sprint, Teleglobe, Verizon, and Deutsche Telekom.

panel 2.6

How the internet works

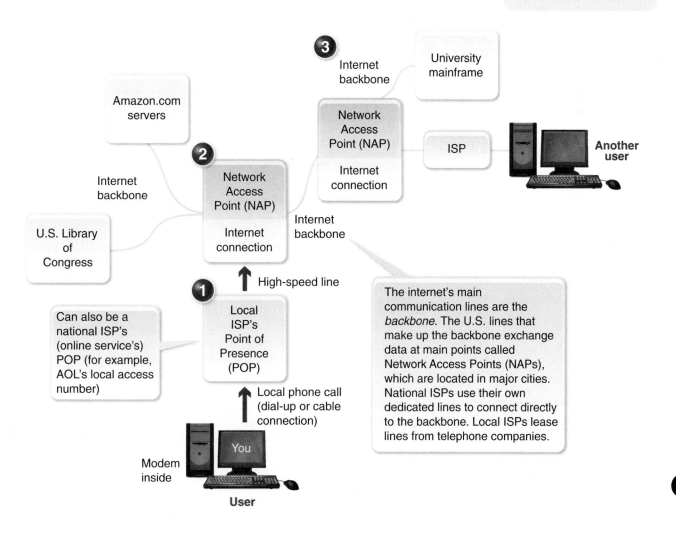

INTERNET2 _Internet2_ **is a cooperative university/business education and research project that enables high-end users to quickly and reliably move huge amounts of data over high-speed networks.** In effect, Internet2 adds "toll lanes" to the older internet to speed things up. The purpose is to advance videoconferencing, research, and academic collaboration—to enable a kind of "virtual university." Presently Internet2 links more than 210 research universities. Requiring state-of-the-art infrastructure, Internet2 operates a high-speed backbone network (formerly called Abiline), which many colleges use.

A rival nonprofit organization is National LamdaRail, a fiber-optic network assembled for colleges' use.

Internet Communications: Protocols, Packets, & Addresses

How do computers understand the data being transmitted over the internet?

When your modem connects to a modem at your ISP's POP location, the two modems go through a process called _handshaking,_ whereby the fastest-available transmission speed is established. Then _authentication_ occurs: your ISP needs to know you are who you say you are, so you will need to provide a user name and a password. These two items will have been established when you opened your account with your ISP.

PROTOCOLS How do computers understand the data being transmitted? The key lies in data following the same **_protocol_, or set of rules, that computers must follow to transmit data electronically. The protocol that enables all computers to use data transmitted on the internet is called _Transmission Control Protocol/Internet Protocol_, or _TCP/IP_,** which was developed in 1978 by ARPA. TCP/IP is used for all internet transactions, from sending email to downloading pictures off a friend's website. Among other things, TCP/IP determines how the sending device will indicate that it has finished sending a message and how the receiving device will indicate that it has received the message.[10]

PACKETS Most important, perhaps, TCP/IP breaks the data in a message into separate **_packets_, fixed-length blocks of data for transmission.** This allows a message to be split up and its parts sent by separate routes yet still all wind up in the same place. IP is used to send the packets across the internet to their final destination, and TCP is used to reassemble the packets in the correct order. The packets do not have to follow the same network routes to reach their destination because all the packets have the same _IP address,_ as we explain next.

IP ADDRESSES An **_Internet Protocol (IP) address_ uniquely identifies every computer and device connected to the internet.** An IP address consists of four sets of numbers between 0 and 255 separated by decimals (called a _dotted quad_)—for example, 1.160.10.240. An IP address is similar to a street address, but street addresses rarely change, whereas IP addresses often do. Each time you connect to your internet access provider, it assigns your computer a new IP address, called a _dynamic IP address,_ for your online session. When you request data from the internet, it is transmitted to your computer's IP address. When you disconnect, your provider frees up the IP address you were using and reassigns it to another user.

A dynamic IP address changes each time you connect to the internet. A _static IP address_ remains constant each time a person logs on to the internet. Established organizational websites—such as your ISP's—have static IP addresses.

It would be simple if every computer that connects to the internet had its own static IP number, but when the internet was first conceived, the architects didn't foresee the need for an unlimited number of IP addresses. Consequently,

The Internet Traffic Report

The Internet Traffic Report monitors the flow of data around the world. It displays values between 0 and 100 for many networks. Higher values indicate faster and more reliable connections. Check out your area at:

www.internettrafficreport.com

Your IP Address

Want to find out what your IP address is while you're online? Go to:

http://whatismyipaddress.com

there are not enough IP numbers to go around. To get around that problem, many internet access providers limit the number of static IP addresses they allocate and economize on the remaining number of IP addresses they possess by temporarily assigning an IP address from a pool of IP addresses.

If your computer is constantly connected to the internet, through a local network at work or school, most likely you have a static IP address. If you have a dial-up connection to the internet or are using a computer that gets connected to the internet intermittently, you're most likely picking up a dynamic IP address from a pool of possible IP addresses at your internet access provider's network during each log-in.

After your connection has been made, your internet access provider functions as an interface between you and the rest of the internet. If you're exchanging data with someone who uses the same provider, the data may stay within that organization's network. Large national internet access providers operate their own backbones that connect their POPs throughout the country. Usually, however, data travels over many different networks before it reaches your computer.

Partial map of the internet based on January 15, 2005, data. Each line is drawn between two nodes, representing two IP addresses. Different colors represent different countries (*http:// commons.wikimedia.org/wiki/ File:Internet_map_1024.jpg*).

Who Runs the Internet?

What does ICANN do?

Although no one owns the internet, everyone on the net adheres to standards overseen by the international Board of Trustees of ISOC, the *Internet Society (www.isoc.org)*. ISOC is a professional, nonprofit society with more than 80 organizational and 28,000 individual members in more than 180 countries. The organizations include companies, governments, and foundations. ISOC provides leadership in addressing issues that confront the future of the internet and is the organizational home for groups responsible for internet infrastructure standards.

In June 1998, the U.S. government proposed the creation of a series of nonprofit corporations to manage such complex issues as fraud prevention, privacy, and intellectual-property protection. The first such group, the **_Internet Corporation for Assigned Names and Numbers (ICANN)_, was established to regulate human-friendly internet domain names—those addresses ending with *.com, .org, .net,* and so on, that overlie IP addresses and identify the website type.**

ICANN (which can be accessed at *www.icann.org*) is a global, private-sector, nonprofit corporation that has no statutory authority and imposes policies through contracts with its world members. Criticized for inefficiency, in 2003 it outlined what it called ICANN 2.0, intended to be a more responsive and agile agency that would consult better with the world internet community about the adoption of standards.[11] One of its improvements is the ICANN Whosis Database, which returns the name and address of any domain name entered (entering *microsoft.com,* for instance, returns the name and address of Microsoft Corp.). However, various groups, including the International Telecommunication Union, a United Nations agency, have suggested that the United States through ICANN has too much control over the internet, and several countries have proposed that an international body take over ICANN. The United States in July 2005 asserted that it intended to retain its role in internet management.[12]

In June 2008, ICANN decided to "increase competition and choice" by allowing perhaps thousands of new internet domain names to join ".com," beginning in 2009. Thus, for instance, new names could cover locations such as ".nyc" (for New York City) and ".berlin" or industries such as ".bank" or companies such as ".ebay." An application would not be allowed if it conflicted with a trademark (such as ".pepsi").[13]

Non-English Domain Names

In October 2009, ICANN approved the use of non-Latin character sets in domain names. This will allow domain names to be written in native character sets, such as Chinese, Arabic, and Greek. ICANN has argued that this change is necessary to expand use of the Web in regions where people don't understand English. This also means that many of us in the USA, for example, will not be able to type such domain names. For more information, try:

www.wired.com/ epicenter/2009/10/icann- international-scripts/

http://news.cnet.com/8301- 1023_3-10387139-93.html

http://arstechnica.com/web/ news/2009/10/domain- extensions-go-global- goodbye-com-welcome.ars

2.3 THE WORLD WIDE WEB

How do the following work: websites, web pages, browsers, URLs, web portals, search tools, and search engines? What are HTML and hyperlinks?

The internet and the World Wide Web, as we have said, are not the same. The internet is a massive network of networks, connecting millions of computers via protocols, hardware, and communications channels. It is the infrastructure that supports not only the web but also other communications systems such as email, instant messaging, newsgroups, and other activities that we'll discuss. The part of the internet called the *web* is a *multimedia-based* technology that enables you to access more than just text. That is, you can also download art, audio, video, and animation and engage in interactive games.

The Face of the Web: Browsers, Websites, & Web Pages

How would I explain to someone the difference between browsers, websites, and web pages?

If a Rip Van Winkle had fallen asleep in 1989—the year computer scientist Tim Berners-Lee developed the web software—and awoke today, he would be completely baffled by the new vocabulary that we now encounter on a daily basis: *browser, website, web page, www.* Let's see how we would explain to him what these and similar web terms mean.

Whence the Word Web?

Why did people perceive the need for a "web," and how did Berners-Lee develop what they needed? Go to:

www.ibiblio.org/pioneers/lee. html

http://en.wikipedia.org/wiki/ Tim_Berners-Lee

Tim Berners-Lee

Tim Berners-Lee was born in London, England; his parents, both mathematicians, were employed together on the team that built the Manchester Mark I, one of the earliest computers. Berners-Lee graduated from the Queen's College of Oxford University, where he built a computer with a soldering iron. In 1980, while an independent contractor at CERN (European Organization for Nuclear Research), Berners-Lee proposed a project based on the concept of hypertext, to facilitate sharing and updating information among researchers. With other researchers, he built a prototype system named Enquire.

After leaving CERN, he used ideas similar to those used in Enquire to create the World Wide Web, for which he designed and built the first browser (called WorldWideWeb and developed into NeXTSTEP). Berners-Lee built the first website at *http://info. cern.ch/* and it was first put online on August 6, 1991. It provided an explanation about what the World Wide Web was, how one could own a browser, how to set up a web server, and so on.

In 1994, Berners-Lee founded the World Wide Web Consortium (W3C) at the Massachusetts Institute of Technology. It comprised various companies willing to create standards and recommendations to improve the quality of the internet. It was not until 2000 and 2001 that popular browsers began to support this standard.

BROWSERS: SOFTWARE FOR SURFING THE WEB A **_browser,_** or *web browser,* **is software that enables you to find and access the various parts of the web.** The two best-known browsers are *Microsoft Internet Explorer,* more commonly used (with a 68% market share), and *Mozilla Firefox* (21%). (● *See Panel 2.7.*) Apple Inc.'s Macintosh computers' *Safari* is third (8%), and Google's *Chrome,* introduced in 2008, is fourth (1%).[14] *Bing,* a new browser from Microsoft, was introduced in 2009.[15] These and other browsers allow you, like riding a wave with a surfboard, to surf the web. **_Surf_ means to explore the web by using your mouse to move via a series of connected paths, or links, from one location, or website, to another.**

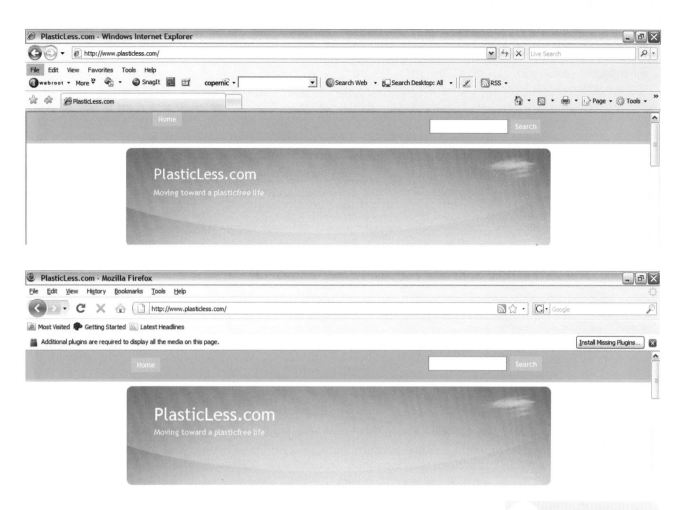

panel 2.7

Internet Explorer (top) and Mozilla Firefox (bottom)
Notice the different tool-bar and tool setups.

WEBSITE: THE LOCATION ON THE COMPUTER A _website_, or simply _site_, is a **location on a particular computer on the web that has a unique address** (called a _URL_, as we'll explain). If you decided to buy books online from bookseller Barnes & Noble, you would visit its website, _www.barnesandnoble.com;_ the website is the location of a computer somewhere on the internet. That computer might be located in Barnes & Noble's offices, but it might be located somewhere else entirely.

WEB PAGES: THE DOCUMENTS ON A WEBSITE A website is composed of a web page or collection of related web pages. **A _web page_ is a document on the World Wide Web that can include text, pictures, sound, and video.** The first page you see at a website is like the title page of a book. This is the **_home page_, or welcome page, which identifies the website and contains links to other pages at the site.** (● _See Panel 2.8, on next page._) If you have your own personal website, it might consist of just one page—the home page. Large websites have scores or even hundreds of pages.

How the Browser Finds Things: URLs

How would I describe how a browser connects?

Now let's look at the details of how the browser finds a particular web page.

URLS: ADDRESSES FOR WEB PAGES Before your browser can connect with a website, it needs to know the site's address, the URL. **The _URL (Uniform Resource Locator)_ is a string of characters that points to a specific piece of information anywhere on the web.** In other words, the URL is the website's unique address.

Survival Tip

Do Home Pages Endure?

The contents of home pages often change. Or they may disappear, and so the connecting links to them in other web pages become links to nowhere. To find out how to view "dead" pages, go to:

http://web.ticino.com/ multilingual/Search.htm

The Internet & the World Wide Web

65

panel 2.8

Home page
This is a website's first page, or welcome page.

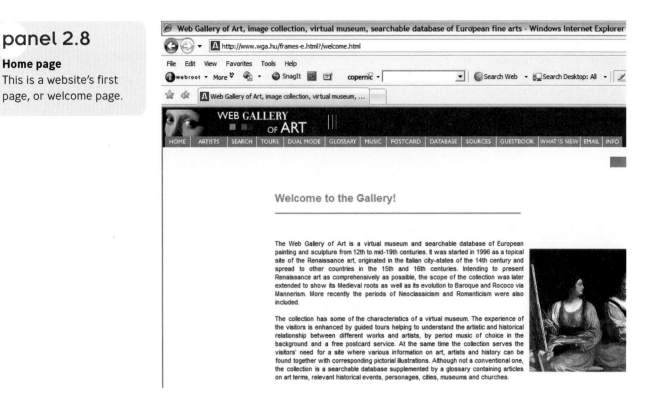

A URL consists of (1) the web *protocol*, (2) the *domain name* or web server name, (3) the *directory* (or folder) on that server, and (4) the *file* within that directory (perhaps with an extension such as *html* or *htm*). Consider the following example of a URL for a website offered by the National Park Service for Yosemite National Park:

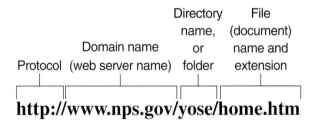

http://www.nps.gov/yose/home.htm

Let's look at these elements.

- **The protocol: http://** As mentioned, a protocol is a set of communication rules for exchanging information. The web protocol, HTTP, was developed by Tim Berners-Lee, and it appears at the beginning of some web addresses (as in *http://www.mcgraw-hill.com*). It stands for ***HyperText Transfer Protocol (HTTP)*, the communications rules that allow browsers to connect with web servers.** (Note: Most browsers assume that all web addresses begin with *http://*, and so you don't need to type this part; just start with whatever follows, such as *www.*)

- **The domain name (web server name): www.nps.gov/A *domain* is simply a location on the internet, the particular web server.** Domain names tell the location and the type of address. Domain-name components are separated by periods (called "dots"). The last part of the domain, called the *top-level domain*, is a three-letter extension that describes the domain type: *.gov, .com, .net, .edu, .org, .mil, .int*—government, commercial, network, educational, nonprofit, military, or international organization. In our example, the *www* stands for "World Wide Web," of course; the *.nps* stands for "National Park Service," and *.gov* is the top-level domain name indicating that this is a government website.

The meanings of other internet top-level domain abbreviations appear in the box on the next page. (● *See Panel 2.9.*) Some top-level domain names also include a two-letter code extension for the country—for example, *.us* for United States, *.ca* for Canada, *.mx* for Mexico, *.uk* for United Kingdom, *.jp* for Japan, *.in* for India, *.cn* for China. These country codes are optional.

- **The directory name: yose/** The *directory* name is the name on the server for the directory, or folder, from which your browser needs to pull the file. Here it is *yose* for "Yosemite." For Yellowstone National Park, it is *yell*.

- **The file name and extension: home.htm** The *file* is the particular page or document that you are seeking. Here it is *home.htm*, because you have gone to the home page, or welcome page, for Yosemite National Park. The *.htm* is an extension to the file name, and this extension informs the browser that the file is an HTML file. Let us consider what HTML means.

URLs & EMAIL ADDRESSES: NOT THE SAME A URL, you may have observed, is *not* the same thing as an email address. The website for the White House (which includes presidential information, history, a tour, and a guide to federal services) is *www.whitehouse.gov.* Some people might type *president@whitehouse.gov* and expect to get a website, but that won't happen. We explain email addresses in another few pages.

Domain Name	Authorized Users	Example
.aero	air-transport industry	director@bigwings.aero
.biz	businesses	ceo@company.biz
.com	originally commercial; now anyone can use	editor@mcgraw-hill.com
.coop	cooperative associations	buyer@greatgroceries.coop
.edu	postsecondary accredited educational and research institutions	professor@harvard.edu
.gov	U.S. government agencies and bureaus	president@whitehouse.gov
.info	generic information service providers	contact@research.info
.int	organizations established by international treaties between governments	sectretary_general@unitednations.int
.jobs	human resources managers	AnnChu@Personnel.jobs
.mil	U.S. military organizations	chief_of_staff@pentagon.mil
.mobi	providers of mobile products and services	user@phonecompany.mobi
.museum	museums	curator@modernart.museum
.name	individuals	joe@smith.name
.net	generic networking organizations	contact@earthlink.net
.org	generic organizations, often non-profit and professional (non-commercial)	director@redcross.org
.post	Universal Postal Union*	manager@UPS.post
.pro	credentialed professionals & related entities	auditor@accountant.pro
tel.	For businesses and individuals to publish their contact data	OurCorporationInfo@MyInc.tel
.travel	travel industry	JoeAgent@flyright.travel
.xxx	adults-only website	proprietor@badtaste.xxx

Note: The number of domain names is expanding; for a list of current domain names, go to *www.iana.org/gtld/gtld.htm.*
*Some groups pay $45,000 or more to ICANN for a particular domain name.

panel 2.9

Internet top-level domain abbreviations and users

Marc Andreessen is best known as a cofounder of Netscape Communications Corporation and coauthor of Mosaic, an early web browser. Andreessen received his bachelor's degree in computer science from the University of Illinois, Urbana-Champaign. As an undergraduate, he interned one summer at IBM in Austin, Texas. He also worked at the university's National Center for Supercomputing Applications, where he became familiar with ViolaWWW, created by Pei-Yuan Wei, which was based on Tim Berners-Lee's open standards for the World Wide Web. These early browsers had been created to work only on expensive Unix workstations, so Andreessen created an improved and more user-friendly version with integrated graphics that would work on personal computers. The resulting code was the Mosaic web browser.

Soon after this development, Mosaic Communications Corporation was in business in Mountain View, California, with Andreessen as vice president. Mosaic Communications changed its name to Netscape Communications, and its flagship web browser became Netscape Navigator, which is available now only in archived versions (not technically supported).

The Nuts & Bolts of the Web: HTML & Hyperlinks

What are HTML and hyperlinks?

The basic communications protocol that makes the internet work, as we described, is *TCP/IP.* The communications protocol used to access that part of the internet called the World Wide Web, we pointed out, is called *HyperText Transfer Protocol (HTTP).* A hypertext document uses *hypertext markup language (HTML),* which uses *hypertext links,* to connect with other documents. The foundations of the World Wide Web, then, are HTML and hypertext links.

HYPERTEXT MARKUP LANGUAGE (HTML) ***Hypertext markup language (HTML)*** **is the set of special instructions (called "tags" or "markups") that are used to specify document structure, formatting, and links to other multimedia documents on the web.** Extensible hypertext markup language (XHTML) is the successor to and the current version of HTML. The need for a stricter version of HTML was perceived primarily because World Wide Web content now needs to be delivered to many devices (such as mobile phones) that have fewer resources than traditional computers have.

HYPERTEXT LINKS ***Hypertext links***—**also called** ***hyperlinks,*** ***hotlinks,*** **or just** ***links***—**are connections to other documents or web pages that contain related information; a word or phrase in one document becomes a connection to a document in a different place.** Hyperlinks appear as underlined or colored words and phrases. On a home page, for instance, the hyperlinks serve to connect the main page with other pages throughout the website. Other hyperlinks will connect to pages on other websites, whether located on a computer next door or one on the other side of the world.

An example of an HTML document with hyperlinks is shown below. (● *See Panel 2.10.*)

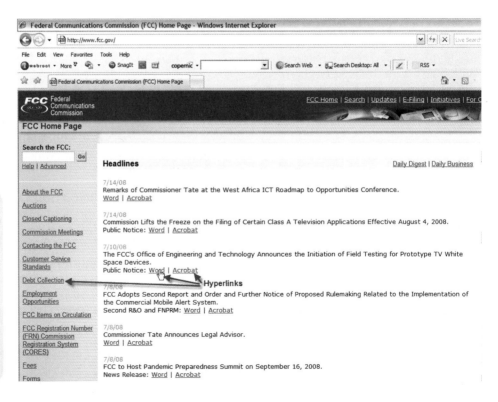

panel 2.10

An HTML document and hyperlinks
Using the mouse to click on the hyperlinked (underlined) text connects you to another location in the same website or at a different site.

Using Your Browser to Get around the Web

What do I need to know to operate my browser?

You can find almost anything you want on the more than 28.1 billion indexed web pages available around the world.[16] In one month alone, one writer reported, he went on the web "to find, among other things, hotel reservations in California, a rose that will grow in the shade, information about volunteer fire departments, a used copy of an obscure novel, two ZIP codes, the complete text of *A Midsummer Night's Dream,* and the news that someone I went to high school with took early retirement. I also heard, out of the blue, from two people I haven't seen in years."[17] Among the droplets of what amounts to a Niagara Falls of information: Weather maps and forecasts. Guitar chords. Recipe archives. Sports schedules. Daily newspapers in all languages. Nielsen television ratings. The Alcoholism Research Data Base. U.S. government phone numbers. The Central Intelligence Agency world map. The daily White House press releases. And on and on. But it takes a browser and various kinds of search tools to find and make any kind of sense of this enormous amount of data.

FIVE BASIC ELEMENTS OF THE BROWSER If you buy a new computer, it will come with a browser already installed. Most browsers have a similar look and feel and similar navigational tools. Note that the web browser screen has five basic elements: *menu bar, toolbar, URL bar, workspace,* and *status bar.* To execute menu-bar and toolbar commands, you use the mouse to move the pointer over the word, known as a *menu selection,* and click the left button of the mouse. This will result in a pull-down menu of other commands for other options. (● *See Panel 2.11.*)

After you've been using a mouse for a while, you may find moving the pointer around somewhat time consuming. As a shortcut, if you click on the right mouse button, you can reach many of the commands on the toolbar (*Back, Forward,* and so on) via a pop-up menu.

STARTING OUT FROM HOME: THE HOME PAGE The first page you see when you start up your browser is the *home page* or *start page.* (You can also start up from just a blank page, if you don't want to wait for the time it takes to connect with a home page.) You can choose any page on the web as your start page, but a good start page offers links to sites you want to visit frequently. Often you may find that the internet access provider with which you arrange your internet connection will provide its own start page. However, you'll no doubt be able to customize it to make it your own personal home page.

Do You Need to Know HTML to Build a Website?

Most general web users do not need to know HTML. If you want to convert a word-processed document to HTML so that someone can post it on a website, applications such as Microsoft Word will convert it for you (for example, using the options Save as, Web page). Also, many website builders offer their services on the web; you can hire them to build a website for you. Many ISPs supply help with building websites and offer website storage on their servers to their subscribers.

If you want to learn more about HTML formatting, try these websites:

www.htmlcodetutorial.com/

www.make-a-web-site.com/

www.w3schools.com/html/ default.asp

panel 2.11

Common tools and functions of a browser

PERSONALIZING YOUR HOME PAGE Want to see the weather forecast for your college and/or hometown areas when you first log on? Or the day's news (general, sports, financial, health, and so on)? Or the websites you visit most frequently? Or a reminder page (as for deadlines or people's birthdays)? You can probably personalize your home page following the directions provided with the first start page you encounter. A customized start page is also provided by Yahoo!, Google, and similar services.

GETTING AROUND: BACK, FORWARD, HOME, & SEARCH FEATURES Driving in a foreign city (or even Boston or San Francisco) can be an interesting experience in which street names change, turns lead into unknown neighborhoods, and signs aren't always evident, so that soon you have no idea where you are. That's what the internet is like, although on a far more massive scale. Fortunately, unlike being lost in Rome, here your browser toolbar provides navigational aids. (● *See Panel 2.12.*) *Back* takes you back to the previous page. *Forward* lets you look again at a page you returned from. If you really get lost, you can start over by clicking on *Home,* which returns you to your home page. *Search* lists various other search tools, as we will describe. Other navigational aids are *history lists* and *favorites* or *bookmarks.*

panel 2.12

More information on common browser functions

Menu bar

◐ **Back:** Moves you to a previous page or site

◑ **Forward:** Lets you visit a page you have just returned from

☒ **Stop:** Halts any ongoing transfer of page information

↕ **Refresh:** If page become stalled or garbled while loading, this will retrieve it again

⌂ **Home:** Returns you to your personal start page

☆☆ **Favorites/Bookmarks:** Lists of sites you have saved so you can remember them and go to them quickly

History ▾ **History:** Names and descriptions of sites most recently visited

🖶 **Print:** Prints the web page you are on

panel 2.13

History list

If you want to return to a previously viewed site in Internet Explorer or Firefox, click on *History.*

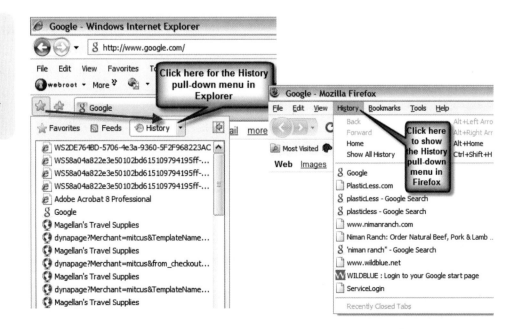

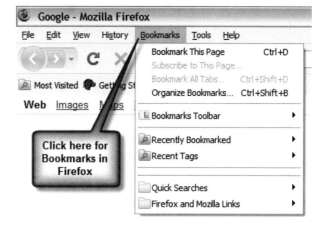

HISTORY LISTS
If you are browsing through many web pages, it can be difficult to keep track of the locations of the pages you've already visited. The *history list* allows you to quickly return to the pages you have recently visited. (● *See Panel 2.13.*)

FAVORITES OR BOOKMARKS
One great helper for finding your way is the Favorites or Bookmarks feature, which lets you store the URLs of web pages you frequently visit so that you don't have to remember and retype your favorite addresses. (● *See Panel 2.14.*) Say you're visiting a site that you really like and that you know you'd like to come back to. You click on *Favorites* (in Internet Explorer) or *Bookmarks* (in Firefox), which displays the URL on your screen, and then click on *Add* or *Bookmark This Page,* which automatically stores the address. Later you can locate the site name on your Favorites menu and click on it, and the site will reappear. (When you want to delete it, you can use the right mouse button and select the *Delete* command.)

INTERACTIVITY: HYPERLINKS, RADIO BUTTONS, & SEARCH BOXES
For any given web page that you happen to find yourself on, there may be one of three possible ways to interact with it—or sometimes even all three on the same page. (● *See Panel 2.15.*)

1. By using your mouse to click on the hyperlinks, which will transfer you to another web page (p. 68).
2. By using your mouse to click on a *radio button* and then clicking on a *Submit* command or pressing the *Enter* key. **Radio buttons are little circles located in front of various options; selecting an option with the mouse places a dot in the corresponding circle.**
3. By typing text in a **_search box_, a fill-in text box,** and then hitting the *Enter* key or clicking on a *Go* or *Continue* command, which will transfer you to another web page.

SCROLLING & FRAMES
To the bottom and side of your screen display you will note **_scroll arrows_, small up/down and left/right arrows. Clicking on scroll arrows with your mouse pointer moves the screen so that you can see the rest of**

panel 2.14
Favorites
If you are at a website you may want to visit again, click on *Favorites* (in Internet Explorer) or *Bookmark* (in Firefox) and choose *Add to Favorites* or *Bookmark This Page.* Later, to revisit the site, go to the Favorites menu, and the site's URL will reappear.

panel 2.15
Radio buttons and text box

Radio buttons
Act like station selector buttons on a car radio

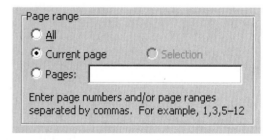

Search (text) boxes
Require you to type in information

Pages: 17-33

the web page, a movement known as _scrolling_. You can also use the arrow keys on your keyboard for scrolling.

Some web pages are divided into different rectangles known as _frames,_ each with its own scroll arrows. **A _frame_ is an independently controllable section of a web page.** A web page designer can divide a page into separate frames, each with different features or options.

LOOKING AT TWO PAGES SIMULTANEOUSLY If you want to look at more than one web page at the same time, you can position them side by side on your display screen. Select _New_ from your File menu to open more than one browser window.

Web Portals: Starting Points for Finding Information

How can I benefit from understanding how portals work?

Using a browser is sort of like exploring an enormous cave with flashlight and string. You point your flashlight at something, go there, and at that location you can see another cave chamber to go to; meanwhile, you're unrolling the ball of string behind you so that you can find your way back.

But what if you want to visit only the most spectacular rock formations in the cave and skip the rest? For that you need a guidebook. There are many such "guidebooks" for finding information on the web, sort of internet superstations known as _web portals._

TYPES OF WEB PORTALS A _web portal_, or simply _portal_, is a type of gateway website that functions as an "anchor site" and offers a broad array of resources and services, online shopping malls, email support, community forums, current news and weather, stock quotes, travel information, and links to other popular subject categories.

In addition, there are _wireless portals,_ designed for web-enabled portable devices. An example is Yahoo! Mobile, which offers Yahoo! oneSearch, Yahoo! Maps, Yahoo! Entertainment, and so on. Yahoo! Mobile users can access not only email, calendar, news, and stock quotes but also Yahoo!'s directory of wireless sites, movies, and auctions.

Portals may be general public portals (horizontal portals or megaportals), such as Yahoo!, Google, Bing (formerly MSN), Lycos, and AOL. (● _See Panel 2.16.)_ There are also specialized portals—called _vertical portals,_ or _vortals,_ which focus on specific narrow audiences or communities—such as iVillage.com for women, Fool.com for investors, Burpee.com for gardeners, and Searchnet working.techtarget.com for network administrators.

LOGGING ON TO A PORTAL When you log on to a portal, you can do three things: (1) check the home page for general information; (2) use the subject guide to find a topic you want; and (3) use a keyword to search for a topic. (● _See Panel 2.17.)_

- **Check the home page for general information:** You can treat a portal's home or start page as you would a newspaper—for example, to get news headings, weather forecasts, sports scores, and stock-market prices.

- **Use the subject guide to find a topic:** Before they acquired their other features, many of these portals began as a type of search tool known as a _subject guide,_ providing lists of several categories of websites classified by topic, such as (with Yahoo!) "Business" or "Entertainment." Such a category is also called a _hypertext index,_ and its purpose is to allow you to access information in specific categories by clicking on a hypertext link.

- **Use search box and keywords to search for a topic:** At the top of each portal's home page is a search box, a blank space into which you can type a _**keyword**_, **the subject word or words of the topic you wish to find.**

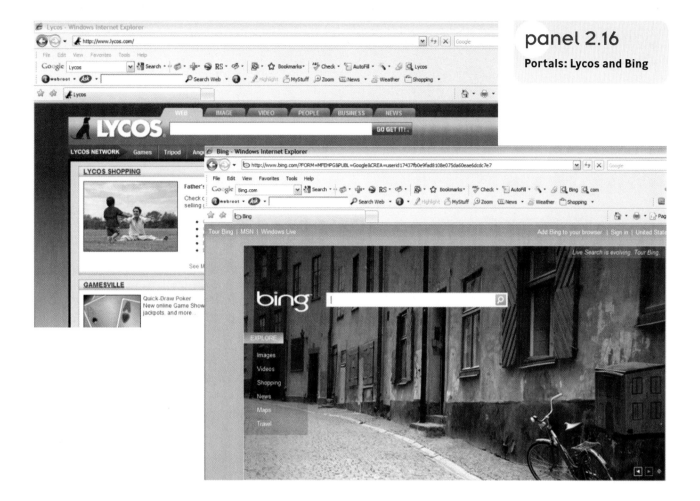

panel 2.17

Yahoo! home page
You can read headlines for news and weather, use the directory to find a topic, or use keywords in the Search text box to research specific topics.

If you want a biography on Apple Computer founder Steve Jobs, then *Steve Jobs* is the keyword. This way you don't have to plow through menu after menu of subject categories. The results of your keyword search will be displayed in a summary of documents containing the keyword you typed.

Some popular portal sites are listed on the next page. (● *See Panel 2.18.*)

Portal Name	Site
AOL	*www.aol.com*
Bing	*www.Bing.com*
Google	*www.google.com*
Lycos	*www.lycos.com*
MSN (part of Bing)	*www.msn.com*
Yahoo!	*www.yahoo.com*

Search Services & Search Engines, & How They Work

How do search services build search engines, and what are the implications for me when I make a search?

Search services **are organizations that maintain databases accessible through websites to help you find information on the internet.** Examples are not only parts of portals such as Yahoo! and Bing/MSN but also Google, Ask.com, and Gigablast, to name just a few. Search services also maintain **search engines**, **programs that enable you to ask questions or use keywords to help locate information on the web.**

Search services compile their databases by using special programs called **spiders**—**also known as** **crawlers, bots** **(for "robots"), or** **agents**—**that crawl through the World Wide Web, following links from one web page to another and indexing the words on that site.** This method of gathering information has two important implications:

A SEARCH NEVER COVERS THE ENTIRE WEB Whenever you are doing a search with a search engine, you are never searching the entire web. As one writer points out, "You are actually searching a portion of the web, captured in a fixed index created at an earlier date."[18] (An exception: Some news databases, such as Yahoo! News or Google Breaking News, offer up-to-the-minute reports on a number of subjects.) In addition, you should realize that there are a lot of databases whose material is not publicly available. Finally, a lot of published material from the 1970s and earlier has never been scanned into databases and made available.

SEARCH ENGINES DIFFER IN WHAT THEY COVER Search engines list their results according to some kind of relevance ranking, and different search engines use different ranking schemes. Some search engines, for instance, rank web pages according to popularity (frequency of visits by people looking for a particular keyword), but others don't.

Four Web Search Tools: Individual Search Engines, Subject Directories, Metasearch Engines, & Specialized Search Engines

What are the differences between the four different web search tools?

There are many types of search tools, but the most popular versions can be categorized as (1) *individual search engines,* (2) *subject directories,* (3) *metasearch engines,* and (4) *specialized search engines.* The most popular search sites, measured in share of visitors, are Google, Yahoo!, Bing, and Ask.[19]

INDIVIDUAL SEARCH ENGINES **An** **individual search engine** **compiles its own searchable database on the web.** You search for information by typing one or more keywords, and the search engine then displays a list of web pages, or "hits," that contain those keywords, ordered from most likely to least likely to contain the information you want. **Hits** **are defined as the sites that a search engine returns after running a keyword search.**

Search Tool	Site
AllTheWeb	www.alltheweb.com
Answers.com	www.answers.com
Ask	www.ask.com
Bing	www.bing.com
Gigablast	www.gigablast.com
Lycos	www.lycos.com
Yahoo!	www.yahoo.com

Search Tool	Site
Beaucoup!	www.beaucoup.com
Galaxy	www.galaxy.com/directory
Google Directory	http://directory.google.com
Open Directory Project	www.dmoz.org
Yahoo! Directory	http://dir.yahoo.com

Examples of this kind of search engine are Ask, Bing, Google, and Yahoo!, as well as AllTheWeb, Gigablast, and Lycos.[20] (● *See Panel 2.19.*) The search engine Ask allows users to ask questions in a natural way, such as "What is the population of the United States?" Answers.com is a site-and-software combination providing instant "one-click" reference answers rather than lists of search engine links.

SUBJECT DIRECTORIES Unlike a search engine, **a *subject directory* is created and maintained by human editors, not electronic spiders, and allows you to search for information by selecting lists of categories or topics,** such as "Health and Fitness" or "Science and Technology." Directories tend to be smaller than search engine databases, usually indexing only the top-level pages of a website. Subject directories are best for browsing and for searches of a more general nature.[21]

Examples of subject directories are Beaucoup!, Galaxy, Google Directory, LookSmart, Open Directory Project, and Yahoo! Directory. (● *See Panel 2.20.*)

METASEARCH ENGINES A *metasearch engine* allows you to search several search engines simultaneously. Metasearch engines are very fast and can give you a good picture of what's available across the web and where it can be found.

Examples are Clusty, Dogpile, Mamma, MetaCrawler, and Webcrawler. (● *See Panel 2.21.*) Clusty organizes search results into groups or clusters. Thus, for example, if you do a search on the word "Indians," the top results will be grouped into clusters such as Tribe, Native Americans, Baseball, and

Search Tool	Site
Clusty	http://clusty.com
Dogpile	www.dogpile.com
Grokker	www.grokker.com
ixquick	www.ixquick.com
Kartoo	www.kartoo.com
Mamma	www.mamma.com
MetaCrawler	www.metacrawler.com
Webcrawler	www.webcrawler.com
Widow	www.widow.com
Zuula	www.zuula.com

Search Tool	Site
Career.com (jobs)	www.career.com
Expedia (travel)	www.expedia.com
Internet Movie Database (movies)	www.imdb.com
Monster Board (jobs)	www.monster.com
Motley Fool (personal investments)	www.fool.com
U.S. Census Bureau (statistics)	www.census.gov
WebMD (health)	www.webmd.com

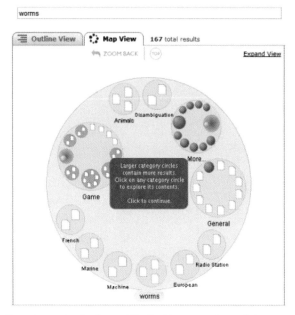

Search results for "worm" in Grokker map view; click on any category circle to explore its contents.

Indian Students. Grokker displays categories in a circular map instead of ranked lists. Searching on the word "Indians" with Grokker produces the categories of Mumbai Indians, American Indians, Cleveland Indians, and Indian Subcontinent, plus General, More, and other clusters.

SPECIALIZED SEARCH ENGINES There are also *specialized search engines,* which help locate specialized subject matter, such as material about movies, health, and jobs. These overlap with the specialized portals, or vortals, we discussed above. (● *See Panel 2.22.*)

Smart Searching: Three General Strategies

How do I find what I want on the web?

The phrase "trying to find a needle in a haystack" will come vividly to mind the first time you type a word into a search engine and back comes a response on the order of "63,173 listings found." Clearly, it becomes mandatory that you have a strategy for narrowing your search. The following are some tips.

IF YOU'RE JUST BROWSING—TWO STEPS If you're just trying to figure out what's available in your subject area, do as follows:

- **Try a subject directory:** First try using a subject directory, such as Yahoo! Directory or Open Directory Project.

- **Try a metasearch engine:** Next enter your search keywords into a metasearch engine, such as Dogpile or Mamma—just to see what else is out there.

  Example: You could type *"search engine tutorial into Yahoo!, then Dogpile."*

IF YOU'RE LOOKING FOR SPECIFIC INFORMATION If you're looking for specific information, you can try Answers.com "one-click" search *(www.answers.com).* Or you can go to a major search engine such as Google or Yahoo! and then go to a specialized search engine.

Example: You could type *"Life expectancy in U.S."* first into Google and then into the Centers for Disease Control and Prevention's search engine *(www.cdc. gov).*

IF YOU'RE LOOKING FOR EVERYTHING YOU CAN FIND ON A SUBJECT If you want to gather up everything you can find on a certain subject, try the same search on several search engines.

Example: You could type *pogonip* (a type of dense winter fog) into more than one search tool. (Of course, you will probably get some irrelevant responses, so it helps to know how to narrow your search, as explained in the box opposite.)

Generalized List of Search Engines

http://searchenginewatch. com/2156241

PRACTICAL ACTION

Evaluating & Sourcing Information Found on the Web

Want to know what a term means? You could try the immensely popular Wikipedia (*http://en.wikipedia.org*), a free online encyclopedia that anyone around the world can contribute to or edit. It has more than 200 million articles in more than 200 languages.

A *wiki,* which founding programmer Ward Cunningham got from the Hawaiian term for "quick" ("wiki wiki") when he created the WikiWiki Web in 1995, is a simple piece of software that can be downloaded for free and used to make a website that can be edited by anyone you like (or don't like). Thus, for example, corporations such as Kodak use business wikis for cross-company collaboration, such as a Word document memo that is worked on by several coworkers simultaneously. That use of wikis is valuable. But the Wikipedia is not considered reliable or authoritative by academics and librarians. As Larry Sanger, Wikipedia's former editor in chief, who now lectures at Ohio State University, says: "The wide-open nature of the internet encourages people to disregard the importance of expertise." As a result, Sanger does not allow his students to use Wikipedia for their papers.[22]

"You can expect to find everything on the web," points out one library director, "silly sites, hoaxes, frivolous and serious personal pages, commercials, reviews, articles, full-text documents, academic courses, scholarly papers, reference sources, and scientific reports."[23] It is "easy to post information on the internet, usually with no editorial oversight whatsoever, and that means it is often of questionable quality," adds a Columbia University instructor. "Few students are able to separate the good research from the bad, which is less of a problem with printed texts."[24]

An alternative to Wikipedia has recently been launched by Google: *Knol.* This is a "monetizable" creation, whereby authors are held accountable for the articles they write (and their names appear). The authors can share in revenue from ads on their page.

If you're relying on web sources for research for a term paper, how do you determine what's useful and what's not?

Guidelines for Evaluating Web Resources

Anyone (including you) can publish anything on the World Wide Web—and all kinds of people do. Here are some ways to assess credibility of the information you find there:[25]

- *On what kind of website does the information appear?* Websites may be *professional sites,* maintained by recognized organizations and institutions. They may be *news and journalistic sites,* which may be anything from *The New York Times* to e-zines (electronic magazines, or small web-based publications) such as *Network Audio Bits.* They may be *commercial sites,* sponsored by companies ranging from the Disney Company to The Happy House Painter. They may be *special-interest sites,* maintained by activists ranging from those of the major political parties to proponents of legalization of marijuana. They may be *blogs* or *personal home pages,* maintained by individuals of all sorts, from professors to children to struggling musicians.

- *Does the website author appear to be a legitimate authority?* What kind of qualifications and credentials does the author have, and what kind of organization is he or she associated with? Does a web search show that the author published in other scholarly and professional publications?

- *Is the website objective, complete, and current?* Is the website trying to sell you on a product, service, or point of view? Is the language balanced and objective, or is it one-sided and argumentative? Does the author cite sources, and do they seem to come from responsible publications?

A variant on these guidelines has been framed by Butler University librarian Brad Matthies as CRITIC. (● *See Panel 2.23, next page*).

Multimedia Search Tools: Image, Audio, & Video Searching

What kind of nontext search engines are available?

Most web searches involve text, but there are many nontext kinds of resources as well, including videos and still images. (● *See Panel 2.24, next page.*)

STILL IMAGES Interested in an image of *Dilbert?* You could go to Yahoo! Search—Image Search (*images.search.yahoo.com*), Google Image Search

panel 2.23

CRITIC

These guidelines will help you think critically about the reliability of online information.

- **C—Claim:** Is the source's claim clear and reasonable, timely and relevant? Or is there evidence of motivationally based language?
- **R—Role of the claimant:** Is the author of the information clearly identifiable? Are there reasons to suspect political, religious, philosophical, cultural, or financial biases?
- **I—Information backing the claim:** Is evidence for the claim presented? Can it be verified, or is the evidence anecdotal or based on testimony? Does the author cite credible references?
- **T—Testing:** Can you test the claim, as by conducting your own quantitative research?
- **I—Independent verification:** Have reputable experts evaluated and verified the claim?
- **C—Conclusion:** After taking the preceding five steps, can you reach a conclusion about the claim?

Source: Adapted from Brad Matthies, "The Psychologist, the Philosopher, and the Librarian: The Information-Literacy Version of CRITIC," *Skeptical Inquirer,* May/June 2005, pp. 49–52.

panel 2.24

Some multimedia search engines

Search Tool	Site
altavista	www.altavista.com/image/default
A9 (Amazon.com)	http://a9.com
Blinkx	www.blinkx.com
Digital Library System	www.fws.gov/dls
Find Sounds	www.findsounds.com/types.html
Google Video	http://video.google.com
Internet Archive for Audio	www.archive.org/details/audio
Internet Archive for Moving Images	www.archive.org/details/movies
Picsearch	www.picsearch.com
Pixsta	www.pixsta.com
The University of Delaware Library	www2.lib.udel.edu/subj/film/resguide/streamingweb.htm
Yahoo! Video	http://video.search.yahoo.com

Citing Web Sources in College Papers

The four principal kinds of styles for citing sources—books, articles, and so on—are (1) the Modern Language Association style (for humanities), (2) the American Psychological Association style (for social science subjects), (3) the University of Chicago Press style, and (4) the Turabian style. To learn the format of these styles—including those for internet sources—go to:

http://library.wustl.edu/ research/citesource.html

www.lib.berkeley.edu/Teaching Lib/Guides/Internet/Style. html

(*http://images.google.com*), or Bing Images (*www.bing.com/images*), where you'll be offered several thousand choices of Dilbert still images. Other good image search engines are Exalead and Picsearch.

AUDIO & VIDEO Other multimedia search engines offer audio as well as image and video searching. If you go to CampaignSearch.com, for instance, and type in keywords of your choosing, the search engine StreamSage will search audio and video broadcasts by analyzing speech. ShadowTV can provide continuous access to live and archived television content via the web. Yahoo! allows users to search for closed captioning associated with a broadcast and then to click for full-motion video of the words being spoken.

Among the audio search engines available are Yahoo! Audio Search, AltaVista Audio Search, BlogDigger, SingingFish, FindSounds, ez2Find, and Blinkx. Among video search engines you can select from are All TheWeb, SingingFish, the Open Video Project, AltaVista Video, Yahoo! Video Search, Google Video Search, and Blinkx Video Search.

MULTIPLE SOURCES, INCLUDING MUSIC A9 culls information from multiple sources, including the web, images from Google, inside-the-book text from Amazon.com, movies (Internet Movie Database), and reference materials from Answers.com. Rocket Mobile has a music search program for cellphones called Song ID. "You can hold your cellphone up to a music source for 10 seconds," says one account, "and it will identify the singer, the song, and the album."[26]

PRACTICAL ACTION
Serious Web Search Techniques

Y ou type *"Bill Gates"* into Google and get around 38,800,000 hits; in Yahoo!, 70,600,000. How useful is that? Following are some tricks of the trade.

- **Choose your search terms well, and watch your spelling:** Use the most precise words possible. If you're looking for information about novelist Thomas Wolfe (author of *Look Homeward Angel,* published 1929) rather than novelist/journalist Tom Wolfe (author of *I Am Charlotte Simmons,* 2005), details are important: *Thomas,* not *Tom; Wolfe,* not *Wolf.* Use *poodle* rather than *dog, Maui* rather than *Hawaii, Martin guitar* rather than *guitar,* or you'll get thousands of responses that have little or nothing to do with what you're looking for. You may need to use alternate words and spellings to explore the topic you're investigating: *e-mail, email, electronic mail.*

- **Type words in lowercase:** Typing words in lowercase will help you find both lowercase and capitalized variations.

- **Use phrases with quotation marks rather than separate words:** If you type *ski resort,* you could get results of (1) everything to do with skis, on the one hand, and (2) everything to do with resorts—winter, summer, mountain, seaside—on the other. Better to put your phrase in quotation marks—*"ski resort"*—to narrow your search.

- **Put unique words first in a phrase:** Better to have *"Tom Wolfe novels"* rather than *"Novels Tom Wolfe."* Or if you're looking for the Hoagy Carmichael song rather than the southern state, indicate "Georgia on My Mind."

- **Use Boolean operators—AND, OR, and NOT:** Most search sites use symbols called *Boolean operators* to make searching more precise. To illustrate how they are used, suppose you're looking for the song "Strawberry Fields Forever."[31]

  AND connects two or more search words and means that all of them must appear in the search results. Example: *Strawberry AND Fields AND Forever.*

  OR connects two or more search words and indicates that any of the two may appear in the results.

Example: *Strawberry Fields OR Strawberry fields.*

  NOT, when inserted before a word, excludes that word from the results. Example: *Strawberry Fields NOT Sally NOT W.C.* (to distinguish from the actress Sally Field and long-ago comedian W.C. Fields).

- **Use inclusion and exclusion operators—plus (+) and minus (−):** With many search engines you can use the *inclusion operator,* the plus sign, and the *exclusion operator,* the minus sign, to take the place of AND and NOT.

  The plus sign (+), like *AND,* precedes a word that must appear. Example: *+ Strawberry + Fields.*

  The minus sign (−), like *NOT,* excludes the word that follows it. Example: *Strawberry Fields–Sally.*

- **Use wildcards—asterisks (*) and question marks (?):** If you want as many results as possible on a keyword, use an asterisk (*) or question mark (?) to mean "anything/everything."

  Example: Type *dance** and you will get hits for *dance, dances, dancers, dancing, dancewear,* and so on.

  If you can't remember how to spell something, use the question mark (?). Example: If you type *Solzhe?,* you will get page matches for the Russian author *Solzhenitsyn.*

- **Read the Help or Search Tips section:** All search sites provide a Help section and tips. This could save you time later.

- **Try an alternate general search site or a specific search site:** As we indicated in the text, if you're looking for very specific information, a general type of search site such as Yahoo! may not be the best way to go. Instead, you should turn to a specific search site. Examples: To explore public companies, try Hoover's Online (*www.hoovers.com*). For news stories, try Yahoo News (*http://dailynews.yahoo.com*) or CNN (*www.cnn.com*). For pay-per-view information from all sorts of articles, journals, and reports, try LexisNexis (*www.lexisnexis.com*) and Factiva (Dow Jones and Reuters at *www.factiva.com*).

SCHOLARLY Google offers Google Scholar *(www.scholar.google.com),* described as "a one-stop shop of scholarly abstracts, books, peer-reviewed papers, and technical papers intended for academics and scientists."[27]

Google has also launched an ambitious project in which it is scanning page by page more than 50 million books (at a cost of about $10 for each book scanned) from several libraries—those at Harvard, Stanford, Oxford, and the University of Michigan, plus the New York Public Library. "This is one of the most transformative events in the history of information distribution since Gutenberg," says New York Public Library CEO Paul LeClerc.[28] The Google Print Library Project, as it is called, is currently being studied by the U.S. Justice Department to see if massive book scanning violates antitrust laws, since authors, campus researchers, and library groups have expressed serious concerns over the move.[29]

Desktop Search: Tools for Searching Your Computer's Hard Disk

How can I find things on my hard disk?

These days an inexpensive desktop computer, points out *BusinessWeek* technology writer Stephen Wildstrom, comes with enough hard-drive storage capacity to store the text of 13,000 copies of the long novel *War and Peace.* "All that space," he observes, "means that anything you save, from Grandma's email messages to a web page for a quaint bed-and-breakfast, is likely to stay there forever. Good luck trying to find it."[30]

The solution: a *desktop search engine,* a tool that extends searching beyond the web to the contents of your personal computer's hard disk. Desktop search allows users to quickly and easily find words and concepts stored on the hard-disk drive, using technology similar to that in web search engines. Desktop tools must be downloaded from the internet, often as part of a toolbar (a bar across the top of the display window on your computer screen, offering frequently executed options or commands). The tools remain in the background on your computer screen until you want to use them. Separate searches are usually required for the web and for the desktop.

AltaVista premiered a version called Discovery in 1998, but the technology failed to catch on. Now all the principal search engine services offer it. (● *See Panel 2.25.*)

Tagging: Saving Links for Easier Retrieval Later

How do I use tags to categorize things I've found on the web?

Once you've found favorite websites, how do you keep them found so that you can get back to them easily? You can always use the bookmarking or favorites feature, but there is also another way called *tagging.* __Tags__ **are do-it-yourself labels that people can put on anything found on the internet, from articles to photos to videos.** Using so-called social-bookmarking websites such as del.icio.us or BlinkList or photo-sharing services such as Flickr, users can tag anything for easy retrieval later. Unlike bookmarks or favorites, these tags can be shared easily with other people, which allows people to share similar interests and ideas.

panel 2.25

Some desktop search tools

Search Tool	Site
Archivarius	*www.likasoft.com/document-search*
Ask.com Desktop Search	*http://sp.ask.com/docs/desktop/ overview.shtml*
Blinkx Pico	*www2.blinkx.com/pico*
Copernic Desktop Search	*www.copernic.com/*
Everything	*www.snapfiles.com*
Professional Google Desktop Search	*http://desktop.google.com*
Yahoo! Desktop Search	*http://us.config.toolbar.yahoo.com/yds*

2.4 EMAIL & OTHER WAYS OF COMMUNICATING OVER THE NET

What are email and webmail, attachments, instant messaging, FTP, newsgroups, listservs, real-time chat, and netiquette?

Once connected to the internet, most people want to immediately join the millions of users—probably 90% of them—who send and receive electronic mail, or email, the principal use of the internet. Your incoming mail is stored in your mailbox on the access provider's computer, usually a server called a *mail server.* Outgoing mail is sent to a *Simple Mail Transfer Protocol (SMTP) server.* (● *See Panel 2.26.)* When you use your email software to retrieve your messages, the email is sent from the server to your computer using Post Office Protocol version 3 (POP3—not the same as "point of presence") or Internet Message Access Protocol (IMAP), which has expanded functions compared to POP3. For example, if your access provider and email software support IMAP,

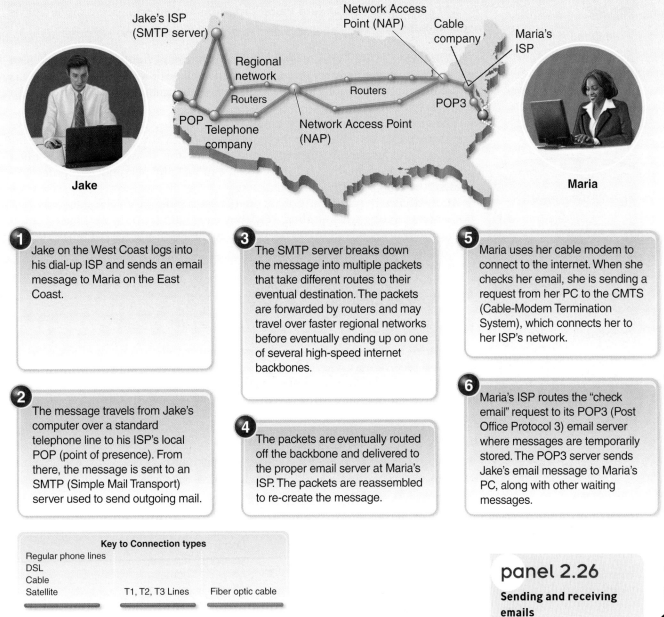

Jake

Maria

1 Jake on the West Coast logs into his dial-up ISP and sends an email message to Maria on the East Coast.

2 The message travels from Jake's computer over a standard telephone line to his ISP's local POP (point of presence). From there, the message is sent to an SMTP (Simple Mail Transport) server used to send outgoing mail.

3 The SMTP server breaks down the message into multiple packets that take different routes to their eventual destination. The packets are forwarded by routers and may travel over faster regional networks before eventually ending up on one of several high-speed internet backbones.

4 The packets are eventually routed off the backbone and delivered to the proper email server at Maria's ISP. The packets are reassembled to re-create the message.

5 Maria uses her cable modem to connect to the internet. When she checks her email, she is sending a request from her PC to the CMTS (Cable-Modem Termination System), which connects her to her ISP's network.

6 Maria's ISP routes the "check email" request to its POP3 (Post Office Protocol 3) email server where messages are temporarily stored. The POP3 server sends Jake's email message to Maria's PC, along with other waiting messages.

Key to Connection types		
Regular phone lines		
DSL		
Cable		
Satellite	T1, T2, T3 Lines	Fiber optic cable

panel 2.26

Sending and receiving emails

you can search through your email messages while they are still on the access provider's server—*before* you download them. Then you can choose which messages to download on your machine.

Two Ways to Send & Receive Email

What's the difference between an email program and web-based email?

There are two ways to send and receive email—via *email program* or via *web-based email.*

EMAIL PROGRAM An _email program_, also called *email client software,* enables you to send email by running email software on your computer, which interacts with an email server at your internet access provider to send and receive email. Your incoming mail is stored on the server in an electronic mailbox. When you access the email server, your incoming messages are sent to your software's *inbox,* where they are ready to be opened and read. Examples of such programs are Microsoft's Outlook Express, now called Windows Mail, and Apple Inc.'s Mail.

The advantage of standard email programs is that you can easily integrate your email with other applications, such as calendar, task list, and contact list.

WEB-BASED EMAIL With _web-based email_, or _webmail_, you send and receive messages by interacting via a browser with a website. The big four email carriers are Yahoo! Mail, Windows Live Hotmail, Gmail (Google), and AOL Mail.[32]

The advantage of web-based email is that you can easily send and receive messages while traveling anywhere in the world. Moreover, because all your outgoing and incoming messages and folders for storing them (explained below) are stored on the mail server, you can use any personal computer and browser to keep up with your email.

Many users will rely mostly on an email program in their personal computer, but when traveling without their PCs, they will switch over to web-based email (using computers belonging to friends or available—for a fee—in airports and hotels) to check messages. Or they use portable devices such as a BlackBerry to do text messaging. (● *See Panel 2.27.*)

How to Use Email

What are some tips for being effective with email?

You'll need an email address, of course, a sort of electronic mailbox used to send and receive messages. All such addresses follow the same approach: *username@domain.* These are somewhat different from web URLs, which do not use the "@" (called "at") symbol. You can check with your internet access provider to see if a certain name is available.

Free Email

For discussion of free email services, go to:

www.emailaddresses.com

panel 2.27

Mobile mail
Portable devices such as this BlackBerry Wireless Handheld allow you to send and receive email messages from many locations.

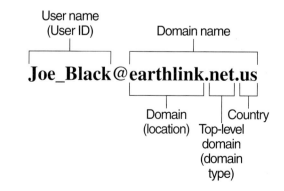

User name (User ID) — Joe_Black

Domain name — @earthlink.net.us

Domain (location) — earthlink

Top-level domain (domain type) — net

Country — us

- **The user name: Joe_Black** The *user name,* or *user ID,* identifies who is at the address—in this case, *Joe_Black* (note the underscore). There are many ways that Joe Black's user name might be designated, with and without capital letters: *Joe_Black, joe_black, joe.black, joeblack, jblack, joeb,* and so on.

- **Domain name: @earthlink** The *domain name,* which is located after the @ ("at") symbol, tells the location and type of address. Domain-name components are separated by periods (called "dots"). The domain portion of the address (such as *Earthlink,* an internet service provider) provides specific information about the location—where the message should be delivered.

- **Top-level domain: .net** The *top-level domain,* or *domain code,* is a three-letter extension that describes the domain type: *.net, .com, .gov, .edu, .org, .mil, .int*—network, commercial, government, educational, nonprofit, military, or international organization.

- **Country: .us** Some domain names also include a two-letter extension for the country—*.us* for United States, *.ca* for Canada, *.mx* for Mexico.

The illustration on the next page shows how to send, receive, and reply to email. (● *See Panel 2.28.*) Here are some tips about using email:

TYPE ADDRESSES CAREFULLY You need to type the address exactly as it appears, including capitalization and all underscores and periods. If you type an email address incorrectly (putting in spaces, for example), your message will be returned to you labeled "undeliverable."

USE THE REPLY COMMAND When responding to an e-message someone has sent you, the easiest way to avoid making address mistakes is to use the Reply command, which will automatically fill in the correct address in the "To" line. Be careful not to use the Reply All command unless you want your reply to be sent to *all* the original email's recipients.

USE THE ADDRESS-BOOK FEATURE You can store the email addresses of people sending you messages in your program's "address book." This feature also allows you to organize your email addresses according to a nickname or the person's real name so that, for instance, you can look up your friend Joe Black under his real name, instead of under his user name, *bugsme2,* which you might not remember. The address book also allows you to organize addresses into various groups—such as your friends, your relatives, club members—so that you can easily send all members of a group the same message with a single command.

DEAL WITH EACH EMAIL ONLY ONCE When a message comes in, delete it, respond to it, or file it away in a folder. Don't use your inbox for storage.

DON'T "BLOAT" YOUR EMAIL Email messages loaded with fancy typestyles, logos, and background graphics take longer to download. Keep messages simple.

Sorting Your Email

How can I keep my emails organized?

On an average day, billions of business and personal emails are sent in North America. If, as many people do, you receive 50–150 emails per day, you'll have to keep them organized so that you don't lose control.

Country Abbreviations

What do you think the country abbreviations are for Micronesia? Botswana? Saint Lucia? Go to:

www.eubank-web.com/William/ Webmaster/c-codes.htm

www.thrall.org/domains.htm

Address Book: Lists email addresses you use most; can be attached automatically to messages

Send: Command for sending messages

cc: For copying ("carbon/courtesy copy") message to others

bcc: For copying others ("blind carbon copy") without the primary recipient knowing it

Message area

You can conclude every message with a custom "signature"

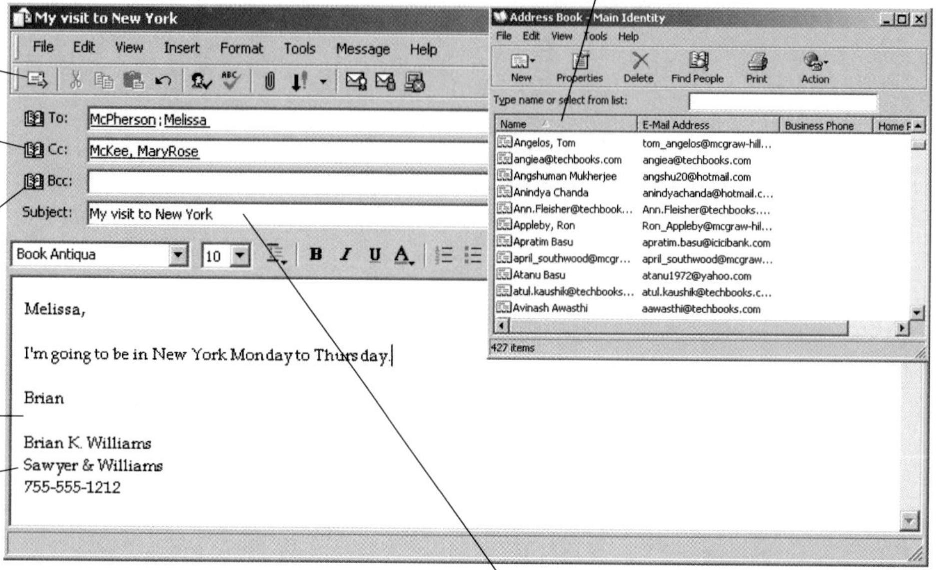

Subject line: Preview incoming email by reviewing the subject lines to see if you really need to read the messages

Receiving email

Reply, Reply All, Forward, Delete: For helping you handle incoming email

Inbox lists messages waiting in email box. (Unopened envelope icon shows unread mail.)

Selected message displayed here

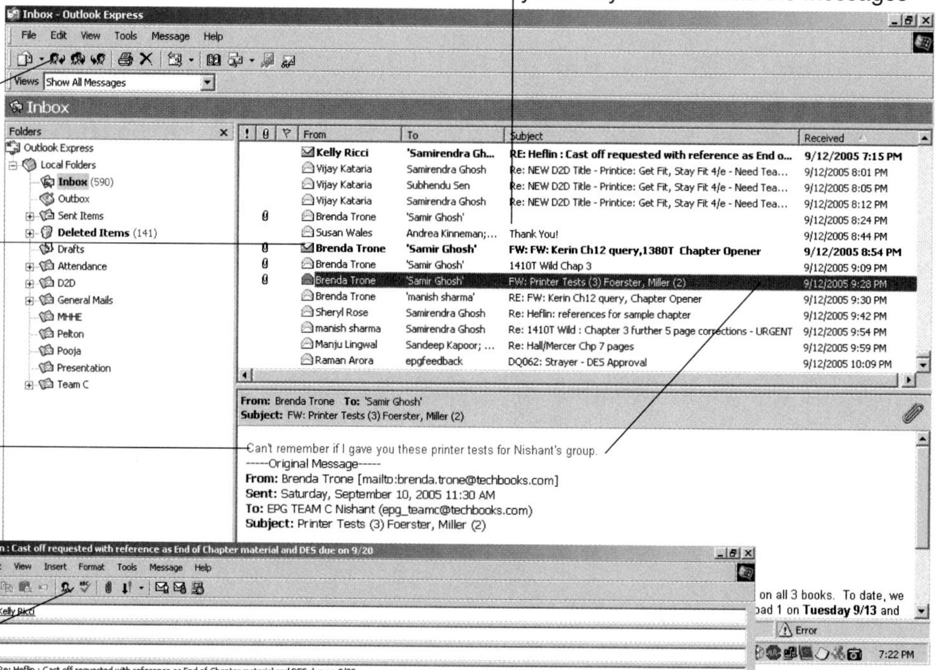

Replying to email

Use the **Reply** command icon, and the email program automatically fills in the To, From, and Subject lines in your reply.

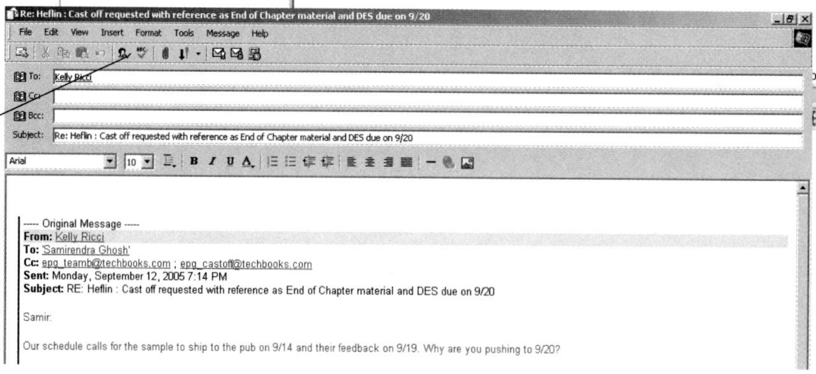

panel 2.28

How to send, receive, and reply with email

One way to stay organized is by using instant organizers, also called *filters,* which sort mail on the basis of the name of the sender or the mailing list and put particular emails into one folder. (● *See Panel 2.29.)* Then you can read emails sent to this folder later when you have time, freeing up your inbox for mail that needs your more immediate attention. Instructions on how to set up such organizers are in your email program's Help section.

Attachments

What are the benefits of being able to do email attachments?

You have written a great research paper and you immediately want to show it off to someone. If you were sending it via the Postal Service, you would write a cover note—"Folks, look at this great paper I wrote about globalization! See attached"—then attach it to the paper, and stick it in an envelope. Email has its own version of this. If the file of your paper exists in the computer from which you are sending email, you can write your email message (your cover note) and then use the Attach File command to attach the document. (● *See Panel 2.30, next page.)* (Note: It's important that the person receiving the email attachment have exactly the same software that created the attached file, such as Microsoft Word, or have software that can read and convert the attached file.) Downloading attachments from the mail server can take a lot of time—so you may want to discourage friends from sending you many attachments. You may also want to use compression software to reduce the size of your attachments.

While you could also copy your document into the main message and send it that way, some email software loses formatting options such as **bold** or *italic* text or special symbols. And if you're sending song lyrics or poetry, the lines of text may break differently on someone else's display screen than they do on

panel 2.29

Sorting email
Email folders

Sending an email attachment

③ Third, use your email software's toolbar buttons or menus to attach the file that contains the attachment.

④ Fourth, click on *Send* to send the email message and attachment.

① First, address the person who will receive the attachment.

② Second, write a "cover letter" email advising the recipient of the attachment.

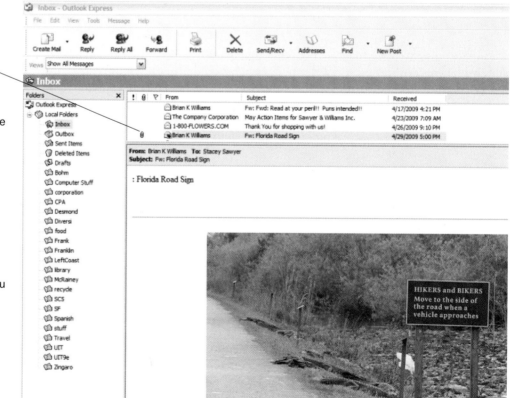

Receiving an email attachment

When you receive a file containing an attachment, you'll see an icon indicating the message contains more than just text. You can click on the icon to see the attachment. If you have the software the attached file was created in, you can open the attachment immediately to read or print, or you can save the attachment in a location of your choice (on your computer). You can also forward the attachment to another person.

panel 2.30

Attach File function

yours. Thus, the benefit of the attachment feature is that it preserves all such formatting, provided the recipient is using the same word processing software that you used. You can also attach pictures, sounds, videos, and other files to your email message.

Important Note: Many *viruses*—those rogue programs that can seriously damage your PC or programs—ride along with email as attached files. Thus, you should *never open an attached file from an unknown source*. (We describe viruses in Chapter 6.)

Instant Messaging

What are the benefits and drawbacks of my using instant messaging?

Instant messages are like a cross between email and phone, allowing communication that is far speedier than conventional email. With **_instant messaging (IM),_ any user on a given email system can send a message and have it pop up instantly on the screen of anyone else logged onto that system.** (Instant messaging should not be confused with *text messaging,* or *texting,* the exchange of messages between mobile phones, as we discuss in Chapter 7. Nor should it be confused with *twittering,* the sending of text-based messages of up to 140 characters.)

As soon as you use your computer or portable device to connect to the internet and log on to your IM account, you see a *buddy* list (or *contacts* list), a list you have created that consists of other IM users you want to communicate with. If all parties agree, they can initiate online typed conversations in real time (in a "chat room"). The messages appear on the display screen in a small **_window_—a rectangular area containing a document or activity**—so that users can exchange messages almost instantaneously while operating other programs.

GETTING INSTANT-MESSAGING CAPABILITY Examples of present instant-message systems are AOL/AIM, MSN, Google Talk, MySpace, Facebook, and Yahoo! Messenger. To get instant messaging, which is often free, you download software and register with the service, providing it with a user name and password. When your computer or portable device is connected to the internet, the software checks in with a central server, which verifies your identity and looks to see if any of your "buddies" are also online. You can then start a conversation by sending a message to any buddy currently online.

THE DOWNSIDE OF IM IM has become a hit with many users. Instant messaging is especially useful in the workplace as a way of reducing long-distance telephone bills when you have to communicate with colleagues who are geographically remote but with whom you must work closely. However, you need to be aware of a few drawbacks:

- **Lack of privacy:** Most IM services lack the basic privacy that most other forms of communication provide. Efforts are under way to develop IM security software and procedures, but for now IM users should be aware that they have virtually no privacy.

- **Lack of common standards:** Many IM products do not communicate with one another. If you're using AOL's AIM, you cannot communicate with a buddy on Yahoo!.

- **Time wasters when you have to get work done:** An instant message "is the equivalent of a ringing phone because it pops up on the recipient's screen right away," says one writer.[33] Some analysts suggest that, because of its speed, intrusiveness, and ability to show who else is online, IM can destroy workers' concentration in some offices. You can put off

Accessing Email while Traveling Abroad

To access your email using a local call while traveling outside North America, get a free email account with Yahoo! (*http://mail.yahoo.com*), Windows Live Hotmail (*www.hotmail.com*), or Mail.com (*www.mail.com*).

acknowledging email, voice mail, or faxes. But instant messaging is "the cyber-equivalent of someone walking into your office and starting up a conversation as if you had nothing better to do," says one critic. "It violates the basic courtesy of not shoving yourself into other people's faces."[34]

You can turn off your instant messages, but that is like turning off the ringer on your phone; after a while people will wonder why you're never available. Buddy lists or other contact lists can also become very in-groupish. When that happens, people are distracted from their work as they worry about staying current with their circle (or being shut out of one). Incidentally, a 2008 survey of 2,134 adults found that although 58% said that email, cellphones, and the internet gave them more control over when to work, 46% also said that these technologies increase the demands that they work more hours, and 49% said that the technologies made it harder to disconnect from work when they should be off.[35]

FTP—for Copying All the Free Files You Want

What does FTP allow me to do?

Many net users enjoy "FTPing"—cruising the system and checking into some of the tens of thousands of FTP sites, which predate the web and offer interesting free or inexpensive files to download. ___FTP (File Transfer Protocol)___ **is a software standard for transferring files between computers with different operating systems. You can connect to a remote computer called an** *FTP site* **and transfer files to your own microcomputer's hard disk via TCI/IP over the internet.** Free files offered cover nearly anything that can be stored on a computer: software, games, photos, maps, art, music, books, statistics. (● *See Panel 2.31.*) You can also set up your own private FTP site (for example, through ShareFile.com) to enable you and other people you allow to use your site to upload and download files that are too large to send as email attachments.

Some FTP files are open to the public (at *anonymous FTP sites*); some are not. For instance, a university might maintain an FTP site with private files (such as lecture transcripts) available only to professors and students with assigned user names and passwords. It might also have public FTP files open to anyone with an email address. You can download FTP files using either your web browser or special software (called an *FTP client program*), such as Fetch and Cute.

FTP CLients & Servers

FTP software programs, called FTP clients, come with many operating systems, including Windows, DOS, Unix, and Linux. Web browsers also come with FTP clients. For lists of FTP clients and FTP servers, go to:

www.answers.com/main/ ntquery? method+4&dsis+2 222&dekey=FTP+client&gwp +ll&curtab+2222

www.thefreecountry.com/web master/freeftpclients.shtml

You can also set up your own FTP site, for example, by going to:

www.sharefile.com

panel 2.31

FTP software

SmartFTP

You are here: Home ▸ Client

- Client
  - Download
  - Features
  - Editions
  - Screenshots
  - Purchase
    - Buy Now
    - Renewal
- FTP Library
  - Download
  - Samples
  - Documentation
  - Purchase
- Support
  - Tutorials
  - Knowledge Base
  - Forums
- Corporate
  - About
  - Contact
- Search

What is SmartFTP?

SmartFTP is an FTP (File Transfer Protocol) client which allows you to transfer files between your local computer and a server on the Internet. With its many basic and advanced Features SmartFTP also offers secure, reliable and efficient transfers that make it a powerful tool. Click here to Download our ftp software.

Download SmartFTP

SmartFTP can be used for:

- Web site publishing and maintenance
- Upload and download of images, documents, movie and music files
- Share your files with your friends and coworkers
- Backups of local or remote files

SmartFTP 3.0 Build 1027 released

What's New

- FIPS 140-2 compliance
  Follows the Federal Information Processing Standards (FIPS) guidelines.
- **Favorites Import from cPanel, DreamHost, Plesk**
  Import all user accounts from your control panel
- **Advanced Filter for Browser Views**
  Filter the files and folders displayed in the list view.
- **Intelligent Folder Monitor**
  Folder monitor processes changes only.

How Do I? 2 of 168513 messages view all »   [+ post your question]

have comments posted
By mark.el - 10:26am - 1 author - 0 replies
My custom domain bought through Blogger is not synchronized
By TomA - 10:22am - 1 author - 0 replies

Something Is Broken 2 of 86334 messages view all »   [+ post your question]

My Blogger account has been suspended :(
By Anna M - 10:07am - 1 author - 0 replies
Mystery author on my blog
By TerriR - 9:57am - 1 author - 0 replies

Publishing Trouble 2 of 57049 messages view all »   [+ post your question]

Newly created blog won't show main page
By Just J - 10:28am - 2 authors - 1 reply
Error on publishing photos
By viewpoint93 - 10:10am - 2 authors - 1 reply

Login Issues 2 of 11474 messages view all »   [+ post your question]

My blog is not deleted nor marked as Spam i Can't access the dashboard ...
By nitecruzr - 10:04am - 3 authors - 7 replies
my blog has been deleted
By Raymond4UNC - 8:51am - 1 author - 0 replies

Layouts & Templates 2 of 36365 messages view all »   [+ post your question]

Template Error
By NattyLou - 10:09am - 3 authors - 4 replies
how do i get back my old template?
By Cruella - 9:55am - 1 author - 0 replies

panel 2.32

Newsgroup message board from the Blogger Help Group, a Google group

Newsgroups—for Online Typed Discussions on Specific Topics

What would probably be my favorite kind of newsgroup?

A **_newsgroup_ (or *forum*) is a giant electronic bulletin board on which users conduct written discussions about a specific subject.** (● *See Panel 2.32.*) There are thousands of internet newsgroups—which charge no fee— and they cover an amazing array of topics. In addition, for a small fee, services such as Meganetnews.com and CoreNews.com will get you access to more than 100,000 newsgroups all over the world. Newsgroups take place on a special network of computers called **_Usenet_, a worldwide public network of servers that can be accessed through the internet** (*www.usenet.com*). To participate, you need a **_newsreader_, a program included with most browsers that allows you to access a newsgroup and read or type messages.** (Messages, incidentally, are known as *articles*.)

One way to find a newsgroup of interest to you is to use a portal such as Yahoo! or Bing to search for specific topics. Or you can use Google's Groups (*http://groups.google.com/grphp?hl+en&ie=UTF-8*), which presents the newsgroups matching the topic you specify. About a dozen major topics, identified by abbreviations ranging from *alt* (alternative topics) to *talk* (opinion and discussion), are divided into hierarchies of subtopics.

Listservs: Email-Based Discussion Groups

Why would I want to sign up for a listserv?

Want to receive email from people all over the world who share your interests? You can try finding a mailing list and then "subscribing"—signing up, just as you would for a free newsletter or magazine. **A _listserv_ is an automatic mailing-list server that sends email to subscribers who regularly participate in discussion topics.** (● *See Panel 2.33, next page.*) Listserv companies include L-Soft's Listserv (*www.lsoft.com*), Majordomo (*www.majordomo.com*), and *http://listserve.com/*. To subscribe, you send an email to the list-server moderator and ask to become a member, after which you will automatically receive email messages from anyone who responds to the server.

Mailing lists are one-way or two-way. A one-way list either accepts or sends information, but the user interacts only with the list server and not other

users. Most one-way mailing lists are used for announcements, newsletters, and advertising (and "spam," discussed shortly). Two-way lists, which are limited to subscribers, let users interact with other subscribers to the mailing list; this is the discussion type of mailing list.

Real-Time Chat—Typed Discussions among Online Participants

What discussion subjects might I like to participate in using RTC?

With mailing lists and newsgroups, participants may contribute to a discussion, go away, and return hours or days later to catch up on others' typed contributions. With **_real-time chat (RTC)_, participants have a typed discussion ("chat") while online at the same time,** just like a telephone conversation except that messages are typed rather than spoken. Otherwise, the format is much like a newsgroup, with a message board to which participants may send ("post") their contributions. To start a chat, you use a service available on your browser such as IRC (Internet Relay Chat) that will connect you to a chat server.

Unlike instant messaging, which tends to involve one-on-one conversation, real-time chat usually involves several participants. As a result, RTC is often like being at a party, with many people and many threads of conversation occurring at once.

Netiquette: Appropriate Online Behavior

What are the rules of courtesy for using email?

You may think etiquette is about knowing which fork to use at a formal dinner. Basically, though, etiquette has to do with politeness and civility—with rules for getting along so that people don't get upset or suffer hurt feelings.

New internet users, known as "newbies," may accidentally offend other people in a discussion group or in an email simply because they are unaware of **_netiquette_, or "network etiquette"—appropriate online behavior.** In

general, netiquette has two basic rules: (1) Don't waste people's time; and (2) don't say anything to a person online that you wouldn't say to his or her face.

Some more specific rules of netiquette are shown below:

- **Consult FAQs:** Most online groups post ***FAQs (frequently asked questions) that explain expected norms of online behavior for a particular group.*** Always read these first—before someone in the group tells you you've made a mistake.

- **Avoid flaming:** A form of speech unique to online communication, ***flaming* is writing an online message that uses derogatory, obscene, or inappropriate language.** Flaming is a form of public humiliation inflicted on people who have failed to read FAQs or have otherwise not observed netiquette (although it can happen just because the sender has poor impulse control and needs a course in anger management). Something that smooths communication online is the use of *emoticons,* keyboard-produced pictorial representations of expressions. (● *See Panel 2.34.)*

- **Don't SHOUT:** Use of all-capital letters is considered the equivalent of SHOUTING. Avoid, except when they are required for emphasis of a word or two (as when you can't use italics in your e-messages).

- **Be careful with jokes:** In email, subtleties are often lost, so jokes may be taken as insults or criticism.

- **Avoid sloppiness, but avoid criticizing others' sloppiness:** Avoid spelling and grammatical errors. But don't criticize those same errors in others' messages. (After all, they may not speak English as a native language.) Most email software comes with spell-checking capability, which is easy to use.

- **Don't send huge file attachments, unless requested:** Your cousin living in the country may find it takes minutes rather than seconds for his or her computer to download a massive file (as of a video that you want to share). Better to query in advance before sending large files as attachments. Also, whenever you send an attachment, be sure the recipient has the appropriate software to open your attachment.

- **When replying, quote only the relevant portion:** If you're replying to just a couple of matters in a long email posting, don't send back the entire message. This forces your recipient to wade through lots of text to find the reference. Instead, edit his or her original text down to the relevant paragraph and then put in your response immediately following.

- **Don't "overforward":** Don't automatically forward emails to your friends without checking if the contents are true and appropriate.

Icon	Meaning
:) :]	smiley or happy face
:D XD	laughing, big grin
:(:c	frown
D: D=	horror, disgust
:) *)	wink
:P :p ::b	tongue sticking out
:O	surprise, shock
:/ :\	skeptical, annoyed, uneasy
:X :#	sealed lips, embarrassed
O:)	innocent
:'(	crying

panel 2.34

Some emoticons

2.5 THE ONLINE GOLD MINE: Telephony, Multimedia, Webcasting, Blogs, E-Commerce, & the Social Web

What are internet telephony, various kinds of multimedia, RSS, and different web feeds (webcasting, blogging, podcasting), types of e-commerce, and the social web?

"For vivid reporting from the enormous zone of tsunami disaster," says a newspaper account, "it was hard to beat the blogs."[36]

Blogs, as technology writer Lee Gomes points out, used to be regarded as web-based "daily diaries of people with no real lives to chronicle in the first place."[37] But the December 2004 Indian Ocean calamity that resulted in over 143,000 people killed and more than 146,000 missing also showed how quick and effective this form of web technology could be in spreading instant news, often beating out the mainstream news media. In particular, the tsunami spurred the distribution of *video blogs,* or *vblogs,* consisting of video footage mostly shot by vacationing foreign tourists during and after the disaster. One video, for example, showed an elderly couple overpowered by a wave, filmed at a beach hotel by a factory worker from Sweden.[38]

The opportunities offered by the internet and the web seem inexhaustible. Here we'll examine several resources available to you.

Telephony: The Internet Telephone & Videophone

Why would I want to make phone calls via the internet?

As we stated earlier, the internet breaks up conversations (as it does any other transmitted data) into "information packets" that can be sent over separate lines and then regrouped at the destination, whereas conventional voice phone lines carry a conversation over a single path. Thus, the internet can move a lot more traffic over a network than the traditional telephone link can.

With ___internet telephony,___ or ***VoIP phoning* (short for *Voice over Internet Protocol*)—using the net to make phone calls, either one to one or for audioconferencing**—you can make long-distance phone calls that are surprisingly inexpensive or even free. (● *See Panel 2.35.*) Indeed, it's possible to do this without owning a computer, simply by picking up your standard telephone and dialing a number that will "packetize" your conversation. However, people also can use a PC with a sound card and a microphone, a modem linked to a standard internet service provider, and internet telephone software such

panel 2.35

Internet telephony ad

as Microsoft NetMeeting and Windows Messenger. VoIP is offered by AT&T, Google Voice, Skype, Vonage, Yahoo! Voice, and scores of other companies. Although sound quality used to be a problem with VoIP systems, the widespread availability of broadband has made call quality no longer an issue.[39]

Besides carrying voice signals, internet telephone software also allows videoconferencing, in which participants are linked by a videophone that will transmit their pictures, thanks to a video camera attached to their PCs.

Multimedia on the Web

How can I get images, sound, video, and animation as well as text?

Many websites (especially those trying to sell you something) employ complicated multimedia effects, using a combination of text, images, sound, video, and animation. While most web browsers can handle basic multimedia elements on a web page, eventually you'll probably want more dramatic capabilities.

PLUG-INS In the 1990s, as the web was evolving from text to multimedia, browsers were unable to handle many kinds of graphic, sound, and video files. To do so, external application files called *plug-ins* had to be loaded into the system. **A _plug-in_ is a program that adds a specific feature to a browser, allowing it to play or view certain files.**

For example, to view certain documents, you may need to download Adobe Acrobat Reader. (● *See Panel 2.36.*) To view high-quality video and hear radio, you may need to download RealPlayer. (● *See Panel 2.37, next page.*) Quick-Time is a media player for the Apple Macintosh. Plug-ins are required by many websites if you want to fully experience their content.

Recent versions of Microsoft Internet Explorer and Firefox can handle a lot of multimedia. Now if you come across a file for which you need a plug-in, the browser will ask whether you want it and then tell you how to go about downloading it, usually at no charge.

DEVELOPING MULTIMEDIA: APPLETS, JAVA, & VISUAL STUDIO.NET How do website developers get all those nifty special multimedia effects? Often web pages contain links to **_applets_, small programs (software) that can be**

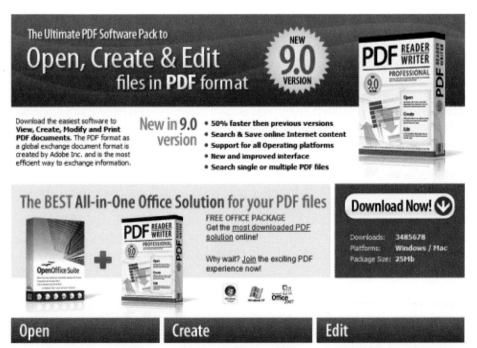

panel 2.36

Adobe Acrobat Reader

quickly downloaded and run by most browsers. Applets are written in **_Java,_** **a complex programming language that enables programmers to create animated and interactive web pages.** Java applets enhance web pages by playing music, displaying graphics and animation, and providing interactive games. Java-compatible browsers such as Internet Explorer automatically download applets from the website and run them on your computer so that you can experience the multimedia effects. Microsoft offers Visual Studio.NET to compete with Java.

TEXT & IMAGES Of course, you can call up all kinds of text documents on the web, such as newspapers, magazines, famous speeches, and works of literature. You can also view images, such as scenery, famous paintings, and photographs. Most web pages combine both text and images.

One interesting innovation is that of aerial maps. Google Earth (*www.google. earth.com*) is a satellite imaging program that Google describes as "part flight simulator, part search tool."[40] You type in your ZIP code or street address and it feels like you're looking down on a high-resolution aerial view of your house from a plane at 30,000 feet. Using Google Local Search, you can search for a business or other attraction in some city, and you'll get an indicator on your satellite image; if you click again, the establishment's web page opens. "Google sightseers can zoom in close enough to see airplanes parked in the desert, the baseball diamond at Wrigley Field, and cars in the Mall of America parking lot," says one writer.[41] Google Earth also extends under the sea. In 2009, the company released a 3-D mapping service "that lets users explore the ocean as if they were dolphins, swimming past submerged volcanoes and through underwater canyons."[42]

ANIMATION **_Animation_** **is the rapid sequencing of still images to create the appearance of motion,** as in most videogames as well as in moving banners displaying sports scores or stock prices.

VIDEO Video can be transmitted in two ways. (1) A file, such as a movie or video clip, may have to be completely downloaded before you can view it. This may take several minutes in some cases. (2) A file may be displayed as streaming video and viewed while it is still being downloaded to your computer. **_Streaming video_** **is the process of transferring data in a continuous flow so that you can begin viewing a file even before the end of the file is sent.** For instance, RealPlayer offers live, television-style broadcasts over the internet as streaming video for viewing on your PC screen. You download and install this software and then point your browser to a site featuring RealVideo. That will produce a streaming-video television image in a window a few inches wide.

A milestone in streaming video occurred in July 2005 when America Online broadcast seven separate live feeds of the Live 8 concerts from London, Philadelphia, Paris, Berlin, Rome, and Toronto, as well as a separate global feed that included footage from four other venues. With more and more American households having the broadband connections that permit streaming video, movies-by-mail firms such as Netflix are moving toward the near-instant delivery of movies streamed to subscribers' TV sets via Net-enabled TV sets, set-top box systems, and Xbox 360 games systems.[43]

AUDIO Audio, such as sound or music files, may also be transmitted in two ways:

- **Downloaded completely before the file can be played:** Many online music services, such as eMusic, iTunes Music Store, MusicMatch, Rhapsody, Virgin, Napster, Connect, and Walmart, offer music for a fee, either by subscription or by the song. Generally, music must be downloaded completely before the file can be played on a computer or portable music player.

- **Downloaded as streaming audio:** Music that is downloaded as **_streaming audio_ allows you to listen to the file while the data is still being downloaded to your computer.** A popular standard for transmitting audio is RealAudio. Supported by most web browsers, it compresses sound so that it can be played in real time, even though sent over telephone lines. You can, for instance, listen to 24-hour-a-day net radio, which features "vintage rock," or English-language services of 19 shortwave outlets from World Radio Network in London. Many large radio stations outside the United States have net radio, allowing people around the world to listen in. (We explain a form of web audio known as *podcasting* shortly.)

The Web Automatically Comes to You: Webcasting, Blogging, & Podcasting

How would I explain webcasting, blogging, and podcasting to someone?

It used to be that you had to do the searching on the web. Now, if you wish, the web will come to you. Let's consider three variations—webcasting, blogging, and podcasting.

PUSH TECHNOLOGY & WEBCASTING The trend began in the late 1990s with **_push technology_, software that automatically downloads information to personal computers** (as opposed to *pull technology*, in which you go to a website and pull down the information you want—in other words, the web page isn't delivered until a browser requests or pulls it). One result of push technology was **_webcasting_, in which customized text, video, and audio are sent to you automatically on a regular basis.**

The idea here is that you choose the categories, or (in Microsoft Internet Explorer) the channels, of websites that will automatically send you updated information. Thus, webcasting saves you time because you don't have to go out searching for the information. Webcasting companies are also called *subscription services,* because they sell on-demand services. However, a lot of push technology fell out of favor because it clogged networks with information that readers often didn't want. Then along came RSS.

BLOGGING—RSS, XML, & THE RISE OF THE BLOGOSPHERE RSS was built to be simpler than push technology. **_RSS newsreaders_, or _RSS aggregators_, are programs that scour the web, sometimes hourly or more frequently,**

and pull together in one place web "feeds" from several websites. The developers of RSS technology don't agree on what the abbreviation stands for, but some say it means "Really Simple Syndication" or "Rich Site Summary," although there are other variations as well.[44] "RSS allows you to play news editor and zero in on the information you really need," says one account, "even as you expand the number of sites you sample."[45] This is because the information is so specifically targeted.

RSS is based on **_XML_, or *extensible markup language*, a web-document tagging and formatting language that is an advance over HTML and that two computers can use to exchange information.** XML, in the form of RSS, has allowed people to have access to a whole new universe of content. One of the earliest adopters, for instance, was the Mormon Church, which used the system to keep in touch with members. Now, however, it has morphed into something called the **_blogosphere_, the total universe of blogs—_blog_ being short for *web log*, a diary-style web page.** (● *See Panel 2.38.*)

"Blogs can be anything their creators want them to be, from newsy to deeply personal, argumentative to poetic," says one writer. "Some are written by individuals. Some are group projects. Some have readerships in the thousands and influence world media. Others are read by a handful of people—or not read at all, because they're all pictures. Bloggers are a new breed of homegrown journal writers and diarists who chronicle life as it happens, with words, photos, sound, and art."[46] Says another dedicated blogger, "Blogging is . . . to writing what extreme sports are to athletics: more free-form, more accident-prone, less formal, more alive. It is, in many ways, writing out loud."[47] Some people have succeeded in turning blogging into successful businesses, with those who receive 100,000 or more unique visitors a month earning an average of $75,000 a year (aided by online ads).[48] But 95% of blogs are essentially abandoned, so the key to building a successful audience for a blog seems to be a nonstop, work-every-day workweek.[49]

Among other variations are *video blogs,* or *vblogs* or *vogs,* which seem to be simply video versions of blogs, and *moblogs,* or *mobile blogs,* in which picture blogs are posted to websites directly from camera-enabled cellphones.

panel 2.38

The blogosphere: one way to create your own blog

PODCASTING <u>*Podcasting*</u> **involves the recording of internet radio or similar internet audio programs.** The term derives not only from *webcasting* but also from the Apple *iPod* portable music player and other mobile listening devices, such as MP3 players.

Blogging and podcasting seem to represent the frontier of personalized media, a subject to which we will return throughout the book, particularly in Chapter 7.

E-Commerce: B2B Commerce, Online Finance, Auctions, & Job Hunting

What are ways I might personally benefit from online e-commerce possibilities?

The explosion in <u>*e-commerce (electronic commerce)*</u>—**conducting business activities online**—is not only widening consumers' choice of products and services but also creating new businesses and compelling established businesses to develop internet strategies. Many so-called brick-and-mortar retailers—those operating out of physical buildings—have been surprised at the success of such online companies as Amazon.com, seller of books, CDs, and other products. As a result, traditional retailers from giant Walmart to very small one-person businesses now offer their products online.

Retail goods can be classified into two categories—hard and soft. *Hard goods* are those that can be viewed and priced online, such as computers, clothes, groceries, and furniture, but are then sent to buyers by mail or truck. *Soft goods* are those that can be downloaded directly from the retailer's site, such as music, software, travel tickets, and greeting cards.

Some specific forms of e-commerce are as follows:

B2B COMMERCE Of course, every kind of commerce has taken to the web, ranging from travel bookings to real estate. One of the most important variations is <u>*B2B (business-to-business) commerce*</u>, **the electronic sale or exchange of goods and services directly between companies, cutting out traditional intermediaries.** Expected to grow even more rapidly than other forms of e-commerce, B2B commerce covers an extremely broad range of activities, such as supplier-to-buyer display of inventories, provision of wholesale price lists, and sales of closed-out items and used materials—usually without agents, brokers, or other third parties.

ONLINE FINANCE: TRADING, BANKING, & E-MONEY The internet has changed the nature of stock trading. Anyone with a computer, a connection to the global network, and the information, tools, and access to transaction systems required to play the stock market can do so online. Companies such as E*Trade have built one-stop financial supermarkets offering a variety of money-related services, including home mortgage loans and insurance. More than 1,000 banks have websites, offering services that include account access, funds transfer, bill payment, loan and credit-card applications, and investments.[50]

AUCTIONS: LINKING INDIVIDUAL BUYERS & SELLERS Today millions of buyers and sellers are linking up at online auctions, where everything is available from comic books to wines.[51] The internet is also changing the tradition-bound art and antiques business (dominated by such venerable names as Sotheby's, Christie's, and Butterfield & Butterfield). There are generally two types of auction sites:

- **Person-to-person auctions:** Person-to-person auctions, such as eBay, connect buyers and sellers for a listing fee and a commission on sold items. (● *See Panel 2.39, next page.*)

- **Vendor-based auctions:** Vendor-based auctions, such as OnSale, buy merchandise and sell it at discount. Some auctions are specialized, such as Priceline, an auction site for airline tickets and other items.

Some Auction Websites

eBay *www.ebay.com*
WeBidz *www.webidz.com*
Overstock.com *http://auctions.overstock.com*

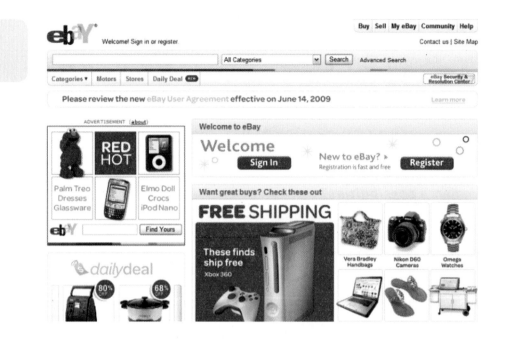

ONLINE JOB HUNTING There are more than 2,000 websites that promise to match job hunters with an employer. Some are specialty "boutique" sites looking for, say, scientists or executives. Some are general sites, the leaders being Monster.com, CareerPath.com, CareerMosaic.com, USAJOBS (U.S. government/federal jobs; *www.usajobs.opm.gov*), and CareerBuilder.com. Job sites can help you keep track of job openings and applications by downloading them to your own computer. Résumé sites such as Employment911.com help you prepare professional-quality résumés.

Relationships: Matchmaking Websites

Would I use a dating website?

A *matchmaking*, or *dating*, *website* **is an online forum that people may join in hopes of meeting compatible potential mates.** People who connect online before meeting in the real world have the chance to base their relationship on personality, intelligence, and sense of humor rather than on purely physical attributes. Five of the biggest and best-known sites are AmericanSingles, eHarmony, Match.com, True, and Yahoo! Personals. Facebook, the social-networking site, also offers the dating site called Are You Interested.[52] Most dating sites charge a fee, but PlentyofFish, OKCupid, MatchDoctor, and BookofMatches are free. Most of the 1,000 or so dating sites are niche or specialty sites for those with different political or religious beliefs, different ethnicities, mature adults, and so on.[53]

Web 2.0 & the Social Web: Social Networking, Media Sharing, Social-Network Aggregation, & Microblogging

What is Web 2.0, and which social-networking, media-sharing, social-network aggregator websites, and microblogging might be useful?

Finally, we come to what is known as **_Web 2.0_, which can be defined as the move toward a more social, collaborative, interactive, and responsive web.**[54] As websites have become easier to use, they allow users to better harness the collective power of people, which has led to a "social web" or "social media," involving not only blogs and wikis (for sharing information) but also social networks and media sharing. The common theme of all these is human interaction.

MYSPACE, FACEBOOK, & OTHER SOCIAL-NETWORKING WEBSITES A _social-networking_ _website_ **is an online community that allows members to keep track of their friends and share photos, videos, music, stories, and ideas with other registered members.** Social-networking websites are led by MySpace (76 million U.S. members) and Facebook (55 million U.S. members) but also include the business-contact site LinkedIn (6.3 million U.S. members).[55] Although 44% of U.S. adults who were online in 2007 did not participate in social networks, according to Forrester Research, another 25% were considered "joiners," who visited social-networking sites such as MySpace; "collectors" consisted of an elite 15% who collected and aggregated information; and the rest were "critics," who posted ratings and reviews, as well as contributed to blogs and forums.[56]

YOUTUBE, FLICKR, & OTHER MEDIA-SHARING WEBSITES A _media-sharing_ _website_ **is a type of online social network in which members share media such as photos, videos, and music.** The most popular example is YouTube, but others are Hulu, Flickr, Shutterfly, Twango, and Yahoo! Video. Forty-eight percent of internet users in 2007 said they had visited video-sharing websites, according to the Pew Internet & American Life Project, and the daily traffic to such sites doubled in a year.[57] Video-sharing sites include YouTube, Flickr, Photobucket, Imageshack, Vimeo, and Veoh. (Incidentally, part of the success of YouTube, where people watch around 3 billion videos a month, is that its founders have kept it pornography-free, using top-secret pattern-recognition software, according to one report.)[58]

Some Top Social-Networking Websites

Bebo
BlackPlanet.com
Facebook
Flixter
Friendster
Last.fm
LinkedIn
MySpace
Ning
Xanga

Some Top Media-Sharing Websites

Flickr
Hulu
Photobucket
Imageshack
Shutterfly
Twango
Yahoo! Video
YouTube

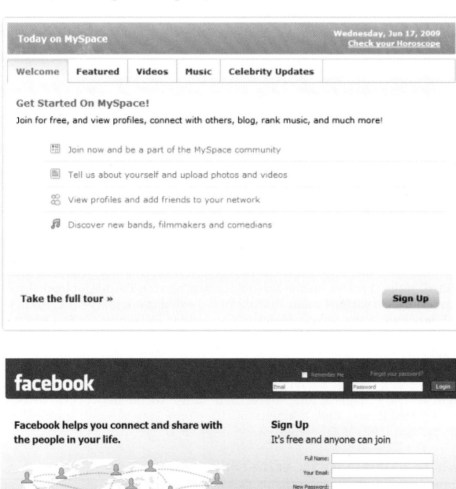

FRIENDFEED, SPOKEO, & OTHER SOCIAL-NETWORK AGGREGATORS Cathy Brooks, 39, of San Francisco is described as a "typically unapologetic Silicon Valley web addict." In one week alone, it's reported, "she produced more than 40 pithy updates on the text messaging service Twitter, uploaded two dozen videos to various video-sharing sites, posted seven graphs on . . . Flickr and one item to the online community calendar Upcoming."[59] She and her friends follow one another's activities by funneling them into a single information broadcast, a content-aggregation system known as FriendFeed.

Social-network aggregators, **or** *social aggregators*, **collect content from all of a user's various social networks profiles into one place, then allow them to track friends and share their other social network activities.** Beside FriendFeed, other examples of "friend-tracking services" are Spokeo, Iminta, Plaxo, Readr, and Mugshot.

TWITTER & TUMBLR SOCIAL NETWORKING & MICROBLOGGING SERVICES As you and your friends track each other's every moment, you can also use services such as Twitter and Tumblr to do "thoughtcasting" or "microblogging"—send a text message from your mobile phone, which your friends will receive on the web/IM or on their phones.[60] (The phenomenon is called *microblogging*, because messages have to be short, 140 characters or less, owing to length restrictions on text messaging.) Tumblr lets you express yourself using multiple media, but in a way that's easier than using traditional blog software.

Some Social-Network Aggregators

FriendFeed
Spokeo
Iminta
Plaxo
Readr
Mugshot

Email is still king at the office, but research suggests that Twitter, Facebook, and other social media have overtaken email to become the fourth-most-popular way people spend time online (after search, portals, and software applications).[61]

2.6 THE INTRUSIVE INTERNET: Snooping, Spamming, Spoofing, Phishing, Pharming, Cookies, & Spyware

How can I protect myself against snoopers, spam, spoofing, phishing, pharming, cookies, and spyware—adware, browser and search hijackers, and key loggers?

"The current internet model is just too wide open," says Orion E. Hill, president of the Napa Valley (California) Personal Computer Users Group, which educates users about PCs. "The internet is just too accessible, and it's too easy for people to make anything they want out of it."[62] Thus, although the internet may be affected to a degree by governing and regulatory bodies, just like society in general, that doesn't mean that it doesn't have its pitfalls or share of users who can do you real harm.

We consider some of the other serious internet issues (such as viruses, worms, and crackers) in Chapter 6 and elsewhere, but here let us touch on a few of immediate concern that you should be aware of: snooping, spam, spoofing, phishing, pharming, cookies, and spyware.

Snooping on Your Email: Your Messages Are Open to Anyone

Who's able to look at my private emails?

The single best piece of advice that can be given about sending email is this: *Pretend every electronic message is a postcard that can be read by anyone.* Because the chances are high that it could be. (And this includes email on college campus systems as well.)

Think the boss can't snoop on your email at work? The law allows employers to "intercept" employee communications if one of the parties involved agrees to the "interception." The party "involved" is the employer.[63] And in the workplace, email is typically saved on a server, at least for a while. Indeed, federal laws require that employers keep some email messages for years.

Think you can keep your email address a secret among your friends? You have no control over whether they might send your e-messages on to someone else—who might in turn forward them again. (One thing you can do for your friends, however, is delete their names and addresses before sending one of their messages on to someone.)

Think your internet access provider will protect your privacy? Often service providers post your address publicly or even sell their customer lists.

If you're really concerned about preserving your privacy, you can try certain technical solutions—for instance, installing software that encodes and decodes messages (discussed in Chapter 6). But the simplest solution is the easiest: Don't put any sensitive or embarrassing information in your email. Even deleted email removed from trash can still be traced on your hard disk. To guard against this, you can use software such as Spytech Eradicator and Webroot's Window Washer to completely eliminate deleted files. (Be aware, however: your email may already have been backed up on the company—or campus—server.)

Spam: Electronic Junk Mail

Is it really possible to manage spam?

Several years ago, Monty Python, the British comedy group, did a sketch in which restaurant customers were unable to converse because people in the background (a group of Vikings, actually) kept chanting "Spam, spam, eggs and spam . . ." The term *spam* was picked up by the computer world to describe another kind of "noise" that interferes with communication. Now ***spam* refers to unsolicited email, or junk mail, in the form of advertising or chain letters.** But the problem of spam has metastasized well beyond the stage of annoyance.

Spam has become so pestiferous that *Smart Computing* magazine refers to it as a "cockroach infestation."[64] In 2001, spam accounted for about 5% of the traffic on the internet; by 2004, it was more than 70%—in some regions more than 90%, more than a hundred billion unsolicited messages.[65] In 2008, the number of spam messages globally was 164 billion per day, using enough electricity to power 2.4 million homes for a year.[66] Spam plagues social networks, such as Facebook. It is even migrating from computers to cellphones, messages that the recipients have to pay for.

Usually, of course, you don't recognize the spam sender on your list of incoming mail, and often the subject line will give no hint, stating something such as "The status of your application" or "It's up to you now." The solicitations can range from money-making schemes to online pornography. To better manage spam, some users get two email boxes. One is used for online shopping, business, research, and the like—which will continue to attract spam. The other is used (like an unlisted phone number) only for personal friends and family—and will probably not receive much spam.

The Practical Action box gives some other tips for fighting spam.

PRACTICAL ACTION
Tips for Fighting Spam[67]

- **Delete without opening the message:** Opening the spam message can send a signal to the spammer that someone has looked at the on-screen message and therefore that the email address is valid—which means you'll probably get more spams in the future. If you don't recognize the name on your inbox directory or the topic on the inbox subject line, simply delete the message without reading it. Or you can use a preview feature in your email program to look at the message without opening it; then delete it.

- **Never reply to a spam message:** The following advice needs to be taken seriously: *Never reply in any way to a spam message!* Replying confirms to the spammer that yours is an active email address. Some spam senders will tell you that if you want to be removed from their mailing list, you should type the word *remove* or *unsubscribe* in the subject line and use the Reply command to send the message back. Invariably, however, all this does is confirm to the spammer that your address is valid, setting you up to receive more unsolicited messages.

- **Opt out:** When you sign up for or buy something online and are asked for an email address, remember to opt out of everything you're sure you don't want to receive. When you register for a website, for example, read its privacy policy to find out how it uses email addresses—and don't give the site permission to pass along yours.

- **Enlist the help of your internet access provider, or use spam filters:** Your IAP may offer a free spam filter to stop the stuff before you even see it. If it doesn't, you can sign up for a filtering service, such as MailWise, for a small monthly charge. Or there are do-it-yourself spam-stopping programs. Examples: Choicemail (*www.digiportal.com*), MailWasher (*www.mailwasher.net/*), Barracuda (*www.barracudanetworks.com*) and McAfee SpamKiller (*http://us.mcafee.com/root/product.asp? productid=msk*). More complicated spam-blocker packages exist for businesses.

  Be warned, however: Even so-called spam killers don't always work. "Nothing will work 100%, short of changing your email address," says the operator of an online service called SpamCop. "No matter how well you try to filter a spammer, they're always working to defeat the filter."[68]

- **Fight back:** If you want to get back at spammers—and other internet abusers—check with abuse.net (*www.abuse.net*) or Ed Falk's Spam Tracking Page (*www.rahul.net/falk*). Spamhaus (*www.spamhaus.org*) tracks the internet's worst spammers and works with ISPs and law enforcement agencies to identify and remove persistent spammers from the internet. These groups will tell you where to report spammers, the appropriate people to complain to, and other spam-fighting tips.

Spoofing, Phishing, & Pharming: Phony Email Senders & Websites

How would I know if I were being spoofed, phished, or pharmed?

A message shows up in your email supposedly from someone named "Sonia Saunders." The subject line reads "Re: Hey there!" It could have been from someone you know, but it's actually a pitch for porn. Or you receive what appears to be an "Urgent notice from eBay," the online auction company, stating that "failure to update billing information will result in cancellation of service" and asking you to go to the web address indicated and update your credit-card information. In the first instance you've been *spoofed*, in the second you've been *phished*.[69]

SPOOFING—USING FAKE EMAIL SENDER NAMES *Spoofing* **is the forgery of an email sender name so that the message appears to have originated from someone or somewhere other than the actual source.** Spoofing is one of the main tactics used by spammers (and virus writers) to induce or trick recipients into opening and perhaps responding to their solicitations. Spoofing is generally not illegal and might even serve a legitimate purpose under some circumstances—say, a "whistle-blowing" employee fearful of retaliation who reports a company's illegalities to a government agency. It is illegal, however, if it involves a direct threat of violence or death.[70]

PHISHING—USING TRUSTED INSTITUTIONAL NAMES TO ELICIT CONFIDENTIAL INFORMATION *Phishing* **(pronounced "fishing" and short for *password harvesting fishing*) is (1) the sending of a forged email that (2) directs recipients to a replica of an existing web page, both of which pretend to belong to a legitimate company. The purpose of the fraudulent sender is to "phish" for, or entice people to share, their personal, financial, or password data.** The names may be trusted names such as Citibank, eBay, or Best Buy.[71] A variant is *spear-phishing*, in which a message seems to originate within your company, as when a "Security Department Assistant" asks you to update your name and password or risk suspension.[72] Thus, you should be suspicious of *any* email that directs you to a website that requests confidential information, such as credit-card or Social Security number.[73]

PHARMING—REDIRECTING YOU TO AN IMPOSTOR WEB PAGE Pharming is a relatively new kind of phishing that is harder to detect. **In *pharming*, thieves implant malicious software on a victim's computer that redirects the user to an impostor web page even when the individual types the correct address into his or her browser.** One way to protect yourself is to make sure you go to special secure web pages, such as any financial website, which begin with *https* rather than the standard *http* and which use encryption to protect data transfer.[74]

Cookies: Convenience or Hindrance?

Do I really want to leave cookies on my computer?

Cookies **are little text files—such as your log-in name, password, and preferences—left on your hard disk by some websites you visit. The websites retrieve the data when you visit again.** A website that welcomes you by name uses cookies.

THE BENEFITS OF COOKIES Cookies can be a convenience. If you visit an online merchant—such as BarnesandNoble.com for a book—and enter all your address and other information, the merchant will assign you an identification number, store your information with that number on its server, and send the number to your browser as a cookie, which stores the ID number on your hard disk. The next time you go to that merchant, the number is sent to the server, which looks you up and sends you a customized web page welcoming you. "Cookies actually

Deciphering Fake Email

For more about spoofing and how to identify origins of fake emails, go to:

www.mailsbroadcast.com/ email.broadcast.faq/46.email. spoofing.htm

Verifying Valid Websites

For more on verifying if you're dealing with a legitimate company website, go to:

www.trustwatch.com

perform valuable services," says technology writer and computer talk-radio-show host Kim Komando. "For instance, they can shoot you right into a site so you don't have to enter your password."[75] Says another writer: "They can also fill in a username on a site that requires logging in, or [help] a weather site remember a ZIP code so that it can show a local forecast on return visits."[76]

THE DRAWBACKS OF COOKIES Cookies are not necessarily dangerous—they are not programs, and they can't transmit computer viruses, for example. However, some websites sell the information associated with your ID number on their servers to marketers, who might use it to target customers for their products. "Unsatisfactory cookies," in Microsoft's understated term, are those that might allow someone access to personally identifiable information that could be used without your consent for some secondary purpose. This can lead to *spyware,* as we describe next. Webroot's Window Washer, among other programs, can clean your computer of cookies.

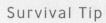

Survival Tip

Control Those Cookies!
You can use your browser's Help function to accept or reject cookies. For instance, in Internet Explorer, go to the Tools menu and click *Internet Options;* on the General tab, click *Settings;* then click *View files,* select the cookie you want to delete, and on the File menu click *Delete.* Software such as Cookie Pal (*www. kburra.com*) will also help block and control cookies, as will Webroot's Window Washer.

Spyware—Adware, Browser & Search Hijackers, & Key Loggers: Intruders to Track Your Habits & Steal Your Data

What should I be afraid of about spyware?

You visit a search site such as Yahoo! or Google and click on a text ad that appears next to your search results. Or you download a free version of some software, such as Kazaa, a file-sharing program. Or you simply visit some web merchant to place an order.

The next thing you know, you seem to be getting **_pop-up ads_, a form of online advertising in which, when you visit certain websites, a new window opens, or "pops up," to display advertisements.** You have just had an encounter with *spyware,* of which pop-up ads are only one form. **_Spyware_ may be defined as deceptive software that is surreptitiously installed on a computer via the web; once installed on your hard disk, it allows an outsider to harvest confidential information,** such as keystrokes, passwords, your email address, or your history of website visits. Spyware was found on the personal computers of 80% of the 329 homes participating in a study conducted by America Online Inc. and the National Cyber Security Alliance.[77] Ways to avoid getting spyware are shown in the more info! in the margin at right.

The most common forms of spyware are the following:

ADWARE OR POP-UP GENERATORS _Adware_, **or _pop-up generators_, is a kind of spyware that tracks web surfing or online buying so that marketers can send you targeted and unsolicited pop-up and other ads.** This is the most common, and benign, type of spyware. Adware can be developed by legitimate companies such as Verizon and Panasonic but also by all kinds of fly-by-night purveyors of pornography and gambling operating from computer servers in Russia, Spain, and the Virgin Islands.

BROWSER HIJACKERS & SEARCH HIJACKERS More damaging kinds of spyware are **_browser hijackers_, which change settings in your browser without your knowledge, often changing your browser's home page and replacing it with another web page, and _search hijackers_, which intercept your legitimate search requests made to real search engines and return results from phony search services designed to send you to sites they run.** "A better name for these programs is scumware," says one writer. "One of them might reset your home page to a porn site or an obscure search engine

Window Washer - Wash Setup ⊗

Wash List - Internet Explorer Wash Items
Washing Internet items protects your privacy by erasing all traces of your Internet activity, such as which Web sites you have visited. Window Washer supports several popular browsers.

Internet Explorer

☑ Address bar history   ☐ Setup log file

☑ Cookies   ☑ Downloaded folder memory

☑ Temporary Internet Files folder (cache)   ☐ Media bar (Media Player) history

☑ History (visited sites)   ☑ Autocomplete form data

☑ Index.dat (Wash with bleach on Windows startup)

[Cancel]   [Apply]

Webroot's Window Washer, among other programs, can clean your computer of cookies.

Fighting Spyware

More information about ways to combat spyware may be found at:

www.microsoft.com/athome/ security/spyware/default. mspx

www.pcpitstop.com

www.spywarewarrior.com/ rogue_anti-spyware.htm

www.webroot.com

www.cleansoftware.org

www.lavasoftusa.com/ software/

Program Name	Site
Ad Aware	www.lavasoftusa.com/software/adaware
AntiSpyware	http://us.mcafee.com
PC Tools Software	www.pctools.com/spyware-doctor/?ref=google77
Pest Patrol	www.ca.com/products/pestpatrol
Spybot Search & Destroy	http://spywaresoftware.net
SpyCatcher	www.tenebril.com
SpyCop	www.spywareinfo.com/downloads.php
Spy Sweeper	www.webroot.com

and then refuse to let you change the page back. Or it might hijack your search requests and then direct them to its own page."[78]

KEY LOGGERS *Key loggers,* **or** *keystroke loggers,* **can record each character you type and transmit that information to someone else on the internet, making it possible for strangers to learn your passwords and other information.** For instance, some may secretly record the keystrokes you use to log in to online bank accounts and then send the information off to who knows where.

In the past, spyware writers have relied on flaws in Microsoft's Internet Explorer. On the PC, you may be protected if you keep your security features updated. Some people believe that getting rid of Internet Explorer and going to Mozilla Firefox, the most popular alternative, is a better solution.[79] Another option is Opera. Internet access providers such as AOL and Earthlink offer scan-and-removal tools, but you can also employ specialized antispyware software. Some of the good ones appear below. (● *See Panel 2.40.*)

One big problem with spyware is that overburdened PCs begin to run more slowly as the hard drives cope with random and uncontrollable processes. If none of the antispyware works, you will need to wipe your hard drive clean of programs and data and start from scratch—a complicated matter that we discuss in Chapter 4.

PRACTICAL ACTION
Tips for Avoiding Spyware

You may not be able to completely avoid spyware, but doing the following may help:

- *Be careful about free and illegal downloads:* Be choosy about free downloads, as from Grokster and Kazaa, or illegal downloads of songs, movies, or TV shows. Often they use a form of spyware. File-sharing programs, which are popular with students, often contain spyware. Pornographic websites also are common carriers of spyware.

- *Don't just say "I agree"; read the fine print:* Sites that offer games, music-sharing videos, screen savers, and weather data often are paid to distribute spyware. When you install their software, you might be asked to agree to certain conditions. If you simply click "I agree" without reading the fine print, you may be authorizing installation of spyware. "People have gotten in the habit of clicking next, next, next, without reading" when they install software, says a manager at McAfee Inc., which tracks spyware and viruses.[80]

- *Beware of unsolicited downloads:* If while you're surfing the net your browser warns you a file is being downloaded and you're asked if you choose to accept, keep clicking *no* until the messages stop.

EXPERIENCE BOX

Web Research, Term Papers, & Plagiarism

No matter how much students may be able to rationalize cheating in college—for example, trying to pass off someone else's term paper as their own (plagiarism)—ignorance of the consequences is not an excuse. Most instructors announce the penalties for cheating at the beginning of the course—usually a failing grade in the course and possible suspension or expulsion from school.

Even so, probably every student becomes aware before long that the World Wide Web contains sites that offer term papers, either for free or for a price. Some dishonest students may download papers and just change the author's name to their own. Others are more likely just to use the papers for ideas. Perhaps, suggests one article, "the fear of getting caught makes the online papers more a diversion than an invitation to wide-scale plagiarism."[81]

How the Web Can Lead to Plagiarism

Two types of term-paper websites are as follows:

- *Sites offering papers for free:* Such a site requires that users fill out a membership form and then provides at least one free student term paper. (Good quality is not guaranteed, since free-paper mills often subsist on the submissions of poor students, whose contributions may be subliterate.)

- *Sites offering papers for sale:* Commercial sites may charge $6–$10 a page, which users may charge to their credit card. (Expense is no guarantee of quality. Moreover, the term-paper factory may turn around and make your $350 custom paper available to others—even fellow classmates working on the same assignment—for half the price.)

How Instructors Catch Cheaters

How do instructors detect and defend against student plagiarism? Professors are unlikely to be fooled if they tailor term-paper assignments to work done in class, monitor students' progress—from outline to completion—and are alert to papers that seem radically different from a student's past work.

One professor of art history requires that papers in his classes be submitted electronically, along with a list of World Wide Web site references. "This way I can click along as I read the paper. This format is more efficient than running around the college library, checking each footnote."[82]

Just as the internet is the source of cheating, it is also a tool for detecting cheaters. Search programs make it possible for instructors to locate texts containing identified strings of words from the millions of pages found on the web. Thus, a professor can input passages from a student's paper into a search program that scans the web for identical blocks of text. Indeed, some websites favored by instructors build a database of papers over time so that students can't recycle work previously handed in by others. One system, Turnitin's Originality Checking, can lock on to a stolen phrase as short as eight words. It can also identify copied material even if it has been changed slightly from the original. Another program professors use is the Self-Plagiarism Detection Tool, or SplaT.

How the Web Can Lead to Low-Quality Papers

William Rukeyser, coordinator for Learning in the Real World, a nonprofit information clearinghouse, points out another problem: The web enables students "to cut and paste together reports or presentations that appear to have taken hours or days to write but have really been assembled in minutes with no actual mastery or understanding by the student."[83]

Philosophy professor David Rothenberg, of New Jersey Institute of Technology, reports that as a result of students' doing more of their research on the web, he has seen "a disturbing decline in both the quality of the writing and the originality of the thoughts expressed."[84] How does an instructor spot a term paper based primarily on web research? Rothenberg offers four clues:

- *No books cited:* The student's bibliography cites no books, just articles or references to websites. Sadly, says Rothenberg, "one finds few references to careful, in-depth commentaries on the subject of the paper, the kind of analysis that requires a book, rather than an article, for its full development."

- *Outdated material:* A lot of the material in the bibliography is strangely out of date, says Rothenberg. "A lot of stuff on the web that is advertised as timely is actually at least a few years old."

- *Unrelated pictures and graphs:* Students may intersperse the text with a lot of impressive-looking pictures and graphs that actually bear little relation to the precise subject of the paper. "Cut and pasted from the vast realm of what's out there for the taking, they masquerade as original work."

- **Superficial references:** "Too much of what passes for information [online] these days is simply advertising for information," points out Rothenberg. "Screen after screen shows you where you can find out more, how you can connect to this place or that." Other kinds of information are detailed but often superficial: "pages and pages of federal documents, corporate propaganda, snippets of commentary by people whose credibility is difficult to assess."

access point (p. 58) Station that sends and receives data to and from a Wi-Fi network. Why it's important: *Many public areas, such as airports and hotels, offer hot spots, or access points, that enable Wi-Fi-equipped users to go online wirelessly.*

adware (p. 105) Also called *pop-up generators:* kind of spyware that tracks web surfing or buying online. Why it's important: *Adware enables marketers to send you targeted and unsolicited pop-up and other ads.*

animation (p. 94) The rapid sequencing of still images to create the appearance of motion, as in a cartoon. Why it's important: *Animation is a component of multimedia; it is used in online video games as well as in moving banners displaying sports scores or stock prices.*

applets (p. 93) Small programs that can be quickly downloaded and run by most browsers. Why it's important: *Web pages contain links to applets, which add multimedia capabilities.*

B2B (business-to-business) commerce (p. 97) Electronic sale or exchange of goods and services directly between companies, cutting out traditional intermediaries. Why it's important: *Expected to grow even more rapidly than other forms of e-commerce, B2B commerce covers an extremely broad range of activities, such as supplier-to-buyer display of inventories, provision of wholesale price lists, and sales of closed-out items and used materials—usually without agents, brokers, or other third parties.*

backbones *See* **internet backbone.**

bandwidth (p. 52) Also known as *channel capacity;* expression of how much data—text, voice, video, and so on—can be sent through a communications channel in a given amount of time. Why it's important: *Different communications systems use different bandwidths for different purposes. The wider the bandwidth, the faster the data can be transmitted.*

bits per second (bps) (p. 52) Eight bits make up a character. Why it's important: *Data transfer speeds are measured in bits per second.*

blog (p. 96) Short for *web log,* an internet journal. Blogs are usually updated daily; they reflect the personality and views of the blogger. Why it's important: *Blogs are becoming important sources of current information.*

blogosphere (p. 96) The total universe of blogs. Why it's important: *The blogosphere has allowed the rise of a new breed of homegrown journal writers and diarists to chronicle life as it happens.*

broadband (p. 52) Very high speed connection. Why it's important: *Access to information is much faster than access with traditional phone lines.*

browser *See* **web browser.**

browser hijacker (p. 105) A damaging kind of spyware that changes settings in your browser without your knowledge. Why it's important: *This spyware can reset your home page to a porn site or obscure search engine or change your home page and replace it with another web page.*

cable modem (p. 57) Device connecting a personal computer to a cable-TV system that offers an internet connection. Why it's important: *Cable modems transmit data faster than do standard modems.*

client (p. 60) Computer requesting data or services. Why it's important: *Part of the client/server network, in which the server is a central computer supplying data or services requested of it to the client computer.*

communications satellite (p. 57) Space station that transmits radio waves called *microwaves* from earth-based stations. Why it's important: *An orbiting satellite contains many communications channels and receives signals from ground microwave stations anywhere on earth.*

cookies (p. 104) Little text files, such as your log-in name, password, and preferences, that are left on your hard disk by some websites you visit; the websites retrieve the data when you visit again. Why it's important: *Cookies can be beneficial in that they put you right into a website without having to enter your password. However, some websites sell the information associated with your ID number on their servers to marketers, who might use it to target you as a customer for their products.*

dial-up connection (p. 53) Use of a telephone modem to connect a computer to the internet. Why it's important: *Cheapest means of online connection and available everywhere.*

domain (p. 66) A location on the internet, the particular web server. Why it's important: *A domain name is necessary for sending and receiving email and for many other internet activities.*

download (p. 53) To transmit data from a remote computer to a local computer. Why it's important: *Downloading enables users to save files on their own computers for later use, which reduces the time spent online and the corresponding charges.*

DSL (digital subscriber line) (p. 55) A hardware and software technology that uses regular phone lines to transmit data in megabits per second. Why it's important: *DSL connections are much faster than regular modem connections.*

e-commerce (electronic commerce) (p. 97) Conducting business activities online. Why it's important: *E-commerce not only is widening consumers' choice of products and services but is also creating new businesses and compelling established businesses to develop internet strategies.*

email program (p. 82) Also called *email client software;* enables you to send email by running email software on your computer, which interacts with an email server at your internet access provider to send and receive email. Why it's important: *With this standard email program, unlike web-based email, you can easily integrate your email with other applications, such as calendar, task list, and contact list.*

FAQs (frequently asked questions) (p. 91) Guides that explain expected norms of online behavior for a particular group. Why it's important: *Users should read a group's/site's FAQs to know how to proceed properly.*

flaming (p. 91) Writing an online message that uses derogatory, obscene, or inappropriate language. Why it's important: *Flaming should be avoided. It is a form of public humiliation inflicted on people who have failed to read FAQs or have otherwise not observed netiquette (although it can happen just because the sender has poor impulse control and needs a course in anger management).*

frame (p. 72) An independently controllable section of a web page. Why it's important: *A web page designer can divide a page into separate frames, each with different features or options.*

FTP (File Transfer Protocol) (p. 88) Method whereby you can connect to a remote computer called an *FTP site* and transfer publicly available files to your own microcomputer's hard disk via TCP/IP over the internet. Why it's important: *The free files offered cover nearly anything that can be stored on a computer: software, games, photos, maps, art, music, books, statistics.*

gigabits per second (Gbps) (p. 52) 1 billion bits per second. Why it's important: *Gbps is a common measure of data transmission speed.*

hit (p. 74) Site that a search engine returns after running a keyword search. Why it's important: *The web pages, or hits, that a search engine returns after you type in a keyword are the beginning of the types of information you are looking for.*

home page (p. 65) Also called *welcome page;* web page that, somewhat like the title page of a book, identifies the website and contains links to other pages at the site. Why it's important: *The first page you see at a website is the home page.*

host computer *See* **server.**

hotspot (p. 58) Public access to Wi-Fi networks. Why it's important: *Hotspots in airports, hotels, and the like enable wireless-equipped users to go online without a physical connection.*

hypertext links (p. 68) Also called *hyperlinks, hotlinks,* or just *links;* connections to other documents or web pages that contain related information. Why it's important: *Allows a word or phrase in one document to become a connection to a document in a different place.*

hypertext markup language (HTML) (p. 68) Set of special instructions (called "tags" or "markups") used to specify web document structure, formatting, and links to other documents. Why it's important: *HTML enables the creation of web pages.*

HyperText Transfer Protocol (HTTP) (p. 66) Communications rules that allow browsers to connect with web servers. Why it's important: *Without HTTP, files could not be transferred over the web.*

individual search engine (p. 74) Type of internet search tool that compiles its own searchable database on the web. You search for information by typing one or more keywords, and the search engine then displays a list of web pages, or "hits," that contain those key words, ordered from most likely to least likely to contain the information you want. Why it's important: *Examples of this kind of search engine are Ask, Bing, Google, and Yahoo!, as well as AllTheWeb, Gigablast, and Lycos. These are the search engines most commonly used by individual users.*

instant messaging (IM) (p. 87) Service that enables any user on a given email system to send a message and have it pop up instantly on the screen of anyone else logged onto that system. Why it's important: *People can initiate online typed conversations in real time. As they are typed, the messages appear on the display screen in a small window.*

internet2 (p. 62) A cooperative university/business education and research project that enables high-end users to quickly and reliably move huge amounts of data over high-speed networks. Why it's important: *Internet2 creates a kind of "virtual university" by advancing videoconferencing, research, and academic collaboration.*

internet access provider (p. 53) Regional, national, or wireless organization or business that connects you to the internet. Why it's important: *This organization is necessary to connect people to the internet.*

internet backbone (p. 61) High-speed, high-capacity transmission lines that use the newest communications technology. Why it's important: *The internet backbone transmits data across the internet.*

Internet Corporation for Assigned Names and Numbers (ICANN) (p. 63) Global, private-sector, nonprofit corporation that was established to regulate human-friendly internet domain names, those addresses ending with.com, .org, .net, and so on, that overlie IP addresses and identify the website type. Why it's important: *This organization helps humans organize and understand websites.*

Internet Protocol (IP) address (p. 62) Uniquely identifies every computer and device connected to the internet; consists of four sets of numbers between 0 and 255 separated by decimals—for example, 1.160.10.240. This address is similar to a street address. However, street addresses rarely change, but IP addresses often do. Why it's important: *Each time you connect to your ISP, the ISP will assign your computer a new IP address, called a* dynamic IP address, *for your online session. When you request data from the internet, it is transmitted to your computer's IP address. When you disconnect, your ISP frees up the IP address you were using and reassigns it to another user.*

internet service provider (ISP) (p. 58) Company that connects you through your communications line to its servers, or central computer, which connects you to the Internet via another company's network access points. Why it's important: *Unless they subscribe to an online information service (such as AOL) or have a direct network connection (such as a TI line), microcomputer users need an ISP to connect to the internet.*

internet telephony (p. 92) Also known as *VoIP phoning,* short for *Voice over Internet Protocol:* using the internet to make phone calls, either one-to-one or for audioconferencing. Why it's important: *Long-distance phone calls by this means are surprisingly inexpensive.*

ISDN (Integrated Services Digital Network) (p. 55) Hardware and software that allow voice, video, and data to be communicated over traditional copper-wire telephone lines (POTS). Why it's important: *ISDN provides faster data transfer speeds than do regular modem connections.*

Java (p. 94) Complex programming language that enables programmers to create animated and interactive web pages using applets. Why it's important: *Java applets enhance web pages by playing music, displaying graphics and animation, and providing interactive games.*

key logger (p. 106) Also known as *keystroke logger;* type of spyware that can record each character you type and transmit that information to someone else on the internet. Why it's important: *A key logger can make it possible for strangers to learn your passwords and other information.*

keyword (p. 72) A keyword is the subject word or words that refer to the topic you wish to find. Why it's important: *You must use keywords to research topics on the internet.*

kilobits per second (Kbps) (p. 52) 1,000 bits per second. Why it's important: *Kbps is a common measure of data transfer speed. The speed of a modem that is 28,800 bps might be expressed as 28.8 Kbps.*

listserv (p. 89) Automatic mailing-list server that sends email to subscribers who regularly participate in discussion topics. To subscribe, the user sends an email to the list-server moderator and asks to become a member, after which he or she automatically receives email messages from anyone who responds to the server. Why it's important: *Anyone connected to the internet can subscribe to listserv services. Subscribers receive information on particular subjects and can post email to other subscribers.*

log on (p. 60) To make a connection to a remote computer. Why it's important: *Users must be familiar with log-on procedures to go online.*

matchmaking website (p. 98) Also called *dating website;* an online forum that people may join in hopes of meeting compatible potential mates. Why it's important: *Matchmaking websites allow people with similar political or religious beliefs, different ethnicities, mature adults, and so on to find others with similar characteristics.*

media-sharing website (p. 99) Type of online social network, such as YouTube, Flickr, and Shutterfly, that allows members to share media. Why it's important: *Members can share their photos, videos, and music with others with great ease and convenience.*

megabits per second (Mbps) (p. 52) 1 million bits per second. Why it's important: *Mbps is a common measure of data transmission speed.*

metasearch engine (p. 75) Type of internet search tool that allows you to search several search engines simultaneously. Why it's important: *A metasearch engine enables you to expand the range of your search.*

modem (p. 53) Device that sends and receives data over telephone lines to and from computers. Why it's important: *The modem provides a means for computers to communicate with one another using the standard copper-wire telephone network, an analog system that was built to transmit the human voice but not computer signals.*

narrowband (p. 53) Low-bandwidth connection, such as dial-up (telephone). Why it's important: *Narrowband connecting technology is inexpensive and widely available.*

netiquette (p. 90) "Network etiquette," or appropriate online behavior. Why it's important: *In general, netiquette has two basic rules: (1) Don't waste people's time, and (2) don't say anything to a person online that you wouldn't say to his or her face.*

network access point (NAP) (p. 61) A routing computer at a point on the internet where several connections come together. Why it's important: *NAPs connect internet service providers to the internet backbone.*

newsgroup (p. 89) Also called *forum;* giant electronic bulletin board on which users conduct written discussions about a specific subject. Why it's important: *There are thousands of newsgroup forums—which charge no fee—and they cover an amazing array of topics.*

newsreader (p. 89) Program included with most browsers that allows users to access a newsgroup and read or type messages. Why it's important: *Users need a newsreader to participate in a newsgroup.*

packet (p. 62) Fixed-length block of data for transmission. Why it's important: *TCP/IP breaks data in a message into separate packets, which allows the message to be split up and its parts sent by separate routes yet still all wind up in the same place.*

password (p. 60) A secret word or string of characters that enables you to log on, or make a connection, to a remote computer. Why it's important: *The password helps keep a computer system secure against intruders.*

pharming (p. 104) A type of phishing in which malicious software is implanted on a victim's computer that redirects the user to an impostor web page even when the individual types the correct address into his or her browser. Why it's important: *The purpose is to trick people into sharing their personal, financial, or password data.*

phishing (p. 104) Short for *password harvesting fishing;* (1) the sending of a forged email that (2) directs recipients to a replica of an existing web page, both of which pretend to belong to a legitimate company. Why it's important: *The purpose of the fraudulent sender is to "phish" for, or entice people to share, their personal, financial, or password data.*

plug-in (p. 93) Program that adds a specific feature to a browser, allowing it to play or view certain files. Why it's important: *To fully experience the contents of many web pages, you need to use plug-ins.*

podcasting (p. 97) Recording of internet radio or similar internet audio programs. Why it's important: *Podcasting is another expression of personalized media.*

point of presence (POP) (p. 61) Collection of modems and other equipment in a local area. Why it's important: *To avoid making their subscribers pay long-distance phone charges, ISPs provide POPs across the country. The POP acts as a local gateway to the ISP's network.*

pop-up ads (p. 105) Form of online advertising in which, when you visit certain websites, a new window opens, or "pops up," to display advertisements. Why it's important: *Pop-up ads are one form of the nuisance known as spyware.*

POTS (plain old telephone system) (p. 54) Traditional kind of connection to the internet. Why it's important: *Slowest method of connecting to the internet.*

protocol (p. 62) Set of communication rules for exchanging information. Why it's important: *Transmission Control Protocol/Internet Protocol (TCP/IP) enables all computers to use data transmitted on the internet. HyperText Transfer Protocol (HTTP) provides the communication rules that allow browsers to connect with web servers.*

push technology (p. 95) Software that automatically downloads information to your computer, as opposed to *pull technology,* in which you go to a website and pull down the information you want. Why it's important: *With little effort, users can obtain information that is important to them.*

radio buttons (p. 71). An interactive tool displayed as little circles in front of options; selecting an option with the mouse places a dot in the corresponding circle. Why it's important: *Radio buttons are one way of interacting with a web page.*

real-time chat (RTC) (p. 90) Typed discussion ("chat") among participants who are online at the same time; it is just like a telephone conversation, except that messages are typed rather than spoken. Why it's important: *RTC provides a means of immediate electronic communication.*

RSS newsreaders (p. 95) Also called *RSS aggregators;* programs that scour the web, sometimes hourly or more frequently, and pull together in one place web "feeds" from several websites. Why it's important: *RSS newsreaders give people access to a whole new universe of content and have led to the creation of the blogosphere.*

scroll arrows (p. 71) Small up/down and left/right arrows located to the bottom and side of your screen display. Why it's important: *Clicking on scroll arrows with your mouse pointer moves the screen so that you can see the rest of the web page, or the content displayed on the screen.*

scrolling (p. 72) Moving quickly upward or downward through text or some other screen display, using the mouse and scroll arrows (or the arrow keys on the keyboard). Why it's important: *Normally a computer screen displays only part of, for example, a web page. Scrolling enables users to view an entire document, no matter how long.*

search (text) box (p. 71) Fill-in text box. Why it's important: *Allows interaction with a web page.*

search engine (p. 74) Search tool that allows you to find specific documents through keyword searches and menu choices, in contrast to directories, which are lists of websites classified by topic. Why it's important: *Search engines enable users to find websites of specific interest or use to them.*

search hijacker (p. 105) A damaging kind of spyware that can intercept your legitimate search requests made to real search engines and return results from phony search services. Why it's important: *Phony search services may send you to sites they run.*

search service (p. 74) Organization that maintains databases accessible through websites. Why it's important: *A search service helps you find information on the internet.*

server (p. 60) Central computer supplying data or services. Why it's important: *Part of the client/server network, in which the central computer supplies data or services requested of it to the client computer.*

site (p. 65) *See* **website.**

social-network aggregator (p. 100) Also called *social aggregator;* this technology collects content from all of a user's various social network profiles into one place. Why it's important: *Aggregators such as FriendFeed and Spokeo are "friend tracking services" that allow members to track friends and share their other social network activities.*

social-networking website (p. 99) An online community that allows members to keep track of their friends and share ideas and media. Why it's important: *Social-networking websites such as MySpace, Facebook, and LinkedIn allow members to easily expand their circle of acquaintances and to exchange photos, videos, music, stories, and ideas with each other.*

spam (p. 102) Unsolicited email in the form of advertising or chain letters. Why it's important: *Spam filters are available that can spare users the annoyance of receiving junk mail, ads, and other unwanted email.*

spider (p. 74) Also known as *crawler, bot,* or *agent;* special program that crawls through the World Wide Web, following links from one web page to another. Why it's important: *A spider indexes the words on each site it encounters and is used to compile the databases of a search service.*

spoofing (p. 104) The forgery of an email sender name so that the message appears to have originated from someone or somewhere other than the actual source. Why it's important: *Spoofing is one of the main tactics used by spammers to induce or trick recipients into responding to their solicitations.*

spyware (p. 105) Deceptive software that is surreptitiously installed on a computer via the web. Why it's important: *Once spyware is installed on your hard disk, it allows an outsider to harvest confidential information, such as keystrokes, passwords, or your email address.*

streaming audio (p. 95) Process of downloading audio in which you can listen to the file while the data is still being downloaded to your computer. Why it's important: *Users don't have to wait until the entire audio is downloaded to the hard disk before listening to it.*

streaming video (p. 94) Process of downloading video in which the data is transferred in a continuous flow so that you can begin viewing a file even before the end of the file is sent. Why it's important: *Users don't have to wait until the entire video is downloaded to the hard disk before watching it.*

subject directory (p. 75) Type of search engine that allows you to search for information by selecting lists of categories or subjects. Why it's important: *Subject directories allow you to look for information by categories such as "Business and Commerce" or "Arts and Humanities."*

surf (p. 64) To explore the web by using your mouse to move via a series of connected paths, or links, from one location, or website, to another. Surfing requires a browser. Why it's important: *Surfing enables you to easily find information on the web that's of interest to you.*

3G (third generation) (p. 58) High-speed wireless technology that does not need access points because it uses the existing cellphone system. Why it's important: *The technology is found in many new smartphones and PDAs that are capable of delivering downloadable video clips and high-resolution games.*

TI line (p. 56) Traditional trunk line that carries 24 normal telephone circuits and has a transmission rate of 1.5 Mbps. Why it's important: *High-capacity TI lines are used at many corporate, government, and academic sites; these lines provide greater data transmission speeds than do regular modem connections.*

tags (p. 80) Do-it-yourself labels that people can put on anything found on the internet, from articles to photos to videos. Why it's important: *A tag is more powerful than a bookmark, because tags can be shared easily with other people.*

Transmission Control Protocol/Internet Protocol (TCP/IP) (p. 62) Protocol that enables all computers to use data transmitted on the internet by determining (1) the type of error checking to be used, (2) the data compression method, if any, (3) how the sending device will indicate that it has finished sending a message, and (4) how the receiving device will indicate that it has received a message. TCP/IP breaks data into *packets,* which are the largest blocks of data that can be sent across the internet (less than 1,500 characters, or 128

kilobytes). IP is used to send the packets across the internet to their final destination, and TCP is used to reassemble the packets in the correct order. Why it's important: *Internet computers use TCP/IP for all internet transactions, from sending email to downloading stock quotes or pictures off a friend's website.*

upload (p. 53) To transmit data from a local computer to a remote computer. Why it's important: *Uploading allows users to easily exchange files over networks.*

URL (Uniform Resource Locator) (p. 65) String of characters that points to a specific piece of information anywhere on the web. A URL consists of (1) the web protocol, (2) the name of the web server, (3) the directory (or folder) on that server, and (4) the file within that directory (perhaps with an extension such as *html* or *htm*). Why it's important: *URLs are necessary to distinguish among websites.*

Usenet (p. 89) Worldwide network of servers that can be accessed through the internet. Why it's important: *Newsgroups take place on Usenet.*

VoIP phoning. *See* **internet telephony.**

Web 2.0 (p. 98) Defined as the move toward a more social, collaborative, interactive, and responsive World Wide Web. Why it's important: *As websites have become easier to use, they allow users to better harness the collective power of people, which has led to a "social web" or "social media," involving blogs, wikis, social networks, and media sharing. The common theme of all these is human interaction.*

web-based email (p. 82) Type of email in which you send and receive messages by interacting via a browser with a website. Why it's important: *Unlike standard email, web-based email allows you to easily send and receive messages while traveling anywhere in the world and to use any personal computer and browser to access your email.*

web browser (browser) (p. 64) Software that enables users to locate and view web pages and to jump from one page to another. Why it's important: *Users can't surf the web without a browser. Examples of browsers are Microsoft Internet Explorer, Netscape Navigator, Mozilla Firefox, Opera, and Apple Macintosh Safari.*

webcasting (p. 95) Service, based on push technology, in which customized text, video, and audio are sent to the user automatically on a regular basis. Why it's important: *Users choose the categories, or the channels, of websites that will automatically send updated information. Thus, webcasting saves time because users don't have to go out searching for the information.*

web page (p. 65) Document on the World Wide Web that can include text, pictures, sound, and video. Why it's important: *A website's content is provided on web pages. The starting page is the home page.*

web portal (p. 72) Type of gateway website that functions as an "anchor site" and offers a broad array of resources and services, online shopping malls, email support, community forums, current news and weather, stock quotes, travel information, and links to other popular subject categories. The most popular portals are America Online, Yahoo!, Google, Microsoft Network, Netscape, and Lycos. Why it's important: *Web portals provide an easy way to access the web.*

website (site) (p. 65) Location of a web domain name in a computer somewhere on the internet. Why it's important: *Websites provide multimedia content to users.*

Wi-Fi (p. 58) Short for "wireless fidelity." The name given to any of several standards—so-called 802.II standards—set by the Institute of Electrical and Electronic Engineers for wireless transmission. Why it's important: *Wi-Fi enables people to use their Wi-Fi-equipped laptops to go online wirelessly in certain areas such as airports that have public access to Wi-Fi networks.*

window (p. 87) A rectangular area on a computer display screen that contains a document or activity. Why it's important: *In instant messaging, a window allows a user to exchange IM messages with others almost simultaneously while operating other programs.*

wireless network (p. 58) Network that uses radio waves to transmit data, such as Wi-Fi. Why it's important: *Wireless networks enable people to access the internet without having a cabled or wired connection, using wireless-equipped laptops and smart cellphones.*

XML (extensible markup language) (p. 96) A Web-document tagging and formatting language that two computers can use to exchange information. Why it's important: *XML is an improvement over HTML and enables the creation of RSS newsreaders.*

CHAPTER REVIEW

STAGE I LEARNING MEMORIZATION

"I can recognize and recall information."

Self-Test Questions

1. Today's data transmission speeds are measured in _____, *Kbps,* _____, and _____.

2. A(n) _____, _____ connects a personal computer to a cable-TV system that offers an internet connection.

3. A space station that transmits data as microwaves is a _____.

4. A company that connects you through your communications line to its server, which connects you to the internet, is a(n) _____.

5. A rectangular area on the computer screen that contains a document or displays an activity is called a(n) _____.

6. _____ is writing an online message that uses derogatory, obscene, or inappropriate language.

7. A(n) _____ is software that enables users to view web pages and to jump from one page to another.

8. A computer with a domain name is called a(n)_____.

9. _____ comprises the communications rules that allow browsers to connect with web servers.

10. A(n) _____ is a program that adds a specific feature to a browser, allowing it to play or view certain files.

11. Unsolicited email in the form of advertising or chain letters is known as _____.

12. The expression of how much data—text, voice, video, and so on—can be sent through a communications channel in a given amount of time is known as _____.

13. A(n) _____ is a string of characters that points to a specific piece of information somewhere on the web.

14. Some websites may leave files on your hard disk that contain information such as your name, password, and preferences; they are called _____.

15. Using trusted institutional names to elicit confidential information is called _____.

16. The kind of spyware that can record each character you type and transmit that information to someone else on the internet, making it possible for strangers to learn your passwords and other information, is called .

Multiple-Choice Questions

1. Kbps means how many bits per second?

   a. I billion

   b. I thousand

   c. I million

   d. I hundred

   e. I trillion

2. A location on the internet is called a
   a. network.
   b. user ID.
   c. domain.
   d. browser.
   e. web.

3. In the email address *Kim_Lee@earthlink.net.us,* Kim_Lee is the
   a. domain.
   b. URL.
   c. site.
   d. user ID.
   e. location.

4. Which of the following is *not* one of the four components of a URL?
   a. web protocol
   b. name of the web server
   c. name of the browser
   d. name of the directory on the web server
   e. name of the file within the directory

5. Which of the following is the fastest method of data transmission?
   a. ISDN
   b. DSL
   c. modem
   d. TI line
   e. cable modem

6. Which of the following is *not* a netiquette rule?
   a. Consult FAQs.
   b. Flame only when necessary.
   c. Don't shout.
   d. Avoid huge file attachments.
   e. Avoid sloppiness and errors.

7. Which protocol is used to retrieve email messages from the server to your computer?
   a. HTTP (HyperText Transfer Protocol)
   b. SMTP (Simple Mail Transfer Protocol)
   c. POP3 (Post Office Protocol version 3)
   d. POP (point of presence)

8. Who owns the internet?
   a. Microsoft
   b. IBM
   c. Apple
   d. U.S. government
   e. No one owns the internet; the components that make up the Internet are owned and shared by thousands of public and private entities.

9. Each time you connect to your ISP, it will assign your computer a new address called a(n)
   a. domain.
   b. IP address.
   c. plug-in.
   d. POP.
   e. URL (Universal Resource Locator).

10. ISPs that don't run their own backbones connect to an internet backbone through a
    a. NAP network access point.
    b. web portal.
    c. web browser.
    d. URL.
    e. TCP/IP.

11. Which of the following is *not* a protocol?
    a. TCP/IP
    b. IE
    c. HTTP
    d. SMTP

12. The sending of phony email that pretends to be from a credit-card company or bank, luring you to a website that attempts to obtain confidential information from you, is called
    a. spoofing.
    b. phishing.
    c. spamming.
    d. keylogging.
    e. cookies.

True/False Questions

T F 1. POP3 is used for sending email, and SMTP is used for retrieving email.

T F 2. A dial-up modem is an ISP (internet service provider).

T F 3. Replying to spam email messages with the statement "remove" will always get spammers to stop sending you unsolicited email.

T F 4. All computer communications use the same bandwidth.

T F 5. A TI line is the slowest but cheapest form of internet connection.

T F 6. A dynamic IP address gives you faster internet access than a static IP address does.

T F 7. A bookmark lets you return to a favorite website quickly.

T F 8. Radio buttons are used for listening to radio stations on the internet.

T F 9. Spoofing means using fake email sender names.

T F 10. Hypertext refers to text presented with very large letters.

"I can recall information in my own terms and explain it to a friend."

Short-Answer Questions

I. Name three methods of data transmission that are faster than a regular modem connection.

2. What does *log on* mean?

3. What is netiquette, and why is it important?

4. Briefly define *bandwidth.*

5. Many web documents are "linked." What does that mean?

6. Compare and contrast a cable modem service to a DSL service.

7. Explain the basics of how the internet works.

8. What expanded functions does IMAP (Internet Message Access Protocol) have?

9. Briefly explain what TCP/IP does.

10. Why was ICANN established?

11. What's the difference between a dynamic IP address and a static IP address?

12. Explain what a blog is.

13. State your answer to a person who asks you the question "Who owns the internet?"

14. What is B2B commerce?

15. List and briefly describe three kinds of spyware.

stage
3 LEARNING APPLYING, ANALYZING, SYNTHESIZING, EVALUATING

"I can apply what I've learned, relate these ideas to other concepts, build on other knowledge, and use all these thinking skills to form a judgment."

Knowledge in Action

I. Distance learning uses electronic links to extend college campuses to people who otherwise would not be able to take college courses. Are you, or is someone you know, involved in distance learning? If so, research the system's components and uses. What hardware and software do students need in order to communicate with the instructor and classmates? What courses are offered? Discuss the pros and cons of distance learning compared to classroom-based learning.

2. It's difficult to conceive how much information is available on the internet and the web. One method you can use to find information among the millions of documents is to use a search engine, which helps you find web pages on the basis of typed keywords or phrases. Use your browser to go to the Google home page, and click in the *Search* box. Type the keywords *"personal computers";* then click on *Google Search,* or press the *Enter* key. How many results did you get?

3. As more and more homes get high-speed broadband internet connections, the flow of data will become exponentially faster and will open up many new possibilities for sharing large files such as video. What types of interactive services can you envision for the future?

4. Draw a diagram of what happens when you log onto your ISP; include all the connections you think possible for your situation.

5. How do the latest cellphones incorporate the internet into their functions? What functions could be improved? Have any of these extra functions affected your daily life?

6. How has the internet affected your life? Start keeping a list.

7. Email and instant messaging (IM) are ways of sending text messages back and forth to other people on the internet. They seem very similar: in both, you compose a message, and when it's ready, you send it; and when someone else sends something to you, you receive it on your device and can read it.

But in practice, email and IM can be surprisingly different; each has its own rhythm, its own strengths and weaknesses, its own sociology, its own etiquette. Instant messaging is like using the telephone, whereas email is more like corresponding by letter.

As you use email and IM during the course of the term, watch for differences between them. Which medium is more appropriate for which kinds of relationships and communications? Which medium is more stressful to use? Which takes more time? Which is more convenient for you? Which one is more useful for getting real work done? Which medium would you use if you knew that whatever you wrote was eventually going to be published in a book? If you were restricted to using only one of these communications methods, which would it be?

8. Internet service providers (ISPs) often place limits on upload speeds, thus making it take much longer to send (upload) a large file than it would take to receive (download) a file of the same size from someone else. Do a comparison between upload and download speeds on your internet connection, perhaps by emailing yourself a file large enough to allow you to notice the difference. Why do you think there is a difference? (Consider both technological and economic factors.)

9. Imagine that an elderly relative wants to start using the internet for the first time. You want to help the person get started, but you need to be careful not to

overwhelm your relative with more information than he or she can use. What three or four things would you tell and show your relative first? What things do you think will be hardest for him or her to master? How do you think using the internet is likely to change this person's life? If possible, seek out such a relative or neighbor and actually introduce him or her to the internet.

10. As we have discussed in this chapter, the internet is both a goldmine and a minefield. There are vast riches of information, entertainment, education, and communication to be found, but there are also snoopers, spam, spoofing, phishing, spyware, adware, browser hijackers, and key loggers. What should you do to avoid these threats?

11. Some websites require you to register before you are allowed to use them. Others require that you have a paid membership. Others allow limited free access to everyone but require payment for further content. Why do you think different sites adopt these different attitudes toward use of their material?

Web Exercises

1. Some websites go overboard with multimedia effects, while others don't include enough. Locate a website that you think makes effective use of multimedia. What is the purpose of the site? Why is the site's use of multimedia effective? Take notes, and repeat the exercise for a site with too much multimedia and one with too little.

2. If you have never done a search before, try this: Find out how much car dealers pay for your favorite cars, what they charge consumers for them, and what you should know about buying a new car. A company called Edmunds publishes a magazine with all that information, but you can get the same information on its website for free.

   Using the Google search engine (*www.google.com*), type *"automobile buyer's guide"* and *Edmunds* in the search box, and hit the *Google Search* button. How many entries did you get? Click on a link to the Edmunds website. Explore the site, and answer the questions at the beginning of this exercise.

3. Ever wanted your own dot-com in your name? Visit these sites to see if your name is still available:

   www.register.com

   www.namezero.com

   www.domainname.com

   www.checkdomain.com/

   www.domaindirect.com/

4. Interested in PC-to-phone calls through your internet connection? Visit these sites and check out their services:

   http://voice.yahoo.com/

   www.net2phonedirect.com

   www.iconnecthere.com

   www.skype.com

   www.voip.com/

5. HTTP (HyperText Transfer Protocol) on the World Wide Web isn't the only method of browsing and transferring data. FTP is the original method and is still a useful internet function. To use FTP, you'll need an FTP client software program, just as you need a web browser to surf the web. Download one of these shareware clients and visit its default FTP sites, which come preloaded:

CuteFtp	www.globalscape.com
WS_FTP	www.ipswitch.com
FTP Voyager	www.ftpvoyager.com
SmartFTP	www.smartftp.com
FileZilla	http://filezilla-project.org/

   You will need an FTP client program to upload files to a server if you ever decide to build a website. Some online website builders have browser uploaders, but the conventional method has always been FTP.

   On some Macintosh computers, an FTP function is built into the Mac OS Finder (for downloading only—you have to use an FTP client to upload).

6. Video chat extensions to chat software are now generally available, and they really constitute at least two-party videoconferencing. These extensions are available through AIM, Yahoo Messenger, MSN Messenger, and Apple's iChat. All you need is a camera, a microphone, and an internet connection. Check out these sites and decide if this type of "video chat" interests you.

7. Visit these websites to learn more about creating websites with HTML:

   www.lissaexplains.com

   www.make-a-web-site.com

   www.htmlgoodies.com/primers/html/

   www.htmlcodetutorial.com/

   www.w3schools.com/html/default.asp

   Or do an internet search for *"html primer," "learn html,"* or *"html tutorial."*

8. To learn more about internet conventions, go to:

   http://members.tripod.com/~paandaa/smiley.htm

   http://research.microsoft.com/~mbj/Smiley/Smiley.html

   http://piology.org/smiley.txt

   www.cygwin.com/acronyms/

9. Some hobbies have been dramatically changed by the advent of the World Wide Web. Particularly affected are the "collecting" hobbies, such as stamp collecting, coin collecting, antique collecting, memorabilia collecting, plate collecting, and so forth. Choose some such hobby that you know something about or have some interest in. Run a web search about the hobby and see if you can find:

   a. a mailing list about the hobby.

   b. an auction site that lists rare items and allows you to bid on them.

   c. a chat room or other discussion forum allowing enthusiasts to gather and discuss the hobby.

   d. a site on which someone's formidable collection is beautifully and proudly displayed.

10. When the web first came into widespread use, the most popular search engine was AltaVista. For several years there were a variety of search engines available, but in recent years one search engine, Google, has become predominant and the word *googling* has entered the

language as a term that means "to use a search engine to find information."

Visit *http://searchenginewatch.com/links/* for a list of many alternative search engines, as well as explanations about how they work and how to get your site listed on them.

11. E-commerce is booming. For any given product you may wish to buy on the web, there may be hundreds or thousands of possible suppliers, with different prices and terms—and not all of them will provide equally reputable and reliable service. The choices can be so numerous that it may sometimes seem difficult to know how to go about choosing a vendor.

Websites that do comparison shopping for you can be a great help. Such a service communicates with many individual vendors' websites, gathering information as it proceeds; it then presents its findings to you in a convenient form. Often, ratings of the various vendors are provided as well, and sales tax and shipping charges are calculated for you.

Here are a few sites that can assist with comparison shopping:

www.epinions.com/

www.bizrate.com/

www.pricescan.com/

http://shopper.cnet.com/

Practice "catch-and-release e-commerce" by researching the best deals you can find for:

a rare or at least out-of-print book that you'd like to have.

a high-end DVD recorder.

a replacement ink or toner cartridge for your laser or inkjet printer.

a pair of athletic shoes exactly like the shoes you currently have.

Pursue each transaction right up to the last step before you would have to enter your credit-card number and actually buy the item, and then quit. (Don't buy it. You can always do that another time.)

12. WebCams, or web cameras, are used by some websites to show pictures of their locations—either live video or still shots. To run your own WebCam site requires a suitable camera and a continuous internet connection. But to look at other people's WebCam sites requires only a web browser.

For example, try searching for "WebCam Antarctica." Or go to *www.webcam-index.com.*

Find and bookmark at least one interesting WebCam site in each of the following places: Africa, Asia, South America, Europe, Australia, Antarctica, Hawaii.

3

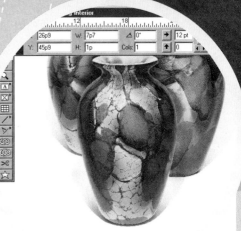

LED APPLE LEAD CRYSTAL VASE
...rh to hold court on your living room mantle,
...vase is infused with shades of yellow,
...specify either the smooth or

B. VOLCANIC LEAD ...
An ever-changing lan...
the surface of ...
redr ...

SOFTWARE

Tools for Productivity & Creativity

Chapter Topics & Key Questions

*W*hat we need is a science called practology, a way of thinking about machines that focuses on how things will actually be used."

So says Alan Robbins, a professor of visual communications, on the subject of *machine interfaces*—the parts of a machine that people actually manipulate.[1] An *interface* is a machine's "control panel," ranging from the volume and tuner knobs on an old radio to all the switches and dials on the flight deck of a jetliner. You may have found, as Robbins thinks, that on too many of today's machines—digital watches, cameras, even stoves—the interface is often designed to accommodate the machine or some engineering ideas rather than the people actually using it. Good interfaces are intuitive—that is, based on prior knowledge and experience—like the twin knobs on a 1950s radio, immediately usable by both novices and sophisticates. Bad interfaces, such as a software program with a bewildering array of menus and icons, force us to relearn the required behaviors every time.

So how well are computer hardware and software makers doing at giving us useful, helpful interfaces? The answer is, They're getting better all the time, but they still have some problematic leftovers from the past. For instance, some interface screens have so many icons that they are confusing instead of helpful. And some microcomputer keyboards still come with a *SysRq* (for System Request) key, which was once used to get the attention of the central computer but now is rarely used. (The Scroll Lock key is also seldom used.)

Improving interfaces is the province of *human-computer interaction (HCI)*, which is concerned with the study, design, construction, and implementation of human-centric interactive computer systems. HCI goes beyond improving screens and menus into the realm of adapting interfaces to human reasoning and studying the long-term effects that computer systems have on humans. HCI encompasses the disciplines of information technology, psychology, sociology, anthropology, linguistics, and others. As computers become more pervasive in our culture, HCI designers are increasingly looking for ways to make interfaces easier, safer, and more efficient.

In time, as interfaces are refined, computers may become no more difficult to use than a car. Until then, however, for smoother computing you need to know something about how software works. Today people communicate one way, computers another. People speak words and phrases; computers process bits and bytes. For us to communicate with these machines, we need an intermediary, an interpreter. This is the function of software, particularly system software.

HCI Careers!

Could you make a career in HCI-associated areas? Go to:

www.sigchi.org

and

www.hfcareers.com/Default. aspx

Do you see some HCI-related areas that you might consider as a major?

Who Was John Tukey?

The term *software* was coined by John Tukey. Who was he? Did he coin any other important computer terms? Do a keyword search on his name and see what you can find out.

3.1 SYSTEM SOFTWARE: The Power behind the Power

What are three components of system software, what does the operating system (OS) do, and what is a user interface?

As we mentioned in Chapter 1, *software,* or *programs,* consists of all the electronic instructions that tell the computer how to perform a task. These instructions come from a software developer in a form (such as a CD or DVD, USB drive, or an internet download) that will be accepted by the computer. **Application software is software that has been developed to solve a particular problem for users—to perform useful work on specific tasks or to provide entertainment. System software enables the application software**

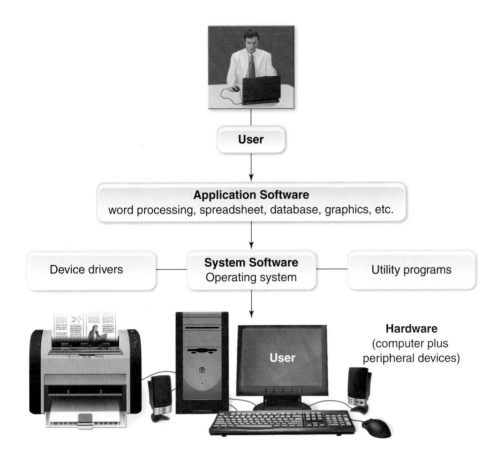

User

Application Software
word processing, spreadsheet, database, graphics, etc.

Device drivers

System Software
Operating system

Utility programs

User

Hardware
(computer plus
peripheral devices)

to interact with the computer and helps the computer manage its internal and external resources.** We interact mainly with the application software, which interacts with the system software, which controls the hardware.

New microcomputers are usually equipped not only with system software
but also with some application software.

There are three basic components of system software that you need to know
about. (● *See Panel 3.1.*)

- **Operating systems:** An operating system is the principal component of
  system software in any computing system.

- **Device drivers:** Device drivers help the computer control peripheral devices.

- **Utility programs:** Utility programs are generally used to support,
  enhance, or expand existing programs in a computer system.

A fourth type of system software, *language translators,* is covered elsewhere.

3.2 THE OPERATING SYSTEM: What It Does

What are the principal functions of the operating system?

The *operating system (OS),* also called the *software platform,* consists of
the low-level, master system of programs that manage the basic operations of the computer.** These programs provide resource management services of many kinds. In particular, they handle the control and use of hardware
resources, including disk space, memory, CPU time allocation, and peripheral
devices. Every general-purpose computer must have an operating system to
run other programs. The operating system allows you to concentrate on your
own tasks or applications rather than on the complexities of managing the
computer. Each application program is written to run on top of a particular
operating system.

If Windows doesn't boot properly, it may go into Safe Mode. You can also get into Safe Mode by pressing the F8 key during the boot process. Safe Mode is used for diagnosing problems and fixing them. When the system is in Safe Mode, only the essential parts of the system work—monitor, mouse, keyboard—and there are no fancy graphics on the screen.

www.computerhope.com/ issues/chsafe.htm

http://computer.howstuffworks. com/question575.htm

Once you are in Safe Mode, you use the Device Manager to help you fix problems:

https://kb.wisc.edu/helpdesk/ page.php?id=502

Going Backward

Another way to get out of a system problem is to use System Restore *(see right)*, found by clicking on the System icon, via Start, Control Panel. Restore System restores the system files to a previous date and/ or time. Your data files (for example, documents) are not affected, and you can customize your System Restore points via the System restore icon.

Different sizes and makes of computers have their own operating systems. For example, Cray supercomputers use UNICOS and COS; IBM mainframes use MVS and VM; PCs run Windows or Linux and Apple Macintoshes run the Macintosh OS. Cellphones have their own operating systems, such as Apple's iPhone OS 3.0, which works with iPhones, or Google and the Open Handset Alliance's Android operating system for mobile devices.[2] In general, an operating system written for one kind of hardware will not be able to run on another kind of machine. In other words, *different operating systems are mutually incompatible.*

Microcomputer users may readily experience the aggravation of such incompatibility when they acquire a new or used microcomputer. Do they get an Apple Macintosh with Macintosh system software, which won't always run PC programs? Or do they get a PC (such as Dell or Hewlett-Packard), which won't run Macintosh programs?

Before we try to sort out these perplexities, we should have an idea of what operating systems do. We consider:

- Booting
- CPU management
- File management
- Task management
- Security management

Booting

What is the boot process?

The work of the operating system begins as soon as you turn on, or "boot," the computer. **_Booting_ is the process of loading an operating system into a computer's main memory.** This loading is accomplished automatically by programs stored permanently in the computer's electronic circuitry (called *read-only memory,* or *ROM,* described in Chapter 4). When you turn on the machine, programs called *diagnostic routines* test the main memory, the central processing unit, and other parts of the system to make sure they

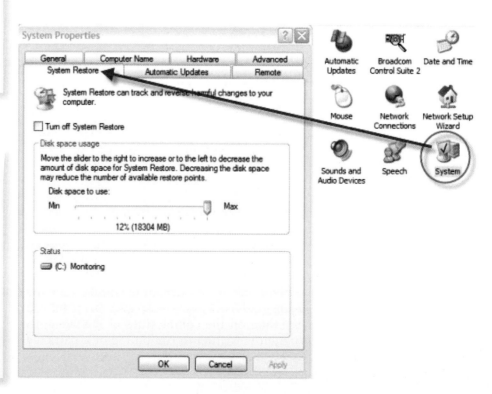

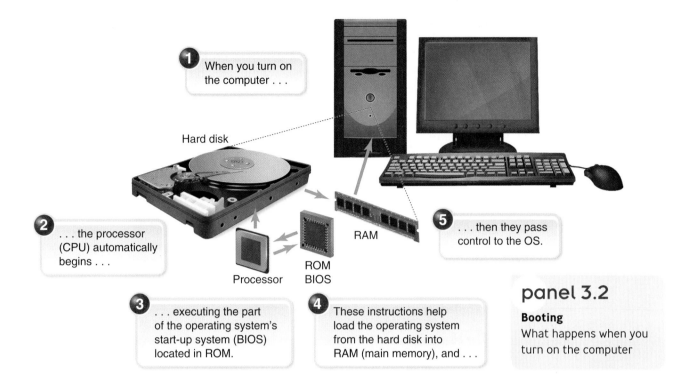

1 When you turn on the computer . . .

2 . . . the processor (CPU) automatically begins . . .

Hard disk

Processor

ROM BIOS

RAM

5 . . . then they pass control to the OS.

3 . . . executing the part of the operating system's start-up system (BIOS) located in ROM.

4 These instructions help load the operating system from the hard disk into RAM (main memory), and . . .

panel 3.2

Booting
What happens when you turn on the computer

are running properly. Next, BIOS (for "basic input/output system") programs are copied to main memory and help the computer interpret keyboard characters or transmit characters to the display screen or to a disk. Then the boot program obtains the operating system, usually from the hard disk, and loads it into the computer's main memory, where it remains until you turn the computer off. (● *See Panel 3.2.*)

COLD BOOTS & WARM BOOTS When you power up a computer by turning on the power "on" switch, this is called a *cold boot.* If your computer is already on and you restart it, this is called a *warm boot* or a *warm start.*

Until recently, computer users have had to endure up to three minutes of waiting while they waited for their machines to boot up. In 2009, however, new software—such as Presto, Hyperspace, and Splashtop—was introduced that allows for "instant on" computing (although there are still problems to be worked out).[3]

THE BOOT DISK Normally, your computer would boot from the hard drive, but if that drive is damaged, you can use a disk called a *boot disk* to start up your computer. A boot disk is a floppy disk or a CD that contains all the files needed to launch the OS. When you insert the boot disk into your computer's floppy or CD drive, you force-feed the OS files to the BIOS, thereby enabling it to launch the OS and complete the start-up routine. After the OS loads completely, you then can access the contents of the Windows drive, run basic drive maintenance utilities, and perform troubleshooting tasks that will help you resolve the problem with the drive.

CPU Management

How does CPU management work?

The central component of the operating system is the supervisor. Like a police officer directing traffic, the ***supervisor,* or *kernel,* manages the CPU** (the central processing unit or processor, as mentioned in Chapter 1). **It remains in memory (main memory or primary storage) while the computer is running and directs other "nonresident" programs (programs that are not in memory) to perform tasks that support application programs.**

Software

MEMORY MANAGEMENT The operating system also manages memory—it keeps track of the locations within main memory where the programs and data are stored. It can swap portions of data and programs between main memory and secondary storage, such as your computer's hard disk, as so-called *virtual memory*. This capability allows a computer to hold only the most immediately needed data and programs within main memory. Yet it has ready access to programs and data on the hard disk, thereby greatly expanding memory capacity.

GETTING IN LINE: QUEUES, BUFFERS, & SPOOLING Programs and data that are to be executed or processed wait on disk in *queues* (pronounced "Qs"). A queue is a first-in, first-out sequence of data and/or programs that "wait in line" in a temporary holding place to be processed. The disk area where the programs or documents wait is called a *buffer*. Print jobs are usually *spooled*—that is, placed—into a buffer, where they wait in a queue to be printed. This happens because the computer can send print jobs to the printer faster than the printer can print them, so the jobs must be stored and then passed to the printer at a rate it can handle. Once the CPU has passed a print job to the buffer, it can take on the next processing task. (The term *spooling* dates back to the days when print jobs were reeled, or copied, onto spools of magnetic tape, on which they went to the printer.)

File Management

What should I know about file management?

A *file* is (1) a named collection of data (data file), or (2) a program (program file) that exists in a computer's secondary storage, such as a hard disk or CD/DVD. Examples of data files are a word processing document, a spreadsheet, images, songs, and the like. Examples of program files are a word processing program or spreadsheet program. (We cover files in more detail in Chapter 4.)

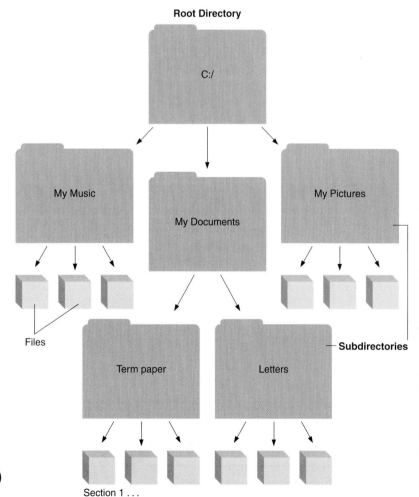

Root Directory
C:/
My Music
My Documents
My Pictures
Files
Subdirectories
Term paper
Letters
Section 1 . . .

FINDING & HANDLING FILES Files containing programs and data are located in many places on your hard disk and other secondary storage devices. The operating system records the storage location of all files. If you move, rename, or delete a file, the operating system manages such changes and helps you locate and gain access to it. For example, you can *copy*, or duplicate, files and programs from one disk to another. You can *back up*, or make a duplicate copy of, the contents of a disk. You can *erase*, or remove, from a disk any files or programs that are no longer useful. You can *rename*, or give new file names to, the files on a disk.

ORGANIZING FILES: DIRECTORIES, SUBDIRECTORIES, & PATHS The operating system's file system arranges files in a hierarchical manner, first into directories (also called *folders*) and then into subdirectories. (● *See Panel 3.3.*) The topmost directory is called the *root directory;* a directory below another directory is called a *subdirectory;* any directory above a subdirectory is called its *parent directory.*

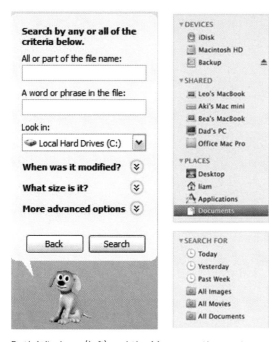

To find a particular file in an operating system's file system, you type in the file's *pathname*. The *path* is the route through the file system. A simple example of a pathname is *C:mydocuments/termpaper/section1.doc.* "C" refers to the hard disk; "mydocuments" is the root directory, or main folder; "term paper" is the subdirectory, or subfolder; "section 1" is the name of the file; and "doc" is a file extension that indicates what type of file it is (document).

Both Windows (*left*) and the Mac operating system (*right*) provide a Find (Search) function for finding files if you don't know the pathname.

Task Management

What is the purpose of task management?

Task Manager

If you want to see a list of processes being executed by your system, open the Task Manager in Windows by holding down the Ctrl, Alt, and Del keys.

A computer is required to perform many different tasks at once (multitasking). In word processing, for example, it accepts input data, stores the data on a disk, and prints out a document—seemingly simultaneously. Most desktop and laptop operating systems are single-user systems that can handle more than one program at the same time—word processing, spreadsheet, database searcher. Each program is displayed in a separate window on the screen. Other operating systems (multiuser systems) can accommodate the needs of several different users at the same time. All these examples illustrate *task management* (*see left*). A *task* is an operation such as storing, printing, or calculating.

MULTITASKING: HANDLING MORE THAN ONE PROGRAM CONCURRENTLY *Multitasking* **is the execution of two or more programs by one user almost at the same time on the same computer with one central processor.** You may be writing a report on your computer with one program while another program plays a music CD. How does the computer handle both programs at once? The answer is that the operating system directs the processor to spend a predetermined amount of time executing the instructions for each program, one at a time. Thus, a small part of the first program is processed, and then the processor moves to the remaining programs, one at a time, processing small parts of each. The cycle is repeated until processing is complete. Because the processor is usually very fast, it may appear that all the programs are being executed at the same time. However, the processor is still executing only one instruction at a time.

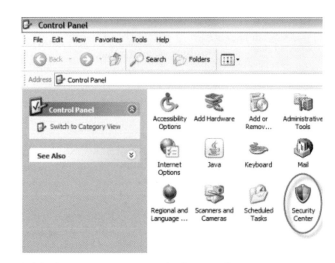

The password is usually displayed as asterisks or dots, so that anyone looking over your shoulder—a "shoulder surfer"—cannot read it.

In Windows, you can access the Security Center via the Control Panel to control additional security features.

Security Management

How does the OS help keep my computer secure?

Operating systems allow users to control access to their computers—an especially important matter when several people share a computer or the same computer network.

Users gain access in the same manner as accessing their email—via a user name (user ID) and a password. As we stated in Chapter 2, a *password* (*above left*) is a special word, code, or symbol required to access a computer system. If you are using a computer at work, you may give yourself a password. When you first boot up a new personal computer, the OS will prompt you to choose a user name and a password. Then, every time after that, when you boot up your computer, you will be prompted to type in your user name and password. Some OSs even allow you to protect individual files with separate access passwords. (The Help feature explains how to change or turn off your password.)

Computer systems and security issues have become complicated and critically important. We discuss this subject in more detail in Chapter 6.

3.3 OTHER SYSTEM SOFTWARE: Device Drivers & Utility Programs

What are the characteristics of device drivers and utility programs?

We said that the three principal parts of system software are the operating system, device drivers, and utility programs. Let's now consider the last two.

Device Drivers: Running Peripheral Hardware

Why do I need device drivers?

<u>Device drivers</u> are specialized software programs that allow input and output devices to communicate with the rest of the computer system. Each device's brand and model are supported by a different driver that works with only one operating system. Many basic device drivers come with the system software when you buy a computer, and the system software will guide you through choosing and installing the necessary drivers. If, however, you buy a new peripheral device, such as a mouse, a scanner, or a printer, the package will include a device driver for the device (probably on a CD or DVD).

Most new operating systems recognize many new hardware devices on their own and automatically install them. If your OS does not recognize your new hardware, it will display a message and ask you to install the driver from the CD that came with your hardware. (● *See Panel 3.4.*)

Utilities: Service Programs

Which utilities would be most important to me?

Utility programs, **also known as** *service programs,* **perform tasks related to the control and allocation of computer resources.** They enhance existing functions or provide services not supplied by other system software programs. Most computers come with built-in utilities as part of the system software. However, they may also be bought separately as external utility programs (such as Norton SystemWorks and McAfee Utilities).

Among the tasks performed by utilities are backing up data, compressing files, recovering lost data, and identifying hardware problems. (*See below.*)

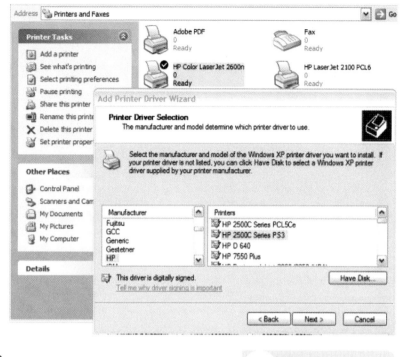

panel 3.4
Device driver selection

PRACTICAL ACTION
Utility Programs

Utility programs are incorporated into the operating system. Others, such as antivirus programs, are sold as stand-alone programs. Some important utility programs are as follows:

Backup

Suddenly your hard-disk drive fails, and you have no more programs or files. Fortunately, we hope, you have used a *backup utility* to make a backup, or duplicate copy, of the information on your hard disk. The backup can be made to an external hard drive, an off-site networked (online) site, or other choices discussed later in the book. Examples of freestanding backup utilities are Norton Ghost (from Symantec) and DT Utilities PC Backup.

Data Recovery

One day in the 1970s, so the story goes, programming legend Peter Norton was working at his computer and accidentally deleted an important file. This was, and is, a common enough error. However, instead of reentering all the information, Norton decided to write a computer program to recover the lost data. He called the program "The Norton Utilities." Ultimately it and other utilities made him very rich.

A *data-recovery utility* is used to restore data that has been physically damaged or corrupted. Data can be damaged by viruses (see following), bad software, hardware failure, and power fluctuations that occur while data is being written/recorded.

Virus Protection

If there's anything that can make your heart sink faster than the sudden failure of your hard disk, it may be the realization that your computer system has been invaded by a virus. A *virus* consists of hidden programming instructions that are buried within an application or system program. Sometimes viruses copy themselves to other programs, causing havoc. Sometimes the virus is merely a simple prank that pops up in a message. Other times, however, it can destroy programs and data and wipe your hard disk clean. Viruses are spread when people exchange disks or CDs, download information from the internet and other computer networks, or open files attached to email. (● *See Panel 3.5.)*

You must, therefore, install antivirus software. *Antivirus software* is a utility program that scans all disks and memory to detect viruses. Some utilities destroy the virus on the spot. Others notify you of possible viral behavior. Because new viruses are constantly being created, you need the type of antivirus software that can detect unknown viruses. Examples of antivirus software are Symantec's Norton Anti-Virus, Bit Defender, Avast!, and McAfee's VirusScan. New viruses appear every day, so it's advisable to look for an antivirus utility that offers frequent online updates without additional cost.

We discuss viruses again in more detail in Chapter 6.

Data Compression

As you continue to store files on your hard disk, it will eventually fill up. You then have several choices: You can delete old files to make room for the new. You can buy a new hard-disk cartridge drive and some cartridges and transfer the old files and programs to those. Or you can use a data compression utility, such as PK Zip, ZipIt, WinZip, or StuffIt. (As a result of the name "Zip," people have come to refer to compressing a file as "zipping" and decompressing a file as "unzipping.")

Data compression utilities remove redundant elements, gaps, and unnecessary data from a computer's storage space so that less space (fewer bits) is required to store or transmit data. With a data compression utility, files can be made more compact for storage on your hard-disk drive. Given today's huge-capacity hard drives, you may never fill yours up. Still, data compression remains an issue.

With the increasing use of large graphic, sound, and video files, data compression is necessary both to reduce the storage space required and to reduce the time required to transmit such large files over a network.

As the use of sophisticated multimedia becomes common, compression and decompression are being increasingly taken over by built-in hardware boards that specialize in this process. That will leave the main processor free to work on other things, and compression/decompression software utilities will become obsolete.

File Defragmentation

Over time, as you delete old files from your hard disk and add new ones, something happens: The files become fragmented. *Fragmentation* is the scattering of portions of files about the disk in nonadjacent areas, thus greatly slowing access to the files.

When a hard disk is new, the operating system puts files on the disk contiguously (next to one another). However, as you update a file over time, new data for that file is distributed to unused spaces. These spaces may not be contiguous to the older data in that file. It takes the operating system longer to read these fragmented files. A *defragmenter* utility program, commonly called a "defragger," will find all the scattered files on your hard disk and reorganize them as contiguous files. Defragmenting the files will speed up the drive's operation.

Disk Scanner (ScanDisk or Check Disk) & Disk Cleanup

These utilities detect and correct certain types of common problems on hard drives and CDs and search for and remove unnecessary files, such as temporary files, or "temp files." Both Windows and the applications you run create temp files needed only for short tasks and system restore (return to normal operating conditions) after certain types of system problems. These files are stored in the Temp folder. For example, when you create a word document, Word will store a temp file version of it in the Temp folder. When you save this document, Word will save it to the location you designated and delete the temp file. The computer should delete temp files when a program is closed, but this doesn't always happen. Also, files will be left in the Temp folder if the computer crashes. Thus temp files can accumulate in the Temp folder and take up space.

Many other utilities exist, such as those for transferring files back and forth between a desktop microcomputer and a laptop and for troubleshooting various types of system problems. Generally, the companies selling utilities do not manufacture the operating system. OS developers usually eventually incorporate the features of a proven utility as part of their product. (Note: Independent, or external, utilities must be compatible with your system software; check the software packaging and user documentation.)

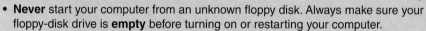

For some unusual utilities, go to:

NimiVisuals *www.mynimi.net*

Defraggler *www.defraggler.com*

FileAlyzer *www.safer-networking. org/en/filealyzer*

Edgeless *www.fxc.btinternet. co.uk/assistive.htm*

Fences *www.stardock.com/ products/fences*

MaxiVista *www.maxivista.com*

FreeOTFE *www.freeotfe.org*

DoubleKiller *www.bigbang enterprises.de/en/doublekiller*

JPEGsnoop *www.impulseadven ture.com/photo/jpeg-snoop.html*

MarxioTimer *www.marxio-tools.net/en/marxio-times.htm*

Edison *www.verdiem.com/edison.asp*

PC Tune-Up: Stop at the Pitstop

To find out what problems your PC has and to learn which utilities might improve its performance, go to:

www.pcpitstop.com/default.asp

and try their free computer scans.

- **If you download** or install **software** from a network server (including the internet), bulletin board, or online service, **always** run **virus scanning software** on the directory you place the new files in before executing them.

- Make sure you have a disk (e.g., **CD**) with your virus program.

- **Do not open any email from unknown sources.**

- **Do not open email attachments** from **unknown** sources.

- **Scan** files attached to email **before** you open them.

- **If your internet** connection is always on (for example, if you have a cable modem), purchase special software called **firewall software** to keep other internet users out of your computer.

- **Never** start your computer from an unknown floppy disk. Always make sure your floppy-disk drive is **empty** before turning on or restarting your computer.

- **Run** virus-scanning software on a new floppy disk or CD **before** executing, installing, or copying its files into your system.

panel 3.5

Preventing viruses

Survival Tip

Free Antivirus Software

For a list of free antivirus software, see:

www.thefreecountry.com/ security/antivirus.shtml

3.4 COMMON FEATURES OF THE USER INTERFACE

What are some common features of the graphical software environment, and how do they relate to the keyboard and the mouse?

The first thing you look at when you call up any system software on the screen is the *user interface*—**the user-controllable display screen that allows you to communicate, or interact, with the computer.** Like the dashboard on a car, the user interface has gauges that show you what's going on and switches and buttons for controlling what you want to do. From this screen, you choose the application programs you want to run or the files of data you want to open.

Using Keyboard & Mouse

How do I use the keys on my keyboard and my mouse as a user interface?

You can interact with the display screen using the keys on your keyboard. As well as having letter, number, and punctuation keys and often a calculator-style numeric keypad, computer keyboards have special-purpose and function keys. (● *See Panel 3.6.*)

SPECIAL-PURPOSE KEYS *Special-purpose keys* **are used to enter, delete, and edit data and to execute commands.** An example is the Esc (for "Escape") key, which tells the computer to cancel an operation or leave ("escape from") the current mode of operation. The Enter, or Return, key, which you will use often, tells the computer to execute certain commands and to start new paragraphs in a document. *Commands* are instructions that cause the software to perform specific actions.

Special-purpose keys are generally used the same way regardless of the application software package being used. Most keyboards include the following special-purpose keys: *Esc, Ctrl, Alt, Del, Ins, Home, End, PgUp, PgDn, Num Lock,* and a few others. (For example, *Ctrl* means "Control," *Del* means "Delete," *Ins* means "Insert.")

FUNCTION KEYS *Function keys,* **labeled "F1," "F2," and so on, are positioned along the top or left side of the keyboard. They are used to execute commands specific to the software being used.** For example, one application software package may use F6 to exit a file, whereas another may use F6 to underline a word.

panel 3.6
Keyboard functions

MACROS Sometimes you may wish to reduce the number of keystrokes required to execute a command. To do this, you use a macro. **A *macro,* also called a *keyboard shortcut,* is a single keystroke or command—or a series**

Escape Key
You can press **Esc** to quit a task you are performing.

Function Keys
These keys let you quickly perform specific tasks. For example, in many programs you can press **F1** to display help information.

Caps Lock and Shift Keys
These keys let you enter text in uppercase (ABC) and lowercase (abc) letters.
Press **Caps Lock** to change the case of all letters you type. Press the key again to return to the original case.
Press **Shift** in combination with another key to type an uppercase letter.

Ctrl and Alt Keys
You can use the **Ctrl** or **Alt** key in combination with another key to perform a specific task. For example, in some programs, you can press **Ctrl** and **S** to save a document.

Windows Key
You can press the **Windows** key to quickly display the Start menu when using many Windows operating systems.

Spacebar
You can press the **Spacebar** to insert a blank space.

of keystrokes or commands—used to automatically issue a longer, predetermined series of keystrokes or commands. Thus, you can consolidate several activities into only one or two keystrokes. The user names the macro and stores the corresponding command sequence; once this is done, the macro can be used repeatedly. (To set up a macro, pull down the Help menu and type in *macro.*)

Although many people have no need for macros, individuals who find themselves continually repeating complicated patterns of keystrokes say they are quite useful.

THE MOUSE & POINTER You will also frequently use your mouse to interact with the user interface. The mouse allows you to direct an on-screen pointer to perform any number of activities. **The _pointer_ usually appears as an arrow, although it changes shape depending on the application. The mouse is used to move the pointer to a particular place on the display screen or to point to little symbols, or icons.** You can activate the function corresponding to the symbol by pressing ("clicking") buttons on the mouse. Using the mouse, you can pick up and slide ("drag") an image from one side of the screen to the other or change its size. (● *See Panel 3.7 on page 132.*)

The GUI: The Graphical User Interface

How does a GUI make life easier for me?

In the beginning, personal computers had *command-driven interfaces,* which required that you type in complicated-looking instructions (such as *copy a:\filename c:* to copy a file from a floppy disk to a hard disk). In the next version, they also had *menu-driven interfaces,* in which you could use the arrow keys on your keyboard (or a mouse) to choose a command from a menu, or a list of activities.

Today the computer's "dashboard" is usually a **_graphical user interface (GUI)_** (pronounced "gooey"), **which allows you to use a mouse or keystrokes**

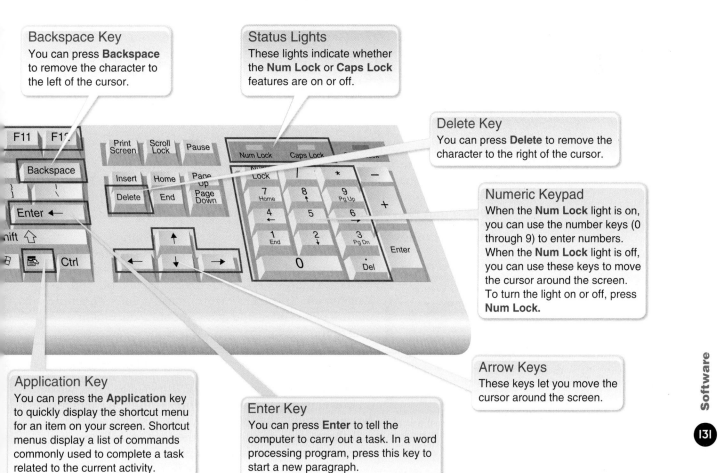

Backspace Key
You can press **Backspace** to remove the character to the left of the cursor.

Status Lights
These lights indicate whether the **Num Lock** or **Caps Lock** features are on or off.

Delete Key
You can press **Delete** to remove the character to the right of the cursor.

Numeric Keypad
When the **Num Lock** light is on, you can use the number keys (0 through 9) to enter numbers. When the **Num Lock** light is off, you can use these keys to move the cursor around the screen. To turn the light on or off, press **Num Lock.**

Arrow Keys
These keys let you move the cursor around the screen.

Application Key
You can press the **Application** key to quickly display the shortcut menu for an item on your screen. Shortcut menus display a list of commands commonly used to complete a task related to the current activity.

Enter Key
You can press **Enter** to tell the computer to carry out a task. In a word processing program, press this key to start a new paragraph.

Term	Action	Purpose
Point	Move mouse across desk to guide pointer to desired spot on screen. The pointer assumes different shapes, such as arrow, hand, or I-beam, depending on the task you're performing.	To execute commands, move objects, insert data, or similar actions on screen.
Click	Press and quickly release left mouse button.	To select an item on the screen.
Double-click	Quickly press and release left mouse button twice.	To open a document or start a program.
Drag and drop	Position pointer over item on screen, press and hold down left mouse button while moving pointer to location in which you want to place item, then release.	To move an item on the screen.
Right-click	Press and release right mouse button.	To display a shortcut list of commands, such as a pop-up menu of options.

to select icons (little symbols) and commands from menus (lists of activities). The GUIs on the PC and on the Apple Macintosh (which was the first easy-to-use personal computer available on a wide scale) are somewhat similar. Once you learn one version, it's fairly easy to learn the other. However, the best-known GUI is that of Microsoft Windows system software. (● *See Panel 3.8.*)

DESKTOP, ICONS, & MENUS Three features of a GUI are the desktop, icons, and menus.

- **Desktop:** After you turn on the computer, the first screen you will encounter is the *desktop (see right),* a term that embodies the idea of folders of work (memos, schedules, to-do lists) on a businessperson's desk. **The *desktop,* which is the system's main interface screen, displays pictures (icons) that provide quick access to programs and information.**

- **Icons and rollovers:** We're now ready to give a formal definition: *Icons* **are small pictorial figures that represent programs, data files, or procedures.** For example, a trash can represents a place to dispose of a file you no longer want. If you click your mouse pointer on a little picture of a printer, you can print out a document. One of the most important icons is the *folder,* a representation of a manila folder; folders hold the files in which you store your documents and other data.

Of course, you can't always be expected to know what an icon or graphic means. **A *rollover* feature, a small text box explaining the icon's function, appears when you roll the mouse pointer over the icon. A rollover may also produce an animated graphic.**

Icon: Symbol representing a program, data file, or procedure. Icons are designed to communicate their function, such as a floppy disk for saving.

Rollover: When you roll your mouse pointer over an icon or graphic (in this case, the "Save" icon), a small box with text appears that briefly explains its function.

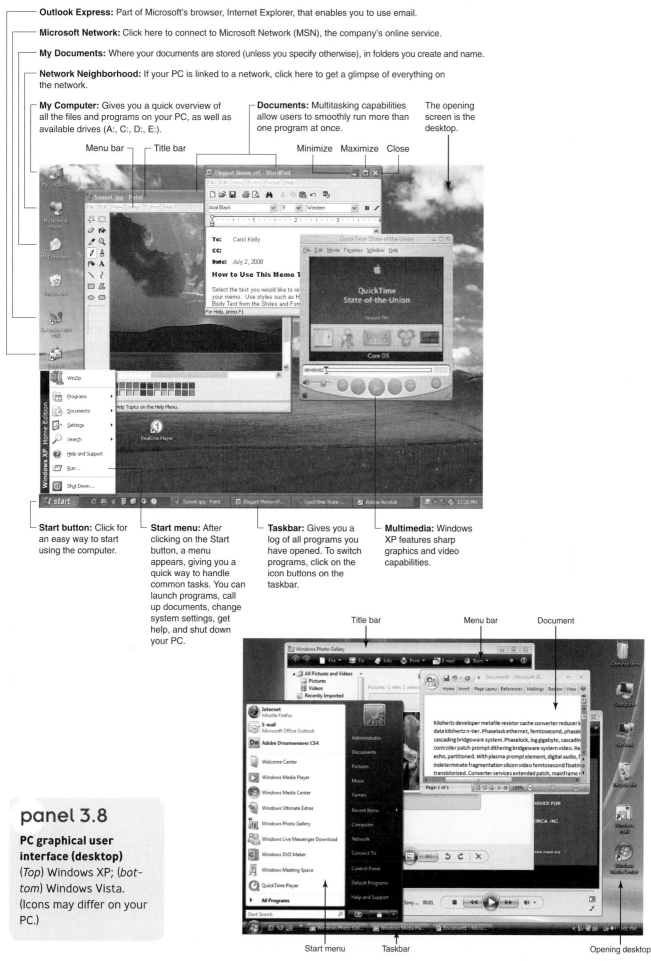

Outlook Express: Part of Microsoft's browser, Internet Explorer, that enables you to use email.

Microsoft Network: Click here to connect to Microsoft Network (MSN), the company's online service.

My Documents: Where your documents are stored (unless you specify otherwise), in folders you create and name.

Network Neighborhood: If your PC is linked to a network, click here to get a glimpse of everything on the network.

My Computer: Gives you a quick overview of all the files and programs on your PC, as well as available drives (A:, C:, D:, E:).

Documents: Multitasking capabilities allow users to smoothly run more than one program at once.

The opening screen is the desktop.

Menu bar   Title bar

Minimize   Maximize   Close

Start button: Click for an easy way to start using the computer.

Start menu: After clicking on the Start button, a menu appears, giving you a quick way to handle common tasks. You can launch programs, call up documents, change system settings, get help, and shut down your PC.

Taskbar: Gives you a log of all programs you have opened. To switch programs, click on the icon buttons on the taskbar.

Multimedia: Windows XP features sharp graphics and video capabilities.

Title bar   Menu bar   Document

panel 3.8

PC graphical user interface (desktop)
(*Top*) Windows XP; (*bottom*) Windows Vista. (Icons may differ on your PC.)

Start menu   Taskbar

Opening desktop screen

Software

Document3 - Microsoft Word

File Edit View Insert Format Tools Table Windo

Can't Undo   Ctrl+Z
Repeat Doc Close   Ctrl+Y
Cut   Ctrl+X
Copy   Ctrl+C
Paste   Ctrl+V
Paste Special...
Paste as Hyperlink
Clear   Del
Select All   Ctrl+A
Find...   Ctrl+F
Replace...   Ctrl+H
Go To...   Ctrl+G
Links...
Object

Pull-down menu: When you click the mouse on the menu bar, a list of options appears or pulls down like a shade.

● **Menus:** Like a restaurant menu, a **_menu_ offers you a list of options to choose from**—in this case, a list of commands for manipulating data, such as Print or Edit. Menus are of several types. Resembling a pull-down window shade, a *pull-down menu,* also called a *drop-down menu,* is a list of options that pulls down from the menu bar at the top of the screen. For example, if you use the mouse to "click on" (activate) a command (for example, File) on the menu bar, you will see a pull-down menu offering further commands.

Choosing one of these options may produce further menus called *cascading menus (left),* menus that seem to fly back to the left or explode out to the right, wherever there is space. A *pull-up menu* is a list of options that pulls up from the menu bar at the bottom of the screen. In Windows XP, a pull-up menu appears in the lower left-hand corner when you click on the Start button.

A *pop-up menu* is a list of command options that can "pop up" anywhere on the screen when you click the right mouse button. In contrast to pull-down or pull-up menus, pop-up menus are not connected to a menu bar.

DOCUMENTS, TITLE BARS, MENU BARS, TOOLBARS, TASKBARS, & WINDOWS (SMALL "W") If you want to go to a document, there are three general ways to begin working from a typical Microsoft Windows GUI desktop: (1) You can click on the *Start* button at the lower left corner and then make a selection from the pull-up menu that appears. (2) Or you can click on the *My Computer* icon on the desktop and pursue the choices offered there. (3) Or you can click on the *My Documents* icon and then on the folder that contains the document you want. In each case, the result is the same: the document is displayed in the window. (● *See Panel 3.9.*)

Pull-up menu: When you click the mouse pointer on the Start button, it produces a pull-up menu offering access to programs and documents.

Cascading menu: Moving the mouse pointer to an option on the pull-up menu produces a flyout menu with more options.

From Start menu

Click on the Start button to produce
Start menu, then go to *Documents* option,
then to *My Documents.* Click on the item you want.

Click on C, which opens a window that provides
access to information stored on your hard disk.

From My Computer

Click on the *My Computer*
icon, which opens a window
that provides access to
information on your computer.

Click on the
My Documents icon,
which opens a window
providing access to
document files
and folders.

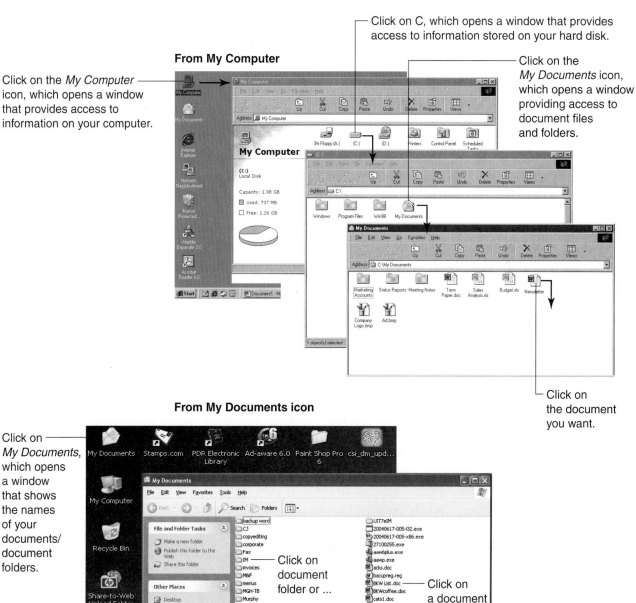

Click on
the document
you want.

From My Documents icon

Click on
My Documents,
which opens
a window
that shows
the names
of your
documents/
document
folders.

Click on
document
folder or ...

Click on
a document
to open it.

Software

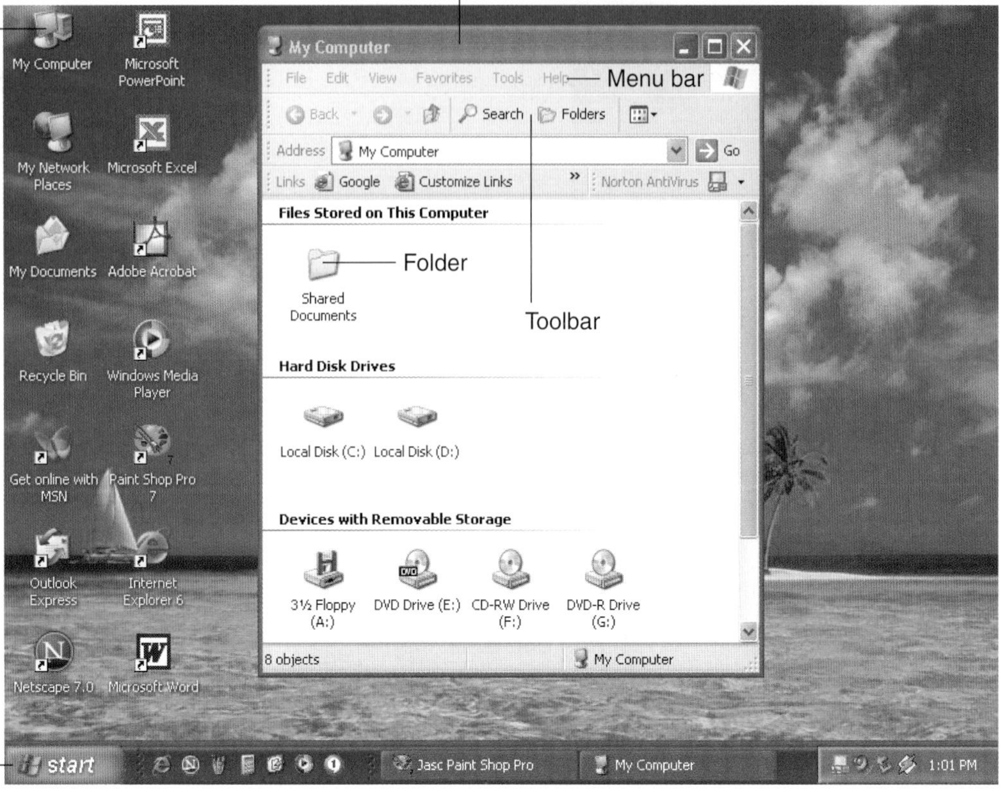

Desktop icons — My Computer, Microsoft PowerPoint, My Network Places, Microsoft Excel, My Documents, Adobe Acrobat, Recycle Bin, Windows Media Player, Get online with MSN, Paint Shop Pro 7, Outlook Express, Internet Explorer 6, Netscape 7.0, Microsoft Word

Title bar — Menu bar — Folder — Shared Documents — Toolbar — Hard Disk Drives — Local Disk (C:) Local Disk (D:) — Devices with Removable Storage — 3½ Floppy (A:) DVD Drive (E:) CD-RW Drive (F:) DVD-R Drive (G:) — 8 objects — My Computer

Windows XP taskbar — start — Jasc Paint Shop Pro — My Computer — 1:01 PM

panel 3.10

"Bars" and windows functions

Once past the desktop—which is the GUI's opening screen—if you click on the *My Computer* icon, you will encounter various "bars" and window functions. (● *See Panel 3.10.*)

- **Title bar:** The _**title bar**_ **runs across the very top of the display window and shows the name of the folder you are in**—for example, "My Computer."

- **Menu bar:** Below the title bar is the _**menu bar,**_ **which shows the names of the various pull-down menus available.** Examples of menus are File, Edit, View, Favorites, Tools, and Help.

- **Toolbar:** The _**toolbar,**_ **below the menu bar, displays menus and icons representing frequently used options or commands.** An example of an icon is the picture of two pages in an open folder with a superimposed arrow, which issues a *Copy to* command.

- **Taskbar:** In Windows, the _**taskbar**_ **is the bar across the bottom of the desktop screen that contains the Start button and that appears by default.** Small boxes appear here that show the names of open files. You can switch among the files by clicking on the boxes.

- **Windows:** When spelled with a capital "W," Windows is the name of Microsoft's system software (Windows 95, 98, Me, XP, Vista, 7, and so on). When spelled with a lowercase "w," a _**window**_ **is a rectangular frame on the computer display screen. Through this frame you can view a file of data—such as a document, spreadsheet, or database—or an application program.**

In the upper right-hand corner of the Windows title bar are some window controls—three icons that represent *Minimize, Maximize and Restore,* and *Close.* By clicking on these icons, you can *minimize* the window (shrink it down to an icon at the bottom of the screen), *maximize* it (enlarge it or restore it to its original size), or *close* it (exit the file and make the window disappear). You can also use the mouse to move the window around the desktop, by clicking on and dragging the title bar.

Minimize to Taskbar
Maximize/ Restore
Close

Type a question for help

Finally, you can create *multiple windows* to show programs running concurrently. For example, one window might show the text of a paper you're working on, another might show the reference section for the paper, and a third might show something you're downloading from the internet. If you have more than one window open, click on the Maximize button of the window you want to be the main window to *restore* it.

The Help Command

What can the Help command do for me?

Don't understand how to do something? Forgotten a command? Accidentally pressed some keys that messed up your screen layout and you want to undo it? Most toolbars contain a **Help command**—**a command generating a table of contents, an index, and a search feature that can help you locate answers.** In addition, many applications have *context-sensitive help,* which leads you to information about the task you're performing. (● *See Panel 3.11.*)

(● *See Panel 3.11.*)

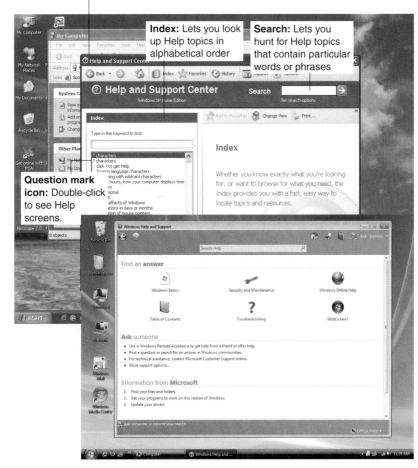

The *Help* menu provides a list of help options.

Index: Lets you look up Help topics in alphabetical order

Search: Lets you hunt for Help topics that contain particular words or phrases

Question mark icon: Double-click to see Help screens.

panel 3.11

Help features

(*Top*) The XP Help command yields a pull-down menu; (*bottom*) the Help screen for Vista

3.5 COMMON OPERATING SYSTEMS

What are some common desktop, network, and portable (embedded) OSs?

The _platform_ is the particular processor model and operating system on which a computer system is based. For example, there are "Mac platforms" (Apple Macintosh) and "Windows platforms" or "PC platforms" (for personal computers such as Dell, Compaq, Lenovo, Gateway, and Hewlett-Packard, which run Microsoft Windows). Sometimes the latter are called *Wintel platforms*, for "Windows + Intel," because they often combine the Windows operating system with the Intel processor chip. (We discuss processors in Chapter 4.)

Despite the dominance of the Windows platform, some so-called *legacy systems* are still in use. A legacy system is an older, outdated, yet still functional technology, such as the _DOS operating system._ **DOS** (rhymes with "boss")—**for *Disk Operating System—was the original operating system produced by Microsoft and had a hard-to-use command-driven user interface.** (● *See Panel 3.12.*) Its initial 1982 version was designed to run on the IBM PC as PC-DOS. Later Microsoft licensed the same system to other computer makers as MS-DOS.

```
C:\WINDOWS\System32\cmd.exe

(C) Copyright 1985-2001 Microsoft Corp.

C:\Documents and Settings\Stacey C. Sawyer>
C:\Documents and Settings\Stacey C. Sawyer>DIR
 Volume in drive C has no label.
 Volume Serial Number is B0EB-7091

 Directory of C:\Documents and Settings\Stacey C. Sawyer

04/25/2003  07:14 PM    <DIR>          .
04/25/2003  07:14 PM    <DIR>          ..
03/01/2003  12:58 PM    <DIR>          .java
03/01/2003  12:58 PM    <DIR>          .jpi_cache
04/25/2003  07:17 PM             1,106 .plugin140_01.trace
08/23/2003  03:31 PM    <DIR>          Desktop
02/11/2003  11:35 AM               831 Eudora.lnk
08/23/2003  03:29 PM    <DIR>          Favorites
08/25/2003  11:48 AM    <DIR>          My Documents
08/25/2003  10:45 AM         3,145,728 ntuser.dat
07/17/2003  10:24 AM    <DIR>          Start Menu
02/28/2002  09:31 PM    <DIR>          WINDOWS
               3 File(s)      3,147,665 bytes
               9 Dir(s)  29,842,452,480 bytes free

C:\Documents and Settings\Stacey C. Sawyer>
```

Here we briefly describe the principal platforms used on *single-user, stand-alone* computers today, both desktops and laptops: the Apple Macintosh OS and Microsoft Windows. We discuss operating systems for *networks* (servers) and for *embedded systems* (handheld computers and some consumer devices) in a few pages.

Macintosh Operating System

What significant contribution has the Mac OS made to personal computing?

The _Macintosh operating system (Mac OS),_ **which runs only on Apple Macintosh computers, set the standard for icon-oriented, easy-to-use graphical user interfaces.** Apple based its new interface on work done at Xerox, which in turn had based its work on early research at Stanford Research Institute (now SRI International). (See the timeline starting on page 166.) The software generated a strong legion of fans shortly after its launch in 1984 and inspired rival Microsoft to upgrade DOS to the more user-friendly Windows operating systems. Much later, in 1998, Apple introduced its iMac computer (the "i" stands for "internet"), which added capabilities such as small-scale networking.

MAC OS X The Mac OS is *proprietary,* meaning that it is privately owned and controlled by a company. Some Mac users still use System 9, introduced in October 1999, which added an integrated search engine, updated the GUI, and improved networking services. The next version of the operating system, Mac OS X ("ex" or "10") broke with 15 years of Mac software to use Unix (discussed shortly) to offer a dramatic new look and feel. (● *See Panel 3.13.*) Many Apple users claim that OS X won't allow software conflicts, a frequent headache with Microsoft's Windows operating systems. (For example, you might install a game and find that it interferes with the device driver for a sound card. Then, when you uninstall the game, the problem persists. With

Mac OS X, when you try to install an application program that conflicts with any other program, the Mac simply won't allow you to run it.) Mac OS X also offers free universal email services, improved graphics and printing, improved security, CD/DVD burning capability, a CD/DVD player, easier ways to find files, and support for building and storing web pages.

Mac OS X also uses:

- **Spotlight—for desktop search:** A desktop search engine, you'll recall from Chapter 2, is a tool that extends searching beyond the web to the contents of your personal computer's hard disk. The Macintosh version, called Spotlight, helps you find information stored in the thousands of files on your hard drive. Spotlight also offers Smart Folders, permanent lists of search results that are automatically updated as files are added or deleted.

- **Dashboard—for creating desktop "widgets":** The Dashboard is a collection of little applications that Apple calls "widgets," such as clock, calculator, weather report, or stock ticker, that can be available on your desktop at any time. Dashboard enables programmers to create customized widgets that provide notification on the desktop whenever there's a newsworthy development, such as a change in stock price, that's important to users—something that "could tame the flood of real-time data that threatens to overwhelm us," says *BusinessWeek*'s Stephen Wildstrom.[4]

- **Automator—for handling repetitive tasks:** Automator is a personal robotic assistant that lets you streamline repetitive tasks into a script that will perform a sequence of actions with a single click, such as checking for new messages from a particular sender, then sending you an alert.

The latest version of OS X, 10.6, or Snow Leopard, was released in 2009. As of 2009, Mac OS X is the second most popular general-purpose operating system in use (almost 10%), after Microsoft Windows (about 88%).[5] (● *See Panel 3.14.*)

WHERE IS MAC KING? Macintosh is still considered king in areas such as desktop publishing, and Macs are still favored in many educational settings. For very specialized applications, most programs are written for

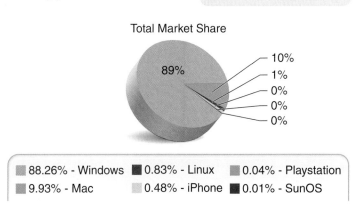

Total Market Share

89%

- 10%
- 1%
- 0%
- 0%
- 0%

88.26% - Windows ■ 0.83% - Linux ■ 0.04% - Playstation
9.93% - Mac 0.48% - iPhone ■ 0.01% - SunOS

the Windows platform. However, programs for games and for common business uses such as word processing and spreadsheets are also widely available for the Mac.

Note that many Macs can work with Microsoft PC (Windows) applications, such as Word—if the Mac version of these applications has been installed on the Mac and the Mac has an Intel processor (Chapter 4). You can also use a PC-formatted disk in many Macs. (The reverse is not true: PCs will not accept Mac-formatted disks.)

Microsoft Windows

What has been the evolution of Windows?

In the 1980s, taking its cue from the popularity of Mac's easy-to-use GUI, Microsoft began working on Windows to make DOS more user-friendly. Also a proprietary system, **_Microsoft Windows_ is the most common operating system for desktop and portable PCs.** Early attempts (Windows 1.0, 2.0, 3.0) did not catch on. However, in 1992, *Windows 3.X* emerged as the preferred system among PC users. (Technically, Windows 3.X wasn't a full operating system; it was simply a layer or "shell" over DOS.)

Bill Gates. The founder of Microsoft has been identified with every PC operating system since the 1980 DOS.

EARLY VERSIONS OF WINDOWS: WINDOWS 95, 98, & ME Windows 3.X evolved into the *Windows 95* operating system, which was succeeded by *Windows 98* and *Windows Me.* Among other improvements over their predecessors, Windows 95, 98, and Me (for *Millennium Edition),* which are still used in many homes and businesses, adhere to a standard called Universal Plug and Play, which is supposed to let a variety of electronics seamlessly network with each other. *Plug and Play* is defined as the ability of a computer to automatically configure a new hardware component that is added to it.

WINDOWS XP **_Microsoft Windows XP_, introduced in 2001, combined elements of Windows networking software and Windows Me with a new GUI.** It has improved stability and increased driver and hardware support. It also features built-in instant messaging; centralized shopping managers to help you keep track of your favorite online stores and products; and music, video, and photography managers. Windows XP comes in many versions: Windows Starter Edition is for new computer users in developing countries; Windows XP Home Edition is for typical home users; Windows XP Professional Edition is for businesses of all sizes and for home users who need to do more than get email, browse the internet, and do word processing; Windows XP Tablet PC Edition is for business notebook computers that support data entry via a special pen used to write on the display screen (● *See Panel 3.15.*); Windows XP Embedded is for embedded systems in portable devices and consumer electronics.

WINDOWS XP MEDIA CENTER EDITION/TV PACK 2008 In late 2004, Microsoft released *Windows XP Media Center Edition 2005*, a media-oriented operating system that supports DVD burning, high-definition television (HDTV), TV tuners, cable TV, and satellite TV and that provides a refreshed user interface. A key feature is support for wireless technology and in particular Media Center Extender, a technology that lets users wirelessly connect up to five TVs and some portable devices to the Media Center PC.

Windows XP Media Center Edition is a premium version of Windows XP, designed to make the PC or the TV the media and entertainment hub of the home. Windows TV Pack 2008 is for Vista (see below). In addition to

performing traditional PC tasks, the system can serve music, pictures, video, and live television to portable devices, stereos, and TVs while also enforcing digital rights set by content owners. Users can access a Windows XP Media Center PC—a combination of special Windows OS and hardware that includes a TV tuner, remote control, and other multimedia equipment—with a remote control through a special user interface on their TV.

WINDOWS VISTA ___Windows Vista___ was introduced to consumers in January 2007 (● *See Panel 3.16.*) It is the equivalent of Windows version 12—preceded by 1.0, 2.0, 3.0, 3.1, NT, 95, NT 4.0, 98, 2000, ME, XP. To create Vista, Microsoft supposedly rebuilt Windows from scratch, and it does indeed have a dazzling interface, glitzier graphics, and improved security tools. However, so much computing power was required to run it that many people found their new PCs ran more slowly than their older, less powerful XP machines.[6] Vista was also criticized for software and hardware incompatibility issues with office suites and some printers, digital cameras, and other devices. So, many businesses decided that, given the downturn in the economy, they wouldn't be upgrading

panel 3.16

Vista desktop screen showing a computer's various storage locations

Software

141

Aerial view of Microsoft's Redmond, Washington, main corporate campus, which spreads over several square miles of the Seattle suburb.

For more on how Media Centers work, go to:

www.microsoft.com/ windows/windows-vista/ features/media-center.aspx

http://on10.net/blogs/ maxpowerhouse7/ CES-2009-Windows- Media-Center-on-Windows- 7-with-Touch/

Survival Tip

OEM

If you buy a computer with Windows (or any other operating system) already installed, the OS is called an *OEM (original equipment manufacturer) version.* If you buy your OS off the shelf, it is called a *retail version.* These two versions are almost identical, except an OEM version will install only on the *specific* machine for which it was intended. A retail version will install on any compatible machine. If you have an OEM version, you have to call the computer manufacturer, not the OS producer, for technical support. Because a retail version is not specifically tailored for your particular computer, Microsoft recommends that, before you buy a retail version of an OS, you run a compatibility check at its website (*http://support. microsoft.com*).

from XP to Vista, because they saw no value in it and because it required buying more powerful PCs and new software.

To spur Vista sales, Microsoft announced it would stop selling Windows XP in June 2008—a move that launched a storm of protest. Microsoft thereupon softened its initial posture and said it would continue to make XP available and would provide extended customer support and fix bugs for XP until 2014.

However, in spite of this change, Vista did not sell well, so Microsoft moved on to Windows 7, or Windows 2009.

WINDOWS 7 <u>*Windows 7*</u> (or Windows 2009), the newest version of Microsoft Windows was released in October 2009. The new operating system includes iPhone-like touch-screen applications called Microsoft Surface, an alternative to the computer mouse. Thus, you can manipulate objects on the screen with your hands, such as enlarge and shrink photos or navigate a city map by stroking the screen. (● *See Panel 3.17.*) Windows 7 is less power-hungry than Vista, boots up more quickly than previous Windows systems, and has improved networking and security features.

As does XP, Windows 7 comes in various versions:

- Starter
- Home Basic
- Home Premium
- Professional
- Enterprise (for multi-user businesses)
- Ultimate (for retail businesses)

Vista and XP users can upgrade to Windows 7, but with some difficulty and some cost. (See **more info!** on the next page.). There are many detailed issues involved with upgrading/changing an operating system. If you are a Windows user and are considering an upgrade, go to Microsoft's support site (*www. support.microsoft.com*) to find out what options are open to you.

A problem for any version of Windows, however, is that it builds off the same core architecture that represents more than 20 years of legacies. Some believe

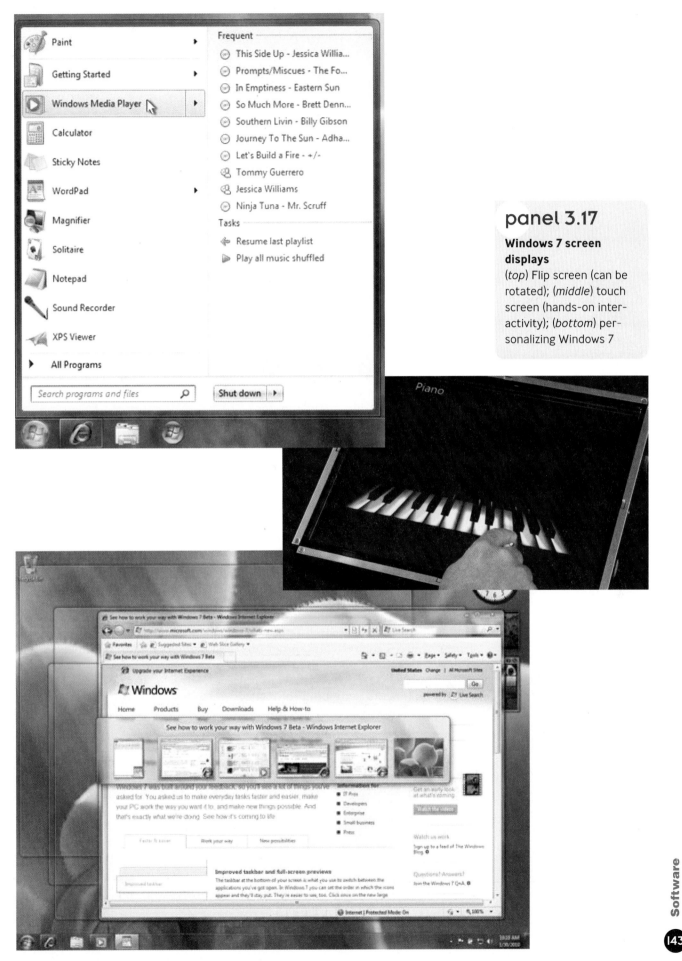

panel 3.17

Windows 7 screen displays
(*top*) Flip screen (can be rotated); (*middle*) touch screen (hands-on interactivity); (*bottom*) personalizing Windows 7

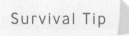

Survival Tip

New Installation

Every time you install or reinstall Windows XP, Vista, or 7 you will have to get Microsoft's permission to activate it. You can do this over the internet or via the phone.

that Microsoft needs to do what Apple did when it introduced its Mac OS X in 2001: start over from scratch. Although this risked alienating some Macintosh users, since it forced them to buy new versions of their existing Mac applications software, it also made the system less vulnerable to crashes. "A monolithic operating system like Windows perpetuates an obsolete design," said one critic. "We don't need to load up our machines with bloated layers we won't use."[7]

Network Operating Systems: NetWare, Windows NT Server, Unix, & Linux

How would I distinguish among the several network OSs?

The operating systems described so far were principally designed for use with stand-alone desktop and laptop machines. Now let's consider the important operating systems designed to work with sizeable networks—NetWare, Windows NT Server, Unix/Solaris, and Linux.

NOVELL'S NETWARE *NetWare* **has long been a popular network operating system for coordinating microcomputer-based local area networks (LANs) throughout a company or a campus.** LANs allow PCs to share programs, data files, and printers and other devices. A network OS is usually located on a main server (see Chapter 1), which controls the connectivity of connected smaller networks and individual computers. Novell, the maker of NetWare, thrived as corporate data managers realized that networks of PCs could exchange information more cheaply than the previous generation of mainframes and midrange computers. The biggest challenge to NetWare has been the Windows' versions of NT and Server. However, Novell is continuing to improve its networking OS with its new version, Open Enterprise Server, which combines Netware with the benefits of a more recently popular operating system, Linux (discussed shortly).

WINDOWS NT & NT SERVER Windows desktop operating systems (95/98/Me/XP/Vista/7) can be used to link PCs in small networks in homes and offices. However, something more powerful was needed to run the huge networks linking a variety of computers—PCs, workstations, mainframes—used by many companies, universities, and other organizations, which previously were served principally by Unix and NetWare operating systems. *Microsoft Windows NT* **(the** *NT* **stands for "New Technology") and now called** *Windows Server 2008,* **is the company's multitasking operating system designed to run on network servers in businesses of all sizes.** It allows multiple users to share resources such as data, programs, and printers and to build web applications and connect to the internet.

The Windows NT/Server networking OS comes in various versions, and some of its functions are built into XP, Vista, and Windows 7.

UNIX, SOLARIS, & BSD Unix (pronounced *"you*-nicks") was developed at AT&T's Bell Laboratories in 1969 as an operating system for minicomputers. By the 1980s, AT&T entered into partnership with Sun Microsystems to develop a standardized version of Unix for sale to industry. Today *Unix* **is a proprietary multitasking operating system for multiple users that has built-in networking capability and versions that can run on all kinds of computers.** (● *See Panel 3.18.*) It is used mostly on mainframes, workstations, and servers, rather than on PCs. Government agencies, universities, research institutions, large corporations, and banks all use Unix for everything from designing airplane parts to currency trading. Because it is particularly stable and reliable, Unix is also used for website management and runs the backbone of the internet. The developers of the internet built their communications system around Unix because it has the ability to keep large systems (with hundreds of processors) churning out transactions day in and day out for years without fail.

```
cerberus (tty1) login: joe
password:
Last login: Wed Jun 15 14:09:20 2005 from 24-205-252.mb-cres.charterpipeline.net
Copyright (c) 1980, 1983, 1986, 1988, 1990, 1991, 1993, 1994
        The Regents of the University of California.  All rights reserved.

FreeBSD 4.7-RELEASE (CERBERUS) #3: Sun Jun  6 09:33:11 PDT 2004

[cerberus:~] % ls -l
total 339
-rw-r-----   1 joe     joe_a          122 Jun 30  2003 archive.tgz
drwxr-xr-x   2 joe     joe_a          512 Apr  7  9:28 finished
lrwxrwx---   1 joe     74              12 Jul  3  2001 dossier -> /ad7/dossier
-rw-------   1 joe     joe_a        13283 Mar 29 13:51 mbox
lrwxr-xr-x   1 root    joe_a           21 Jun  9  2002 public_html -> /ulS/WWW/
drwxr-xr-x   2 joe     joe_a          512 Jun 15 17:49 work
web/cfcl/joe
[cerberus:~] % cd work
[cerberus:~/work] % ls
page1.out       page1.txt       page2.out       page2.txt
page3.txt       page3.out       page4.txt       process.pl
[cerberus:~/work] % ./process.pl <page4.txt >page4.out
[cerberus:~/work] %
```

PRACTICAL ACTION
Get a PC or Get a Mac? Security Issues

Nervous about spam, spyware, phishing, viruses, and other threats to your computer? That's certainly been the case for many Windows PC users.

"Microsoft has paid so little attention to security over the years," says distinguished technology writer Walter Mossberg, "that consumers who use Windows have been forced to spend more and more of their time and money fending off" these invasive demons.[8]

In late 2004, the software giant rolled out a major, free operating system upgrade called *Service Pack 2,* or *SP2.* Among other things, this was supposed to reduce the risk to Microsoft's Internet Explorer web browser of online attacks that had frustrated users and slowed businesses. However, the company conceded that SP2 interfered with about 50 known programs, including corporate products and a few games. And a couple of months later, Microsoft issued several "security advisories" urging consumers and businesses to patch 21 new flaws in Windows software products. In February 2005 it said that it was upgrading its Internet Explorer against malicious software and expected to include security defenses in its new operating system, Vista. Service Pack 3 (2008) was supposed to "cure" some more Windows security ills, but many users remain critical of Windows' vulnerability to viruses and the like.

Microsoft's Service Packs versus Patches

As we have mentioned, a *service pack* (sometimes called a "service release") is a collection of files for various updates, software bug fixes, and security improvements. A *patch* (sometimes called a "hotfix") is an update that occurs between service packs; most patches are built to correct security vulnerabilities. Service packs are planned, or strategic, releases. Patches are unplanned, interim solutions.

A new service pack is supposed to "roll up" all previous service packs and patches. Microsoft recommends installing both packs and patches as they become available but also checking the online bulletin accompanying every new patch to see what vulnerability risks it poses to your particular hardware and software configuration.

It would appear, however, that the pack-and-patch approach to security for Microsoft products will be with us for a long time. "We don't feel like we've ever crossed the finish line," says Windows' lead product manager. "We have to keep outrunning the bad guys."[9]

Switch to Mac?

Perhaps because Apple Macintosh has a smaller percentage of the market share for microcomputers, it seems to have eluded most of the attention of the hackers and virus writers. Similarly, for whatever reasons, Linux-based computers hardly get infected or invaded at all.

Big-business users, it's suggested, have too much money invested in Windows machines to think of switching to Macintoshes; the costs of making the change would be astronomical. Individual users, however, might wish to give it some thought.

What if you already have Microsoft Office files, such as Microsoft Word or Microsoft Excel, on a PC and want to move them to a Mac? In that case, you'll need the current version of Microsoft Office for the Mac, which will handle the PC version, and a Mac with an Intel processor. Apple's OS X also comes with a program called *Mail* and a word processor called *Text Edit* that will deal with Microsoft Word documents that come to you online. You can also get a Macintosh version of Internet Explorer, which is, in fact, considered safer than the Windows versions.

Check out *www.macvswindows.com/index.php?title= Main_Page,* or do keyword searches for "Mac vs. Windows" and "Mac vs. PC."

DAPPLED APPLE LEAD CRYSTAL VASE
B. VOLCANIC LEAD CRYSTA

Software

145

Some Common Unix Commands

^h, [backspace]	erase previously typed character
^u	erase entire line of input typed so far
cp	copy files
whoami	who is logged on to this terminal
mkdir	make new directory
mv	change name of directory
mail	read/send email
gzip, gunzip	compress, recompress a file
lpr	send file to printer
wc	count characters, words, and lines in a file
head	show first few lines of a file
tail	show last few lines of a file
find	find files that match certain criteria

- **Versions of Unix:** Sun Microsystems' *Solaris* is a version of Unix that is popular for handling large e-commerce servers and large websites. Another interesting variant is *BSD,* free software derived from Unix. BSD began in the 1970s in the computer science department of the University of California, Berkeley, when students and staff began to develop their own derivative of Unix, known as the Berkeley Software Distribution, or BSD. There are now three variations, which are distributed online and on CD. Other Unix variations are made by Hewlett-Packard (HP-UX) and IBM (AIX).

- **Unix interface—command or shell?** Like MS-DOS, Unix uses a command-line interface (but the commands are different for each system). Some companies market Unix systems with graphical interface *shells* that make Unix easier to use.

LINUX It began in 1991 when programmer Linus Torvalds, a graduate student in Finland, posted his free Linux operating system on the internet. Linux (pronounced "*linn*-uks") is the rising star of network software. **_Linux_ is a free (nonproprietary) version of Unix, and its continual improvements result from the efforts of tens of thousands of volunteer programmers.** (• *See Panel 3.19.*) Whereas Windows NT/Server is Microsoft's proprietary product, Linux is **_open-source software_—meaning any programmer can download it from the internet for free and modify it with suggested improvements.** The only qualification is that changes can't be copyrighted; they must be made available to all and remain in the public domain. From these beginnings, Linux has attained cultlike status. "What makes Linux different is that it's part of the internet culture," says an IBM general manager. "It's essentially being built by a community."[10]

panel 3.19

Linux screen (*inset*)

- **Linux and China:** In 2000, the People's Republic of China announced that it was adopting Linux as a national standard for operating systems because it feared being dominated by the OS of a company of a foreign power—namely, Microsoft. In 2005, Red Flag Software Company, Ltd., the leading developer of Linux software in China, joined the Open Source Development Labs, a global consortium dedicated to accelerating the adoption of Linux in the business world. In 2007, OSDL and the Free Standards Group merged to form The Linux Foundation (*http://osdl.org/en/Main_Page*), narrowing their respective focuses to that of promoting Linux in competition with Microsoft Windows.

- **The permutations of Linux:** If Linux belongs to everyone, how do companies such as Red Hat Software—a company that bases its business on Linux—make money? Their strategy is to give away the software but then sell services and support. Red Hat, for example, makes available an inexpensive application software package that offers word processing, spreadsheets, email support, and the like for users of its PC OS version. It also offers more powerful versions of its Linux OS for small and medium-size businesses, along with applications, networking capabilities, and support services.

- **Google Chrome:** In late 2008, Google launched its Chrome internet browser. Based on Linux, this browser is intended for people who do most of their computer activities on the web. However, most of the operating systems that computers run on were designed in an era when there was no web; so in July 2009, Google introduced the Chrome OS. This operating system is a lightweight, open-source Linux-based system with a new windowing arrangement that has initially been targeted at netbooks. The user interface is minimal, and internet connection is fast and secure. As with the Chrome browser, this OS has been created for people who spend most of their computer time on the web. Chrome does not support Microsoft Office, which will limit its usability in business, educational, and professional environments, but it does support OpenOffice, Google email, Google Docs, and cloud computing. The full version of Chrome OS was supposed to become available in 2010.

  Dell Computers now offers a Linux-based operating system, Ubuntu (the Zulu word for "humanity"), on some of its products. Some companies, such as Ibex, make dual-boot PCs that can switch back and forth between Windows and Linux by rebooting. Win4Lin, Inc., a leading supplier of specialized operating systems that run on Linux, has released Win4Lin Desktop 5, which runs Windows and Windows applications on Linux. More recently, several varieties of Linux have been introduced to run on the low-end kind of computers known as netbooks. They include Ubuntu, Hewlett-Packard's Mi (which is based on Ubuntu), and Intel Corp.'s Mobilin.[11]

- **Linux in the future:** Because it was originally built for use on the internet, Linux is more reliable than Windows for online applications. Hence, it is better suited to run websites and e-commerce software. Its real growth, however, may come as it reaches outward to other applications and, possibly, replaces Windows in many situations. IBM, Red Hat, Motorola Computing, Panasonic, Sony, and many other companies have formed the nonprofit, vendor-neutral Embedded Linux Consortium, which now, as part of The Linux Foundation, is working to make Linux a top operating system of choice for developers designing embedded systems, as we discuss next.

The three major microcomputer operating systems are compared in the box on the next page. (● *See Panel 3.20.*)

China's Red Flag

To learn more about China's Red Flag Software Company, go to:

www.redflag-linux.com/egyhq. html

http://en.wikipedia.org/wiki/ Red_Flag_Linux

Linux versus Windows

Do you think Linux will overtake Windows? Will more users switch to Mac OS X? To research Linux, go to:

www.kernel.org

http://news.softpedia.com/ cat/Linux/

www.lwn.net

For Mac OS, go to:

www.macosrumors.com

http://news.softpedia.com/ cat/Apple/, www.macrumors. com

For Windows, go to:

www.winsupersite.com

www.neowin.net

www.winbeta.org

http://news.softpedia.com/ cat/Microsoft/

For general OS matters, go to:

www.betanews.com

www.osnews.com

Windows XP	Linux	Mac OS X
Pros:	*Pros:*	*Pros:*
Runs on a wide range of hardware	Runs on a wide range of hardware	Easy to install
Has largest market share	Has largest number of user interface types	Best GUI
Has many built-in utilities	Can be used as server or desktop PC open source software; anyone can fix bugs	Secure and stable
Cons:		*Cons:*
Security problems	*Cons:*	Supports only Apple computers
Not efficient used as a server OS	Limited support for games	Base hardware more expensive than other platforms
Have to reboot every time a network configuration is changed	Limited commercial applications available	Fewer utilities available
	Can be difficult to learn	Fewer games than for Windows
Proprietary software; only company programmers can fix bugs		Proprietary software; only company programmers can fix bugs

More on OS Comparisons

For more details on OS comparisons, go to:

www.iterating.com/ productclasses/ Operating-Systems

Open-Source Search

Open-source utilities—some command-line interfaces, some GUIs—are available for Linux and Mac systems. What keywords could you use to find these utilities?

Embedded Operating Systems for Handhelds: Palm OS & Windows CE

What are some different embedded OSs for handheld computers and PDAs?

An *embedded system* is any electronic system that uses a CPU chip but that is not a general-purpose workstation, desktop, or laptop computer. It is a specialized computer system that is part of a larger system or a machine. Embedded systems are used, for example, in automobiles, planes, trains, barcode scanners, fuel pumps, space vehicles, machine tools, watches, appliances, cellphones, PDAs, and robots. Handheld computers and personal digital assistants rely on specialized operating systems, embedded operating systems, that reside on a single chip. Such operating systems include the Palm OS and Windows CE.

PALM OS—THE DOMINANT OS FOR HANDHELDS The Linux-based *Palm OS*, also known as *Garnet OS* and *webOS*, developed by Palm Inc., is a popular operating system for mobile devices, including smartphones, wrist watches, handheld gaming consoles, barcode readers and GPS devices. In 1994, Jeff Hawkins took blocks of mahogany and plywood into his garage and emerged with a prototype for the

Palm Prē OS screen

Palm OS launcher screen

Microsoft OS for HP iPAQ

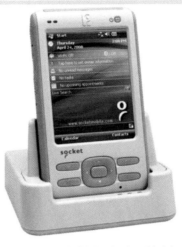

Microsoft OS for Socket Mobile

info!

Palm OS

For updates on the Palm OS for Palm PDAs and Treo Smart-phones, try:

www.versiontracker.com/ palmos/

www.freeware-palm.com/
and

http://kb.palm.com/wps/ portal/kb/na/centro/ centro/sprint/downloads/ page_en.html

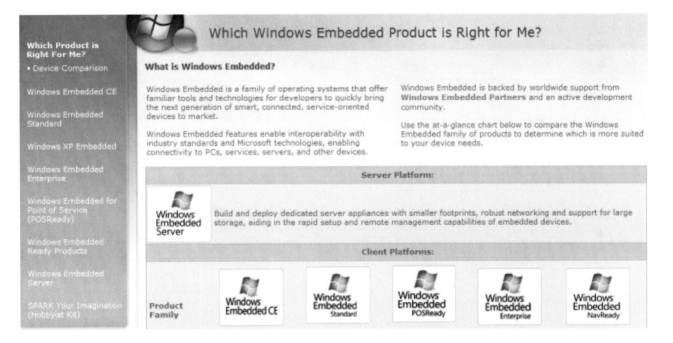

PalmPilot, which led to the revolution in handheld computing. Palm Inc. sells the popular Pre⁻ Smartphone, the Centro Smartphone, and the Treo Pro Smartphone, as well as various models of PDAs. (Smartphones are cellular phones that have built-in music players and video recorders and that run com-puterlike applications and support internet activities beyond just email. We discuss them in detail in Chapter 7.)

Early versions of handhelds cannot be upgraded to run recent versions of Palm OS. If you buy a PDA or a smartphone, therefore, you need to make sure that the OS is a current version and that the manufacturer plans to continue to support it.

WINDOWS EMBEDDED—MICROSOFT WINDOWS FOR HANDHELDS & EMBEDDED SYSTEMS In 1996, Microsoft released *Microsoft Windows CE,* now known as *Windows Embedded,* **a slimmed-down version of Windows, for handhelds** such as those made by Garmin, ASUS, Dell, and Hewlett-Packard. The Windows handheld OS has the familiar Windows look and feel and includes mobile

Software

149

versions of word processing, spreadsheet, email, web browsing, text messaging, and other software. Windows Mobile, based on CE, is used in certain smartphones. Special versions of Windows CE are also used in embedded systems such as ATMs, barcode scanners, kiosks, gaming devices, and set-top boxes.

3.6 APPLICATION SOFTWARE: Getting Started

What are five ways of obtaining application software, tools available to help me learn to use software, three common types of files, and the types of software?

At one time, just about everyone paid for microcomputer application software. You bought it as part of the computer or in a software store, or you downloaded it online with a credit card charge. Now, other ways exist to obtain software.

Application Software: For Sale, for Free, or for Rent?

What are the various ways I can obtain software?

Although most people pay for software, usually popular brands that they can use with similar programs owned by their friends and coworkers, it's possible to rent programs or get them free. (● *See Panel 3.21.*) Let's consider these categories.

COMMERCIAL SOFTWARE *Commercial software,* also called *proprietary software* or *packaged software,* is software that's offered for sale, such as Microsoft Word, Microsoft Office XP, or Adobe PhotoShop. Although such software may not show up on the bill of sale when you buy a new PC, you've paid for some of it as part of the purchase. And, most likely, whenever you order a new game or other commercial program, you'll have to pay for it. This software is copyrighted. A *copyright* is the exclusive legal right that prohibits copying of intellectual property without the permission of the copyright holder.

Software manufacturers don't sell you their software; rather, they sell you a license to become an authorized user of it. What's the difference? In paying for a **_software license_, you sign a contract in which you agree not to make copies of the software to give away or resell.** That is, you have bought only the company's permission to use the software and not the software itself. This legal nicety allows the company to retain its rights to the program and limits the way its customers can use it. The small print in the licensing agreement usually allows you to make one copy *(backup copy* or *archival copy)* for your own use. (Each software company has a different license; there is no industry standard.)

Several types of software licenses exist:

- *Site licenses* allow the software to be used on all computers at a specific location.

- *Concurrent-use licenses* allow a certain number of copies of the software to be used at the same time.

Survival Tip

What to Set Up First?

When setting up a new microcomputer system, install your peripherals first—first your printer, any external storage drives, scanner, and so on. Test each one separately by restarting the computer. Then install the next peripheral. After this, install your applications software, again testing each program separately.

panel 3.21

Choices among application software

Types	Definition
Commercial software	Copyrighted. If you don't pay for it, you can be prosecuted.
Public-domain software	Not copyrighted. You can copy it for free without fear of prosecution.
Shareware	Copyrighted. Available free, but you should pay to continue using it.
Freeware	Copyrighted. Available free.
Rentalware	Copyrighted. Lease for a fee.

- A *multiple-user license* specifies the number of people who may use the software.

- A *single-user license* limits software use to one user at a time.

Most personal computer software licenses allow you to run the program on only one machine and make copies of the software only for personal backup purposes. Personal computer users often buy their software in shrink-wrapped packages; once you have opened the shrink wrap, you have accepted the terms of the software license.

Every year or so, software developers find ways to enhance their products and put forth new versions or new releases. A *version* is a major upgrade in a software product, traditionally indicated by numbers such as 1.0, 2.0, 3.0—for example, Adobe 8.0 and Adobe 9.0. More recently, other notations have been used. After 1995, Microsoft labeled its Windows and Office software versions by year instead of by number, as in Microsoft's Office 97, Office 2000, Office 2003, and Office 2007. A *release,* which now may be called an "add" or "addition," is a minor upgrade. Often this is indicated by a change in number after the decimal point. (For instance, 8.0 may become 8.1, 8.2, and so on.) Some releases are now also indicated by the year in which they are marketed. And, unfortunately, some releases are not clearly indicated at all. (These are "patches," which may be downloaded from the software maker's website, as can version updates.) Once you have purchased an application, the manufacturer will usually allow you to download small patches for free but will charge for major new versions.

More recently, Apple Inc. has enjoyed huge success with its online Apple App Store, offering more than 1,600 business applications that can be downloaded directly to your cellphone.[12] Other "stores" offering downloadable applications are BlackBerry App World, Google Android Market, Palm Software Store, and Microsoft's Windows Mobile Store.[13]

PUBLIC-DOMAIN SOFTWARE *Public-domain software* **is not protected by copyright and thus may be duplicated by anyone at will.** Public-domain programs—sometimes developed at taxpayer expense by government agencies—have been donated to the public by their creators. They are often available through sites on the internet. You can download and duplicate public-domain software without fear of legal prosecution.

SHAREWARE *Shareware* **is copyrighted software that is distributed free of charge, but users are required to make a monetary contribution, or pay a registration fee, to continue using it**—in other words, you can try it before you buy it. Once you pay the fee, you usually get supporting documentation, access to updated versions, and perhaps some technical support. Shareware is distributed primarily through the internet, but because it is copyrighted, you cannot use it to develop your own program that would compete with the original product. If you copy shareware and pass it along to friends, they are expected to pay the registration fee also, if they choose to use the software.

FREEWARE *Freeware* **is copyrighted software that is distributed free of charge,** today most often over the internet. Why would any software creator let his or her product go for free? Sometimes developers want to see how users respond, so that they can make improvements in a later version. Sometimes they want to further some scholarly or humanitarian purpose—for instance, to create a standard for software on which people are apt to agree. In its most recent form, freeware is made available by companies trying to make money some other way—as, by attracting viewers to their advertising. (The web browsers Internet Explorer and Mozilla Firefox are of this type.) Freeware developers generally retain all rights to their programs; technically, you are not supposed to duplicate and redistribute the programs. (Freeware is different

Part of a software license

Public Domain Software

For information on public domain software and where to obtain it, go to:

www.gnu.org/philosophy/ categories.html

www.webcrawler.com/ webcrawler30l/ws/results/ web/public+domain+ software/l/4l7/topnavigation/ relevance/iq=true/ zoom=off/_iceurlflag=7?_ice url=true&gclid=ckiklifjspscfr wdagodtafvpa

Shareware & Freeware

What kinds of shareware and freeware are available? To find out, go to:

www.searchalot.com/Top/ Computers/Software/

www.shareware.com

www.tucows.com

www.freewarehome.com

www.download.com

www.sharewareking.com

from free software, or public-domain software, which has no restrictions on use, modification, or redistribution.)

More about ASPs

If you want to learn more about ASPs, go to:

www.aspnews.com

www.dmoz.org/Computers/ Software/Business/ E-Commerce/Business-to- Business/Application_ Service_Providers//

RENTALWARE: ONLINE SOFTWARE *Rentalware* **is online software that users lease for a fee and download whenever they want it.** This is the concept behind *application service providers (ASPs)*, or *software-as-a-service (SaaS) technology*, the idea of leasing software over the internet. The ASP stores the software on its servers and supplies users with support and other services. Today online software accounts for only a small part of business-software sales, but it could represent the wave of the future, because it frees businesses from having to buy computer servers and hire a staff to maintain them. Some business owners find that present-day online software isn't as good as the traditional software available. However, online software represents a stage in what in Chapter 1 we called "cloud computing," the idea of obtaining computing resources from the network of computers sitting beyond a user's own four walls.[14] Some experts believe that future software is more apt to be available in a variety of ways: through traditional licensing, through online rentalware, through ad-supported online means, and even through open-source means.[15]

PIRATED SOFTWARE *Pirated software* **is software obtained illegally,** as when you get a CD/DVD from a friend who has made an illicit copy of, say, a commercial video game. Sometimes pirated software can be downloaded off the internet. Sometimes it is sold in retail outlets in foreign countries. If you buy such software, not only do the original copyright owners not get paid for their creative work, but you risk getting inferior goods and, worse, picking up a virus. To discourage software piracy, many software manufacturers, such as Microsoft, require that users register their software when they install it on their computers. If the software is not registered, it will not work properly.

ABANDONWARE "Abandonware" does not refer to a way to obtain software. It refers to software that is no longer being sold or supported by its publisher. U.S. copyright laws state that copyrights owned by corporations are valid for up to 95 years from the date the software was first published. Copyrights are not considered abandoned even if they are no longer enforced. Therefore, abandoned software does not enter the public domain just because it is no longer supported. Don't copy it.

CUSTOM SOFTWARE Occasionally, companies or individuals need software written specifically for them, to meet unique needs. This software is called *custom software*, and it's created by software engineers and programmers. Recently many people who have never written a line of computer code have been inspired to learn programming as a possible way to make money developing applications for downloading off the popular Apple iPhone.[16]

Tutorials & Documentation

How could software tutorials and documentation be helpful to me?

How are you going to learn a given software program? Most commercial packages come with tutorials and documentation.

TUTORIALS A *tutorial* is an instruction book or program that helps you learn to use the product by taking you through a prescribed series of steps. For instance, our publisher offers several how-to books that enable you to learn different kinds of software. Tutorials may also form part of the software package.

DOCUMENTATION *Documentation* is all information that describes a product to users, including a user guide or reference manual that provides a narrative and graphical description of a program. Although documentation may

Tutorial: Microsoft Office training

First page of downloaded documentation for Adobe Acrobat 8

be print-based, today it is usually available on CD, as well as via the internet. Documentation may be instructional, but features and functions are usually grouped by category for reference purposes. For example, in word processing documentation, all features related to printing are grouped together so that you can easily look them up.

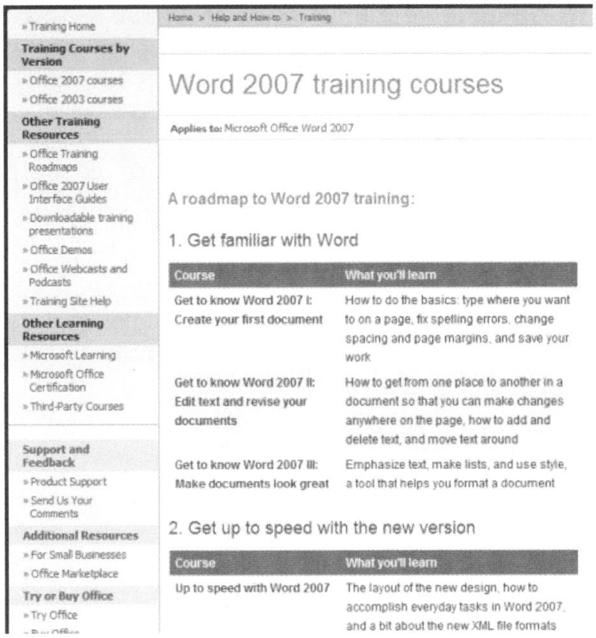

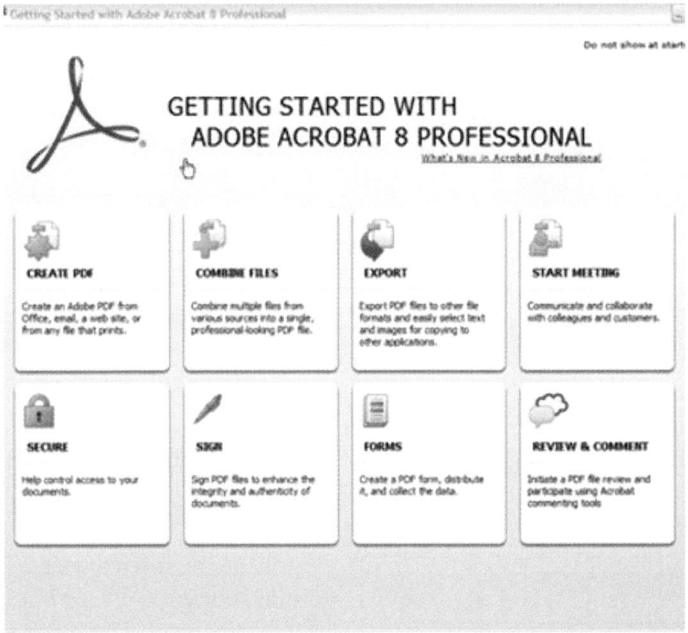

A Few Facts about Files & the Usefulness of Importing & Exporting

What are three types of files, and what do importing and exporting mean?

There is only one reason for having application software: to take raw data and manipulate it into useful files of information. A *file,* as we said earlier, is (1) a named collection of data (data file) or (2) a program (program file) that exists in a computer's secondary storage, such as hard disk, keychain (Chapter 4), or CD/DVD.

THREE TYPES OF DATA FILES Three well-known types of data files are these:

- **Document files:** Document files are created by word processing programs and consist of documents such as reports, letters, memos, and term papers.
- **Worksheet files:** Worksheet files are created by electronic spreadsheets and usually consist of collections of numerical data such as budgets, sales forecasts, and schedules.
- **Database files:** Database files are created by database management programs and consist of organized data that can be analyzed and displayed in various useful ways. Examples are student names and addresses that can be displayed according to age, grade-point average, or home state.

EXCHANGING FILES: IMPORTING & EXPORTING It's useful to know that often files can be exchanged—that is, imported and exported—between programs.

- **Importing: *Importing* is defined as getting data from another source and then converting it into a format compatible with the program in**

which you are currently working. For example, you might write a letter in your word processing program and include in it—that is, import—a column of numbers from your spreadsheet program. The ability to import data is very important in software applications because it means that one application can complement another.

- **Exporting:** *Exporting* **is defined as transforming data into a format that can be used in another program and then transmitting it.**
  For example, you might work up a list of names and addresses in your database program and then send it—export it—to a document you wrote in your word processing program. Exporting implies that the sending application reformats the data for the receiving application; importing implies that the receiving application does the reformatting.

Types of Application Software

What is productivity software?

Application software can be classified in many ways—for entertainment, personal, education/reference, productivity, and specialized uses. (● *See Panel 3.22.*)

In the rest of this chapter we will discuss types of ***productivity software***— **such as word processing programs, spreadsheets, and database managers— whose purpose is to make users more productive at particular tasks.** Some productivity software comes in the form of an *office suite,* which bundles several applications together into a single large package. Microsoft Office, for example, includes (among other things) Word, Excel, and Access—word processing, spreadsheet, and database programs, respectively. (Office is available

panel 3.22

Types of application software

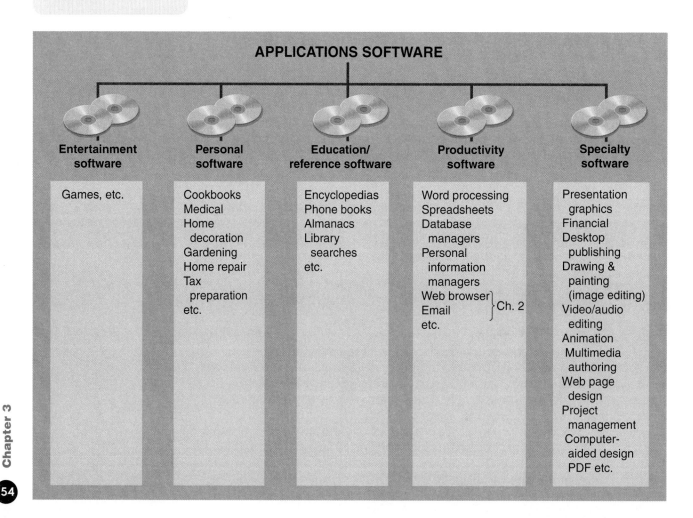

APPLICATIONS SOFTWARE

Entertainment software	Personal software	Education/ reference software	Productivity software	Specialty software
Games, etc.	Cookbooks Medical Home decoration Gardening Home repair Tax preparation etc.	Encyclopedias Phone books Almanacs Library searches etc.	Word processing Spreadsheets Database managers Personal information managers Web browser Email } Ch. 2 etc.	Presentation graphics Financial Desktop publishing Drawing & painting (image editing) Video/audio editing Animation Multimedia authoring Web page design Project management Computer-aided design PDF etc.

for both the PC and the Mac platforms.) Corel Corp. offers similar programs, such as the WordPerfect word processing program. Other productivity software, such as Lotus Notes, is sold as *groupware*—online software that allows several people to collaborate on the same project and share some resources. Google offers a free suite of applications called Google Aps (from *www.google.com/apps*).[17]

We now consider the three most important types of productivity software: word processing, spreadsheet, and database software (including personal information managers). We then discuss more specialized software: presentation graphics, financial, desktop-publishing, drawing and painting, project management, computer-aided design, web page design, image/video/audio editing, and animation software.

3.7 WORD PROCESSING

What can I do with word processing software that I can't do with pencil and paper?

After a long and productive life, the typewriter has gone to its reward. Indeed, it is practically as difficult today to get a manual typewriter repaired as to find a blacksmith. Word processing software offers a much-improved way of dealing with documents.

Word processing software allows you to use computers to create, edit, format, print, and store text material, among other things. Word processing is the most common software application. The best-known word processing program is Microsoft Word, but there are others, such as Corel WordPerfect, Apple Pages, Google Apps (a free download from *www.google.com/apps*), and Zoho Writer (a free download from *www.zoho.com*).[18] There is even a full-fledged word processor, known as Quickoffice, that can be used on the Apple iPhone.[19] Word processing software allows users to work through a document and *delete, insert,* and *replace* text, the principal edit/correction activities. It also offers such additional features as *creating, formatting, printing,* and *saving.*

To clean your printer, first open the top by pressing the button on the left side near the top. Swing the lid

Cursor

Scrolling

Creating Documents

What are word processing features I would use when creating a document?

Creating a document means entering text using the keyboard or the dictation function associated with speech-recognition software. Word processing software has three features that affect this process—the *cursor, scrolling,* and *word wrap.*

CURSOR The _cursor_ is the movable symbol on the display screen that shows you where you may next enter data or commands. The symbol is often a blinking rectangle or an I-beam. You can move the cursor on the screen using the keyboard's directional arrow keys or a mouse. The point where the cursor is located is called the *insertion point.*

SCROLLING _Scrolling_ means moving quickly upward, downward, or sideways through the text or other screen display. A standard computer screen displays only 20–22 lines of standard-size text. Of course, most documents are longer than that. Using the directional arrow keys, or the mouse and a scroll bar located at the side of the screen, you can move ("scroll") through the display screen and into the text above and below it.

WORD WRAP _Word wrap_ automatically continues text to the next line when you reach the right margin. That is, the text "wraps around" to the next line. You don't have to hit a "carriage-return" key or Enter key, as was necessary with a typewriter.

SOME OTHER To help you organize term papers and reports, the *Outline View* feature puts tags on various headings to show the hierarchy of heads—for example, main head, subhead, and sub-subhead. Word processing software also allows you to insert footnotes that are automatically numbered and renumbered when changes are made. The basics of word processing are shown in the illustration at right. (● *See Panel 3.23.*)

Editing Documents

What are various kinds of editing I can do in a word processing document?

Editing is the act of making alterations in the content of your document. Some features of editing are *insert* and *delete, undelete, find and replace, cut/copy and paste, spelling checker, grammar checker,* and *thesaurus.* Some of these commands are in the Edit pull-down menu and icons on the toolbar.

INSERT & DELETE *Inserting* is the act of adding to the document. Simply place the cursor wherever you want to add text and start typing; the existing characters will be pushed along. If you want to write over (replace) text as you write, press the *Insert* key before typing. When you're finished typing, press the *Insert* key again to exit Insert mode.

Deleting is the act of removing text, usually using the *Delete* key or the *Backspace* key.

The *Undo command* allows you to change your mind and restore text that you have deleted. Some word processing programs offer as many as 100 layers of "undo," so that users who delete several paragraphs of text, but then change their minds, can reinstate the material.

FIND & REPLACE The *Find,* or *Search, command* allows you to find any word, phrase, or number that exists in your document. The *Replace command* allows you to automatically replace it with something else.

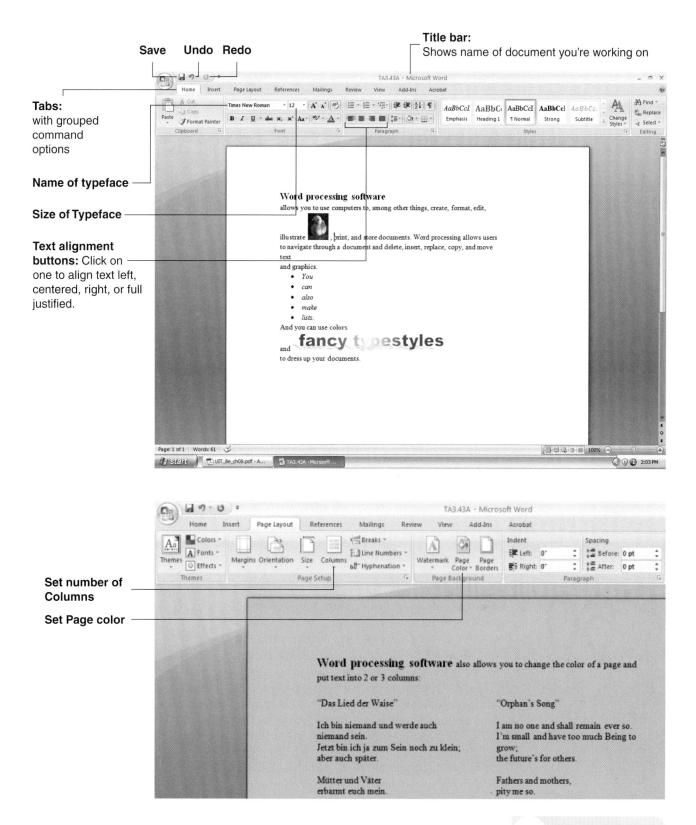

Save Undo Redo

Title bar:
Shows name of document you're working on

Tabs:
with grouped command options

Name of typeface

Size of Typeface

Text alignment buttons: Click on one to align text left, centered, right, or full justified.

Set number of Columns

Set Page color

CUT/COPY & PASTE Typewriter users who wanted to move a paragraph or block of text from one place to another in a manuscript used scissors and glue to "cut and paste." With word processing, moving text takes only a few keystrokes. You select (highlight with the mouse) the portion of text you want to copy or move. Then you use the *Copy* or *Cut command* to move it to the *clipboard,* a special holding area in the computer's memory. From there, you use *Paste* to transfer the material to any point (indicated with the cursor) in the existing document or in a new document. The clipboard retains its material, so repeated pastes of the same item will work without your having to recopy each time.

panel 3.23
Some word processing functions

SPELLING CHECKER Most word processors have a *spelling checker,* which tests for incorrectly spelled words. As you type, the spelling checker indicates (perhaps with a squiggly line) words that aren't in its dictionary and thus may be misspelled. (● *See Panel 3.24 at right.*) Special add-on dictionaries are available for medical, engineering, and legal terms.

In addition, programs such as Microsoft Word have an Auto Correct function that automatically fixes such common mistakes as transposed letters—replacing "teh" with "the," for instance.

GRAMMAR CHECKER A *grammar checker* highlights poor grammar, wordiness, incomplete sentences, and awkward phrases. The grammar checker won't fix things automatically, but it will flag (perhaps with a different-color squiggly line) possible incorrect word usage and sentence structure. (● *See Panel 3.25.*)

THESAURUS If you find yourself stuck for the right word while you're writing, you can call up an on-screen *thesaurus,* which will present you with the appropriate word or alternative words.

Formatting Documents with the Help of Templates & Wizards

What are some types of formatting I can do?

In the context of word processing, *formatting* means determining the appearance of a document. You can always format your documents manually, but word processing programs provide a helpful device to speed the process up and make it more sophisticated. **A *template,* called a *wizard* in older Office versions, is a preformatted document that provides basic tools for shaping a final document**—the text, layout, and style for a letter, for example. Simply put, it is a style guide for documents. Because most documents are fairly standard in format, every word processing program comes with at least a few standard templates. When you use a template, you're actually opening a copy of the template. In this way you'll always have a fresh copy of the original template when you need it. After you open a copy of the template and add your text, you save this version of the template under the filename of your choice. In this way, for example, in a letterhead template, your project's name, address, phone number, and web address are included every time you open your letterhead template file.

Among the many aspects of formatting are these:

FONT You can decide what *font*—typeface and type size—you wish to use. For instance, you can specify whether it should be Arial, Courier, or Freestyle Script. You can indicate whether the text should be, say, 10 points or 12 points in size and the headings should be 14 points or 16 points. (There are 72 points in an inch.) You can specify what parts should be underlined, *italic,* or **boldface.**

SPACING & COLUMNS You can choose whether you want the lines to be *single-spaced* or *double-spaced* (or something else). You can specify whether you want text to be *one column* (like this page), *two columns* (like many magazines and books), or *several columns* (like newspapers).

MARGINS & JUSTIFICATION You can indicate the dimensions of the margins—left, right, top, and bottom—around the text. You can specify the text *justification*—how the letters and words are spaced in each line. To *justify* means to align text evenly between left and right margins, as in most newspaper columns and this text. To *left-justify* means to align text evenly on the left. (Left-justified text has a "ragged-right" margin, as do many business letters.) *Centering* centers each text line in the available white space between the left and right margins.

Word can help you choose templates

10 point
Times Roman

**14 point
Arial Black**

16 point
Courier

60

(60 point Arial)

Left-justified

Justified

Centered

Right-justified

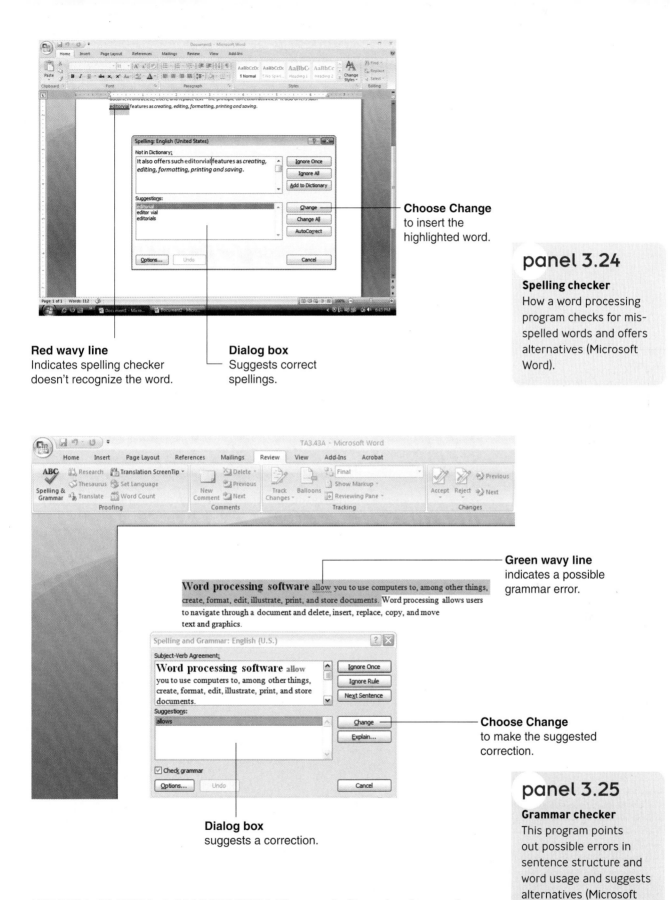

Choose Change
to insert the
highlighted word.

panel 3.24

Spelling checker
How a word processing
program checks for mis-
spelled words and offers
alternatives (Microsoft
Word).

Red wavy line
Indicates spelling checker
doesn't recognize the word.

Dialog box
Suggests correct
spellings.

Green wavy line
indicates a possible
grammar error.

Choose Change
to make the suggested
correction.

panel 3.25

Grammar checker
This program points
out possible errors in
sentence structure and
word usage and suggests
alternatives (Microsoft
Word).

Dialog box
suggests a correction.

HEADERS, FOOTERS, & PAGE NUMBERS You can indicate headers or footers and include page numbers. A *header* is common text (such as a date or document name) printed at the top of every page. A *footer* is the same thing printed at the bottom of every page. If you want page numbers, you can determine what number to start with, among other things.

Software

OTHER FORMATTING You can specify *borders* or other decorative lines, *shading*, *tables*, and *footnotes*. You can import *graphics* or drawings from files in other software programs, including *clip art*—collections of ready-made pictures and illustrations available online or on CDs/DVDs.

DEFAULT SETTINGS Word processing programs (and indeed most forms of application software) come from the manufacturer with default settings. ***Default settings* are the settings automatically used by a program unless the user specifies otherwise, thereby overriding them.** Thus, for example, a word processing program may automatically prepare a document single-spaced, left-justified, with 1-inch right and left margins, unless you alter these default settings.

Output Options: Printing, Faxing, or Emailing Documents

What are some of my output options?

Most word processing software gives you several options for printing. For example, you can print *several copies* of a document. You can print *individual pages* or a *range of pages*. You can even preview a document before printing it out. *Previewing (print previewing)* means viewing a document on-screen to see what it will look like in printed form before it's printed. Whole pages are displayed in reduced size.

You can also send your document off to someone else by fax or email attachment if your computer has the appropriate communications link.

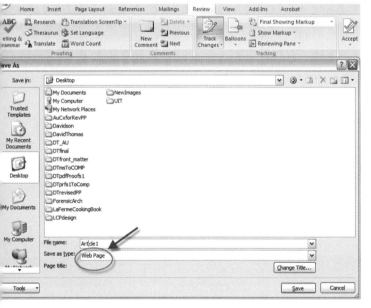

Saving a document as a web page in Word 2007

Tracking in Word 2007

Saving Documents

How can I save a document?

***Saving* means storing, or preserving, a document as an electronic file permanently**—on your hard disk or a CD, for example. Saving is a feature of nearly all application software. Having the document stored in electronic form spares you the tiresome chore of retyping it from scratch whenever you want to make changes. You need only retrieve it from the storage medium and make the changes you want. Then you can print it out again. (Always save your documents often while you are working; don't wait!)

Web Document Creation

How do I format a document to put it on the web?

Most word processing programs allow you to automatically format your documents into HTML so that they can be used on the web. To do this in Microsoft Word, open *File, Save As, Save As Type: Web page (*.htm, *.html)*.

Tracking Changes & Inserting Comments

How do I and any cowriters make changes visible in a document?

What if you have written an important document and have asked other people to edit it? Word processing software allows editing changes to be *tracked* by highlighting them, underlining additions, and crossing out deletions. Each person working on the document can choose a different color so that you can tell who's done what and when. And anyone can insert hidden questions or comments that become visible when you pass the mouse pointer over yellow-highlighted words or punctuation. An edited document can be printed out showing all the changes, as well as a list of comments keyed to the text by numbers. Or it can be printed out "clean," showing the edited text in its new form, without the changes.

3.8 SPREADSHEETS

What can I do with an electronic spreadsheet that I can't do with pencil and paper and a standard calculator?

What is a spreadsheet? Traditionally, it was simply a grid of rows and columns, printed on special light-green paper, that was used to produce financial projections and reports. A person making up a spreadsheet spent long days and weekends at the office penciling tiny numbers into countless tiny rectangles. When one figure changed, all other numbers on the spreadsheet had to be erased and recomputed. Ultimately, there might be wastebaskets full of jettisoned worksheets.

In 1978, Daniel Bricklin was a student at the Harvard Business School. One day he was staring at columns of numbers on a blackboard when he got the idea for computerizing the spreadsheet. He created the first electronic spreadsheet, now called simply a spreadsheet. **The _spreadsheet_ allows users to create tables and financial schedules by entering data and formulas into rows and columns arranged as a grid on a display screen.** Before long, the electronic spreadsheet was the most popular small business program. Unfortunately for Bricklin, his version (called VisiCalc) was quickly surpassed by others. Today the principal spreadsheets are Microsoft Excel, Corel Quattro Pro, and IBM's Lotus 1-2-3. Spreadsheets are used for maintaining student grade books, tracking investments, creating and tracking budgets, calculating loan payments, estimating project costs, and creating other types of financial reports.

The Basics: How Spreadsheets Work

What are the basic principles involved with manipulating a spreadsheet?

A spreadsheet is arranged as follows. (● *See Panel 3.26, next page.*)

HOW A SPREADSHEET IS ORGANIZED A spreadsheet's arrangement of columns, rows, and labels is called a *worksheet*.

- **Column headings:** In the worksheet's frame area (work area), lettered *column headings* appear across the top ("A" is the name of the first column, "B" the second, and so on).

- **Row headings:** Numbered *row headings* appear down the left side ("1" is the name of the first row, "2" the second, and so forth).

- **Labels:** *Labels* are any descriptive text that identifies categories, such as APRIL, RENT, or GROSS SALES.

You use your computer's keyboard to type in the various headings and labels. Each Office 2007 worksheet has 16,384 columns and 1,048,576 rows, and each spreadsheet file can technically hold up to 650 related worksheets—but the computer's memory will not likely hold more than about 200.

CELLS: WHERE COLUMNS & ROWS MEET Each worksheet has more than 17 million cells.

- **Cells & cell addresses: A _cell_ is the place where a row and a column intersect; its position is called a _cell address_.** For example, "A1" is the cell address for the top left cell, where column A and row 1 intersect.

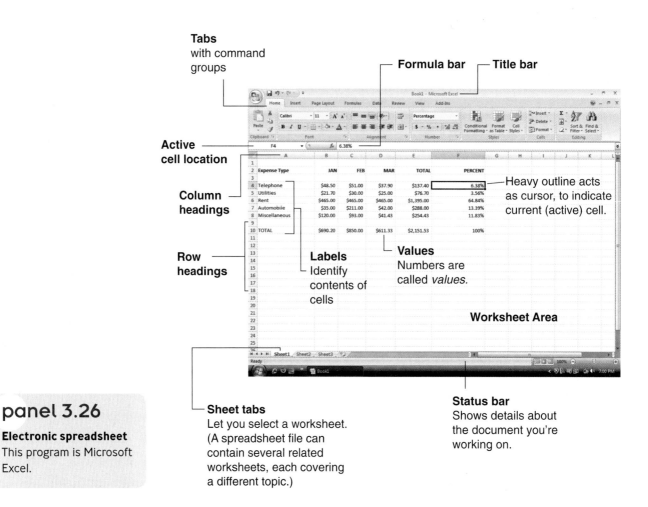

Tabs with command groups

Formula bar

Title bar

Active cell location

Column headings

Row headings

Heavy outline acts as cursor, to indicate current (active) cell.

Labels Identify contents of cells

Values Numbers are called *values*.

Worksheet Area

Sheet tabs Let you select a worksheet. (A spreadsheet file can contain several related worksheets, each covering a different topic.)

Status bar Shows details about the document you're working on.

panel 3.26

Electronic spreadsheet This program is Microsoft Excel.

- **Ranges:** A *range* is a group of adjacent cells—for example, A1 to A5.

- **Values:** **A number or date entered in a cell is called a *value*.** The values are the actual numbers used in the spreadsheet—dollars, percentages, grade points, temperatures, or whatever. Headings, labels, and formulas also go into cells.

- **Cell pointer:** A *cell pointer,* or *spreadsheet cursor,* indicates where data is to be entered. The cell pointer can be moved around like a cursor in a word processing program.

FORMULAS, FUNCTIONS, RECALCULATION, & WHAT-IF ANALYSIS Why has the spreadsheet become so popular? The reasons lie in the features known as formulas, functions, recalculation, and what-if analysis.

- **Formulas:** ***Formulas* are instructions for calculations; they define how one cell relates to other cells.** For example, a formula might be =SUM(A5:A15) or @SUM(A5:A15), meaning "Sum (that is, add) all the numbers in the cells with cell addresses A5 through A15."

- **Functions:** ***Functions* are built-in formulas that perform common calculations.** For instance, a function might average a range of numbers or round off a number to two decimal places.

- **Recalculation:** After the values have been entered into the worksheet, the formulas and functions can be used to calculate outcomes. However, what was revolutionary about the electronic spreadsheet was its ability to easily do recalculation. ***Recalculation* is the process of recomputing values,** either as an ongoing process as data is entered or afterward, with the press of a key. With this simple feature, the hours of mind-numbing work required to manually rework paper spreadsheets has become a thing of the past.

- **What-if analysis:** The recalculation feature has opened up whole new possibilities for decision making. In particular, ***what-if analysis* allows the user to see how changing one or more numbers changes the outcome of the calculation.** That is, you can create a worksheet, putting in formulas and numbers, and then ask, "What would happen if we change that detail?"—and immediately see the effect on the bottom line.

WORKSHEET TEMPLATES You may find that your spreadsheet software makes worksheet templates available for specific tasks. *Worksheet templates* are forms containing formats and formulas custom-designed for particular kinds of work. Examples are templates for calculating loan payments, tracking travel expenses, monitoring personal budgets, and keeping track of time worked on projects. Templates are also available for a variety of business needs—providing sales quotations, invoicing customers, creating purchase orders, and writing a business plan.

MULTIDIMENSIONAL SPREADSHEETS Most spreadsheet applications are *multidimensional*, meaning that you can link one spreadsheet to another. A three-dimensional spreadsheet, for example, is like a stack of spreadsheets all connected by formulas. A change made in one spreadsheet automatically affects the other spreadsheets.

Mooving data. A dairy farmer enters feeding data into a spreadsheet.

Analytical Graphics: Creating Charts

What are analytical graphics?

You can use spreadsheet packages to create analytical graphics, or charts. ***Analytical graphics*, or *business graphics*, are graphical forms that make numeric data easier to analyze than it is when organized as rows and columns of numbers.** Whether viewed on a monitor or printed out, analytical graphics help make sales figures, economic trends, and the like easier to comprehend and visualize. In Excel, you enter your data to the worksheet, select the data, and use the Chart wizard to step through the process of choosing the chart type and various options.

Examples of analytical graphics are *column charts, bar charts, line graphs, pie charts,* and *scatter charts.* (● *See Panel 3.27.*) If you have a color printer, these charts can appear in color. In addition, they can be displayed or printed out so that they look three-dimensional. Spreadsheets can even be linked to more exciting graphics, such as digitized maps.

panel 3.27

Analytical graphics
Bar charts, line graphs, and pie charts are used to display numbers in graphical form.

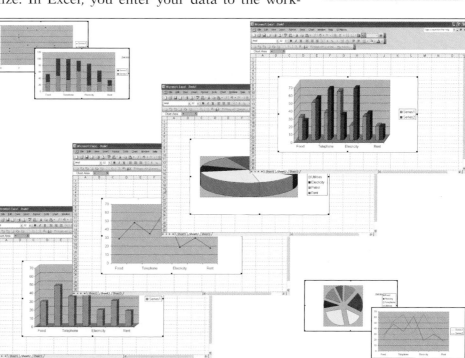

163

3.9 DATABASE SOFTWARE

What is database software, and what is personal information management software?

In its most general sense, a database is any electronically stored collection of data in a computer system. In its more specific sense, a **_database_ is a collection of interrelated files in a computer system.** These computer-based files are organized according to their common elements, so that they can be retrieved easily. Sometimes called a *database manager* or *database management system (DBMS)*, **_database software_ is a program that sets up and controls the structure of a database and access to the data.**

The Benefits of Database Software

What are two advantages of database software over the old ways of organizing files?

When data is stored in separate files, the same data will be repeated in many files. In the old days, each college administrative office—registrar, financial aid, housing, and so on—might have a separate file on you. Thus, there was *redundancy*—your address, for example, was repeated over and over. This means that when you changed addresses, all the college's files on you had to be updated separately. Thus, database software has two advantages.

INTEGRATION With database software, the data is not in separate files. Rather, it is *integrated*. Thus, your address need only be listed once, and all the separate administrative offices will have access to the same information.

INTEGRITY For that reason, information in databases is considered to have more *integrity*. That is, the information is more likely to be accurate and up to date.

Databases are a lot more interesting than they used to be. Once they included only text. Now they can also include pictures, sound, and animation. It's likely, for instance, that your personnel record in a future company database will include a picture of you and perhaps even a clip of your voice. If you go looking for a house to buy, you will be able to view a real estate agent's database of video clips of homes and properties without leaving the realtor's office.

Today the principal microcomputer database programs are Microsoft Access and Corel Paradox. (In larger systems, Oracle is a major player.)

The Basics: How Databases Work

What are the basic principles involved with manipulating a database?

Let's consider some basic features of databases:

HOW A RELATIONAL DATABASE IS ORGANIZED: TABLES, RECORDS, & FIELDS The most widely used form of database, especially on PCs, is the **_relational database_, in which data is organized into related tables.** Each table contains rows and columns; the rows are called *records*, and the columns are called *fields*. An example of a record is a person's address—name, street address, city, and so on. An example of a field is that person's last name; another field would be that person's first name; a third field would be that person's street address; and so on. (● *See Panel 3.28.*)

Just as a spreadsheet may include a workbook with several worksheets, so a relational database might include a database with several tables. For instance, if you're running a small company, you might have one database

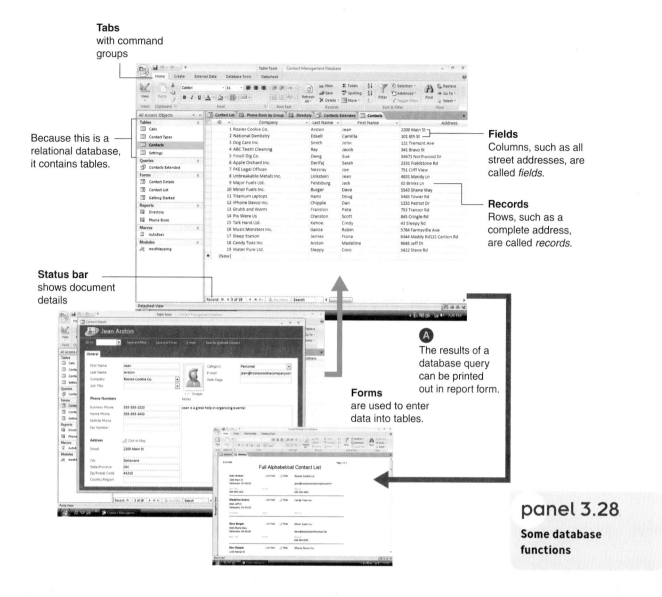

Tabs
with command groups

Because this is a relational database, it contains tables.

Status bar
shows document details

Fields
Columns, such as all street addresses, are called *fields*.

Records
Rows, such as a complete address, are called *records*.

A
The results of a database query can be printed out in report form.

Forms
are used to enter data into tables.

panel 3.28

Some database functions

headed *Employees,* containing three tables—*Addresses, Payroll,* and *Benefits.* You might have another database headed *Customers,* with *Addresses, Orders,* and *Invoices* tables.

LINKING RECORDS, USING A KEY In relational databases a **_key_—also called _key field, sort key, index,_ or _keyword_—is a field used to sort data.** For example, if you sort records by age, then the age field is a key. The most frequent key field used in the United States is the Social Security number, but any unique identifier, such as employee number or student number, can be used. Most database management systems allow you to have more than one key so that you can sort records in different ways. One of the keys is designated the *primary key* and must hold a unique value for each record. A key field that identifies records in different tables is called a *foreign key.* Foreign keys are used to cross-reference data among relational tables.

FINDING WHAT YOU WANT: QUERYING & DISPLAYING RECORDS The beauty of database software is that you can locate records quickly. For example, several offices at your college may need access to your records but for different reasons: registrar, financial aid, student housing, and so on. Any of these offices can *query records*—locate and display records—by calling them up on a computer screen for viewing and updating. Thus, if you move, your address field will need to be corrected for all relevant offices of the college. A person making a search might make the query, *"Display the address of [your name]."* Once a record is displayed, the address field can be changed. Thereafter, any office calling up your file will see the new address.

SORTING & ANALYZING RECORDS & APPLYING FORMULAS With database software you can easily find and change the order of records in a table—in other words, they can be *sorted* in different ways—arranged alphabetically, numerically, geographically, or in some other order. For example, they can be rearranged by state, by age, or by Social Security number.

In addition, database programs contain built-in mathematical *formulas* so that you can analyze data. This feature can be used, for example, to find the grade-point averages for students in different majors or in different classes.

PUTTING SEARCH RESULTS TO USE: SAVING, FORMATTING, PRINTING, COPYING, OR TRANSMITTING Once you've queried, sorted, and analyzed the records and fields, you can simply save them to your hard disk, CD, or other secondary storage medium. You can format them in different ways, altering headings and typestyles. You can print them out on paper as reports, such as an employee list with up-to-date addresses and phone numbers. A common use is to print out the results as names and addresses on *mailing labels*—adhesive-backed stickers that can be run through your printer and then stuck on envelopes. You can use the Copy command to copy your search results and then paste them into a paper produced on your word processor. You can also cut and paste data into an email message or make the data an attachment file to an email, so that it can be transmitted to someone else.

Personal Information Managers

How could a personal information manager be valuable to me?

Pretend you are sitting at a desk in an old-fashioned office. You have a calendar, a Rolodex-type address file, and a notepad. Most of these items could also be found on a student's desk. How would a computer and software improve on this arrangement?

Many people find ready uses for specialized types of database software known as personal information managers. **A _personal information manager (PIM)_ is software that helps you keep track of and manage information you use on a daily basis, such as addresses, telephone numbers, appointments, to-do lists, and miscellaneous notes.** Some programs feature phone dialers, outliners (for roughing out ideas in outline form), and ticklers (or reminders). With a PIM, you can key in notes in any way you like and then retrieve them later based on any of the words you typed.

Popular PIMs are Microsoft Outlook and Lotus SmartSuite Organizer (PC), and Contactizer Pro and Yojimbo (Mac). Microsoft Outlook, for example, has

panel 3.29

Timeline
Developments in software

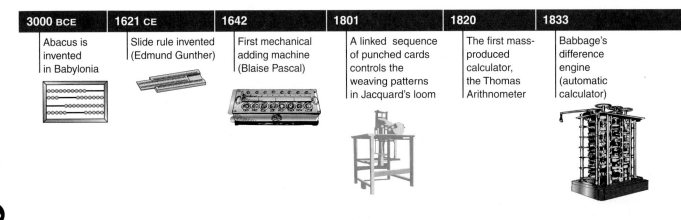

3000 BCE	1621 CE	1642	1801	1820	1833
Abacus is invented in Babylonia	Slide rule invented (Edmund Gunther)	First mechanical adding machine (Blaise Pascal)	A linked sequence of punched cards controls the weaving patterns in Jacquard's loom	The first mass-produced calculator, the Thomas Arithmometer	Babbage's difference engine (automatic calculator)

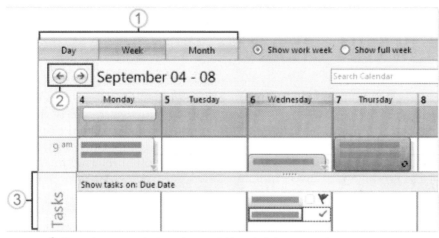

1 Bigger buttons make it easier to quickly switch between daily, weekly, and monthly calendar views.

2 **Back** and **Forward** buttons let you quickly go to the next day, week, or month in the calendar.

3 Also new is a **Tasks** area. You can use this area to track your accomplishments. Completed items on this list appear crossed out and "stick" to the day; tasks not marked as complete will automatically be carried over to the next day, until you complete them.

sections such as Inbox, Calendar, Contacts, Tasks (to-do list), Journal (to record interactions with people), Notes (scratchpad), and Files. (● *See Panel 3.30.*)

3.10 SPECIALTY SOFTWARE

What are the principal uses of specialty software?

After learning some of the productivity software just described, you may wish to become familiar with more specialized programs. For example, you might first learn word processing and then move on to desktop publishing, or first learn spreadsheets and then learn personal-finance software. We will consider the following kinds of software, although they are but a handful of the thousands of specialized programs available: *presentation graphics, financial, desktop-publishing, drawing and painting, project management, computer-aided design, video/audio editing, animation,* and *web page design software.*

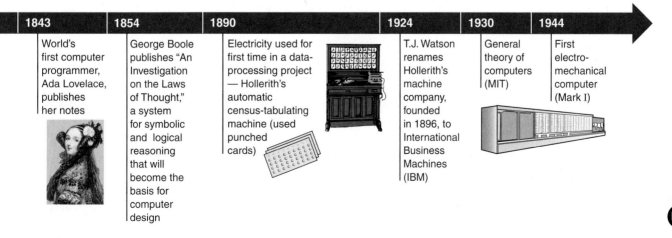

1843	1854	1890	1924	1930	1944
World's first computer programmer, Ada Lovelace, publishes her notes	George Boole publishes "An Investigation on the Laws of Thought," a system for symbolic and logical reasoning that will become the basis for computer design	Electricity used for first time in a data-processing project — Hollerith's automatic census-tabulating machine (used punched cards)	T.J. Watson renames Hollerith's machine company, founded in 1896, to International Business Machines (IBM)	General theory of computers (MIT)	First electro-mechanical computer (Mark I)

Presentation Graphics Software

How could I do a visual presentation, using presentation graphics software?

Presentation graphics software is intended primarily for the business user, for creating slide-show presentations, overhead transparencies, reports, portfolios, and training materials. ***Presentation graphics software* uses graphics, animation, sound, and data or information to make visual presentations.** Presentation graphics are much more fancy and complicated than are analytical graphics. Pages in presentation software are often referred to as *slides,* and visual presentations are commonly called *slide shows.* They can consist, however, not only of 35-mm slides but also of paper copies, overhead transparencies, video, animation, and sound. Completed presentations are frequently published in multiple formats, which may include print, the web, and electronic files.

Most often, presentation projects are used in live sessions. They are commonly projected onto large screens or printed on overhead transparencies. The slides may be distributed in printed form as handouts to accompany the live presentation. Slides are generally intended to be followed in an ordered sequence, although some presentations may utilize interactive forms of navigation. More and more of this software now has the ability to export to HTML for posting presentations on the web.

You may already be accustomed to seeing presentation graphics because many college instructors now use such software to accompany their lectures. Well-known presentation graphics packages include Microsoft PowerPoint, Corel Presentations, Harvard Graphics, and Presentation Graphics SDK. (● *See Panel 3.31.*) Companies such as Presentation Load specialize in professional templates for sophisticated business presentations.

Presentation graphics packages often come with slide sorters, which group together a dozen or so slides in miniature. The person making the presentation can use a mouse or a keyboard to bring the slides up for viewing or even start a self-running electronic slide show. You can also use a projection system from the computer itself.

PowerPoint provides three types of movements: Entrance, emphasis, and exit of elements on a slide itself are controlled by what PowerPoint calls *Custom Animations. Transitions* are movements between slides. These can be animated in a variety of ways. Custom animation can be used to create small story boards by *animating pictures to enter, exit, or move.* Speech bubbles with edited text can be set on and off to create speech.

Just as word processing programs offer templates for faxes, business letters, and the like, presentation graphics programs offer templates to help you organize your presentation, whether it's for a roomful of people or over the internet. Templates are of two types: design and content.

- **Design templates:** These offer formats, layouts, background patterns, and color schemes that can apply to general forms of content material.

- **Content templates:** These offer formats for specific subjects. For instance, PowerPoint offers templates for "Selling Your Ideas," "Facilitating a Meeting," and "Motivating a Team."

1946	1967	1969–1971	1970
First programmable electronic computer in United States (ENIAC)	A graphical user interface (GUI) is a main theme of Jeff Raskin, who later became an Apple Macintosh team leader; handheld calculator	Unix is developed and released by Bell Laboratories	Microprocessor chips come into use; floppy disk introduced for storing data

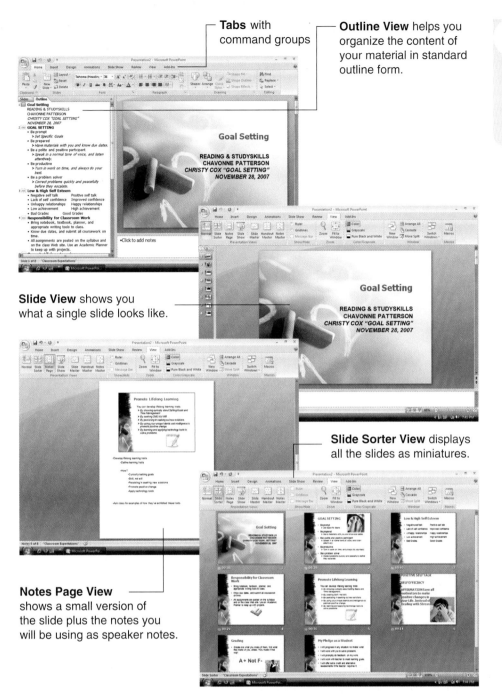

Tabs with command groups

Outline View helps you organize the content of your material in standard outline form.

Slide View shows you what a single slide looks like.

Slide Sorter View displays all the slides as miniatures.

Notes Page View shows a small version of the slide plus the notes you will be using as speaker notes.

DRESSING UP YOUR PRESENTATION Presentation software makes it easy to dress up each visual page ("slide") with artwork by pulling in ("dragging and dropping") clip art from other sources. Although presentations may make use of some basic analytical graphics—bar, line, and pie charts—they generally use much more sophisticated elements. For instance, they may display different

1973	1975	1976	1977
Xerox PARC develops an experimental PC that uses a mouse and a GUI	Bill Gates and Paul Allen start Microsoft in Albuquerque, N.M. (move to Seattle in 1979); first microcomputer (MITS Altair 8800)	Apple I computer (first personal computer sold in assembled form)	Apple II's floppy disk drive leads to writing of many software programs

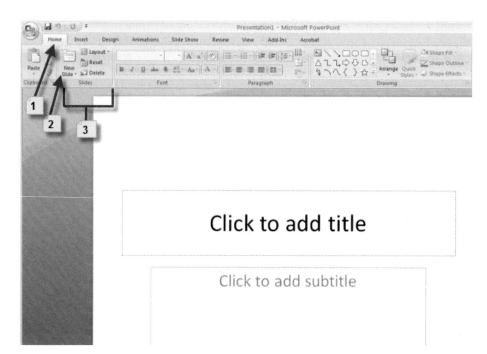

Getting started in Microsoft Office PowerPoint 2007: [1] Tabs are designed to be task-oriented; [2] groups within each tab break a task into subtasks; [3] command buttons in each group carry out a command or display a menu of commands.

Adding Clip Art

For information on adding clip art to presentation slides, check out:

www.communicateusing technology.com/articles/ using_clip_art_photo.htm

www.clipartpress.com/43

http://presentationsoft. about.com/od/nextstepsin powerpoint/ss/add_pics.htm

For information on obtaining clip art, go to:

www.clipartinc.com

http://dir.yahoo.com/ Computers_and_Internet/ Graphics/Clip_art/

http://office.microsoft.com/ en-us/clipart/default.aspx

textures (speckled, solid, cross-hatched), color, and three-dimensionality. In addition, you can add sound clips, special visual effects (such as blinking text), animation, and video clips. (You can, in fact, drag and drop art and other enhancements into desktop-publishing, word processing or other standard PC applications.)

Financial Software

What are the features of financial software that could be useful to me?

___Financial software___ **is a growing category that ranges from personal-finance managers to entry-level accounting programs to business financial-management packages.**

Consider the first of these, which you may find particularly useful. ___Personal-finance managers___ **let you keep track of income and expenses, write checks, do online banking, and plan financial goals.** (● *See Panel 3.32.*) Such programs don't promise to make you rich, but they can help you manage your money. They may even get you out of trouble. Many personal-finance programs, such as Quicken and Microsoft Money, include a calendar and a calculator.

FEATURES OF FINANCIAL SOFTWARE The principal features are these:

- **Tracking of income and expenses:** The programs allow you to set up various account categories for recording income and expenses, including credit card expenses.

1978	1980	1981	1982	1983	1984
The first electronic spreadsheet, VisiCalc, is introduced; WordStar, the first commercial word processor for consumers, is introduced	Microsoft obtains DOS version that becomes PC-DOS for IBM PC.	Xerox introduces mouse-operated icons, buttons, and menus on the Star computer; IBM introduces personal computer (IBM PC)	Portable computers	Bill Gates announces the first version of the Windows operating system (and releases it two years later)	Apple Macintosh; first personal laser printer; the Apple Macintosh introduces the first widely used GUI; Mac System 1.0 is introduced

Financial software
Microsoft Money can be used for all sorts of money-related management. It includes guidance tips for setting up your accounts.

- **Checkbook management:** All programs feature checkbook management, with an on-screen check-writing form and check register that look like the ones in your checkbook. Checks can be purchased to use with your computer printer.

- **Reporting:** All programs compare your actual expenses with your budgeted expenses. Some will compare this year's expenses to last year's.

- **Income tax:** All programs offer tax categories, for indicating types of income and expenses that are important when you're filing your tax return.

- **Other:** Some of the more versatile personal-finance programs also offer financial-planning and portfolio-management features.

GOING BEYOND PERSONAL FINANCE Besides personal-finance managers, financial software includes small business accounting and tax software programs, which provide virtually all the forms you need for filing income taxes. Tax programs such as TaxCut and TurboTax make complex calculations, check for mistakes, and even unearth deductions you didn't know existed. Tax programs can be linked to personal-finance software to form an integrated tool.

Many financial software programs may be used in all kinds of enterprises. For instance, accounting software such as Intuit Quickbooks and Sage Software's Peachtree automates bookkeeping tasks, while payroll software keeps records of employee hours and produces reports for tax purposes.

Some programs go beyond financial management and tax and accounting management. For example, Business Plan Pro and Small Business Management Pro can help you set up your own business from scratch.

1985	1986	1987	1988	1990	1991
Aldus PageMaker becomes the first integrated desktop publishing program; Microsoft Windows 1.0 is released; Mac System 2.0	Mac System 3.0	Microsoft's Excel program introduced; Mac system 4.0, then 5.0	Mac System 6.0	Microsoft introduces Windows 3.0 in May, intensifying its legal dispute with Apple over the software's "look and feel" resemblance to the Macintosh operating system	Linus Torvalds introduces Linux; Mac System 7.0

Desktop-publishing software.
Named after the subatomic particle proposed as the building block for all matter, the Quark company was founded in Colorado in 1981. QuarkXPress was released in 1987 and made an immediate impact on the fledgling desktop publishing business. QuarkXPress introduced precision typography, layout, and color control to the desktop computer.

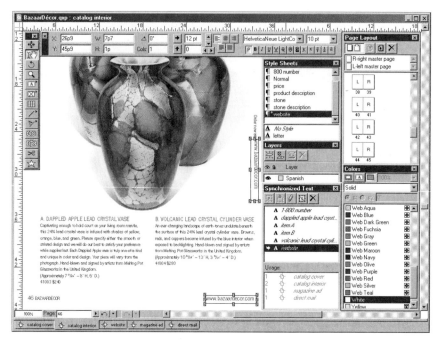

Finally, there are investment software packages, such as StreetSmart Pro from Charles Schwab and Online Xpress from Fidelity, as well as various retirement-planning programs.

Desktop Publishing

What are the principal features of desktop-publishing software?

Adobe Systems was founded in 1982, when John Warnock and Charles Geschke began to work on solving some of the long-standing problems that plagued the relationship between microcomputers and printers. Collaboration with Apple Computers produced the first desktop-publishing package, using Adobe Post-Script, a printer language that can handle many fonts and graphics, in 1984. By 1987, Adobe had agreements with IBM, Digital, AST Research, Hewlett-Packard, and Texas Instruments for them to use PostScript in their printers.

Desktop publishing (DTP) involves mixing text and graphics to produce high-quality output for commercial printing, using a microcomputer and mouse, scanner, laser or ink-jet printer, and DTP software. Often the printer is used primarily to get an advance look before the completed job is sent to a typesetter service bureau for even higher-quality output. Service bureaus have special machines that convert the DTP files to film, which can then be used to make plates for offset printing. Offset printing produces higher-quality documents, especially if color is used, but is generally more expensive than laser printing.

1992	1993	1994	1995	1997	1998
Microsoft's Access database program released	Multimedia desktop computers PDF software	Apple and IBM introduce PCs with full-motion video built in; wireless data transmission for small portable computers; Netscape's first web browser is introduced (based on Mosaic, introduced in 1993)	Windows 95 is released	Mac OS 8 sells 1.25 million copies in its first two weeks; Mac System 8.0	Windows 98 is released

FEATURES OF DESKTOP PUBLISHING Desktop publishing has these characteristics:

- **Mix of text with graphics:** Desktop-publishing software allows you to precisely manage and merge text with graphics. As you lay out a page on-screen, you can make the text "flow," liquidlike, around graphics such as photographs. You can resize art, silhouette it, change the colors, change the texture, flip it upside down, and make it look like a photo negative.

- **Varied type and layout styles:** As do word processing programs, DTP programs support a variety of fonts, or typestyles, from readable Times Roman to staid Tribune to wild Jester and Scribble. Additional fonts can be purchased on disk or downloaded online. You can also create all kinds of rules, borders, columns, and page-numbering styles.

- **Use of files from other programs:** It's usually not efficient to do word processing, drawing, and painting with the DTP software. As a rule, text is composed on a word processor, artwork is created with drawing and painting software, and photographs are input using a scanner and then modified and stored using image-editing software. Prefabricated art to illustrate DTP documents may be obtained from clip-art sources. The DTP program is used to integrate all these files. You can look at your work on the display screen as one page, as two facing pages (in reduced size), or as "thumbnails." Then you can see it again after it has been printed out. (● *See Panel 3.33.*)

panel 3.33

How desktop publishing uses other files

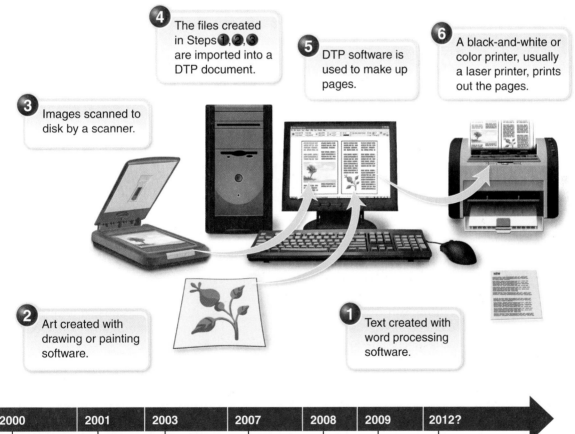

3 Images scanned to disk by a scanner.

4 The files created in Steps ❶,❷,❸ are imported into a DTP document.

5 DTP software is used to make up pages.

6 A black-and-white or color printer, usually a laser printer, prints out the pages.

2 Art created with drawing or painting software.

1 Text created with word processing software.

9	2000	2001	2003	2007	2008	2009	2012?
Adobe InDesign	Windows 2000 (ME) is released; Mac System 9.0	Windows XP becomes available; Mac OS X ships	Microsoft Vista OS (Pre-Beta) first introduced; Windows Mobile released	Windows Vista commercially availiable; Mac OS X.5 (Leopard) available	Cloud computing starts to take off	Windows 7	Most software will be open-source; 3-D user interface

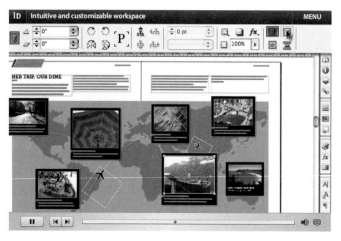

Page design and layout in Adobe InDesign

BECOMING A DTP PROFESSIONAL Not everyone can be successful at desktop publishing, because many complex layouts require experience, skill, and knowledge of graphic design. Indeed, use of these programs by nonprofessional users can lead to rather unprofessional-looking results. Nevertheless, the availability of microcomputers and reasonably inexpensive software has opened up a career area formerly reserved for professional typographers and printers.

QuarkXPress and Adobe InDesign are professional DTP programs. Microsoft Publisher is a "low-end," consumer-oriented DTP package. Some word processing programs, such as Word and WordPerfect, also have many DTP features, although still not at the sophisticated level of the specialized DTP software. DTP packages, for example, give you more control over typographical characteristics and provide more support for full-color output.

Drawing & Painting Programs

How do drawing and painting programs differ?

It may be no surprise to learn that commercial artists and fine artists have largely abandoned the paintbox and pen-and-ink for software versions of palettes, brushes, and pens. However, even nonartists can produce good-looking work with these programs.

There are two types of computer art programs, also called *illustration software*—drawing and painting.

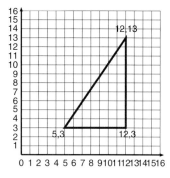

Vector image

DRAWING PROGRAMS A *drawing program* is graphics software that allows users to design and illustrate objects and products. Some drawing programs are CorelDRAW, Adobe Illustrator, and Macromedia Freehand.

Drawing programs create *vector images*—images created from geometrical formulas. Almost all sophisticated graphics programs use vector graphics.

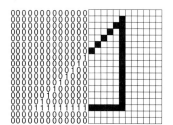

Bit-mapped image

PAINTING PROGRAMS *Painting programs* are graphics programs that allow users to simulate painting on-screen. A mouse or a tablet stylus is used to simulate a paintbrush. The program allows you to select "brush" sizes, as well as colors from a color palette. Examples of painting programs are Adobe PhotoShop, Microsoft Photo Editor, Corel Photopaint, and JASC's PaintShop Pro.

Painting programs produce *bit-mapped images*, or *raster images*, made up of little dots.

Painting software is also called *image-editing software* because it allows you to retouch photographs, adjust the contrast and the colors, and add special effects, such as shadows.

SOME GRAPHICS FILE FORMATS When you create an image, it's important to choose the most appropriate graphics file format, which specifies the method of organizing information in a file. Among the most important graphics formats you are apt to encounter are these:

File Formats

For a complete list of file formats, go to:

http://en.wikipedia.org/wiki/ List_of_file_formats

- **.bmp (BitMaP):** This bitmap graphic file format is native to Microsoft Windows and is used on PCs. Microsoft Paint creates .bmp file formats.

- **.gif (Graphic Interchange Format):** This format is used in Web pages and for downloadable online images.

- **.jpeg (Joint Photographic Experts Group):** Pronounced *"jay-peg,"* this bitmap format is used for websites and for photos and other high-resolution images.

- **.tiff (Tagged Image File Format):** This bitmap format is used on both PCs and Macs for high-resolution files that will be printed.
- **.png (Portable Network Graphics):** This file format was specifically created for web page images and can be used as a public domain alternative to .gif for compression.

Video/Audio Editing Software

Could I benefit from using video/audio editing software?

The popularity of digital camcorders ("camera recorders") has caused an increase in sales of video-editing software. This software allows you to import video footage to your PC and edit it, for example, deleting parts you don't want, reordering sequences, and adding special effects. Popular video-editing software packages include Adobe Premiere, Sony Pictures Digital Vegas, Apple Final Cut Express, Pinnacle Studio DV, and Ulead VideoStudio.

Audio-editing software provides similar capabilities for working with sound tracks, and you can also clean up background noise (called *artifacts*) and emphasize certain sound qualities. Sound-editing software includes Windows Sound Recorder, Sony Pictures Digital Sound Forge, Audacity (freeware), Felt Tip Software's Sound Studio (shareware), GoldWave, and WavePad.

Video and audio are covered in more detail in Chapter 5.

Animation Software

How does animation software differ from video software?

Animation **is the simulation (illusion) of movement created by displaying a series of still pictures, or frames, very quickly in sequence.** *Computer animation* refers to the creation of moving images by means of a computer. Whereas video devices record continuous motion and break it up into discrete frames, animation starts with independent pictures and puts them together to form the illusion of continuous motion. Animation is one of the chief ingredients of multimedia presentations and is commonly used on web pages. There are many software applications that enable you to create animations that you can display on a computer monitor.

The first type of animation to catch on for web use was called *GIF* (for Graphics Interchange Format) animation, and it is still very popular today. GIF files contain a group of images that display very quickly to simulate movement when a web page viewer clicks on the file icon. Animated GIF Construction Professional enables users to easily create animation via the use of a wizard. It

Survival Tip

Compressing Web & Audio Files

Video and audio files tend to be very large, so they need to be edited down and compressed to be as short as possible, especially if they are to be used on web pages. Your software documentation will explain how to do this.

About Animation

For sources about animation, go to:

http://webreference.com/3d/

For schools offering training in computer-based graphics, including animation, check out:

www.computertrainingschool. com/?googleanimation= y&got=3d_animation_ training&t=30

Sophisticated application software. Animation artist at work at the Studio Ghibli, Mitaka, Japan.

Screen from a GIF animation program

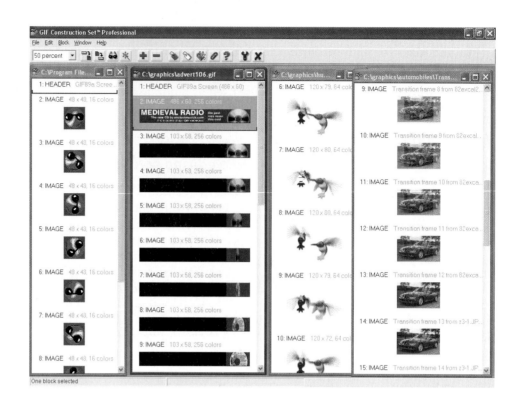

allows the creation of many special effects and supports compression, as well as offering tutorials. Among the many other GIF animation software packages are 3D GIF Designer and The Complete Animator.

Multimedia Authoring Software

What is multimedia authoring software?

**Multimedia authoring software** **combines text, graphics, video, animation, and sound in an integrated way to create stand-alone multimedia applications.** Content can be burned to CDs/DVDs or delivered via the web. Until the mid-1990s, multimedia applications were relatively uncommon, owing to the expensive hardware required. With increases in performance and decreases in price, however, multimedia is now commonplace. Nearly all microcomuters are capable of displaying video, though the resolution available depends on the power of the computer's video adapter and CPU. Macromedia Director and Macromedia Authorware are two popular multimedia authoring packages.

Many websites, as well as business training centers and educational institutions, use multimedia to develop interactive applications.

Web Page Design/Authoring Software

How could using web page design software be to my benefit?

**Web page design/authoring software** **is used to create web pages with sophisticated multimedia features.** A few of these packages are easy enough for beginners to use. Some of the best-known are Adobe Dreamweaver, Adobe Flash, Coffee Cup Visual Site designer, RealMac Rapid Weaver, Microsoft Expression Web 2, and Dynamic HTML Editor. These tools generate the necessary HTML coding (and other,

Explore new dimensions in rich multimedia authoring

Adobe® Director® 11 and Adobe Shockwave® Player software help you create and publish compelling interactive games, demos, prototypes, simulations, and eLearning courses for the web, Mac and Windows® desktops, DVDs, and CDs. Integrate virtually any major file format, including video created with Adobe Flash® software and native 3D content, for the greatest return on your creativity.

Adobe Director 11

Reall's HTML/WYSIWYG Editor IE5.5+ only

to use this free html editor..... wait until page loads fully......

Normal | impact | 7 (36 pt) | **B** *I* <u>U</u> S̶ | A | x₂ x²

```
<p><font face="Verdana" size="2">Reall's HTML Editor is an online
html/WYSIWYG editor to use for editing our templates.<br /><br />If
you're not a customer of ours, then please feel free to use this editor
if it helps you understand and learn HTML.</font> </p><p /><p><font
face="Verdana" size="2">To start using our Editor, you need to highlight
all of the text here and then delete it. </font></p><p /><p /><p><font
face="Verdana" size="2">At the moment you are viewing this html in <font
color="#ff0000" size="2"><strong>WYSIWYG</strong></font> mode. If you
have a template of ours, simply delete this and then in code view paste
your template. To see how it looks, toggle back to the WYSIWYG
mode.</font></p><p /><p /><p><font face="Verdana" size="2">To see your
template in html view, you need to find and push the &lt; &gt; icon
button above (bottom row - right hand side) to see your html source
code.</font></p><p /><p /><p><font face="Verdana" size="2">If you get
stuck at any stage, just hit refresh in your browser window and this
text will appear again. With our Editor you can change images, insert
hyperlinks, add tables and so on, you could even create an entire
website..</font></p><p /><p /><p><font face="Verdana" size="2">Then
simply right click and then copy and paste this code into your file for
the page, and upload it to your server.</font><font
```

You are in TEXT MODE. Use the [<>] button to switch back to WYSIWYG.

Reall's HTML/WYSIWYG Editor IE5.5+ only

to use this free html editor..... wait until page loads fully......

— format — | — font — | — size — | **B** *I* <u>U</u> S̶ | x₂ x²

Reall's HTML Editor is an online html/WYSIWYG editor to use for editing our templates.

If you're not a customer of ours, then please feel free to use this editor if it helps you understand and learn HTML.

To start using our Editor, you need to highlight all of the text here and then delete it.

At the moment you are viewing this html in **WYSIWYG** mode. If you have a template of ours, simply delete this and then in code view paste your template. To see how it looks, toggle back to the WYSIWYG mode.

To see your template in html view, you need to find and push the < > icon button above (bottom row - right hand side) to see your html source code.

panel 3.34

(*Top*) HTML coded text; (*bottom*) the same text translated into WYSIWYG form by Reall's HTML WYSIWYG Editor

Web Authoring

This site offers a lot of information on web authoring tools:

http://webdesign.about.com/ od/htmleditors/HTML_ Editors_Web_Page_ Authoring_Tools.htm

For 5 basic steps of web design, go to:

www.grantasticdesigns. com/5rules.html

For information on becoming a professional website designer, try:

http://designeducation. allgraphicdesign.com/

http://websitetips.com/ business/education/

www.sessions.edu/courses/ index.asp

www.tuj.ac.jp/newsite/main/ cont-ed/certificate/graphic_ design.html

newer language coding) based on the user's design and content and present everything to the design in a WYSIWYG ("what you see is what you get") form. (● *See Panel 3.34.*)

Internet access providers also offer some free, easy-to-use web-authoring tools for building simple websites. They help you create web pages, using icons and menus to automate the process; you don't need to know hypertext markup language (HTML, Chapter 2) to get the job done. These automated tools let you select a prepared, template web page design, type a few words, add a picture or two—and you're done. To save the pages and make them accessible on the internet, the provider grants you a certain amount of space on its web servers.

Website design can include much more than text: for example, animation, video, sound, interactivity, search-engine functions. But before creating a website, the designer must first plan exactly what is needed in the website—define the audience, as well as the purpose and the content. Once a web site is completed, it must be uploaded (published) in order to be available to internet

Software

PRACTICAL ACTION
Help in Building Your Web Page

Local and national internet access providers often offer web-page-building tools, as well as space on their servers for storing your web page. Other sources of information for designing and building web pages are these:

For Novices

- **Yahoo!:** Yahoo! offers web-page-building tools and templates under the name SiteBuilder (*http://webhosting.yahoo.com/ps/sb/index.php*), which enables you to add music and other special effects to your web pages and have components that track how many people visit your site. For a fee, Yahoo! offers unlimited storage for your website and will help you determine your URL (website address).

- **Lycos:** Lycos offers templates and tools, and it also offers tutorials to help you get started if you want to build your own pages from scratch. Lycos also offers free space in its Tripod area (*www.tripod.lycos.com*). As with Yahoo!, you will have advertisements on your pages unless you pay a small fee to get rid of them.

- **Google Sites:** Google offers this free online tool that makes it easy for anyone to create and publish web pages in just minutes. You can see what your pages will look like, and you can edit your pages right in your browser. Google will host your web pages on your own site at *www.sites.google.com*.

Once you've created your website, you'll need to "publish" it—upload it to a web server for viewing on the internet. You can get upload instructions from your online service or internet access provider, which may also provide space (for free or for a fee) on its servers. (Or, as we mention below, if you have a powerful, large-storage-capacity microcomputer that has an always-on internet connection, you can use it to host your own website.)

For much more information about building and storing your own web pages, just do a keyword search using "build web page" or "website design" in any good search engine.

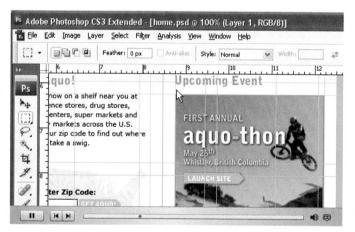

Inserting an Adobe Photoshop photo file into a Dreamweaver web page that is being designed

users via a browser. Some people with powerful personal computers and an always-on internet connection, such as cable, leave their websites on their own computers; the website is accessed by users typing in the site's URL (web address; Chapter 2) in their browsers. Most people, however, use FTP software (Chapter 2) to upload their website files to a server host, where, for a fee, the website is stored for access.

Complicated business websites are created and maintained by professional website developers.

Project Management Software
Should I learn to use project management software?

As we have seen, a personal information manager (PIM) can help you schedule your appointments and do some planning. That is, it can help you manage your own life. But what if you need to manage the lives of others in order to accomplish a full-blown project, such as steering a political campaign or handling a nationwide road tour for a band? Strictly defined, a *project* is a one-time operation involving several tasks and multiple resources that must be organized toward completing a specific goal within a given period of time. The project can be small, such as an advertising campaign for an in-house

panel 3.35

Project management software: Microsoft Project

advertising department, or large, such as construction of an office tower or a jetliner.

Project management software is a program used to plan and schedule the people, costs, and resources required to complete a project on time. *(See • Panel 3.35.)* For instance, the associate producer on a feature film might use such software to keep track of the locations, cast and crew, materials, dollars, and schedules needed to complete the picture on time and within budget. The software would show the scheduled beginning and ending dates for a particular task—such as shooting all scenes on a certain set—and then the date that task was actually completed. Examples of project management software are Mindjet MindManager Pro 8, MindView, Intuit, Microsoft Project, FastTrackSchedule, and Project KickStart.

Portable Document Format (PDF)

Why is PDF useful?

Short for *Portable Document Format,* **PDF is a file format developed by Adobe Systems. PDF captures text, graphic, and formatting information from a variety of applications on different platforms making it possible to send documents and have them appear on the recipient's monitor (or printer) as they were intended to be viewed.** *(See • Panel 3.36, next page.)* A properly prepared PDF file maintains the original fonts, images, colors, and graphics, as well as the exact layout of the file.

Originally, PDF was mostly used by graphic artists, designers, and publishers for producing color page proofs. Today, however PDF is used for virtually any data that needs to be exchanged among applications and users. Individuals, businesses, and government agencies around the world trust and rely on PDF to communicate. PDF files are widely used on websites and are also used to distribute electronic documents over networks and via email.

panel 3.36

Screen from the Adobe Acrobat PDF tutorial; (lower right corner) Adobe PDF file icon. Any file in the PDF format will have this icon next to the filename.

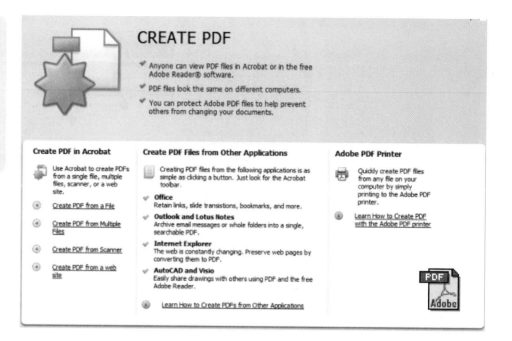

A PDF file can be shared, viewed, and printed by anyone using the free downloadable Adobe Reader software regardless of the operating system and original application used. PDF can also be used on mobile devices. In addition, many applications, such as Microsoft Word, enable users to save their files in a PDF version. To be able to create and work with all of Adobe's PDF features, you need to purchase the complete Adobe Acrobat Suite.

Computer-Aided Design

What could I do with a CAD program?

Computers have long been used in engineering design. ***Computer-aided design (CAD)*** **programs are intended for the design of products, structures, civil engineering drawings, and maps.** CAD programs, which are available for microcomputers, help architects design buildings and workspaces and help engineers design cars, planes, electronic devices, roadways, bridges, and subdivisions. CAD and drawing programs are similar. However, CAD programs provide precise dimensioning and positioning of the elements being drawn, so they can be transferred later to computer-aided manufacturing (CAM) programs. Also, CAD programs lack some of the special effects for illustrations that come with drawing programs. One advantage of CAD software is that the product can be drawn in three dimensions and then rotated on the screen, so the designer can see all sides. (● *See Panel 3.36.*) Examples of popular CAD programs are Autodesk, AutoCAD, TurboCAD, Alibre Design, and PowerCADD.

Computer-aided design/computer-aided manufacturing (CAD/CAM) software allows products designed with CAD to be input into an automated manufacturing system that makes the products. For example, CAD/CAM systems brought a whirlwind of enhanced creativity and efficiency to the fashion industry. The designs and specifications are then input into CAM systems that enable robot pattern-cutters to automatically cut thousands of patterns from fabric with only minimal waste. Whereas previously the fashion industry worked about a year in advance of delivery, CAD/CAM has cut that time to less than 8 months—a competitive edge for a field that feeds on fads.

The Ultimate CAD Directory

This directory has information about all sorts of CAD products to suit every type of need:

www.tenlinks.com/CAD

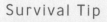

Survival Tip

Try before You Buy

Free trial versions of software are often offered as downloads from company sites.

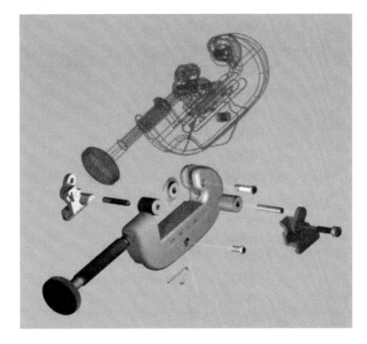

panel 3.37

CAD

CAD software is used for nearly all three-dimensional designing. (*Top*) TurboCAD; (*bottom*) Autodesk.

EXPERIENCE BOX
The Mysteries of Tech Support

Your screen flashes "Fatal Error." Your new software upgrade totals your printer. You can't connect to your internet access provider. No wonder one online survey found that nearly 20% of the respondents admitted they'd dropped a computer on the floor out of anger.[20] Because of the complicated mesh of elements—software, hardware, communications, people—Murphy's Law ("If anything can go wrong, it will") seems to apply in computing as almost nowhere else. Thus, one of the most valuable tasks you can learn is how to deal with tech support—getting technical help on the phone or online when things don't work. (There's no need to be shy. One survey found that nearly half of all U.S. tech users said they needed assistance with their new gadgets.)[21]

What's Wrong with Tech Support?

It has been found that for every $1 the typical company spends buying information technology, it will spend $4–$10 making it all work.[22] Thus, more than two decades after Apple Computer revolutionized PC software with intuitive, easy-to-use designs, software companies have begun to get the message about the importance of usability.[23]

Simultaneously, technology companies have also had to try to improve their tech support operations, which customers said were falling down on the job. The result was tedious delays on help lines and complaints about unhelpful tech advice, among other things.

Two problems seem to affect the tech support industry:

- *Information technology is becoming more complex:* The more personal computers and other infotech devices are expected to do—music, video, photos, DVDs, home networking, and so on—the more complex the interaction between the components and the harder it is to figure out what's wrong. In addition, points out technology writer Edward C. Baig, "The severe outbreak of viruses, worms, and spyware makes the support task more daunting."[24]

- *Manufacturers practice a "blame game":* One computer user found he had a possible online virus (a rogue program that can damage a computer) when he started up his PC. He first called the computer manufacturer, who said it was a software issue, but the software maker could provide help only if he went online, which his affected computer didn't allow him to do. Later he discovered the antivirus manufacturer had tech support phone numbers, but there was a charge ($3.95 a minute) for their use. Eventually a friend had to help him out. This kind of experience is not uncommon.

Improving Your Chances for Avoiding Tech Support Hassles

Wouldn't it be wonderful if you never had to go through tech support agony in the first place? Here are three things technology writer Baig suggests that you can do *in advance* to improve your chances:[25]

- *Never upgrade, and never add software:* "If your PC is working fine and you have no ambitions for doing more," says Baig, "don't mess around" by adding new hardware accessories or new software. Many problems occur, for instance, because of conflicts between the operating system and special software (known as *drivers*) that arise when people do upgrades or add software that didn't come with the original system. (Of course, this would seem to defeat one of the purposes of having a computer in the first place—that you can save money by readily adding new things to it. If you must do so, ask the retailer from whom you buy them to handle the installation. But you probably can't do this if you ordered your original equipment from an online seller.)

- *Use the web to research a manufacturer's tech support before you buy:* If you decide to upgrade/add anyway, go to the manufacturer's website and look at tech support resources to see "how coherent and easily accessible" they are, advises Baig. This will also give you some feel for the kinds of problems customers are having.

- *Call tech support before you buy:* Calling tech support in advance of purchasing may cost you something in long-distance charges, but you'll also find out how confusing the voice menu is and how long it takes to reach a live human.

We would add some other tips:

- *Create a fact sheet with your computer's important specs:* When you get a computer, create a fact sheet listing the important technical specifications and attach it to the outside of the case. This will provide you with the kind of information that tech support personnel are apt to ask should you call on them. Take a copy along with you whenever you buy a game or other video- and sound-intensive application to make sure it is compatible with the rest of your system.[26]

- *If you have a communication problem, hang up and call again:* Many companies now hire people in offshore call centers as tech support specialists, and sometimes you may have trouble with foreign accents. If this happens to you, hang up and call again.

Company	Price	Services
AAATechSupport.com 800-392-5938 www.aaatechsupport.com	First 2 minutes free. $2.79 per minute after that.	Support for most computer products
Ask Dr. Tech 800-AskDrTech www.AskDrTech.com	$149 per year, $39 per month, $19 per call	Phone, email, or online chat support for PCs and peripherals
geeks to go! Toll free: 888-433-5435 www.geekstogo.com/	free	Live chat support with consultants and forums for numerous software and hardware problems
Live Repair www.liverepair.com/com/ individual.asp	Varies	Tech support via web-based chat for PCs, phone, and email
Speak With A Geek 866-933-HELP www.speakwithageek.com	Individual plan $34.95 per month	Phone, email, or online chat PC support
Geek Squad 1-800-433-5778 www.geeksquad.com	From $29 to about $300, depending on the problem; at your location, one of their stores, or at a Best Buy store	Almost any problem related to computers, electronics, and networks
Geeks on Call 1-800-905-GEEK www.geeksoncall.com	Varies, depending on the problem	Same as above
Nerds On Site 1-877-696-3737 www.nerdsonsite.us	Same as above	Same as above
iYogi 866-242-4609 www.iyogi.net/tollfree1/ tech-support	$120 per year	24/7 PC and peripherals support
Mac Help 954-726-9525 www.lookatmymac.com/? gclid=CNiy7oW61JQCFR GiiQodggG5kA	$1.50 per minute or $90 per hour phone/live chat support; on-site $120 per hour	Support for Mac-related issues
JustAnswer.mac http://mac.justanswer.com/ mac	Create an account and name your price for an answer to your problem; email and live chat	Same as above

panel 3.38

Some individual technical support services
800 and 888 numbers are toll-free. Most services are available 24 hours a day, 7 days a week. Note that not all operations serve Macintosh users, and not all have a phone option—which can be a handicap when you're not able to go online.

Finding Your Own Personal Tech Support

Can't get any satisfaction from Microsoft (whose tech support might charge you $35 per incident), Apple, Dell, or the like? Maybe you should turn to your own personal support service—for instance, to Support Freaks, iYogi, BluePhone, or Speak With a Geek. (● *See Panel 3.38.*) Because these services don't have a stake in any particular kind of software or hardware, you are more apt to avoid the blame-game problem. "We'll support your Gateway talking to your Compaq talking to your scanner talking to your digital camera," says a representative of Speak With a Geek.[27] However, because most of these operations are small, you may find yourself waiting while whoever answers the phone or online inquiry tracks down an on-call consultant to help you. If you're prepared to pay, however, companies such as Geek Squad, as well as local specialists, will come to your house or office. Personalized tech support can be paid for on an hourly basis, service-call basis, or subscription basis, as the chart shows.

Other Sources of Help

Although usually less specific in solving your problem, there are nonetheless a number of other sources of help to be aware of:

- *Help: instruction manuals, software, and online:* User guides or instruction manuals printed on paper have traditionally accompanied software. Now most software publishers rely more on Help programs on a CD/DVD or in downloadable PDF manuals. Help programs are also available through the internet. The problem with this approach, of course, is, How do you go online to solve the problem of your computer not working if your computer isn't working? (It helps to have two computers.)

- *Commercial how-to books:* How-to books are the kind of books found both in computer stores and in general bookstores such as Barnes & Noble or Borders and on Amazon.com. Examples are the "For Dummies" or "Complete Idiot's" books (such as *PCs for Dummies* and *The Complete Idiot's Guide to Microsoft Office*).

- *Knowledgeable friends:* Believe it or not, nothing beats having a knowledgeable friend: your instructor, a student more advanced than you, or someone with a technical interest in computers. We can't stress enough how important it is to get to know people—from your classes, from computer user groups (including online internet groups), from family, friends, or whatever—who can lend aid and expertise when your computer software gives you trouble.

analytical graphics (p. 163) Also called *business graphics;* graphical forms that make numeric data easier to analyze than it is when organized as rows and columns of numbers. The principal examples of analytical graphics are bar charts, line graphs, and pie charts. Why it's important: *Whether viewed on a monitor or printed out, analytical graphics help make sales figures, economic trends, and the like easier to comprehend and analyze.*

animation (p. 175) The simulation (illusion) of movement created by displaying a series of still pictures, or frames, very quickly in sequence. Why it's important: *Animation is used in video games, movies, special-effects presentations, and even in email, to make it more interesting.*

application software (p. 120) Software that has been developed to solve a particular problem for users—to perform useful work on specific tasks or to provide entertainment. Why it's important: *Application software consists of most of the software you are familiar with and use on a daily basis.* (Compare **system software**.)

booting (p. 122) Loading an operating system into a computer's main memory. Why it's important: *Without booting, computers could not operate. The programs responsible for booting are stored permanently in the computer's electronic circuitry. When you turn on the machine, programs called* diagnostic routines *test the main memory, the central processing unit, and other parts of the system to make sure they are running properly. Next, BIOS (basic input/output system) programs are copied to main memory and help the computer interpret keyboard characters or transmit characters to the display screen or to a diskette. Then the boot program obtains the operating system, usually from the hard disk, and loads it into the computer's main memory, where it remains until you turn the computer off.*

cell (p. 161) Place where a row and a column intersect in a spreadsheet worksheet; its position is called a *cell address.* Why it's important: *The cell is the smallest working unit in a spreadsheet. Data and formulas are entered into cells. Cell addresses provide location references for spreadsheet users.*

computer-aided design (CAD) (p. 180) Programs intended for the design of products, structures, civil engineering drawings, and maps. Why it's important: *CAD programs, which are available for microcomputers, help architects design buildings and workspaces and help engineers design cars, planes, electronic devices, roadways, bridges, and subdivisions. While similar to drawing programs, CAD programs provide precise dimensioning and positioning of the elements being drawn, so they can be transferred later to computer-aided manufacturing programs; however, they lack special effects for illustrations. One advantage of CAD software is that three-dimensional drawings can be rotated on-screen, so the designer can see all sides of the product.*

cursor (p. 156) Movable symbol on the display screen that shows where the user may next enter data or commands. The symbol is often a blinking rectangle or an I-beam. You can move the cursor on the screen using the keyboard's directional arrow keys or a mouse. The point where the cursor is located is called the *insertion point.* Why it's important: *All application software packages use cursors to show the current work location on the screen.*

database (p. 164) Collection of interrelated files in a computer system. These computer-based files are organized according to their common elements, so that they can be retrieved easily. Why it's important: *Businesses and organizations build databases to help them keep track of and manage their affairs. In addition, online database services put enormous resources at the user's disposal.*

database software (p. 164) Also called *database manager* or *database management system (DBMS);* application software that sets up and controls the structure of a database and access to the data. Why it's important: *Database software allows users to organize and manage huge amounts of data.*

default settings (p. 160) Settings automatically used by a program unless the user specifies otherwise, thereby overriding them. Why it's important: *Users need to know how to change default settings in order to customize documents.*

desktop (p. 132) The operating system's main interface screen. Why it's important: *The desktop displays pictures (icons) that provide quick access to programs and information.*

desktop publishing (DTP) (p. 172) Application software and hardware system that involves mixing text and graphics to produce high-quality output for commercial printing, using a microcomputer and mouse, scanner, laser or ink-jet printer, and DTP software (such as QuarkXPress and In Design or, at a more consumer-oriented level, Microsoft Publisher). Often the printer is used primarily to get an advance look before the completed job is sent to a typesetter for even higher-quality output. Some word processing programs, such as Word and WordPerfect, have rudimentary DTP features. Why it's important: *Desktop publishing has reduced the number of steps, the time, and the money required to produce professional-looking printed projects.*

device drivers (p. 126) Specialized software programs—usually components of system software—that allow input and output devices to communicate with the rest of the computer system. Why it's important: *Drivers are needed so that the computer's operating system can recognize and run peripheral hardware.*

DOS (Disk Operating System) (p. 138) Original operating system produced by Microsoft, with a hard-to-use command-driven user interface. Its initial 1982 version was designed to run on the IBM PC as PC-DOS. Later Microsoft licensed the same system to other computer makers as MS-DOS. Why it's important: *DOS used to be the most common microcomputer operating system, and it is still used on some microcomputers. Today the most popular operating systems use GUIs.*

exporting (p. 154) Transforming data into a format that can be used in another program and then transmitting it. Why it's important: *Users need to know how to export many types of files.*

file (p. 124) A named collection of data (data file) or a program (program file) that exists in a computer's secondary storage, such as on a hard disk or CD. Why it's important: *Dealing with files is an inescapable part of working with computers. Users need to be familiar with the different types of files.*

financial software (p. 170) Application software that ranges from personal-finance managers to entry-level accounting programs to business financial-management packages. Why it's important: *Financial software provides users with powerful management tools (personal-finance managers) as well as small business programs. Moreover, tax programs provide virtually all the forms needed for filing income taxes, make complex calculations, check for mistakes, and even unearth deductions you didn't know existed. Tax programs can also be integrated with personal finance software to form an integrated tool. Accounting software automates bookkeeping tasks, while payroll software keeps records of employee hours and produces reports for tax purposes. Some programs allow users to set up a business from scratch. Financial software also includes investment software packages and various retirement planning programs.*

formulas (p. 162) In a spreadsheet, instructions for calculations entered into designated cells. Why it's important: *When spreadsheet users change data in one cell, all the cells linked to it by formulas automatically recalculate their values.*

freeware (p. 151) Copyrighted software that is distributed free of charge, today most often over the internet. Why it's important: *Freeware saves users money.*

function keys (p. 130) Keys labeled "F1," "F2," and so on, positioned along the top or left side of the keyboard. Why it's important: *They are used to execute commands specific to the software being used.*

functions (p. 162) In a spreadsheet, built-in formulas that perform common calculations. Why it's important: *After the values have been entered into the worksheet, formulas and functions can be used to calculate outcomes.*

graphical user interface (GUI) (p. 131) User interface in which icons and commands from menus may be selected by means of a mouse or keystrokes. Why it's important: *GUIs are easier to use than command-driven interfaces.*

Help command (p. 137) Command generating a table of contents, an index, and a search feature that can help users locate answers to questions about the software. Why it's

important: *Help features provide a built-in electronic instruction manual.*

icons (p. 132) Small pictorial figures that represent programs, data files, or procedures. Why it's important: *Icons have simplified the use of software. The feature represented by the icon can be activated by clicking on the icon.*

importing (p. 153) Getting data from another source and then converting it into a format compatible with the program in which the user is currently working. Why it's important: *Users will often have to import files.*

key (p. 165) Also called *key field, sort key, index,* or *keyword;* field used to sort data in a database. For example, if users sort records by age, then the age field is a key. Why it's important: *Key fields are needed to identify and retrieve specific items in a database. Most database management systems allow you to have more than one key so that you can sort records in different ways. One of the keys is designated the primary key and must hold a unique value for each record. A key field that identifies records in different tables is called a foreign key. Foreign keys are used to cross-reference data among relational tables. The most frequent key field used in the United States is the Social Security number, but any unique identifier, such as employee number or student number, can be used.*

Linux (p. 146) Free (open-source) version of the Unix OS, supported by the efforts of thousands of volunteer programmers. Why it's important: *Linux is an inexpensive, open-source operating system useful for online applications and to PC users who have to maintain a web server or a network server.*

Macintosh operating system (Mac OS) (p. 138) System software that runs only on Apple Macintosh computers. Why it's important: *Although Macs are not as common as PCs, many people believe they are easier to use. Macs are often used for graphics and desktop publishing.*

macro (p. 130) Also called *keyboard shortcut;* a single keystroke or command—or a series of keystrokes or commands—used to automatically issue a longer, predetermined series of keystrokes or commands. Why it's important: *Users can consolidate several activities into only one or two keystrokes. The user names the macro and stores the corresponding command sequence; once this is done, the macro can be used repeatedly.*

menu (p. 134) Displayed list of options—such as commands—to choose from. Why it's important: *Menus are a feature of GUIs that make software easier to use.*

menu bar (p. 136) Bar across the top of the display window, below the title bar. Why it's important: *It shows the names of the various pull-down menus available.*

Microsoft Windows (p. 140) Most common operating system for desktop and portable microcomputers. Windows 95 was succeeded by Windows 98, Windows 2003, Windows Me, Windows XP, Vista, and, most recently, Windows 7 (Windows 2009). Why it's important: *Windows supports the most applications written for microcomputers.*

Microsoft Windows Embedded (p. 149) Previously known as *Windows CE*; operating system for handhelds. *Why it's important: Windows Embedded offers pocket versions of Word and Excel that let users read standard word processing and spreadsheet files sent as email attachments from their PCs. It also enables web functions. A version of Windows Embdedded, Windows Mobile, is used in certain smartphones.*

Microsoft Windows NT (p. 144) *NT* stands for "New Technology"; Microsoft's multitasking OS designed to run on network servers in businesses of all sizes. *Why it's important: It allows multiple users to share resources such as data, programs, and printers and to build web applications and connect to the internet.*

Microsoft Windows Vista (p. 141) Introduced to consumers in January 2007, the Vista operating system is the equivalent of Windows version 12—preceded by 1.0, 2.0, 3.0, 3.1, NT, 95, NT 4.0, 98, 2000, ME, XP. *Why it's important: To create Vista, Microsoft supposedly rebuilt Windows from scratch, with an interesting interface, glitzier graphics, and improved security tools. However, so much computing power was required to run it that many new PCs ran more slowly than older, less powerful XP machines. Vista was also criticized for software and hardware incompatibility issues with office suites and some printers, digital cameras, and other devices. Many businesses decided that they would not upgrade from XP to Vista, because they saw no value in it and because it required buying more powerful PCs and new software. For that reason, Microsoft turned to developing Windows 7.*

Microsoft Windows XP (p. 140) Recent Microsoft operating system for PCs. *Why it's important: With this OS version, Microsoft finally gave up the last of the Windows software carried forward from the aging DOS programming technology. Windows XP was being replaced by Windows Vista but now is being replaced by Windows 7, Microsoft's newest operating system.*

Microsoft Windows 7 (2009) (p. 142) Newest operating system developed by Microsoft; it follows Vista. *Why it's important: Windows 7 is less power-hungry than Vista, boots up more quickly than previous Windows systems, and has improved networking and security features.*

multimedia authoring software (p. 176) Application software that combines text, graphics, video, animation, and sound in an integrated way to create stand-alone multimedia applications. *Why it's important: Multimedia is now commonplace. Nearly all PCs are capable of handling multimedia.*

multitasking (p. 125) Feature of OS software that allows the execution of two or more programs concurrently by one user almost at the same time on the same computer with one CPU. For instance, you might write a report on your computer with one program while another plays a music CD. *Why it's important: Multitasking allows the computer to switch rapidly back and forth among different tasks. The user is generally unaware of the switching process and thus can work in more than one application at a time.*

NetWare (p. 144) Long-popular network operating system for coordinating microcomputer-based local area networks (LANs) throughout an organization. *Why it's important: LANs allow PCs to share programs, data files, and printers and other devices.*

open-source software (p. 146) Software that any programmer can download from the internet free and modify with suggested improvements. The only qualification is that changes can't be copyrighted; they must be made available to all and remain in the public domain. *Why it's important: Because this software is not proprietary, any programmer can make improvements, which can result in better-quality software.*

operating system (OS) (p. 121) Also called *software platform*; low-level master system of programs that manage the basic operations of the computer. *Why it's important: These programs provide resource management services of many kinds. In particular, they handle the control and use of hardware resources, including disk space, memory, CPU time allocation, and peripheral devices. The operating system allows users to concentrate on their own tasks or applications rather than on the complexities of managing the computer.*

Palm OS (p. 148) Palm Source's operating system for handhelds. *Why it's important: Because it is not a Windows derivative but was specifically designed for handhelds, Palm OS is a smoother-running operating system.*

PDF *See* **portable document format.**

personal-finance manager (p. 170) Application software that lets users keep track of income and expenses, write checks, do online banking, and plan financial goals. *Why it's important: Personal-finance software can help people manage their money more effectively.*

personal information manager (PIM) (p. 166) Software that helps users keep track of and manage information they use on a daily basis, such as addresses, telephone numbers, appointments, to-do lists, and miscellaneous notes. Some programs feature phone dialers, outliners (for roughing out ideas in outline form), and ticklers (or reminders). *Why it's important: PIMs can help users better organize and manage daily business activities.*

pirated software (p. 152) Software that is obtained illegally. *Why it's important: If you buy such software, not only do the original copyright owners not get paid for their creative work but you risk getting inferior goods and, worse, picking up a virus. To discourage software piracy, many software manufacturers require that users register their software when they install it on their computers. If the software is not registered, it will not work properly.*

platform (p. 138) Particular processor model and operating system on which a computer system is based. *Why it's important: Generally, software written for one platform will not run on any other. Users should be aware that there are Mac platforms (Apple Macintosh) and Windows platforms, or "PC platforms" (for personal computers such as Dell, Compaq, Gateway, Hewlett-Packard, or IBM that run Microsoft Windows). Sometimes the latter are called* Wintel platforms, *for*

Chapter 3

186

"Windows + Intel," because they often combine the Windows operating system with the Intel processor chip.

pointer (p. 131) Indicator that usually appears as an arrow, although it changes shape depending on the application. The mouse is used to move the pointer to a particular place on the display screen or to point to little symbols, or icons. Why it's important: *Manipulating the pointer on the screen by means of the mouse is often easier than typing commands on a keyboard.*

portable document format (PDF) (p. 179) File format developed by Adobe Systems. PDF captures text, graphic, and formatting information from a variety of applications on different platforms, making it possible to send documents and have them appear on the recipient's monitor (or printer) as they were intended to be viewed. Why it's important: *A properly prepared PDF file maintains the original fonts, images, colors, and graphics, as well as the exact layout of the file. A PDF file can be shared, viewed, and printed by anyone using the free downloadable Adobe Reader software. PDF can also be used on mobile devices.*

presentation graphics software (p. 168) Software that uses graphics, animation, sound, and data or information to make visual presentations. Why it's important: *Presentation graphics software provides a means of producing sophisticated graphics.*

productivity software (p. 154) Application software such as word processing programs, spreadsheets, and database managers. Why it's important: *Productivity software makes users more productive at particular tasks.*

project management software (p. 179) Program used to plan and schedule the people, costs, and resources required to complete a project on time. Why it's important: *Project management software increases the ease and speed of planning and managing complex projects.*

public-domain software (p. 151) Software, often available on the internet, that is not protected by copyright and thus may be duplicated by anyone at will. Why it's important: *Public-domain software offers lots of software options to users who may not be able to afford much commercial software. Users may download such software from the internet free and make as many copies as they wish.*

range (p. 162) A group of adjacent cells in a spreadsheet—for example, A1 to A5. Why it's important: *Ranges help sort data for calculation or reports.*

recalculation (p. 162) The process of recomputing values in a spreadsheet, either as an ongoing process as data is entered or afterward, with the press of a key. Why it's important: *With this simple feature, the hours of mind-numbing work required to manually rework paper spreadsheets has become a thing of the past.*

relational database (p. 164) Database in which data is organized into related tables. Each table contains rows and columns; the rows are called *records,* and the columns are called

fields. An example of a record is a person's address—name, street address, city, and so on. An example of a field is that person's last name; another field would be that person's first name; a third field would be that person's street address; and so on. Why it's important: *The relational database is a common type of database.*

rentalware (p. 152) Software that users lease for a fee and download whenever they want it. Why it's important: *This is the concept behind application service providers (ASPs).*

rollover (p. 132) Icon feature in which a small textbox explaining the icon's function appears when you roll the mouse pointer over the icon. A rollover may also produce an animated graphic. Why it's important: *The rollover gives the user an immediate explanation of an icon's meaning.*

saving (p. 160) Storing, or preserving, a document as an electronic file permanently—on diskette, hard disk, or CD-ROM, for example. Why it's important: *Saving is a feature of nearly all application software. Having the document stored in electronic form spares users the tiresome chore of retyping it from scratch whenever they want to make changes. Users need only retrieve it from the storage medium and make the changes, then resave it and print it out again.*

scrolling (p. 156) Moving quickly upward, downward, or sideways through the text or other screen display. Why it's important: *A standard computer screen displays only 20–22 lines of standard-size text; however, most documents are longer than that. Using the directional arrow keys, or the mouse and a scroll bar located at the side of the screen, users can move ("scroll") through the display screen and into the text above and below it.*

shareware (p. 151) Copyrighted software that is distributed free of charge but requires that users make a monetary contribution in order to continue using it. Shareware is distributed primarily through the internet. Because it is copyrighted, you cannot use it to develop your own program that would compete with the original product. Why it's important: *Like public-domain software and freeware, shareware offers an inexpensive way to obtain new software.*

software license (p. 150) Contract by which users agree not to make copies of software to give away or resell. Why it's important: *Software manufacturers don't sell people software; they sell them licenses to become authorized users of the software.*

special-purpose keys (p. 130) Keys used to enter, delete, and edit data and to execute commands. For example, the *Esc* (for "Escape") key tells the computer to cancel an operation or leave ("escape from") the current mode of operation. The Enter, or Return, key tells the computer to execute certain commands and to start new paragraphs in a document. Why it's important: *Special-purpose keys are essential to the use of software.*

spreadsheet (p. 161) Application software that allows users to create tables and financial schedules by entering data and formulas into rows and columns arranged as a grid on a display screen. Why it's important: *When data is changed in one cell, values in other cells in the spreadsheet are automatically recalculated.*

supervisor (p. 123) Also called *kernel;* the central component of the operating system that manages the CPU. Why it's important: *The supervisor remains in main memory while the computer is running. As well as managing the CPU, it directs other nonresident programs to perform tasks that support application programs.*

system software (p. 120) The software that helps the computer perform essential operating tasks and enables the application software to run. The most important component of system software is the *operating system,* the master control program that runs the computer. Examples of operating system software for the PC are various Microsoft programs (such as Windows XP, Vista, and 7), Apple Macintosh OS X, Unix, and Linux. Why it's important: *Computers cannot run application software without having system software.*

taskbar (p. 136) Graphic toolbar that appears at the bottom of the Windows screen. Why it's important: *The taskbar presents the applications that are running.*

template (p. 158) In word processing, a preformatted document that provides basic tools for shaping a final document—the text, layout, and style for a letter, for example. Why it's important: *Templates make it very easy for users to prepare professional-looking documents, because most of the preparatory formatting is done.*

title bar (p. 136) Bar across the very top of the display window. Why it's important: *It shows the name of the folder the user is in.*

toolbar (p. 136) Bar across the top of the display window, below the menu bar. It displays menus and icons representing frequently used options or commands. Why it's important: *Toolbars make it easier to identify and execute commands.*

Unix (p. 144) Proprietary multitasking operating system for multiple users that has built-in networking capability and versions that can run on all kinds of computers. Why it's important: *Government agencies, universities, research institutions, large corporations, and banks all use Unix for everything from designing airplane parts to currency trading. Unix is also used for website management. The developers of the internet built their communication system around Unix because it has the ability to keep large systems (with hundreds of processors) churning out transactions day in and day out for years without fail.*

user interface (p. 129) User-controllable display screen that allows the user to communicate, or interact, with his or her computer. Why it's important: *The interface determines the ease of use of hardware and software. The three types of user interface are command-driven, menu-driven, and graphical (GUI), which is now the most common. Without user interfaces, no one could operate a computer system.*

utility programs (p. 127) Also known as *service programs;* system software components that perform tasks related to the control and allocation of computer resources. Why it's important: *Utility programs enhance existing functions or provide services not supplied by other system software programs. Most computers come with built-in utilities as part of the system software; they usually include backup, data recovery, virus protection, data compression, and file defragmentation, along with check (scan) disk and disk cleanup.*

value (p. 162) A number or date entered in a spreadsheet cell. Why it's important: *Values are the actual numbers used in the spreadsheet—dollars, percentages, grade points, temperatures, or whatever.*

web page design/authoring software (p. 176) Software used to create web pages with sophisticated multimedia features. Why it's important: *Allows beginners as well as professional web designers to create web pages, which have become extremely important communications tools on the internet, for all sorts of purposes.*

what-if analysis (p. 163) Spreadsheet feature that employs the recalculation feature to investigate how changing one or more numbers changes the outcome of the calculation. Why it's important: *Users can create a worksheet, putting in formulas and numbers, and then ask, "What would happen if we change that detail?"—and immediately see the effect.*

window (p. 136) Rectangular frame on the computer display screen. Through this frame users can view a file of data—such as a document, spreadsheet, or database—or an application program. Why it's important: *Using windows, users can display at the same time portions of several documents and/or programs on the screen.*

Windows Mobile *See* **Microsoft Windows Embedded.**

word processing software (p. 155) Application software that allows users to use computers to format, create, edit, print, and store text material, among other things. Why it's important: *Word processing software allows users to maneuver through a document and delete, insert, and replace text, the principal correction activities. It also offers such additional features as creating, editing, formatting, printing, and saving.*

word wrap (p. 156) Special feature that automatically continues text to the next line by "wrapping around" when the user reaches the right margin. Why it's important: *You don't have to hit a "carriage-return" key or Enter key to move to the next line.*

"I can recognize and recall information."

Self-Test Questions

1. _____ software enables the computer to perform essential operating tasks.

2. _____ _____ is the term for programs designed to perform specific tasks for the user.

3. _____ is the activity in which a computer works on more than one process at a time.

4. _____ is the scattering of portions of files about the disk in nonadjacent areas, thus greatly slowing access to the files.

5. Windows and Mac OS are generally used on _____ computers.

6. _____ is the process of loading an operating system into a computer's main memory.

7. A(n) _____ is a utility that will find all the scattered files on your hard disk and reorganize them as contiguous files.

8. The _____ is the component of system software that comprises the master system of programs that manage the basic operations of the computer.

9. The _____ is the user-controllable display screen that allows you to communicate, or interact, with your computer.

10. Disk scanner and disk cleanup utilities detect and correct certain types of common problems on hard disks, such as removing unnecessary files called _____ files that are created by Windows only for short tasks and system restore after system problems.

11. OSs allow users to control access to their computers via use of a _____ and a _____.

12. Software or hardware that is _____ means that it is privately owned and controlled by a company.

13. Linux is _____-_____ software—meaning any programmer can download it from the internet for free and modify it with suggested improvements.

14. When you power up a computer by turning on the power "on" switch, this is called a _____ boot. If your computer is already on and you restart it, this is called a _____ boot.

15. _____ software allows you to create and edit documents.

16. _____ is the activity of moving upward or downward through the text or other screen display.

17. Name four editing features offered by word processing programs: _____, _____, _____, _____.

18. In a spreadsheet, the place where a row and a column intersect is called a _____.

19. The _____ is the movable symbol on the display screen that shows you where you may next enter data or commands.

20. When you buy software, you pay for a _____, a contract by which you agree not to make copies of the software to give away or resell.

21. Records in a database are sorted according to a _____.

22. _____ involves mixing text and graphics to produce high-quality output for commercial printing.

23. A _____ allows users to create tables and do "what-if" financial analyses by entering data and formulas into rows and columns arranged as a grid on a display screen.

24. _____ automatically continues text to the next line when you reach the right margin.

25. Settings that are automatically used by a program unless the user specifies otherwise are called _____. _____.

26. _____ - _____ software is not protected by copyright and may be copied by anyone.

27. _____ _____ are specialized software programs that allow input and output devices to communicate with the rest of the computer system.

28. The _____ format allows documents to be sent to almost any platform and be opened without losing any of their characteristics (text, colors, graphics, formatting).

Multiple-Choice Questions

1. Which of the following are functions of the operating system?

   a. file management

   b. CPU management

   c. task management

   d. booting

   e. all of these

2. Which of the following was the first major microcomputer OS?

   a. Mac OS

   b. Windows

   c. DOS

   d. Unix

   e. Linux

3. Which of the following is a prominent network operating system?

   a. Linux

   b. Ubuntu

   c. Windows NT

   d. DOS

   e. Mac OS

4. Which of the following is the newest Microsoft Windows operating system?

   a. Windows Vista

   b. Windows XP

   c. Windows 7

   d. Windows NT

   e. Windows CE

5. Which of the following refers to the execution of two or more programs by one user almost at the same time on the same computer with one central processor?

   a. multitasking

   b. multiprocessing

   c. time-sharing

   d. multiprogramming

   e. coprocessing

6. Which of the following are specialized software programs that allow input and output devices to communicate with the rest of the computer system?

   a. multitasking

   b. boot-disks

   c. utility programs

   d. device drivers

   e. service packs

7. Which of the following is *not* an advantage of using database software?

   a. integrated data

   b. improved data integrity

   c. lack of structure

   d. elimination of data redundancy

8. Which of the following is *not* a feature of word processing software?

   a. spelling checker

   b. cell address

   c. formatting

   d. cut and paste

   e. find and replace

9. What is the common consumer computer interface used today?

   a. command-driven interface

   b. graphical user interface

   c. menu-driven interface

   d. electronic user interface

   e. biometric user interface

10. Which type of software can you download and duplicate without any restrictions whatsoever and without fear of legal prosecution?

    a. commercial software

    b. shareware

    c. public-domain software

    d. pirated software

    e. rentalware

True/False Questions

T F 1. The supervisor manages the CPU.

T F 2. The first graphical user interface was provided by Microsoft Windows.

T F 3. All operating systems are mutually compatible.

T F 4. *Font* refers to a preformatted document that provides basic tools for shaping the final document.

T F 5. Unix crashes often and thus is not normally used for running important large systems.

T F 6. Windows NT is the most recent Microsoft OS.

T F 7. Spreadsheet software enables you to perform what-if calculations.

T F 8. Public-domain software is protected by copyright and so is offered for sale by license only.

T F 9. The records within the various tables in a database are linked by a key field.

T F 10. QuarkXPress and Adobe InDesign are professional desktop-publishing programs.

T F 11. The best-known graphical user interface is the command-driven one.

T F 12. Microsoft PowerPoint is an example of financial software.

T F 13. Drawing programs create vector images, and painting programs produce bit-mapped images.

T F 14. General computer users can design their own web pages using Adobe Dreamweaver, Adobe Flash, and Microsoft FrontPage.

"I can recall information in my own terms and explain it to a friend."

Short-Answer Questions

1. Briefly define *booting.*

2. What is the difference between a command-driven interface and a graphical user interface (GUI)?

3. Why can't you run your computer without system software?

4. Why is multitasking useful?

5. What is a device driver?

6. What is a utility program?

7. What is a platform?

8. What are the three components of system software? What is the basic function of each?

9. What is open-source software?

10. What does defragmenting do?

11. What is an embedded system?

12. What are the following types of application software used for?
    a. project management software
    b. desktop-publishing software
    c. database software
    d. spreadsheet software
    e. word processing software

13. Which program is more sophisticated, analytical graphics or presentation graphics? Why?

14. How are the following different from one another? Pop-up menu; pull-down menu; cascading menu.

15. What is importing? Exporting?

16. Briefly compare drawing programs and painting programs.

17. Explain what computer-aided design (CAD) programs do.

18. Discuss the various software licenses: site licenses, concurrent-use licenses, multiple-user licenses, single-user license.

"I can apply what I've learned, relate these ideas to other concepts, build on other knowledge, and use all these thinking skills to form a judgment."

Knowledge in Action

1. Here's a Windows XP exercise in defragmenting your hard-disk drive. Defragmenting is a housekeeping procedure that will speed up your system and often free up hard-disk space.

   Double-click on *My Computer* on your Windows desktop (opening screen). Now use your right mouse button to click on *C drive,* then right-click on *Properties,* then left-click on the *General* tab, and you will see how much free space there is on your hard disk. Next left-click on the *Tools* tab; to clear out any errors, click the *Check Now* button; this will run a scan.

   Once the scan is complete, return to the *Tools* window and click the *Defragment Now* button. Click on *Show Details.* This will visually display on the screen the process of your files being reorganized into a contiguous order.

   Many times when your PC isn't performing well, such as when it's sluggish, running both ScanDisk (Check Now) and Defragment will solve the problem.

2. Ray Kurzweil is, among other things, the author of *The Age of Intelligent Machines; The Age of Spiritual Machines, When Computers Exceed Human Intelligence; and The Singularity Is Near: When Humans Transcend Biology.* He has said: "We are entering a new era. I call it 'the Singularity.' It's a merger between human intelligence and machine intelligence that is going to create something bigger than itself. It's the cutting edge of evolution on our planet" (*www.edge.org/3rd_culture/kurzweil_singularity/kurzweil_singularity_index.html;* accessed July 1, 2009). He envisions a future in which information technologies have advanced so far that they enable humans to transcend their biological limitations (*www.singularity.com*).

   What is "singularity"? Will it hurt? Will we hate it? Will we be able to notice it? Search the terms "Kurzweil" and "Singularity" on *www.singularity.com, www.kurzweilai.net,* and other sites, and see if you can explain the concept to friends within 5 minutes or so.

3. What do you think is the future of Linux? Experts currently disagree about whether Linux will become a serious competitor to Windows. Research Linux on the web. Which companies are creating application software to run on Linux? Which businesses are adopting Linux as an OS? What are the predictions about Linux use?

4. How do you think you will obtain software for your computer in the future? Explain your answer.

5. Design your own handheld. Draw what your ideal handheld would look like, and draw screens of what your user interface would look like. Describe the key features of your handheld.

6. What sorts of tasks do operating systems *not* do that you would like them to do?

7. If you were in the market for a new microcomputer today, what application software would you want to use on it? Why? What are some "dream" applications that you would like that have not yet been developed?

8. Several websites include libraries of shareware programs. Visit the *www.5star-shareware.com* site and identify three shareware programs that interest you. State the name of each program, the operating system it runs on, and its capabilities. Also, describe the contribution you must make to receive technical support. What about freeware? Check out *www.freewarehome.com.*

9. What is your opinion of downloading free music from the web to play on your own PC and/or CDs? Much attention has been given lately to music download-ing and copyright infringement. Research this topic in library magazines and newspapers or on the internet, and take a position in a short report.

10. How do you think you could use desktop publishing at home? For personal items? Family occasions? Holidays? What else? What hardware and software would you have to buy?

11. Think of three new ways that software companies could prevent people from pirating their software.

12. What is your favorite application software program of all? Why?

13. Did your computer come with a Windows Startup disk, and have you misplaced it? If your computer crashes, you'll need this disk to reinstall the operating system.

    To learn the benefits of having a Startup disk, visit *www.microsoft.com.* Type *startup* in the "search for" box; then click on the links that interest you.

Web Exercises

1. Go to *http://list.driverguide.com/list/company243/* and identify the drivers that correspond to equipment you use. How does this website let you know which devices the drivers are for and which operating systems are compatible with them? If you own your own com-puter, go to the manufacturer's website and locate its resource for updating drivers. Does the manufacturer recommend any driver updates that you could use?

2. Use a web search tool such as Google or Yahoo! to find some online antivirus sites—sites where users can regularly download updates for their antivirus software. Do you know what kind of antivirus software is installed on your computer?

3. Microsoft offers "patches," or updates, for its Windows OS. Go to *www.microsoft.com* and search for the list of updates. What kinds of problems do these updates fix? Do you need any?

4. The History of Operating Systems: Visit the following websites to get an overview of the evolution and his-tory of the theory and function of operating systems:

    www.microsoft.com/windows/winhistoryintro.mspx

www.computinghistorymuseum.org/teaching/papers/ research/history_of_operating_system_Moumina.pdf

www.osdata.com/kind/history.htm

www.answers.com/topic/history-of-operating-systems

5. Security Issue: Read about some security flaws and limitations of Microsoft Windows operating systems:

    www.sans.org/top20/

    www.zdnetasia.com/news/ security/0,39044215,39242898,00.htm

6. Some people are fascinated by the error message com-monly referred to as the "Blue Screen of Death" (BSOD) or "Doom." Run a search on the internet and find websites that sell T-shirts with the BSOD image on it, photo galleries of public terminals displaying the BSOD, fictional stories of BSOD attacks, and various other forms of entertainment based on the infamous error message.

    Do a search on the web to find users' hypotheses of why the BSOD occurs, and find methods to avoid it. Here are a few sites:

    www.errornerds.com/error/blue-screen-of-death.php? gclid=COL79bfTtZsCFRMUagodfAZOOw

    http://bluescreenofdeathfixer.com/

    http://bsod.org/

    http://bbspot.com/News/2000/9/bsod_death.html

7. Using Microsoft Excel or another spreadsheet program, make a food shopping list incorporating the estimated price for each item, and then have Excel calculate the overall cost. Then go buy your groceries and compare Excel's price with the supermarket's price. What else could Excel help you with?

8. The Windows operating system comes with a basic word processing program called *Wordpad.* Go to the Microsoft home page and to *http://en.wikipedia.org/ wiki/WordPad* and find out how Wordpad differs from Microsoft Word. Then use a keyword search in a search engine to get more information about these programs. Which one is right for you?

9. Curriculum Data Wales (CDW) is a public/private partnership that has been charged by the Welsh Assembly Government with the task of design-ing, building, and maintaining the National Grid for Learning Cymru as a bilingual service to schools and colleges in Wales. CDW's website includes some short tutorials on desktop-publishing (DTP), spread-sheet, word processing, and database management software:

    www.ngfl-cymru.org.uk/vtc-home/vtc-ks4-home/ vtc-ks4-ict/vtc-ks4-ict-application_software.htm

    Work through the tutorials. Did they expand your knowledge of these applications?

    Do a search for *"application software" & tutorials.* What other useful tutorials did you find?

4

HARDWARE: THE CPU & STORAGE   How to Choose a
Multimedia Computer System

Chapter Topics & Key Questions

4.1   **Microchips, Miniaturization, & Mobility**   What are the differences between transistors, integrated circuits, chips, and microprocessors?

4.2   **The System Unit: The Basics**   How is data represented in a computer, what are the components of the system cabinet, and what are processing speeds?

4.3   **More on the System Unit**   How do the processor and memory work, and what are some important ports, buses, and cards?

4.4   **Secondary Storage**   What are the features of floppy disks, hard disks, optical disks, magnetic tape, smart cards, flash memory, and online secondary storage?

4.5   **Future Developments in Processing & Storage**   What are some forthcoming developments that could affect processing power and storage capacity?

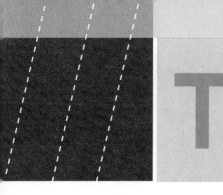

he microprocessor was "the most important invention of the 20th century," says Michael Malone, author of The Microprocessor: A Biography.[1]

Quite a bold claim, considering the incredible products that issued forth during those 100 years. More important than the airplane? More than television? More than atomic energy?

According to Malone, the case for the exalted status of this thumbnail-size information-processing device is demonstrated, first, by its pervasiveness in the important machines in our lives, from computers to transportation. Second, "The microprocessor is, intrinsically, something special," he says. "Just as [the human being] is an animal, yet transcends that state, so too the microprocessor is a silicon chip, but more." Why? Because it can be programmed to recognize and respond to patterns in the environment, as humans do. Malone writes: "Implant [a microprocessor] into a traditional machine—say an automobile engine or refrigerator—and suddenly that machine for the first time can learn, it can adapt to its environment, respond to changing conditions, become more efficient, more responsive to the unique needs of its user."[2]

4.1 MICROCHIPS, MINIATURIZATION, & MOBILITY

What are the differences between transistors, integrated circuits, chips, and microprocessors?

The microprocessor has presented us with gifts that we may only barely appreciate—*portability* and *mobility* in electronic devices.

In 1955, for instance, portability was exemplified by the ads showing a young woman holding a Zenith television set over the caption: IT DOESN'T TAKE A MUSCLE MAN TO MOVE THIS LIGHTWEIGHT TV. That "lightweight" TV weighed a hefty 45 pounds. Today, by contrast, there is a handheld Casio 2.3-inch color TV weighing a mere 6.7 ounces.

Had the transistor not arrived, as it did in 1947, the Age of Portability and consequent mobility would never have happened. To us a "portable" telephone might have meant the 40-pound backpack radio-phones carried by some American GIs during World War II, rather than the 3-ounce shirt-pocket cellular models available today.

From Vacuum Tubes to Transistors to Microchips

How do transistors and integrated circuits differ, and what does a semiconductor do?

A *circuit* is a closed path followed or capable of being followed by an electric current. Without circuits, electricity would not be controllable, and so we would not have electric or electronic appliances. Old-time radios used vacuum tubes—small lightbulb-size electronic tubes with glowing filaments, or wire circuits, inside them—to facilitate the transmission (flow) of electrons.

One computer with these tubes, the ENIAC, was switched on in 1946 at the University of Pennsylvania and employed about 18,000 of them. Unfortunately, a tube failure occurred on average once every 7 minutes. Since it took more than 15 minutes to find and replace the faulty tube, it was difficult to get any useful computing work done—during a typical week, ENIAC was down for about one-third of the time. Moreover, the ENIAC was enormous, occupying

1,800 square feet and weighing more than 30 tons. ENIAC could perform about 5,000 calculations per second—more than 10,000 times *slower* than modern PCs. Yet even at that relatively slow speed, ENIAC took about 20 seconds to complete a problem that had taken experts 1 or 2 days to complete manually.

THE TRANSISTOR ARRIVES The transistor changed all that. **A _transistor_ is essentially a tiny electrically operated switch, or gate, that can alternate between "on" and "off" many millions of times per second.** The transistor was developed by Bell Labs in 1947. The first transistors were one-hundredth the size of a vacuum tube, needed no warm-up time, consumed less energy, and were faster and more reliable. (● *See Panel 4.1.*) Moreover, they marked the beginning of a process of miniaturization that has not ended yet. In 1960 one transistor fit into an area about a half-centimeter square. This was sufficient to permit Zenith, for instance, to market a transistor radio weighing about 1 pound (convenient, the company advertised, for "pocket or purse"). Today more than 6 million transistors can be squeezed into a centimeter, and a Sony headset radio, for example, weighs only 4.3 ounces. Hewlett-Packard is working on a transistor about 0.1 nanometer square. One nanometer is 1 billionth of a meter; a human hair is about 80,000 nanometers thick.

In the old days, transistors were made individually and then formed into an electronic circuit with the use of wires and solder. Today transistors are part of an **_integrated circuit_—an entire electronic circuit, including wires, formed on a single "chip," or piece, of special material, usually silicon,** as part of a single manufacturing process. Integrated circuits were developed by Jack Kilby at Texas Instruments, who demonstrated the first one in 1958. (● *See the timeline, Panel 4.2, next page.*)

An integrated circuit embodies what is called solid-state technology. **In a _solid-state device_, the electrons travel through solid material**—in this case, silicon. They do not travel through a vacuum, as was the case with the old radio vacuum tubes.

SILICON & SEMICONDUCTORS What is silicon, and why use it? **_Silicon_ is an element that is widely found in clay and sand. It is used not only because its abundance makes it cheap but also because it is a semiconductor.**

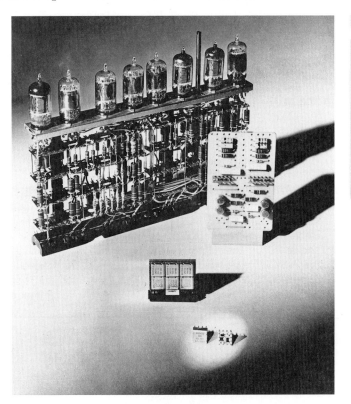

panel 4.1

Shrinking components
The lightbulb-size 1940s vacuum tube was replaced in the 1950s by a transistor one-hundredth its size. Today's transistors are much smaller, being microscopic in size.

A _semiconductor_ **is a material whose electrical properties are intermediate between a good conductor of electricity and a nonconductor of electricity.** (An example of a good conductor of electricity is the copper in household wiring; an example of a nonconductor is the plastic sheath around that wiring.) Because it is only a semiconductor, silicon has partial resistance to electricity. As a result, highly conducting materials can be overlaid on the silicon to create the electronic circuitry of the integrated circuit. (● _See Panel 4.3._)

Silicon alone has no processing power. **A _chip_, or _microchip_, is a tiny piece of silicon that contains millions of microminiature integrated electronic circuits.** Chip manufacture requires very clean environments, which is why chip manufacturing workers appear to be dressed for a surgical operation. Such workers must also be highly skilled, which is why chip makers are not found everywhere in the world.

Modern chip with etched transistors. This chip would be about 1/2 inch by 1/2 inch and be several layers deep, with transistors etched on each level.

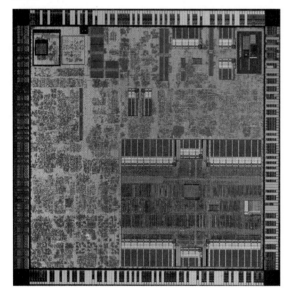

Miniaturization Miracles: Microchips, Microprocessors, & Micromachines

What is a microprocessor?

Microchips—"industrial rice," as the Japanese call them— are responsible for the miniaturization that has revolutionized consumer electronics, computers, and communications. They store and process data in all the electronic gadgetry we've become accustomed to—from microwave ovens to videogame controllers to music synthesizers to cameras to automobile fuel-injection systems to pagers to satellites.

There are different kinds of microchips—for example, microprocessor, memory, logic, communications, graphics, and math coprocessor chips. We discuss some of these later in this chapter. Perhaps the most important is the microprocessor chip. **A _microprocessor_ ("microscopic processor" or "processor on a chip") is the miniaturized circuitry of a computer processor—the CPU, the part that processes, or manipulates, data into information.** When modified for use in machines other than computers, microprocessors are called _microcontrollers_ or _embedded computers_.

Mobility

How have microprocessors helped make information technology more mobile?

Smallness in TVs, phones, radios, camcorders, CD players, and computers is now largely taken for granted. In the 1980s, portability, or mobility,

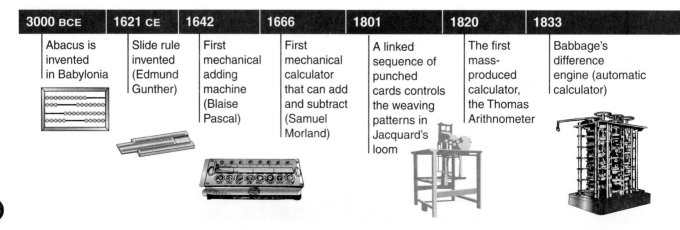

3000 BCE	1621 CE	1642	1666	1801	1820	1833
Abacus is invented in Babylonia	Slide rule invented (Edmund Gunther)	First mechanical adding machine (Blaise Pascal)	First mechanical calculator that can add and subtract (Samuel Morland)	A linked sequence of punched cards controls the weaving patterns in Jacquard's loom	The first mass-produced calculator, the Thomas Arithnometer	Babbage's difference engine (automatic calculator)

1. A large drawing of the electrical circuitry is made; it looks something like the map of a train yard. The drawing is photographically reduced hundreds of times, to microscopic size.

2. That reduced photograph is then duplicated many times so that, like a sheet of postage stamps, there are multiple copies of the same image or circuit.

3. That sheet of multiple copies of the circuit is then printed (in a printing process called *photolithography*) and etched onto a round slice of silicon called a *wafer*. Wafers have gone from 4 inches in diameter to 6 inches to 8 inches, and now are moving toward 12 inches; this allows semiconductor manufacturers to produce more chips at lower cost.

4. Subsequent printings of layer after layer of additional circuits produce multilayered and interconnected electronic circuitry built above and below the original silicon surface.

5. Later an automated die-cutting machine cuts the wafer into separate *chips,* which are usually less than 1 centimeter square and about half a millimeter thick. A *chip,* or microchip, is a tiny piece of silicon that contains millions of microminiature electronic circuit components, mainly transistors. An 8-inch silicon wafer will have a grid of nearly 300 chips, each with as many as 5.5 million transistors.

6. After testing, each chip is mounted in a protective frame with protruding metallic pins that provide electrical connections through wires to a computer or other electronic device.

Chip designers checking out an enlarged drawing of chip circuits

(above) Pentium 4 microprocessor chip mounted in protective frame with pins that can be connected to an electronic device such as a microcomputer.

A wafer imprinted with many microprocessors.

panel 4.3

Making of a chip
How microscopic circuitry is put onto silicon.

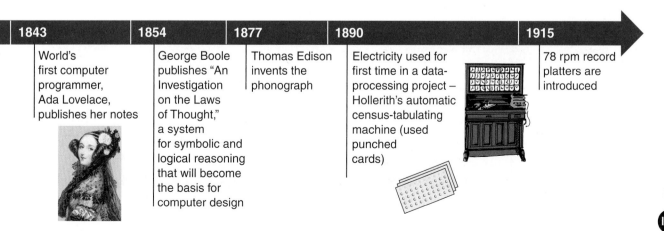

1843	1854	1877	1890	1915
World's first computer programmer, Ada Lovelace, publishes her notes	George Boole publishes "An Investigation on the Laws of Thought," a system for symbolic and logical reasoning that will become the basis for computer design	Thomas Edison invents the phonograph	Electricity used for first time in a data-processing project – Hollerith's automatic census-tabulating machine (used punched cards)	78 rpm record platters are introduced

meant trading off computing power and convenience in return for smaller size and less weight. Today, however, we are getting close to the point where we don't have to give up anything. As a result, experts have predicted that small, powerful, wireless personal electronic devices will transform our lives far more than the personal computer has done so far. "The new generation of machines will be truly personal computers, designed for our mobile lives," wrote one reporter back in 1992. "We will read office memos between strokes on the golf course, and answer messages from our children in the middle of business meetings."[3] Today, of course, such activities are commonplace.

Choosing an Inexpensive Personal Computer: Understanding Computer Ads

What kind of features does a multimedia personal computer have?

You're in the market for a new PC and are studying the ads. What does "1 GB DDR SDRAM" mean? How about "160 GB SATA 7200 RPM Hard Drive"? Let's see how to interpret a typical computer ad. (● *See Panel 4.4.*)

Most desktop computers are *multimedia computers*, with sound and graphics capability. As we explained in Chapter 1, the word *multimedia* means "combination of media"—the combination of pictures, video, animation, and sound in addition to text. A multimedia computer features such equipment as a fast processor, DVD drive, sound card, graphics card, and speakers; and you may also wish to have headphones and a microphone. (Common peripherals are printer, scanner, sound recorder, and digital camera.)

Let us now go through the parts of a computer system so that you can understand what you're doing when you buy a new computer. First we look at how the system processes data. In the remainder of this chapter, we will consider the *system unit* and *storage devices*. In Chapter 5, we look at *input devices* and *output devices*.

4.2 THE SYSTEM UNIT: The Basics

How is data represented in a computer, what are the components of the system cabinet, and what are processing speeds?

Computers run on electricity. What is the most fundamental thing you can say about electricity? Electricity is either *on* or *off*. This two-state situation allows computers to use the binary system to represent data and programs.

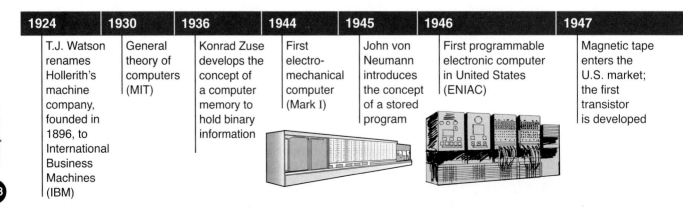

1924	1930	1936	1944	1945	1946	1947
T.J. Watson renames Hollerith's machine company, founded in 1896, to International Business Machines (IBM)	General theory of computers (MIT)	Konrad Zuse develops the concept of a computer memory to hold binary information	First electro-mechanical computer (Mark I)	John von Neumann introduces the concept of a stored program	First programmable electronic computer in United States (ENIAC)	Magnetic tape enters the U.S. market; the first transistor is developed

Great PC BUY!

- 7-Bay Mid-Tower Case
- Intel Pentium Dual-Core Processor 2.80 GHz
- 2 GB DDR2 SDRAM
- 3 MB L2 Cache
- 6 USB 2.0 Ports
- 256 MB DDR2 Nvidia GeForce PCI Graphics
- Sound Blaster Digital Sound Card
- 56 Kbps Internal Modem
- 320 GB SATA 7200 RPM Hard Drive
- 24X DVD/CD-RW Combo Drive
- Full-Sized Keyboard with Numeric Keypad
- Microsoft IntelliMouse
- 17" Flat Panel Display
- HP Officejet Pro K5400

Details of this ad are explained throughout this chapter and the next. See the little magnifying glass:

panel 4.4

Advertisement for a PC

The terminology in microcomputer ads generally does not change as quickly as the numbers; users will continue to need most of these components for a while, but the speeds and capacities change quickly, as do methods of connection.

The Binary System: Using On/Off Electrical States to Represent Data & Instructions

What does a computer's binary system do, and what are some binary coding schemes?

The decimal system that we are accustomed to has 10 digits (0, 1, 2, 3, 4, 5, 6, 7, 8, 9). By contrast, the **binary system** **has only two digits: 0 and 1.** Thus, in the computer, the 0 can be represented by the electrical current being off and the 1 by the current being on. Although the use of binary systems is not restricted to computers, *all data and program instructions that go into the computer are represented in terms of these binary numbers. (● See Panel 4.5.)*

For example, the letter "G" is a translation of the electronic signal 01000111, or off-on-off-off-off-on-on-on. When you press the key for "G" on the computer keyboard, the character is automatically converted into the series of electronic impulses that the computer can recognize. Inside the computer, the character "G" is represented by a combination of eight *transistors* (as we will describe). Some are off, or closed (representing the 0s), and some are on, or open (representing the 1s).

1947–1948	1949	1952	1954	1956	1958	1962	1963
Magnetic drum memory is introduced as a data storage device for computers	45 rpm record platters are introduced	UNIVAC computer correctly predicts election of Eisenhower as U.S. President	Texas Instruments introduces the silicon transistor	First computer hard disk is used	Stereo records are produced	Integrated circuit is nicknamed the "chip"; timesharing becomes common	The American National Standards Institute accepts ASCII-7 code for information exchange

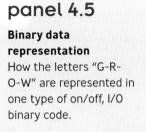

panel 4.5

Binary data representation
How the letters "G-R-O-W" are represented in one type of on/off, I/O binary code.

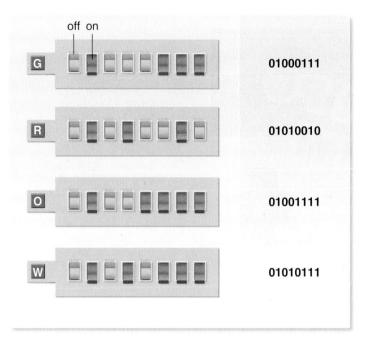

off on

G   01000111

R   01010010

O   01001111

W   01010111

MEASURING CAPACITY How many representations of 0s and 1s can be held in a computer or a storage device such as a hard disk? Capacity is denoted by *bits* and *bytes* and multiples thereof:

- **Bit:** In the binary system, **each 0 or 1 is called a _bit_, which is short for "binary digit."**

- **Byte:** To represent letters, numbers, or special characters (such as ! or *), bits are combined into groups. **A group of 8 bits is called a _byte_, and a byte represents one character, digit, or other value.** (As we mentioned, in one scheme, 01000111 represents the letter "G.") The capacity of a computer's memory or of a floppy disk is expressed in numbers of bytes or multiples such as kilobytes and megabytes. (There are 256 combinations of 8 bits available: 28 = 256.)

- **Kilobyte:** A _kilobyte (K, KB)_ **is about 1,000 bytes.** (Actually, it's precisely 1,024 bytes, but the figure is commonly rounded.) The kilobyte was a common unit of measure for memory or secondary storage capacity on older computers. 1 KB equals about one-half page of text.

- **Megabyte:** A _megabyte (M, MB)_ **is about 1 million bytes** (1,048,576 bytes). Measures of microcomputer primary storage capacity today are expressed in megabytes. 1 MB equals about 500 pages of text.

- **Gigabyte:** A _gigabyte (G, GB)_ **is about 1 billion bytes** (1,073,741,824 bytes). This measure was formerly used mainly with "big iron"

1964	1965	1968	1969	1970
IBM introduces 360 line of computers; IBM's seven-year long Sabre project, allowing travel agents anywhere to make airline reservations via terminals, is fully implemented; Control Data Corp.'s CDC 6600, designed by Seymour Cray, becomes the first commercially successful supercomputer	Audio cassette tape introduced; Gordon Moore pronounces "Moore's Law"	Robert Noyce, Andy Grove, and Gordon Moore establish Intel, Inc.	Klass Compaan conceives idea for CD	Microprocessor chips come into use; floppy disk introduced for storing data; a chip ¹/₁₀ inches square contains 1,000 transistors; the first and only patent on the smart card is filed

(mainframe) computers, but it is typical of the secondary storage (hard-disk) capacity of today's microcomputers. One gigabyte equals about 500,000 pages of text.

- **Terabyte:** A _terabyte (T, TB)_ **represents about 1 trillion bytes** (1,009,511,627,776 bytes). 1 TB equals about 500,000,000 pages of text. Some high-capacity disk storage is expressed in terabytes.

- **Petabyte:** A _petabyte (P, PB)_ **represents about 1 quadrillion bytes** (1,048,576 gigabytes). The huge storage capacities of modern databases are now expressed in petabytes.

- **Exabyte:** An _exabyte (EB)_ **represents about 1 quintillion bytes**—that's _1 billion billion_ bytes (1,024 petabytes—or 1,152,921,504,606,846,976 bytes). This number is seldom used. It is estimated that all the printed material in the world represents about 5 exabytes.[4]

BINARY CODING SCHEMES Letters, numbers, and special characters are represented within a computer system by means of binary coding schemes. (● _See Panel 4.6._) That is, the off/on 0s and 1s are arranged in such a way that they can be made to represent characters, digits, or other values.

- **EBCDIC:** Pronounced "_eb_-see-dick," **EBCDIC (Extended Binary Coded Decimal Interchange Code) is a binary code used with large**

Bigger Than an Exabyte?

How big is a zettabyte? A yottabyte? Do an online search to find out.

Survival Tip

Decimal to Binary Conversion

Use the Windows Calculator for quick decimal to binary conversions. Open Windows Calculator by choosing _Start, All programs, Accessories, Calculator._ Or you could just go to _Start, Run, Calc._ When the calculator opens, choose _View, Scientific._ This will change your calculator interface from a standard calculator to a scientific calculator. Type in your number, and click the circle that says _BIN._ Also, while having the calculator on the Bin setting, you can type in any combination of 0s and 1s and convert them to decimal form by clicking on the _DEC_ circle.

Character	EBCDIC	ASCII-8	Character	EBCDIC	ASCII-8
A	1100 0001	0100 0001	N	1101 0101	0100 1110
B	1100 0010	0100 0010	O	1101 0110	0100 1111
C	1100 0011	0100 0011	P	1101 0111	0101 0000
D	1100 0100	0100 0100	Q	1101 1000	0101 0001
E	1100 0101	0100 0101	R	1101 1001	0101 0010
F	1100 0110	0100 0110	S	1110 0010	0101 0011
G	1100 0111	0100 0111	T	1110 0011	0101 0100
H	1100 1000	0100 1000	U	1110 0100	0101 0101
I	1100 1001	0100 1001	V	1110 0101	0101 0110
J	1101 0001	0100 1010	W	1110 0110	0101 0111
K	1101 0010	0100 1011	X	1110 0111	0101 1000
L	1101 0011	0100 1100	Y	1110 1000	0101 1001
M	1101 0100	0100 1101	Z	1110 1001	0101 1010
0	1111 0000	0011 0000	5	1111 0101	0011 0101
1	1111 0001	0011 0001	6	1111 0110	0011 0110
2	1111 0010	0011 0010	7	1111 0111	0011 0111
3	1111 0011	0011 0011	8	1111 1000	0011 1000
4	1111 0100	0011 0100	9	1111 1001	0011 1001
!	0101 1010	0010 0001	;	0101 1110	0011 1011

panel 4.6

Binary coding schemes: ASCII and EBCDIC

1971	1972	1973	1974	1975	1976	1978
First pocket calculator; the Intel 4004 microprocessor is developed—a "computer on a chip"	Intel 8008 8-bit microprocessor	Large-scale integration: 10,000 components are placed on a 1-sq.-cm. chip	A DRAM chip becomes available	First microcomputer (MITS Altair 8800)	Apple I computer (first personal computer sold in assembled form); has 512 KB RAM	5¼" floppy disk; Atari home videogame; Intel's first 16-bit microprocessor, the 8086, debuts

computers, such as mainframes. It was deveoped in 1963–1964 by IBM and uses 8 bits (1 byte) for each character.

- **ASCII:** Pronounced "*ask*-ee," **_ASCII (American Standard Code for Information Interchange)_ is the binary code most widely used with microcomputers.** Depending on the version, ASCII uses 7 or 8 bits (1 byte) for each character. Besides having the more conventional characters, the version known as Extended ASCII includes such characters as math symbols and Greek letters. ASCII's 256 characters, however, are not enough to handle such languages as Chinese and Japanese, with their thousands of characters.

- **Unicode:** Developed in the early 1990s, **_Unicode_ uses 2 bytes (16 bits) for each character, rather than 1 byte (8 bits).** Instead of having the 256 character combinations of ASCII, Unicode can handle 65,536 character combinations. Thus, it allows almost all the written languages of the world to be represented using a single character set.

Machine Language

How would I define machine language?

Every brand of computer has its own binary language, called *machine language.* **_Machine language_ is a binary-type programming language built into the CPU that the computer can run directly.** The machine language is specific to the particular CPU model; this is why, for example, software written for a Macintosh will not run on a Dell PC. To most people, an instruction written in machine language, consisting only of 0s and 1s, is incomprehensible. To the computer, however, the 0s and 1s represent precise storage locations and operations.

How do people-comprehensible program instructions become computer-comprehensible machine language? Special system programs called *language translators* rapidly convert the instructions into machine language. This translating occurs virtually instantaneously, so you are not aware it is happening.

Because the type of computer you will most likely be working with is the microcomputer, we'll now take a look at what's inside the microcomputer's system unit.

The Computer Case: Bays, Buttons, & Boards

What is a bay used for?

The *system unit* houses the motherboard (including the processor chip and memory chips), the power supply, and storage devices. (● *See Panel 4.7.*) In computer ads, the part of the system unit that is the empty box with just the power supply is called the *case* or *system cabinet.*

For today's desktop PC, the system unit may be advertised as something like a "4-bay mini-tower case" or an "8-bay mid-tower case." **A _bay_ is a shelf**

1979	1981	1982	1983	1984	1985
Motorola introduces the 68000 chip, which later will support the Mac	IBM introduces personal computer (with 8088 CPU and 16 KB RAM)	Portable computers 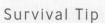	The capacity of floppy disks is expanded to 360 KB; CDs are introduced to U.S. market	Apple Macintosh; first personal laser printer; Sony and Philips introduce the CD-ROM; Intel's 80286 chip is released	Intel's 80386 32-bit micro-processor is introduced

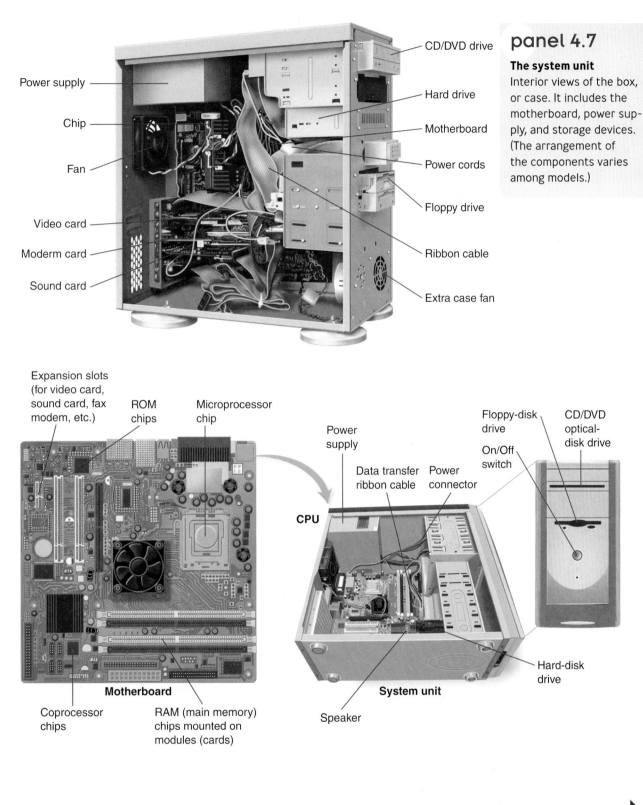

panel 4.7

The system unit
Interior views of the box, or case. It includes the motherboard, power supply, and storage devices. (The arrangement of the components varies among models.)

Power supply

Chip

Fan

Video card

Moderm card

Sound card

CD/DVD drive

Hard drive

Motherboard

Power cords

Floppy drive

Ribbon cable

Extra case fan

Expansion slots (for video card, sound card, fax modem, etc.)

ROM chips

Microprocessor chip

Coprocessor chips

RAM (main memory) chips mounted on modules (cards)

Motherboard

Power supply

Data transfer ribbon cable

Power connector

CPU

Floppy-disk drive

On/Off switch

CD/DVD optical-disk drive

Hard-disk drive

Speaker

System unit

1986	1988	1989	1990
The 3½" diskette is introduced for the Mac and becomes popular for the PC as well	Motorola's 32-bit 88000 series of RISC microprocessors is introduced	Double-sided, double-density floppy disks come on the market, increasing the 5¼" diskette to 1.2 MB and the 3½" diskette to 1.4 MB; Intel's 80486 chip with 1.2 million transistors is introduced; first portable Mac	Motorola's 68040 and Intel's 1486 chips are released

A line from the PC ad on page 199

7-Bay Mid-Tower Case

or an opening used for the installation of electronic equipment, generally storage devices such as a hard drive or DVD drive. A computer may come equipped with four to eight bays. Empty bays are covered by a panel.

A *tower* is a cabinet that is tall, narrow, and deep (so that it can sit on the floor beside or under a table) rather than short, wide, and deep. Originally a tower (full tower) was considered to be 24 inches high. Mini- (micro) and mid-towers may be less than half that size. At 6.5 inches square and 2 inches high, the Mac mini (Chapter 1, p. 23) is the smallest desktop microcomputer.

The number of buttons on the outside of the computer case will vary, but the on/off power switch will appear somewhere, probably on the front. There may also be a "sleep" switch; this allows you to suspend operations without terminating them, so that you can conserve electrical power without the need for subsequently "rebooting," or restarting, the computer.

Inside the case—not visible unless you remove the cabinet—are various electrical circuit boards, chief of which is the motherboard, as we'll discuss.

Power Supply

What does a computer's power supply do?

The electricity available from a standard wall outlet is alternating current (AC), but a microcomputer runs on direct current (DC). **The _power supply_ is a device that converts AC to DC to run the computer.** The on/off switch in your computer turns on or shuts off the electricity to the power supply. Because electricity can generate a lot of heat, a fan inside the computer keeps the power supply and other components from becoming too hot.

Electrical power drawn from a standard AC outlet can be quite uneven. For example, a sudden surge, or "spike," in AC voltage can burn out the low-voltage DC circuitry in your computer ("fry the motherboard"). Instead of plugging your computer directly into a wall electrical outlet, it's a good idea to plug it into a power protection device. The three principal types are surge protectors, voltage regulators, and UPS units:

SURGE PROTECTOR A *surge protector,* or *surge suppressor,* is a device that protects a computer from being damaged by surges (spikes) of high voltage. The computer is plugged into the surge protector, which in turn is plugged into a standard electrical outlet. (*See the Practical Action box on page 205.*)

VOLTAGE REGULATOR A *voltage regulator,* or line conditioner, is a device that protects a computer from being damaged by insufficient power—"brownouts" or "sags" in voltage. Brownouts can occur when a large machine such as a power tool starts up and

Surge protector

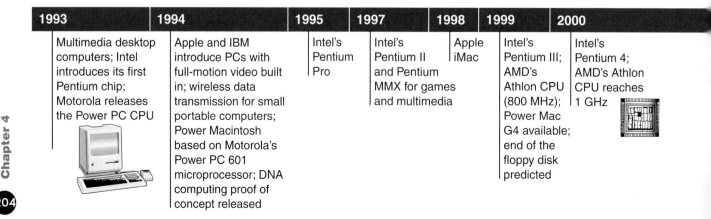

1993	1994	1995	1997	1998	1999	2000
Multimedia desktop computers; Intel introduces its first Pentium chip; Motorola releases the Power PC CPU	Apple and IBM introduce PCs with full-motion video built in; wireless data transmission for small portable computers; Power Macintosh based on Motorola's Power PC 601 microprocessor; DNA computing proof of concept released	Intel's Pentium Pro	Intel's Pentium II and Pentium MMX for games and multimedia	Apple iMac	Intel's Pentium III; AMD's Athlon CPU (800 MHz); Power Mac G4 available; end of the floppy disk predicted	Intel's Pentium 4; AMD's Athlon CPU reaches 1 GHz

PRACTICAL ACTION

Power Issues: Problems with Electrical Power to Your Computer

Ben Veligdan, a Brooklyn, New York, music teacher, wondered why his monthly electric bill exceeded $100 a month when his household consisted only of himself, his wife, and his cat. Then he looked around his modest one-bedroom apartment and thought, Could it be the computer? When he decided to unplug it while sleeping or not working, his electric bill fell almost immediately.[5]

You need power to run your computer, of course, but electricity can be very problematic: Leaving a computer turned on all the time is expensive. Having a computer on your thighs can quickly become hot and uncomfortable. Sudden power surges can devastate your hardware. Sudden power drops can wipe out your data.

Here are a few things you can do to deal with these problems:

- *To reduce your electricity bill, turn off your computer when you're not using it:* It's not just your computer. Many electronic gadgets—cellphone chargers, microwave ovens, and so on—suck electricity when they're not being used (it's called a "phantom" load). Indeed, it amounts to 5%–10% every year in American homes.[6] Leaving PCs on overnight costs U.S. companies $2.8 billion a year.[7] Devices are coming to market that can detect when an appliance is in standby mode (not working).[8] But the best thing you can do is to plug your computer into some variant of a power strip (discussed below), so that you can turn off the on-off switch when your PC is not in use.

- *If a laptop's heat on your thighs is uncomfortable, put it on a "cool tray" with fan:* A computer on your lap can generate heat that can quickly make you uncomfortable. Some companies now offer pads and so-called cool trays ($30–$50) with fans that you can slide under your laptop and can cool off both the machine and your lap. Devices are marketed by Logitech, Belkin, Kensington, and Microsoft.[9]

- *Back up data regularly:* You should faithfully make backup (duplicate) copies of your data every few minutes as you're working. Then, if your computer has power

problems, you'll be able to get back in business fairly quickly once the machine is running again.

- *Use a surge protector to protect against too much electricity:* Plug all your hardware into a surge protector (suppressor), which will prevent damage to your equipment if there is a power surge. (You'll know you've experienced a power surge when the lights in the room suddenly get very bright.) Surge protectors cost $10–$35.

- *Use a voltage regulator to protect against too little electricity:* Plug your computer into a voltage regulator (line conditioner) to adjust for power sags or brownouts. If power is too low for too long, it's as though the computer had been turned off.

- *Consider using a UPS to protect against complete absence of electricity:* Consider plugging your computer into a UPS, or uninterruptible power supply (available at electronics stores for $35–$200). The UPS is kind of a short-term battery that, when the power fails, will keep your computer running long enough (5–30 minutes) for you to save your data before you turn off the machine. It also acts as a surge protector.

- *Turn ON highest-power-consuming hardware first:* When you turn on your computer system, you should turn on the devices that use the most power first. This will avoid causing a power drain on smaller devices. The most common advice is to turn on (1) printer, (2) other external peripherals, (3) system unit, (4) monitor—in that order.

- *Turn OFF lowest-power-consuming hardware first:* When you turn off your system, follow the reverse order. This avoids a power surge to the smaller devices.

- *Unplug your computer system during lightning storms:* Unplug all your system's components—including phone lines—during thunder and lightning storms. If lightning strikes your house or the power lines, it can ruin your equipment.

2001	2002	2003	2004	2005	2006
Pentium 4 reaches 2 GHz; USB 2.0 is introduced	Pentium 4 reaches 3.06 GHz; Power Mac has 2 1-GHz Power PC CPUs; about 1 billion PCs have been shipped worldwide since the mid-70s	Intel's Pentium M/Centrino for mobile computing; 64-bit processors	Intel Express chipsets for built-in sound and video capabilities (no cards needed); IBM sells its PC computing division to Lenovo Group	Perpendicular recording for disk drives	Intel and AMD introduce dual-core processors; 64-bit processors enter the market

causes the lights in your house to dim. They also may occur on very hot summer days when the power company has to lower the voltage in an area because too many people are running their air conditioners all at once.

UPS A *UPS (uninterruptible power supply)* is a battery-operated device that provides a computer with electricity if there is a power failure. The UPS will keep a computer going for 5–30 minutes or more. It goes into operation as soon as the power to your computer fails.

Power supply units are usually rated in *joules,* named after a 19th-century English physicist. The higher the number of joules, the better the power protection. (One hundred joules of energy keep a 100-watt light going for 1 second.)

UPS

The Motherboard & the Microprocessor Chip

How is the motherboard important, and what are types of processor chips?

As we mentioned in Chapter 1, the *motherboard,* or *system board,* is the main circuit board in the system unit. The motherboard consists of a flat board that fills one side of the case. It contains both soldered, nonremovable components and sockets or slots for components that can be removed—microprocessor chip, RAM chips, and various expansion cards, as we explain later. (● *See Panel 4.8, next page.*)

Making some components removable allows you to expand or upgrade your system. **_Expansion_ is a way of increasing a computer's capabilities by adding hardware to perform tasks that are beyond the scope of the basic system.** For example, you might want to add video and sound cards. **_Upgrading_ means changing to newer, usually more powerful or sophisticated versions,** such as a more powerful microprocessor or more memory chips.

THE MICROPROCESSOR CHIP The motherboard may be thought of as your computer's central nervous system. The brain of your computer is the microprocessor chip. As we described in Chapter 1, a *microprocessor* is the miniaturized circuitry of a computer processor, contained on a small silicon chip. It stores program instructions that process, or manipulate, data into information.

processors

modem card in slot

data transfer ribbon

CPU

fan

Mac motherboard

expansion slots

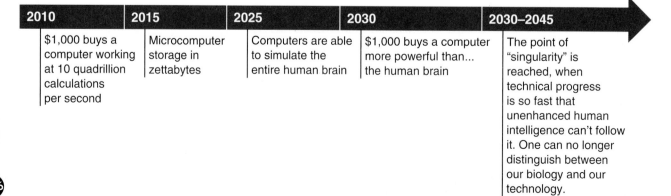

2010	2015	2025	2030	2030–2045
$1,000 buys a computer working at 10 quadrillion calculations per second	Microcomputer storage in zettabytes	Computers are able to simulate the entire human brain	$1,000 buys a computer more powerful than... the human brain	The point of "singularity" is reached, when technical progress is so fast that unenhanced human intelligence can't follow it. One can no longer distinguish between our biology and our technology.

RAM (main memory) chips mounted on modules (cards)

Cards in expansion slots

Microprocessor chip (with CPU)

panel 4.8

The motherboard
This main board offers slots or sockets for removable components: microprocessor chip, RAM chips, and various expansion cards.

- **Transistors—key parts of a chip:** The key parts of the microprocessor are transistors. *Transistors,* we said, are tiny electronic devices that act as on/off switches, which process the on/off (1/0) bits used to represent data. According to *Moore's law,* named for legendary Intel cofounder Gordon Moore, the number of transistors that can be packed onto a chip doubles about every 18 months, while the price stays the same, which has enabled the industry to shrink the size and cost of things such as computers and cellphones while improving their performance. In 1961 a chip had only 4 transistors. In 1971 it had 2,300; in 1979 it had 30,000; and in 1997 it had 7.5 million. In 2008, Intel announced a new Itanium chip with 2 billion transistors.[10]

- **The chipset—chips for controlling information among system components:** **The _chipset_ consists of groups of interconnected chips on the motherboard that control the flow of information between the microprocessor and other system components connected to the motherboard.** The chipset determines what types of processors, memory, and video card ports will work on the same motherboard. It also establishes the types of multimedia, storage, network, and other hardware the motherboard supports.

TRADITIONAL MICROCOMPUTER MICROPROCESSORS Most personal computers in use today have one of two types of microprocessors— one for the PC, one for the Macintosh. The leading chip makers have been Intel, AMD, IBM, and Motorola/Freescale.

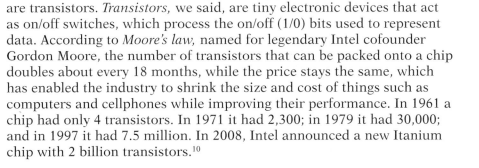

Intel Pentium Dual-Core Processor 2.80 GHz

- **Intel-type processors for PCs—Intel and AMD chips:** Most PCs use CPUs manufactured by Intel Corporation or Advanced Micro Devices (AMD). Indeed, the Microsoft Windows operating system was designed to run on Intel chips. **_Intel-type chips_ have a similar internal design and are made to run PCs.** They are used by manufacturers such as Dell and Hewlett-Packard in their PC microcomputers.

  Since 1993, Intel has marketed its chips under such names as "Pentium," "Pentium Pro," "Pentium II," and "Pentium III." New computers usually have a "Pentium 4" (P4), "Celeron," "Xeon," or "Itanium" processor. Less expensive PCs use Pentium or Celeron processors; workstations and low-end servers use Xeon or Itanium

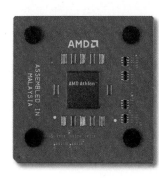

Dell Inspiron Mini 9 netbook

processors. AMD's Opteron processors compete with Intel's Xeon and Itanium families, and its Athlon processors compete with Intel's Pentium and Celeron families. In 2008, Intel introduced a line of chips dubbed Atom, for use in so-called nettops and netbooks, Intel's terms for low-priced desktop ($200–$300) and notebook ($200–$350) computers. AMD announced Puma as a new chip to help the company maintain its share in the laptop market.[11]

- **Motorola/Freescale and IBM processors for Macintoshes:** Apple computers have used a design different from Intel-type processors. For many years, ***Motorola-type chips* were made by Motorola and later its subsidiary Freescale Semiconductor for Apple Macintosh computers up to and including the Apple Mac G4.** PowerMac G5 Macintoshes used the PowerPC family of processors, which were originally developed in a cooperative effort by Apple, Freescale, and IBM. Apple MacBooks use Intel Core 2 Duo processors, and the Mac Pros use Quad Core Intel Xeon processors.

Motorola processor

RECENT MICROCOMPUTER MICROPROCESSORS Some recent developments in chips have had significant effects:

- **Intel processors for Macintoshes:** In mid-2005, Apple announced that it would end its current line of products based on PowerPC chips from IBM and Freescale and would switch its machines to Intel chips. Although risky for Apple, the advantage of this major switch is that an Intel processor gives Mac users access to the vast array of Windows-based games and programs (at least those users who are willing to run a Windows OS as well as Mac OS on their systems). This appeals to Windows users who are attracted to Apple's designs but have stayed away from Macs because they didn't run Windows programs.[12]

Even Windows users benefit, suggests well-known technology journalist Walter Mossberg, because, as the most innovative major computer maker, Apple's impact on the industry is vastly greater than its market share. "Almost everything it does is later copied by the Windows PC makers," he points out, "so keeping Apple strong and innovating is good for Windows users, too."[13]

- **Multicore processors for PCs—dual core and quadcore:** "You'll be typing along on an email when suddenly the PC stops responding to your keystrokes, then catches up a few seconds later," wrote *BusinessWeek*'s Stephen Wildstrom. "Or a program that used to load in a few seconds inexplicably takes three times as long. Processors are faster than ever, but the demands of even routine computing are overwhelming them."[14]

The reason computers bog down is that, as Wildstrom explained, "no matter how fast a processor runs, it can do only one thing at a time." Adding more transistors doesn't help, because they generate too much heat. Enter a new kind of microcomputer chip—**the *multicore processor*, designed to let the operating system divide the work over more than one processor, with two or more processor "cores" on a single piece of silicon.**

The concept is not new; large computer systems, such as IBM's Blue Gene/L supercomputer, have featured as many as 65,000 processors working in unison.[15] But the beauty of having two or more cores is that chips can take on several tasks at once, eliminating the annoying pauses that Wildstrom mentioned.

For desktop personal computers, Intel offers a Pentium Dual-Core, a Core 2 Duo, a Core 2 Extreme, and a Core 2 Quad (four processors). AMD offers the Athlon 64 FX/X2 Dual-Core. For servers, Intel offers a Xeon Dual-Core and Quad-Core Xeon, and AMD offers a Dual-Core Opteron a Quad-Core Opteron. In early 2009, Intel said it was developing an eight-core processor, the "Enterprise" Xeon processor, which would carry 2.3 billion transistors.[16] (The multicore technology takes advantage of a technology called *hyperthreading*, explained in a few pages.)

- **Processors for portable devices:** Chip makers have been rushing to produce processors for a new breed of portable devices—*mobile internet devices* (Chapter 1), *netbooks* (Intel's term), and other electronics, from cellphones to MP3 players to handheld game systems to household appliances. Among the contenders making processors for this market are Nvidia (with its Tegra system-on-a-chip), Qualcomm (Snapdragon), Texas Instruments (OMAP4), Via Technologies (the Via C7), and Intel (Atom and Moorestown, and the forthcoming Medfield).[17] What all such chips have in common is energy efficiency; Nvidia's Tegra, for instance, can hold a battery charge five times longer than Intel's Atom.[18]

- **Graphics processing units—specialized processors for 3-D graphics:** A ***graphics processing unit (GPU)* is a specialized processor used to manipulate three-dimensional (3-D) computer graphics.** Unlike a general-purpose CPU, a GPU is able to perform a range of complex algorithms (problem-solving steps). GPUs are found in personal computers, workstations, cellphones, and game consoles. The first company to develop the GPU was Nvidia, whose GeForce 256 GPU has over 22 million transistors (compared to 9 million in the Pentium III) and can process billions of calculations per second.

Processing Speeds: From Megahertz to Picoseconds

How does the system clock work in my computer, and how is its speed measured?

Often a PC ad will say something like "Intel Celeron processor 1.80 GHz," "Intel Pentium 4 processor 2.80 GHz," or "AMD Athlon 64 X2 processor 2.30 GHz." *GHz* stands for "gigahertz." These figures indicate how fast the microprocessor can process data and execute program instructions.

Every microprocessor contains a ***system clock*, which controls how fast all the operations within a computer take place.** The system clock uses fixed vibrations from a quartz crystal to deliver a steady stream of digital pulses or "ticks" to the CPU. These ticks are called *cycles*. Faster *clock speeds* will result in faster processing of data and execution of program instructions, as long as the computer's internal circuits can handle the increased speed.

There are four main ways in which processing speeds are measured, as follows.

FOR MICROCOMPUTERS: MEGAHERTZ & GIGAHERTZ Older microcomputer microprocessor speeds are expressed in ***megahertz (MHz),* a measure of frequency equivalent to 1 million cycles (ticks of the system clock) per second.** The original IBM PC had a clock speed of 4.77 megahertz, which equaled 4.77 million cycles per second. The latest-generation processors from AMD and Intel operate in ***gigahertz (GHz)*—a billion cycles per second.** Intel's Pentium 4 operates at up to 3.60 gigahertz, or 3.60 billion cycles per second. Some experts predict that advances in microprocessor technology will produce a 50-gigahertz processor by 2010, the kind of power that will be required to support such functions as true speech interfaces and real-time speech translation. However, unfortunately, the faster a CPU runs, the more power it consumes and the more waste heat it produces. Thus, rather than increasing clock speeds, which requires smaller transistors and creates tricky engineering problems, chip makers such as Intel and AMD are now employing additional

Which Intel Processor Is Better?

Which is the better Intel processor, Pentium or Celeron, for basic word processing and web surfing versus video games and complex applications? Find out by doing a web search.

Year	Processor Name	Clock Speed	Transistors
2008	Intel Core i7	2.66 GHz (each core)	410 million (each core; 4 cores usually used)
2008	Intel Tukwila Quad Core	2 GHz (each core)	2 billion
2007	Intel Core Quad	2.4–2.7 HZ	582 million
2006	Intel Pentium EE 840 dual core	3.2 GHZ (each core)	230 million
2005	Intel Pentium 4 660	3.6–3.7 GHz	169 million
2005	AMD Athlon 64 X2 dual core	2 GHz (each core)	105.9 million
2005	Intel Itanium 2 Montecito dual core	2 GHz (each core)	1.7 billion
2004	IBM PowerPC 970FX (G5)	2.2 GHz	58 million
2003	AMD Opteron	2–2.4 GHz	37.5 million
2002	Intel Itanium 2	1 GHz and up	221 million
2002	AMD Athlon MP	1.53–1.6 GHz	37.5 million
2001	Intel Xeon	1.4–2.8 GHz	140 million
2001	Intel Mobile Pentium 4	1.4–3.06 GHz	55 million
2001	AMD Athlon XP	1.33–1.73 GHz	37.5 million
2001	Intel Itanium	733–800 MHz	25.4–60 million
2000	Intel Pentium 4	1.4–3.06 GHz	42–55 million
1999	Motorola PowerPC 7400 (G4)	400–500 MHz	10.5 million

CPU cores and running them in parallel—dual core or multicore technology, as we've described.[19]

As for you, since a new high-speed processor can cost many hundred dollars more than a previous-generation chip, experts often recommend that buyers fret less about the speed of the processor (since the work most people do on their PCs doesn't even tax the limits of the current hardware) and more about spending money on extra memory. (However, game playing *does* tax the system. Thus, if you're an avid computer game player, you may want to purchase the fastest processor.)

FOR WORKSTATIONS & MAINFRAMES: MIPS Processing speed can also be measured according to the number of instructions per second that a computer can process. **_MIPS_ stands for "millions of instructions per second."** MIPS is used to measure processing speeds of mainframes and workstations. A workstation might perform at 100 MIPS or more; a mainframe at as much as 981,024 MIPS.

FOR SUPERCOMPUTERS: FLOPS The abbreviation **_flops_ stands for "floating-point operations per second."** A *floating-point operation* is a special kind of mathematical calculation. This measure, used mainly with supercomputers, is expressed as *megaflops* (*mflops,* or millions of floating-point operations per second), *gigaflops* (*gflops,* or billions), and *teraflops* (*tflops,* or trillions). IBM's Blue Gene/L (for "Lite") supercomputer cranks out 280.6 teraflops, or 280.6 trillion calculations per second. (With the previous top speed of 70.72 teraflops, a person able to complete one arithmetic calculation every second would take more than a million years to do what Blue Gene/L does in a single second.) The latest champion supercomputer, Roadrunner, developed by Los Alamos National Laboratory and IBM (Chapter 1), has a speed of 1,105 teraflops, or more than a *petaflop* (1,000 trillion operations per second).[20]

FOR ALL COMPUTERS: FRACTIONS OF A SECOND Another way to measure cycle times is in fractions of a second. A microcomputer operates in microseconds, a supercomputer in nanoseconds or picoseconds—thousands or millions of times faster. A *millisecond* is one-thousandth of a second. A *microsecond* is one-millionth of a second. A *nanosecond* is one-billionth of a second. A *picosecond* is one-trillionth of a second.

4.3 MORE ON THE SYSTEM UNIT

How do the processor and memory work, and what are some important ports, buses, and cards?

Technology moves on—toward simplifying on the one hand, toward mastering more complexity on the other.

An example of simplifying: How about a $100 laptop that could be put into the hands of billions of schoolchildren in the world's poorest nations? Nicholas Negroponte of the Media Lab at the Massachusetts Institute of Technology has proposed just such a "world computer," the One Laptop Per Child project's XO laptop. The XO, which weighs 3.2 pounds, has no hard drive or expensive display system, comes with less capable batteries and a hand crank for charging them, and stretches wireless networks with a technology that lets each computer in a third-world village in Peru or Mexico, for example, relay data to the others. Originally intended to sell for $100, the initial generation of XOs cost $188, depending on whether it used Linux or (for about $20 more) a version of Windows.[21] The One Laptop effort has led to competing low-cost computers, such as the itty-bitty 2-pound Eee PC from Asus, available for as little as $299.[22]

An example of mastering more complexity: IBM, Sony, and Toshiba announced a processor chip called Cell that has nine processing units, or cores, each of which can work independently, allowing the processor to tackle nine tasks at once. Cell's processing power of 48 gigaflops is such that it would have been among the top 500 supercomputers in 2002, but a version of the chip was released in a Toshiba notebook in 2008.[23]

To understand the different ways computers are diverging, let's take a deeper look at how the system unit works.

How the Processor or CPU Works: Control Unit, ALU, Registers, & Buses

How do the CPU and its parts work?

Once upon a time, the processor in a computer was measured in feet. A processing unit in the 1946 ENIAC (which had 20 such processors) was about 2 feet wide and 8 feet high. Today, computers are based on *micro*processors, less than 1 centimeter square. It may be difficult to visualize components so tiny. Yet it is necessary to understand how microprocessors work if you are to grasp what PC advertisers mean when they throw out terms such as "2 GB DDR-SDRAM" or "1 MB Level 2 Advanced Transfer Cache."

WORD SIZE Computer professionals often discuss a computer's word size. **_Word size_ is the number of bits that the processor may process at any one time.** The more bits in a word, the faster the computer. A 32-bit computer—that is, one with a 32-bit-word processor—will transfer data within each microprocessor chip in 32-bit chunks, or 4 bytes at a time. (Recall there are 8 bits in a byte.) A 64-bit-word computer is faster; it transfers data in 64-bit chunks, or 8 bytes at a time.

THE PARTS OF THE CPU A processor is also called the *CPU*, and it works hand in hand with other circuits known as *main memory* to carry out processing. **The _CPU (central processing unit)_ is the "brain" of the computer; it follows the instructions of the software (program) to manipulate data into information. The CPU consists of two parts—(1) the control unit and**

CPU on motherboard
(enlarged representation)

Registers
High-speed storage
areas used by control
unit and ALU to
speed up processing

Control unit
Directs electronic
signals between main
memory and ALU

Arithmetic/logic unit (ALU)
Performs arithmetic
and logical operations

Buses
Electrical data roadways
that transmit data within
CPU and between CPU
and main memory and
peripherals

Bus

Main memory
(Random Access
Memory, or RAM)

Bus

**Expansion
slots
on motherboard**

panel 4.9

**The CPU and main
memory**

The two main CPU com-
ponents on a micropro-
cessor are the control
unit and the ALU, which
contain working storage
areas called *registers* and
are linked by a kind of
electronic roadway called
a *bus*.

(2) the arithmetic/logic unit (ALU), both of which contain registers, or high-speed storage areas (as we discuss shortly). All are linked by a kind of electronic "roadway" called a *bus*. (● *See Panel 4.9.*)

- **The control unit—for directing electronic signals: The _control unit_ deciphers each instruction stored in the CPU and then carries out the instruction.** It directs the movement of electronic signals between main memory and the arithmetic/logic unit. It also directs these electronic signals between main memory and the input and output devices.

  For every instruction, the control unit carries out four basic operations, known as the *machine cycle*. In the _**machine cycle,**_ **the CPU (1) fetches an instruction, (2) decodes the instruction, (3) executes the instruction, and (4) stores the result.** (● *See Panel 4.10, opposite.*)

- **The arithmetic/logic unit— for arithmetic and logical operations: The _arithmetic/logic unit (ALU)_ performs arithmetic operations and logical operations and controls the speed of those operations.**

  As you might guess, *arithmetic operations* are the fundamental math operations: addition, subtraction, multiplication, and division.

  Logical operations are comparisons. That is, the ALU compares two pieces of data to see whether one is equal to ($=$), greater than ($>$), greater than or equal to ($>=$), less than ($<$), less than or equal to ($<=$), or not equal to ($\neq$) the other.

- **Registers—special high-speed storage areas:** The control unit and the ALU also use registers, special CPU areas that enhance the computer's performance. _**Registers**_ **are high-speed storage areas that temporarily store data during processing.** They may store a program instruction while it is being decoded, store data while it is being processed by the ALU, or store the results of a calculation.

  All data must be represented in a register before it can be processed. For example, if two numbers are to be multiplied, both numbers must be in registers, and the result is also placed in a register. (The register can contain the address of a memory location where data is stored rather than the actual data itself.)

  The number of registers that a CPU has and the size of each (number of bits) help determine the power and speed of a CPU. For example, a 32-bit CPU is one in which each register is 32 bits wide. Therefore, each CPU instruction can manipulate 32 bits of data. (There are several types of registers, including *instruction register, address register, storage register,* and *accumulator register.*)

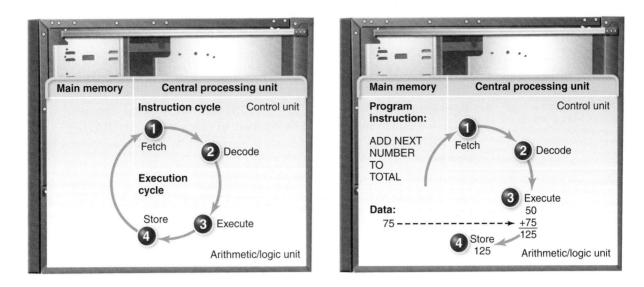

- **Buses—data roadways:** _Buses_, or *bus lines*, **are electrical data roadways through which bits are transmitted within the CPU and between the CPU and other components of the motherboard.** A bus resembles a multilane highway: The more lanes it has, the faster the bits can be transferred. The old-fashioned 8-bit-word bus of early microprocessors had only eight pathways. Data is transmitted four times faster in a computer with a 32-bit bus, which has 32 pathways, than in a computer with an 8-bit bus. Intel's Pentium chip is a 64-bit processor, as are Intel's dual-core and quad-core processors. Supercomputers usually have 128-bit processors.

We return to a discussion of buses in a few pages.

How Memory Works: RAM, ROM, CMOS, & Flash

How do I distinguish among the four principal types of memory chips?

So far we have described only the kinds of chips known as microprocessors. But other silicon chips called *memory chips* are attached to the motherboard. The four principal types of memory chips are *RAM, ROM, CMOS,* and *flash.*

RAM CHIPS—TO TEMPORARILY STORE PROGRAM INSTRUCTIONS & DATA Recall from Chapter 1 that there are two types of storage: primary and secondary. Primary storage is temporary or working storage and is often called *memory* or *main memory.* Secondary storage, usually called just *storage,* is relatively permanent storage. *Memory* refers to storage media in the form of chips, and *storage* refers to media such as disks and tape.

RAM (random access memory) chips **temporarily hold (1) software instructions and (2) data before and after it is processed by the CPU.** Think of RAM as the primary workspace inside your computer. When you open a file, a copy of the file transfers from the hard disk to RAM, and this copy in RAM is the one that changes as you work with the file. When you activate the Save command, the changed copy transfers from RAM back to permanent storage on the hard drive.

Because its contents are temporary, RAM is said to be _volatile_—**the contents are lost when the power goes off or is turned off.** This is why you should *frequently*—every 5–10 minutes, say—transfer (save) your work to a secondary storage medium such as your hard disk, in case the electricity goes off while you're working. (However, there is one kind of RAM, called *flash RAM,* that is not temporary, as we'll discuss shortly.)

Need More RAM?

If your system is giving you low-system-resources messages, you may need more memory. For detailed information on your system, go to:
www.crucial.com
www.kingston.com
www.tomshardware.com

2 GB DDR2 SDRAM

info!

RAM-ifications

To find out more about how RAM works, go to:

http://computer.howstuffworks. com/ram.htm

Several types of RAM chips are used in personal computers—*DRAM, SDRAM, SRAM,* and *DDR-SDRAM:*

- **DRAM:** The first type (pronounced "dee-ram"), *DRAM (dynamic RAM),* must be constantly refreshed by the CPU or it will lose its contents.

- **SDRAM:** The second type of RAM is *SDRAM (synchronous dynamic RAM),* which is synchronized by the system clock and is much faster than DRAM. Often in computer ads the speed of SDRAM is expressed in megahertz.

- **SRAM:** The third type, *static RAM,* or *SRAM* (pronounced "ess-ram"), is faster than DRAM and retains its contents without having to be refreshed by the CPU.

- **DDR-SDRAM:** The fourth type, *DDR-SDRAM (double-data rate synchronous dynamic RAM),* is the current standard of RAM chip in PCs used at home; the speed is measured in megahertz. An even faster version is *DDR2 SDRAM,* the most recent entry, which is found on gaming machines and multimedia machines, where speed is needed.

Microcomputers come with different amounts of RAM, which is usually measured in megabytes or gigabytes. An ad may list "256 MB SDRAM," but you can get more. The Mac Pro, for instance, can provide up to 32 gigabytes of RAM. The more RAM you have, the more efficiently the computer operates and the better your software performs. *Having enough RAM is a critical matter.* Before you buy a software package, look at the outside of the box or check the manufacturer's website to see how much RAM is required. Microsoft Office XP, for instance, states that a minimum of 128 megabytes of RAM is required, depending on the operating system, plus 8 megabytes of RAM for *each* application the user plans to run simultaneously. Windows Vista requires 512 megabytes to 1 gigabyte minimum RAM, as does Apple's OS X version 10.6.

If you're short on memory capacity, you can usually add more RAM chips by plugging a RAM *memory module* into the motherboard. A memory module is a small fiberglass circuit board that can be plugged into an expansion slot on the motherboard. There are two types of such modules: SIMMs and the newer DIMMs.

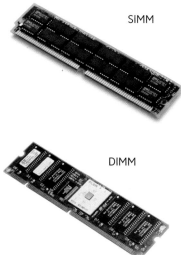

SIMM

DIMM

- **SIMM:** A *SIMM (single inline memory module)* has RAM chips on only one side. SIMMs are available in either FPM (fast page mode) or EDO (extended data output) speeds, with EDO being the faster of the two. SIMMs are more expensive than modern memory modules because they are no longer in demand, which also makes them difficult to obtain.

- **DIMM:** A *DIMM (dual inline memory module)* has RAM chips on both sides. DIMMs are the most popular and common type of RAM used today.

ROM CHIPS—TO STORE FIXED START-UP INSTRUCTIONS Unlike RAM, to which data is constantly being added and removed, **ROM (read-only memory) cannot be written on or erased by the computer user without special equipment. ROM chips contain fixed start-up instructions.** That is, ROM chips are loaded, at the factory, with programs containing special instructions for basic computer operations, such as those that start the computer (BIOS) or put characters on the screen. These chips are nonvolatile; their contents are not lost when power to the computer is turned off.

In computer terminology, **_read_ means to transfer data from an input source into the computer's memory or CPU. The opposite is _write_—to transfer data from the computer's CPU or memory to an output device.**

Thus, with a ROM chip, *read-only* means that the CPU can retrieve programs from the ROM chip but cannot modify or add to those programs. A variation is *PROM (programmable read-only memory)*, which is a ROM chip that allows you, the user, to load read-only programs and data. However, this can be done only once.

CMOS CHIPS—TO STORE FLEXIBLE START-UP INSTRUCTIONS Pronounced "*see*-moss," **_CMOS (complementary metal-oxide semiconductor) chips_ are powered by a battery and thus don't lose their contents when the power is turned off.** CMOS chips contain flexible start-up instructions—such as time, date, and calendar—that must be kept current even when the computer is turned off. Unlike ROM chips, CMOS chips can be reprogrammed, as when you need to change the time for daylight savings time. (Your system software may prompt you to do this; newer systems do it automatically.)

FLASH MEMORY CHIPS—TO STORE FLEXIBLE PROGRAMS Also a nonvolatile form of memory, **_flash memory chips_ can be erased and reprogrammed more than once** (unlike PROM chips, which can be programmed only once). Flash memory, which doesn't require a battery and which can range from 128 megabytes to 32 gigabytes and up in capacity, is used to store programs not only in personal computers but also in pagers, cellphones, MP3 players, Palm organizers, printers, and digital cameras. Flash memory is also used in newer PCs for BIOS instructions; they can be updated electronically on flash memory—the chip does not need to be replaced, as a ROM chip would. One flash memory chip called the EcoRAM (from Spansion) has been developed that might replace DRAM chips, because it can record data faster yet consumes one-eighth the power of DRAM; this might enable customers to replace four DRAM-based servers with one system using EcoRAM chips.[24]

How Cache Works

How do cache and virtual memory differ?

Because the CPU runs so much faster than the main system RAM, it ends up waiting for information, which is inefficient. To reduce this effect, we have cache. Pronounced "cash," **_cache_ temporarily stores instructions and data that the processor is likely to use frequently. Thus, cache speeds up processing.** SRAM chips are commonly used for cache.

THREE KINDS OF CACHE There are three kinds of cache, as follows:

- **Level 1 (L1) cache—part of the microprocessor chip:** *Level 1 (L1) cache,* also called *internal cache,* is built into the processor chip. Ranging from 8 to 256 kilobytes, its capacity is less than that of Level 2 cache, although it operates faster.

- **Level 2 (L2) cache—not part of the microprocessor chip:** This is the kind of cache usually referred to in computer ads. *Level 2 (L2) cache,* also called *external cache,* resides outside the processor chip, and consists of SRAM chips. Capacities range from 64 kilobytes to 2 megabytes. (In Intel ads, L2 is called *Advanced Transfer Cache.*) L2 cache is generally quite a bit larger than L1 cache (most new systems have at least 1 megabyte of L2 cache) and is the most commonly cited type of cache when measuring PC performance.

3 MB L2 Cache

- **Level 3 (L3) cache—on the motherboard:** *Level 3 (L3) cache* is a cache separate from the processor chip on the motherboard. It is found only on very high-end computers, only those that use L2 Advanced Transfer Cache.

Cache is not upgradable; it is set by the type of processor purchased with the system.

VIRTUAL MEMORY In addition to including cache, most current computer operating systems allow for the use of ___virtual memory___—**that is, some free hard-disk space is used to extend the capacity of RAM.** The processor searches for data or program instructions in the following order: first L1, then L2, then RAM, then hard disk (or CD). In this progression, each kind of memory or storage is slower than its predecessor.

Other Methods of Speeding Up Processing

What are interleaving, bursting, pipelining, superscalar architecture, and hyperthreading?

The placement of memory chips on the motherboard has a direct effect on system performance. Because RAM must hold all the information the CPU needs to process, the speed at which the data can travel between memory and the CPU is critical to performance. And because the exchanges of data between the CPU and RAM are so intricately timed, the distance between them becomes another critical performance factor. Ways to speed up data traveling between memory and CPU are *interleaving, bursting, pipelining, superscalar architecture,* and *hyperthreading.* When you see these terms in a computer ad, you'll know that the processor's speed is being boosted.

INTERLEAVING The term *interleaving* refers to a process in which the CPU alternates communication between two or more memory banks. Interleaving is generally used in large systems such as servers and workstations. For example, SDRAM chips are each divided into independent cell banks. Interleaving between the two cell banks produces a continuous flow of data.

BURSTING The purpose of *bursting* is to provide the CPU with additional data from memory based on the likelihood that it will be needed. So, instead of the CPU retrieving data from memory one piece at a time, it grabs a block of information from several consecutive addresses in memory. This saves time because there's a statistical likelihood that the next data address the CPU will request will be sequential to the previous one.

PIPELINING *Pipelining* divides a task into a series of stages, with some of the work completed at each stage. That is, large tasks are divided into smaller overlapping ones. The CPU does not wait for one instruction to complete the machine cycle before fetching the next instruction. Pipelining is available in most PCs; each processor can pipeline up to four instructions.

SUPERSCALAR ARCHITECTURE & HYPERTHREADING *Superscalar architecture* means the computer has the ability to execute more than one instruction per clock cycle (a 200-MHz processor executes 200 million clock cycles per second). One type of such architecture is hyperthreading. With *hyperthreading,* software and operating systems treat the microprocessor as though it's two microprocessors. This technology lets the microprocessor handle simultaneous requests from the OS or from software, initially improving performance by around 30%–40%. A processor using hyperthreading technology manages the incoming data instructions in parallel by switching between the instructions every few nanoseconds, essentially letting the processor handle two separate threads of code at once.

Ports & Cables

What ports will I probably use most?

A ___port___ **is a connecting socket or jack on the outside of the system unit into which are plugged different kinds of cables.** (● *See Panel 4.11.*) A port allows you to plug in a cable to connect a peripheral device, such as a monitor, printer, or modem, so that it can communicate with the computer system.

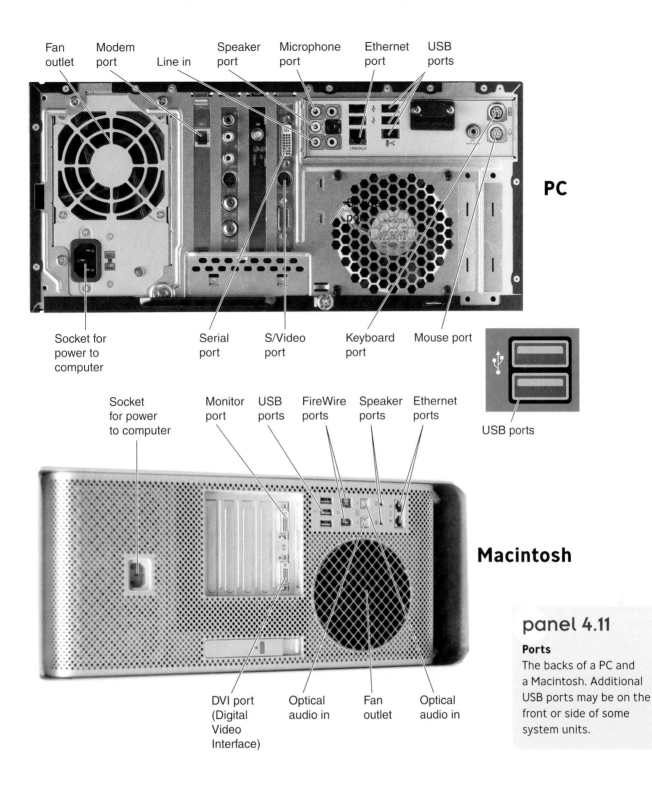

Fan outlet | Modem port | Line in | Speaker port | Microphone port | Ethernet port | USB ports

PC

Socket for power to computer | Serial port | S/Video port | Keyboard port | Mouse port

Socket for power to computer | Monitor port | USB ports | FireWire ports | Speaker ports | Ethernet ports

USB ports

Macintosh

DVI port (Digital Video Interface) | Optical audio in | Fan outlet | Optical audio in

Ports are of several types, as follows.

DEDICATED PORTS—FOR KEYBOARD, MOUSE, MONITOR, AUDIO, & MODEM/ NETWORK CONNECTION *Dedicated ports* are ports for special purposes, such as the round ports for connecting the keyboard and the mouse (if they're not USB), the monitor port, the audio ports (green for speakers or headphones, pink for microphone, yellow for home stereo connection), the modem port to connect your computer to a phone line, and a network port for a high-speed internet connection. (There is also one connector that is not a port at all—the power plug socket, into which you insert the power cord that brings electricity from a wall plug.)

SERIAL, PARALLEL, & SCSI PORTS Most ports other than the dedicated ones just described are generally multipurpose. We consider serial, parallel, and SCSI ports:

- **Serial ports—for transmitting slow data over long distances: A line connected to a _serial port_ will send bits one at a time, one after another,** like cars on a one-lane highway. Because individual bits must follow each other, a serial port is usually used to connect devices that do not require fast transmission of data, such as keyboard, mouse, monitors, and dial-up modems. It is also useful for sending data over a long distance.

- **Parallel ports—for transmitting fast data over short distances: A line connected to a _parallel port_ allows 8 bits (1 byte) to be transmitted simultaneously,** like cars on an eight-lane highway. Parallel lines move information faster than serial lines do, but they can transmit information efficiently only up to 15 feet. Thus, parallel ports are used principally for connecting printers or external disk or magnetic-tape backup storage devices.

- **SCSI ports—for transmitting fast data to up to seven devices in a daisy chain:** Pronounced "scuzzy," a **_SCSI (small computer system interface) port_ allows data to be transmitted in a "daisy chain" to up to seven devices connected to a single port at speeds higher (32 bits at a time) than those possible with serial and parallel ports.** Among the devices that may be connected are external hard-disk drives, CD drives, scanners, and magnetic-tape backup units. The term _daisy chain_ means that several devices are connected in series to each other, so that data for the seventh device, for example, has to go through the other six devices first. Sometimes the equipment on the chain is inside the computer, an internal daisy chain; sometimes it is outside the computer, an external daisy chain. (● _See Panel 4.12._)

USB PORTS—FOR TRANSMITTING DATA TO UP TO 127 DEVICES IN A DAISY CHAIN A single _USB (universal serial bus) port_ can theoretically connect

panel 4.12

Daisy chains

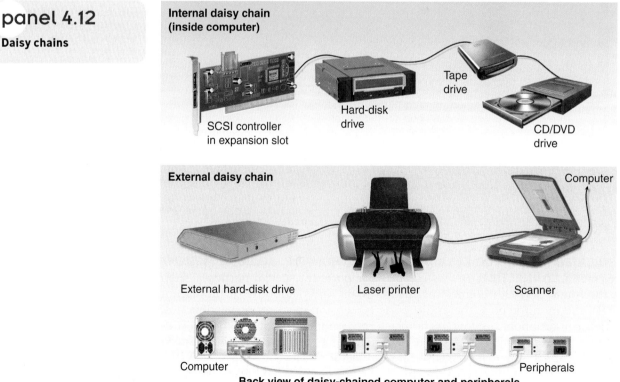

Internal daisy chain (inside computer)

Tape drive

SCSI controller in expansion slot

Hard-disk drive

CD/DVD drive

External daisy chain

Computer

External hard-disk drive

Laser printer

Scanner

Computer

Peripherals

Back view of daisy-chained computer and peripherals

up to 127 peripheral devices in a daisy chain. USB ports are multipurpose, useful for all kinds of peripherals, and are included on all new computers.

6 USB 2.0 Ports

- **The goals of USB:** The designers of the USB standard had several goals in mind. They wanted it to . . .

  1. Be low-cost so that it could be used in cheap peripherals such as mice and game controllers.
  2. Be able to connect lots of devices and have sufficient speed that it could replace all the different ports on computers with a single standard.
  3. Be "hot swappable" or "hot pluggable," meaning that it could allow USB devices to be connected or disconnected even while the PC is running.
  4. Permit _**plug and play**_—**to allow peripheral devices and expansion cards to be automatically configured while they are being installed**—to avoid the hassle of setting switches and creating special files, as was required of early users.

  USB has fulfilled these goals, so now just about every peripheral is available in a USB version, and it's expected that soon microcomputers will have nothing but USB ports.

- **USB connections—daisy chains, hubs, and wireless:** Can you really connect up to 127 devices on a single chain? An Intel engineer did set a world record at an industry trade show before a live audience by connecting 111 peripheral devices to a single USB port on a personal computer. But many USB peripherals do not support such long daisy chains. Thus, because some PCs contain only two USB ports, it's worth shopping around to find a model with more than two.

  USB hub connectors

  You can also hook up a USB hub to one of the USB ports. A _USB hub_ typically has four USB ports. You plug the hub into your computer, and then plug your devices—or other hubs—into that. By chaining hubs together, you can build up dozens of available USB ports on a single computer. However, using a hub weakens data signals, so some peripherals, such as cable modems, work better when plugged directly into one of the computer's USB ports.

  Individual USB cables can run as long as 5 meters (about 5.4 yards). With hubs, devices can be up to 30 meters (about 32.8 yards) away. Each USB cable has an A connector, which plugs into the computer, and a B connector, which plugs into the peripheral USB device.

  Wireless USB technology was introduced in 2004, and wireless USB products became available in 2006. This connection technology is useful in home and office networks in ranges of 9 to about 30 feet.

- **USB standards:** Just about every peripheral made now comes in a USB version. Common USB standards are _USB 1.1_ and the more recent _USB 2.0._ Nearly all new PCs have USB 2.0 ports. Users with an older PC with USB 1.1 ports will have to buy a 2.0 add-on upgrade card to be able to hook up 2.0 peripherals. (USB 2.0 data "throughput"—the speed at which data passes through the cable—is 2–13 times faster than USB 1.1.) Windows 95 and Windows NT do not support USB.

  Super-speed USB 3.0 was released by Intel and its partners in November 2008. According to Intel, bus speeds will be 10 times faster than USB 2.0 owing to the inclusion of a fiber-optic link that works with traditional copper connectors.

- **USB connectors:** There are four types of USB connectors: A, B, Mini B, and Mini A. USB 1.1 specifies the Type A and Type B. USB 2.0 specifies the Type A, Type B, and Mini B. The Mini A connector was developed as part of the USB OTG (an enhancement to USB) specification and is used for smaller peripherals, such as cellphones.

FireWire port
USB port

Parallel printer port on a notebook computer

Infrared port

Bluetooth logo

SPECIALIZED EXPANSION PORTS—FIREWIRE, MIDI, IRDA, BLUETOOTH, & ETHERNET Some specialized expansion ports are these:

- **FireWire ports—for camcorders, DVD players, and TVs:** FireWire was created by Apple Computer and later standardized as IEEE-1394 (IEEE is short for Institute of Electrical and Electronics Engineers). It actually preceded USB and had similar goals. The difference is that **_FireWire (IEEE-1394)_ is intended for devices working with lots of data—not just mice and keyboards but digital video recorders, DVD players, gaming consoles, and digital audio equipment.** Like USB, FireWire is a serial bus. However, whereas USB is limited to 12 megabits per second, FireWire currently handles up to 400 megabits per second. USB can handle 127 devices per bus, while FireWire handles 63. Both USB and FireWire allow you to plug and unplug devices at any time.

  FireWire doesn't always require the use of a PC; you can connect a FireWire camcorder directly to a digital TV, for example, without a PC in the middle. Like USB devices, FireWire devices can be powered or unpowered, and they are also hot pluggable. FireWire requires a special card in the PC.

- **MIDI ports—for connecting musical instruments: A _MIDI_ (pronounced _"mid_-dee" and short for _Musical Instrument Digital Interface_) _port_ is a specialized port used in creating, recording, editing, and performing music.** It is used for connecting amplifiers, electronic synthesizers, sound cards, drum machines, and the like.

- **IrDA ports—for cableless connections over a few feet:** When you use a handheld remote unit to change channels on a TV set, you're using invisible radio waves of the type known as infrared waves. **An _IrDA_, or _infrared_, _port_ allows a computer to make a cableless connection with infrared-capable devices,** such as some printers. (_IrDA_ stands for "Infrared Data Association," which sets the standards.) This type of connection requires an unobstructed line of sight between transmitting and receiving ports, and they can be only a few feet apart.

- **Bluetooth ports—for wireless connections up to 30 feet: _Bluetooth_ technology consists of short-range radio waves that transmit up to 30 feet.** It is used to connect cellphones to computers but also to connect computers to printers, keyboards, headsets, and other appliances (including refrigerators).

- **Ethernet—for LANs:** Developed by the Xerox Corporation in the mid-1970s, **_Ethernet_ is a network standard for linking all devices in a local area network.** (The name comes from the concept of "ether.") It's commonly used to connect microcomputers, cable modems, and printers. (To use Ethernet, the computer must have an Ethernet network interface card, and special Ethernet cables are required.

  Bluetooth and Ethernet are also discussed in Chapter 6.

MULTIMEDIA PORTS "The trend toward multimedia notebooks has introduced a whole slew of port types you may not be familiar with, but that you might need," states a computer magazine.[25] These include ports for connecting your computer to the following: gaming consoles or camcorders (Composite In/RCA ports); cable boxes, TVs, or VCRs, so you can watch and record TV content on your computer (TV tuner/75-ohm coaxial port); speakers or stereo receivers to play digital audio (S/PDIF ports); digital projectors to LCD panels to display in large format video content or a PowerPoint presentation (DVI port); digital cameras to display video stored on the cameras (S-video In port); and plasma or newer TV so you can view video content streaming from the computer (S-Video Out).

Expandability: Buses & Cards

What is the purpose of expansion buses and cards?

Today many new microcomputer systems can be expanded. As mentioned earlier, *expansion* is a way of increasing a computer's capabilities by adding hardware to perform tasks that are not part of the basic system. *Upgrading* means changing to a newer, usually more powerful or sophisticated version. (Computer ads often make no distinction between expansion and upgrading. Their main interest is simply to sell you more hardware or software.)

CLOSED & OPEN ARCHITECTURE Whether a computer can be expanded depends on its "architecture"—closed or open. *Closed architecture* means a computer has no expansion slots; *open architecture* means it does have expansion slots. (An alternative definition is that closed architecture is a computer design whose specifications are not made freely available by the manufacturer. Thus, other companies cannot create ancillary devices to work with it. With open architecture, the manufacturer shares specifications with outsiders.)

    Expansion slots **are sockets on the motherboard into which you can plug expansion cards.** ***Expansion cards***—**also known as** *expansion boards, adapter cards, interface cards, plug-in boards, controller cards, add-ins,* **or** *add-ons*—**are circuit boards that provide more memory or that control peripheral devices.** (● *See Panel 4.13.*)

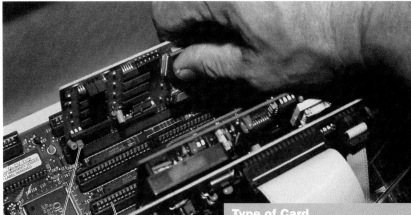

Expansion   Expansion
card   slot

panel 4.13

Expandability
(Left) How an expansion card fits into an expansion slot. *(Below)* Types of cards.

Type of Card (Board)	What It Does
Accelerator board	Speeds up processing; also known as turbo board or upgrade board
Cache card	Improves disk performance
Coprocessor board	Contains specialized processor chips that increase processing speed of computer system
Disk controller card	Allows certain type of disk drive to be connected to computer system
Emulator board	Permits microcomputer to be used as a terminal for a larger computer system
Fax modem board	Enables computer to transmit and receive fax messages and data over telephone lines
Graphics (video) adapter board	Permits computer to have a particular graphics standard
Memory expansion board	Enables additional RAM to be added to computer system
Sound board	Enables certain types of systems to produce sound output

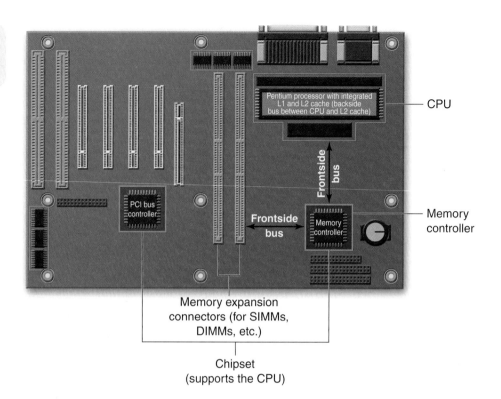

Memory expansion
connectors (for SIMMs,
DIMMs, etc.)

Chipset
(supports the CPU)

COMMON EXPANSION CARDS & BUSES Common expansion cards connect to the monitor (graphics card), speakers and microphones (sound card), and network (network card), as we'll discuss. Most computers have four to eight expansion slots, some of which may already contain expansion cards included in your initial PC purchase.

Expansion cards are made to connect with different types of buses on the motherboard. As we mentioned, *buses* are electrical data roadways through which bits are transmitted. The bus that connects the CPU within itself and to main memory is the *frontside bus*, also called the *memory bus* or the *local bus*. (● *See Panel 4.14.*) The buses that connect the CPU with expansion slots on the motherboard and thus with peripheral devices are *expansion buses*. We already described the universal serial bus (USB), whose purpose, in fact, is to *eliminate* the need for expansion slots and expansion cards, since you can just connect USB devices in a daisy chain outside the system unit.

Some expansion buses to be aware of are these:

- **PCI bus—for high-speed connections: At 32- or 64-bits wide, the _PCI (peripheral component interconnect) bus_ is a high-speed bus** that has been widely used to connect PC graphics cards, sound cards, modems, and high-speed network cards. A more recent standard is the *PCI Express (PCIe),* as we explain below.

- **AGP bus—for even higher speeds and 3-D graphics:** The PCI bus was adequate for many years, providing enough bandwidth for all the peripherals most users wanted to connect—except graphics cards. In the mid-1990s, however, graphics cards were becoming more powerful, and three-dimensional (3-D) games were demanding higher performance. Because the PCI bus couldn't handle all the information passing between the main processor and the graphics processor, Intel developed the AGP bus. **The _AGP (accelerated graphics port) bus_, which transmits data at twice the speed of a PCI bus, is designed to support video and 3-D graphics.**

- **PCIe Express bus—for outperforming AGP:** In 2004, Intel developed the **_PCIe (PCI Express) bus_, which can outperform AGP and is more**

reliable. PCIe is the latest standard for expansion cards available on mainstream personal computers.

TYPES OF EXPANSION CARDS Among the types of expansion cards are graphics, sound, modem, and network interface cards. A special kind of card is the PC card.

- **Graphics cards—for monitors:** Graphics cards are included in all PCs. **Also called a** *video card, video RAM (VRAM), or video adapter, a graphics card converts signals from the computer into video signals that can be displayed as images on a monitor.* Each graphics card has its own memory chips, a graphics BIOS ROM chip, and a dedicated processor, the graphics processing unit (GPU), discussed earlier. The GPU works in tandem with the computer's CPU to ease the load, resulting in faster overall speed. Some computers (such as Toshiba's Qosimio X305-Q708 laptop) have more than one GPU, so that one GPU is used for normal activities such as word processing and email and then the machine kicks in with another GPU for superfast gaming.[26]

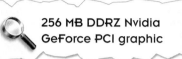

256 MB DDRZ Nvidia GeForce PCI graphic

- **Sound cards—for speakers and audio output:** A *sound card* **is used to convert and transmit digital sounds through analog speakers, microphones, and headsets.** Sound cards come installed on most new PCs. Cards such as PCI wavetable sound cards are used to add music and sound effects to computer videogames. *Wavetable synthesis* is a method of creating music based on a wave table, which is a collection of digitized sound samples taken from recordings of actual instruments. The sound samples are then stored on a sound card and are edited and mixed together to produce music. Wavetable synthesis produces higher-quality audio output than other sound techniques.

Sound Blaster Digital Sound Card

- **Modem cards—for remote communication via phone lines:** Occasionally you may still see a modem that is outside the computer. Most new PCs, however, come with internal modems— modems installed inside as circuit cards. The modem not only sends and receives digital data over telephone lines to and from other computers but can also transmit voice and fax signals. (Modems are discussed in more detail in later chapters.)

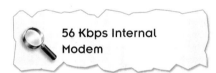

56 Kbps Internal Modem

- **Network interface cards—for remote communication via cable:** A *network interface card (NIC)* **allows the transmission of data over a cable network,** which connects various computers and other devices such as printers. (Various types of networks are covered in Chapter 6.)

- **PC cards—for laptop computers:** Originally called *PCMCIA cards* (for the Personal Computer Memory Card International Association), *PC cards* **are thin, credit card–size flash memory devices used principally on laptop computers to expand capabilities,** such as to access the internet wirelessly. (● *See Panel 4.15.) ExpressCard modules* are used as removable flash memory devices; they can be used to add communications, multimedia, and memory capabilities.

panel 4.15

PC card
Example of a PC card used in a laptop

4.4 SECONDARY STORAGE

What are the features of floppy disks, hard disks, optical disks, magnetic tape, smart cards, flash memory, and online secondary storage?

You're on a trip with your laptop, or maybe just a cellphone or a personal digital assistant, and you don't have a crucial file of data. Or maybe you need to look up a phone number that you can't get through the phone company's directory assistance. Fortunately, you backed up your data online, using any one of several storage services (for example, Driveway, *www.driveway.com; eSureIT,* www.intronis. com; or X:Drive, *www.xdrive.com*), and are able to access it through your modem.

Here is yet another example of how the World Wide Web is offering alternatives to traditional computer functions that once resided within stand-alone machines. We are not, however, fully into the all-online era ("the cloud") just yet. Let us consider more traditional forms of ***secondary storage hardware,*** **devices that permanently hold data and information as well as programs.** We look at these types of secondary storage devices:

- Floppy disks
- Hard disks
- Optical disks
- Magnetic tape
- Smart cards
- Flash memory
- Online secondary storage

Floppy Disks

Are floppy disks still being used?

Although floppy disks are almost obsolete, some microcomputer systems still offer the inclusion of an internal floppy disk drive, and external floppy disk

Floppy disk

drives are still available. Floppies are still used for emergency boots in aging systems that may lack support for CD-ROMs and USB devices, and you may come across them in older (legacy) computer systems used by certain companies.

A *floppy disk,* often called a *diskette* or simply a *disk,* is a removable flat piece of mylar plastic packaged in a 3.5-inch plastic case. Data and programs are stored on the disk's coating by means of magnetized spots, following standard on/off patterns of data representation (such as ASCII). The plastic case protects the mylar disk from being touched by human hands. Originally, when most disks were larger (5.25 inches) and covered in paper, the disks actually were "floppy"; now only the disk inside the rigid plastic case is flexible, or floppy. Floppy disks each store about 1.44 megabytes, the equivalent of 400 typewritten pages.

HOW FLOPPY DISKS WORK Floppy disks are inserted into a floppy-disk drive, a device that holds, spins, reads data from, and writes data to a floppy disk. *Read* means that the data in secondary storage is converted to electronic signals and a copy of that data is transmitted to the computer's memory (RAM). *Write* means that a copy of the electronic information processed by the computer is transferred to secondary storage.

- **Tracks, sectors, and clusters:** On the diskette, **data is recorded in concentric recording bands called *tracks*.** Unlike on a vinyl phonograph record, these tracks are neither visible grooves nor a single spiral. Rather, they are closed concentric rings; each track forms a full circle on the disk. **When a disk is formatted, the disk's storage locations are divided into wedge-shaped sections, which break the tracks into small arcs called _sectors_.** When you save data from your computer to a diskette, the data is distributed by tracks and sectors on the disk. That is, the system software uses the point at which a sector intersects a track to reference the data location. The smallest unit of disk space that holds data is called a cluster. A _cluster_ is a group of sectors on a storage device. Tracks, sectors, and clusters are also used in hard disks, as we'll discuss.

- **The read/write head:** When you insert a floppy disk into the slot (the _drive gate_ or _drive door_) in the front of the disk drive, the disk is fixed in place over the spindle of the drive mechanism. **The _read/write head_ is used to transfer data between the computer and the disk.** When the disk spins inside its case, the read/write head moves back and forth over the _data access area_ on the disk. When the disk is not in the drive, a metal or plastic shutter covers this access area. An access light goes on when the disk is in use. After using the disk, you can retrieve it by pressing an eject button beside the drive.

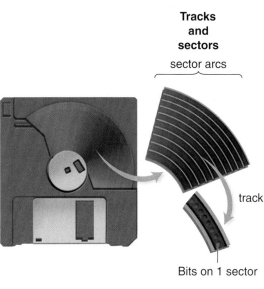

Tracks and sectors

sector arcs

track

Bits on 1 sector

Hard Disks

How does the hard disk in my computer work?

320 GB SATA 7200 RPM Hard Drive

Floppy disks use flexible plastic, but hard disks are rigid. **_Hard disks_ are thin but rigid metal, glass, or ceramic platters covered with a substance that allows data to be held in the form of magnetized spots.** Most hard-disk drives have at least two platters; the greater the number of platters, the larger the capacity of the drive. The platters in the drive are separated by spaces and are clamped to a rotating spindle that turns all the platters in unison. Hard disks are tightly sealed within an enclosed hard-disk-drive unit to prevent any foreign matter from getting inside. Data may be recorded on both sides of the disk platters. (● _See Panel 4.16._)

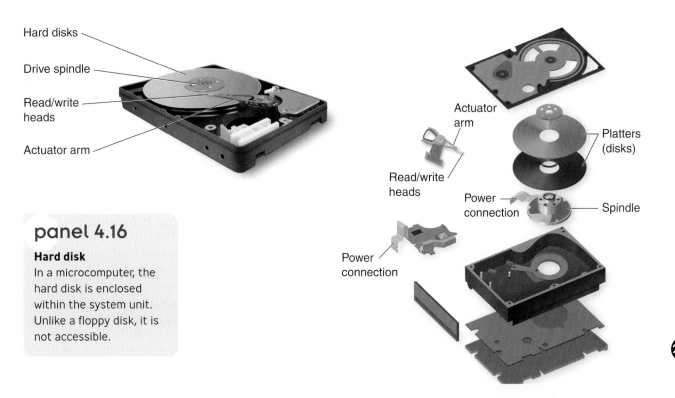

Hard disks

Drive spindle

Read/write heads

Actuator arm

Actuator arm

Read/write heads

Power connection

Platters (disks)

Spindle

Power connection

panel 4.16

Hard disk

In a microcomputer, the hard disk is enclosed within the system unit. Unlike a floppy disk, it is not accessible.

Relative size of a hard-disk drive

KEEPING TRACK OF DATA: THE VIRTUAL FILE ALLOCATION TABLE Like floppy disks, hard disks store data in *tracks, sectors,* and *clusters.* Computer operating systems keep track of hard-disk sectors according to clusters. The Windows operating system assigns a unique number to each cluster and then keeps track of files on a disk by using a kind of table, a *Virtual File Allocation Table (VFAT),* as a method for storing and keeping track of files according to which clusters they use. (The VFAT was called a FAT in earlier operating systems.) That is, the VFAT includes an entry for each cluster that describes where on the disk the cluster is located.

Occasionally, the operating system numbers a cluster as being used even though it is not assigned to any file. This is called a *lost cluster.* You can free up lost clusters and thus increase disk space in Windows by using the ScanDisk utility.

HEAD CRASHES Hard disks are sensitive devices. The read/write head does not actually touch the disk but rather rides on a cushion of air about 0.000001 inch thick. (● *See Panel 4.17, opposite page.*) The disk is sealed from impurities within a container, and the whole apparatus is manufactured under sterile conditions. Otherwise, all it would take is a human hair, a dust particle, a fingerprint smudge, or a smoke particle to cause what is called a head crash. A *head crash* happens when the surface of the read/write head or particles on its surface come into contact with the surface of the hard-disk platter, causing the loss of some or all of the data on the disk. A head crash can also happen when you bump a computer too hard or drop something heavy on the system cabinet. An incident of this sort could, of course, be a disaster if the data has not been backed up. There are firms that specialize in trying to retrieve data from crashed hard disks (for a hefty price), though this cannot always be done.

Bits on disk. Magnetic bits on a disk surface, caught by a magnetic force microscope. The dark stripes are 0 bits; the bright stripes are I bits.

NONREMOVABLE HARD DISKS An internal *nonremovable hard disk,* also known as a *fixed disk,* is housed in the microcomputer system unit and is used to store nearly all programs and most data files. Usually it consists of several metallic or glass platters, from 1 to 5.25 inches (most commonly 3.5 inches) in diameter, stacked on a spindle, with data stored on both sides. Read/write heads, one for each side of each platter, are mounted on an access arm that moves back and forth to the right location on the platter. The entire apparatus is sealed within an airtight case to protect it from contaminants such as dust.

The storage capacities of nonremovable hard drives for microcomputers range from 40 to 500 gigabytes. In large computer systems, a hard drive might hold 1.5 terabytes. A gigabyte holds around 20,000 pages of regular text, but video and sound files often run to 30 megabytes or more.

A hard disk spins many times faster than a floppy disk, allowing faster access. Computer ads frequently specify hard-disk speeds in *revolutions per minute (rpm),* usually 5,400–7,200 rpm. Whereas a floppy-disk drive rotates at only 360 rpm, a 7,200-rpm hard drive is going about 300 miles per hour. (Newer hard dives can spin at 15,000 rpm.)

PORTABLE HARD-DRIVE SYSTEMS: EXTERNAL & REMOVABLE HARD DISKS Two types of portable hard-drive systems are available:

● **External hard disk:** An *external hard disk* is a freestanding hard-disk drive enclosed in an airtight case, which is connected by cable to the computer system unit through a FireWire, USB, or other port. Storage capacities run as high as 2 terabytes. They are used not only by businesses but also by households that want to back up files from all the computers in a home, allowing music, photos, videos, and other files to be accessed

Storage in the Old Days

In 1978, a pioneering drive for home computers, the external Shugart SA4000, weighed 35 pounds, wholesaled for $2,550, and stored only 14.5 megabytes. Hard drives began to become popular with PC users in 1983, when Seagate made one that fit into the PC case. For more history, go to:

www.computerhistory.org

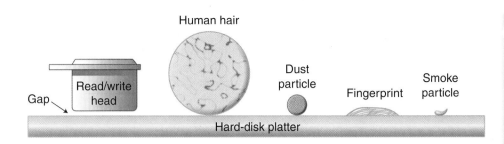

Human hair

Dust particle

Read/write head

Smoke particle

Gap

Fingerprint

Hard-disk platter

from all over the house. Such drives are made by Western Digital, Seagate, Iomega, Netgear, and Data Robotics, to name a few.[27]

- **Removable hard disk:** A *removable hard disk,* or *hard-disk cartridge,* consists of one or two platters enclosed along with read/write heads in a hard plastic case, which is inserted into a cartridge drive built into the microcomputer's system unit. Cartridges, which have storage capacities of 80–160 gigabytes and more, are frequently used to back up and transport huge files of data, such as those for large spreadsheets or desktop-publishing files.

HARD-DISK CONTROLLERS When advertising hard-disk drives, computer ads may specify the type of *hard-disk controller* used, a special-purpose circuit board that positions the disk and read/write heads and manages the flow of data and instructions to and from the disk. The hard-disk controller may be part of the hard disk or an adapter card located inside the system unit. Two hard-disk controllers for connecting external hard-disk drives are FireWire and USB. Other standards are as follows:

- **EIDE:** *EIDE (Enhanced Integrated Drive Electronics)* can support up to four hard disks at 137 gigabytes per disk. EIDE controllers are marketed under such names as SATA (for "Serial Advanced Technology Attachment"), Fast ATA, Ultra ATA, Fast IDE, ATA-2, ATA/100, and Serial ATA. Nowadays consumers are advised to buy SATA or Serial ATA, which have faster data transfer and less magnetic interference.

- **SCSI:** *SCSI (small computer system interface),* pronounced "scuzzy," supports several disk drives as well as other peripheral devices by linking them in a daisy chain. SCSI controllers are faster and have more storage capacity than EIDE controllers; they are typically found in servers and workstations.

- **Fibre Channel:** *Fibre Channel* is an up-and-coming standard that is not expected to be used much with personal computers, though it may some day replace SCSI. This standard has the advantage of very fast data speeds and so will probably be used with host computers and high-end servers.

HARD-DISK TECHNOLOGY FOR LARGE COMPUTER SYSTEMS: RAID Large databases, such as those maintained by insurance companies or AOL, require far bigger storage systems than the fixed-disk drives we've been describing, which send data to a computer along a single path. A *RAID (redundant array of independent [or inexpensive] disks) storage system,* which links any number of disk drives within a single cabinet or connected along a SCSI chain, sends data to the computer along several parallel paths simultaneously. Response time is thereby significantly improved.

Optical Disks: CDs & DVDs

Why would I prefer an optical disk over other forms of secondary storage?

Everyone who has ever played an audio CD is familiar with optical disks. **An *optical disk* is a removable disk, usually 4.75 inches in diameter and less**

RAID unit

Optical disk

than one-twentieth of an inch thick, on which data is written and read through the use of laser beams. An audio CD holds up to 74 minutes (2 billion bits' worth) of high-fidelity stereo sound. Some optical disks are used strictly for digital data storage, but many are used to distribute multimedia programs that combine text, visuals, and sound.

HOW OPTICAL-DISK STORAGE WORKS With an optical disk, there is no mechanical arm, as with floppy disks and hard disks. Instead, a high-power laser beam is used to write data by burning tiny pits or indentations into the surface of a hard plastic disk. To read the data, a low-power laser light scans the disk surface: Pitted areas are not reflected and are interpreted as 0 bits; smooth areas are reflected and are interpreted as 1 bits. (● *See Panel 4.18.*) Because the pits are so tiny, a great deal more data can be represented than is possible in the same amount of space on a diskette and many hard disks. An optical disk can hold about 6 gigabytes of data, the equivalent of about 1.3 million typewritten pages.

Nearly every PC marketed today contains a CD/DVD drive, which can also read audio CDs. These, along with their recordable and rewritable variations, are the two principal types of optical-disk technology used with computers.

CD-ROM—FOR READING ONLY The first kind of optical disk for microcomputers was the CD-ROM. ***CD-ROM (compact disk read-only memory)*** **is an**

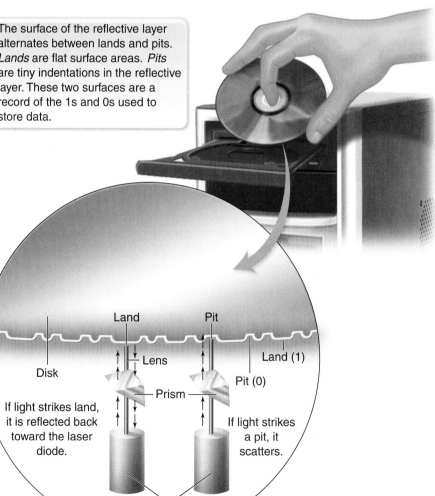

The surface of the reflective layer alternates between lands and pits. *Lands* are flat surface areas. *Pits* are tiny indentations in the reflective layer. These two surfaces are a record of the 1s and 0s used to store data.

Land — Lens

Pit

Land (1)

Disk

Pit (0)

Prism

If light strikes land, it is reflected back toward the laser diode.

If light strikes a pit, it scatters.

Laser diode

Chapter 4

228

optical-disk format that is used to hold prerecorded text, graphics, and sound. Like music CDs, a CD-ROM is a read-only disk. *Read-only* means the disk's content is recorded at the time of manufacture and cannot be written on or erased by the user. As the user, you have access only to the data imprinted by the disk's manufacturer. A CD-ROM disk can hold up to 650 megabytes of data, equal to over 300,000 pages of text.

A CD-ROM drive's speed is important because, with slower drives, images and sounds may appear choppy. In computer ads, drive speeds are indicated by the symbol "X," as in "56X," which is a high speed. *X* denotes the original data-transfer rate of 150 kilobytes per second. The data-transfer rate is the time the drive takes to transmit data to another device. A 56X drive runs at 56 times 150, or 8,400 kilobytes (8.4 megabytes) per second. If an ad carries the word *Max,* as in "56X Max," this indicates the device's maximum speed. Drives range in speed from 16X to 75X; the faster ones are more expensive.

CD-R—FOR RECORDING ONLY ONCE <u>**CD-R (compact disk–recordable) disks**</u> **can be written to only once but can be read many times.** This allows users to make their own CD disks. Once recorded, the information cannot be erased. CD-R is often used by companies for archiving—that is, to store vast amounts of information. If you're still using a film camera, for example, once you've shot a roll of color film, you can take it for processing to a photo shop, which can produce a disk containing your images. You can view the disk on any personal computer with a CD-ROM drive and the right software.

CD-RW—FOR REWRITING MANY TIMES A <u>**CD-RW (compact disk–rewritable) disk,**</u> also known as an *erasable optical disk,* **allows users to record and erase data, so the disk can be used over and over again.** CD-RW drives are becoming more common on microcomputers. CD-RW disks are useful for archiving and backing up large amounts of data or work in multimedia production or desktop publishing. CD-RW disks cannot be read by CD-ROM drives. CD-RW disks commonly have a capacity of 650–700 megabytes.

DVD-ROM—THE VERSATILE VIDEO DISK A <u>**DVD-ROM (digital versatile disk or digital video disk, with read-only memory)**</u> **is a CD-style disk with extremely high capacity, able to store 9.4 or more gigabytes.** How is this done? Like a CD or CD-ROM, the surface of a DVD contains microscopic pits, which represent the 0s and 1s of digital code that can be read by a laser. The pits on the DVD, however, are much smaller and grouped more closely together than those on a CD, allowing far more information to be represented. Also, the laser beam used focuses on pits roughly half the size of those on current audio CDs. In addition, the DVD format allows for two layers of data-defining pits, not just one. Finally, engineers have succeeded in squeezing more data into fewer pits, principally through data compression.

24X DVD/CD-RW Combo Drive

Most new computer systems now come with a DVD drive as standard equipment. A great advantage is that these drives can also take standard CD-ROM disks, so now you can watch DVD movies and play CD-ROMs using just one drive. DVDs are replacing CDs for archival storage, mass distribution of software, and entertainment. They not only store far more data but are different in quality from CDs. As one writer points out, "DVDs encompass much more: multiple dialogue tracks

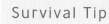

Did You Back Up Your Files?

According to the Consumer Electronics Association, a 2008 study ("Amassing Digital Fortunes: A Digital Storage Study") shows that nearly one in three (33%) of U.S. consumers don't see the need to back up their files, while nearly a quarter (22%) say they aren't backing up files because it's too time consuming. Generally, consumers don't know how to back up their data and if they do, they're failing to back up data because they claim it takes too much time. The average American adult has 1,800 digital files.[28]

How about you? Will you be able to get your files back if something goes wrong with your computer system?

CD/DVD, label side up

Slide-out tray for DVD/CD disk drive

and screen formats, and best of all, smashing sound and video."[29] The theater-quality video and sound, of course, are what made DVD a challenger to videotape as a vehicle for movie rentals.

Like CDs, DVDs have their recordable and rewritable variants:

- **DVD-R—recordable DVDs:** ***DVD-R (DVD-recordable) disks* allow one-time recording by the user.** That is, they cannot be reused—written on more than once.

- **DVD-RW, DVD-RAM, DVD+RW—reusable DVDs:** Three types of reusable disks are *DVD-RW (DVD-rewritable), DVD-RAM (DVD–random access memory),* and *DVD+RW (DVD+rewritable),* all of which can be recorded on and erased (except for video) many times. DVD-R disks have a capacity of 4.7 (single-sided) to 9.4 (double-sided) gigabytes.

BLU-RAY: THE NEXT-GENERATION OPTICAL DISK *Blu-ray,* also known as *Blu-ray Disc (BD),* is the name of a next-generation optical-disk format jointly developed by the Blu-ray Disc Association (BDA), a group of consumer electronics and PC companies (including Dell, Hitachi, HP, JVC, LG, Mitsubishi, Panasonic, Pioneer, Philips, Samsung, Sharp, Sony, TDK, and Thomson). **The *Blu-ray* optical format was developed to enable recording, rewriting, and playback of high-definition video, as well as storing of large amounts of data.** A decision by Blu-ray rival Warner Brothers to withdraw support for its competing HD DVD optical disc format appeared to hand the future of home entertainment to Blu-ray.[30]

A single-layer Blu-ray Disc can hold 25 gigabytes, which can be used to record over 2 hours of HDTV (or more than 13 hours of standard-definition TV). There are also dual-layer versions of the disks that can hold 50 gigabytes.

While current optical-disk technologies such as DVD, DVD-R, DVD-RW, and DVD-RAM use a red laser to read and write data, the new format uses a blue-violet laser instead, hence the name Blu-ray. Blu-ray products are backward-compatible and allow use of CDs and DVDs. The benefit of using a blue-violet laser is that it has a shorter wavelength than a red laser, which makes it possible to focus the laser spot with even greater precision. This allows data to be packed more tightly and stored in less space, so it's possible to fit more data on the disk even though it's the same size as a CD/DVD.

Not all the optical-disk drives and different types of optical media (read-only, rewritable, and so on) are mutually compatible. Thus, you need to check the product information before you buy to make sure you get what you want.

THE WORLD'S DVD ZONES As a way to maximize movie revenues, the film industry decided to split the world up into six DVD zones. This is to prevent the DVD version of a movie made in one country from being sold in another country in which the theater version has not yet opened. DVD disks with a particular region code will play only on DVD players with that region code. However, some of the newest DVD players are code-free—they are not "region locked." (Thus, if you plan to travel and use a DVD player for foreign movies, check out the compatibility restrictions.)

Sony's first Blu-ray disc recorder

Common DVD Capacities

Type	Sides	Layers	Capacity	Type	Sides	Layers	Capacity
Read only				**Rewritable (100,000 cycles)**			
DVD-Video	1	1	4.7 GB (DVD-5)	DVD-RAM Ver. 1	1	1	2.6 GB
and	1	2	8.5 GB (DVD-9)	DVD-RAM Ver. 1	2	1	5.2 GB
DVD-ROM	2	1	9.4 GB (DVD-10)	DVD-RAM Ver. 2	1	1	4.7 GB
	2	2	17.0 GB (DVD-18)	DVD-RAM Ver. 2	2	1	9.4 GB
HD DVD	1	1	15.0 GB	DVD-RAM (80 mm)	1	1	1.46 GB
HD DVD	1	2	30.0 GB	DVD-RAM (80 mm)	2	1	2.92 GB
Write once				Blu-ray	1	1	25.0 GB
DVD-R (A)	1	1	3.95 GB	Blu-ray	1	2	50.0 GB
DVD-R (A)	1	1	4.7 GB	HD DVD	1	1	20.0 GB
DVD-R (G)	1	1	4.7 GB	HD DVD	1	2	32.0 GB
DVD-R (G)	2	1	9.4 GB	**Re-recordable (1,000 cycles)**			
DVD + R	1	1	4.7 GB	DVD-RW	1	1	4.7 GB
				DVD + RW	1	1	4.7 GB
				DVD + RW	2	1	9.4 GB

Six DVD regions. The DVD world is basically divided into six regions. This means that DVD players and DVDs are encoded for operation in a specific geographical region. For example, the U.S. is in region 1; thus all DVD players sold in the U.S. are made to region 1 specifications. As a result, region 1 players can play only region 1 DVDs. On the back of each DVD package, you will find a region number (1 through 6).

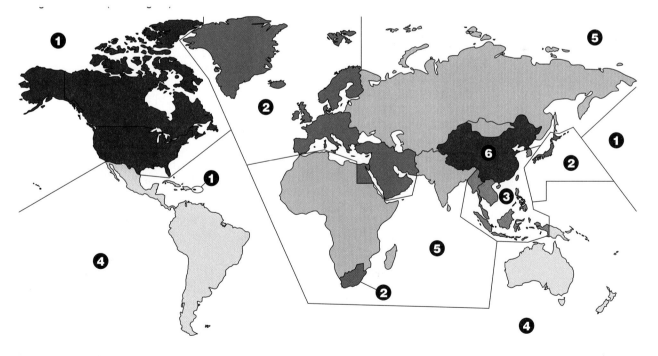

Magnetic Tape

Would I find magnetic tape storage useful?

Similar to the tape used on an audio tape recorder (but of higher density), **_magnetic tape_ is thin plastic tape coated with a substance that can be magnetized. Data is represented by magnetized spots (representing 1s)**

or nonmagnetized spots (representing 0s). Today, "mag tape" is used mainly for backup and archiving—that is, for maintaining historical records—where there is no need for quick access.

On large computers, tapes are used on magnetic-tape units or reels and in special cartridges. These tapes offer terabytes of storage. On microcomputers, tape is used in the form of ***tape cartridges,*** **modules resembling audiocassettes that contain tape in rectangular, plastic housings.** These cartridges can store up to 3.2 gigabytes; in groups, or arrays, they can store up to about 1.6 terabytes. The two most common types of tape drives are DAT (digital audio tape) from Hewlett-Packard, Sony, and Maxwell, for example, and Travan TR-3. (● *See Panel 4.19.*) An internal or external tape drive is required to use tape media.

Tape fell out of favor for a while, supplanted by such products as Iomega's Jaz and Zip-disk cartridge drives (since discontinued). Moreover, as hard drives swelled to multigigabyte size, using Zip disks for backup became less convenient. Today, as we mentioned, CD-R and DVD-R are becoming the most popular backup methods.

Smart Cards

Would I ever have occasion to use smart cards?

Today in the United States, most credit cards are old-fashioned magnetic-strip cards. A *magnetic-strip card* has a strip of magnetically encoded data on its back and holds about 0.2–0.9 kilobytes (KB) of data. The encoded data might include your name, account number, and PIN (personal identification number). The strip contains information needed to use the card, but the strip also has drawbacks. First, it can degrade over time, making the data unreadable. Second, the magnetic strip doesn't hold much information. Third, such data as the magnetic strip does contain is easy to access and duplicate, raising the risk of fraud.

Two other kinds of cards, smart cards and optical cards, which hold far more information, are already popular in Europe. Manufacturers are betting they will become more popular in the United States.

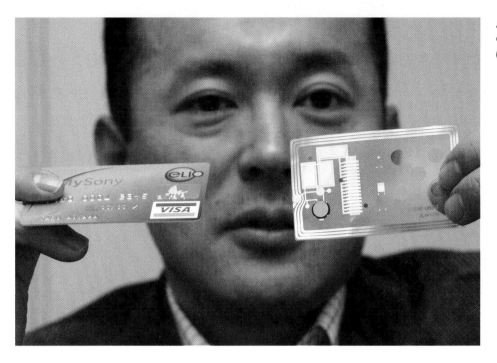

SMART CARDS A *smart card* **is a plastic card the size of a credit card with an integrated circuit—a microprocessor and memory chips—built into it.** Most smart cards have been designed with the look and feel of a credit or debit card but can function on at least three levels: credit, debit, and personal information. Smart cards include data storage capacity of around 10 megabytes. Owing to the portability and the size of smart cards, they are seen as the next generation of data exchange.

Smart cards contain an operating system just like personal computers. Smart cards can store and process information and are fully interactive. Advanced smart cards also contain a file structure. Some smart cards can be reloaded for reuse. When inserted into a reader, a smart card transfers data to and from a central computer. It is more secure than a magnetic-strip card and can be programmed to self-destruct if the wrong password is entered too many times. As a financial transaction card, it can be loaded with digital money and used as a traveler's check, except that variable amounts of money can be spent until the balance is zero.

Smart cards are well suited for prepaid, disposable applications such as cash cards or telephone debit cards. For example, when you're using a phone card, which is programmed to contain a set number of available minutes, you insert the card into a slot in the phone, wait for a tone, and dial the number. The length of your call is automatically calculated on the card, and the corresponding charge is deducted from the balance. Other uses of smart cards are as student cards, building-entrance cards, bridge-toll cards, and (as in Germany) national health care cards.

Different forms of smart-card technology are available:

● **Contact smart cards:** These kinds of cards, which must be swiped through card readers, are less prone to misalignment and being misread, but they tend to wear out from the contact.

● **Contactless smart cards:** These cards, which are read when held in front of a low-powered laser, can be used in mobile applications, as by automated toll-collecting devices reading cards as drivers pass through toll booths without stopping.

OPTICAL MEMORY CARDS Optical cards use the same type of technology as music compact disks but look like silvery credit cards. *Optical memory cards*

are plastic, laser-recordable, wallet-type cards used with an optical-card reader. Optical health cards have room not only for the individual's medical history and health-insurance information but also for digital images, such as electrocardiograms.

One form of optical memory card technology, the LaserCard, is used by the U.S. Immigration and Naturalization Service as new Permanent Resident and Border Crossing cards because of its highly secure, counterfeit-resistant features. In addition, LaserCards containing shipping manifest data are attached to shipping containers and sea vans, speeding up receipt processing considerably.

Flash & Solid State Memory

How useful is flash and sold state memory to me?

Disk drives, whether for diskettes, hard disks, or CD-ROMs, all involve moving parts—and moving parts can break. By contrast, *flash memory*, which is a variation on conventional computer memory chips, has no moving parts. Flash memory is also nonvolatile—it retains data even when the power is turned off. A drawback, however, is that flash memory circuits wear out after repeated use, limiting their life span.

Flash memory media are available in three forms: *flash memory cards*, *flash memory sticks*, and *flash memory drives*.

FLASH MEMORY CARDS <u>*Flash memory cards*</u>, or *flash RAM cards*, **are removable storage media that are inserted into a flash memory port in a digital camera, handheld PC, smartphone, or other mobile device.** Unlike smart cards, flash memory cards have no processor; they are useful only for storage. Flash memory cards store up to 16 gigabytes.

FLASH MEMORY STICKS Smaller than a stick of chewing gum, **a <u>*flash memory stick*</u> is a form of flash memory media**

(*Above*) A collection of flash drives; (*right*) Swiss Army knife with a flash drive that folds out.

that plugs into a memory stick port in a digital camera, camcorder, notebook PC, photo printer, and other devices. It holds up to 4 gigabytes of data.

FLASH MEMORY DRIVES A *flash memory drive*, also called a *USB flash drive, keychain drive,* or *key drive,* consists of a finger-size module of flash memory that plugs into the USB ports of nearly any PC or Macintosh. It has storage capacities up to 64 gigabytes, making the device extremely useful if you're traveling from home to office, say, and don't want to carry a laptop. When you plug the device into your USB port, it shows up as an external drive on the computer screen.

SOLID-STATE MEMORY DRIVES Instead of hard disk drives, some newer laptops (such as Apple's MacBook Air laptop) now feature **solid-state drives, which have far greater capacity than flash memory drives or keychain drives; like flash drives, they have no moving parts to break down,** as hard disk drives do. Some solid-state drives use SDRAM instead of flash memory, but in either case such drives are lighter and use less power than conventional disk drives and can better withstand bumps and bangs. The drawback, however, is that so far solid-state drives are much more expensive than hard disk drives.[31]

Survival Tip

What's the Life Span of Storage Media?

Hard drives: 3–6 years
CD/DVD-R: 2–15 years
CD/DVD-RW: 25–30 years
Flash drives: 10 years

Online Secondary Storage

Would I ever use an online storage service?

Online storage services, mentioned at the start of this section, allow you to use the internet to back up your data. Some services are free; others charge a small fee. Examples are Syncplicity, Dropbox, Mozy, Carbonite, iDrivePro, iDrive.com, and (for business) iBackup.com and eSureIt Business.[32] Asustek Computer, maker of the low-cost ($300) Eee PC, offers free online storage.[33] When you sign up, you obtain software that lets you upload whatever files you wish to the company's server. For security, you are given a password, and the files are supposedly encrypted to guard against unwanted access.

Incidentally, you should know that if you lose your cellphone, all those phone numbers in your address book are wirelessly backed up on a regular schedule by your cellphone carrier.[34]

Online Storage

Examples of online storage services:

Backup, *www.atbackup.com*
Connected Online Backup, *www.connected.com*
Digital Iron Mountain, *www.ironmountain.com/digital/*
Driveway, *www.driveway.com*
eSureIT, *www.intronis.com*
MagicalDesk.com, *www.magicaldesk.com*
X:Drive, *www.xdrive.com*

4.5 FUTURE DEVELOPMENTS IN PROCESSING & STORAGE

What are some forthcoming developments that could affect processing power and storage capacity?

Computer developers are obsessed with speed and power, constantly seeking ways to promote faster processing and more main memory in a smaller area. IBM, for instance, came up with a manufacturing process (called *silicon-on-insular,* or *SOI*) that had the effect of increasing a chip's speed and reducing its power consumption. This increasing power, says physicist Michio Kaku, is the reason you can get "a musical birthday card that contains more processing power than the combined computers of the Allied Forces in World War II."[35]

Does this mean that Moore's law—Intel cofounder Gordon Moore's 1965 prediction that the number of circuits on a silicon chip would keep doubling every 18 months—will never be repealed? After all, the smaller circuits get, the

PRACTICAL ACTION
Starting Over with Your Hard Drive: Erasing, Reformatting, & Reloading

There may come a time when your hard drive is so compromised by spyware and other parasites and slows down your computer so much it's as though you had lost two cylinders on your car engine. (This situation might have been avoided had you been running antispyware software, such as, for example, Ad-aware, AntiSpyware, CounterSpy, PestPatrol, Spybot Search & Destroy, SpyCatcher, or Spy Sweeper. But many people don't do this, which is why one study found that 80% of computers were infected with spyware.)[36] Or perhaps you've installed a new application, such as a speech-recognition program or new piece of hardware, whose drivers have the effect of causing such chaos in your system that you wish you'd never acquired the new item.

What should you do now? Give up your computer, buy a new one (if you can afford it), and transfer all your old data to it? (Some people actually do this.) Or erase everything on your hard drive and reinstall your software and data files? Here's what to do.[37]

Make a List of Everything in Your System & Tech Support Phone Numbers

The first thing you need to do is take paper and pencil and make a list of all (I) hardware components, (2) software registration codes, and (3) technical support phone numbers for your computer maker and your internet access provider, in case you run into problems while rebuilding your system.

Make Sure You Have Disks with Copies of Your Software

See if you have the original disks for all your software (your program files), including the Windows installation disks that came with your computer. If you don't, create CD/DVD copies. Or contact your computer maker for new ones (for which the company will probably charge you).

Make Backup Copies of Your Data Files

There are several different ways to back up your data files, those listed under My Documents, My Pictures, and My Music:

- **Copy to a server:** If you're on a network, you can save all your data files to a networked folder.

- **Copy to CDs or DVDs:** Using a CD/DVD drives, you can back up your data files onto writable CDs or DVDs. (A 5-gigabyte DVD may be sufficient. Or you may use several CDs, which hold about 700 megabytes each.)

- **Copy to a keychain drive or an MP3 player:** You can save all your data files to a keychain drive, an MP3 player, or another external hard drive and then transfer them to another computer to copy them onto CD/DVD disks.

You might wish to make two copies of your backed-up files—just in case.

Reformat Your Hard Drive & Reinstall Your Operating System

Insert your operating system CD-ROM installation disks into the CD drive. When your computer asks you if you want to reformat your hard dive, answer yes. When it advises that if you continue all files will be deleted, respond that this is okay. It will take perhaps 60 minutes to reformat the hard disk. You will then be asked to fill in your name, time zone, country, and type of internet connection. Probably at this point you should also download any operating system updates (patches) from the manufacturer's website. Reboot your computer.

Reinstall Your Programs & Drivers

Reinstall all your programs, such as Microsoft Office, and all the drivers for your printer, camera, CD burner, and other peripherals. (Drivers may not be needed, because new OSs can recognize almost anything and find the driver online.)

Install Security Software & Firewall

To be sure you're starting over with a secure system, now you should install updated security software (such as McAfee Virus Protection, Norton AntiVirus, Avast!, or ZoneAlarm Antivirus), which contains antivirus software and a firewall that prevents unauthorized users from gaining access to your network. Reboot your computer.

Reinstall All Your Data Files

Copy your saved data files from the backup source. Run scans on everything, using the security software. Reboot. By now, it's hoped, you will have gotten rid of all your spyware and other nuisances.

more chip manufacturers bump up against material limits. "The fact that chips are made of atoms has increasingly become a problem for us," said Moore in 2000. "In the next two or three generations, it may slow down to doubling every five years. People are predicting we will run out of gas in about 2020,

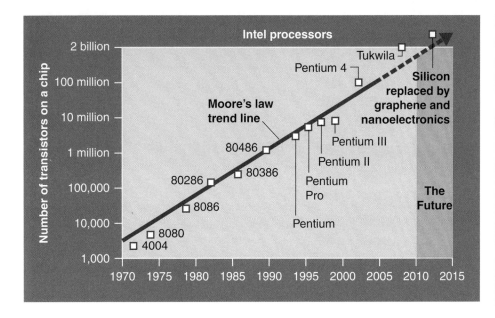

Intel processors

Number of transistors on a chip

- 2 billion
- 100 million
- 10 million
- 1 million
- 100,000
- 10,000
- 1,000

1970 · 1975 · 1980 · 1985 · 1990 · 1995 · 2000 · 2005 · 2010 · 2015

4004 · 8080 · 8086 · 80286 · 80386 · 80486 · Moore's law trend line · Pentium · Pentium Pro · Pentium II · Pentium III · Pentium 4 · Tukwila · Silicon replaced by graphene and nanoelectronics · The Future

panel 4.20

Moore's law: How much longer?

Miraculously, Gordon Moore's prediction that the number of transistors on a silicon chip will double every 18 months has held up since the 1960s. Eventually transistors will become so tiny that their components will approach the size of molecules, and the laws of physics will no longer allow this kind of doubling.

and I don't see how we get around that."[38] Later, in 2005, he said, "I think we've got quite a bit more to go . . . but then I can never see more than 10 years."[39] (● *See Panel 4.20.*)

Scientists have assumed that silicon chips can't be made infinitely smaller because of leakage of electrons across boundaries that are supposed to serve as insulators. In addition, engineers are creating three-dimensional chips that consist of a multistory silicon stack that can run faster and cooler than ordinary chips. Still, chip makers continue to refine the technology. Intel, for example, has changed the materials used in its chips—using metal instead of silicon in a key component called a gate and replacing silicon dioxide as an insulating layer in its transistors with hafnium—to reduce energy consumption and increase processing speed. (This is known as "high-k" technology.) It is also reducing chip size from 180 nanometers (a nanometer is a billionth of a meter) in 1999 to an expected 32 nanometers in late 2009. IBM is working on a 22-nanometer memory chip.[40]

For now, RAM is volatile, but researchers have developed new nonvolatile forms of RAM that may soon be available. One form is *M-RAM*—the *M* stands for "magnetic"—which uses minuscule magnets rather than electric charges to store the 0s and 1s of binary data. M-RAM uses much less power than current RAM, and whatever is in memory when the computer's power is turned off or lost will remain there. A second type, *OUM (ovonic unified memory)* or *phase-change memory,* stores bits by generating different levels of low and high resistance on a glossy material.

Magnetic RAM

M-RAM is the focus of the website at:

http://mram-info.com

Future Developments in Processing

What are ways that processing power could be increased in the future?

What are the possible directions in which processors can go? Let us consider some of them:

SELLING PROCESSING POWER OVER THE INTERNET In 2002, IBM launched a service, Virtual Linux Service, selling computer processing power on an as-needed basis, in the same way that power companies sell electricity. When, for example, a company wants to update its email or other programs, instead of buying more servers or the latest hardware to provide processing power, it rents the processing time on Linux servers. By now, many companies have gone into the business of what is now called *application virtualization.*

panel 4.21

Nanotechnology: A matter of scale

The world of nanotechnology is so small it defies imagination.

Each bar represents 1,000th of the bar above it

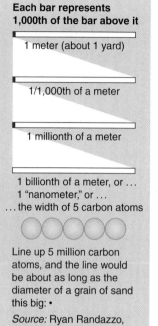

1 meter (about 1 yard)

1/1,000th of a meter

1 millionth of a meter

1 billionth of a meter, or …
1 "nanometer," or …
…the width of 5 carbon atoms

Line up 5 million carbon atoms, and the line would be about as long as the diameter of a grain of sand this big: •

Source: Ryan Randazzo, "Science of Small," *Reno-Gazette Journal,* June 16, 2002, pp. 1E, 8E; Knight-Ridder.

An ant carrying a I-millimeter-square microchip illustrates the kind of scale involved in nanotechnology.

Nokia's nanotech Morph telephone

More about Nanotechnology

Is nanotechnology really here? To begin to find out, check out nanotechnology's leading forum, the Foresight Institute (*www.foresight.org*), and leading critic, ETC (*www.etcgroup.org*). Also, what effects might nanoparticles have on the body's systems? Go to:

www.cdc.gov/niosh/topics/ nanotech/

NANOTECHNOLOGY Nanotechnology, nanoelectronics, nanostructures, nanofabrication—all start with a measurement known as a *nanometer,* a billionth of a meter, which means we are operating at the level of atoms and molecules. (● See Panel *4.21.*)

In *nanotechnology,* molecules are used to create tiny machines for holding data or performing tasks. Experts attempt to do nanofabrication by building tiny nanostructures one atom or molecule at a time. When applied to chips and other electronic devices, the field is called *nanoelectronics.*

Today scientists are trying to simulate the on/off of traditional transistors by creating transistor switches that manipulate a single electron, the subatomic particle that is the fundamental unit of electricity. In theory, a trillion of these electrons could be put on a chip the size of a fingernail—a chip made not of silicon, which has its physical limits, but of cylindrical wisps of carbon atoms known as carbon nanotubes. IBM has built some working nanocircuits, but it will probably not be until 2015 that factory chipmakers will be able to make them in huge quantities.[41]

OPTICAL COMPUTING Today's computers are electronic; tomorrow's might be optical, or optoelectronic—using light, not electricity. With optical technology, a machine using lasers, lenses, and mirrors would represent the on/off codes of data with pulses of light.

Light is much faster than electricity. Indeed, fiber-optic networks, which consist of hair-thin glass fibers instead of copper wire, can move information at speeds 3,000 times faster than conventional networks. However, the signals get bogged down when they have to be processed by silicon chips. Optical chips would remove that bottleneck. It's suggested that mass-produced versions of optical chips could not only slash costs of voice and data networks but also become a new type of technology for delivering high-bandwidth movies, music, and games.

DNA COMPUTING Potentially, biotechnology could be used to grow cultures of bacteria that, when exposed to light, emit a small electrical charge,

Dr. Milan Stojanovik of Columbia University developed the first game-playing DNA computer, called Maya.

for example. The properties of this "biochip" could be used to represent the on/off digital signals used in computing. Or a strand of synthetic DNA might represent information as a pattern of molecules, and the information might be manipulated by subjecting it to precisely designed chemical reactions that could mark or lengthen the strand. For instance, instead of using binary, it could manipulate the four nucleic acids (represented by *A, T, C, G*), which holds the promise of processing big numbers. This is an entirely *nondigital* way of thinking about computing.[42]

QUANTUM COMPUTING Sometimes called the "ultimate computer," the *quantum computer* is based on quantum mechanics, the theory of physics that explains the erratic world of the atom. Whereas an ordinary computer stores information as 0s and 1s represented by electrical currents or voltages that are either high or low, a quantum computer stores information by using states of elementary particles. Scientists envision using the energized and relaxed states of individual atoms to represent data. For example, hydrogen atoms could be made to switch off and on like a conventional computer's transistors by moving from low energy states (off) to high energy states (on).[43]

EXTENDING BATTERY & RECHARGING TECHNOLOGY Where is the weak link in our high-tech world? Says one writer, "Computer chips double in speed every two years—your current BlackBerry is as powerful as your desktop computer once was—but the batteries powering these devices are improving only about 8% per year."[44] Laptop, cellphone, and iPod users are tired of having their devices run out of electric charge after only a few hours. And claims that a laptop will get up to 5 hours and 40 minutes of battery life are "not even close," says one expert.[45]

Among the areas of research: Intel is working on developing wireless charging, freeing gadgets from their recharging cords.[46] Companies are also experimenting with developing new lithium-ion batteries, which may extend battery life.[47] Silver-zinc batteries may provide up to 30% higher capacity compared to existing lithium-ion batteries.[48] Tiny fuel-cell batteries, powered by combustible liquids or gases, could potentially power a laptop for days between refills.[49] Marvell Technology Group, which makes chips, is promoting the idea of "plug computers," computing devices that plug into electrical sockets and that are about the same size yet would have enough power to manage people's digital media.[50]

ETHICAL MATTERS Of these future developments, nanotechnology has probably received the most attention, and indeed the U.S. government has launched the National Nanotechnology Initiative. In fact, however, nanotechnology and other important fields have been melding into a new field of science vital to U.S. security and economic development. This field is known by the acronym *NBIC* (pronounced either "*en*-bick" or "*nib*-bick"), which represents the convergence of nanotechnology, biotechnology, information technology, and cognitive (brain) science. "NBIC are the power tools of the 21st century," says James Canton, president of a technology trends research firm in San Francisco called Institute for Global Futures.[51]

But is there a possibility of "Gray Goo"? This is a scenario hypothesized in *Wired* magazine in which self-replicating molecule-size robots run amok and transform all earthly matter into nanobots. (It is also the plot for Michael Crichton's science-fiction thriller *Prey*.) People concerned about adverse effects of nanotechnology worry that the tiny particles might embed themselves in live tissue, with unknown harmful effects.[52]

Future Developments in Secondary Storage

What are ways that secondary storage could be increased in the future?

As for developments in secondary storage, when IBM introduced the world's first disk drive in 1956, it was capable of storing 2,000 bits per square inch. Today the company is shipping hard disks with densities of 14.3 billion bits, or 1.43 gigabits, per square inch. But that, too, is sure to change.

HIGHER-DENSITY DISKS With 700 megabytes of storage space, and prices well under $1 each, blank CDs have replaced floppy disks and Zip disk cartridges as the most cost-effective storage medium. Present DVD disks currently hold up to 9.4 gigabytes of data. We mentioned the Blu-ray, which uses a blue-violet laser to record information; Blu-ray disks are able (at 25 gigabytes) to record more than 13 hours of standard TV programming and over 2 hours of digital high-definition video.

Hard drive makers have begun employing a technology known as *perpendicular recording technology*, which involves stacking magnetic bits vertically on the surface of a platter (instead of horizontally, as is usual). Based on this innovation, Seagate Technology makes a 1.5 terabyte hard drive, the Barracuda, for desktop PCs, servers, and external storage. Also using perpendicular recording, Hitachi Ltd's Ultrastar can store up to 1,000 gigabytes (1 trillion bytes). (● *See Panel 4.22.*)

Another promising technology is the *micro-holographic* disk being developed by General Electric Co., which GE says could store 540 gigabytes, or the content of 100 standard DVDs, on a single DVD (equivalent to 20 single-layer Blu-ray disks). Holographic technology can store data beneath the surface of a disk,

panel 4.22

Conventional versus perpendicular recording technologies

Conventional (Longitudinal) Recording

Each bit of information is represented by a collection of magnetized particles, with their north and south poles oriented in one direction or the other. In longitudinal recording, the particles' north and south poles are lined up parallel to the disk's surface in a ring around its center. Magnetic repulsion limits how closely packed those bits can be and still maintain data integrity.

Perpendicular Recording

In this type of recording, the poles are arranged perpendicular to the disk's surface, which allows more bits to be packed onto a disk and reduces problems from magnetic interference.

whereas CDs, DVDs, and Blu-ray disks store data only on the surface.[53] A team of Australian researchers is going beyond this to develop "five-dimensional" storage, which would permit a 10-terabyte disk, the equivalent of storing 10,000 standard-definition movies on one disk.[54]

MOLECULAR ELECTRONICS—STORAGE AT THE SUBATOMIC LEVEL An emerging field, molecular electronics, may push secondary storage into another dimension entirely. Some possibilities include polymer memory, holograms, molecular magnets, subatomic lines, and bacteria.

Polymer memory involves developing an alternative to silicon to create chips that store data on polymers, or plastics, which are cheaper than silicon devices. A bonus with polymers is that, unlike conventional RAM memory, it is nonvolatile—it retains information even after the machine is shut off. Polymer memory involves storing data based on the polymer's electrical resistance. IBM is also developing so-called *probe storage* that uses tiny probes to burn pits in a Plexiglas-like polymer, in which each hole is about 10 nanometers wide, resulting in an experimental storage device of 200 gigabits per square inch. IBM has said that some day it expects as many as 25 million pages of text will be stored in an area no larger than a postage stamp.

EXPERIENCE BOX
How to Buy a Laptop

"Choosing a laptop computer is trickier than buying a desktop PC," says Wall Street Journal technology writer Walter Mossberg.[55] The reason: laptops are more diverse and more personal and include "a mind-boggling array of computers, from featherweight models that are great for travel to bulky multimedia machines that double as TV sets." In addition, desktop "generic boxes" tend to be similar, at least within a price class. Trying to choose among the many Windows-based laptops is a particularly brow-wrinkling experience. Macintosh laptops tend to be more straightforward.

Nevertheless, here are some suggestions:[56]

Purpose. What are you going to use your laptop for? You can get one that's essentially a desktop replacement and won't be moved much. If you expect to use the machine a lot in class, in libraries, or on airplanes, however, weight and battery life are important.

Whatever kind of computer you get (whether laptop or desktop), you want to be sure it works with your school's system. Some departments within a college may require a specific computer configuration or software, so check beforehand. Certainly it should be up to date and able to get internet access through Ethernet and wireless connections. "Don't bring clunkers [to college]," says one article. "Older computers tend to be buggy, and often lack protection against viruses and other malicious software."[57]

Basics. Writer Mossberg advises that if you're buying an Apple laptop, 2 gigabytes of memory is plenty. If you're using Microsoft Vista Home Premium, get 3 gigabytes for best performance. And make sure that you install antivirus and firewall software right away.

Budget & Weight. Laptops range from $300 (with rebates) to $3,000, with high-end brands aimed mainly at business-people, hard-core videogamers, and people doing video production. Weight can range from about 3 pounds to over 10 pounds. Windows laptops are often less expensive than Apple laptops, and they tend to have a greater variety of ports and slots and come in more styles and sizes. But Apple laptops are considered to have a more reliable operating system, to work faster, and to be more secure.

- *Low-budget:* Laptops costing in the $350–$1,000 range weigh from 2.2 pounds to 7.5 pounds, have 8.9-, 13.3-, or 15.4-inch screens, run on an Intel Pentium, Celeron, or Atom chip, have 1–2 gigabytes of RAM, and have 60- to 80-gigabyte hard drives. Be sure the laptop comes with a CD burner (drive) or CD burner/DVD-ROM combination and Wi-Fi connection. Examples of this level of laptop are the Dell Inspiron 1525 and the ASUS Eee PC 900.

- *Middle range:* Generally priced at $1,000–$2,000 and weighing 4–7 pounds, these laptops have a dual-core processor, a 17-inch screen, 2 gigabytes of RAM, a 160-gigabyte hard drive, and a CD/DVD-RW drive. Dell, Hewlett-Packard, Compaq, Sony, and Apple, among others, all sell middle-range laptops.

- *Lightweight ultraportables:* Weighing under 4 pounds, ultraportable laptops have screen sizes ranging from 8.9 inches to 12.1 inches, 1.0- to 1.8-gigahertz processors, 1–2 gigabytes of RAM, and 160-gigabyte hard drives. Some models lack internal CD or DVD drives. Battery life varies from 2 to 4 or so hours. Cost is generally $1,300–$2,500. Examples of lightweight laptops are Hewlett-Packard's HP 2133 Mini-Note and the Apple MacBook Air.

- *High-end desktop replacements:* Weighing 7–10 pounds and costing $2,500–$3,000, high-end laptops are bulky machines designed to be desktop replacements. Their 15.1- to 20-inch display screens with wide viewing angles allow four or five people to watch at once. These machines feature graphics processors, 2–4 gigabytes of RAM, 250-gigabyte hard drives, high-speed DVD-RW drives, and perhaps even TV tuners for watching TV on the display screen. Examples are the fully loaded Dell XPS M2010, the Apple MacBook Pro, and Toshiba's Qosmio X305.

Batteries: The Life–Weight Trade-Off. You should strive to find a laptop that will run for at least 3 hours on its battery. A rechargeable lithium-ion battery lasts longer than the nickel-metal hydride battery. Even so, a battery in the less expensive machines will usually run continuously for only about 2¼ hours. (DVD players are particularly voracious consumers of battery power, so it's the rare laptop that will allow you to finish watching a 2-hour movie.)

The trade-off is that heavier machines usually have longer battery life. The lightweight machines tend to get less than 2 hours, and toting extra batteries offsets the weight savings. (A battery can weigh a pound or so.)[58]

Software. Laptops might come with less software than you would get with a typical desktop, though what you get will probably be adequate for most student purposes. For instance, notebook PCs might offer Microsoft Works rather than the more powerful Microsoft Office to handle word processing, spreadsheets, databases, and the like.

Keyboards & Pointing Devices. The keys on a laptop keyboard are usually the same size as those on a desktop machine, although they can be smaller. However, the up-and-down action feels different, and the keys may feel wobbly. In addition, some keys may be omitted altogether, or keys may do double duty or appear in unaccustomed arrangements.

Most laptops have a small touch-sensitive pad in lieu of a mouse—you drag your finger across the touchpad to move the cursor. Others use a pencil-eraser-size pointing stick in the middle of the keyboard. (But be sure to carry a regular mouse with your laptop, so when you are working on a large flat surface, you can just plug the mouse connector into the mouse port on the laptop and use it as you would on a desktop computer.)

Screens. If you're not going to carry the notebook around much, go for a big, bright screen. Most people find they are comfortable with a 13- to 15-inch display, measured diagonally, though screens can be as small as 8 inches and as large as 17 or 20 inches (which is better for viewing movies).

Memory, Speed, & Storage Capacity. If you're buying a laptop to complement your desktop, you may be able to get along with reduced memory, slow processor, small hard disk, and no CD-ROM. Otherwise, all these matters become important.

Memory (RAM) is the most important factor in computer performance, even though processor speed is more heavily hyped. Most laptops have at least 1 gigabyte of memory, but

2–3 gigabytes of high-speed DDR SDRAM is best. A microprocessor running 1.6 gigaherz should be adequate. (But if you plan to work with a lot of graphics and/or video, get more RAM and a higher-speed processor, as well as a laptop with a separate video card inside with its own additional memory.)

A hard drive of 160 gigabytes or more is sufficient for most people, and make sure that you have an internal CD/DVD drive, for backing up your files and to play movies and the like.

Wireless. Most laptops come with Wi-Fi for wireless networking; 802.11b technology is fine for ordinary use, but try to buy a laptop with the newer and faster "n" version.

For more information about buying computers, go to *www.zdnet.com/computershopper,* *www.computerhistory.org/?gclid=CMeF-f7I6JQCFSkViQodlk2iSA,* and *http://compreviews.about.com/od/buyers/bb/DesktopPCs.htm.*

Also, go green: look for manufacturers that sell Energy Star systems and provide instructions for recycling old computer equipment.

AGP (accelerated graphics port) bus (p. 222) Bus that transmits data at very high speeds; designed to support video and three-dimensional (3-D) graphics. Why it's important: *An AGP bus is twice as fast as a PCI bus.*

arithmetic/logic unit (ALU) (p. 212) Part of the CPU that performs arithmetic operations and logical operations and controls the speed of those operations. Why it's important: *Arithmetic operations are the fundamental math operations: addition, subtraction, multiplication, and division. Logical operations are comparisons such as "equal to," "greater than," or "less than."*

ASCII (American Standard Code for Information Interchange) (p. 202) Binary code used with microcomputers. Besides having the more conventional characters, the Extended ASCII version includes such characters as math symbols and Greek letters. Why it's important: *ASCII is the binary code most widely used in microcomputers.*

bay (p. 202) Shelf or opening in the computer case used for the installation of electronic equipment, generally storage devices such as a hard drive or DVD drive. Why it's important: *Bays permit the expansion of system capabilities. A computer may come equipped with four or eight bays.*

binary system (p. 199) A two-state system used for data representation in computers; has only two digits—0 and 1. Why it's important: *In the computer, 0 can be represented by electrical current being off and 1 by the current being on. All data and program instructions that go into the computer are represented in terms of these binary numbers.*

bit (p. 200) Short for "binary digit," which is either a 0 or a 1 in the binary system of data representation in computer systems. Why it's important: *The bit is the fundamental element of all data and information processed and stored in a computer system.*

bluetooth (p. 220) Wireless technology that consists of short-range radio waves that transmit up to 30 feet. Why it's important: *It is used to connect cellphones to computers but also to connect computers to printers, keyboards, headsets, and other appliances.*

Blu-ray (p. 230) The Blu-ray optical format was developed to enable recording, rewriting, and playback of high-definition video, as well as storing of large amounts of data. Why it's important: *It's possible to fit more data on a Blu-ray disk even though it's the same size as a CD/DVD.*

bus (p. 213) Also called *bus line;* electrical data roadway through which bits are transmitted within the CPU and between the CPU and other components of the motherboard. Why it's important: *A bus resembles a multilane highway: The more lanes it has, the faster the bits can be transferred.*

byte (p. 200) Group of 8 bits. Why it's important: *A byte represents one character, digit, or other value. It is the basic unit used to measure the storage capacity of main memory and secondary storage devices (kilobytes and megabytes).*

cache (p. 215) Special high-speed memory area on a chip that the CPU can access quickly. It temporarily stores instructions and data that the processor is likely to use frequently. Why it's important: *Cache speeds up processing.*

CD-R (compact disk–recordable) disk (p. 229) Optical-disk form of secondary storage that can be written to only once but can be read many times. Why it's important: *This format allows consumers to make their own CD disks, though it's a slow process. Once recorded, the information cannot be erased. CD-R is often used by companies for archiving—that is, to store vast amounts of information. A variant is the Photo CD, an optical disk developed by Kodak that can digitally store photographs taken with an ordinary 35-millimeter camera.*

CD-ROM (compact disk read-only memory) (p. 228) Optical-disk form of secondary storage that is used to hold prerecorded text, graphics, and sound. Why it's important: *Like music CDs, a CD-ROM is a read-only disk. Read-only means the disk's content is recorded at the time of manufacture and cannot be written on or erased by the user. A CD-ROM disk can hold up to 650–700 megabytes of data, equal to over 300,000 pages of text.*

CD-RW (compact disk–rewritable) disk (p. 229) Also known as *erasable optical disk;* optical-disk form of secondary storage that allows users to record and erase data, so the disk can be used over and over again. Special CD-RW drives and software are required. Why it's important: *CD-RW disks are useful for archiving and backing up large amounts of data or work in multimedia production or desktop publishing; however, they are relatively slow.*

chip (p. 196) Also called a *microchip,* or *integrated circuit;* consists of millions of microminiature electronic circuits printed on a tiny piece of silicon. Silicon is an element widely found in sand that has desirable electrical (or "semiconducting") properties. Why it's important: *Chips have made possible the development of small computers.*

chipset (p. 207) Groups of interconnected chips on the motherboard that control the flow of information between the microprocessor and other system components connected to the motherboard. Why it's important: *The chipset determines what types of processors, memory, and video-card ports will work on the same motherboard. It also establishes the types of multimedia, storage, network, and other hardware the motherboard supports.*

CMOS (complementary metal-oxide semiconductor) chips (p. 215) Battery-powered chips that don't lose their contents when the power is turned off. Why it's important: *CMOS chips contain flexible start-up instructions—such as time, date, and calendar—that must be kept current even when the computer is turned off. Unlike ROM chips, CMOS chips can be* *reprogrammed, as when you need to change the time for daylight savings time.*

control unit (p. 212) Part of the CPU that deciphers each instruction stored in it and then carries out the instruction. Why it's important: *The control unit directs the movement of electronic signals between main memory and the arithmetic/logic unit. It also directs these electronic signals between main memory and the input and output devices.*

CPU (central processing unit) (p. 211) The processor; it follows the instructions of the software (program) to manipulate data into information. The CPU consists of two parts—(1) the control unit and (2) the arithmetic/logic unit (ALU), both of which contain registers, or high-speed storage areas. All are linked by a kind of electronic "roadway" called a *bus.* Why it's important: *The CPU is the "brain" of the computer.*

DVD-R (DVD-recordable) disks (p. 230) DVD disks that allow one-time recording by the user. Why it's important: *Recordable DVDs offer the user yet another option for storing large amounts of data.*

DVD-ROM (digital versatile disk or digital video disk, with read-only memory) (p. 229) CD-type disk with extremely high capacity, able to store 4.7 or more gigabytes. Why it's important: *It is a powerful and versatile secondary storage medium.*

EBCDIC (Extended Binary Coded Decimal Interchange Code) (p. 201) Binary code used with large computers. Why it's important: *EBCDIC is commonly used in mainframes.*

ethernet (p. 220) Network standard for linking all devices in a local area network. Why it's important: *It's commonly used to connect microcomputers, cable modems, and printers. (To use Ethernet, the computer must have an Ethernet network interface card, and special Ethernet cables are required.)*

exabyte (EB) (p. 201) Approximately 1 quintillion bytes—1 billion billion bytes (1,024 petabytes—or 1,152,921,504,606,846,976 bytes). Why it's important: *Although this number is seldom used, it is estimated that all the printed material in the world represents about 5 exabytes.*

expansion (p. 206) Way of increasing a computer's capabilities by adding hardware to perform tasks that are beyond the scope of the basic system. Why it's important: *Expansion allows users to customize and/or upgrade their computer systems.*

expansion card (p. 221) Also known as *expansion board, adapter card, interface card, plug-in board, controller card, add-in,* or *add-on;* circuit board that provides more memory or that controls peripheral devices. Why it's important: *Common expansion cards connect to the monitor (graphics card), speakers and microphones (sound card), and network (network card). Most computers have four to eight expansion slots, some of which may already contain expansion cards included in your initial PC purchase.*

expansion slot (p. 221) Socket on the motherboard into which the user can plug an expansion card. Why it's important: *See expansion card.*

FireWire (p. 220) A specialized serial-bus port intended to connect devices working with lots of data, such as digital video recorders, DVD players, gaming consoles, and digital audio equipment. Why it's important: *Whereas the USB port handles only 12 megabits per second, FireWire handles up to 400 megabits per second.*

flash memory card (p. 234) Also known as *flash RAM cards;* form of secondary storage consisting of circuitry on credit-card-size cards that can be inserted into slots connecting to the motherboard on notebook computers. Why it's important: *Flash memory is nonvolatile, so it retains data even when the power is turned off.*

flash memory chip (p. 215) Chip that can be erased and reprogrammed more than once (unlike PROM chips, which can be programmed only once). Why it's important: *Flash memory, which can range from 32 to 128 megabytes in capacity, is used to store programs not only in personal computers but also in pagers, cellphones, printers, and digital cameras. Unlike standard RAM chips, flash memory is nonvolatile—data is retained when the power is turned off.*

flash memory drive (p. 235) Also called a *USB flash drive, keychain drive,* or *key drive;* a finger-size module of flash memory that plugs into the USB ports of nearly any PC or Macintosh. Why it's important: *They generally have storage capacities up to 64 gigabytes, making the device extremely useful if you're traveling from home to office and don't want to carry a laptop. When you plug the device into your USB port, it shows up as an external drive on the computer.*

flash memory stick (p. 234) Smaller than a stick of chewing gum, a form of flash memory media that plugs into a memory stick port in a digital camera, camcorder, notebook PC, photo printer, and other devices. Why it's important: *It holds up to 4 gigabytes of data and is very convenient to transport and use.*

flops (p. 210) Stands for "floating-point operations per second." A *floating-point operation* is a special kind of mathematical calculation. This measure, used mainly with supercomputers, is expressed as *megaflops* (*mflops,* or millions of floating-point operations per second), *gigaflops* (*gflops,* or billions), and *teraflops* (*tflops,* or trillions). Why it's important: *The measure is used to express the processing speed of supercomputers.*

gigabyte (G, GB) (p. 200) Approximately 1 billion bytes (1,073,741,824 bytes); a measure of storage capacity. Why it's important: *This measure was formerly used mainly with "big iron" (mainframe) computers but is typical of the secondary storage (hard-disk) capacity of today's microcomputers.*

gigahertz (GHz) (p. 209) Measure of speed used for the latest generation of processors: 1 billion cycles per second. Why it's important: *Since a new high-speed processor can cost many hundred dollars more than a previous-generation chip, experts often recommend that buyers fret less about the speed of the processor (since the work most people do on their PCs doesn't even tax the limits of the current hardware) and more about spending money on extra memory.*

graphics processing unit (GPU) (p. 209) Specialized processor used to minipulate three-dimensional (3-D) computer graphics. Why it's important: Unlike a general-purpose CPU, a GPU is able to perform a range of complex algorithms (problem-solving steps). GPUs are found in personal computers, workstations, cellphones, and game consoles.

graphics card (p. 223) Also called a *video card* or *video adapter;* expansion card that converts signals from the computer into video signals that can be displayed as images on a monitor. Why it's important: *The power of a graphics card, often expressed in megabytes, as in 8-, 16-, or 32- MB, determines the clarity of the images on the monitor.*

hard disk (p. 225) Secondary storage medium; thin but rigid metal, glass, or ceramic platter covered with a substance that allows data to be stored in the form of magnetized spots. Hard disks are tightly sealed within an enclosed hard-disk-drive unit to prevent any foreign matter from getting inside. Data may be recorded on both sides of the disk platters. Why it's important: *Hard disks hold much more data than do floppy disks. All microcomputers use hard disks as their principal storage medium.*

integrated circuit (p. 195). An entire electronic circuit, including wires, formed on a single "chip," or piece, of special material, usually silicon. Why it's important: *In the old days, transistors were made individually and then formed into an electronic circuit with the use of wires and solder. An integrated circuit is formed as part of a single manufacturing process.*

Intel-type chip (p. 207) Processor chip originally made for PCs; made principally by Intel Corp. and Advanced Micro Devices (AMD), but also by Cyrix, DEC, and others. Why it's important: *These chips are used by manufacturers such as Compaq, Dell, Gateway, Hewlett-Packard, and IBM. Since 1993, Intel has marketed its chips under the names "Pentium," "Pentium Pro," "Pentium MMX," "Pentium II," "Pentium III," "Pentium 4," "Xeon," "Itanium," and "Celeron." Many ads for PCs contain the logo "Intel inside" to show that the systems run an Intel microprocessor. New Apple Macs use Intel dual-core and quad-core processors.*

IrDA port (p. 220) Port that allows a computer to make a cableless connection with infrared-capable devices, such as some printers. Why it's important: *Infrared ports eliminate the need for cabling.*

kilobyte (K, KB) (p. 200) Approximately 1,000 bytes (1,024 bytes); a measure of storage capacity. Why it's important: *The kilobyte was a common unit of measure for memory or secondary storage capacity on older computers.*

machine cycle (p. 212) Series of operations performed by the control unit to execute a single program instruction. It (1) fetches an instruction, (2) decodes the instruction, (3) executes the instruction, and (4) stores the result. *The machine cycle is the essence of computer-based processing.*

machine language (p. 202) Binary code (language) that the computer uses directly. The 0s and 1s represent precise storage locations and operations. Why it's important: *For a program to run, it must be in the machine language of the computer that is executing it.*

magnetic tape (p. 231) Thin plastic tape coated with a substance that can be magnetized. Data is represented by magnetized spots (representing 1s) or nonmagnetized spots (representing 0s). Why it's important: *Today, "mag tape" is used mainly for backup and archiving—that is, for maintaining historical records—where there is no need for quick access.*

megabyte (M, MB) (p. 200) Approximately 1 million bytes (1,048,576 bytes); measure of storage capacity. Why it's important: *Microcomputer primary storage capacity is expressed in megabytes.*

megahertz (MHz) (p. 209) Measure of microcomputer processing speed, controlled by the system clock; 1 million cycles per second. Why it's important: *Generally, the higher the megahertz rate, the faster the computer can process data. A 550-MHz Pentium III–based microcomputer, for example, processes 550 million cycles per second.*

microprocessor (p. 196) Miniaturized circuitry of a computer processor. It stores program instructions that process, or manipulate, data into information. The key parts of the microprocessor are transistors. Why it's important: *Microprocessors enabled the development of microcomputers.*

MIDI port (p. 220) Pronounced "*mid*-dee," and short for *Musical Instrument Digital Interface.* A specialized port used in creating, recording, editing, and performing music. Why it's important: *It is used for connecting amplifiers, electronic synthesizers, sound cards, drum machines, and the like.*

MIPS (p. 210) Stands for "millions of instructions per second"; a measure of processing speed. Why it's important: *MIPS is used to measure processing speeds of mainframes, minicomputers, and workstations. A workstation might perform at 100 MIPS or more, a mainframe at up to 981,024 MIPS.*

Motorola-type chips (p. 208) Microprocessors made by Motorola for Apple Macintosh computers. Why it's important: *From 1993 until the arrival of the PowerPC, Motorola provided an alternative to the Intel-style chips made for PC microcomputers. New Apple Macs now use Intel processors.*

multicore processor (p. 208) Microcomputer chip such as Intel's dual-core and quad-core processors and AMD's Athlon X2 processor, with two or more processor "cores" on a single piece of silicon. Why it's important: *Chips can take on several tasks at once because the operating system can divide its work over more than one processor.*

network interface card (NIC) (p. 223) Expansion card that allows the transmission of data over a cable network. Why it's important: *Installation of a network interface card in the computer enables the user to connect with various computers and other devices such as printers.*

optical disk (p. 227) Removable disk, usually 4.75 inches in diameter and less than one-twentieth of an inch thick, on which data is written and read through the use of laser beams. Why it's important: *An audio CD holds up to 74 minutes (2 billion bits' worth) of high-fidelity stereo sound. Some optical disks are used strictly for digital data storage, but many are* used to distribute multimedia programs that combine text, visuals, and sound.

optical memory card (p. 233) Plastic, laser-recordable, wallet-type card used with an optical-card reader. Why it's important: *Because optical cards can cram so much data into so little space, they may become more popular in the future. For instance, a health card based on an optical card would have room not only for the individual's medical history and health-insurance information but also for digital images, such as electrocardiograms.*

parallel port (p. 218) A connector for a line that allows 8 bits (I byte) to be transmitted simultaneously, like cars on an eight-lane highway. Why it's important: *Parallel lines move information faster than serial lines do. However, because they can transmit information efficiently only up to I5 feet, they are used principally for connecting printers or external disk or magnetic-tape backup storage devices.*

PC card (p. 223) Thin, credit card-size (2.I- by 3.4-inch) hardware device. Why it's important: *PC cards are used principally on laptop computers to expand capabilities.*

PCI (peripheral component interconnect) bus (p. 222) High-speed bus; at 32- or 64-bits wide. Why it's important: *PCI has been widely used in microcomputers to connect graphics cards, sound cards, modems, and high-speed network cards.*

PCIe (PCi Express) (p. 222) Intel's PCI Express bus. Why it's important: *PCIe is the latest standard for expansion card available on mainstream personal computers and is faster and more reliable than AGP.*

petabyte (P, PB) (p. 20I) Approximately I quadrillion bytes (I,048,576 gigabytes); measure of storage capacity. Why it's important: *The huge storage capacities of modern databases are now expressed in petabytes.*

plug and play (p. 219) USB peripheral connection standard that allows peripheral devices and expansion cards to be automatically configured while they are being installed. Why it's important: *Plug and play avoids the hassle of setting switches and creating special files, which plagued earlier users.*

port (p. 216) A connecting socket or jack on the outside of the system unit into which are plugged different kinds of cables. Why it's important: *A port allows the user to plug in a cable to connect a peripheral device, such as a monitor, printer, or modem, so that it can communicate with the computer system.*

power supply (p. 204) Device that converts AC to DC to run the computer. Why it's important: *The electricity available from a standard wall outlet is alternating current (AC), but a microcomputer runs on direct current (DC).*

RAM (random access memory) chips (p. 2I3) Also called *primary storage* and *main memory;* chips that temporarily hold software instructions and data before and after it is processed by the CPU. RAM is a volatile form of storage. Why it's impor-

tant: *RAM is the working memory of the computer. Having enough RAM is critical to users' ability to run many software programs.*

read (p. 2I4) To transfer data from an input source into the computer's memory or CPU. Why it's important: *Reading, along with writing, is an essential computer activity.*

read/write head (p. 225) Mechanism used to transfer data between the computer and the disk. When the disk spins inside its case, the read/write head moves back and forth over the data access area on the disk. Why it's important: *The read/write head enables the essential activities of reading and writing data.*

registers (p. 2I2) High-speed storage areas that temporarily store data during processing. Why it's important: *Registers may store a program instruction while it is being decoded, store data while it is being processed by the ALU, or store the results of a calculation.*

ROM (read-only memory) (p. 2I4) Memory chip that cannot be written on or erased by the computer user without special equipment. Why it's important: *ROM chips contain fixed start-up instructions. They are loaded, at the factory, with programs containing special instructions for basic computer operations, such as starting the computer or putting characters on the screen. These chips are nonvolatile; their contents are not lost when power to the computer is turned off.*

SCSI (small computer system interface) port (p. 2I8) Pronounced "scuzzy," a connector that allows data to be transmitted in a "daisy chain" to up to seven devices at speeds (32 bits at a time) higher than those possible with serial and parallel ports. The term *daisy chain* means that several devices are connected in series to each other, so that data for the seventh device, for example, has to go through the other six devices first. Why it's important: *A SCSI enables users to connect external hard-disk drives, CD-ROM drives, scanners, and magnetic-tape backup units.*

secondary storage hardware (p. 224) Devices that permanently hold data and information as well as programs. Why it's important: *Secondary storage—as opposed to primary storage—is nonvolatile; that is, saved data and programs are permanent, or remain intact, when the power is turned off.*

sectors (p. 225) The small arcs created in tracks when a disk's storage locations are divided into wedge-shaped sections. Why it's important: *The system software uses the point at which a sector intersects a track to reference the data location.*

semiconductor (p. I96) Material, such as silicon (in combination with other elements), whose electrical properties are intermediate between a good conductor and a nonconductor of electricity. When highly conducting materials are laid on the semiconducting material, an electronic circuit can be created. Why it's important: *Semiconductors are the materials from which integrated circuits (chips) are made.*

serial port (p. 218) A connector for a line that sends bits one after another, like cars on a one-lane highway. Why it's important: *Because individual bits must follow each other, a serial port is usually used to connect devices that do not require fast transmission of data, such as keyboard, mouse, monitors, and modems. It is also useful for sending data over a long distance.*

silicon (p. 195) An element that is widely found in clay and sand and is used in the making of solid-state integrated circuits. Why it's important: *It is used not only because its abundance makes it cheap but also because it is a good semiconductor. As a result, highly conducting materials can be overlaid on the silicon to create the electronic circuitry of the integrated circuit.*

smart card (p. 233) Wallet-type card that looks like a credit card but has a microprocessor and memory chips embedded in it. When inserted into a reader, it transfers data to and from a central computer. Why it's important: *Unlike conventional credit cards, smart cards can hold a fair amount of data and can store some basic financial records. Thus, they are used as telephone debit cards, health cards, and student cards.*

solid-state device (p. 195) Electronic component, such as an integrated circuit, made of solid materials with no moving parts. Why it's important: *Solid-state integrated circuits are far more reliable, smaller, and less expensive than electronic circuits made from several components.*

solid-state drive (p. 235) Secondary storage device that has far greater capacity than flash memory drives or keychain drives; like flash drives, they have no moving parts to break down, as hard disk drives do. Why it's important: Some newer laptops (such as Apple's MacBook Air laptop) now feature solid-state drives. These drives are lighter and use less power than conventional disk drives and can better withstand bumps and bangs.

sound card (p. 223) Expansion card used to convert and transmit digital sounds through analog speakers, microphones, and headsets. Why it's important: *Cards such as PCI wavetable sound cards are used to add music and sound effects to computer video games.*

system clock (p. 209) Internal timing device that uses fixed vibrations from a quartz crystal to deliver a steady stream of digital pulses or "ticks" to the CPU. These ticks are called *cycles.* Why it's important: *Faster clock speeds will result in faster processing of data and execution of program instructions, as long as the computer's internal circuits can handle the increased speed.*

tape cartridge (p. 232) Module resembling an audiocassette that contains tape in a rectangular plastic housing. The two most common types of tape drives are DAT and Travan TR-3. Why it's important: *Tape cartridges are used for secondary storage on microcomputers and also on some large computers. Tape is used mainly for archiving purposes and backup.*

terabyte (T, TB) (p. 201) Approximately 1 trillion bytes (1,009,511,627,776 bytes); measure of storage capacity. Why it's important: *Some high-capacity disk storage is expressed in terabytes.*

tracks (p. 224) The rings on a diskette along which data is recorded. Why it's important: See *sectors.*

transistor (p. 195) Tiny electronic device that acts as an on/off switch, switching between "on" and "off" millions of times per second. Why it's important: *Transistors are part of the microprocessor.*

Unicode (p. 202) Binary coding scheme that uses 2 bytes (16 bits) for each character, rather than 1 byte (8 bits). Why it's important: *Instead of the 256 character combinations of ASCII, Unicode can handle 65,536 character combinations. Thus, it allows almost all the written languages of the world to be represented using a single character set.*

upgrading (p. 206) Changing to newer, usually more powerful or sophisticated versions, such as a more powerful microprocessor or more memory chips. Why it's important: *Through upgrading, users can improve their computer systems without buying completely new ones.*

USB (universal serial bus) port (p. 218) Port that can theoretically connect up to 127 peripheral devices daisy-chained to one general-purpose port. Why it's important: *USB ports are useful for peripherals such as digital cameras, digital speakers, scanners, high-speed modems, and joysticks. Being "hot pluggable" or "hot swappable" means that USB allows such devices to be connected or disconnected even while the PC is running.*

virtual memory (p. 216) Type of hard-disk space that mimics primary storage (RAM). Why it's important: *When RAM space is limited, virtual memory allows users to run more software at once, provided the computer's CPU and operating system are equipped to use it. The system allocates some free disk space as an extension of RAM; that is, the computer swaps parts of the software program between the hard disk and RAM as needed.*

volatile (p. 213) Temporary; the contents of volatile storage media, such as RAM, are lost when the power is turned off. Why it's important: *To avoid data loss, save your work to a secondary storage medium, such as a hard disk, in case the electricity goes off while you're working.*

word size (p. 211) Number of bits that the processor may process at any one time. Why it's important: *The more bits in a word, the faster the computer. A 32-bit computer—that is, one with a 32-bit-word processor—will transfer data within each microprocessor chip in 32-bit chunks, or 4 bytes at a time. A 64-bit computer transfers data in 64-bit chunks, or 8 bytes at a time.*

write (p. 214) To transfer data from the computer's CPU or memory to an output device. Why it's important: See *read.*

CHAPTER REVIEW

stage 1 LEARNING MEMORIZATION

"I can recognize and recall information."

Self-Test Questions

1. A(n) _____ is about 1,000 bytes; a(n) _____ is about 1 million bytes; a(n) _____ is about 1 billion bytes.

2. The _____ is the part of the microprocessor that tells the rest of the computer how to carry out a program's instructions.

3. The process of retrieving data from a storage device is referred to as _____; the process of copying data to a storage device is called _____.

4. To avoid losing data, users should always _____ their files.

5. Formatted disks have _____ and _____ that the system software uses to reference data locations.

6. The _____ is often referred to as the "brain" of a computer.

7. The electrical data roadways through which bits are transmitted are called _____.

8. A cable connected to a _____ port sends bits one at a time, one after the other; a cable connected to a _____ port sends 8 bits simultaneously.

9. Part of the disk-drive mechanism, the _____ transfers data between the computer and the disk.

10. _____ chips, also called *main memory,* are critical to computer performance.

11. _____ operations are the fundamental math operations: addition, subtraction, multiplication, and division. _____ operations are comparisons such as "equal to," "greater than," or "less than."

12. A group of 8 bits is a _____.

13. The extra bit attached to the end of a byte for error checking is a _____ bit.

14. A tiny electronic device that acts as an on/off switch, switching between "on" and "off" millions of times per second, is called a _____.

15. _____ is a form of flash memory media that plugs into a special port in a digital camera, camcorder, notebook PC, or photo printer and holds up to 1 gigabyte of data.

Multiple-Choice Questions

1. Which of the following is another term for primary storage?
   a. ROM
   b. ALU
   c. CPU
   d. RAM
   e. CD-R

2. Which of the following is *not* included on a computer's motherboard?
   a. RAM chips
   b. ROM chips
   c. keyboard
   d. microprocessor
   e. expansion slots

3. Which of the following is used to hold data and instructions that will be used shortly by the CPU?
   a. ROM chips
   b. peripheral devices
   c. RAM chips
   d. CD-R
   e. hard disk

4. Which of the following coding schemes is widely used on microcomputers?
   a. EBCDIC
   b. Unicode
   c. ASCII
   d. Microcode
   e. Unix

5. Which of the following is used to measure processing speed in microcomputers?
   a. MIPS
   b. flops
   c. picoseconds
   d. megahertz
   e. millihertz

6. Which expansion bus specializes in graphics processing?
   a. PCI
   b. ROM
   c. CMOS
   d. AGP
   e. AMR

7. Which element is commonly used in the making of solid-state integrated circuits?
   a. pentium
   b. lithium

c. copper

d. iron

e. silicon

8. DVD-Rs allow

  a. repeated rewriting.

  b. one-time recording by the user; they cannot be written on more than once.

  c. no writing; they are read-only.

True/False Questions

T F   I. A bus connects a computer's control unit and ALU.

T F   2. The machine cycle comprises the instruction cycle and the execution cycle.

T F   3. Magnetic tape is the most common secondary storage medium used with microcomputers.

T F   4. Main memory is nonvolatile.

T F   5. Pipelining is a method of speeding up processing.

T F   6. Today's laptop computers can perform more calculations per second than the ENIAC, an enormous machine occupying more than 1,800 square feet and weighing more than 30 tons.

T F   7. USB can theoretically connect up to 127 peripheral devices.

T F   8. A petabyte is approximately 1 quadrillion bytes.

T F   9. Online secondary storage services test your computer's RAM capacity.

T F   10. Keychain memory is a pipelining device.

---

stage 2 LEARNING   COMPREHENSION

"I can recall information in my own terms and explain it to a friend."

Short-Answer Questions

1. What is ASCII, and what do the letters stand for?

2. Why should measures of capacity matter to computer users?

3. What's the difference between RAM and ROM?

4. What is the significance of the term *megahertz?*

5. What is a motherboard? Name at least four components of a motherboard.

6. What are the most convenient forms of backup storage? Why?

7. Why is it important for your computer to be expandable?

8. What are three uses of a smart card?

9. What is nanotechnology?

10. What are the uses of a surge protector, voltage regulator, and UPS, and why are these devices important?

11. Explain the binary system.

12. What is Unicode?

13. Why is silicon used in the manufacture of microprocessors?

14. What is Blu-ray used for?

---

stage 3 LEARNING   APPLYING, ANALYZING, SYNTHESIZING, EVALUATING

"I can apply what I've learned, relate these ideas to other concepts, build on other knowledge, and use all these thinking skills to form a judgment."

Knowledge in Action

1. If you're using Windows XP, you can easily determine what microprocessor is in your computer and how much RAM it has. To begin, click the *Start* button in the Windows desktop pull-up menu bar and then choose *Control Panel.* Then locate the System icon in the Control Panel window and double-click on the icon.

    The System Properties dialog box will open. It contains several tabs: General, Computer Name, Hardware, System Restore, Automatic Updates, and Advanced. The name of your computer's microprocessor will display on the General tab, as well as its speed and your computer's RAM capacity.

2. Visit a local computer store and note the system requirements listed on five software packages. What are the requirements for processor? RAM? Operating system? Available hard-disk space? CD/DVD speed? Audio/video cards? Are there any output hardware requirements?

3. Develop a binary system of your own. Use any two objects, states, or conditions, and encode the following statement: "I am a rocket scientist."

4. The floppy drive no longer comes as a standard component of microcomputers. What do you think will be the next "legacy" device to be abandoned?

5. Storing humans: If the human genome is 800 million bytes (according to Raymond Kurzweil), how many humans could you fit on a 120-GB hard drive?

6. What are the predictions about how long Moore's Law will continue to apply? Do a web search for four opinions; list the website sources and their predictions, and state how reliable you believe the sites are, and why.

Web Exercises

1. The objective of this project is to introduce you to an online encyclopedia that's dedicated to computer technology. The *www.webopedia.com* website is a good resource for deciphering computer ads and clearing up difficult concepts. For practice, visit the site and type *processor* into the Search text box and then press the *Enter* key or click on the *Go!* button. Click on some of the links that are displayed. Search for information on other topics of interest to you.

2. You can customize your own PC through a brand-name company such as Dell or Gateway, or you can create your own personal model by choosing each component on your own. Decide which method is best for you.

    Go to the following sites and customize your ideal PCs:

    www.dell.com

    www.gateway.com

    www.compaq.com

    www.hpshopping.com

    http://store.apple.com/us

    Write down the prices for your ideal customized PCs. Then go to

    www.pricewatch.com

    www.dealsdepot.com/Shop/Control/fp/SFV/14930/ view_page/custom/RID/118778?engine=adwords+ 1&keyword=custom+1

    http://store.sysbuilder.com/desktop.html

    and see if you could save money by putting your own PC together piece by piece. (This includes purchasing each component separately and verifying compatibility of all components.)

    For a tutorial on building your own computer, go to *www.pcmech.com/build.htm.*

3. DVD formats: DVD + R, DVD-R, DVD + RW, DVD-RW, so many formats! Are they all the same? Visit these websites to get current information on the issues surrounding recordable DVD media:

    www.webopedia.com/DidYouKnow/Hardware_ Software/2003/DVDFormatsExplained.asp

    www.dvddemystified.com/dvdfaq.html#4.3

    www.plextor.com/english/support/faqs/G00015.htm

    www.videohelp.com/dvd

4. What is a Qubit? You've learned about binary digits in this chapter; now learn about the Qubit, the basic unit of information in a quantum computer. Beware: When you step into the realm of quantum theory, things become bizarre.

    http://whatis.techtarget.com/ wsearchResults/1,290214,sid9,00.html?query=qubit#

    www.thefreedictionary.com/quantum+bit

    www.qubit.org/

    www.answers.com/topic/qubit?method=6

    www.worldwidewords.org/turnsofphrase/tp-qub1.htm

5. DNA computing: Visit the following websites to learn more about DNA software and computing:

    www.arstechnica.com/reviews/2q00/dna/dna-1.html

    http://expertvoices.nsdl.org/cornell- cs322/2008/03/29/dna-computing/

    www.tribuneindia.com/2008/200807111/science.htm

    http://computer.howstuffworks.com/dna-computer.htm

6. You mean the Matrix was real? Visit this website for analysis of real-world applications of concepts from the movie *Matrix: www.kurzweilai.net/index. html?flash=2.*

SECURITY

7. Security issue—credit card fraud: When buying parts or making any kind of purchase over the internet, always make sure that the web address says HTTPS to let you know it is an encrypted SSL (Secured Socket Layer) website. Visit these sites for safety tips when using your credit card online.

    http://money.howstuffworks.com/personal-finance/ debt-management/credit-card4.htm

    www.creditcards.com/credit-card-news/credit-card- fraud-and-online-shopping-1282.php

    http://idtheft.about.com/od/preventionpractices/a/ OnlineShopping.htm

5

HARDWARE: INPUT & OUTPUT Taking Charge of Computing & Communications

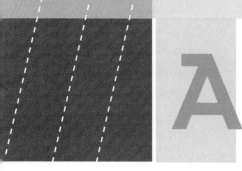

Automated teller machines have become so common, it now seems there are almost as many places to get cash as to spend it," says one account.[1]

Not only are *automated teller machines (ATMs),* or cash machines, in office buildings, convenience stores, nightclubs, and even the lobbies of some big apartment buildings; they are also becoming something quite different from simple devices for people who need fast cash. They are migrating into different kinds of *kiosks* (pronounced "*key*-osks"), computerized booths or small standing structures providing any number of services, from electronic banking options to corporate job benefits, from tourism advice to garage-sale permits. (• *See Panel 5.1.)*

In Tampa, Florida, Kimberly Ruggiero, 22, a hospital inventory tracker, avoids a 30-minute bank line on Fridays by stopping at a 7-Eleven and using an ATM-like kiosk to cash her paycheck. "It's extremely convenient and fast," she says, "and I don't have to wait in line."[2] In New York City, kiosks can be used by citizens to pay parking tickets and check for building-code violations. In San Antonio, they provide information on animals available for adoption. In Seattle, commuters at car-ferry terminals view images of traffic conditions on major highways. In Nevada, motorists can use kiosks at the Department of Motor Vehicles to get a driver history printout.[3] Many colleges and universities use kiosks to provide students with information about classes, schedules, activity locations, maps, and so on.[4]

Kiosks also sell stamps, print out checks, and issue movie and plane tickets. Many grocery stores have video-rental kiosks offering movie rentals for $1 a night.[5] Alamo car rental offices have kiosks at which travelers can print out directions, get descriptions of hotel services, and obtain restaurant menus and reviews—in four languages. At MainStay Suites, guests may not even find front-desk clerks; kiosks have replaced them at many locations. Many kiosks have been transformed into full-blown multimedia centers, offering publicized corporate and governmental activities, job listings, and benefits, as well as ads, coupons, and movie previews.

The kiosk presents the two faces of the computer that are important to humans: It allows them to *input data* and to *output information.* For example, many kiosks use touch screens (and sometimes also keyboards) for input and thermal printers for output. In this chapter, we discuss what the principal input and output devices are and how you can make use of them.

panel 5.1

Kiosks

(Left) The Bell Atlantic public internet access kiosk at T. F. Green airport in Warwick, Rhode Island. *(Right)* Check-cashing kiosk at a 7-Eleven store.

5.1 INPUT & OUTPUT

How is input/output hardware used by a computer system?

Recall from Chapter 1 that *input* refers to data entered into a computer for processing—for example, from a keyboard or from a file stored on disk. Input includes program instructions that the CPU receives after commands are issued by the user. Commands can be issued by typing keywords, defined by the application program, or pressing certain keyboard keys. Commands can also be issued by choosing menu options or clicking on icons. Finally, input includes user responses—for example, when you reply to a question posed by the application or the operating system, such as "Are you sure you want to put this file in the Recycle Bin?" *Output* refers to the results of processing—that is, information sent to the screen or the printer or to be stored on disk or sent to another computer in a network. Some devices combine input and output functions, examples being not only ATMs and kiosks, as we just mentioned, but also combination scanner-printer-fax devices.

This chapter focuses on the common input and output devices used with a computer. (● *See Panel 5.2.*) ***Input hardware* consists of devices that translate data into a form the computer can process.** The people-readable form of the data may be words like those on this page, but the computer-readable form consists of binary 0s and 1s, or off and on electrical signals.

***Output hardware* consists of devices that translate information processed by the computer into a form that humans can understand.** The computer-processed information consists of 0s and 1s, which need to be translated into words, numbers, sounds, and pictures.

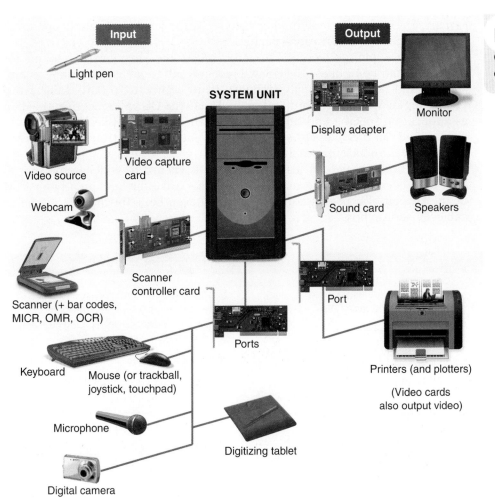

panel 5.2

Common input and output devices

Input

Light pen

Video source

Video capture card

Webcam

SYSTEM UNIT

Display adapter

Monitor

Output

Sound card

Speakers

Scanner controller card

Scanner (+ bar codes, MICR, OMR, OCR)

Keyboard

Mouse (or trackball, joystick, touchpad)

Microphone

Digital camera

Ports

Digitizing tablet

Port

Printers (and plotters)

(Video cards also output video)

5.2 INPUT HARDWARE

What are the three categories of input hardware, what devices do they include, and what are their features?

Consider the *joystick,* a vertical lever mounted on a base that is used as a pointing device in videogames or flying or driving simulators. The joystick's translation of human movement into machine movement elegantly satisfies the three virtues of an input device—simplicity, efficiency, and control.

The pointing device, however, is only one of three types of input hardware devices: *keyboards, pointing devices,* and *source data-entry devices. (● See Panel 5.3.)* Quite often a computer system will combine all three.

Keyboards

How do traditional and specialty keyboards differ?

A _keyboard_ is a device that converts letters, numbers, and other characters into electrical signals that can be read by the computer's processor. The keyboard does this with its own processor and a grid of circuits underneath the keys.

When you press a key or combination of keys, the current flowing through the circuits is interrupted. The processor determines where the break occurs and compares the location information with a character map (organized by *x,y* coordinates) located on the keyboard's ROM chip. The character information is briefly stored in the keyboard's memory, which usually holds about 16 bytes. The keyboard then sends the data in a stream to the PC via a wired or wireless connection. (Laptops use an internal wired connection.) The computer has a keyboard controller, an integrated circuit whose job it is to process all the data that comes from the keyboard and forward it to the operating system. The operating system checks to see if the keyboard data is operating system-specific or application-specific.

If, for example, you press *Ctrl+Alt+Delete*—the keyboard command for rebooting your computer—the OS will recognize the data as operating-system-specific and react accordingly (reboot). If, in contrast, you are doing word processing in Microsoft Word and press *Alt+F,* the OS will recognize the data as application-specific and send it along to the current application, Word, to be executed. All this happens so quickly that you notice no time lapse between pressing keys and seeing results.

The keyboard may look like a typewriter keyboard to which some special keys have been added. Alternatively, it may look like the keys on a bank ATM or the keypad of a pocket computer. It may even be a Touch-Tone phone or cable-TV set-top box.

panel 5.3

Three types of input devices

Keyboards	Pointing Devices	Source Data-Entry Devices
Traditional computer keyboards	Mice, trackballs, pointing sticks, touchpads	Scanner devices: imaging systems, barcode readers, mark- and character-recognition devices (MICR, OMR, OCR), fax machines
Specialty keyboards and terminals: dumb terminals, intelligent terminals (ATMs, POS terminals), internet terminals	Touch screens	Audio-input devices
	Pen-based computer systems, light pens, digitizers (digitizing tablets)	Webcams and video-input devices
	Optical sensor technology remotes, such as for Wii	Digital cameras
		Speech-recognition systems
		Sensors
		Radio-frequency identification
		Human-biology input devices

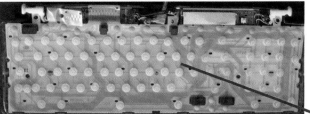

Inside a computer keyboard. In most keyboards, each key sits over a small, flexible rubber dome with a hard carbon center. When the key is pressed, a plunger on the bottom of the key pushes down against the dome. This pushes the carbon center down, which presses against the keyboard circuitry to complete an electrical circuit and send a signal to the computer.

Let's look at *traditional computer keyboards* and various kinds of *specialty keyboards and terminals.*

TRADITIONAL COMPUTER KEYBOARDS Picking up where we left off with the PC ad presented in Chapter 4 (Panel 4.4 on p. 199), we see that the seller lists a "full-sized keyboard with numeric keypad." Conventional computer keyboards have all the keys on old typewriter keyboards, plus other keys unique to computers. This generally totals 104–108 keys for desktop computers and 80–85 keys for laptops. Newer keyboards include extra keys for special activities such as instant web access, CD/DVD controls, and Windows shortcut keys.

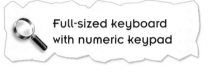

Full-sized keyboard with numeric keypad

Wired keyboards connect a cable to the computer via a serial port or a USB port. Wireless keyboards use either infrared-light (IR) technology or radio frequency (RF) technology to transmit signals to a receiver device plugged into the computer, usually via a USB port. Infrared wireless keyboards have a transmission range of 6–10 feet and cannot have any obstacles in the transmission path (called the *line of sight*). (Some laptop/notebook computers and printers come with built-in IR ports.) Radio-based keyboards have a range of up to 100 feet and have no line-of-sight problems. A final interesting variation is the VKB Virtual Keyboard. The size of a writing pen, it uses light (laser) to project a full-size computer keyboard onto almost any surface; the image disappears when not in use. The Virtual Keyboard can be used with PDAs and smartphones, allowing

Wireless keyboard

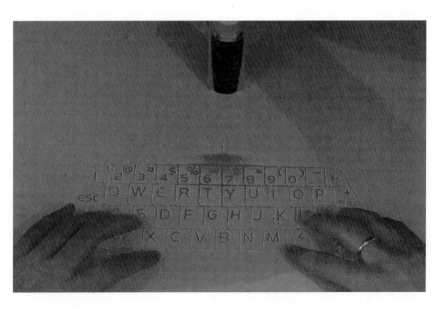

Seeing the light. The Virtual Keyboard uses light to project a full-size computer keyboard onto almost any surface. Used with smartphones and PDAs, this technology provides a way to do email, word processing, and other basic tasks without one's having to carry a notebook computer.

users a practical way to do email and word processing without having to take along a laptop computer.[6]

The keyboard illustration in Chapter 3 shows keyboard and numeric keypad functions. *(Refer back to Panel 3.6, pp. 130–131.)*

SPECIALTY KEYBOARDS & TERMINALS Specialty keyboards range from Touch-Tone telephone keypads to keyboards featuring pictures of food for use in fast-food restaurants. Here we will consider dumb terminals, intelligent terminals, and internet terminals:

- **Dumb terminals: A _dumb terminal_, also called a *video display terminal (VDT)*, has a display screen and a keyboard and can input and output but cannot process data.** Usually the output is text only. For instance, airline reservations clerks use these terminals to access a mainframe computer containing flight information. Dumb terminals cannot perform functions independent of the mainframe to which they are linked.[7]

- **Intelligent terminals: An _intelligent terminal_ has its own memory and processor, as well as a display screen and a keyboard.** Such a terminal can perform some functions independent of any mainframe to which it is linked. One example is the familiar *automated teller machine (ATM),* the self-service banking machine that is connected through a telephone network to a central computer. Another example is the *point-of-sale (POS) terminal,* used to record purchases at a store's checkout counter. Intelligent terminals can be connected to the main (usually mainframe) computer system wirelessly or via cables.

  A third example of an intelligent terminal is the *mobile data terminal (MDT),* a rugged notebook PC found in police cruisers, which must endure high-speed chases and nonstop use. MDTs may run Windows operating systems but use specialized software that lets officers track dispatch information, search for local and national warrants, verify license plate and vehicle registration, check criminal records, and more. Some systems, such as that used by the Tulsa, Oklahoma, police department, let officers complete reports online to avoid time-consuming in-office paperwork.

Terminals. (*Left*) A dumb terminal at an airline check-in counter. (*Right*) A point-of-sale (POS) terminal at a retail store. It records purchases and processes the buyer's credit card.

- **Internet terminals: An _internet terminal_ provides access to the internet**—that is, it powers up directly into a browser. There are several variants: (1) _internet TV,_ which distributes TV via the internet; (2) _internet-ready TV,_ TV sets that allow viewers to also go online; (3) the _network computer,_ a cheap, stripped-down computer that connects people to networks; (4) the _online game player,_ which not only lets the user play games but also connects to the internet; and (5) the _wireless pocket PC_ or _personal digital assistant (PDA),_ a handheld computer with a tiny keyboard that can do two-way wireless messaging; most smartphones also act as internet terminals.

Internet terminals—PDAs

SPECIAL KEYBOARDS FOR HANDHELDS Users of PDAs generally use a penlike device (a stylus, as we'll describe) to enter data and commands. Some PDAs do include a small keyboard, but it is usually limited in function and hard to use. However, there are alternatives:

- **Foldable PDA keyboards:** Many manufacturers offer foldable keyboards for PDAs. One example is Think Outside's Stowaway Portable Keyboard, which folds up to roughly the size of a PDA and then unfolds into a full-size keyboard. Once the keyboard driver is installed, you can simply clip the PDA onto the keyboard, which runs off the PDA's power, thus requiring no external power source. Wireless foldable keyboards are also available.

- **One-hand PDA keyboards:** The FrogPad is a 20-key gadget designed to be used with just the five fingers of one hand. A clamshell allows people to plug in a smartphone and use the whole kit like a mini-laptop.

Stowaway Portable Keyboard for PDAs. This keyboard folds up to roughly the size of a PDA (3.8 inches wide × 5.1 inches deep × 0.8 inch thick) and unfolds into a full-size keyboard measuring 13.8 inches wide × 5.1 inches deep × 0.4 inch thick. To use the keyboard, you simply unfold it and slide the sections together.

FrogPad one-hand, 20-key keyboard for PDAs. Keys are the same size as those on a regular computer keyboard. Fifteen keys represent letters, numbers, and punctuation marks; four keys alternate the symbols for each key; a Shift key is for capital letters. The keyboard can also handle page navigation.

Pointing Devices

How do pointing devices work, such as the mouse and its variants, touch screens, and pen-based systems?

One of the most natural of all human gestures, the act of pointing, is incorporated in several kinds of input devices. **_Pointing devices_ control the position of the cursor or pointer on the screen and allow the user to select options displayed on the screen.** Pointing devices include the *mouse* and its variants, the *touch screen*, and various forms of *pen input*. We also describe recent innovations in *handwriting input*.

THE MOUSE The principal pointing tool used with microcomputers is the **_mouse_, a device that is rolled about on a desktop mouse pad and directs a pointer on the computer's display screen.** Making its first appearance at a demonstration in San Francisco in 1968, the mouse's name is derived from the device's shape, which is a bit like a mouse, with the cord to the computer being the tail.[8] The mouse went public in 1984 with the introduction of the Apple Macintosh. (● *See the timeline, Panel 5.4.*) Once Microsoft Windows 3.1 made the GUI the PC standard, the mouse also became a standard input device.

- **How the mouse works:** When the mouse is moved, a ball inside the mouse touches the desktop surface and rolls with the mouse. Two rollers inside the mouse touch the ball. One of the rollers detects motions in the x direction, and the other roller detects motions in the y direction (90 degrees opposite from the x direction). The rollers connect to a shaft that spins a disk with holes in it. On either side of the disk there is an infrared light-emitting diode (LED) and an infrared sensor. The holes in the disk break the beam of light coming from the LED so that the infrared sensor sees pulses of light. A processor chip in the mouse reads the pulses and turns them into binary data that the computer can understand. The chip sends the data to the computer through the mouse cord (serial, USB, or PS/2) or through a wireless connection (infrared or radio transmission).

- **Mechanical versus optical mouse:** A mouse pad—a rectangular rubber/foam pad—provides traction for the traditional mouse, often called a *mechanical mouse* or a *wheeled mouse.* Newer mice are *optical;* that is, they use laser beams and special chips to encode data for the computer. Optical mice have no moving parts, have a smoother response, and don't require a mouse pad.

Microsoft IntelliMouse

Mouse on a mouse pad—the cord looks a bit like a tail.

info!

Hands-Free Mice

If your mouse is causing arm and wrist pain, you could try the hands-free voice mouse models at:

www.fentek-ind.com/ergmouse. htm

3000 BCE	1621 CE	1642	Late 1700s	1814	1820
Abacus is invented in Babylonia	Slide rule invented (Edmund Gunther)	First mechanical adding machine (Blaise Pascal)	First attempts to produce human speech by machine made by Ch.G. Kratzenstein, professor of physiology in Copenhagen—he produced vowel sounds using resonance tubes connected to organ pipes; Wolfgang von Kempelen produces the first mechanical speaking machine in Vienna	First photographic image	The first mass-produced calculator, the Thomas Arithnometer

panel 5.4

Timeline: developments in input/output

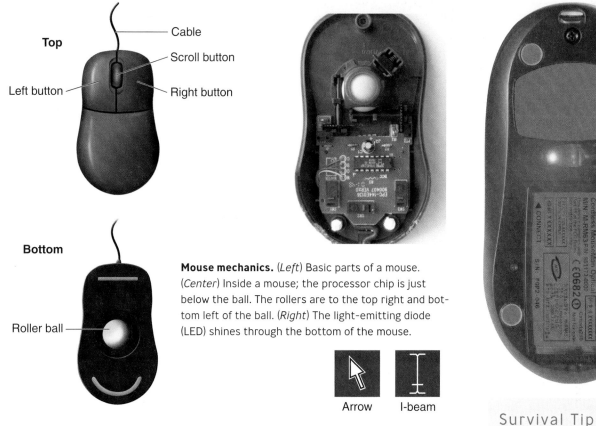

Top
Cable
Scroll button
Left button
Right button

Bottom
Roller ball

Mouse mechanics. (*Left*) Basic parts of a mouse. (*Center*) Inside a mouse; the processor chip is just below the ball. The rollers are to the top right and bottom left of the ball. (*Right*) The light-emitting diode (LED) shines through the bottom of the mouse.

Arrow   I-beam

- **Mouse pointers and buttons:** The *mouse pointer*—an arrow, a rectangle, a pointing finger—is the symbol that indicates the position of the mouse on the display screen or that activates icons. When the mouse pointer changes to the shape of an I-beam, it shows the place where text may be inserted or selected for special treatment.

  On the top side of the mouse are one to five buttons. The first button is used for common functions, such as clicking and dragging. The functions of the other buttons are determined by the software you're using. Some mice have a scroll wheel on top to make it easier for you to scroll down the screen.

- **Specialty mice:** Many specialty mice versions are available. For example, the APC Biometric Mouse has a sensor that reads the user's index fingerprint and keeps unauthorized people from using the system.

Survival Tip

Setting Mouse Properties

From the Start menu in Windows, go to *Settings, Control Panel, Mouse* to get a dialog box with several tabs that allow you to set mouse properties, such as setting the mouse buttons for left-handed use, adjusting the speed at which the pointer moves across the screen, and changing the shape of the mouse pointer.

1821	1829	1843	1844	1876	1877
First microphone	William Austin patents the first workable typewriter in America	World's first computer programmer, Ada Lovelace, publishes her notes; facsimile transmission (faxing) over wires invented by Alexander Bain, Scottish mechanic (via telegraph wires)	Samuel Morse sends a telegraph message from Washington to Baltimore	A. G. Bell patents the electric telephone	Thomas Edison patents the phonograph

Hardware: Input & Output

261

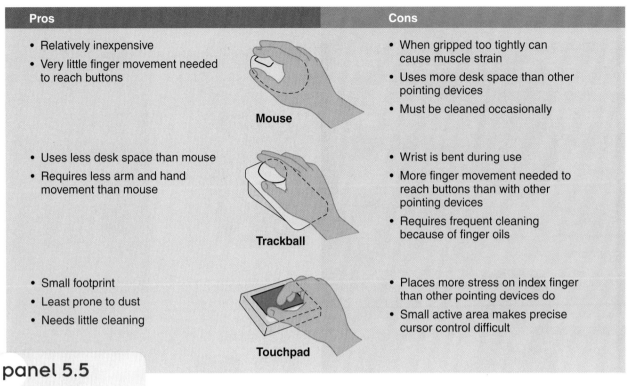

Pros	Cons
• Relatively inexpensive • Very little finger movement needed to reach buttons **Mouse**	• When gripped too tightly can cause muscle strain • Uses more desk space than other pointing devices • Must be cleaned occasionally
• Uses less desk space than mouse • Requires less arm and hand movement than mouse **Trackball**	• Wrist is bent during use • More finger movement needed to reach buttons than with other pointing devices • Requires frequent cleaning because of finger oils
• Small footprint • Least prone to dust • Needs little cleaning **Touchpad**	• Places more stress on index finger than other pointing devices do • Small active area makes precise cursor control difficult

panel 5.5

Mouse, trackball, touchpad

Trackball

Interlinks Electronics makes the DuraPoint Mouse the "world's toughest mouse," with stainless-steel casing that can survive almost anything, including being dropped five stories, being used as a hockey puck, and being run over by an 18-wheel truck. Immune to liquids, gases, dirt, and dust, the DuraPoint is ideal for industrial, manufacturing, and field-computing environments and any home with especially curious kids.

Boost Technology's Tracer mouse can be used by people who have trouble using their hands. It's worn on and controlled by the head via a tiny gyroscope and radio waves.

VARIATIONS ON THE MOUSE: TRACKBALL, POINTING STICK, & TOUCH-PAD There are three main variations on the mouse. (● *See Panel 5.5.*)

- **Trackball: The *trackball* is a movable ball, mounted on top of a stationary device, that can be rotated using your fingers or palm.** In fact, the trackball looks like the mouse turned upside down. Instead of moving the mouse around on the desktop, you move the trackball with the tips of your fingers. A trackball is not as accurate as a mouse, and it requires more frequent cleaning, but it's a good alternative when desktop space is limited. Trackballs come in wired and wireless versions, and newer optical trackballs use laser technology.

1897	1898	1912	1924	1927
Karl Ferdinand Braun, German physicist, invents the first cathode-ray tube (CRT), the basis of all TV and computer monitors	First telephone answering machine	Motorized movie camera replaces hand-cranked movie camera	T.J. Watson renames Hollerith's machine company, founded in 1896, to International Business Machines (IBM); first political convention photos faxed via AT&T telephone fax technology	The first electronic TV picture is transmitted

- **Pointing stick:** A _pointing stick_ **looks like a pencil eraser protruding from the keyboard between the G, H, and B keys. When you move the pointing stick with your finger, the screen pointer moves accordingly.** IBM developed the pointing stick for use with its notebook computers. (A forerunner of the pointing stick is the joystick, which consists of a vertical handle like a gearshift lever mounted on a base with one or two buttons.)

Pointing stick

- **Touchpad:** A _touchpad_ **is a small, flat surface over which you slide your finger, using the same movements as you would with a mouse.** The cursor follows the movement of your finger. You "click" by tapping your finger on the pad's surface or by pressing buttons positioned close by the pad. Touchpads are most often found on laptop computers, but freestanding touchpads are available for use with PCs.

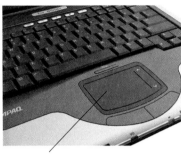

Touchpad

TOUCH SCREEN A _touch screen_ **is a video display screen that has been sensitized to receive input from the touch of a finger.** (● _See Panel 5.6._) The specially coated screen layers are covered with a plastic layer. Depending on the type of touch screen, the pressure of the user's finger creates a connection of electrical current between the layers, decreases the electrical charge at the touched point, or otherwise disturbs the electrical field. The change in electrical current creates a signal that is sent to the computer. You can input requests for information by pressing on displayed buttons or

panel 5.6

Touch screens
(_Left_) Touch screen menus at a Holiday Inn restaurant; they can keep track of the charges, as well as the carbs and the calories. (_Right_) Touch screen used to operate a sewing machine.

1931	1936	1939	1944	1946	1959
Reynold B. Johnson, a Michigan high-school science teacher, invents a test-scoring machine that senses conductive pencil marks on answer sheets	Bell Labs invents the voice-recognition machine	First electrical speech-producing machine—New York World's Fair; computer technology takes over speech synthesis in about 1970	First electro-mechanical computer (Mark I)	First programmable electronic computer in United States (ENIAC)	General Electric produces the first system to process checks in a banking application via magnetic-ink character recognition (MICR)

panel 5.7

Touch-screen menus
(Left) Touch-screen menu on a self-scanning checkout system. *(Right)* Touch-screen voter's ballot.

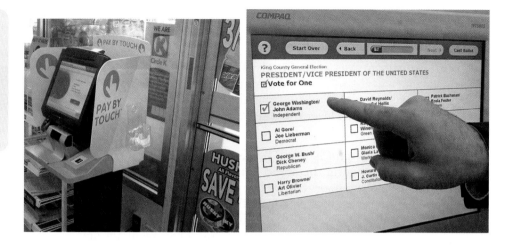

Survival Tip

Games & Wireless Input

If you're a serious game fan, you're advised to stick with wired input devices. Wireless devices tend to lag during data transmission, which will slow down your game response. (The lag time is called *latency.*)

menus. (● *See Panel 5.7.*) The answers to your requests are then output as displayed words or pictures on the screen. (There may also be sound.)

Already found in ATMs, Apple iPhones, and campus information kiosks, touch screens look very much like the wave of the future. Hewlett-Packard, Dell, Asus-Tek, and others are producing several touch-screen products, using the same type of finger-tapping interface made popular by the iPhone.[9] One is AsusTek's Eee Top touch-sensitive computer designed for use in kitchens, which are generally not friendly to computers.[10] Microsoft has added touch-screen capabilities to its latest operating system, Windows 7. Touch screens have become standard for Global Positioning System devices, e-book readers, and most especially cellphones.[11] Incidentally, women with long fingernails will find that nails hitting the screen don't work; you have to use the flesh part of the finger.[12]

PEN INPUT Some input devices use variations on an electronic pen. Examples are *pen-based systems, light pens, digitizers,* and *digital pens:*

- **Pen-based computer systems:** **_Pen-based computer systems_ allow users to enter handwriting and marks onto a computer screen by means of a penlike stylus rather than by typing on a keyboard.**
  A *stylus* is a penlike device that is used to write text or draw lines on a touch-sensitive surface as input to a computer. Pen computers use *handwriting-recognition* software that translates handwritten characters made by the stylus into data that is usable by the computer. **_Handwriting recognition_ refers to the ability of a computer to receive intelligible written input.** The system requires special software that interprets the movements of the stylus across the writing surface and translates the resulting cursive writing into digital information. (Alternatively, written text may be

1960	1962	1963	1967	1968	1970
DEC introduces the PDP-1, the first commercial computer with a monitor for output and a keyboard for input	Bell Laboratories develops software to design, store, and edit synthesized music	Ivan Sutherland uses the first interactive computer graphics in his Ph.D. thesis, which used a light pen to create engineering graphics	Hand-held calculator	World debut of the computer mouse, in development since 1965 by Doug Engelbart at Stanford Research Institute (SRI)	Microprocessor chips come into use; floppy disk introduced for storing data; barcodes come into use; the daisy wheel printer makes its debut

Chapter 5

scanned from a piece of paper, using optical character recognition, as we describe in the next section.)

panel 5.8

Pen-based computer systems
Handheld tablet PCs

Handwriting recognition is commonly used as an input method for PDAs. Earlier attempts to allow written input—the Apple Newton, IBM's Thinkpad tablet computer, and Microsoft Windows for Pen—were not commercially successful. Then Palm launched a successful series of PDAs based on the Graffiti recognition system. A currently successful handwriting-recognition system is Microsoft's version of the Windows operating system for the Tablet PC. The Tablet PC is Microsoft's version of a *tablet PC,* a special notebook computer outfitted with a digitizer tablet and a stylus that allows a user to handwrite text on the unit's screen. (● *See Panel 5.8.*) A Mac version is the Modbook from Axiotron.[13] A stylus can take the place of a keyboard when users use an on-screen input panel or tap letters and numbers directly on an on-screen keyboard. Some tablets (such as ViewSonic and Motion Computing) also include a standard keyboard so that the computer can function as a laptop when the screen is repositioned. We discuss tablet PCs further in Chapter 7.

Although handwriting recognition has become a popular input form, it is still generally accepted that keyboard input is both faster and more reliable.

● **Light pen: The _light pen_ is a light-sensitive penlike device that uses a wired connection to a computer terminal.** The user brings the pen to a desired point on the display screen and presses the pen button, which identifies that screen location to the computer. Light pens are used by engineers, graphic designers, and illustrators. They also are used in the health, food service, and chemical fields in situations in which users' hands need to be covered. (● *See Panel 5.9, next page.*)

● **Digitizer: A _digitizer_ uses an electronic pen or a mouselike copying device called a *puck* that can convert drawings and photos to digital**

1973	1974	1976	1984	1990
The Alto, an experimental PC that uses a mouse and a GUI, is developed at Xerox PARC	Simple version of optical character recognition (OCR) developed	IBM develops the ink-jet printer	Apple Macintosh; first personal laser printer	Dragon speech-recognition program recognizes 30,000 words; SVGA video standard

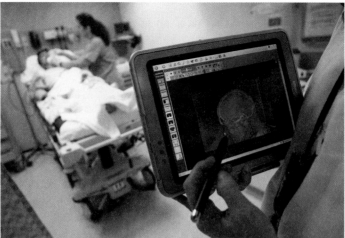

panel 5.9

Light pen
This person is using a light pen to input medical information to the computer.

panel 5.10

Digitizing tablet
Such tablets are often used in engineering and architectural applications.

data. One form of digitizer is **the *digitizing tablet*, used in engineering and architecture applications, in which a specific location on an electronic plastic board corresponds to a location on the screen.** *(● See Panel 5.10.)*

● **Digital pen: A *digital pen* is a writing instrument that allows users to write on paper and send the writing as an image file to the computer.** *(● See Panel 5.11.)* Basically, there are two kinds of digital pens. The first version, such as Logitech's Io pen and Leapfrog's FLY Fusion pen,

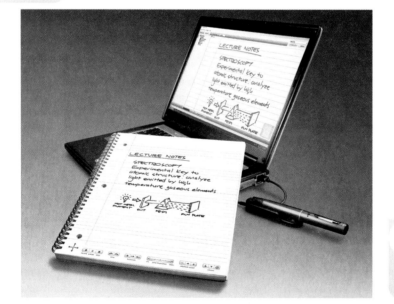

panel 5.11

Handwritten notes via electronic pen

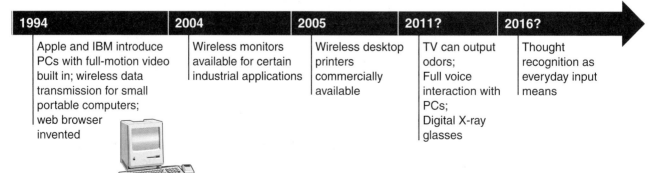

1994	2004	2005	2011?	2016?
Apple and IBM introduce PCs with full-motion video built in; wireless data transmission for small portable computers; web browser invented	Wireless monitors available for certain industrial applications	Wireless desktop printers commercially available	TV can output odors; Full voice interaction with PCs; Digital X-ray glasses	Thought recognition as everyday input means

FLY Fusion™ Pentop Computer

Convert handwritten essays to digital text or write an email with pen and paper. Find important class notes using the key word search feature.

Customize your FLY Fusion Pentop Computer by using the FLY World™ Application to download and manage the software that you need.

Use the FLY Fusion Notebook to capture your notes and get step-by-step help solving homework problems.

The FLY Fusion Pentop Computer works only with FLY™ Paper. FLY paper and software sold separately. FLY Fusion Pentop Computer is not compatible with FLY I.0 products.

When you write with the FLY Fusion™ Pentop Computer on FLY™ Paper, everything is automatically captured and digitized. You can then upload it to your PC and convert to a document. Touch your pentop computer to FLY Paper, and you can quiz yourself on history, get help with a quadratic equation, or even play your favorite MP3. And when you're ready for new software, simply connect to your PC again to purchase and download custom homework and gaming applications directly to your FLY Fusion Pentop Computer.

Finally, technology designed for your Life, School, Music and Fun! This is Pentop Computing, the next generation of high-speed digital processing, developed to deliver high-speed homework help—in the palm of your hand.

How FLY Fusion works; it uses special paper to enable the pen to track positions of characters (*www.leap frog.com/en/ families/fly_fusion/learning_ systems/ff_Pentop.html*).

requires you to write on special paper that's been printed with millions of nearly invisible microdots. A tiny camera in the pen tip learns its position, and a microchip in the pen converts the pen to digital ink, which can be transmitted to a PC.[14] Recent pens such as the LiveScribe Pulse and the Nokia Digital Pen SU-27W also require special paper.[15] The second version, such as the Mobile Digital Scribe, doesn't need preprinted paper. Instead, you attach a small "clip" with an LCD screen to your standard paper notepad, and the pen signals its position to the clip using ultrasonic pulses and invisible infrared light. You then connect the clip to your computer to transfer the notes.[16]

Scanning & Reading Devices

How is source data entry different from keyboard entry?

In old-fashioned grocery stores, checkout clerks read the price on every can and box and then enter those prices on the keyboard—a wasteful, duplicated effort. In most stores, of course, the clerks merely wave the products over a scanner, which automatically enters the price (from the bar code) in digital form. This is the difference between keyboard entry and source data entry.

Source data-input devices do not require keystrokes (or require only a few keystrokes) to input data to the computer. In most cases, data is entered directly from the source, without human intervention. **_Source data-entry devices_ create machine-readable data on magnetic media or paper or feed it directly into the computer's processor.** One type of source data-entry device includes scanning and reading devices—scanners, bar-code readers, mark- and character-recognition devices, and fax machines.

SCANNERS *Scanners,* **or** *optical scanners,* **use light-sensing (optical) equipment to translate images of text, drawings, photos, and the like into digital form.** (● *See Panel 5.12, next page.*) The images can then be processed by a computer, displayed on a monitor, stored on a storage device, or transmitted to another computer.

Scanners have led to a whole new industry called *electronic imaging,* the software-controlled integration and manipulation of separate images, using scanners, digital cameras, and advanced graphic computers. This technology has become invaluable for all kinds of reasons, such as to digitize and preserve

Survival Tip

Can Your PC Connect Your New Scanner?

No USB ports on your PC? Then no USB scanner. Connections must be compatible.

Hardware: Input & Output

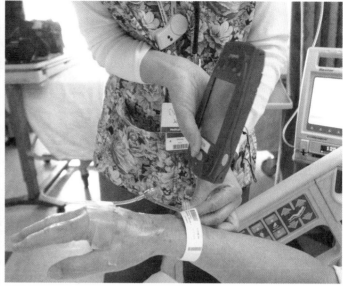

Choosing a Scanner

- In scanner resolution, the first number is the number of sensors the scanner uses to capture the image. The second number is the number of points the scanner stops at. The two numbers are usually the same.
- Look for a high first number. Because the first number measures the number of sensors, it's the more important number. Some scanners will advertise a resolution of 1,200 by 2,400, but these scanners do not necessarily produce a higher quality image than a scanner with a resolution of 1,200 by 1,200.
- Consider the resolution of your printer before buying a scanner. If you're scanning images primarily to print them, note the resolution of your printer. Purchasing a scanner with a higher resolution than your printer is a waste, because the quality of your images will be limited by your printer.
- Settle for a 300 by 300 resolution scanner for text. If you need to capture only text with your scanner, you can save some money and get a low-end scanner with a low resolution.
- Move up to a 600 by 600 resolution scanner for most image applications. While more expensive scanners offer resolutions of 1,200 by 1,200 or 2,400 by 2,400, a resolution of 600 by 600 is adequate for capturing images for quality 4 by 6 or 5 by 7 prints.
- Get a 1,200 by 1,200 or greater scanner only if you need to capture large images. Resolutions this high are not necessary unless you need to print 8 by 10 or larger images.
(Adapted from *www.ehow.com/how_2105727_choose-scanner-resolution.html*)

old books and manuscripts (for example, relics from the golden age of Timbuktu) that would otherwise fall into decay.[17] PC users can get a decent scanner with good software for less than $100 or a fantastic one for about $1,000.

- **Dots and bitmaps:** Scanners are similar to photocopy machines except they create electronic files of scanned items instead of paper copies. The system scans each image—color or black and white—with light and breaks the image into rows and columns of light and dark dots or color dots. Dots are stored in computer memory as digital code called a *bitmap*, a grid of dots. A *dot* is the smallest identifiable part of an image, and each dot is represented by one or more bits. The more bits in each dot, the more shades of gray and the more colors that can be represented. The amount of information stored in a dot is referred to as *color depth*, or *bit depth*. Good scanners have a 48-bit color depth.

- **Resolution:** Scanners vary in resolution. In general, **_resolution_ refers to the clarity and sharpness of an image and**

Flatbed: Costs $60–$400. The type most PC users have. Operates like a photocopier—image lies atop glass, which is scanned by scanning beam. Useful for single-sheet documents, books, photos. Some models scan transparencies, slides.

Sheet-fed: Costs $300–$500. Also popular for desktops because of compact size, which is smaller than flatbed. Operates similarly except sheet with image being scanned is fed into a slot and drawn past sensor. Useful only for single-page documents, photos; some accept slides.

Handheld: Costs $130–$160. Popular for use in factory and field settings and student and research use because of portability. Handheld scanners are physically dragged by hand across a document. Most models are pen-shaped and scan in swaths 5 inches wide or less, and special software "knits" strips of images together into a complete image. Some models translate single words into other languages. Images can be transmitted to a PC, PDA, or cellphone via serial, infrared (IR), or USB connection.

Drum: Costs in tens of thousands of dollars. Used by publishing industry to capture extremely detailed images. Image to be scanned is mounted on a glass cylinder, inside of which are sensors (photomultiplier tubes) that convert light signals into digital images.

is measured in <u>*dots per inch*</u> *(dpi)*—**the number of columns and rows of dots per inch.** The higher the number of dots, the clearer and sharper the image—that is, the higher the resolution. Popular color desktop scanners currently vary in dpi from 300 × 200 up to 2,400 × 2,400; some commercial scanners operate at 4,800 × 9,600 dpi. The quality of the scanner's optical equipment also affects the quality of the scanned images.

- **Types of scanners:** One of the most popular types of scanners is the <u>*flatbed scanner,*</u> **or** *desktop scanner,* **which works much like a photocopier—the image being scanned is placed on a glass surface, where it remains stationary, and the scanning beam moves across it.** Three other types of scanners are *sheet-fed, handheld,* and *drum.* The four types are compared below. (● *See Panel 5.13.)* Other single-purpose scanners are available, such as business-card, slide, and photo scanners. There are even scanner pens, such as the DocuPen, that can scan text from books and articles.

BAR-CODE READERS On June 26, 1974, a customer at Marsh's Supermarket in Troy, Ohio, made the first purchase of a product with a bar code—a pack of Wrigley's Juicy Fruit chewing gum (which pack is now in the Smithsonian National Museum of National History in Washington, D.C.). <u>*Bar codes*</u> **are the vertical, zebra-striped marks you see on most manufactured retail products**—everything from candy to cosmetics to comic books. (● *See Panel 5.14, next page.)* In North America, supermarkets, food manufacturers, and others have agreed to use a bar-code system called the *Universal Product Code (UPC),* established by the Uniform Code Council (UCC). Other kinds of bar-code systems are used on everything from FedEx and Postal Service packages to railroad cars, video-store videos, and the jerseys of long-distance runners.

- **Bar-code readers:** <u>*Bar-code readers*</u> **are photoelectric (optical) scanners that translate the symbols in the bar code into digital code.** In this system, the price of a particular item is set within the store's computer. Once the bar code has been scanned, the corresponding price appears on the salesclerk's point-of-sale terminal and on your receipt. Records of sales from the bar-code readers are input to the store's computer and used for accounting, restocking store inventory, and weeding out products that don't sell well.

"Want to skip long lines?" asks one writer. "Be your own cashier."[18] The reference is to self-scanning, which is becoming increasingly available in

panel 5.13

Types of scanners compared

What Is TWAIN?

Maybe "Technology Without An Interesting Name"? It's a driver that's a go-between for a scanner and the applications on the computer. Borrowing from a Rudyard Kipling poem ("and never the twain [that is, two] shall meet," about Eastern and Western cultures), someone used the word *TWAIN* to express the difficulty, at the time, of connecting scanners and personal computers, although this is no longer the case.

Do a web search for *TWAIN.* When was it developed, and how does it work?

panel 5.14

Bar code and bar-code reader
This bar-code reader is being used to update inventory, by scanning in the information on the stickers put on the boxes coming into the warehouse.

panel 5.15

Self-Scanning System
The NCR FastLane self-service scanning system allows consumers to check themselves out of the supermarket. The shopper begins the process by touching the computer's welcome screen. Then the computer's voice output provides the shopper with instructions about how to scan the items and where to place them once they've been scanned. When the shopper scans in an item, the item's bar code provides the computer with the information it needs to determine what item is being scanned, its weight, and its price. The system also deactivates any security tags on the items. The shopper places the items in shopping bags sitting on security scales, so the system can check that heavy items were not substituted for light ones.

stores throughout the United States. Do-it-yourself checkout is an automated process that enables shoppers to scan, bag, and pay for their purchases without human assistance. The self-scanning checkout lane looks like a traditional checkout lane except that the shopper interacts with a computer's user interface instead of a store employee. (● *See Panel 5.15.*) Self-scanning has become popular in Walmart, Home Depot, Kroger, and many other name-brand stores.

The next evolution in bar codes and groceries is the Ikan, a countertop appliance designed to eliminate trips to the grocery store. This device, which has a laser scanner and a Wi-Fi antenna that connects to your home wireless network, enables you to scan the bar code of an empty container,

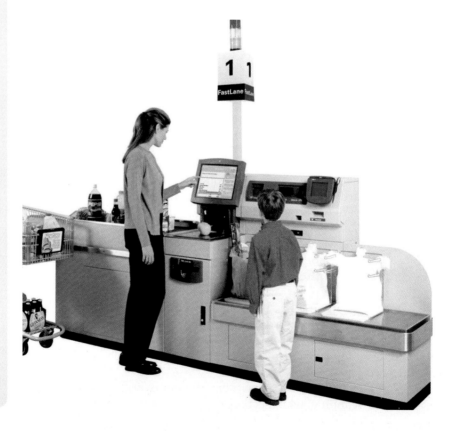

whether it's for milk, paper towels, or dog food; this enters the product into a database. After a few days of entering products, you can review your list online (at Ikan.net), then click to have everything delivered to your house at a time of your choosing.[19]

TYPES OF BAR CODES Bar codes may be 1-D, 2-D, or 3-D.

- *1-D* codes, today's ordinary vertical bar codes, can hold up to 16 ASCII characters. These are the bar codes commonly used by supermarkets.

- *2-D* bar codes, composed of different-size rectangles, with data recorded along both the height and the length of each rectangle, can hold 1,000–2,000 ASCII characters. 2-D codes are used on medication containers and for other purposes in which there is limited space for a bar-code label. Shipping company UPS uses a special 2-D bar code (based on hexagons). Many airlines now use 2-D bar codes on boarding passes that passengers can display on cellphones instead of paper documents.[21] A new use for this bar code is as a label on packages of fruit, so that customers can locate the farms that grew the fruit and find out their location and records of food safety.[20] And new 2-D bar codes (such as those created by ScanLife and Jagtag) are being rushed out that can be photographed with your cellphone camera, so that it acts as a magic wand to extract digital content from a variety of objects, such as magazine articles.[22]

- *3-D* bar codes, used on items such as automobile tires, are called "bumpy" bar codes because they are read by a scanner that differentiates by symbol height. 3-D codes are used on metal, hard rubber, and other surfaces to which ordinary bar codes will not adhere.

  Soon store 1-D bar codes may yield to so-called *smart tags*, radio-frequency identification (RFID) tags already now employed for the tracking of cattle or of electronic components in a warehouse. We discuss RFID on page 279.

MARK-RECOGNITION/CHARACTER-RECOGNITION DEVICES There are three types of scanning devices that sense marks or characters. They are usually referred to by their abbreviations—MICR, OMR, and OCR:

- **Magnetic-ink character recognition:** ***Magnetic-ink character recognition (MICR)* is a character-recognition system that uses magnetizable ink and special characters.** When an MICR document needs to be read, it passes through a special scanner that magnetizes the special ink and then translates the magnetic information into characters. MICR technology is used by banks. Numbers and characters found on the

More Types of Bar Codes

What are these proprietary bar codes used for: Aztec Code, Data Matrix, Code I, Snowflake Code, QR Code? Go to:

www.adamsl.com/pub/ russadam/stack.html

and find out.

Conventional I-D bar code

2-D bar code

Maxicode is a 2-D bar code used by United Parcel Service (UPS).

The ModelMaker 3-D scanning system can scan all types of surfaces in all sorts of lighting. It is used, among other things, to scan cars and motorcycles, or specific components, into a CAD/CAM system so that new models can be created.

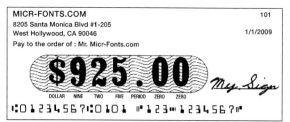

bottom of checks (usually containing the check number, sort number, and account number) are printed with a laser printer that accepts MICR toner. MICR provides a secure, high-speed method of scanning and processing information.

- **Optical mark recognition:** ***Optical mark recognition (OMR)* uses a special scanner that reads "bubble" marks and converts them into computer-usable form.** The best-known example is the OMR technology used to read students' answers to the College Board Scholastic Aptitude Test (SAT) and the Graduate Record Examination (GRE). In these cases, the scanner reads pencil marks that fill in circles, or bubbles, on specially designed documents. OMR is also used in forms and surveys.

- **Optical character recognition:** These days almost all scanners come with OCR software. ***Optical character recognition (OCR)* software converts scanned text from images (pictures of the text) to an editable text format (usually ASCII) that can be imported into a word processing application and manipulated.** Special OCR characters appear on utility bills and price tags on department-store merchandise. The wand reader is a common OCR scanning device. (● *See Panel 5.16.*)

  OCR software can deal with nearly all printed characters, but script fonts and handwriting still present problems. In addition, OCR accuracy varies with the quality of the scanner—a text with 1,200 dpi will take longer to scan than one with 72 dpi, but the accuracy will be higher. Some OCR programs are better than others, with lesser versions unable to convert tables, boxes, or other extensive formatting; high-quality OCR software can read such complex material without difficulty. Users wanting to scan text with foreign-language (diacritical) marks, such as French accents, should check the OCR package to see if the program can handle this.

FAX MACHINES A *fax machine*—or *facsimile transmission machine*—**scans an image and sends it as electronic signals over telephone lines to a receiving fax machine, which prints out the image on paper.**

  There are two types of fax machines—dedicated fax machines and fax modems:

- **Dedicated fax machines:** *Dedicated fax machines* are specialized devices that do nothing except send and receive fax documents. These are what we usually think of as fax machines. They are found not only in offices

panel 5.16

Optical character recognition

OCR is often used in stores to encode and read price tags. A hand-held wand is used as a reading device.

OCR-A	
NUMERIC	0123456789
ALPHA	ABCDEFGHIJ
SYMBOLS	KLMNOPQRST
	UVWXYZ
	>$/-+-#"

OCR-B	
NUMERIC	00123456789
ALPHA	ACENPSTVX
SYMBOLS	<+>-¥

and homes but also alongside regular phones in public places such as airports.

- **Fax modems:** A *fax modem* is installed as a circuit board inside the computer's system cabinet. It is a modem with fax capability that enables you to send signals directly from your computer to someone else's fax machine or computer fax modem. With this device, you don't have to print out the material from your printer and then turn around and run it through the scanner on a fax machine. The fax modem allows you to send information more quickly than you could if you had to feed it page by page into a machine.

  The fax modem is another feature of mobile computing; it's especially powerful as a receiving device. Fax modems are installed inside portable computers, including pocket PCs and PDAs. If you link up a cellular phone to a fax modem in your portable computer, you can send and receive wireless fax messages no matter where you are in the world.

Dedicated fax machine

Why, you might wonder, does fax technology still exist in the era of email? Although email is certainly faster and cheaper (in terms of the cost of supplies), the fax machine is still more reliable, more secure, and cheaper in its equipment cost (a fax machine costs only $100 whereas the cost of a computer and monitor is more).[23]

Fax modem circuit board, which plugs into an expansion slot inside the computer

Audio-Input Devices

What are ways of digitizing audio input?

An _audio-input device_ **records analog sound and translates it for digital storage and processing.** An analog sound signal is a continuously variable wave within a certain frequency range. For the computer to process them, these variable waves must be converted to digital 0s and 1s. The principal use of audio-input devices is to produce digital input for multimedia computers.

TWO WAYS OF DIGITIZING AUDIO An audio signal can be digitized in two ways—by a *sound board* or a *MIDI board:*

PC fax modem card, which plugs into a USB port on a notebook computer

- **Sound board:** Analog sound from a cassette player or a microphone goes through a special circuit board called a *sound board*. **A _sound board_ is an add-on circuit board in a computer that converts analog sound to digital sound and stores it for further processing and/or plays it back, providing output directly to speakers or an external amplifier.**

- **MIDI board:** A _MIDI board_—**MIDI, pronounced "middie," stands for "Musical Instrument Digital Interface"—uses a standard for the interchange of musical information between musical instruments, synthesizers, and computers.**

MICROPHONES Also supporting audio input are *microphones,* devices that take varying air pressure waves created by voice or other sound sources and convert them into varying electric signals. Many new microcomputers and notebooks come with built-in microphones; stand-alone microphones can be connected via USB or some other connection. Microphones are used in speech-recognition input (discussed on page 276).

Webcams & Video-Input Cards

What are my options in video input?

Are you the type who likes to show off for the camera? Maybe, then, you'd like to acquire a **_webcam_, a video camera attached to a computer to record live moving images that can then be posted on a website in real time.**

panel 5.17

Webcam in use
The cameras are mounted on the top of the screens.

Coffee Pot Cam

The first webcam was the "Trojan room coffee pot cam." What was this? Search the web to find out.

(● *See Panel 5.17.*) Webcam connections require special software, usually included with the camera, and a USB or video cable or a wireless radio-frequency connection.

Initially intended for personal videoconferencing, the webcam has become popular with web users. You can join thousands of other webcam users out there who are hosting such riveting material as a live 24-hour view of the aquarium of a turtle named Pixel. Or you might show your living quarters or messy desk for all to see. Twenty20's VholdR Helmet Camera Camcorder is a digital video camera with a lens that straps onto your helmet—perfect for capturing your moves as you ski down a black-diamond trail.

As with sound, most film and videotape traditionally has been in analog form; the signal is a continuously variable wave. For computer use, the signals that come from a VCR or camcorder must be converted to digital form through a special digitizing card—a *video-capture card* or simply *video card*—that is installed in the computer. There are two types of video cards—frame-grabber and full-motion.

FRAME-GRABBER VIDEO CARD The *frame-grabber video card* can capture and digitize only a single frame at a time.

FULL-MOTION VIDEO CARD The *full-motion video card* can convert analog to digital signals at rates up to 30 frames per second, giving the effect of a continuously flowing motion picture. (● *See Panel 5.18.*)

Digital Cameras

How does a digital camera differ from a film camera?

Digital cameras, which now greatly outsell film cameras in the United States, are particularly interesting because they have changed the entire industry of photography. The environmentally undesirable stage of chemical development required for conventional film is completely eliminated.

Instead of using traditional (chemical) film, **a _digital camera_ uses a light-sensitive processor chip to capture photographic images in digital form and store them on a small diskette inserted into the camera or on flash memory cards.** (● *See Panel 5.19.*) The bits of digital information can then be copied right into a computer's hard disk for manipulation, emailing, posting on websites, and printing out.

Many digital cameras can be connected to a computer by a USB or FireWire connection (discussed in Chapter 6), so your computer's operating system

Survival Tip

Your Choice: More Colors or More Resolution?

You can't have the best of both. A video card may let you have 16.8 million colors at 800 × 600 resolution or 65,536 colors at 1,600 × 1,200 resolution.

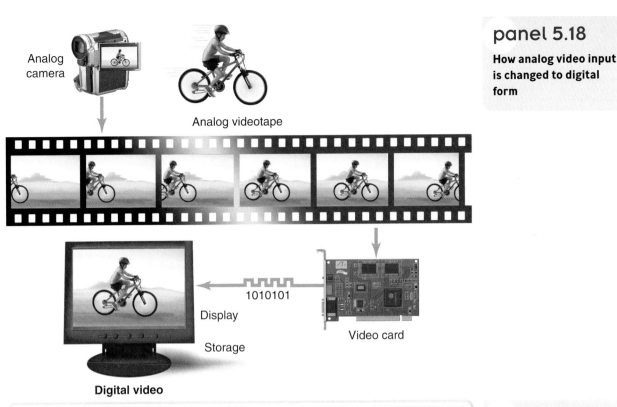

Analog camera

Analog videotape

1010101

Display

Storage

Video card

Digital video

Video input: **Analog to Digital**
Full-motion video is accomplished by taking multiple pictures in sequence. Movie theater film uses 24 frames per second, which is the minimum frequency required to eliminate the perception of moving frames and make the images appear visually fluid to the eye. TV video generates 30 interlaced frames per second, which is actually transmitted as 60 half frames ("fields" in TV lingo) per second.

Video that has been digitized and stored in the computer can be displayed at varying frame rates, depending on the speed of the computer. The slower the computer, the jerkier the movement.

panel 5.19

Digital cameras and how they work
(*Below*) This digital camera is attached to a desktop computer in order to download its images to the computer.

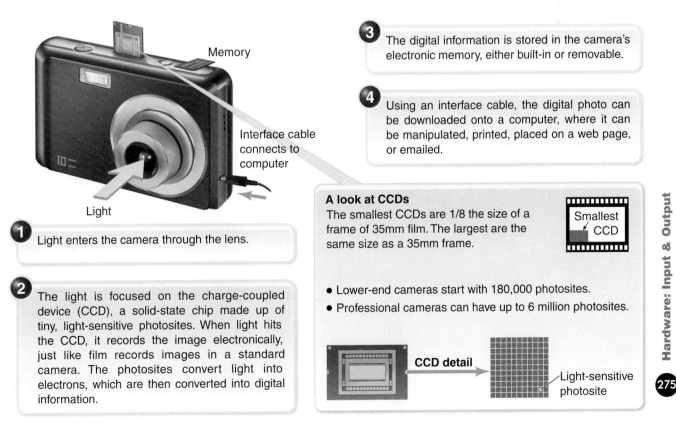

Memory

Interface cable connects to computer

Light

1 Light enters the camera through the lens.

2 The light is focused on the charge-coupled device (CCD), a solid-state chip made up of tiny, light-sensitive photosites. When light hits the CCD, it records the image electronically, just like film records images in a standard camera. The photosites convert light into electrons, which are then converted into digital information.

3 The digital information is stored in the camera's electronic memory, either built-in or removable.

4 Using an interface cable, the digital photo can be downloaded onto a computer, where it can be manipulated, printed, placed on a web page, or emailed.

A look at CCDs
The smallest CCDs are 1/8 the size of a frame of 35mm film. The largest are the same size as a 35mm frame.

Smallest CCD

- Lower-end cameras start with 180,000 photosites.
- Professional cameras can have up to 6 million photosites.

CCD detail

Light-sensitive photosite

Hardware: Input & Output

275

must support these connections to recognize the camera's driver. Most cameras store picture data on flash memory cards and memory sticks, from which later you can transmit photo data to your computer through a USB cable. Popular software applications for sophisticated digital photo manipulation include Adobe Photoshop, Corel Snapfire, Jasc Paint Shop Pro, and Microsoft Picture It! Digital Image Pro.

CAMERA CAVEATS Three facts that all digital-camera users should be aware of:

- **Don't use the "delete" function:** Instead of using a camera's "delete" function to remove images you don't want from the camera's memory card each night, you should download all the images to your computer and then reformat the card. This will prevent possible fragmentation and loss of your pictures.

Digital photo in an HP Photosmart digital camera; the dock sends pictures to the computer.

- **Use a photo shop for printing:** Photos printed out on standard computer printers do not last nearly as long as photos printed in the usual manner—that is, by a photo shop on good-quality paper.

- **Be aware of limitations of storage media:** If you store your photos on such secondary storage media as CDs, be aware that such media may very well not be usable by information technology equipment 20 or 30 years from now.

CAMERA PHONES Digital-camera technology has, of course, migrated to cellphones (which can also be used for web surfing, playing games, and downloading music), enabling you to visually share your vacation experiences in real time. You compose the shot on your phone's color LCD screen, point and shoot, then wait a minute or so for the picture to "develop," and then send it. We discuss camera phones further in Chapter 7.

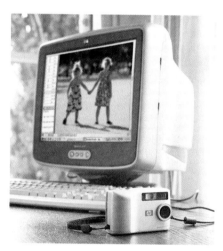

Speech-Recognition Systems

How might I use a speech-recognition system?

Can your computer tell whether you want it to "recognize speech" or "wreck a nice beach"? **A _speech-recognition system_, using a microphone (or a telephone) as an input device, converts a person's speech into digital signals by comparing the electrical patterns produced by the speaker's voice with a set of prerecorded patterns stored in the computer.** (● *See Panel 5.20.*) Most of today's speech-recognition packages have a database of about 200,000 words from which they try to match the words you say. These programs let you accomplish two tasks: turn spoken dictation into typed text and issue oral commands (such as "Print file" or "Change font") to control your computer.

Speech-recognition systems have had to overcome many difficulties, such as different voices, pronunciations, and accents. Recently, however, the systems have measurably improved, at least up to a point.[24] Major recognition

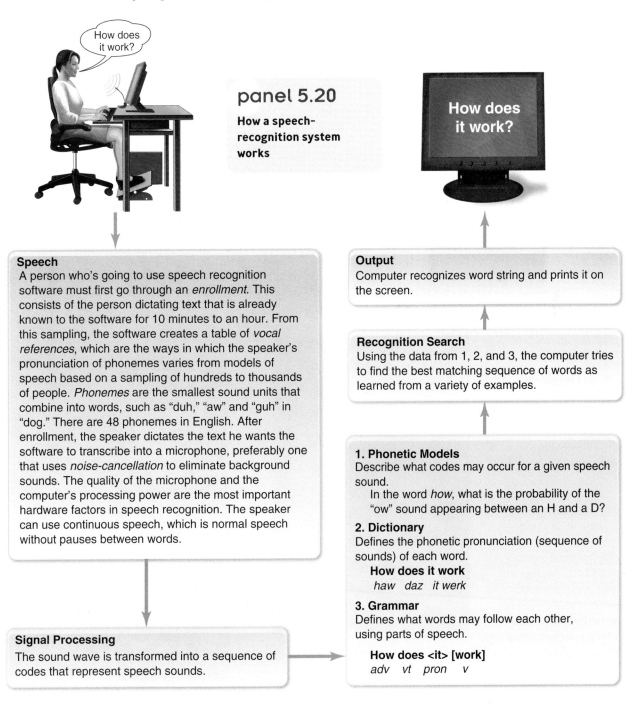

panel 5.20

How a speech-recognition system works

Speech
A person who's going to use speech recognition software must first go through an *enrollment*. This consists of the person dictating text that is already known to the software for 10 minutes to an hour. From this sampling, the software creates a table of *vocal references*, which are the ways in which the speaker's pronunciation of phonemes varies from models of speech based on a sampling of hundreds to thousands of people. *Phonemes* are the smallest sound units that combine into words, such as "duh," "aw" and "guh" in "dog." There are 48 phonemes in English. After enrollment, the speaker dictates the text he wants the software to transcribe into a microphone, preferably one that uses *noise-cancellation* to eliminate background sounds. The quality of the microphone and the computer's processing power are the most important hardware factors in speech recognition. The speaker can use continuous speech, which is normal speech without pauses between words.

Signal Processing
The sound wave is transformed into a sequence of codes that represent speech sounds.

Output
Computer recognizes word string and prints it on the screen.

Recognition Search
Using the data from 1, 2, and 3, the computer tries to find the best matching sequence of words as learned from a variety of examples.

1. Phonetic Models
Describe what codes may occur for a given speech sound.
　　In the word *how*, what is the probability of the "ow" sound appearing between an H and a D?

2. Dictionary
Defines the phonetic pronunciation (sequence of sounds) of each word.
　　How does it work
　　haw　daz　it werk

3. Grammar
Defines what words may follow each other, using parts of speech.

　　How does <it> [work]
　　adv　vt　pron　v

systems are Dragon Naturally Speaking and speech-recognition software built into Windows Vista.[25] Other systems are ScanSoft and Nuance, Fonix Speech, Aculab, and Verbio. Special speech-recognition software is available for specific professions, such as law, medicine, and public safety.

Speech-recognition systems are finding many uses. Warehouse workers are able to speed inventory taking by recording inventory counts verbally. Traders on stock exchanges can communicate their trades by speaking to computers. Radiologists can dictate their interpretations of X rays directly into transcription machines. Nurses can fill out patient charts by talking to a computer. Users can do online voice searches on their cellphones, using programs such as Google Mobile App, Yahoo OneSearch with Voice, Vlingo, and ChaCha.[26] Speakers of Chinese can speak to machines that will print out Chinese characters. And for many individuals with disabilities, a computer isn't so much a luxury or a productivity tool as a necessity, providing freedom of expression, independence, and empowerment.

Sensors

What are various kinds of uses for sensors?

A _sensor_ is an input device that collects specific data directly from the environment and transmits it to a computer. Although you are unlikely to see such input devices connected to a PC in an office, they exist all around us, often in nearly invisible form and as part of some larger electronic system. Sensors can be used to detect all kinds of things: speed, movement, weight, pressure, temperature, humidity, wind, current, fog, gas, smoke, light, shapes, images, and so on. An electronic device is used to measure a physical quantity such as temperature, pressure, or volume and convert it into an electronic signal of some kind (for instance, a voltage).

Adidas markets a running shoe with a sensor that adjusts cushioning for different surfaces. (● *See Panel 5.21.*) Building security systems use sensors to detect movement. Sensors are used to detect the speed and volume of traffic and adjust traffic lights. They are used on highways in wintertime in Iowa as weather-sensing devices to tell workers when to roll out snowplows and on Interstate 95 to give drivers from New Jersey to North Carolina access to

panel 5.21

Sensors

(*Left*) On October 9, 2003, the 2,080-pound Liberty Bell made a 963-foot journey to a new home on Independence Mall in Philadelphia. High-tech sensors monitored the famous crack, to make sure it did not get larger. (*Right*) The Adidas-I running shoe was advertised as the world's first "intelligent shoe." A microprocessor beneath the arch sends instructions to a small battery-powered motor that adjusts the cushioning level of the shoe.

real-time information on traffic flows, crashes, and travel time to help them anticipate delays.[27] In aviation, sensors are used to detect ice buildup on airplane wings or to alert pilots to sudden changes in wind direction. In California, sensors have been planted along major earthquake fault lines in an experiment to see whether scientists can predict major earth movements.[28] Also in California, environmental scientists have hooked up a network of sensors, robots, cameras, and computers to produce an ecological picture of a lush world that is home to more than 30 rare and endangered species.[29]

Radio-Frequency Identification Tags

Is there any way I could benefit from RFID technology?

Radio-frequency identification (RFID) tags are based on an identifying tag bearing a microchip that contains specific code numbers. These code numbers are read by the radio waves of a scanner linked to a database. RFID tags range in size "from small chips on paper labels to palm-size plastic boxes," in one description.[30] *Active RFID tags* have their own power source and can transmit signals over a distance to a reader device. *Passive RFID tags* have no battery power of their own and must be read by some sort of scanner.

RFID tags of both types are used for a wide range of purposes. Drivers with RFID tags breeze through tollbooths without having to even roll down their windows; the toll is automatically charged to their accounts. Radio-wave-readable ID tags are also used by the Postal Service to monitor the flow of mail, by stores for inventory control and warehousing, and in the railroad industry to keep track of rail cars. The Food and Drug Administration (FDA) and drug companies are working on tagging popular drugs with RFID devices to guard against counterfeit medicines. The technology is used to make supposedly "thiefproof" keys in millions of Fords, Toyotas, and Nissans (although researchers have succeeded in cracking the security).[31] Gambling casinos have put RFID tags inside gambling chips to help them track the betting habits of high rollers.[32] Visa and MasterCard "no-swipe" or "wave-and-pay" credit cards have been developed with embedded RFID technology that means cards don't have to be swiped across a magnetic-strip reader but can just be waved near a scanner, which could help speed up lines in stores.[33] Walmart has required that all its vendors replace bar codes with RFID technology in order to improve inventory control. In the long run, the tags could end up on every product we buy, so that in the future we will no longer wait for a checkout counter but will breeze past readers that will scan our purchases in milliseconds.[34]

Of great significance, all U.S. passports now must have RFID tags embedded in them. Machines can read the personal information in these passports—

RFID. (*Left, center*) Drivers can buy RFID tags to drive past tollbooths without having to stop; the tolls are automatically charged to their account, usually established with a credit card. FastTrack is a common tollbooth RFID program. (*Right*) RFID tags are starting to replace bar codes.

aiding customs and immigration officials but also, unfortunately making passport information vulnerable to terrorists and other criminals.[35] But concerns about the use of RFID technology go beyond this. First, tiny transmitters were installed in things ranging from cars to National Park Service cactuses to help authorities track thefts.[36] Then pet owners began putting RFID tags in their dogs and cats, to allow veterinarians with the right scanning equipment to identify the animals if they became separated from their owners. Then an epidemic of kidnappings led wealthy and some middle-class Mexicans to start implanting geolocator tags that can pinpoint their location by satellite.[37]

In the United States, the FDA improved implantation of an implantable chip, the VeriChip, for medical purposes, on the premise that patient-specific information stored in the chip could speed vital information about a person's medical history. However, privacy advocates fear that the technology could be used to track people's movements and put sensitive personal information at risk to hackers. "If privacy protections aren't built in at the outset," says a policy analyst with the Health Privacy Project, "there could be harmful consequences for patients.[38]

Human-Biology-Input Devices

Have I ever seen biometrics in use?

Security concerns following the terrorist attacks of September 11, 2001, on the New York World Trade Center and the Pentagon made more people aware of ***biometrics*, the science of measuring individual body characteristics.** Biometric security devices identify a person through a fingerprint; hand, eye, or facial characteristics; voice intonation; or some other biological trait. (● *See Panel 5.22.*) Hewlett-Packard, Toshiba, and Lenovo have produced notebook computers equipped with biometric sensors that read fingerprints, instead of passwords, before allowing access to networks.[39] A new system helps a U.S. traveler flying overseas avoid customs lines at a foreign airport by swiping a digital ID card embedded with an image of his or her eye to verify the traveler's identity.[40]

5.3 OUTPUT HARDWARE

What are the two categories of output hardware, what devices do they include, and what are their features?

Computer output gets more innovative all the time. Ready to move up from one screen to two when you're working at your computer? "As every office worker knows," writes reporter Farhad Manjoo, "trying to get anything done on a computer that's connected to the internet can be a test of wills."[41]

panel 5.22

Some types of biometric devices
(*Left*) Palm print recognition. (*Right*) Screen from a face recognition program.

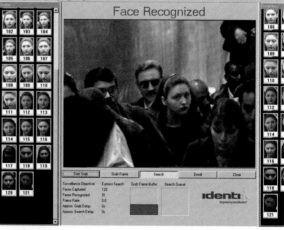

Softcopy Devices	Hardcopy Devices	Other Devices
CRT display screens	Impact printers: dot-matrix printer	Sound output
Flat-panel display screen (e.g., liquid-crystal display)	Nonimpact printers: laser, ink-jet, thermal	Voice output
		Video output

panel 5.23

Types of output devices

Hardcopy

Softcopy

With only a single display screen, you find yourself switching back and forth between, say, a word processing document, email, and web searches. Multiple monitors reduce distractions. Indeed, a study shows that people who use *two* display screens, rather than one, are 44% more productive at certain text-editing operations.[42] "The study reveals multi-screen users get on task quicker, work faster, and get more work done with fewer errors editing documents, spreadsheets, and graphic files in comparison with single screen users," said one of the study authors.[43] A cost-effective arrangement is to get two 22-inch monitors, one placed vertically, the other horizontally.[44]

In this section, we discuss monitors and other output hardware, devices that convert machine-readable information, obtained as the result of processing, into people-readable form. The principal kinds of output are softcopy and hardcopy. (● *See Panel 5.23.*)

- **Softcopy:** *Softcopy* **is data that is shown on a display screen or is in audio or voice form; it exists only electronically.** This kind of output is not tangible; it cannot be touched. It's like music: You can see musical scores and touch CDs and tapes, but the music itself is intangible. Similarly, you can touch floppy disks on which programs are stored, but the software itself is intangible. *Soft* is also used to describe things that are easily changed or impermanent. In contrast, *hard* is used to describe things that are relatively permanent.

- **Hardcopy:** *Hardcopy* **is printed output.** The principal examples are printouts, whether text or graphics, from printers. Film, including microfilm and microfiche, is also considered hardcopy output.

There are several types of softcopy and hardcopy output devices. In the following three sections, we discuss, first, traditional *softcopy* output—*display screens;* second, traditional *hardcopy* output—*printers;* and, third, *mixed* output—including *sound, voice,* and *video.*

Traditional Softcopy Output: Display Screens

What are the principal things I need to know to make a good choice of display screen?

Display screens—**also variously called** *monitors* **or simply** *screens*—**are output devices that show programming instructions and data as they are being input and information after it is processed.** The monitor is the component that displays the visual output from your computer as generated by the video card. It is responsible not for doing any real computing but rather for showing the results of computing.

As with TV screens, the size of a computer screen is measured diagonally from corner to corner in inches. For desktop microcomputers, the most common sizes are 15 inches to 30 inches. For laptop computers, they are 12 inches to 18 inches. Increasingly, computer ads state the actual display area, called the *viewable image size (vis),* which may be an inch or so less. A 15-inch monitor may have a 13.8-inch vis; a 17-inch monitor may have a 16-inch vis. The 22-inch wide display, available for around $200, is fast becoming the industry's standard. (If you want to run two screens at once, you'll need to install a video card to get them to work.)

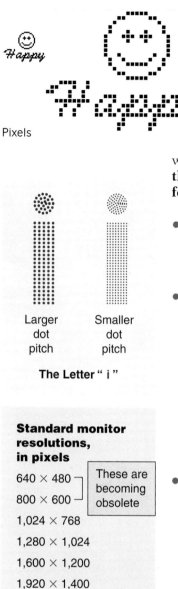

Pixels

Larger dot pitch   Smaller dot pitch

The Letter " i "

Standard monitor resolutions, in pixels

640 × 480 ⎤
            ⎥ These are becoming obsolete
800 × 600 ⎦

1,024 × 768

1,280 × 1,024

1,600 × 1,200

1,920 × 1,400

Standard bit depths for color

4-bit—16 colors

8-bit—256 colors

16-bit—65,536 colors

24-bit—10 million colors

In deciding which display screen to buy, you will need to consider issues of screen clarity (dot pitch, resolution, color depth, and refresh rate), type of display technology (active-matrix flat panel versus passive-matrix flat panel), and color and resolution standards.

SCREEN CLARITY: DOT PITCH, RESOLUTION, COLOR DEPTH, & REFRESH RATE Among the factors affecting screen clarity (often mentioned in ads) are *dot pitch, resolution, color depth,* and *refresh rate.* These relate to the individual dots on the screen known as *pixels,* which represent the images on the screen. **A _pixel_, for "*picture element,*" is the smallest unit on the screen that can be turned on and off or made different shades.** Pixels are tiny squares, not circles.

- **Dot pitch: _Dot pitch (dp)_ is the amount of space between the centers of adjacent pixels; the closer the pixels, the crisper the image.** For a .25-dp monitor, for instance, the dots (pixels) are 25/100ths of a millimeter apart. Generally, a dot pitch of .25 dp will provide clear images.

- **Resolution:** Here _resolution_ **refers to the image sharpness of the display screen; the more pixels, or dots, there are per square inch, the finer the level of detail.** As with scanners, resolution is expressed in *dots per inch (dpi),* the number of columns and rows of dots per inch. The higher the number of dots, the clearer and sharper the image. Resolution clarity is measured by the formula *horizontal-row pixels × vertical-row pixels.* For example, a 1,024 × 768 screen displays 1,024 pixels on each of 768 lines, for a total of 786,432 pixels. On color monitors, each pixel is assigned some red, some green, some blue, or particular shades of gray. (Note that higher resolutions appear crisper on a small screen and fuzzier on a large screen.)

- **Color depth:** As we said about scanners, _color depth_, or *bit depth*, **is the amount of information, expressed in bits, that is stored in a dot.** The more bits in a dot or pixel, the more shades of gray and colors can be represented. With 24-bit color depth, for example, 8 bits are dedicated to each primary color—red, green, and blue. Eight-bit color is standard for most of computing; 24-bit, called *true color,* requires more resources, such as video memory.

- **Refresh rate: _Refresh rate_ is the number of times per second that the pixels are recharged so that their glow remains bright.** That is, refresh rate refers to the number of times that the image on the screen is redrawn each second. The higher the refresh rate, the more solid the image looks on the screen—that is, the less it flickers. In general, displays are refreshed 56–120 times per second, or *hertz (Hz),* with speeds of 70–87 hertz being common. A high-quality monitor has a refresh rate of 90 hertz—the screen is redrawn 90 times per second. A low-quality monitor will be under 72 hertz, which will cause noticeable flicker and lead to headaches and eyestrain. (The measurement *hertz* was named after the German professor of physics Heinrich Rudolf Hertz [1847–1894], who was the first to broadcast and receive radio waves.)

panel 5.24

CRT *(left)* **versus flat-panel displays**

TWO TYPES OF MONITORS: CRT & FLAT PANEL Display screens are of two types: CRT and flat panel. (*Note:* Advertisements for desktop computers often *do not* include a monitor as part of the system. You need to be prepared to spend a few hundred dollars extra for the monitor.) (● *See Panel 5.24.*)

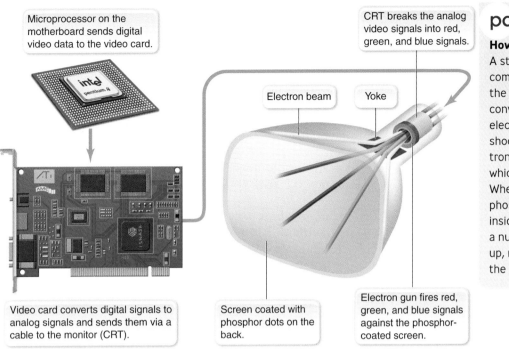

Microprocessor on the motherboard sends digital video data to the video card.

CRT breaks the analog video signals into red, green, and blue signals.

Electron beam

Yoke

Video card converts digital signals to analog signals and sends them via a cable to the monitor (CRT).

Screen coated with phosphor dots on the back.

Electron gun fires red, green, and blue signals against the phosphor-coated screen.

panel 5.25

How a CRT works

A stream of bits from the computer's CPU is sent to the electron gun, which converts the bits into electrons. The gun then shoots a beam of electrons through the yoke, which deflects the beam. When the beam hits the phosphor coating on the inside of the CRT screen, a number of pixels light up, making the image on the screen.

- **CRT:** A *__CRT (cathode-ray tube)__* **is a vacuum tube used as a display screen in a computer or video display terminal.** (● *See Panel 5.25.*) The same kind of technology is found not only in older desktop computers but also in older television sets and flight-information monitors in airports.

- **Flat panel:** Compared to CRTs, flat-panel displays are much thinner, weigh less, and consume less power, which is why they are used in portable computers. *__Flat-panel displays__* **are made up of two plates of glass separated by a layer of a substance in which light is manipulated. One flat-panel technology is *__liquid crystal display (LCD)__*, in which molecules of liquid crystal line up in a way that alters their optical properties, creating images on the screen by transmitting or blocking out light.**

  CRTs are still cheaper, but flat-panel prices have come down, and they have been matched by technical advances that make flat panels a better choice. The best flat-panel displays can also now do double duty as desktop television sets.

17" Flat-Panel Display

ACTIVE-MATRIX VERSUS PASSIVE-MATRIX PANEL DISPLAYS Flat-panel screens are either active-matrix or passive-matrix displays, according to where their transistors are located.

- **Active matrix:** In an *__active-matrix display__*, **also known as *TFT (thin-film transistor) display*, each pixel on the flat-panel screen is controlled by its own transistor.** Active-matrix screens are much brighter and sharper than passive-matrix screens, but they are more complicated and thus more expensive. They also require more power, affecting the battery life in laptop computers.

- **Passive matrix:** In a *__passive-matrix display__*, **a transistor controls a whole row or column of pixels on the flat-screen display.** Passive matrix provides a sharp image for one-color (monochrome) screens but is more subdued for color. The advantage is that passive-matrix displays are less expensive and use less power than active-matrix displays, but they aren't as clear and bright and can leave "ghosts" when the display changes quickly. Passive-matrix displays go by the abbreviations *HPA, STN,* or *DSTN.*

New flat-panel displays

COLOR & RESOLUTION STANDARDS FOR MONITORS: SVGA & XGA As mentioned earlier, PCs come with *graphics cards* (also known as *video cards* or *video adapters*) that convert signals from the computer into video signals that can be displayed as images on a monitor. The monitor then separates the video signal into three colors: red, green, and blue signals. Inside the monitor, these three colors combine to make up each individual pixel. Video cards have their own memory, video RAM, or VRAM, which stores the information about each pixel. The more VRAM you have, which can range from 2 to 64 megabytes, the higher the resolution you can use. Video gamers and desktop publishers (Photoshop users) will want a video card with lots of VRAM.

The common color and resolution standards for monitors are *XGA, SXGA, UXGA, QXGA, WXGA, and WUXGA*. (● *See Panel 5.26.*)

- **XGA:** *XGA (extended graphics array)* **has a resolution of up to 1,024 × 768 pixels, with 65,536 possible colors.** It is used mainly with 15- and 17-inch CRT monitors. It's useful for simple applications plus spreadsheets and graphics software.

- **SXGA:** *SXGA (super extended graphics array)* **has a resolution of up to 1,280 × 1,024 pixels.** It is often used with 15-inch LCD monitors.

- **UXGA:** *UXGA (ultra extended graphics array)* **has a resolution of up to 1,600 × 1,200 pixels and supports up to 16.8 million colors.** It is commonly used with 1,280 × 1,024 15- and 17-inch CRT monitors and 17- and 19-inch LCD monitors. Common applications for it include CAD (computer-aided design) and business presentations, such as trade show displays.

- **QXGA:** *QXGA (quantum extended graphics array)* **uses a resolution of up to 2,048 × 1,536 pixels.** Still relatively uncommon and very expensive in 2008, QXGA is being used for large LCD screens for computer users needing to view extreme detail in advanced graphics, for businesspeople needing to enlarge images that will still be crisp in big-screen presentations, for high-definition television (discussed in Chapter 7), and for special applications involving viewing multiple images on a single screen.

A single pixel

panel 5.26

Video graphics standards compared for pixels

Common Display Standards and Resolutions

- *1,024 x 768 15- and 17-inch CRT monitors:* XGA (Extended Graphics Array)
- *15-inch LCD monitors:* SXGA (Super XGA)
- *1,280 x 1,024 15-and 17-inch CRT monitors / 17- and 19-inch LCD monitors:* UXGA (Ultra XGA)
- *1,600 x 1,200 19-, 20-, 21-inch CRT monitors / 20-inch LCD monitors:* QXGA (Quad XGA)
- *2,048 x 1,536 21-inch and larger CRT monitors / 1,280 x 800 Wide Aspect 15.4-inch laptops:* WXGA (Wide XGA)
- *1,680 x 1,050 Wide Aspect 20-inch LCD monitors / 1,920 x 1,200 Wide Aspect 22-inch and larger LCD monitors:* WUXGA (Wide Ultra XGA)

- **WXGA and WUXGA:** *WXGA (wide aspect [wide screen] extended graphics array)* and *WUXGA (wide aspect ultra extended graphics array)* are the newest VGA standards, wide-screen versions of XGA and UXGA. WXGA has a resolution of 1,366 × 768, and WUXGA 1,920 × 1,200; these standards are used with high-definition (HD) TVs and HD movies and with wide-screen notebook computers.

Traditional Hardcopy Output: Printers

What kind of options do I have in printers?

The prices in ads for computer systems often do not include a printer. Thus, you will need to budget an additional $100–$1,000 or more for a printer. **A *printer* is an output device that prints characters, symbols, and perhaps graphics on paper or another hardcopy medium.** As with scanners, the resolution, or quality of sharpness, of the printed image is indicated by *dots per inch (dpi)*, a measure of the number of rows and columns of dots that are printed in a square inch. For microcomputer printers, the resolution is in the range of 600 × 600 to 5,760 × 1,440, with 1,200 × 1,200 being most common.

HP Officejet Pro K5400

Printers can be separated into two categories, according to whether or not the image produced is formed by physical contact of the print mechanism with the paper. *Impact printers* do have contact with paper; *nonimpact printers* do not. We will also consider plotters and multifunction printers.

IMPACT PRINTERS Impact printers, an old printing technology, are most functional in specialized environments where low-cost printing is essential. **An *impact printer* forms characters or images by striking a mechanism such as a print hammer or wheel against an inked ribbon, leaving an image on paper.** The most common form of impact printer is the dot-matrix printer. A *dot-matrix printer* contains a print head of small pins that strike an inked ribbon against paper, to form characters or images. Print heads are available with 9, 18, or 24 pins; the 24-pin head offers the best quality. Dot-matrix printers can print *draft quality,* a coarser-looking 72 dpi; or *near-letter-quality (NLQ),* a crisper-looking 240 dpi. The machines print 40–300 characters per second and can handle graphics as well as text.

Impact printers are the only desktop printers that can use multilayered forms to print "carbon copies." A disadvantage, however, is the noise they produce, because of the print head striking the paper. Nowadays such printers are more commonly used with mainframes than with personal computers.

NONIMPACT PRINTERS Nonimpact printers are faster and quieter than impact printers because no print head strikes paper. ***Nonimpact printers* form characters and images without direct physical contact between the printing mechanism and paper.** Two types of nonimpact printers often used with microcomputers are *laser printers* and *inkjet printers.* A third kind, the *thermal printer,* is seen less frequently.

Laser printer

- **Laser printers:** Like a dot-matrix printer, a ***laser printer* creates images with dots. However, as in a photocopying machine, these images are produced on a drum, treated with a magnetically charged inklike toner (powder),**

5 Intense heat is applied by rollers to fuse the toner to the paper.

2 Using patterns of small dots, a laser beam conveys information from the computer to a rotating mirror. The laser recreates the image on the rotating drum.

1 As sheets of paper are fed into the printer, the photosensitive drum rotates.

panel 5.27

Laser printer
How a laser printer works.

4 The toner is transferred from the drum to the paper as the drum rotates.

3 The laser alters the electrical charge on the drum, which causes toner, a powdery substance, to stick to the drum.

and then transferred from drum to paper. (● *See Panel 5.27.*) (Laser printers are still sometimes called *page printers,* because they print one page at a time.)

Laser printers run with software called a <u>*page description language (PDL)*</u>. This software tells the printer how to lay out the printed page, and it supports various fonts. A laser printer comes with one of two types of PDL: PostScript (developed by Adobe) or PCL (Printer Control Language, developed by Hewlett-Packard). In desktop publishing, PostScript is the preferred PDL. Laser printers have their own CPU, ROM, and memory (RAM), usually 16 megabytes (expandable generally up to 512 megabytes for higher-cost printers). When you need to print out graphics-heavy color documents, your printer will need more memory.

There are good reasons that laser printers are among the most common types of nonimpact printer. They produce sharp, crisp images of both text and graphics. They are quiet and fast—able to print 11–33 pages per minute (ppm) in color and 10.5–37 black-and-white pages per minute for individual microcomputers and up to 200 pages per minute for mainframes. They can print in different *fonts*—that is, sets of typestyles and type sizes. The more expensive models can print in different colors. Laser printers usually have a dpi of 1,200 × 1,200.

● **Inkjet printers: <u>*Inkjet printers*</u> spray onto paper small, electrically charged droplets of ink from four nozzles through holes in a matrix at high speed.** (● *See Panel 5.28.*) Like laser and dot-matrix printers,

1 Four removable ink cartridges are attached to print heads with 64 firing chambers and nozzles apiece.

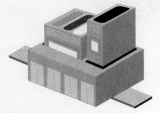

2 As the print heads move back and forth across the page, software instructs them where to apply dots of ink, what colors to use, and in what quantity.

3 To follow those instructions, the printer sends electrical pulses to thin resistors at the base of the firing chambers behind each nozzle.

Resistor
Vapor bubble
Ink

5 A matrix of dots forms characters and pictures. Colors are created by layering multiple color dots in varying densities.

4 The resistor heats a thin layer of ink, which in turn forms a vapor bubble. That expansion forces ink through the nozzle and onto the paper at a rate of about 6,000 dots per second.

panel 5.28

Inkjet printer
How an inkjet printer works.

inkjet printers form images with little dots. Inkjet printers commonly have a dpi of 4,800 × 1,200 (but can be as high as 9,600 × 2,400); they spray ink onto the page a line at a time, in both high-quality black-and-white text and high-quality color graphics. (To achieve impressive color images, you should use high-quality, high-gloss paper, which prevents inkjet-sprayed dots from *feathering,* or spreading.) Inkjet cartridges come in various combinations: a single cartridge for black and all color inks, two separate black and color cartridges, or separate cartridges for black and each color. Some cartridges also include the print head, which is apt to wear out before the rest of the machine.

The advantages of inkjet printers are that they can print in color, are quiet, and are generally less expensive than color laser printers. The disadvantages have been that they print a bit less precisely than laser printers do and traditionally they have been slower.

Another disadvantage is that inkjet cartridges have to be replaced more often than laser-toner cartridges do and so may cost more in the long run. Moreover, a freshly inkjet-printed page is apt to smear unless handled carefully. For users who print infrequently, laser printers (which use toner, a dry powder) have the advantage of not drying out. Laser owners don't have to deal with dried-out cartridges clogging nozzles and wasting expensive ink and time—a common problem for inkjet users.

Still, experts maintain that users who want the best-quality photo output should get a photo inkjet printer. Laser printers in general are known for their mediocre photo output, with cheap personal laser printers often doing an especially poor job.

Laser printers are known for handling a much higher volume of printouts than inkjet printers. Buyers who do a lot of printing should pay

Hardware: Input & Output

Homaro Cantu, chef at Chicago's Moto Restaurant, prints sushi on a Canon inkjet printer using edible paper made of soybeans and cornstarch and food-based inks of his own concoction. He then flavors the back of the paper with powdered soy sauce and seaweed. Even Mr. Cantu's menu is edible; diners crunch it up into soups.

Thermal printed cash-register receipt

close attention to a printer's monthly duty cycle, which determines how many printouts a printer can comfortably handle in a month. Going over this can often shorten the life of a printer. In general, cheaper printers have much lower duty cycles than the higher-end printers.

- **Thermal printers:** *__Thermal printers__* **are low- to medium-resolution printers that use a type of coated paper that darkens when heat is applied to it.** The paper is moved past a line of heating elements that burn dots onto the paper. This technology is typically used in business for bar-code label applications and for printing cash register receipts. Until about 2000, most fax machines used direct thermal printing, though now only the cheapest models use it, the rest having switched to thermal wax-transfer, laser, or inkjet printing.

- **Thermal wax-transfer printers:** *Thermal wax-transfer printers* print a wax-based ink onto paper. As the paper and ribbon travel in unison beneath the thermal print head, the wax-based ink from the transfer ribbon melts onto the paper. After it becomes cool, the wax adheres permanently to the paper. Although such printers are highly reliable, because of the small number of moving parts, they don't compare with modern inkjet printers and color laser printers. However, because of their waterfastness, they find uses in industrial label printing.

  Wax-transfer printers are faster and less expensive to use than photo printers, but the dye-sublimation photo printers produce photo-realistic quality. Recently Polaroid introduced an inkless photo printer that prints 2 × 3-inch photos sent to it via Bluetooth-enabled devices such as cellphones or from plugged-in digital cameras.[45]

Wax-transfer thermal printed label

PRACTICAL ACTION
Buying a Printer

Some questions to consider when you're buying a printer:

- *Do I need color, or will black-only do?* Are you mainly printing text, or will you need to produce color charts and illustrations (and, if so, how often)? If you print lots of black text, consider getting a laser printer. If you might occasionally print color, get an inkjet that will accept cartridges for both black and color. Unless you are in the publishing or design business, you will probably not need an expensive color laser printer.

- *Do I have other special output requirements?* Do you need to print envelopes or labels? Special fonts (type styles)? Multiple copies? Transparencies or on heavy paper? Unusual paper size? Find out if the printer comes with envelope feeders, sheet feeders holding at least 100 sheets, or whatever will meet your requirements.

- *Is the printer easy to set up?* Can you easily pull the unit together, plug in the hardware, and adjust the software (the driver programs) to make the printer work with your computer?

- *Is the printer easy to operate?* Can you add paper, replace ink/toner cartridges or ribbons, and otherwise operate the printer without much difficulty?

- *Does the printer provide the speed and quality I want?* A laser printer prints about 11–37 pages per minute (ppm); a color inkjet prints about 17–34 ppm. Colors and graphics take longer to print. Are the blacks dark enough and the colors vivid enough?

- *Will I get a reasonable cost per page?* Special paper, ink or toner cartridges (especially color), and ribbons are all ongoing costs. Inkjet color cartridges, for example, may last 100–500 pages and cost $2–$30 new. Laser toner cartridges can cost up to $100 each but last much longer. Ribbons for dot-matrix printers are inexpensive. Ask the seller what the cost per page works out to.

- *Does the manufacturer offer a good warranty and good telephone technical support?* Find out if the warranty for a printer lasts at least 2 years. See if the printer's manufacturer offers telephone support in case you have technical problems. The best support systems offer toll-free numbers and operate evenings and weekends as well as weekdays. (If you can, try calling tech support before you buy and see what happens.)

- **Photo printers:** *Photo printers* are specialized machines for printing continuous-tone photo prints (typically 3 × 5 or 4 × 6 inches), using special dye-receptive paper and ribbons with special transparent color dyes. Paper and ribbon pass together over the printhead, which contains thousands of heating elements producing varying amounts of heat. The hotter the element, the more dye is released, and as the temperature is varied, shades of each color can be overlaid on top of one another. The dyes are transparent and blend (sublimate) into continuous-tone color. Some inexpensive ($150–$200) photo printers are designed to be unplugged and taken on the go; in fact, they connect directly to a digital camera.[46]

Dye-sublimation photo printer

PLOTTERS A *plotter* is a specialized output device designed to produce large, high-quality graphics in a variety of colors. (● *See Panel 5.29, next page.*) Plotter lines are not made up of dots; they are actually drawn.

The plotter was the first computer output device that could not only print graphics but also accommodate full-size engineering, three-dimensional, and architectural drawings, as well as maps. Using different colored pens, it was also able to print in color long before inkjet printers became an alternative. Plotters are still the most affordable printing device for computer-aided design (CAD) and offer much higher resolutions than desktop printers do. Plotters are controlled by PCL and HPCL (Hewlett-Packard Control Language).

The three principal kinds of plotters are pen, electrostatic, and large-format:

- **Pen:** A *pen plotter* uses one or more colored pens to draw on paper or transparencies.

  - **Electrostatic:** In an *electrostatic plotter,* paper lies partially flat on a tablelike surface, and toner is used in a photocopier-like manner.

  - **Large-format:** *Large-format plotters* operate somewhat like an inkjet printer but on a much larger scale. This type of plotter is often used by graphic artists.

MULTIFUNCTION PRINTERS: PRINTERS THAT DO MORE THAN PRINT <u>*Multifunction printers*</u> **combine several capabilities, such as printing, scanning, copying, and faxing.** (● *See Panel 5.30.*) Brother, Canon, Epson, and Hewlett-Packard make machines in a price range of $89–$266 that combine a photocopier, fax machine, scanner, and inkjet printer. Hewlett-Packard also offers an all-in-one printer that connects wirelessly to the Internet, allowing users to bypass their computer and print out Web content in paper form.[47] Multifunction printers take up less space and cost less than the four separate office machines that they replace. The drawback is that if one component breaks, nothing works.

panel 5.30

Multifunction device
This machine combines four functions in one—printer, copier, fax machine, and scanner.

Proofreader Ed Kochanowski proofreads a Braille edition of *Beowulf* at the National Braille Press in Boston.

SPECIALTY PRINTERS Specialty printers exist for such purposes as printing certain types of labels, tickets, and text in Braille.

Mixed Output: Sound, Voice, & Video

How would I explain sound, voice, and video output?

Most PCs are now multimedia computers, capable of displaying and printing not only traditional softcopy and hardcopy text and graphics but also sound, voice, and video, as we consider next.

SOUND OUTPUT <u>*Sound-output devices*</u> **produce digitized sounds, ranging from beeps and chirps to music.** To use sound output, you need appropriate software and a sound card. The sound card could be Sound Blaster or, since that brand has become a de facto standard, one that is "Sound Blaster–compatible." Well-known brands include Creative Labs, Diamond, and Turtle Beach. The sound card plugs into an expansion slot in your computer; on newer computers, it is integrated with the motherboard.

Not too long ago, the audio emerging from a computer had the crackly sound of an old vacuum-tube radio. Then, in 1997, audio in personal computers began to shift to three-dimensional sound. Now, a PC with two speakers can sound more like a "surround sound" movie house. Unlike conventional stereo sound, 3-D audio describes an expanded field of sound—a broad arc starting at the right ear and curving around to the left. Thus, in a video game, you might hear a rocket approach, go by, and explode off your right shoulder. The effect is achieved by boosting certain frequencies that provide clues to a sound's location in the room or by varying the timing of sounds from different speakers. You can augment your computer's internal speakers with external speakers for high-quality sound.

VOICE OUTPUT _Voice-output devices_ **convert digital data into speechlike sounds.** You hear such forms of voice output on telephones ("Please hang up and dial your call again"), in soft-drink machines, in cars, in toys and games, and in mapping software for vehicle-navigation devices. Voice portals read news and other information to users on the go.

One form of voice output that is becoming popular is _text-to-speech (TTS) systems,_ which convert computer text into audible speech. TTS benefits not only the visually impaired but also anyone with a computer system sound card and speakers who wants to reduce reading chores (and eyestrain) and do other tasks at the same time. Windows XP offers a TTS program called Narrator; Windows Vista offers Speech API. Others are CoolSpeech, CrazyTalk, and Digalo. AOL, Yahoo!, and MapQuest have licensed a high-quality TTS program developed by the AT&T Natural Voices Lab to read email, give driving directions, provide stock quotes, and more.

VIDEO OUTPUT _Video_ **consists of photographic images, which are played at 15–29 frames per second to give the appearance of full motion.** Video is input into a multimedia system using a video camera or VCR and, after editing, is output on a computer's display screen. Because video files can require a great deal of storage—a 3-minute video may require 1 gigabyte of storage—video is often compressed. Good video output requires a powerful processor as well as a video card.

Another form of video output is _videoconferencing_, in which people in different geographic locations can have a meeting—can see and hear one another—using computers and communications. Videoconferencing systems range from videophones to group conference rooms with cameras and multimedia equipment to desktop systems with small video cameras, microphones, and speakers. (We discuss videoconferencing further in Chapter 6.)

5.4 INPUT & OUTPUT TECHNOLOGY & QUALITY OF LIFE: Health & Ergonomics

What are the principal health and ergonomic issues relating to computer use?

Danielle Weatherbee, 29, of Seattle, a medical supplies saleswoman who's on the road constantly, spends much of her time hunched over the keyboard of her notebook computer on planes, in coffee shops, in bed, and even in taxicabs. Her neck and wrists constantly ache. Her doctor has said she has the skeletal health of a 50-year-old. "But what can I do?" Weatherbee says. "My laptop is the only way to go for my work. I couldn't live without it."[48]

Health Matters

How could information technology adversely affect my health?

The computer clearly has negative health consequences for some people. College students, for example, may be susceptible to back, shoulder, wrist, and neck aches because they often use laptops, which—unlike desktop computers—have keyboard and screen too close to each other. "When you use a laptop, you can make your head and neck comfortable, or you can make your hands and arms comfortable, but it's impossible to do both," says Tom Albin of the Human Factors and Ergonomics Society, an organization that issues standards on the use of computers.[49] Observes another expert about students, "They sit in lecture halls with built-in tables, hunched over their laptops eight hours a day, and you can see it's very uncomfortable with them. Even if they could move their chairs, that would be a help.[50]

Let's consider some of the adverse health effects of computers. These may include repetitive strain injuries, eyestrain and headache, and back and neck pains. We will also consider the effects of electromagnetic fields and noise.

REPETITIVE STRESS INJURIES *Repetitive stress (or strain) injuries (RSIs)* **are wrist, hand, arm, and neck injuries resulting when muscle groups are forced through fast, repetitive motions.** Most victims of RSI are in dentistry, meatpacking, automobile manufacturing, poultry slaughtering, and clothing manufacturing, which require awkward wrist positions. Musicians, too, are often troubled by RSI (because of long hours of practice).

People who use computer keyboards—some superstar data-entry operators reportedly regularly average 15,000 keystrokes an hour—account for some RSI cases that result in lost work time. Before computers came along, typists would stop to make corrections or change paper. These motions had the effect of providing many small rest breaks. Today keyboard users must devise their own mini-breaks to prevent excessive use of hands and wrists (or install a computer program that uses animated characters to remind users to take breaks and provide suggestions for exercises). People who use a mouse for more than a few hours a day—graphic designers, desktop-publishing professionals, and the like—are also showing up with increased RSI injuries. The best advice is to find a mouse large enough so that your hand fits comfortably over it, and don't leave your hand on the mouse when you are not using it. Some cordless mice, such as the Logitech MX1000 and the MediaPlay cordless mouse, are said to offer relief to aching fingers.[51] You might also try using function keys instead of the mouse whenever possible.[52]

Among the various RSIs, some, such as muscle strain and tendinitis, are painful but usually not crippling. These injuries may be cured by rest, anti-inflammatory medication, and change in typing technique. One type of RSI, carpal tunnel syndrome, is disabling and often requires surgery. *Carpal tunnel syndrome (CTS)* **is a debilitating condition caused by pressure on the median nerve in the wrist, producing damage and pain to nerves and tendons in the hands.** It is caused by short repetitive movements, such as typing, knitting, and using vibrating tools for hours on end. The lack of rest in between these motions irritates and inflames the flexor tendons that travel with the median nerve to the hand through an area in the wrist called the "carpal tunnel," which is surrounded by bones and a transverse ligament. The inflamed tendons squeeze the nerve against the ligament.

It must be pointed out, however, that there is some dispute as to whether continuous typing is necessarily a culprit in CTS. A 2003 study by researchers in Denmark found no association between computer use and CTS, and a 2001 Mayo Clinic study found that even 7 hours a day of computer use didn't increase the disorder.[53] Other researchers have found limitations in both studies.[54] There is little clinical data to prove whether repetitive and forceful movements of the hand and wrist during work or leisure activities can cause carpal tunnel syndrome. Repeated motions performed in the course of normal work or other daily activities can result in repetitive motion disorders such as bursitis and tendonitis. Writer's cramp—a condition in which a lack of fine motor skill coordination and ache and pressure in the fingers, wrist, or forearm is brought on by repetitive activity—is not a symptom of carpal tunnel syndrome.[55]

EYESTRAIN & HEADACHES Vision problems are actually more common than RSI problems among computer users. Computers compel people to use their eyes at close range for a long time. However, our eyes were made to see most efficiently at a distance. It's not surprising, then, that people develop what's called *computer vision syndrome.*

***Computer vision syndrome (CVS)* consists of eyestrain, headaches, double vision, and other problems caused by improper use of computer display screens.** By "improper use," we mean not only staring at the screen for too long but also failing to correct faulty lighting and screen glare and using screens with poor resolution.

BACK & NECK PAINS Improper chairs or improper positioning of keyboards and display screens can lead to back and neck pains. All kinds of adjustable, special-purpose furniture and equipment are available to avoid or diminish such maladies.

ELECTROMAGNETIC FIELDS Like kitchen appliances, hairdryers, and television sets, many devices related to computers and communications generate low-level electromagnetic field emissions. ***Electromagnetic fields (EMFs)* are waves of electrical energy and magnetic energy.**

In recent years, stories have appeared in the mass media reflecting concerns that high-voltage power lines, cellphones, wireless mice, and CRT-type computer monitors might be harmful. There have been worries that monitors might be linked to miscarriages and birth defects and that cellphones and power lines might lead to some types of cancers.

Is there anything to this? The answer, so far, is that no one is sure. The evidence seems scant that weak electromagnetic fields, such as those used for cellphones and found near high-voltage lines, cause cancer. Still, handheld cellphones do put the radio transmitter next to the user's head. This causes some health professionals concern about the effects of radio waves entering the brain as they seek out the nearest cellular transmitter. Thus, in the United Kingdom, the Independent Expert Study Group on Mobile Phones recommended that children should use cellphones only when necessary, and Norway's Ombudsman for Children has said that children under the age of 13 should not have their own mobile phones. Dr. Lief Salford of Lund University in Sweden, who has called the evolution of wireless phones "the largest biological experiment in the history of the world," reported that cellphone radiation damaged neurons in the brains of young rats.[56] Another study found that cellphone users face a 50% greater risk of developing tumors of the parotid gland than do people who do not use cellphones.[57] However, an August 2005 study found no increased risk of brain tumors associated with using a cellphone for at least 10 years.[58] Cancer researcher Ronald Herberman suggests that, until conclusive data arrives in another couple of years, it's prudent to consider cellphone use a health risk and consumers should buy phones (such as the Motorola Razr V3x) that emit low radiation.[59]

The Federal Communications Commission (FCC) has created a measurement called *Specific Absorption Rate (SAR)* to give consumers data on the radiation levels their phones produce. Currently, the Motorola V195s and the Motorola W385 cellphones have the highest SAR levels (1.6 and 1.54 SAR), and the Motorola Razr V3x and the Samsung SGH-G800 have the lowest levels (0.14 and 0.23 SAR). The World Health Organization has said that further research is needed for long-term health assessment.

As for CRT monitors, those made since the early 1980s produce very low emissions. Even so, users are advised to work no closer than arm's length to a CRT monitor. The strongest fields are emitted from the sides and backs of terminals. Alternatively, you can use laptop computers, because their liquid crystal display (LCD) screens emit negligible radiation.

The current advice from the Environmental Protection Agency is to exercise *prudent avoidance.* That is, we should take precautions that are relatively easy.

More on CVS

Do you have CVS? What are computer eyeglasses? Find out at:

www.allaboutvision.com/cvs/faqs.htm

Ergonomics for Kids

To learn how to set up an ergonomic workstation for children, go to:

www.businessweek.com/ magazine/content/02_51/ b3813121.htm

For more general government ergonomic guidelines, go to:

www.osha.gov

and then search for *computer workstations.*

However, we should not feel compelled to change our whole lives or to spend a fortune minimizing exposure to electromagnetic fields. Thus, we can take steps to put some distance between ourselves and a CRT monitor. However, it is probably not necessary to change residences because we happen to be living near some high-tension power lines.

NOISE The chatter of impact printers or hum of fans in computer power units can be psychologically stressful to many people. Sound-muffling covers are available for impact printers. Some system units may be placed on the floor under the desk to minimize noise from fans.

Ergonomics: Design with People in Mind
Why is ergonomics important?

Previously, workers had to fit themselves to the job environment. However, health and productivity issues have spurred the development of a relatively new field, called *ergonomics,* that is concerned with fitting the job environment to the worker.

    The purpose of _ergonomics_ is to make working conditions and equipment safer and more efficient. It is concerned with designing hardware and software that are less stressful and more comfortable to use, that blend more smoothly with a person's body or actions. Examples of ergonomic hardware are tilting display screens, detachable keyboards, and keyboards hinged in the middle to allow the users' wrists to rest in a more natural position.

    We address some further ergonomic issues in the Experience Box at the end of this chapter.

5.5 THE FUTURE OF INPUT & OUTPUT
What are some examples of future input and output technology?

Biologists studying wildlife at the James San Jacinto Mountains Reserve in southern California found out something interesting about squirrels. It seems the little rodents chew on moss for the moisture. No one had known that before, but researchers learned it when the animals tripped motion sensors spread around a patch of wilderness, which activated tiny wireless cameras, which in turn were linked to a speedy wireless network.[60] Other scientists are using "smart dust," grids of simple, low-powered devices called "motes" to monitor the environment and wirelessly pass along collected data.[61] Birds outfitted with sensors have surprised scientists by their speed and routes during their migrations from the United States to Central and South America.[62]

    The uses of such "intelligent sensors"—digital sensors placed in all kinds of places and linked by wireless networks—"could be bigger than the internet," suggests one expert.[63] Not only do they allow squirrels and other inhabitants of the natural world to communicate with the digital realm; they are also used for many other purposes—security, for example. Sensors that can detect biological agents have been placed in thousands of locations across the United States to provide warnings of bioterror attacks.[64] Networks of sensors have been used to detect undersea intruders and accidents, as when the Russian submarine *Kursk* sank in August 2000.[65] A "virtual fence" consisting of sensors and cameras is planned for the Arizona border to catch illegal immigrants and drug runners.[66] Sensors could also occupy a big role in the rebuilding of U.S. bridges, roads, and the electrical grid, where wireless communications and computing power could lead to a "smarter" infrastructure.[67]

    As these examples show, input technology seems headed in two directions: (1) toward more input devices in remote locations and (2) toward more refinements in source data automation. Output is distinguished by (1) more output in remote locations and (2) increasingly realistic—even lifelike—forms, as we discuss in a few pages.

Science Sensors

Want to see how biologists study 30 acres of nature with wireless-network-linked sensors? Go to:

www.jamesreserve.edu

Toward More Input from Remote Locations

How can data be input from anywhere?

The linkage of computers and telecommunications means that data may be input from nearly anywhere. For instance, X-ray machines are now going digital, which means that a medical technician in the jungles of South America can take an X ray of a patient and then transmit a perfect copy of it by satellite uplink to a hospital in Boston. Visa and MasterCard are moving closer to using "smart cards," or stored-value cards, for internet transactions.

Toward More Source Data Automation

How might source data automation be of help to me?

Increasingly, input technology is being designed to capture data at its source, which will reduce the costs and mistakes associated with copying or otherwise preparing data in a form suitable for processing. We mentioned some possible innovations in high-capacity bar codes, more sophisticated scanners, smarter smart cards, and widespread use of sensors. Some reports from elsewhere on the input-technology front:

INPUT HELP FOR THE DISABLED Some devices now available for people with physical disabilities, such as paraplegics, may portend new ways of entering and manipulating data input. For example, in one system a camera and special software enable users to operate the on-screen pointer with their eye movements instead of their hands.[68] In another hands-free system, a camera tracks the user's body movements and the system converts them into mouse-pointer movements on the screen. In yet another system, the user's breathing controls the screen pointer. In a fourth, the nose is used to direct the cursor on a computer screen. There is also a system that can be attached to a baseball cap, enabling head movements to control the pointer. There is a Web-based application called Web Anywhere that provides verbal feedback and enables blind people to use any internet-connected computer, allowing them to type up a quick email at an internet café or check a flight time on a public computer at the airport.[69] Tongue movement alone, it's been suggested, could become an input device for assisting with computers, home appliances, and wheelchair control.[70] Finally, there are ideas about implanting video cameras behind the false eyeball of those who have lost an eye.[71]

MORE SOPHISTICATED TOUCH DEVICES As we mentioned, touch screens are becoming more and more popular. Microsoft, for instance, has developed the Surface tabletop computer, an interactive, 30-inch touch-responsive table that can be used to order meals or display maps. It is now in use at Harrah's Rio hotel in Las Vegas and in AT&T phone stores. Microsoft executives see surface computing as an alternative to the mouse and keyboard, one that could have far-reaching effects on the office, living room, and car. ("Multi-Touch" technology is included in Windows 7.) A highly coveted form of touch technology among educators is interactive whiteboards, essentially giant touchscreens.[72]

Researchers in what is known as *hepatic*—active touch—systems are exploring how to create devices that will allow people to feel what isn't there. With this kind of "virtual touch," a dental student could train in drilling down into the decay of a simulated tooth without fear of destroying a real healthy tooth. Doctors would have new surgical

Mouse-Pointer Systems for the Disabled

To learn more about this subject, use the following keywords to search the web: *Quick Glance Eye-Gaze Tracking System, CameraMouse, Quadjoy, Cordless Gyro-HeadMouse.*

(*Top*) One-handed keyboard. (*Bottom*) Special mouse/digitizer and pointing stick to press keys.

tools, videogames would be made more realistic, and drivers would be able to manipulate dials and knobs without taking their eyes off the road.

BETTER SPEECH RECOGNITION It's possible that speech recognition may someday fulfill world travelers' fondest dream: You'll be able to speak in English, and a speech-recognition device will instantly translate your remarks into another language, whether French, Swahili, or Japanese. At the moment, translation programs such as Easy Translator can translate text on web pages (English to Spanish, French, and German and the reverse), although they do so imperfectly. Research is also going forward on speech-recognition software that can decode slight differences in pitch, timing, and amplitude, so that computers can recognize anger and pain, for example.[73] And already voice-recognition techniques have been applied to animal sounds, so that, for instance, farmers can be alerted to unrest in the pigpen or cows in heat.[74]

IMPROVED DIGITAL CAMERAS Digital still cameras and video cameras are now commonplace. Now manufacturers are also bringing out compact digital camcorders, some that are coat-pocket size. Some will also produce both still photos and respectable video. Olympus has a camera with a 40-gigabyte hard drive that can store both photos and music.

Microsoft has invented a wide-angle, fish-eye lens digital camera that can be worn like a badge, recording all the still and video images of the wearer's daily life.[75] A boon to bird-watchers, sports spectators, and opera goers is the appearance of binoculars with built-in digital cameras, so that one can bring home photos or digital movies.[76] The newest development is the camera-on-a-chip, which contains all the control components necessary to take a photograph or make a movie. Such a device, called an *active pixel sensor,* based on NASA space technology, is now being made by Micron and by Photobit.

A future feature of cellphone cameras is exploitation of a branch of a field of computer science called *augmented reality*—which gave us yellow first-down lines (which really don't exist) on the field of televised football games—which will enable camera users to "see information about nearby restaurants, ATMs, and available jobs in front of buildings that house them," in one description.[77]

GESTURE RECOGNITION In the movie *Minority Report,* Tom Cruise, playing a police officer who fights crimes occurring in the future, gestures into the air and calls up computer images. Researchers have been trying to apply gesturing to computing input devices for decades, and we have already seen the development of the *accelerometer,* a motion sensor that allows machines to respond to movement without waiting for humans to push a button. The Apple iPhone and Nintendo's Wii game console, for instance, currently feature similar technology, and many cellphones, computers, and other gadgets are being produced that are sensitive to motion.[78] In 2010, we should see gesture-reading technology incorporated in TVs, PCs, and similar devices.[79]

Gesture recognition also is a key component in the idea of *pervasive computing,* which refers to having access to computing tools any place at any time. For example, a display could appear on a wall or wherever you want. To make pervasive computing work, however, users need to have an input device available wherever they are, a process often referred to as *human-centric computing.* Through human-centric computing, the user is always connected to computing tools. Gesture-recognition technology could provide the needed input capabilities for both types of computing.

PATTERN-RECOGNITION & BIOMETRIC DEVICES Would you believe a computer could read people's emotions, such as surprise and sadness, from changes in their facial patterns? Such devices are being worked on at Georgia Institute of Technology and elsewhere. (● *See Panel 5.31.*) Indeed, you can buy a face-recognition program so that you can have your computer respond only to your smile.

Camera on a chip. Active pixel sensor, a digital camera (exclusive of the opticals) on a single I cm² chip. It can set the desired exposure time and control any number of imaging modes.

Gesture Recognition

For an update on the progress in gesture-recognition technology, go to:

www.gesturecentral.com

www.engineerlive.com/Asia-Pacific-Engineer/Automotive-Design/Gesture_%26lsq uo%3Brecognition%26rs quo%3B_could_improve_ automotive_safety/16927/ gesture+recognition+ automotive

www.igesture.org/

With the shift to digital cameras, people are accumulating thousands of photographs—so many that they often fail to label them. Google's genealogy site MyHeritage and a handful of young companies (Eyealike, GazoPa, ILovePhotos, Like.com, Picasa, VideoSurf) have adopted image-recognition tech-

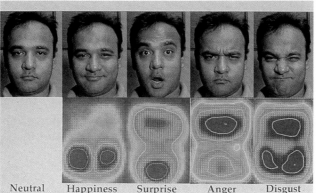

Neutral　Happiness　Surprise　Anger　Disgust

nology to help people sort through and label their photos, using facial recognition techniques to group photos in which a similar person appears in different locations or wearing different clothes.[80]

BRAINWAVE DEVICES Perhaps the ultimate input device analyzes the electrical signals of the brain and translates them into computer commands. In one experiment, 100 tiny sensors were implanted in the brain of a 25-year-old quadriplegic who, using just his thoughts, was able to control a computer well enough to operate a TV, open email, and play Pong with 70% accuracy.[81] At the University of Pittsburgh, macaque monkeys with electrical sensors in their brains have learned to feed themselves with robotic arms, an experiment billed as the first successful use of a "brain-machine interface" to control a robotic limb for a practical function.[82] Users have successfully moved a cursor on the screen through the sheer power of thought.[83] Emotiv Systems of San Francisco even offers a noninvasive technology that allows players to manipulate objects in video games simply with their thoughts.[84]

Quadriplegic Matt Nagle is connected to a computer by a cable that is screwed into his head. The 4-millimeter square chip, which is placed on the surface of the motor cortex area of the brain, contains 100 electrodes, each thinner than a hair, that detect neural electrical activity. The sensor is then connected to a computer via a small wire attached to a pedestal mounted on the skull. Nagle has been able to check email and play computer games simply by using thoughts. He can also turn lights on and off and control a television, all while talking and moving his head.

Toward More Output in Remote Locations

How could information be output in far-flung places?

Clearly, output in remote locations is the wave of the future. As TV and the personal computer converge, we can expect more scenarios like this: Your PC

Suitor (Simple User Internet Tracker) eye-gaze technology is an *attentive system* that pays attention to what users do so it can attend to what users need. Suitor tracks computer users according to what they look at and how often they look at it.

continually receives any websites covering topics of interest to you—CNN's home page for news on Afghanistan, for example—which are stored on your hard disk for later viewing. The information, on up to 5,000 websites a day, is transmitted from a television broadcast satellite to an 18-inch satellite dish on your roof. Interested? The technology is available now with direct-broadcast services such as DirecTV Inc.

Another idea of future remote output, being developed at Stanford University, is a *digital nagging device,* a PDA or smart cellphone that reminds people to walk briskly for 150 minutes a week, make better diet choices, and similar health advice.[85]

Toward More Realistic Output

In what way is output being made more realistic?

Another interesting new output technology: so-called *audio spotlight* or *directed-sound technology* projects sound in a focused beam so that only people in a certain spot can hear it. Court TV used the technology in New York and Atlanta bookstores to promote a murder mystery show. When customers tripped a motion sensor, they would suddenly hear a voice whispering a 30-second message that said in part: "Don't turn around. Do you ever think about murder? Committing the ultimate crime? I do. All the time." Directed-sound devices use narrow beams of ultrasound waves that can't be heard by human ears; the beam distorts air as it passes through, generating sound people can hear. The biggest use of such technology, unfortunately, is for advertising, so that messages could be sent to customers in grocery store checkout lines without disturbing the store's staff.[86]

Clearly, we are seeing increased realism appearing in all forms of output. Let's consider what's coming into view.

E Ink's flexible screen on 0.3-millimeter thick electronic "paper" with millions of tiny capsules with black and white pigment chips and transmitting electrodes.

DISPLAY SCREENS: BETTER & CHEAPER Computer screens are becoming crisper, brighter, bigger, and cheaper. Newer LCD monitors, for instance, have as high a resolution as previous larger CRT monitors, and the prices have dropped significantly.

New gas-plasma technology is being employed to build flat-panel hang-on-the-wall screens as large as 50 inches from corner to corner. Using a technique known as *microreplication,* researchers have constructed a thin transparent sheet of plastic prisms that allows builders of portable computer screens to halve the amount of battery power required.

PRINTERS: REDUCING PRINTER INK Xerox is hoping to help companies survive with fewer printers and copiers and less paper through a new technology they call *erasable paper.* The idea here is that you would print out a document you need only temporarily, then feed it through a machine with a heating element, which would make the document images disappear—so that you could reuse the paper for something else.[87] Another company, called Zink (short for "zero ink"), hopes to get rid of ink entirely. Its approach is to encode paper with billions of dye crystals. To produce an image, a print head emits heat pulses that melt the dye crystals, turning them into the desired colors.[88]

VIDEO: MOVIE QUALITY FOR PCS Today the movement of many video images displayed on a microcomputer comes across as fuzzy and jerky, with a person's lip movements out of sync with his or her voice. This is because currently available equipment often is capable of running only about eight frames a second.

New technology based on digital wavelet theory, a complicated mathematical theory, has led to software that can compress digitized pictures into fewer bytes and do it more quickly than current standards. Indeed, the technology can display 30–38 frames a second—"real-time video." Images have the look and feel of a movie.

In addition, advanced graphics chips from firms such as Nvidia and NTI are increasing the realism of animation, making possible lifelike imagery. Nvidia's computer-generated mermaid named Nalu, for instance, is described as having "a cloud of golden tresses that realistically seem to reflect dappled light and flow with the water [and] rosy, unusually lifelike skin."[89] Such images use geometric building blocks called *polygons*, and Nalu is composed of 300,000 of them—far more than most video images today have.

THREE-DIMENSIONAL OUTPUT In the 1930s, radiologists tried to create three-dimensional images by holding up two slightly offset X rays of the same object and crossing their eyes. Now the same effects can be achieved by computers. With 3-D technology, flat, cartoonlike images give way to rounded objects with shadows and textures. Artists can even add "radiosity," so that a dog standing next to a red car, for instance, will pick up a red glow.

In the early 21st century, we have 3-D versions of films such as *Monsters vs. Aliens, My Bloody Valentine,* and *Up* becoming hits in theaters. Indeed, for some of the top Hollywood filmmakers (such as *Titanic* director James Cameron, maker of the 2009 *Avatar*), digital 3-D looks like the future of movies.[90] But 3-D is also a reality in home theaters, with many companies selling what they call "3-D ready" TV sets.[91] In addition, Nvidia markets the GeForce 3D Vision system, which consists of software and special glasses that connect wirelessly to your PC, which can be used for existing games and other software as well as movies.[92]

But the same technology that makes images pop off movie screens is now being used for all kinds of other purposes as well.[93] Three-dimensional printers using inkjet printer heads are able to output layer after layer of images printed on starch or plaster, producing 3-D objects. In the future, this technology may be used to print on plastics and metals to produce electronic components, such as transistors. Indeed, military engineers have developed something called a Mobile Parts Hospital in which technicians use workstations and robotic machine tools to fabricate replacement parts, such as bolts or machine-gun mounts, that lasers then will "print" as powdered metal, layer by layer.[94] Medical researchers have even used 3-D printing technology to print layers of cells, building intricate tissue structures. Indeed, researchers have used older-model inkjet printers to spray cells onto a gauze scaffolding to create living tissue—artificial skin that may be of help to burn victims.

Using the Smithsonian

What kind of technology does the Smithsonian Museum in Washington, D.C., have on display? Find the museum's website and enter keywords of computer terms.

EXPERIENCE BOX
Good Habits: Protecting Your Computer System, Your Data, & Your Health

Whether you set up a desktop computer and never move it or tote a portable PC from place to place, you need to be concerned about protecting not only your computer but yourself. You don't want your computer to get stolen or zapped by a power surge. You don't want to lose your data. And you certainly don't want to lose your health for computer-related reasons. Here are some tips for taking care of these vital areas.

Guarding against Hardware Theft & Loss

Portable computers are easy targets for thieves. Obviously, anything conveniently small enough to be slipped into your briefcase or backpack can be slipped into someone else's. Never leave a portable computer unattended in a public place.

It's also possible to simply lose a portable—for example, forgetting it's in the overhead-luggage bin in an airplane. To help in its return, use a wide piece of clear tape to tape a card with your name and address to the outside of the machine. You should tape a similar card to the inside also. In addition, scatter a few such cards in the pockets of the carrying case.

Desktop computers are also easily stolen. However, for under $25, you can buy a cable and lock, like those used for bicycles, and secure the computer, monitor, and printer to a work area. If your hardware does get stolen, its recovery may be helped if you have inscribed your driver's license number or home address on each piece. Some campus and city police departments lend inscribing tools for such purposes. Finally, insurance to cover computer theft or damage is surprisingly cheap. Look for advertisements in computer magazines. (If you have standard tenants' or homeowners' insurance, it may not cover your computer. Ask your insurance agent.)

Guarding against Damage to Hardware

Because desktop computers aren't moved around much, they are less susceptible to damage. Laptops, however, are another story. According to a survey of 714 information technology managers, physical damage to laptops with data loss resulted from the following causes: 34% from spilled food or liquids on them, 28% from dropping them, 25% from not protecting them during travel, and 13% from worker anger.[95] (Special "ruggedized" laptops exist, such as the Hewlett-Packard EliteBook 2530p and the Panasonic Toughbook F8, which are built to be shock resistant.)[96]

Guarding against Damage to Software

Systems software and applications software generally come on CD-ROM disks. The unbreakable rule is simply this: copy the original disk, either onto your hard-disk drive or onto another disk. Then store the original disk in a safe place. If your computer gets stolen or your software destroyed, you can retrieve the original and make another copy.

Protecting Your Data

Computer hardware and commercial software are nearly always replaceable, although perhaps with some expense and difficulty. Data, however, may be major trouble to replace or even be irreplaceable. If your hard-disk drive crashes, do you have the same data on a backup disk? Almost every microcomputer user sooner or later has the experience of accidentally wiping out or losing material and having no copy. This is what makes people true believers in backing up their data—making a duplicate in some form. If you're working on a research paper, for example, it's fairly easy to copy your work onto a CD or keychain memory at the end of your work session. Then store the copy in a safe place.

Protecting Your Health

Could a computer put you in the emergency room? Actually, the number of injuries caused by computers in the home, caused by people tripping over wires or getting hit by falling equipment, rose 732% from 1994 to 2006.[97] The leading cause of injury for small children and adults over 60 was tripping or falling over computer equipment.

But injuries are also caused by not setting up computers correctly. Many people, for instance, set up their computers, particularly laptops, on a desk or table. This means "the keyboard is too high, which makes your arms reach up, your shoulders hunch and your wrists bend down," says one report. "The monitor is too low, which pulls your head and neck forward and down and puts a strain on your neck."[98] (It's best to separate the keyboard and the monitor so each can be placed at the proper height.)

With a computer, it's important to sit with both feet on the floor, thighs at right angles to your body. The chair should be adjustable and support your lower back. Your forearms should be parallel to the floor. You should look down slightly at the screen. (● *See Panel 5.32.*) This setup is particularly important if you are going to be sitting at a computer for hours at a time.

To avoid wrist and forearm injuries, keep your wrists straight and hands relaxed as you type. Instead of putting the keyboard on top of a desk, put it on a low table or in a keyboard drawer under the desk. Otherwise the nerves in your wrists will rub against the sheaths surrounding them, possibly leading to RSI pains. Or try setting an hourly alarm on your watch or on an alarm clock; when the alarm goes off, take a short break and rotate your wrists and hands a bit.

Eyestrain and headaches usually arise because of improper lighting, screen glare, and long shifts staring at the screen. Make sure that your windows and lights don't throw a glare on the screen and that your computer is not framed by an uncovered window.

Head Directly over shoulders, without straining forward or backward, about an arm's length from screen.

Neck Elongated and relaxed.

Shoulders Kept down, with the chest open and wide.

Back Upright or inclined slightly forward from the hips. Maintain the slight natural curve of the lower back.

Elbows Relaxed, at about a right angle, try to keep forearms parallel to floor.

Wrists Relaxed, and in a neutral position, without flexing up or down.

Knees Slightly lower than the hips.

Light source Should come from behind the head.

Screen At eye level or slightly lower. Use an anti-glare screen.

Fingers Gently curved.

Keyboard Best when kept flat (for proper wrist positioning) and at or just below elbow level. Computer keys that are far away should be reached by moving the entire arm, starting from the shoulders, rather than by twisting the wrists or straining the fingers. Take frequent rest breaks.

Feet Firmly planted on the floor. Shorter people may need a footrest.

Chair Sloped slightly forward to facilitate proper knee position.

Keep wrists above the pad, and tilt the keyboard downward.

Yes

Use both hands to type combination key strokes.

Yes

Don't rest on the wrist pad.

No

Don't bend your hand in awkward angles to type key combinations.

No

Twisting your hands puts strain on them. Resting on a wrist rest, the table, or arm rests while typing forces you to twist your hand to reach some keys. Instead, keep your hands moving freely above the keyboard, letting the strong muscles of your arms move your hands.

It is also a bad idea to contort your hands in other ways. Your hand should be flat and parallel to the keyboard, without twisting. there should not be any pressure on your wrist or forearms while you type. You should NOT rest your wrists on a wrist rest except while taking a very short break from typing. A wrist rest of the proper height (level with the space bar) can serve as a reminder to keep your wrists straight. If you feel your wrist touching the rest, you know that your wrists are starting to dip.

Back and neck pains occur because furniture is not adjusted correctly or because of heavy computer use, especially on laptops. Adjustable furniture and frequent breaks should provide relief.

panel 5.32

How to set up your computer work area

active-matrix display (p. 283) Also known as *TFT (thin-film transistor) display;* flat-panel display in which each pixel on the screen is controlled by its own transistor. Why it's important: *Active-matrix screens are much brighter and sharper than passive-matrix screens, but they are more complicated and thus more expensive. They also require more power, affecting the battery life in laptop computers.*

audio-input device (p. 273) Hardware that records analog sound and translates it for digital storage and processing. Why it's important: *Analog sound signals are continuous variable waves within a certain frequency range. For the computer to process them, these variable waves must be converted to digital 0s and 1s. The principal use of audio-input devices is to produce digital input for multimedia computers. An audio signal can be digitized in two ways—by an audio board or a MIDI board.*

bar-code reader (p. 269) Photoelectric (optical) scanner that translates bar codes into digital codes. Why it's important: *With bar-code readers and the appropriate software system, store clerks can total purchases and produce invoices with increased speed and accuracy, and stores and other businesses can monitor inventory and services with increased efficiency.*

bar codes (p. 269) Vertical, zebra-striped marks imprinted on most manufactured retail products. Why it's important: *Bar codes provide a convenient means of identifying and tracking items. In North America, supermarkets, food manufacturers, and others have agreed to use a bar-code system called the Universal Product Code (UPC). Other kinds of bar-code systems are used on everything from FedEx packages to railroad cars to the jerseys of long-distance runners.*

biometrics (p. 280) Science of measuring individual body characteristics. Why it's important: *Biometric security devices identify a person through a fingerprint, voice intonation, or some other biological characteristic. For example, retinal-identification devices use a ray of light to identify the distinctive network of blood vessels at the back of the eyeball.*

carpal tunnel syndrome (CTS) (p. 292) Debilitating condition caused by pressure on the median nerve in the wrist, producing damage and pain to nerves and tendons in the hands. Why it's important: *CTS can be caused by overuse or misuse of computer keyboards.*

color depth (p. 282) Also called *bit depth;* the amount of information, expressed in bits, that is stored in a dot. Why it's important: *The more bits in a dot or pixel, the more shades of gray and colors can be represented. With 24-bit color depth, for example, 8 bits are dedicated to each primary color—red, green, and blue. Eight-bit color is standard for most of computing; 24-bit, called true color, requires more resources, such as video memory.*

computer vision syndrome (CVS) (p. 293) Eyestrain, headaches, double vision, and other problems caused by improper use of computer display screens. Why it's important: *CVS can be prevented by not staring at the display screen for too long, by correcting faulty lighting, by avoiding screen glare, and by not using screens with poor resolution.*

CRT (cathode-ray tube) (p. 283) Vacuum tube used as a display screen in a computer or video display terminal. Why it's important: *This technology is found not only in the screens of some desktop computers but also in television sets and flight-information monitors in airports.*

digital camera (p. 274) Electronic camera that uses a light-sensitive processor chip to capture photographic images in digital form and store them on a small diskette inserted into the camera or on flash memory chips (cards). Why it's important: *The bits of digital information—the snapshots you have taken, say—can be copied right onto a computer's hard disk for manipulation and printing out. The environmentally undesirable stage of chemical development required for conventional film is completely eliminated.*

digital pen (p. 266) Writing instrument that allows users to write on paper and send the writing as an image file to the computer. Why it's important: *You can easily store your handwritten notes in digital form.*

digitizer (p. 265) Input unit based on an electronic pen or a mouselike copying device called a *puck* that converts drawings and photos to digital data. Why it's important: See *digitizing tablet.*

digitizing tablet (p. 266) One form of digitizer; an electronic plastic board on which each specific location corresponds to a location on the screen. When the user uses a puck, the tablet converts his or her movements into digital signals that are input to the computer. Why it's important: *Digitizing tablets are often used to make maps and engineering drawings, as well as to trace drawings.*

display screen (p. 281) Also called *monitor, CRT,* or simply *screen;* output device that shows programming instructions and data as they are being input and information after it is processed. Why it's important: *Screens are needed to display softcopy output.*

dot pitch (dp) (p. 282) Amount of space between the centers of adjacent pixels; the closer the pixels (dots), the crisper the image. Why it's important: *Dot pitch is one of the measures of display-screen crispness. For a .25dp monitor, for instance, the dots are 25/100ths of a millimeter apart. Generally, a dot pitch of .25dp will provide clear images.*

dots per inch (dpi) (p. 269) Measure of the number of columns and rows of dots per inch. For microcomputer printers, resolution is usually in the range 1,200 × 1,200 dpi. Why it's important: *The higher the dpi, the better the resolution.* (See also *resolution.*)

dumb terminal (p. 258) Also called *video display terminal (VDT);* display screen and a keyboard hooked up to a computer system. It can input and output but not process data. Why it's important: *Dumb terminals are used, for example, by airline reservations clerks to access a mainframe computer containing flight information.*

electromagnetic fields (EMFs) (p. 293) Waves of electrical energy and magnetic energy. Why it's important: *Some people have worried that CRT monitors might be linked to miscarriages and birth defects and that cellphones and power lines might lead to some types of cancers. However, the evidence is unclear.*

ergonomics (p. 294) Study, or science, of working conditions and equipment with the goal of improving worker safety and efficiency. Why it's important: *On the basis of ergonomic principles, stress, illness, and injuries associated with computer use may be minimized.*

fax machine (p. 272). Also called a *facsimile transmission machine;* input device that scans an image and sends it as electronic signals over telephone lines to a receiving fax machine, which prints the image on paper. Two types of fax machines are dedicated fax machines and fax modems. Why it's important: *Fax machines permit the transmission of text or graphic data over telephone lines quickly and inexpensively. They are found not only in offices and homes but also alongside regular phones in some public places such as airports.*

flat-panel display (p. 283) Display screen that is much thinner, weighs less, and consumes less power than a CRT. Flat-panel displays are made up of two plates of glass separated by a layer of a substance in which light is manipulated. Why it's important: *Flat-panel displays are essential to portable computers, and are commonly used for desktop computers as well.*

flatbed scanner (p. 269) Also called *desktop scanner;* the image being scanned is placed on a glass surface, where it remains stationary, and the scanning beam moves across it. Three other types of scanners are *sheet-fed, handheld,* and *drum.* Why it's important: *Flatbed scanners are one of the most popular types of scanner.*

handwriting recognition (p. 264) System in which a computer receives intelligible written input, using special software to interpret the movement of a stylus across a writing service and translating the resulting cursive writing into digital information. Why it's important: *Handwriting recognition is a commonly used input method for PDAs, some handheld videogames, and tablet PCs.*

hardcopy (p. 281) Printed output. The principal examples are printouts, whether text or graphics, from printers. Film, including microfilm and microfiche, is also considered hardcopy output. Why it's important: *Hardcopy is an essential form of computer output.*

impact printer (p. 285) Printer that forms characters or images by striking a mechanism such as a print hammer or wheel against an inked ribbon, leaving an image on paper. Why it's important: *Nonimpact printers are more commonly used than impact printers, but dot-matrix printers are still used in some businesses.*

inkjet printer (p. 286) Printer that sprays onto paper small, electrically charged droplets of ink from four nozzles through holes in a matrix at high speed. Like laser and dot-matrix printers, inkjet printers form images with little dots. Why it's important: *Because they produce high-quality images on special paper, inkjet printers are often used in graphic design and desktop publishing. However, traditionally inkjet printers have been slower than laser printers and they print at a lower resolution on regular paper.*

input hardware (p. 255) Devices that translate data into a form the computer can process. Why it's important: *Without input hardware, computers could not function. The computer-readable form consists of Os and Is, represented as off and on electrical signals. Input hardware devices are categorized as three types: keyboards, pointing devices, and source data-entry devices.*

intelligent terminal (p. 258) Hardware unit with its own memory and processor, as well as a display screen and keyboard, hooked up to a larger computer system. Why it's important: *Such a terminal can perform some functions independent of any mainframe to which it is linked. Examples include the automated teller machine (ATM), a self-service banking machine connected through a telephone network to a central computer, and the point-of-sale (POS) terminal, used to record purchases at a store's customer checkout counter. Recently, many intelligent terminals have been replaced by personal computers.*

internet terminal (p. 259) Terminal that provides access to the internet. There are several variants of internet terminal: (I) the set-top box or web terminal, which displays web pages on a TV set; (2) the network computer, a cheap, stripped-down computer that connects people to networks; (3) the online game player, which not only lets you play games but also connects to the Internet; (4) the full-blown PC/TV (or TV/PC), which merges the personal computer with the television set; and (5) the wireless pocket PC or personal digital assistant (PDA), a handheld computer with a tiny keyboard that can do two-way wireless messaging. Why it's important: *In the near future, most likely, internet terminals will be everywhere.*

keyboard (p. 256) Input device that converts letters, numbers, and other characters into electrical signals that can be read by the computer's processor. Why it's important: *Keyboards are the most popular kind of input device.*

laser printer (p. 285) Nonimpact printer that creates images with dots. As in a photocopying machine, images are produced on a drum, treated with a magnetically charged inklike toner (powder), and then transferred from drum to paper. Why it's important: *Laser printers produce much better image quality than do dot-matrix printers and can print in many more colors; they are also quieter. Laser printers, along with page description languages, enabled the development of desktop publishing.*

light pen (p. 265) Light-sensitive penlike device connected by a wire to the computer terminal. The user brings the pen to a desired point on the display screen and presses the pen button, which identifies that screen location to the computer. Why it's important: *Light pens are used by engineers, graphic designers, and illustrators.*

liquid crystal display (LCD) (p. 283) Flat-panel display in which molecules of liquid crystal line up in a way that alters their optical properties, creating images on the screen by transmitting or blocking out light. Why it's important: *LCD is useful not only for portable computers but also as a display for various electronic devices, such as watches and radios.*

magnetic-ink character recognition (MICR) (p. 271) Scanning technology that reads magnetized-ink characters printed at the bottom of checks and converts them to digital form. Why it's important: *MICR technology is used by banks to sort checks.*

MIDI board (p. 273) *MIDI,* pronounced "middie," stands for "Musical Instrument Digital Interface." MIDI sound boards use this standard. Why it's important: *MIDI provides a standard for the interchange of musical information between musical instruments, synthesizers, and computers.*

mouse (p. 260) A pointing device that is rolled about on a desktop mouse pad and directs a pointer on the computer's display screen. The name is derived from the device's shape, which is a bit like a mouse, with the cord to the computer being the tail. Why it's important: *The mouse is the principal pointing tool used with microcomputers.*

multifunction printer (p. 290) Hardware device that combines several capabilities, such as printing, scanning, copying, and faxing. Why it's important: *Multifunction printers take up less space and cost less than the four separate office machines that they replace. The downside, however, is that if one component breaks, nothing works.*

nonimpact printer (p. 285) Printer that forms characters and images without direct physical contact between the printing mechanism and paper. Two types of nonimpact printers often used with microcomputers are laser printers and inkjet printers. A third kind, the thermal printer, is seen less frequently. Why it's important: *Nonimpact printers are faster and quieter than impact printers.*

optical character recognition (OCR) (p. 272) Software technology that converts scanned text from images (pictures of the text) to an editable text format (usually ASCII) that can be imported into a word processing application and manipulated. Why it's important: *Special OCR characters appear on utility bills and price tags on department-store merchandise. The wand reader is a common OCR scanning device. These days almost all scanners come with OCR software.*

optical mark recognition (OMR) (p. 272) Scanning technology that reads "bubble" marks and converts them into computer-usable form. Why it's important: *OMR technology is used to read the College Board Scholastic Aptitude Test (SAT) and the Graduate Record Examination (GRE).*

output hardware (p. 255) Hardware devices that convert machine-readable information, obtained as the result of processing, into people-readable form. The principal kinds of output are softcopy and hardcopy. Why it's important: *Without output devices, people would have no access to processed data and information.*

page description language (PDL) (p. 286) Software that describes the shape and position of characters and graphics to the printer. PostScript and PCL are common page description

languages. Why it's important: *Page description languages are essential to desktop publishing.*

passive-matrix display (p. 283) Flat-panel display in which a transistor controls a whole row or column of pixels. Passive matrix provides a sharp image for one-color (monochrome) screens but is more subdued for color. Why it's important: *Passive-matrix displays are less expensive and use less power than active-matrix displays, but they aren't as clear and bright and can leave "ghosts" when the display changes quickly. Passive-matrix displays go by the abbreviations HPA, STN, or DSTN.*

pen-based computer system (p. 264) Input system that allows users to enter handwriting and marks onto a computer screen by means of a penlike stylus rather than by typing on a keyboard. Pen computers use handwriting-recognition software that translates handwritten characters made by the stylus into data that is usable by the computer. Why it's important: *Many handheld computers and PDAs have pen input, as do digital notebooks.*

pixel (p. 282) Short for "picture element"; the smallest unit on the screen that can be turned on and off or made different shades. Why it's important: *Pixels are the building blocks that allow text and graphical images to be displayed on a screen.*

plotter (p. 289) Specialized output device designed to produce high-quality graphics in a variety of colors. The inkjet plotter employs the same principle as an inkjet printer; the paper is output over a drum, enabling continuous output. In an electrostatic plotter, paper lies partially flat on a tablelike surface, and toner is used in a photocopier-like manner. Why it's important: *Plotters are used to create hardcopy items such as maps, architectural drawings, and three-dimensional illustrations, which are usually too large for regular printers.*

pointing device (p. 260) Hardware that controls the position of the cursor or pointer on the screen. It includes the mouse and its variants, the touch screen, and various forms of pen input. Why it's important: *In many contexts, pointing devices permit quick and convenient data input.*

pointing stick (p. 263) Pointing device that looks like a pencil eraser protruding from the keyboard between the G, H, and B keys. The user moves the pointing stick with a forefinger. Why it's important: *Pointing sticks are used principally in video games, in computer-aided design systems, and in robots.*

printer (p. 285) Output device that prints characters, symbols, and perhaps graphics on paper or another hardcopy medium. Why it's important: *Printers provide one of the principal forms of computer output.*

QXGA (quantum extended graphics array) (p. 284) Expensive display standard with a resolution of up to 2,048 × 1,536 pixels. Why it's important: *QXGA is used for large LCD screens for computer users needing to view extreme detail, for businesspeople needing to enlarge images that will still be crisp in big-screen presentations, for high-density television, and for special applications involving viewing multiple images on a single screen.*

radio-frequency identification (RFID) tags (p. 279) Source data-entry technology based on an identifying tag bearing a microchip that contains specific code numbers. These code numbers are read by the radio waves of a scanner linked to a database. Why it's important: *Drivers with RFID tags can breeze through tollbooths without having to even roll down their windows; the toll is automatically charged to their accounts. Radio-wave-readable ID tags are also used by the Postal Service to monitor the flow of mail, by stores for inventory control and warehousing, and in the railroad industry to keep track of rail cars.*

refresh rate (p. 282) Number of times per second that screen pixels are recharged so that their glow remains bright. In general, displays are refreshed 56–120 times per second. Why it's important: *The higher the refresh rate, the more solid the image looks on the screen—that is, the less it flickers.*

repetitive stress (or strain) injuries (RSIs) (p. 292) Several wrist, hand, arm, and neck injuries resulting when muscle groups are forced through fast, repetitive motions. They include muscle strain and tendinitis, which are painful but usually not crippling, and carpal tunnel syndrome, which is disabling and often requires surgery. Why it's important: *People who use computer keyboards account for some of the RSI cases that result in lost work time.*

resolution (pp. 269, 282) Clarity or sharpness of display-screen/scanned/printed images; the more pixels (dots) there are per square inch, the finer the level of detail attained. Resolution is expressed in terms of the formula: horizontal pixels × vertical pixels. Each pixel can be assigned a color or a particular shade of gray. Standard screen resolutions are 1,024 × 768, 1,280 × 1,024, and 1,600 × 1,200 pixels. Common scanner resolutions are 300 × 200, 600 × 600, 600 × 1,200, 1,200 × 1,200, and 1,200 × 2,400. Why it's important: *Users need to know what resolution is appropriate for their purposes.*

scanner (p. 267) Source data-input device that uses light-sensing (optical) equipment to translate images of text, drawings, photos, and the like into digital form. Why it's important: *Scanners simplify the input of complex data. The images can be processed by a computer, displayed on a monitor, stored on a storage device, or communicated to another computer.*

sensor (p. 278) Input device that collects specific data directly from the environment and transmits it to a computer. Why it's important: *Although you are unlikely to see such input devices connected to a PC in an office, they exist all around us, often in nearly invisible form. Sensors can be used to detect all kinds of things: speed, movement, weight, pressure, temperature, humidity, wind, current, fog, gas, smoke, light, shapes, images, and so on. In aviation, for example, sensors are used to detect ice buildup on airplane wings and to alert pilots to sudden changes in wind direction.*

softcopy (p. 281) Data on a display screen or in audio or voice form. This kind of output is not tangible; it cannot be touched. Why it's important: *This term is used to distinguish nonprinted output from printed (hardcopy) output.*

sound board (p. 273) An add-on circuit board in a computer that converts analog sound to digital sound and stores it for further processing and/or plays it back, providing output directly to speakers or an external amplifier. Why it's important: *The sound board enables users to work with audible sound.*

sound-output device (p. 290) Hardware that produces digitized sounds, ranging from beeps and chirps to music. Why it's important: *To use sound output, the user needs appropriate software and a sound card. Such devices are used to produce the sound effects when the user plays a CD-ROM, for example.*

source data-entry devices (p. 267) Data-entry devices that create machine-readable data on magnetic media or paper or feed it directly into the computer's processor, without the use of a keyboard. Categories include scanning devices (imaging systems, bar-code readers, mark- and character-recognition devices, and fax machines), audio-input devices, video input, photographic input (digital cameras), voice-recognition systems, sensors, radio-frequency identification devices, and human-biology-input devices. Why it's important: *Source data-entry devices lessen reliance on keyboards for data entry and can make data entry more accurate.*

speech-recognition system (p. 276) Input system that uses a microphone (or a telephone) as an input device and converts a person's speech into digital signals by comparing the electrical patterns produced by the speaker's voice with a set of prerecorded patterns stored in the computer. Why it's important: *Voice-recognition technology is useful in situations where people are unable to use their hands to input data or need their hands free for other purposes.*

SXGA (super extended graphics array) (p. 284) Graphics board standard that supports a resolution of 1,280 × 1,024 pixels. Why it's important: *SXGA is often used with 15-inch LCD monitors.*

thermal printer (p. 288) Printer that uses colored waxes and heat to produce images by burning dots onto special paper. The colored wax sheets are not required for black-and-white output. Thermal printers are expensive, and they require expensive paper. Why it's important: *For people who want the highest-quality color printing available with a desktop printer, thermal printers are the answer.*

touch screen (p. 263) Video display screen that has been sensitized to receive input from the touch of a finger. The screen is covered with a plastic layer, behind which are invisible beams of infrared light. Why it's important: *Users can input requests for information by pressing on buttons or menus displayed. The answers to requests are displayed as output in words or pictures on the screen. (There may also be sound.) Touch screens are found in kiosks, ATMs, airport tourist directories, hotel TV screens (for guest checkout), and campus information kiosks making available everything from lists of coming events to (with proper ID and personal code) student financial-aid records and grades.*

touchpad (p. 263) Input device; a small, flat surface over which the user slides a finger, using the same movements as those used with a mouse. The cursor follows the movement of the finger. The user "clicks" by tapping a finger on the pad's surface or by pressing buttons positioned close by the pad.

Why it's important: *Touchpads let users control the cursor/ pointer with a finger, and they require very little space to use. Most laptops have touchpads.*

trackball (p. 262) Movable ball, mounted on top of a stationary device, that can be rotated by the user's fingers or palm. It looks like the mouse turned upside down. Instead of moving the mouse around on the desktop, you move the trackball with the tips of your fingers. Why it's important: *A trackball requires less space to use than does a mouse.*

UXGA (ultra extended graphics array) (p. 284) Graphics board standard that supports a resolution of 1,600 × 1,200 pixels, producing up to 16.8 million colors. Why it's important: *UXGA is popular with graphic artists, engineering designers, and others using 15- and 19-inch LCD monitors.*

video (p. 291) Output consisting of photographic images played at 15–29 frames per second to give the appearance of full motion. Why it's important: *Video is input into a multimedia system using a video camera or VCR and, after editing, is output on a computer's display screen. Because video files can require a great deal of storage—a 3-minute video may require 1 gigabyte of storage—video is often compressed. Digital video has revolutionized the movie industry, as in the use of special effects.*

videoconferencing (p. 291) Form of video output in which people in different geographic locations can have a meeting— can see and hear one another—using computers and communications. Why it's important: *Many organizations use videoconferencing to take the place of face-to-face meetings. Videoconferencing systems range from videophones to group conference rooms with cameras and multimedia equipment to desktop systems with small video cameras, microphones, and speakers.*

voice-output device (p. 291) Hardware that converts digital data into speechlike sounds. Why it's important: *We hear such voice output on telephones ("Please hang up and dial your call again"), in soft-drink machines, in cars, in toys and games, and recently in mapping software for vehicle-navigation devices. For people with physical challenges, computers with voice output help to level the playing field.*

webcam (p. 273) A video camera attached to a computer to record live moving images that can then be posted on a website in real time. Why it's important: *The webcam is an affordable tool that enables users to have videoconferencing capabilities and may change the future of communications.*

XGA (extended graphics array) (p. 284) Graphics board display standard with a resolution of up to 1,024 × 768 pixels, corresponding to 65,536 possible colors. Why it's important: *XGA is used mainly on 15- and 17-inch CRT monitors for simple applications plus spreadsheets and graphics software.*

CHAPTER REVIEW

stage 1 LEARNING MEMORIZATION

"I can recognize and recall information."

Self-Test Questions

1. A(n) _____ terminal is entirely dependent for all its processing activities on the computer system to which it is connected.

2. The two main categories of printer are _____ and _____.

3. _____ is the study of the physical relationships between people and their work environment.

4. A(n) _____ is an input device that is rolled about on a desktop and directs a pointer on the computer's display screen.

5. _____ consists of devices that translate information processed by the computer into a form that humans can understand.

6. _____ is the science of measuring individual body characteristics.

7. CRT is short for _____.

8. LCD is short for _____.

9. An _____ is software that describes the shape and position of characters and graphics to the printer.

10. When people in different geographic locations can have a meeting using computers and communications, it is called _____.

11. _____-matrix screens are much brighter and sharper than _____-matrix screens, but they are more complicated and thus more expensive.

12. A debilitating condition caused by pressure on the median nerve in the wrist, producing damage and pain to nerves and tendons in the hands, is called _____.

13. The measure of the number of dots that are printed in a linear inch is called _____ or _____.

14. A printer that forms characters or images by striking a mechanism such as a print hammer or wheel against an inked ribbon, leaving images on a paper, is called a(n) _____ printer.

15. _____ printers enabled the development of desktop publishing.

Multiple-Choice Questions

1. Which of the following is *not* a pointing device?
   a. mouse

b. touchpad

c. keyboard

d. joystick

2. Which of the following is not a source data-entry device?

   a. bar-code reader

   b. sensor

   c. digital camera

   d. scanner

   e. mouse

3. Which of the following display standards has the highest screen resolution?

   a. XGA

   b. UXGA

   c. VGA

   d. SVGA

   e. QXGA

4. Which of the following *isn't* considered hardcopy output?

   a. spreadsheet printout

   b. microfilm

   c. fax report

   d. Word document computer file

   e. printed invoice

5. Which of the following factors does *not* affect the quality of a screen display?

   a. refresh rate

   b. speed

   c. resolution

d. pixels

e. color depth

True/False Questions

T F 1. On a computer screen, the more pixels that appear per square inch, the higher the resolution.

T F 2. Photos taken with a digital camera can be downloaded to a computer's hard disk.

T F 3. Resolution is the amount of space between the centers of adjacent pixels.

T F 4. The abbreviation *dpi* stands for "dense pixel intervals."

T F 5. Pointing devices control the position of the cursor on the screen.

T F 6. Output hardware consists of devices that translate information processed by the computer into a form that humans can understand.

T F 7. Optical character-recognition software reads "bubble" marks and converts them into computer-usable form.

T F 8. The lower the refresh rate, the more solid the image looks on the screen.

T F 9. CRTs consume more power than flat-panel displays do.

T F 10. Computer users have no need to be concerned about ergonomics.

T F 11. It has been proven that electromagnetic fields pose no danger to human beings.

T F 12. Plotters are used to print architectural drawings and in computer-aided design.

2 LEARNING   **COMPREHENSION**

"I can recall information in my own terms and explain it to a friend."

Short-Answer Questions

1. What is a common use of dumb terminals?

2. What characteristics determine the clarity of a computer screen?

3. Describe two situations in which scanning is useful.

4. What is source data entry?

5. What is *pixel* short for? What is a pixel?

6. Briefly describe RSI and CTS. Why are they problems?

7. What is a font?

8. Discuss the different types of printers and their features.

9. Explain the differences between CRT monitors and LCD monitors.

10. What is OCR used for?

3 LEARNING   **APPLYING, ANALYZING, SYNTHESIZING, EVALUATING**

"I can apply what I've learned, relate these ideas to other concepts, build on other knowledge, and use all these thinking skills to form a judgment."

Knowledge in Action

1. Cut out several advertisements from newspapers or magazines that feature new microcomputer systems. Circle all the terms that are familiar to you now that

you have read the first five chapters of this text. Define these terms on a separate sheet of paper. Is this computer expandable? How much does it cost? Is a monitor included in the price? A printer?

2. *Paperless office* is a term that has been around for some time. However, the paperless office has not yet been achieved. Do you think the paperless office is a good idea? Do you think it's possible? Why do you think it has not yet been achieved?

3. Many PC warranties do not cover protection against lightning damage, which is thought to be an "act of God." Does your PC warranty provide coverage for "acts of God"? Read it to find out.

4. Compare and contrast the pros and cons of different types of monitors. Decide which one is best for you and explain why. Do some research on how each monitor type creates displayed images.

5. Do you have access to a computer with (a) speech-recognition software, and (b) word processing software that determines writing level (such as eighth grade, ninth grade, and so on)? Dictate a few sentences about your day into the microphone. After your speech is encoded into text, use the word processing software to determine the grade level of your everyday speech.

6. A pixel is the smallest unit on the screen that can be turned on and off. In most high-quality digital photos, you can't see the pixilation unless you zoom in real close. However, even when you don't zoom in, you know that the pixilation is there, a series of different pixels all plotted on a grid. How can you relate this to our experience of reality? Via high-tech microscopes we see that everything is made of smaller particles not visible to the naked eye, such as atoms, subatomic particles, and quarks. How are the basic building blocks of computer imaging and the basic building blocks of physical matter alike, and how are they different?

7. Biometrics: Which form of biometric technology do you prefer for identification purposes: fingerprints, voice intonation, facial characteristics, or retinal identification? Which do you think will become most commonly used in the future?

Web Exercises

1. Visit an online shopping site such as *www.yahoo.com*. Click on *Shopping;* then type *Printers* in the Shopping search box. Investigate five different types of printers by clicking on the printer names and then on Full Specifications. Note (a) the type of printer, (b) its price, (c) its resolution, and (d) its speeds for black-and-white printing and for color printing, if applicable. Which operating system is each printer compatible with? Which printer would you choose? Why?

2. There is an abundance of information about electronic devices on the internet. People write all kinds of reviews either raving about the device that made their lives better or lamenting the device that became their evil nemesis. Go to *www.consumerreports.org/cro/search.htm?query=reviews* and find out how people at ConsumerReports.org rate some of your favorite electronic devices.

3. Go to *www.touchscreens.com* and find a touch screen that appeals to you.

4. Concerned about electromagnetic radiation? For a question-and-answer session on electromagnetic frequencies, go to *www.u-g-h.com/2007/02/28/emf-dangerous-or-not/* and *www.articlesbase.com/article-tags/emf-danger.*

5. Do you see any ethical problems involved with self-scanning checkout? Can people cheat the system? Are store jobs being lost to automation? Are people without credit cards and/or computer experience being excluded? Do a keyword search for *self-scanning* and *self-checkout* and other terms related to these issues. Do you think self-scanning is a good idea?

6. Research the development of Smart Labels. Visit these websites for more information on radio-frequency tagging:

    http://smart-labels.vista-files.org/

    www.answers.com/topic/rfid-tag

7. The human cyborg: Visit Professor Kevin Warwick's website to learn about the implant microchips he has been creating and surgically implanting in his body to allow it to communicate with a computer. Investigate the many applications he has been working on. After visiting his site, run a search on *"Kevin Warwick"* to read what others have to say about him and his ideas.

    www.kevinwarwick.com/

    www.kevinwarwick.com/Cyborgl.htm

    www.wired.com/wired/archive/8.02/warwick.html (Kevin Warwick outlines his plan to become one with his computer)

8. PostScript is the most important page description language in desktop publishing. Read the information at Answer.com, *www.answers.com/topic/postscript-l?hl=postscript&hl=printing,* and find out why. You almost certainly will need some familiarity with PostScript.

9. What is the difference between a screen font and a printer font? Go to Answers.com and Wikipedia to find out. What does *WYSIWYG* mean?

10. How many images can the newest digital cameras hold? Do a web search and find out.

6

COMMUNICATIONS, NETWORKS, & SAFEGUARDS
The Wired & Wireless World

Chapter Topics & Key Questions

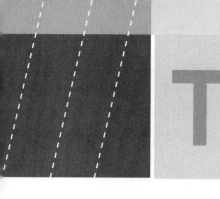

he essence of all revolution, stated philosopher Hannah Arendt, is the start of a new story in human experience.

Before the 1950s, computing devices processed data into information, and communications devices communicated information over distances. The two streams of technology developed pretty much independently, like rails on a railroad track that never merge. Now we have a new story, a revolution.

For us, the new story has been *digital convergence*—the gradual merger of computing and communications into a new information environment, in which the *same information is exchanged among many kinds of equipment, using the language of computers.* (● *See Panel 6.1.*) At the same time, there has been a convergence of several important industries—computers, telecommunications, consumer electronics, entertainment, mass media—producing new electronic products that perform multiple functions.

panel 6.1

Digital convergence— the fusion of computer and communications technologies
Today's new information environment came about gradually from the merger of two separate streams of technological development—computers and communications.

Computer Technology

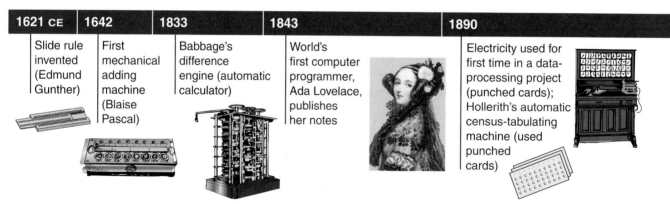

1621 CE	1642	1833	1843		1890
Slide rule invented (Edmund Gunther)	First mechanical adding machine (Blaise Pascal)	Babbage's difference engine (automatic calculator)	World's first computer programmer, Ada Lovelace, publishes her notes		Electricity used for first time in a data-processing project (punched cards); Hollerith's automatic census-tabulating machine (used punched cards)

Communications Technology

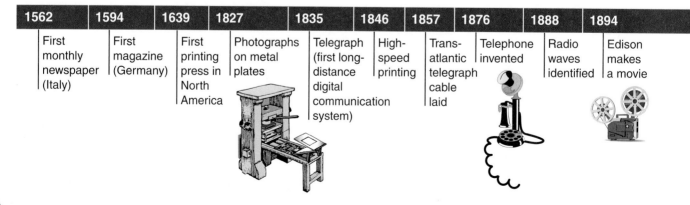

1562	1594	1639	1827	1835	1846	1857	1876	1888	1894
First monthly newspaper (Italy)	First magazine (Germany)	First printing press in North America	Photographs on metal plates	Telegraph (first long-distance digital communication system)	High-speed printing	Trans-atlantic telegraph cable laid	Telephone invented	Radio waves identified	Edison makes a movie

6.1 FROM THE ANALOG TO THE DIGITAL AGE

How do digital data and analog data differ, and what does a modem do?

Why have the worlds of computers and of telecommunications been so long in coming together? Because *computers are digital, but most of the world has been analog.* Let's take a look at what this means. We will elaborate on two subjects we introduced earlier—digital signals and modems.

The Digital Basis of Computers: Electrical Signals as Discontinuous Bursts

What does "digital" mean?

Computers may seem like incredibly complicated devices but, as we've seen, their underlying principle is simple. Because they are based on on/off electrical states, they use the *binary system*, which consists of only two digits—0 and 1. At their most basic level computers can distinguish between just these two values, 0 and 1, or off and on. There is no simple way to represent all the values in between, such as 0.25. All data that a computer processes must be encoded digitally, as a series of 0s and 1s.

In general, *digital* means "computer-based." Specifically, **_digital_ describes any system based on discontinuous data or events; in the case of computers, it refers to communications signals or information represented in a two-state (binary) way using electronic or electromagnetic signals. Each 0 and 1 signal represents a** *bit*.

1930	1944	1946	1949	1952	1964	1967	1969
General theory of computers (MIT)	First electro-mechanical computer (Mark I)	First program-mable electronic computer in United States (ENIAC)	First theories for self-replicating programs (viruses)	UNIVAC computer correctly predicts election of Eisenhower as U.S. President	IBM introduces 360 line of computers	Hand-held calcu-lator	ARPANet estab-lished, led to internet

1895	1907	1912	1915	1928	1939	1946	1947	1948	1950
Marconi develops radio; motion-picture camera invented	First regular radio broadcast from New York	Motion pictures become a big business	AT&T long-distance service reaches San Francisco	First TV demonstrated; first sound movie	Commercial TV broad-casting	Color TV demon-strated	Transistor invented	Reel-to-reel tape recorder	Cable TV

The Analog Basis of Life: Electrical Signals as Continuous Waves

What does "analog" mean?

"The shades of a sunset, the flight of a bird, or the voice of a singer would seem to defy the black or white simplicity of binary representation," points out one writer.[1] Indeed, these and most other phenomena of the world are **_analog_**, **continuously varying in strength and/or quality—fluctuating, evolving, or continually changing.** Sound, light, temperature, and pressure values, for instance, can be anywhere on a continuum or range. The highs, lows, and in-between states have historically been represented with analog devices rather than in digital form. Examples of analog devices are a speedometer, a thermometer, and a tire-pressure gauge, all of which can measure continuous fluctuations.

Humans experience most of the world in analog form—our vision, for instance, perceives shapes and colors as smooth gradations. But most analog events can be simulated digitally. A newspaper photograph, viewed through a magnifying glass, is made up of an array of dots—so small that most newspaper readers see the tones of the photograph as continuous (that is, analog).

Traditionally, electronic transmission of telephone, radio, television, and cable-TV signals has been analog. The electrical signals on a telephone line, for instance, have been analog-data representations of the original voices, transmitted in the shape of a wave (called a *carrier wave*). Why bother to change analog signals into digital ones, especially since the digital representations are only *approximations* of analog events? The reason is that *digital signals are easier to store and manipulate electronically.*

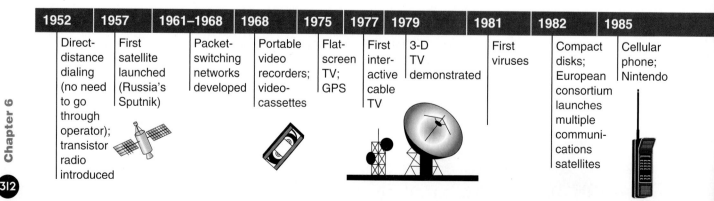

1970	1971	1973	1975	1976	1978	1981	1982	1984
Micro-processor chips come into use; floppy disk introduced for storing data	First pocket calculator	FTP is developed	First micro-computer (MITS Altair 8800)	Apple I computer (first personal computer sold in assembled form); has 512 KB RAM	5¼" floppy disk; Atari home videogame	IBM introduces personal computer	Portable computers; TCP/IP is established as an internet standard; *internet* is coined	Apple Macintosh; first personal laser printer; desktop publishing takes hold; Domain Name System (DNS) is introduced

1952	1957	1961–1968	1968	1975	1977	1979	1981	1982	1985
Direct-distance dialing (no need to go through operator); transistor radio introduced	First satellite launched (Russia's Sputnik)	Packet-switching networks developed	Portable video recorders; video-cassettes	Flat-screen TV; GPS	First inter-active cable TV	3-D TV demonstrated	First viruses	Compact disks; European consortium launches multiple communi-cations satellites	Cellular phone; Nintendo

Purpose of the Dial-Up Modem: Converting Digital Signals to Analog Signals & Back

How does a telephone modem change analog to digital signals and the reverse?

Michelle Philips, an Indianapolis real-estate agent, used to drive to her office at odd hours just to check her email messages and search the web on her company's high-speed internet lines because her dial-up connection at home was too slow. "At home, I can do laundry, take a shower, and wash dishes while the computer is logging on to the internet," she said with a laugh.[2] No wonder so many Americans have switched from the slower dial-up means of access to high-speed connections. Nevertheless, let's stick with the telephone modem for a moment to help illustrate the differences between digital and analog transmission.

Consider a graphic representation of an on/off digital signal emitted from a computer. Like a regular light switch, this signal has only two states—on and off. Compare this with a graphic representation of a wavy analog signal emitted as a signal. The changes in this signal are gradual, as in a dimmer switch, which gradually increases or decreases brightness.

Because telephone lines have traditionally been analog, you need to have a dial-up modem if your computer is to send communications signals over a telephone line. As we've seen, the modem translates the computer's digital signals into the telephone line's analog signals. The receiving computer also needs a modem to translate the analog signals back into digital signals. (● *See Panel 6.2, next page.*)

How, in fact, does a modem convert the continuous analog wave to a discontinuous digital pulse that can represent 0s and 1s? The modem can make

Computer Technology

1993	1994	1997	2000	2001	2003	2005	2047?
Multimedia desktop computers; personal digital assistants	Apple and IBM introduce PCs with full-motion video built in; wireless data transmission for small portable computers; web browser Mosaic invented	Network computers; Pathfinder robot lands on Mars	Microsoft .NET announced; BlackBerry	Windows XP; Mac OS X; MP3	Mac G5; iPod	Mac mini; Apple video iPod	By this date, some experts predict, all electronically encodable information will be in cyberspace

Communications Technology

1986	1991	1994	1997	2000	2001	2004	2005	2007	2010?
First computer virus in the public sphere	CD-ROM games (Sega)	FCC selects HDTV standard	Internet telephone-to-telephone service	Napster popular; 3.8% of music sales online	2.5G wireless services; Wi-Fi and Bluetooth	Facebook launched; MySpace in operation	3G wireless services	112 million blogs are tracked	Power rationing due to grid shortage

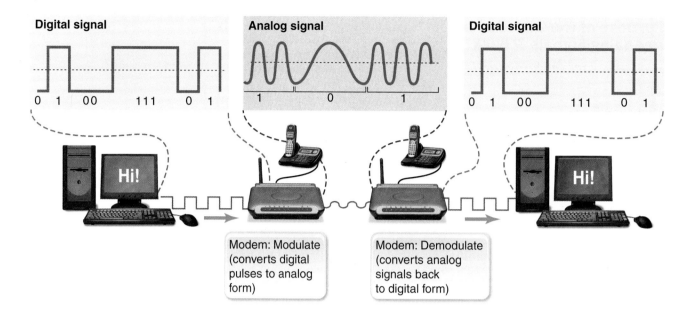

Digital signal

0 1 00 111 0 1

Analog signal

1   0   1

Digital signal

0 1 00 111 0 1

Modem: Modulate
(converts digital
pulses to analog
form)

Modem: Demodulate
(converts analog
signals back
to digital form)

panel 6.2

**Analog versus digital
signals, and the modem**
Note that an analog
signal represents a con-
tinuous electrical signal
in the form of a wave.
A digital signal is discontinuous, expressed as
discrete bursts of on/off
electrical pulses.

adjustments to the frequency—the number of cycles per second, or the number
of times a wave repeats during a specific time interval (the fastness/slowness).
Or it can make adjustments to the analog signal's amplitude—the height of the
wave (the loudness/softness). Thus, in frequency, a slow wave might represent
a 0 and a quick wave might represent a 1. In amplitude, a low wave might represent a 0 and a high wave might represent a 1. (● *See Panel 6.3.*)

<u>*Modem*</u> **is short for "*mo*dulate/*dem*odulate." A sending modem modu-
lates digital signals into analog signals for transmission over phone lines.
A receiving modem demodulates the analog signals back into digital signals.** The modem provides a means for computers to communicate with one
another using the standard copper-wire telephone network, an analog system
that was built to transmit the human voice but not computer signals.

Our concern, however, goes far beyond telephone transmission. How can
the analog realities of the world be expressed in digital form? How can light,
sounds, colors, temperatures, and other dynamic values be represented so that
they can be manipulated by a computer? Let us consider this.

panel 6.3

**How analog waves are
modified to resemble
digital pulses**

The continuous, even
cycle of an analog wave ...

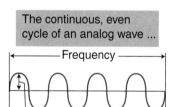

Frequency

Amplitude

OR

... is converted to digital form through
frequency modulation—the frequency
of the cycle increases to represent a 1
and stays the same to represent a 0.

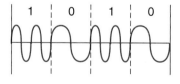

1   0   1   0

... or is converted to digital form through
amplitude modulation—the height of the
wave is increased to represent a 1 and
stays the same to represent a 0.

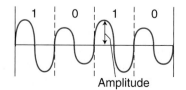

1   0   1   0

Amplitude

Converting Reality to Digital Form

How is sampling used to express analog reality in digital form?

Suppose you are using an analog tape recorder to record a singer during a performance. The analog wave from the microphone, which is recorded onto the tape as an analog wave as well, will produce a near duplicate of the sounds—including distortions, such as buzzings and clicks, or electronic hums if an amplified guitar is used.

The digital recording process is different. The way that music is captured for digital audio CDs, for example, does not provide a duplicate of a musical performance. Rather, the digital process uses a device (called an *analog-to-digital converter*) to record *representative selections*, or *samples*, of the sounds and convert the analog waves into a stream of numbers that the computer then uses to express the sounds. To play back the music, the stream of numbers is converted (by a *digital-to-analog converter*) back into an analog wave. The samples of sounds are taken at regular intervals—nearly 44,100 times a second—and the copy obtained is virtually exact and free from distortion and noise. The sampling rate of 44,100 times per second and the high precision fool our ears into hearing a smooth, continuous sound.

Digital photography also uses sampling: A computer takes samples of values such as brightness and color. The same is true of other aspects of real-life experience, such as pressure, temperature, and motion.

Does digital sampling cheat us out of our experience of "reality" by allowing computers to sample sounds, images, and so on? Actually, people willingly made this compromise years ago, before computers were invented. Movies, for instance, carve up reality into 24 frames a second. Conventional television pictures (before high-definition TV) were drawn at 30 frames per second. These processes happen so quickly that our eyes and brains easily jump the visual gaps. Digital processing of analog experience is just one more way of expressing or translating reality.

Turning analog reality into digital form provides tremendous opportunities. One of the most important is that *all kinds of multimedia can now be changed into digital form and transmitted as data to all kinds of devices.*

Now let us examine the digital world of telecommunications. We begin with the subject of networks and then discuss how networks are connected—first by wired means, then by wireless means.

info!

Sampling

For detailed information, go to:

www.informit.com/articles/ article.aspx?p=372009

http://en.wikipedia.org/wiki/ Digitizing

6.2 NETWORKS

What are the benefits of networks, and what are their types, components, and variations?

More and more people are now designing their homes to accommodate networks. For instance, when Lisa Guernsey and her husband, Rob Krupicka, were planning their new house, they wanted modern conveniences without the modern-day headaches. "We didn't want to face another nest of tangled cables or to see speaker wires snaking beneath the rugs," Guernsey said. "What Rob and I wanted was . . . a so-called networked home with 'digital plumbing' for internet and television connections hidden behind walls, and just enough equipment to make tapping into video and audio as easy as filling a glass of water."[3]

Whether wired or wireless or both, **a _network_, or *communications network*, is a system of interconnected computers, telephones, or other communications devices that can communicate with one another and share applications and data.** The tying together of so many communications devices in so many ways is changing the world we live in.

The Benefits of Networks

What are five ways I might benefit from networks?

People and organizations use networks for the following reasons, the most important of which is the sharing of resources.

Internet cafe in Laos

SHARING OF PERIPHERAL DEVICES Peripheral devices such as laser printers, disk drives, and scanners can be expensive. Consequently, to justify their purchase, management wants to maximize their use. Usually the best way to do this is to connect the peripheral to a network serving several computer users.

SHARING OF PROGRAMS & DATA In most organizations, people use the same software and need access to the same information. It is less expensive for a company to buy one word processing program that serves many employees than to buy a separate word processing program for each employee.

Moreover, if all employees have access to the same data on a shared storage device, the organization can save money and avoid serious problems. If each employee has a separate machine, some employees may update customer addresses while others remain ignorant of the changes. Updating information on a shared server is much easier than updating every user's individual system.

Finally, network-linked employees can more easily work together online on shared projects.

BETTER COMMUNICATIONS One of the greatest features of networks is electronic mail. With email, everyone on a network can easily keep others posted about important information.

SECURITY OF INFORMATION Before networks became commonplace, an individual employee might have been the only one with a particular piece of information, which was stored in his or her desktop computer. If the employee was dismissed—or if a fire or flood demolished the office—the company would lose that information. Today such data would be backed up or duplicated on a networked storage device shared by others.

ACCESS TO DATABASES Networks enable users to tap into numerous databases, whether private company databases or public databases available online through the internet.

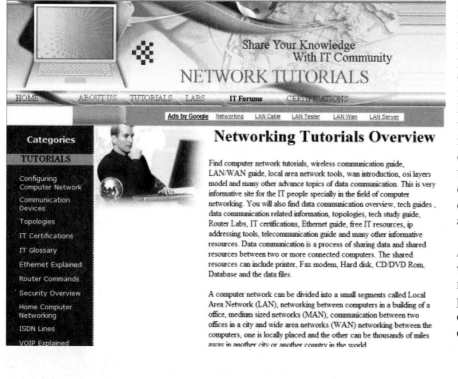

Types of Networks: WANs, MANs, LANs, HANs, PANs, & Others

How do the sizes of networks differ?

Networks, which consist of various combinations of computers, storage devices, and communications devices, may be divided into several main categories, differing primarily in their geographic range and purposes.

WIDE AREA NETWORK A *wide area network (WAN)* **is a communications network that covers a wide geographic area, such as a country or the world.** Most long-distance and regional telephone companies are WANs. A WAN may use a combination of satellites, fiber-optic cable, microwave, and copper-wire connections and link a variety of computers, from mainframes to terminals. (● *See Panel 6.4.*)

WANs are used to connect local area networks (see below) together, so that users and computers in one location can communicate with users and computers in other locations. A wide area network may be privately owned or rented, but the term usually connotes the inclusion of public (shared-user) networks. The best example of a WAN is the internet.

METROPOLITAN AREA NETWORK A *metropolitan area network (MAN)* **is a communications network covering a city or a suburb.** The purpose of a MAN is often to bypass local telephone companies when accessing long-distance services. Many cellphone systems are MANs.

LOCAL AREA NETWORK A *local area network (LAN)*, or *local net*, **connects computers and devices in a limited geographic area, such as one office, one building, or a group of buildings close together.** LANs are the basis for most office networks. The LANs of different offices on a university campus may also be linked together into a so-called *campus-area network*.

HOME AREA NETWORK A *home area network (HAN)* **uses wired, cable, or wireless connections to link a household's digital devices**—not only multiple computers, printers, and storage devices but also VCRs, DVDs, televisions,

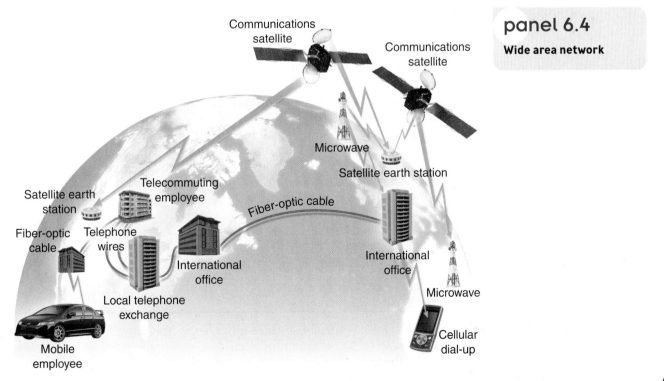

fax machines, videogame machines, and home security systems.[4] (A variant of the HAN is the GAN—the *garden area network*—which can be used to link watering systems, outdoor lights, and alarm systems.)

PERSONAL AREA NETWORK Slightly different from a HAN because it doesn't use wires or cables, **a _personal area network (PAN)_, or _wireless personal area network (WPAN)_, uses short-range wireless technology to connect an individual's personal electronics,** such as cellphone, PDA, MP3 player, notebook PC, and printer. PANs are made possible with such inexpensive, short-range wireless technologies as Bluetooth, ultra wideband, and wireless USB, which have a range of 30 feet or so, as we will describe.

HOME AUTOMATION NETWORK A _home automation network_ **relies on very inexpensive, very short-range, low-power wireless technology in the under-200-Kbps range to link switches and sensors around the house.**[5] Such networks, which use wireless standards such as Insteon, ZigBee, and Z-Wave, as we will describe, run on inexpensive AA batteries and use wireless remotes, in-wall touch screens, and PDAs, along with special software, to control lights and switches, thermostats and furnaces, smoke alarms and outdoor floodlights.

How Networks Are Structured: Client/Server & Peer to Peer

What's the difference between client/server and peer-to-peer networks?

Two principal ways in which networks are structured are *client/server* and *peer to peer*. (● *See Panel 6.5.*)

CLIENT/SERVER NETWORKS A _client/server network_ **consists of _clients_, which are microcomputers that request data, and _servers_, which are computers used to supply data.** The server is a powerful microcomputer that manages shared devices, such as laser printers. It runs server software for applications such as email and web browsing. Different servers may be used to manage different tasks. A *file server* is a computer that acts like a disk drive, storing the programs and data files shared by users on a LAN. A *database server* is a computer in a LAN that stores data but doesn't store programs. A *print server* controls one or more printers and stores the print-image output from all the microcomputers on the system. *Web servers* contain web pages that can be viewed using a browser. *Mail servers* manage email.

PEER-TO-PEER NETWORKS The word *peer* denotes one who is equal in standing with another (as in the phrases "peer pressure" and "jury of one's peers"). **In a _peer-to-peer (P2P) network_, all microcomputers on the network communicate directly with one another without relying on a server.** Every computer can share files and peripherals with all other computers on the network, given that all are granted access privileges. Peer-to-peer networks are less expensive than client/server networks and work effectively for up to 25 computers. Beyond that, they slow down under heavy use. They are appropriate for small networks, such as *home networks*.

Intranets, Extranets, & VPNs

What are the differences among intranets, extranets, and VPNs?

Early in the Online Age, businesses discovered the benefits of using the World Wide Web to get information to customers, suppliers, or investors. For example, in the mid-1990s, FedEx found it could save millions by allowing customers to click through web pages to trace their parcels, instead of having

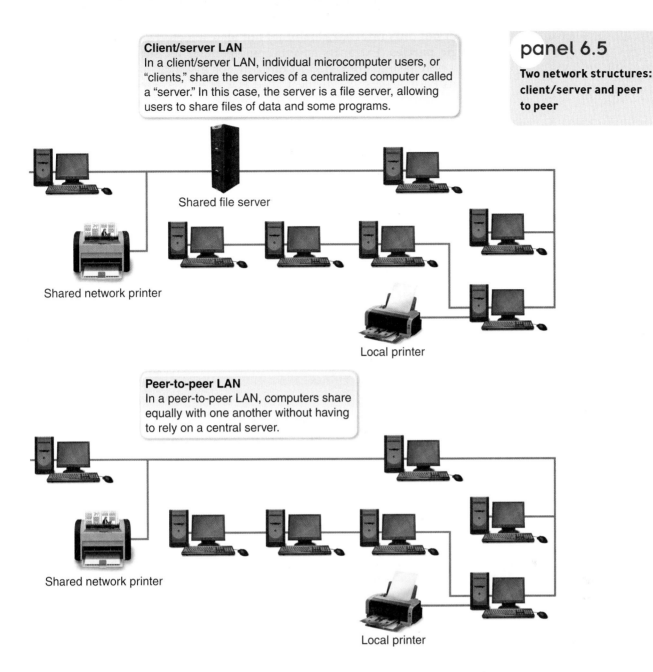

Client/server LAN
In a client/server LAN, individual microcomputer users, or "clients," share the services of a centralized computer called a "server." In this case, the server is a file server, allowing users to share files of data and some programs.

Shared file server

Shared network printer

Local printer

Peer-to-peer LAN
In a peer-to-peer LAN, computers share equally with one another without having to rely on a central server.

Shared network printer

Local printer

FedEx customer-service agents do it. From there, it was a short step to the application of the same technology inside companies—in internal internet networks called *intranets*.

INTRANETS: FOR INTERNAL USE ONLY An *intranet* **is an organization's internal private network that uses the infrastructure and standards of the internet and the web.** When a corporation develops a public website, it is making selected information available to consumers and other interested parties. When it creates an intranet, it enables employees to have quicker access to internal information and to share knowledge so that they can do their jobs better. Information exchanged on intranets may include employee email addresses and telephone numbers, product information, sales data, employee benefit information, and lists of jobs available within the organization.

EXTRANETS: FOR CERTAIN OUTSIDERS Taking intranet technology a few steps further, extranets offer security and controlled access. As we have seen, intranets are internal systems, designed to connect the members of a specific group or a single company. By contrast, *extranets* **are private intranets that**

connect not only internal personnel but also selected suppliers and other strategic parties. Extranets have become popular for standard transactions such as purchasing. Ford Motor Company, for instance, has an extranet that connects Ford dealers worldwide. Called FOCALpt, the extranet supports sales and servicing of cars, with the aim of improving service to Ford customers.

Tunneling

For a short tutorial on VPNs, go to:

http://computer.howstuffworks. com/vpn.htm

VIRTUAL PRIVATE NETWORKS Because wide area networks use leased lines, maintaining them can be expensive, especially as distances between offices increase. To decrease communications costs, some companies have established their own ***virtual private networks (VPNs)***, **private networks that use a public network (usually the internet) to connect remote sites.** Company intranets, extranets, and LANs can all be parts of a VPN.

Components of a Network

What are the various parts of a network?

Regardless of size, networks all have several components in common.

WIRED AND/OR WIRELESS CONNECTIONS Networks use a wired or wireless connection system. Wired connections may be twisted-pair wiring, coaxial cable, or fiber-optic cable, and wireless connections may be infrared, microwave (such as Bluetooth), broadcast radio (such as Wi-Fi), or satellite, as we describe shortly.

HOSTS & NODES A client/server network has a ***host computer***, **a mainframe or midsize central computer that controls the network.** The other devices on the network are called nodes. **A *node* is any device that is attached to a network—for example, a microcomputer, terminal, storage device, or printer.** For instance, a device called a *wireless access point (WAP)* when attached to a network essentially extends the range of the network by offering several wireless nodes, enabling you, say, to wirelessly connect a computer in a back bedroom to a network at the front of the house.

PACKETS Electronic messages are sent as packets. **A *packet* is a fixed-length block of data for transmission.** A sending computer breaks an electronic message apart into packets, each of which typically contains 1,000–1,500 bytes. The various packets are sent through a communications network—often using different (and most expedient) routes, at different speeds, and sandwiched in between packets from other messages. Once the packets arrive at their destination, the receiving computer reassembles them into proper sequence to complete the message.

PROTOCOLS **A *protocol*, or *communications protocol*, is a set of conventions governing the exchange of data between hardware and/or software components in a communications network.** Every device connected to a network has an internet protocol (IP) address so that other computers on the network can properly route data to that address. Sending and receiving devices must follow the same set of protocols.

Protocols are built into the hardware or software you are using. The protocol in your communications software, for example, will specify how receiver devices will acknowledge sending devices, a matter called *handshaking*. Handshaking establishes the fact that the circuit is available and operational. It also establishes the level of device compatibility and the speed of transmission. In addition, protocols specify the type of electrical connections used, the timing of message exchanges, and error-detection techniques.

A packet, or electronic message, carries four types of information that will help it get to its destination—namely, the sender's address (the IP), the intended receiver's address, how many packets the message has been broken into, and the number of the individual packet. The packets carry the data in the protocols that the internet uses—that is, TCP/IP.

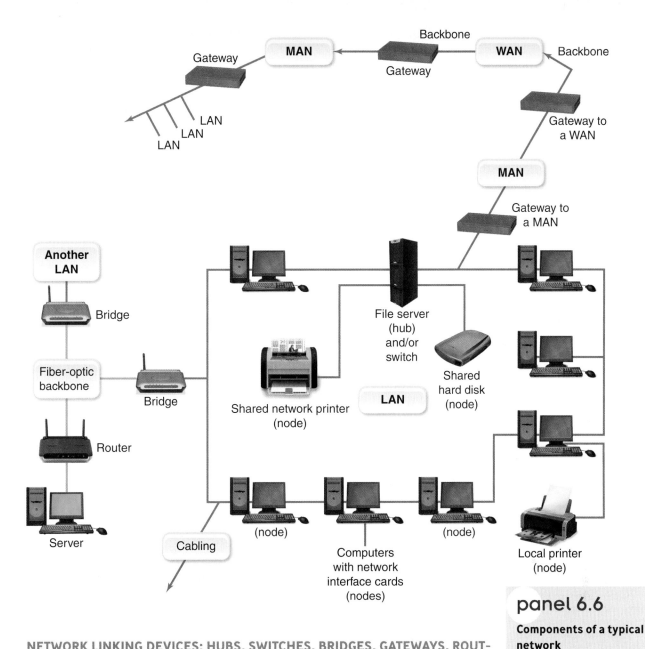

Backbone

Gateway

MAN

WAN

Backbone

LAN
LAN
LAN

Gateway

Gateway

Gateway to
a WAN

MAN

Gateway to
a MAN

**Another
LAN**

Bridge

Fiber-optic
backbone

Bridge

Router

Server

Cabling

Shared network printer
(node)

File server
(hub)
and/or
switch

Shared
hard disk
(node)

LAN

(node)

Computers
with network
interface cards
(nodes)

(node)

Local printer
(node)

panel 6.6

**Components of a typical
network**

**NETWORK LINKING DEVICES: HUBS, SWITCHES, BRIDGES, GATEWAYS, ROUT-
ERS, & BACKBONES** Networks are often linked together—LANs to MANs
and MANs to WANs, for example. The means for connecting them are hubs,
switches, bridges, routers, and gateways. (● *See Panel 6.6.*)

- **Hubs:** In general, a hub is the central part of a wheel where the spokes
  come together. In computer terminology, a **_hub_ is a common connection
  point for devices in a network—a place of convergence where
  data arrives from one or more directions and is forwarded out in
  one or more other directions.** With hubs, bandwidth is shared by all
  components. Hubs are commonly used to connect segments of a LAN.
  A hub contains multiple ports. When a packet arrives at one port, it is
  copied to the other ports so that all segments of the LAN can see all
  packets. A hub is a *half-duplex* device, meaning it transmits data in both
  directions but only in one direction at a time.

- **Switches: A _switch_ is a device that connects computers to a network.**
  Unlike a hub, it sends messages only to a computer that is the intended
  recipient. A switch is a *full-duplex* device, meaning data is transmitted
  back and forth at the same time, which improves the performance of
  the network. Switches allow each component full use of the bandwidth.

Switches are used only in certain configurations; hubs and switches can be used in combination.

- **Bridges: A _bridge_ is an interface used to connect the same types of networks.** For instance, similar local area networks can be joined together to create larger area networks.

- **Gateways: A _gateway_ is an interface permitting communication between dissimilar networks**—for instance, between a LAN and a WAN or between two LANs based on different network operating systems or different layouts. Gateways can be hardware, software, or a combination of the two.

- **Routers: A _router_ is a special computer that directs communicating messages when several networks are connected together.** High-speed routers can serve as part of the internet backbone, or transmission path, handling the major data traffic.

- **Backbones: The _backbone_ consists of the main highway—including gateways, routers, and other communications equipment—that connects all computer networks in an organization.** People frequently talk about the _internet backbone,_ the central structure that connects all other elements of the internet. As we discussed in Chapter 2, several commercial companies provide these major high-speed links across the country; these backbones are connected at network access points (NAPs).

NETWORK INTERFACE CARDS As we stated in Chapter 4, a _network interface card (NIC)_ enables the computer to send and receive messages over a cable network. The network card can be inserted into an expansion slot in a microcomputer. Alternatively, a network card in a stand-alone box may serve a number of devices. New computers often come with network cards already installed.

NETWORK OPERATING SYSTEM The _network operating system (NOS)_ is the system software that manages the activity of a network. The NOS supports access by multiple users and provides for recognition of users based on passwords and terminal identifications. Depending on whether the LAN is client/server or peer-to-peer, the operating system may be stored on the file server, on each microcomputer on the network, or on a combination of both.

Examples of popular NOS software are Novell NetWare, Microsoft Windows Server 2008, Solaris, Unix, and Linux. Peer-to-peer networking can also be accomplished with Microsoft Windows 95/98/Me/XP/Vista/7.

Network Topologies: Bus, Ring, & Star

What are three popular configurations for networks?

Networks can be laid out in different ways. **The logical layout, or shape, of a network is called a _topology_.** The three basic topologies, or configurations, are _bus, ring,_ and _star._

BUS NETWORK The bus network works like a bus system at rush hour, with various buses pausing in different bus zones to pick up passengers. In a bus network, all communications devices are connected to a common channel. (● _See Panel 6.7._) That is, **in a _bus network,_ all nodes are connected to a single wire or cable, the _bus,_ which has two endpoints. Each communications device on the network transmits electronic messages to other devices.** If some of those messages collide, the sending device waits and tries to transmit again.

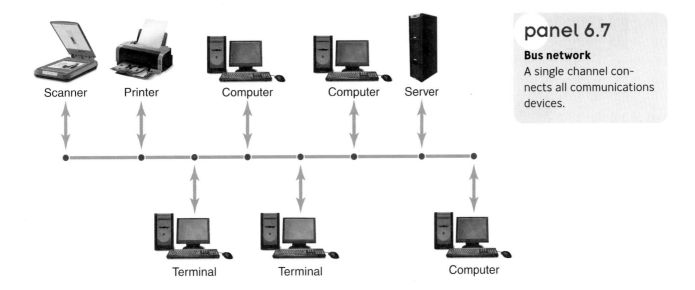

Scanner Printer Computer Computer Server

Terminal Terminal Computer

The advantage of a bus network is that it may be organized as a client/server or peer-to-peer network. The disadvantage is that extra circuitry and software are needed to avoid collisions between data. Also, if a connection in the bus is broken—as when someone moves a desk and knocks the connection out—the entire network may stop working. This arrangement connects the network's devices in a closed loop.

RING NETWORK A _ring network_ **is one in which all microcomputers and other communications devices are connected in a continuous loop.** (● _See Panel 6.8.)_ There are no endpoints.

Electronic messages are passed around the ring until they reach the right destination. There is no central server. An example of a ring network is IBM's Token Ring Network, in which a bit pattern (called a "token") determines which user on the network can send information, as we'll discuss.

The advantage of a ring network is that messages flow in only one direction. Thus, there is no danger of collisions. The disadvantage is that if a connection is broken, the entire network stops working.

STAR NETWORK A _star network_ **is one in which all microcomputers and other communications devices are directly connected to a central server.** (● _See Panel 6.9, next page.)_ Electronic messages are routed through the central hub to their destinations. The central hub monitors the flow of traffic. A PBX system—a private telephone system, such as that found on a college campus, that connects telephone extensions to each other—is an example of a star network. Traditional star networks are designed to be easily expandable because hubs can be connected to additional hubs of other networks.

The advantage of a star network is that the hub prevents collisions between messages. Moreover, if a connection is broken between any communications device and the hub, the rest of the devices on the network will continue operating. However, if the hub goes down, the entire network stops.

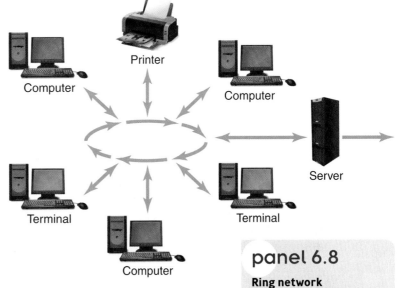

Computer Printer Computer

Terminal Server Terminal

Computer

panel 6.8

Ring network

This arrangement connects the network's devices in a closed loop.

Communications, Networks, & Safeguards

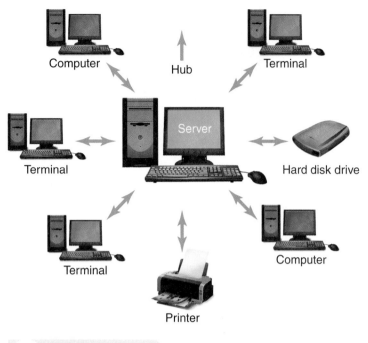

Computer   Hub   Terminal

Terminal   Server   Hard disk drive

Terminal   Computer

Printer

panel 6.9

Star network

This arrangement connects at the network's devices to a central host computer, through which all communications must pass.

Two Ways to Prevent Messages from Colliding: Ethernet & Token Ring

How do the two methods of keeping messages from colliding work?

When you deal with small LANs, especially when they use wired or cable (twisted-pair, coaxial, or fiber-optic) connections, you may hear about Ethernet and Token Ring, two LAN protocols, or technologies, used to keep messages from bumping into one another along the transmission line.

ETHERNET In 1973, at Xerox Corporation's Palo Alto Research Center (more commonly known as PARC), researcher Bob Metcalfe designed and tested the first Ethernet network. While working on a way to link a particular computer to a printer, Metcalfe developed the physical method of cabling that connected devices on the Ethernet as well as the standards that governed communication on the cable. Ethernet has since become the most popular and most widely deployed network technology in the world.

Ethernet **is a LAN technology that can be used with almost any kind of computer and that describes how data can be sent in packets in between computers and other networked devices usually in close proximity.** When two nodes try to send data at the same time that might collide, Ethernet instructs the nodes to resend the data one packet at a time. It is frequently used in a star topology.

Ethernet devices used to be able to have only a few hundred meters of cable between them, making it impractical to connect geographically dispersed locations. Modern advances have increased these distances considerably, allowing Ethernet networks to span tens of kilometers.

The most common version (called _10Base-T_) handles about 10 megabits per second. A newer version, _Fast Ethernet_ (or _100Base-T_) transfers data at 100 megabits per second. The newest version, _Gigabit Ethernet_ (or _1000Base-T_) transmits data at the rate of 1 gigabit (1,000 megabits) per second. Most new microcomputers come equipped with an Ethernet card and an Ethernet port (Chapter 4).

TOKEN RING A technology developed by IBM, _Token Ring_ is a LAN technology that transmits a special control message or message frame, called a "token," around a network to each node, signaling the node that it can then send a message. The node then

Traders work on the floor of the heavily networked New York Stock Exchange.

sends the token on to the next node, thus guaranteeing that each computer or device on the network will transmit at regular intervals. The Token Ring standard is mainly used in star or ring topologies. The advantage of Token Ring is that broken cable connections are easily detected and thus easily fixed.

6.3 WIRED COMMUNICATIONS MEDIA

What are types of wired communications media?

It used to be that two-way individual communications were accomplished mainly in two ways. They were carried by the medium of (1) a telephone wire or (2) a wireless method such as shortwave radio. Today there are many kinds of communications media, although they are still wired or wireless. ***Communications media***, or *communications channels*, **carry signals over a** *communications path*, **the route between two or more communications media devices.** The speed, or data transfer rate, at which transmission occurs—and how much data can be carried by a signal—depends on the media and the type of signal.

Wired Communications Media: Wires & Cables

What is the difference between the three types of wired communications media?

Three types of wired communications media are *twisted-pair wire* (conventional telephone lines), *coaxial cable*, and *fiber-optic cable*. The various kinds of wired internet connections discussed in Chapter 2—dial-up modem, DSL, ISDN, cable modem, T1 lines, as well as internet backbones—are created by using these wired communications media.

TWISTED-PAIR WIRE The telephone line that runs from your house to the pole outside, or underground, is probably twisted-pair wire. ***Twisted-pair wire*** **consists of two strands of insulated copper wire, twisted around each other. This twisted-pair configuration (compared to straight wire) somewhat reduces interference (called "crosstalk") from electrical fields.** Twisted-pair is relatively slow, carrying data at the rate of 1–128 megabits per second (normally 56 Kbps). Moreover, it does not protect well against electrical interference. However, because so much of the world is already served by twisted-pair wire, it will no doubt be used for years to come, both for voice messages and for modem-transmitted computer data (dial-up connections).

Twisted-pair wire

The prevalence of twisted-pair wire gives rise to what experts call the "last-mile problem." That is, it is relatively easy for telecommunications companies to upgrade the physical connections between cities and even between neighborhoods. But it is expensive for them to replace the "last mile" of twisted-pair wire that connects to individual houses.

COAXIAL CABLE ***Coaxial cable***, **commonly called "co-ax," is a high-frequency transmission cable that consists of insulated copper wire wrapped in a solid or braided metal shield and then in an external plastic cover.** Co-ax is widely used for cable television and cable internet connections. Thanks to the extra insulation, coaxial cable is much better than twisted-pair wiring at resisting noise. Moreover,

Coaxial cable

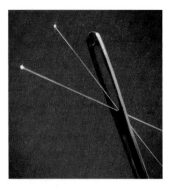

Fiber-optic strands

it can carry voice and data at a faster rate (up to 200 megabits per second; residential cable, 4–10 megabits per second). Often many coaxial cables are bundled together.

FIBER-OPTIC CABLE A *fiber-optic cable* consists of dozens or hundreds of thin strands of glass or plastic that transmit pulsating beams of light rather than electricity. These strands, each as thin as a human hair, can transmit up to about 2 billion pulses per second (2 gigabits); each "on" pulse represents 1 bit. When bundled together, fiber-optic strands in a cable 0.12 inch thick can support a quarter- to a half-million voice conversations at the same time. Moreover, unlike electrical signals, light pulses are not affected by random electromagnetic interference in the environment. Thus, fiber-optic cable has a much lower error rate than normal telephone wire and cable. In addition, fiber-optic cable is lighter and more durable than twisted-pair wire and co-ax cable, although it is more expensive. A final advantage is that it cannot easily be wiretapped, so transmissions are more secure.

Wired Communications Media for Homes: Ethernet, HomePNA, & HomePlug

What is the difference between the three types of wired communications media used for home networks?

Many households now have more than one computer, and many have taken steps to link their equipment in a home network. Indeed, some new high-tech homes include network technology that links as many as 12 televisions positioned around the house plus computers, telephones, lights, audio, and alarm systems.

Traditionally, wired media have been used to connect equipment. Three wired network technologies are *Ethernet, HomePNA,* and *HomePlug.*

ETHERNET Most personal PCs come with Ethernet capability. Homes wanting to network with this technology use the kind of cabling (Cat5) that permits either regular Ethernet data speeds (10 megabits per second) or Fast Ethernet speeds (100 megabits per second). Besides cabling, which will have to be installed throughout the house (by you or by a professional installer), a home Ethernet network may require a router and a hub, which may be available from your internet access provider.

HOMEPNA: USING THE HOME'S EXISTING TELEPHONE WIRING Does your house have a phone jack in every room in which you have a computer? Then you might be interested in setting up a *phoneline network,* using conventional phonelines to connect the nodes in a network. The means for doing this is **HomePNA (HPNA) technology, an alliance of leading technology companies working to ensure the adoption of a single, unified existing wire (telephone and cable) home-networking standard that transmits data at about 320 megabits per second.**

HOMEPLUG: USING THE HOME'S EXISTING ELECTRIC-POWER WIRING Alternatively, you might want to set up a *power-line network,* using conventional power lines in a home to connect the nodes in a network, using HomePlug. **HomePlug technology is a standard that allows users to send data over a home's existing electrical (AC) power lines,** which can be transmitted at up to 200 megabits per second. This kind of communications medium has an advantage, of course, in that there is at least one power outlet in every room.

Some households have a combination of wired and wireless networks, but more are going over to all-wireless.

Do We Need More Fiber Optics?

Google has long been buying up data communications capacity, especially fiber-optics. Its search engine works by making copies of nearly every page of the internet in its own data centers. That requires Google to move a huge amount of data around the world on a regular basis. And its plans to deliver applications over the internet will use even more bandwidth (*www.googlizationofeverything. com/2007/09/do_we_need_ more_fiberoptic_cab.php,* accessed August 13, 2009).

PRACTICAL ACTION
Telecommuting & Telework: The Nontraditional Workplace

Christie Thomas, 33, of Morgan Hill, California, is a "mompreneur." A loan officer and independent contractor for Pacific West Financial, she does loan work and research while her 2-year-old daughter sleeps and when her husband, a teacher, gets home from work. "It's very lucrative," says Thomas, who also manages other loan officers. However, she adds, "You do have to manage your time very well. I can work in my pajamas."[6]

Home-based working moms, or mompreneurs, are the beneficiaries of technology such as high-speed internet access, the widespread availability of personal computers, and the willingness of budget-conscious companies to rely on home-based free agents. But if this kind of "home work" was once primarily the province of technical employees, it is also now moving into senior management ranks.[7]

The rise of remote working arrangements may be part of a larger trend. "Powerful economic forces are turning the whole labor force into an army of freelancers—temps, contingents, and independent contractors and consultants," says business strategy consultant David Kline. The result, he believes, is that "computers, the net, and telecommuting systems will become as central to the conduct of 21st-century business as the automobile, freeways, and corporate parking lots were to the conduct of mid-20th-century business."[8] The transformation gathered momentum during the 2008–2009 economic downturn, when companies looked to save money on office real estate costs.[9]

Two offshoots of nontraditional office work are telecommuting and telework.

Telecommuting: Working from Home

Working at home while in telecommunication with the office is called *telecommuting*. In the United States, telecommuting has been gaining favor for several years. According to one research group, in 2008 17.2 million Americans were working at least one day a month for their employer remotely or at home, an increase of 74% since 2005.[10] A great many of these workers were employees who telecommute to traditional offices.

Telecommunication can have many benefits. The advantages to society are reduced traffic congestion, energy consumption, and air pollution. The advantages to employees are lower commuting and workplace-wardrobe costs and more choices about how they handle their time. The advantage to employers, it's argued, is increased productivity, because telecommuters may experience fewer distractions at home than in the office and can work flexible hours. Absenteeism may be reduced, teamwork improved, and the labor pool expanded because hard-to-get employees don't have to uproot themselves from where they want to live. Costs for office space, parking, insurance, and other overhead are reduced.

Despite the advantages, however, telecommuting has some drawbacks. Employees sometimes feel isolated, even deserted, or they are afraid that working outside the office will hinder their career advancement. They also find the arrangements blur the line between office and home, straining family life. Employers may feel telecommuting causes resentments among office-bound employees, and they may find it difficult to measure employees' productivity. In addition, with teamwork now more of a workplace requirement, managers may worry that telecommuters cannot keep up with the pace of change. Finally, some employers are concerned that telecommuters create more opportunities for security breaches by hackers or equipment thieves.[11]

Telework: Working from Anywhere

More recently, the term *telework* (or *virtual office*) has been adopted to replace the term "telecommuting" because it encompasses not just working from home but working from anywhere: "a client's office, a coffee shop, an airport lounge, a commuter train," in one description. "With cellphones, broadband at home, Wi-Fi, virtual private networks, and instant messaging becoming ubiquitous, telework has become easier than ever."[12]

Employees at big high-tech companies work from their homes, cars, and other nontraditional work sites. Thus, the workplace exists more in virtual than physical space, and the actual office may be little more than a computer, a high-bandwidth connection, and a cellphone, with most communication with the outer world being through a voice mail system, an email address, a web page, and a post office box. (Indeed, you can live anywhere you want in the world but have a local business presence with a prestigious physical mailing address and local phone number by hiring a virtual office web service such as Officescape, whose staff can handle all your office information locally and forward your physical mail and packages.)

Despite the history of productivity, some managers fear losing control over employees who become teleworkers, picturing them at home watching TV instead of working. The way to avoid that, suggests Robert Smith, director of ITAC (formerly the International Telework Association & Council), is for companies to install ways of measuring productivity. "Good organizations put into place performance requirements," he says. "They have a process in which managers can set performance goals and properly evaluate whether those goals are met. If you have that in place, you'll have a more effective organization, whether an employee is 10 feet or 10 miles away."[13]

6.4 WIRELESS COMMUNICATIONS MEDIA

What are types of wireless communications media, both long distance and short distance?

Wireless connection has become increasingly popular, with 56% of Americans reporting in 2009 they got on the internet through wireless, many (39%) through a laptop, others (32%) through a mobile device, such as a cellphone.[14] Wireless, mobile technology has led to a new class of worker that scholars David Pauleen and Brian Harmer have dubbed *nanobots:* "Empowered by their mobile devices and remote access to the corporate network, nanobots put in long hours, sometimes seven days a week—just not at their office desks. Different from mobile workers, who usually stay in close contact with managers, nanobots thrive on their driven natures and on the personal freedom with which they are entrusted." [15]

Cellphones are only one kind of wireless communication. We consider (1) the electromagnetic spectrum, (2) the five types of long-distance wireless communications media, (3) long-distance wireless, and (4) short-distance wireless.

The Electromagnetic Spectrum, the Radio-Frequency (RF) Spectrum, & Bandwidth

What is the electromagnetic spectrum, and how do electromagnetic waves differ?

Often it's inefficient or impossible to use wired media for data transmission, and wireless transmission is better. To understand wireless communication, we need to understand transmission signals and the electromagnetic spectrum.

THE ELECTROMAGNETIC SPECTRUM Telephone signals, radar waves, microwaves, and the invisible commands from a garage-door opener all represent

panel 6.10

The radio-frequency spectrum

The radio-frequency spectrum, which carries most communications signals, appears as part of the electromagnetic spectrum.

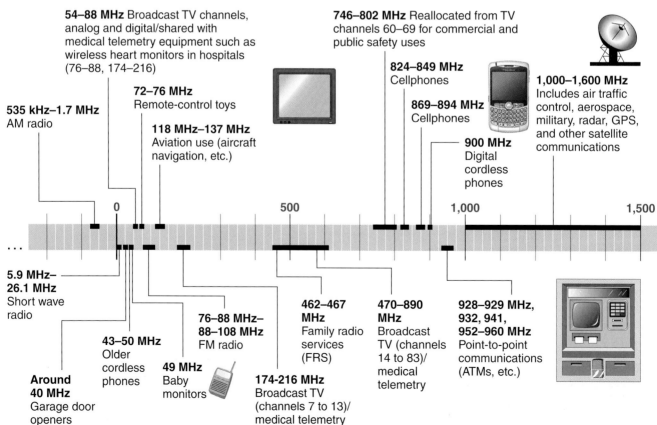

54–88 MHz Broadcast TV channels, analog and digital/shared with medical telemetry equipment such as wireless heart monitors in hospitals (76–88, 174–216)

72–76 MHz Remote-control toys

535 kHz–1.7 MHz AM radio

118 MHz–137 MHz Aviation use (aircraft navigation, etc.)

746–802 MHz Reallocated from TV channels 60–69 for commercial and public safety uses

824–849 MHz Cellphones

869–894 MHz Cellphones

900 MHz Digital cordless phones

1,000–1,600 MHz Includes air traffic control, aerospace, military, radar, GPS, and other satellite communications

5.9 MHz–26.1 MHz Short wave radio

43–50 MHz Older cordless phones

49 MHz Baby monitors

76–88 MHz– 88–108 MHz FM radio

462–467 MHz Family radio services (FRS)

470–890 MHz Broadcast TV (channels 14 to 83)/ medical telemetry

928–929 MHz, 932, 941, 952–960 MHz Point-to-point communications (ATMs, etc.)

Around 40 MHz Garage door openers

174–216 MHz Broadcast TV (channels 7 to 13)/ medical telemetry

different waves on what is called the electromagnetic spectrum of radiation. The _**electromagnetic spectrum of radiation**_ **is the basis for** _all_ **telecommunications signals, carried by both wired and wireless media.**

Part of the electromagnetic spectrum is the _**radio-frequency (RF) spectrum**_, **fields of electrical energy and magnetic energy that carry most communications signals.** (● _See Panel 6.10._) Internationally, the RF spectrum is allocated by the International Telecommunications Union (ITU) in Geneva, Switzerland. Within the United States, the RF spectrum is further allocated to nongovernment and government users.

The Federal Communications Commission (FCC), acting under the authority of Congress, allocates and assigns frequencies to nongovernment users. The National Telecommunications and Information Administration (NTIA) is responsible for departments and agencies of the U.S. government.

Electromagnetic waves vary according to _frequency_—the number of times a wave repeats, or makes a cycle, in a second. The radio-frequency spectrum ranges from low-frequency waves, such as those used for garage-door openers (40 megahertz), through the medium frequencies for certain cellphones (824–849 megahertz) and air-traffic control monitors (960–1,215 megahertz), to deep-space radio communications (2,290–2,300 megahertz). Frequencies at the very ends of the spectrum take the forms of infrared rays, visible light, ultraviolet light, X rays, and gamma rays.

BANDWIDTH **The** _**bandwidth**_ **is the range, or** _band_, **of frequencies that a transmission medium can carry in a given period of time.** For analog signals, bandwidth is expressed in _hertz (Hz)_, or _cycles per second_. For example, certain cellphones operate within the range 824–849 megahertz—that is, their bandwidth is 25 megahertz. _The wider a medium's bandwidth, the more frequencies it can use to transmit data and thus the faster the transmission._

There are two general classes of bandwidth—narrow and broad—which can be expressed in hertz but also in _bits per second (bps):_

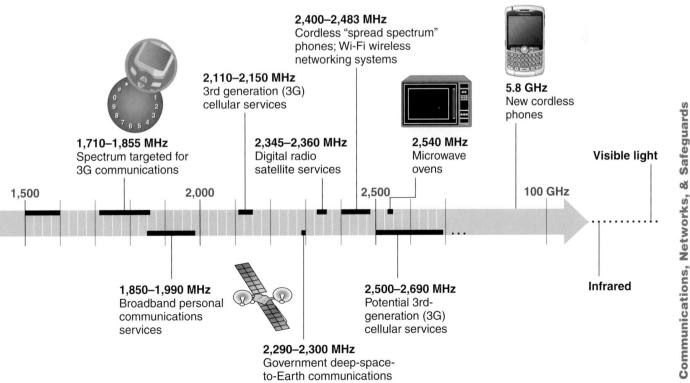

- **Narrowband:** _Narrowband,_ **also known as** _voiceband,_ **is used for regular telephone communications**—that is, for speech, faxes, and data. Transmission rates are usually 1.5 megabits per second or less. Dial-up modems use this bandwidth.

- **Broadband:** _Broadband_ **is used to transmit high-speed data and high-quality audio and video.** Transmission speeds are 1.5 megabits per second to (for super-broadband and ultra-broadband) 1 gigabit per second or more.

Currently, the average download speed in the United States is 4.9 megabits per second, compared with 63.6 megabits per second for Japan. That's why the United States ranks 15 out of 30 in broadband deployment, trailing such countries as South Korea and Japan, with their blinding megabit speeds.[16]

WAP: WIRELESS APPLICATION PROTOCOL Wireless handheld devices such as cellphones use the Wireless Application Protocol for connecting wireless users to the World Wide Web. Just as the protocol TCP/IP gives you a wired connection to your internet access provider, **the** _Wireless Application Protocol (WAP)_ **is designed to link nearly all mobile devices to your telecommunications carrier's wireless network and content providers.**

Five Types of Wireless Communications Media

What are the differences between the five types of wireless communications media?

The five types of wireless media are _infrared transmission, broadcast radio, cellular radio, microwave radio,_ and _communications satellite._

INFRARED TRANSMISSION _Infrared wireless transmission_ **sends data signals using infrared-light waves at a frequency too low (1–16 megabits per second) for human eyes to receive and interpret.** Infrared ports can be found on some laptop computers, PDAs, digital cameras, and printers, as well as wireless mice. TV remote-control units use infrared transmission. The drawbacks are that _line-of-sight_ communication is required—there must be an unobstructed view between transmitter and receiver—and transmission is confined to short range.

BROADCAST RADIO When you tune in to an AM or FM radio station, you are using **_broadcast radio,_ a wireless transmission medium that sends data over long distances at up to 2 megabits per second—between regions, states, or countries.** A transmitter is required to send messages and a receiver to receive them; sometimes both sending and receiving functions are combined in a _transceiver._

In the lower frequencies of the radio spectrum, several broadcast radio bands are reserved not only for conventional AM/FM radio but also for broadcast television, CB (citizens band) radio, ham (amateur) radio, cellphones, and private radio-band mobile services (such as police, fire,

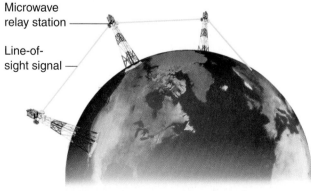

Microwave relay station —

Line-of-sight signal —

and taxi dispatch). Some organizations use specific radio frequencies and networks to support wireless communications. For example, UPC (Universal Product Code) bar-code readers are used by grocery-store clerks restocking store shelves to communicate with a main computer so that the store can control inventory levels. In addition, there are certain web-enabled devices that follow standards such as *Wi-Fi (wireless fidelity),* as we discuss in a few pages.

CELLULAR RADIO Actually a form of broadcast radio, ***cellular radio* is widely used for cellphones and wireless modems, using high-frequency radio waves to transmit voice and digital messages.** Unlike CB (citizens band) radio, used by truck drivers, which has a few radio channels that everyone must share, cellular radio channels are reused simultaneously in nearby geographic areas, yet customers do not interfere with each others' calls.[17]

We discuss cellphones in more detail starting on p. 336.

MICROWAVE RADIO *Microwave radio* **transmits voice and data at 45 megabits per second through the atmosphere as superhigh-frequency radio waves called** *microwaves,* **which vibrate at 2.4 gigahertz (2.4 billion hertz) per second or higher.** These frequencies are used not only to operate microwave ovens but also to transmit messages between ground-based stations and satellite communications systems. One short-range microwave standard used for communicating data is *Bluetooth,* as we shall discuss.

Nowadays horn-shaped microwave reflective dishes, which contain transceivers and antennas, are nearly everywhere—on towers, buildings, and hilltops. Why, you might wonder, do we have to interfere with nature by putting a microwave dish on top of a mountain? As with infrared waves, microwaves are line-of-sight; they cannot bend around corners or around the earth's curvature, so there must be an unobstructed view between transmitter and receiver. Thus, microwave stations need to be placed within 25–30 miles of each other, with no obstructions in between. The size of the dish varies with the distance (perhaps 2–4 feet in diameter for short distances, 10 feet or more for long distances). In a string of microwave relay stations, each station will receive incoming messages, boost the signal strength, and relay the signal to the next station.

More than half of today's telephone systems use dish microwave transmission. However, the airwaves are becoming so saturated with microwave signals that future needs will have to be satisfied by other channels, such as satellite systems.

COMMUNICATIONS SATELLITES To avoid some of the limitations of microwave earth stations, communications companies have added microwave "sky stations"— communications satellites. ***Communications satellites* are microwave relay stations in orbit around the earth.** Transmitting a signal from a ground station to a satellite is called *uplinking;* the reverse is called *downlinking.* The delivery process will be slowed if, as is often the case, more than one satellite is required to get the message delivered. Satellites cost from $300 million to $700 million each. A satellite launch costs between $50 million and

Microwave towers on buildings in Shanghai

Communications satellites

Satellite launch in India

GEO

Orbit:
22,300 miles
at the equator

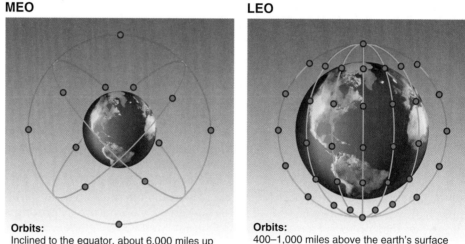

MEO

Orbits:
Inclined to the equator, about 6,000 miles up

LEO

Orbits:
400–1,000 miles above the earth's surface

$400 million. Communications satellites are the basis for the *Global Positioning System (GPS)*, as we shall discuss.

Satellite systems may occupy one of three zones in space: *GEO, MEO,* and *LEO.*

- **GEO:** The highest level, known as *geostationary earth orbit (GEO)*, is 22,300 miles and up and is always directly above the equator. Because the satellites in this orbit travel at the same speed as the earth, they appear to an observer on the ground to be stationary in space—that is, they are geostationary. Consequently, microwave earth stations are always able to beam signals to a fixed location above. The orbiting satellite has solar-powered transceivers to receive the signals, amplify them, and retransmit them to another earth station. At this high orbit, fewer satellites are required for global coverage; however, their quarter-second delay makes two-way conversations difficult.

- **MEO:** The *medium-earth orbit (MEO)* is 5,000–10,000 miles up. It requires more satellites for global coverage than does GEO.

- **LEO:** The *low-earth orbit (LEO)* is 200–1,000 miles up and has no signal delay. LEO satellites may be smaller and are much cheaper to launch.

Long-Distance Wireless: One-Way Communication

How do the Global Positioning System and one-way pager systems work?

Mobile wireless communications have been around for some time. The Detroit Police Department started using two-way car radios in 1921. Mobile telephones were introduced in 1946. Today, however, we are in the midst of an explosion in mobile wireless use that is making worldwide changes.

There are essentially two ways to move information through the air long distance on radio frequencies—one way and two way. *One-way communications*, discussed below, is typified by the satellite navigation system known as the Global Positioning System and by some pagers. *Two-way communications*, described on page 335, is exemplified by cellphones.

THE GLOBAL POSITIONING SYSTEM Doreen Rosimos of Marlborough, New Hampshire, who heads a firm that funds microenterprises, sometimes brings along her Rottweiler, Zelda, when she takes business trips. One day in Kentucky when Zelda became sick, Rosimos quickly typed "veterinarian" in her car's global positioning device and found one nearby within minutes.[18]

A $10 billion infrastructure developed by the military, the ___Global Positioning System (GPS)___ **consists of 24–32 MEO earth-orbiting satellites continuously transmitting timed radio signals that can be used to identify earth locations.**

This blind woman is using a GPS unit with a Braille keyboard and voice output to find her way around a park.

- **How GPS works:** The U.S. military developed and implemented this satellite network in the 1970s as a military navigation system, but on May 1, 2000, the federal government opened it up to everyone else. Each of these 3,000- to 4,000-pound, solar-powered satellites circles the earth twice a day at an altitude of 11,000 nautical miles. A GPS receiver—handheld or mounted in a vehicle, plane, or boat—can pick up transmissions from any four satellites, interpret the information from each, and pinpoint the receiver's longitude, latitude, and altitude. (● *See Panel 6.11 on the next page.*) The system is accurate within 3–50 feet, with 10 feet being the norm. About half of the mobile phones in the United States have GPS.[19]

- **The uses of GPS:** Besides being the technology behind car onboard navigation systems, the GPS is used for such activities as tracking trucks, buses, and taxis; locating stolen cars; orienting hikers; and aiding in surveying. An aerial camera connected to a GPS receiver can automatically tag photos with GPS coordinates, showing where the photograph was taken, which can be useful to surveyors, forestry managers, search-and-rescue teams, and archaeologists. GPS has been used by scientists to keep a satellite watch over a Hawaiian volcano, Mauna Loa, and to capture infinitesimal movements that may be used to predict eruptions. In one technology, cellular carriers have E911 (for "Enhanced 911") capability that is able to locate, through tiny GPS receivers embedded in users' digital cellphones, the position of every person making an emergency 911 call.[20]

The RoamEO Location System is designed for pet owners to quickly and accurately locate their pets by using GPS technology. Up to three dogs can each wear a GPS-equipped collar; the collars are tracked by the dog walker's handheld GPS unit.

Many cars come with GPS units to guide users to their destinations.

The ABCs of GPS

Developed by the U.S. military to aid ship and plane navigation, the Global Positioning System has evolved to serve a variety of purposes, with GPS receivers in everything from cars to handheld devices. The system has three main components—a satellite constellation, ground control, and receivers.

Space
There are about 24–32 satellites orbiting the Earth at an altitude of 11,000 nautical miles. Each is equipped with an atomic clock that keeps time to three-billionths of a second. The satellites send time-stamped radio signals to Earth at the speed of light. The signals include information about each satellite's exact position.

Ground control
Five stations around the world monitor the satellites and send them information about their orbital position. The main control center is in Colorado Springs, Colorado.

The receiver
The receiver must pick up signals from at least four satellites. It calculates its distance from each satellite by comparing the time stamp of the signal to the time it reached the receiver. The receiver's clock isn't nearly as accurate as the atomic clocks in the satellites, but mathematical adjustments are made to account for inaccuracies.

Connect four
The basic premise of GPS is a concept called triangulation. Using this concept, the exact location of a golf ball on a two-dimensional course can be calculated by determining its distance from three pins.

The distance from pin 1 reveals possible locations anywhere along the edge of an imaginary circle.

The distances from pins 1 and 2 reveal two possible ball locations—the point where the circles intersect.

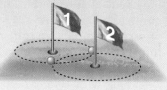

The distances from pins 1, 2, and 3 reveal one possible location—the point where all three circles intersect.

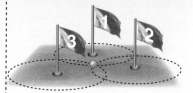

Triangulation works the same way in three-dimensional space, but with spheres instead of circles and a fourth reference point is needed.

panel 6.11

GPS
The Global Positioning System uses 24 satellites, developed for military use, to pinpoint a location on the earth's surface.

● **"Geocaching"** hobbyists practice an activity in which they hide a metal or plastic receptacle (a cache) filled with pens, pins, pliers, and other inexpensive trinkets; give the location a funny name ("Indiana Jones Fortress of Doom"); and post the GPS coordinates on the official geocachers' website *(www. geocaching.com)*. Cache hunters then punch the coordinates into their handheld GPS units ($90–$700 at sporting-goods and electronics stores) and follow electronic prompts to the site, where they sign a log and replace some trinkets with gewgaws of their own.

- **The limitations of GPS:** Not all services based on GPS technology are reliable, as any frequent user of online mapping systems (such as those of MapQuest, MSN Maps and Directions, Google Earth, and Yahoo Maps) knows by now. Indeed, about 1 in 50 computer-generated directions is a dud, according to Doug Richardson, executive director of the Association of American Geographers, mostly because of inaccurate road information. "You have to have the latest data about road characteristics—things like one-way streets, turns, and exits in order for it to generate accurate directions," he says.[21]

Brian Sniatkowski holds a GPS unit in the Kekeout Reservoir Forest while geo-caching, engaging in a high-tech treasure hunt for GPS users. Participants set up caches all over the world and share the locations via the internet. GPS users can then use the location coordinates to find the caches. Each cache may provide the finder with a variety of rewards; each finder is asked to put something new in the cache.

Emergency operators answering E911 cellphone calls have also often found some unsettling results, in which the information giving the caller's location either didn't appear or was inaccurate. The Federal Communications Commission has ordered that wireless carriers must meet standards of accuracy for 95% of E911 systems by September 2012.[22]

PAGERS Known as *beepers,* for the sound they make when activated, **_pagers_ are simple radio receivers that receive data sent from a special radio transmitter.** The radio transmitter broadcasting to the pager sends signals over a specific frequency. All of the pagers for that particular network have a built-in receiver that is tuned to the same frequency broadcast from the transmitter. The pagers listen to the signal from the transmitter constantly as long as the pager is turned on.

Although generally obsolete, pagers are still used in areas where cellphones are unreliable or prohibited, such as large hospital complexes. They are also used to reach some emergency personnel and to control traffic signals and some irrigation systems.

Pager

Long-Distance Wireless: Two-Way Communication

How do I distinguish among five types of long-distance wireless technologies?

Residential home phone users have been doing "cord cutting" to the point where in the United States in 2009 about 20% of homes had only cellphones compared with 17% with landlines but no cellphones.[23] About a third of people ages 18–24 live in households with only cellphones. Worldwide, in 2008 there were more than three times as many mobile phone subscriptions as fixed telephone lines—4.1 billion versus 1.1 billion.[24]

Two-way wireless communications devices have evolved over time from two-way pagers and wireless email devices such as the original BlackBerry, which has become an all-in-one wireless data and voice device, so popular among users that it has earned the nickname "CrackBerry."[25] The categories

BlackBerry

of long-distance wireless devices we will discuss use the transmission medium known as cellular radio, which has several levels: 1G, 2G, 3G, and 4G.

IG (FIRST-GENERATION) CELLULAR SERVICE: ANALOG CELLPHONES "In the fall of 1985," wrote *USA Today* technology reporter Kevin Maney, "I went to Los Angeles to research a story about a new phenomenon called a cellphone. I got to use one for a day. The phones then cost $1,000 and looked like field radios from *M*A*S*H*. Calls were 45 cents a minute, and total cellphone users in the world totaled 200,000."[26] By 2013, it is estimated, there will be 6.5 billion cellphones in use worldwide.[27]

Inside a cellphone

Cellphones are essentially two-way radios that operate using either analog or digital signals. ***Analog cellphones* are designed primarily for communicating by voice through a system of ground-area cells. Each cell is hexagonal in shape, usually 8 miles or less in diameter, and is served by a transmitter-receiving tower.** Communications are handled in the bandwidth of 824–894 megahertz. Calls are directed between cells by a mobile-telephone switching office (MTSO). Movement between cells requires that calls be "handed off" by this switching office. (• *See Panel 6.12.*) This technology is known as *1G,* for "first generation."

panel 6.12

Cellular connections

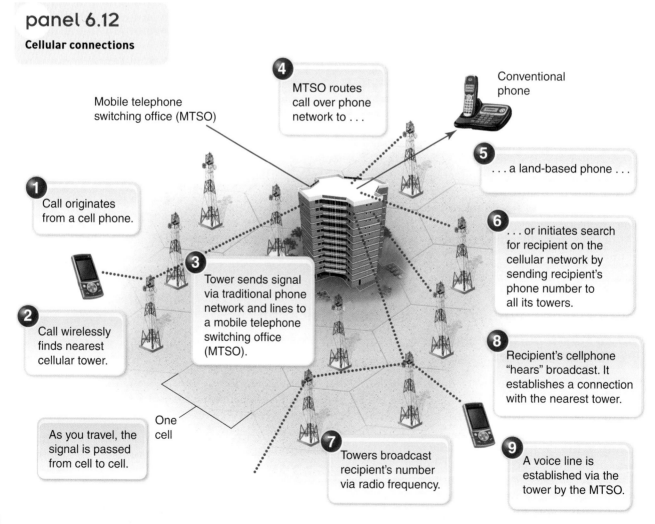

Mobile telephone switching office (MTSO)

4 MTSO routes call over phone network to . . .

Conventional phone

1 Call originates from a cell phone.

5 . . . a land-based phone . . .

2 Call wirelessly finds nearest cellular tower.

3 Tower sends signal via traditional phone network and lines to a mobile telephone switching office (MTSO).

6 . . . or initiates search for recipient on the cellular network by sending recipient's phone number to all its towers.

8 Recipient's cellphone "hears" broadcast. It establishes a connection with the nearest tower.

One cell

As you travel, the signal is passed from cell to cell.

7 Towers broadcast recipient's number via radio frequency.

9 A voice line is established via the tower by the MTSO.

Handing off voice calls between cells poses only minimal problems. However, handing off data transmission (where every bit counts), with the inevitable gaps and pauses on moving from one cell to another, is much more difficult.

2G (SECOND-GENERATION) WIRELESS SERVICES: DIGITAL CELLPHONES & PDAs *Digital wireless services*—**which support digital cellphones and personal digital assistants—use a network of cell towers to send voice communications and data over the airwaves in digital form.** Known as *2G,* for "second-generation," technology, digital cellphones began replacing analog cellphones during the 1990s as telecommunications companies added digital transceivers to their cell towers. *2G (second-generation)* technology was the first digital voice cellular network; data communication was added as an afterthought, with data speeds ranging from 9.6 to 19.2 kilobits per second. 2G technology not only dramatically increased voice clarity; it also allowed the telecommunications companies to cram many more voice calls into the same slice of bandwidth.

3G (THIRD-GENERATION) WIRELESS DIGITAL SERVICES 3G cellphones look more like PDAs. *3G (third-generation) wireless digital services,* often called *broadband technology,* are based on the U.S. GSM standard and support devices that are "always on," carry data at high speeds (144 kilobits per second up to 2.4 megabits per second), accept emails with attachments, provide internet and web access, are able to display color video and still pictures, and play music.

There are several 3G standards. (● *See Panel 6.13.*)

4G (FOURTH-GENERATION) WIRELESS DIGITAL SERVICES: WIMAX The latest standard, 4G (fourth-generation) wireless services, uses the standard known as WiMax (for Worldwide Interoperability for Microwave Access), a wireless standard capable of transmitting at a typical range of 6–10 miles at up to 20 megabits per second. (Wi-Fi, the popular short-range standard, is similar to WiMax but doesn't transmit as far.) There are two varieties of WiMax, one fixed and one mobile.

Sprint Nextel Corp. launched the first WiMax 4G network in Baltimore in October 2008.[28] Atlanta, Charlotte, Chicago, Dallas, Ft. Worth, Honolulu, Las Vegas, Philadelphia, Portland, and Seattle were scheduled to have Spring 4G rollouts by the end of 2009, and residents of Boston, Houston, New York, San Francisco, and Washington, DC were supposed to receive the service in 2010.[29]

Short-Range Wireless: Two-Way Communication

How do I distinguish among the three types of short-range wireless technologies?

We have discussed the standards for high-powered wireless digital communications in the 800–1,900 megahertz part of the radio-frequency spectrum, which are considered long-range waves. Now let us consider low-powered wireless communications in the 2.4–7.5 gigahertz part of the radio spectrum, which are short-range and effective only within several feet of a wireless

Standard	Speed in Kbps
GSM (Global System for Mobile Communication)	About 9.6
UMTS (Universal Mobile Telecommunications System)	220–320
GPRS (General Packet Radio Service)	30–50
CDMA (Code Division Multiple Access)	About 14.4
EDGE (Enhanced Data for Global Evolution)	Up to 236
EVDO (Evolution Data Optimized)	400–700

panel 6.13

3G standards

access point—generally between 30 and 250 feet. This band is available globally for unlicensed, low-power uses and is set aside as an innovation zone where new devices can be tested without the need for a government license; it's also used for industrial, scientific, and medical devices.

There are three kinds of networks covered by this range:

- **Local area networks—range 100–228 feet:** These include the popular Wi-Fi standards.

- **Personal area networks—range 30–32 feet:** These use Bluetooth, ultra wideband, and wireless USB.

- **Home automation networks—range 100–150 feet:** These use the Insteon, ZigBee, and Z-Wave standards.

SHORT-RANGE WIRELESS FOR LOCAL AREA NETWORKS: WI-FI B, A, G, & N Wi-Fi is known formally as an *802.11 network,* named for the wireless technical standard specified by the Institute of Electrical and Electronics Engineers (IEEE). As we mentioned in Chapter 2, *Wi-Fi*—short for *"wireless fidelity"*—is a short-range wireless digital standard aimed at helping portable computers and handheld wireless devices to communicate at high speeds and share internet connections at distances of 100–228 feet. You can find Wi-Fi connections, which operate at 2.4–5 gigahertz, inside offices, airports, and internet cafés, and some enthusiasts have set up transmitters on rooftops, distributing wireless connections throughout their neighborhoods. (● *See Panel 6.14.)*

Wi-Fi camera

Wi-Fi

A land-based internet connection (DSL, cable modem, TI line, etc.) . . .

. . . is connected to an antenna, also known as an *access point.* The access point translates the internet signal into radio waves and broadcasts them over an area about the size of a house.

Cable

Access point

Anyone within range who has a receiving antenna, usually attached to a notebook computer, can pick up the signal.

Notebook computer

Receiving antenna

panel 6.14
Wi-Fi

There are four varieties of Wi-Fi standards—Wi-Fi a, Wi-Fi b, Wi-Fi g, and Wi-Fi n:

- **Wi-Fi b, a, and g:** Named for variations on the IEEE 802.11 standard (802.11b, 802.11a, 802.11g), these all typically transmit at data rates ranging from 11 megabits per second up to about 126 feet indoors (for Wi-Fi b, the older and slower version) to 54 megabits per second up to 120 feet (for Wi-Fi a and g).

- **Wi-Fi n with MIMO:** Wi-Fi n—when used with a technology called *MIMO* (pronounced "my-moh" and short for "multiple input multiple output"), which extends the range of Wi-Fi by using multiple transmitting and receiving antennas (instead of the one transmit and two receive antennas typical for most Wi-Fi)—is able to transmit at 108–320 megabits per second up to about 228 feet.

Increasingly, people are installing Wi-Fi networks in their homes, going online through wireless hot spots at Starbucks and other establishments, or bringing a device called a MiFi on their travels, a 2-ounce, credit-card-size gadget that acts as a private Wi-Fi network. [30] Some airlines also offer Wi-Fi connections on certain planes and routes.[31] Whatever the means of connection, it's extremely important to make sure the Wi-Fi connection is secure against cyberspying. "If you're using a mobile connection, you may not even be aware that you're connected to an unverified access point because the connection can be made without your knowledge," says one writer. "Disable your Wi-Fi software, instead of leaving it on to autoconnect, whenever you're not using it. This will keep you from unknowingly connecting to a fraudulent network and wasting your laptop's battery."[32] We give some more security tips in another few pages.

SHORT-RANGE WIRELESS FOR PERSONAL AREA NETWORKS: BLUETOOTH, ULTRA WIDEBAND, & WIRELESS USB As we stated, personal area networks (PANs) use short-range wireless technology to connect personal electronics, such as cellphones, PDAs, MP3 players, and printers in a range of 30–32 (sometimes up to 320) feet. The principal wireless technology used so far has been Bluetooth, which is now being joined by ultra wideband (UWB) and wireless USB.

- **Bluetooth:** **_Bluetooth_ is a short-range wireless digital standard aimed at linking cellphones, PDAs, computers, and peripherals up to distances of about 30 feet.** (The name comes from Harald Bluetooth, the 10th-century Danish king who unified Denmark and Norway.) Now transmitting up to 3 megabits per second, the original version of Bluetooth was designed to replace cables connecting PCs to printers and PDAs or wireless phones and to overcome line-of-sight problems with infrared transmission. When Bluetooth-capable devices come within range of one another, an automatic electronic "conversation" takes place to determine whether they have data to share, and then they form a mini-network to exchange that data. (• *See Panel 6.15, next page.*) Bluetooth 2.1 has a data rate of about 3 megabits per second, faster than the original Bluetooth, although not as high-speed as Wi-Fi g or n. This version also has lower battery consumption than the older version. *Bluetooth 3.0 + HS*, released in April 2009, has a data rate of around 24 megabits per second, considerably faster and useful in transferring large amounts of data.

  Bluetooth technology is found in many Palm PDAs, Pocket PCs, and some cellphones.

- **Ultra wideband (UWB):** Developed for use in military radar systems, **_ultra wideband (UWB)_ is a promising technology operating in the range of 480 megabits per second up to about 30 feet that uses a low-power**

info!

Lastest Bluetooth Devices

What are the newest Bluetooth devices? See:

www.bluetooth.com

Bluetooth symbol on a notebook computer

Communications, Networks, & Safeguards

339

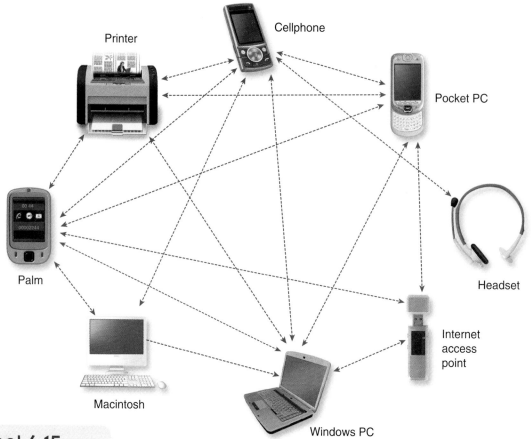

Printer

Cellphone

Pocket PC

Palm

Headset

Macintosh

Internet access point

Windows PC

panel 6.15

Bluetooth
Bluetooth allows two devices to interact wirelessly in sometimes novel ways. A Bluetooth-equipped notebook, for example, can connect through a similarly enabled cellphone or internet access point to send and receive email. In addition to the links shown, Bluetooth can be used to network similar devices—for example, to send data from PC to PC, as long as they are up to 33–320 feet apart. Line of sight is not required.

Meshing

The following websites provide more information about these mesh technologies:

www.insteon.net
www.zigbee.org
www.z-wavealliance.com.

source to send out millions of bursts of radio energy every second over many different frequencies, which are then reassembled by a UWB receiver. It operates over low frequencies not used by other technologies, making it a candidate to replace many of the cables that now currently connect household and office devices. UWB systems tend to be short-range and indoor applications. High-data-rate UWB can enable wireless monitors, the efficient transfer of data from digital camcorders, wireless printing of digital pictures from a camera without the need for an intervening personal computer, and the transfer of files among cellphones and other handheld devices such as personal digital audio and video players.

Although UWB is 100 times as fast as Bluetooth and should be a natural successor to Wi-Fi, unfortunately the industry committee that is supposed to be setting specifications for it has been deadlocked between two technical approaches and has failed to agree on a standard. Thus, some predict that UWB is effectively dead in consumer and computer markets.[33]

- **Wireless USB:** _Wireless USB (WUSB)_ **has a typical range of 32 feet and a maximum data rate of 480 megabits per second.** Wireless USB is used in game controllers, printers, scanners, digital cameras, MP3 players, hard disks, and flash drives.

SHORT-RANGE WIRELESS FOR HOME AUTOMATION NETWORKS: INSTEON, ZIGBEE, & Z-WAVE Home automation networks—those that link switches and sensors around the house and yard—use low-power, narrowband wireless technology, which operate in a range of 100–150 feet but at relatively slow data rates of 13.1–250 kilobits per second. The current standards are Insteon, ZigBee, and Z-Wave. All three are so-called *mesh technologies*—networked devices equipped with two-way radios that can communicate with each other rather than just with the controller, the device that serves as central command for the network.

- **Insteon:** *Insteon* combines electric power line and wireless technologies and is capable of sending data at 13.1 kilobits a second at a typical range of 150 feet. With this kind of technology, you might drive up to your house, and the garage door device would recognize your car and open to let you in. The lights would come on and your favorite radio station would start playing.

- **ZigBee:** *ZigBee* is an entirely wireless, very power-efficient technology that can send data at 128 kilobytes per second at a range of about 250 feet. It is primarily touted as sensor network technology and can be used in everything from automatic meter readers and medical sensing and monitoring devices to wireless smoke detectors and TV remote controls. One of the best features is that it can run for years on inexpensive batteries, eliminating the need to be plugged into an electric power line.

- **Z-Wave:** *Z-Wave* is also an entirely wireless, power-efficient technology, which can send data at 127 kilobits per second to a range of 100 feet. With a Z-Wave home, you could program the lights to go on when the garage door opens. You could program devices remotely, turning the thermostat up on the drive home from work.

Curious about Networked Homes?

For starters, try:

www.sciencedaily.com/ releases/2007/12/ 071221215021.htm

www.technewsworld.com/ story/Home-Automation-The-Unfulfilled-Promise-66973.html?wlc=1250196188

6.5 CYBERTHREATS, HACKERS, & SAFEGUARDS

SECURITY

What are areas I should be concerned about for keeping my computer system secure?

San Francisco internet executive Lew Tucker found his desktop computer so compromised by internet-borne infections that he was spending time every week dealing with them. Rather than get rid of the offending programs, however, he took a radical step: He threw out the whole computer. "I was losing the battle," he says. "It was cheaper and faster to go to the store and buy a low-end PC."[34]

Is throwing your virus-overrun computer in the dumpster a rational response? Many would disagree. However, there's no question that the ongoing dilemma of the Digital Age is balancing convenience against security. *Security* is a system of safeguards for protecting information technology against unauthorized access and systems failures that can result in damage or loss. Security matters are a never-ending problem, with attacks on computers and data becoming more powerful and more complex.[35]

We consider the following aspects of security as it relates to telecommunications:

- **Cyber threats:** denial-of-service attacks, worms, viruses, and Trojan horses

- **Perpetrators of cyber mischief:** hackers and crackers

- **Computer safety:** antivirus software, firewalls, passwords, biometric authentication, and encryption

Cyber Threats: Denial-of-Service Attacks, Worms, Viruses, & Trojan Horses

What are denial-of-service attacks, worms, viruses, and Trojan horses?

Internet users, especially home users, are not nearly as safe as they believe, according to a study by McAfee and the nonprofit National Cyber Security Alliance.[36] Consumers suffer from complacency and a lack of expert advice on keeping their computer systems secure. The study found that 92% of 378 adults believed that they were safe from viruses; however, only 51% had up-to-date virus software. And 73% thought they had a firewall installed, but only 64% actually had it enabled. Little more than half had anti-spyware protection, and only about 12% had phishing protection. As we will explain, these kinds of protections are musts in guarding against important cyber threats such as denial-of-service attacks, worms, viruses, and Trojan horses and other kinds of "malware."

DENIAL-OF-SERVICE ATTACKS A ***denial-of-service (DoS) attack*, or *distributed denial-of-service (DDoS) attack*, consists of making repeated requests of a computer system or network, thereby overloading it and denying legitimate users access to it.** Because computers are limited in the number of user requests they can handle at any given time, a DoS onslaught will tie them up with fraudulent requests that cause them to shut down. The assault may come from a single computer or from hundreds or thousands of computers that have been taken over by those intending harm.

WORMS Worms, viruses, and Trojan horses are three forms of *malware,* or malicious software, that attack computer systems. The latest Symantec Internet Security Threat Report identified over 1.6 million instances of "malicious code" (worms and viruses) in 2008, a 165% increase over 2007.[37]

A *worm* is a program that copies itself repeatedly into a computer's memory or onto a disk drive. Sometimes it will copy itself so often it will cause a computer to crash. Among some famous worms are Code Red, Nimda, Klez, Sasser, Bagle, Blaster, Sobig, and Melissa. The 2002 worm Klez, dubbed the most common worm ever, spread its damage through Microsoft products by being inside email attachments or part of email messages themselves, so that merely opening an infected message could infect a computer running Outlook or Outlook Express. (● *See Panel 6.16.*) The Sasser worm was estimated to account for 26% of all virus infections in the first half of 2004. Incredibly, one person, Sven Jaschan, 18, who admitted programming the Sasser and other worms and who was arrested in Germany in May 2004, was responsible for 70% of the virus infections in the early part of that year.[38]

In 2008–2009, a worm known as Conficker or Downadup, spread through a Microsoft Windows vulnerability that allowed guessing of network passwords and by people hand-carrying such gadgets as USB keys, infected millions of computers. The Conficker authors cleverly updated the worm through several versions, playing a cat-and-mouse game that kept them one step ahead of security experts. Some researchers feared that Conficker could be turned into a powerful offensive weapon that could disrupt the internet itself. April 1,

panel 6.16

How one worm works
This is the Klez worm, but others work in similar ways. If you don't recognize the sender of an email message and you don't open the message, but instead just immediately delete it, your PC will not be infected.

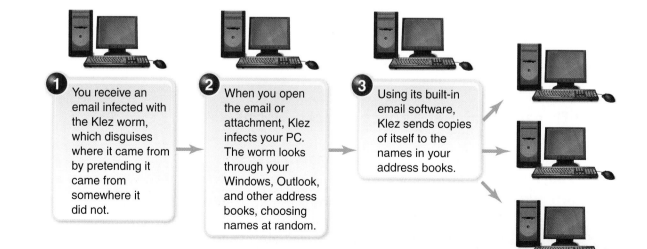

1. You receive an email infected with the Klez worm, which disguises where it came from by pretending it came from somewhere it did not.

2. When you open the email or attachment, Klez infects your PC. The worm looks through your Windows, Outlook, and other address books, choosing names at random.

3. Using its built-in email software, Klez sends copies of itself to the names in your address books.

- **Boot-sector virus:** The boot sector is that part of the system software containing most of the instructions for booting, or powering up, the system. The boot-sector virus replaces these boot instructions with some of its own. Once the system is turned on, the virus is loaded into main memory before the operating system. From there it is in a position to infect other files. Any diskette that is used in the drive of the computer then becomes infected. When that diskette is moved to another computer, the contagion continues. Examples of boot-sector viruses: AntCMOS, AntiEXE, Form.A, NYB (New York Boot), Ripper, Stoned.Empire.Monkey.

- **File virus:** File viruses attach themselves to executable files—those that actually begin a program. (In DOS these files have the extensions .com and .exe.) When the program is run, the virus starts working, trying to get into main memory and infecting other files.

- **Multipartite virus:** A hybrid of the file and boot-sector types, the multipartite virus infects both files and boot sectors, which makes it better at spreading and more difficult to detect. Examples of multipartite viruses are Junkie and Parity Boot.

  A type of multipartite virus is the *polymorphic virus,* which can mutate and change form just as human viruses can. Such viruses are especially troublesome because they can change their profile, making existing antiviral technology ineffective.

  A particularly sneaky multipartite virus is the *stealth virus,* which can temporarily remove itself from memory to elude capture. An example of a multipartite, polymorphic stealth virus is One Half.

- **Macro virus:** Macro viruses take advantage of a procedure in which miniature programs, known as macros, are embedded inside common data files, such as those created by email or spreadsheets, which are sent over computer networks. Until recently, such documents have typically been ignored by antivirus software. Examples of macro viruses are Concept, which attaches to Word documents and email attachments, and Laroux, which attaches to Excel spreadsheet files. Fortunately, the latest versions of Word and Excel come with built-in macro virus protection.

- **Logic bomb:** Logic bombs, or simply bombs, differ from other viruses in that they are set to go off at a certain date and time. A disgruntled programmer for a defense contractor created a bomb in a program that was supposed to go off two months after he left. Designed to erase an inventory tracking system, the bomb was discovered only by chance.

- **Trojan horse:** The Trojan horse covertly places illegal, destructive instructions in the middle of a legitimate program, such as a computer game. Once you run the program, the Trojan horse goes to work, doing its damage while you are blissfully unaware. An example of a Trojan horse is FormatC.

- **Email hoax:** These are really not virus programs; they are email messages sent by usually well-meaning people to warn others about a new virus they have read or heard of. These false warning messages often say "be sure to send this to everyone you know." Hoax virus warnings can cause huge amounts of internet traffic and unnecessary worry. Users should check with knowledgeable sources before forwarding such messages.

2009, was supposed to be the day the worm would launch a massive cyber attack, but the day came and went without incident.[39]

VIRUSES A *virus* is a "deviant" program, stored on a computer floppy disk, hard drive, or CD, that can cause unexpected and often undesirable effects, such as destroying or corrupting data. (● *See Panel 6.17.*) The famous email Love Bug (its subject line was I LOVE YOU), which originated in the Philippines in May 2000 and did perhaps as much as $10 billion in damage worldwide, was both a worm and a virus, spreading faster and causing more damage than any other bug before it. The Love Bug was followed almost immediately by a variant virus. This new Love Bug didn't reveal itself with an I LOVE YOU line but changed to a random word or words each time a new computer was infected. More recent viruses have targeted Twitter, YouTube, website advertising, and digital photo-holding frames.[40] A virus called Koobface attacked Facebook.[41] Fast-spreading Clampi took aim at business financial accounts.[42] A fired computer programmer embedded a malicious virus in servers run by financial institution Fannie Mae.[43]

The virus usually attaches itself to your hard disk. It might then display annoying messages ("Your PC is stoned—legalize marijuana") or cause Ping-Pong balls to bounce around your screen and knock away text. More seriously, it might add garbage to your files and then erase or destroy your system

panel 6.17

Types of worms and viruses

Free Online Virus & Security Check

Go to Symantec.com at:

http://security.symantec.com/ sscv6/home.asp?langid=ie& venid=sym&plfid=23&pkj=IH QYJABOKQYWTFVRHRM

and run the check. What are your results? What do you plan to do next?

software. It may evade your detection and spread its havoc elsewhere, infecting every floppy disk, CD/DVD, and even digital-camera flash memory used by the system.

TROJAN HORSES If, as a citizen of Troy around 1200–1500 B.C.E., you looked outside your fortified city and saw that the besieging army of Greeks was gone but a large wooden horse was left standing on the battlefield, what would you think? Maybe you would decide it was a gift of the gods, as the Trojans did, and haul it inside the city gates—and be unpleasantly surprised when late at night several Greek soldiers climbed out of the horse and opened the gates for the invading army. This is the meaning behind the illegal program known as a Trojan horse, which, though not technically a virus, can act like one.

A _Trojan horse_ is a program that pretends to be a useful program, usually free, such as a game or screen saver, but carries viruses, or destructive instructions, that perpetrate mischief without your knowledge. One particularly malicious feature is that a Trojan horse may allow so-called backdoor programs to be installed. A _backdoor program_ is an illegal program that allows illegitimate users to take control of your computer without your knowledge. An example is the kind of program that records what people type, logging individual keystrokes, paying particular attention to user names and passwords, which can be used to access and even open bank accounts online.

HOW MALWARE IS SPREAD Worms, viruses, and Trojan horses are passed in the following ways:

- **By infected floppies or CDs:** The first way is via an infected floppy disk or CD, perhaps from a friend or a repair person.

- **By opening unknown email attachments:** The second way is from an email attachment. This is why a basic rule of using the internet is: _Never_ click on an email attachment that comes from someone you don't know. This advice also applies to unknown downloaded files, as for free video games or screen savers.

- **By clicking on infiltrated websites:** Some crackers "seed" web pages with contagious malware that enables them to steal personal data, so that by simply clicking on a website you can unwittingly compromise your PC. The risk can be minimized if you have a firewall and keep antivirus software on your computer up to date, as we describe below. (You might also consider switching to Mozilla Firefox from Internet Explorer as your browser.)

- **Through infiltrated Wi-Fi hot spots:** As mentioned earlier, if you're a user of Wi-Fi wireless access points, or hot spots, you have to be aware that your laptop or PDA could be exposed to wireless transmitted diseases from illegal users. Many hot spots do not require passwords; which means that anyone with a wireless connection and hacking know-how can hop aboard the network. Here, too, having wireless firewalls can reduce risks.

CELLPHONE MALWARE A recent concern is that worms and viruses have been found to attack cellphones. A cellphone virus is basically the same thing as a computer virus: an unwanted executable file that "infects" a device and then copies itself to other devices. But whereas a computer virus or worm spreads through email attachments and internet downloads, a cellphone virus or worm spreads via internet downloads, MMS (multimedia messaging service) attachments, and Bluetooth transfers. The most common type of cellphone infection right now occurs when a cellphone downloads an infected file from a PC or the internet, but phone-to-phone viruses are on the rise. Infected files usually show up disguised as applications such as games, security patches, add-on functionalities, and, of course, erotica and free stuff. Here are some steps you can take to decrease your chances of installing a virus:

PRACTICAL ACTION
Ways to Minimize Virus Attacks

Some tips for minimizing the chances of infecting your computer are as follows:

- Don't open, download, or execute any files, email messages, or email attachments if the source is unknown or if the subject line of an email is questionable or unexpected.

- Delete all spam and email messages from strangers. Don't open, forward, or reply to such messages.

- Use webmail (HTML email) sparingly, since viruses can hide in the HTML coding of the email. Even the simple act of previewing the message in your email program can activate the virus and infect your computer.

- Don't start your computer with a floppy disk in the floppy-disk drive (drive A).

- Back up your data files regularly, and keep the backup CD or whatever in a location separate from your computer (or use an online backup service). Then if a virus (or a fire) destroys your work files, your data won't be totally devastated.

- Make sure you have virus protection software, such as McAfee VirusScan *(www.mcafee.com)* or Norton AntiVirus *(www.symantec.com/nav)* activated on your machine. You can download it from these companies; then follow the installation instructions.

- Buying a new computer with antivirus software on it does not mean you are automatically protected. The software could be six months old and not cover new viruses. You have to register it with the designer company, and you need to receive antivirus updates.

- Scan your entire system with antivirus software the first time it's installed; then scan it regularly after that. Often the software can be set to scan each time the computer is rebooted or on a periodic schedule. Also scan any new CDs and the like before using them.

- Update your antivirus software regularly. There are virus and security alerts almost every day. Most antivirus software is automatically linked to the internet and will add updated antivirus code to your system whenever the software vendor discovers a new threat.

- If you discover you have a virus, you can ask McAfee or Norton to scan your computer online. Then follow the company's directions for cleaning or deleting it.

Cellphone viruses currently target Symbian Series 60 phones with Bluetooth and MMS capabilities, like the Nokia 6620. Future possibilities include viruses that bug phones—so someone can see every number you call and listen to your conversations—and viruses that steal financial information, which would be a serious issue if smartphones end up being used as common payment devices. Ultimately, more connectivity means more exposure to viruses and faster spreading of infection.

- **Turn off Bluetooth discoverable mode:** Set your phone to "hidden" so other phones can't detect it and send it the virus. You can do this on the Bluetooth options screen.

- **Check security updates to learn about filenames you should keep an eye out for.** It's not foolproof—the Commwarrior program generates random names for the infected files it sends out, so users can't be warned not to open specific filenames—but many viruses can be easily identified by the filenames they carry. Security sites with detailed virus information include F-Secure, McAfee, and Symantec. Some of these sites will send you email updates with new virus information as it gets posted.

- **Install some type of security software on your phone:** Numerous companies are developing security software for cellphones, some for free download, some for user purchase, and some intended for cellphone service providers.

Now let's consider the people who perpetrate cyber threats—hackers and crackers.

Some Cyber Villains: Hackers & Crackers
What are the various kinds of hackers and crackers?

The popular press uses the word *hacker* to refer to people who break into computer systems and steal or corrupt data, but this is not quite the exact definition. Perhaps it helps to distinguish between hackers and crackers, although the term *cracker* has never caught on with the general public.

HACKERS *Hackers* **are defined (1) as computer enthusiasts, people who enjoy learning programming languages and computer systems, but also (2) as people who gain unauthorized access to computers or networks, often just for the challenge of it.**
Considering the second kind of hacker, those who break into computers for relatively benign reasons, we can say there are probably two types:

- **Thrill-seeker hackers:** *Thrill-seeker hackers* are hackers who illegally access computer systems simply for the challenge of it. Although they penetrate computers and networks illegally, they don't do any damage or steal anything; their reward is the achievement of breaking in.

- **White-hat hackers:** *White-hat hackers* are usually computer professionals who break into computer systems and networks with the knowledge of their owners to expose security flaws that can then be fixed.[44] (The term "white hat" refers to the hero in old Western movies, who often wore a white hat, as opposed to the villain, who usually wore a black hat—see below.) Kevin Mitnik, for instance, became a tech security consultant after serving five years in prison for breaking into corporate computer systems in the mid-1990s.

CRACKERS As opposed to hackers, who do break-ins for more or less positive reasons, *crackers* **are malicious hackers, people who break into computers for malicious purposes**—to obtain information for financial gain, shut down hardware, pirate software, steal people's credit information, or alter or destroy data.
There seem to be four classes of crackers:

- **Script kiddies:** On the low end are *script kiddies,* mostly teenagers without much technical expertise who use downloadable software or source code to perform malicious break-ins. Script kiddies (or "script bunnies") use published source code to construct viruses. Although releasing the viruses themselves is illegal, publishing the code for viruses is not; it is allowed under the First Amendment right to free speech.

- **Hacktivists:** *Hacktivists* are "hacker activists," people who break into a computer system for a politically or socially motivated purpose. For example, they might leave a highly visible message on the home page of a website that expresses a point of view that they oppose.

- **Black-hat hackers:** *Black-hat hackers* are those who break into computer systems to steal or destroy information or to use it for illegal profit. They are usually not bored, crafty teenagers but often professional criminals, the people behind the increase in cyberattacks on corporate networks, the Russian cybercrooks, such as the one nicknamed A-Z, who target high bank balances online and pull off Web scams on a vast scale.[45] Recently, such hackers have gone after cellphones and Twitter.[46]

- **Cyberterrorists:** Cyberterrorism, according to the FBI, is any "premeditated, politically motivated attack against information, computer systems, computer programs, and data which results in violence against noncombatant targets by sub-national groups or clandestine agents."[47] Thus, *cyberterrorists* are politically motivated persons who attack computer systems so as to bring physical or financial harm to a lot of people or destroy a lot of information. Particular targets are power plants, water systems, traffic control centers, banks, and military installations. Cyberattacks on U.S. government computer networks climbed 40% in 2008.[48] Recently, U.S. and South Korean officials reported cyberwarfare on government and commercial websites, probably by China and/or North Korea.[49]

The most flagrant cases of cracking are met with federal prosecution. For instance, Jeffrey Lee Parson of Hopkins, Minnesota, was an 18-year-old high school senior when he unleashed a variant of the Blaster internet worm in 2003 that crippled an estimated 48,000 computers—a crime for which he could have been sentenced to 10 years in prison and fined $250,000. Because Parson was a minor at the time of the crime, however, a federal district court judge gave him 18 months in prison.[50]

Online Safety: Antivirus Software, Firewalls, Passwords, Biometric Authentication, & Encryption

What should I be doing to keep my computer safe against cyber threats?

Now let us consider a few things you can do to try to keep your computer system safe: antivirus software, firewalls, passwords, biometric authentication, and encryption.

ANTIVIRUS SOFTWARE A variety of virus-fighting programs are available. *Antivirus software* **scans a computer's hard disk, CDs, and main memory to detect viruses and, sometimes, to destroy them.** Such virus watchdogs operate in two ways. First, they scan disk drives for "signatures," characteristic strings of 1s and 0s in the virus that uniquely identify it. Second, they look for suspicious viruslike behavior, such as attempts to erase or change areas on your disks.

Examples of antivirus programs are McAfee VirusScan, Norton AntiVirus, Pc-cillin Internet Security, Avast!, and ZoneAlarm with Antivirus. Others worth considering are CA Internet Security Suite Plus, Panda Antivirus Platinum, and McAfee Virex for Macs.[51]

Other ways of protecting your computer against viruses are given in the Practical Action box on page 345.

FIREWALLS A *firewall* **is a system of hardware and/or software that protects a computer or a network from intruders.** The firewall software monitors all internet and other network activity, looking for suspicious data and preventing unauthorized access. Always-on internet connections such as cable modem, satellite, and DSL, as well as some wireless devices, are particularly susceptible to unauthorized intrusion.

- **If you have one computer—software firewall:** If you have just one computer, a software firewall is probably enough to protect you while you're connected to the internet. (Windows XP/Windows Vista and Mac OS X have built-in software firewalls that can be activated quickly.)

- **If you have more than one computer—hardware firewall:** If you have more than one computer and you are linked to the internet by a cable modem or DSL, you probably need a hardware firewall, such as a hub/router, which is available for as little as $50.

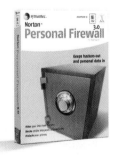

Firewall software

Survival Tip

Firewalls

Windows XP/Vista/7 and Mac OS X have built-in firewalls. Many companies sell their own firewall versions. If you buy separate firewall software, turn off the operating system's firewall.

PASSWORDS When New York's World Trade Center was destroyed during the September 11, 2001, terrorist attack, debt-trading firm Cantor Fitzgerald lost 700 of its 1,000 employees—and no one knew the deceased workers' *passwords,* the special words, codes, or symbols required to access a computer system. Although records had been backed up and existed in another location, to maintain its customers' confidence, the company realized it had to be back up and running within two days. That meant discovering the passwords needed to get into essential files. What was it to do? According to one account, what surviving employees did was this: "They sat around in a group and recalled everything they knew about their colleagues, everything they had done, everywhere they had been, and everything that had ever happened to them. *And they managed to guess the passwords.*[52]

As this story shows, protecting your internet access accounts and files with a password isn't enough. Passwords (and PINs, too) can be guessed, forgotten, or stolen. To foil a stranger's guesses, experts say, you should never choose a real word or variations of your name, your birth date, or those of your friends or family. Instead you should mix letters, numbers, and punctuation marks in an oddball sequence of no fewer than eight characters. Examples of some good passwords are *2b/orNOT2b%* and *Alfred!E!Newman7.* Or you can also choose an obvious and memorable password but shift the position of your hands on the keyboard, creating a meaningless string of characters—the best kind of password. (Thus, *ELVIS* becomes *R;BOD* when you move your fingers one position right on the keyboard.)

Some other practical advice about passwords is given in the Practical Action box on page 349.

BIOMETRIC AUTHENTICATION A hacker or cracker can easily breach a computer system with a guessed or stolen password. But some forms of identification can't be easily faked—such as your physical traits. ***Biometrics,* the science of measuring individual body characteristics,** tries to use these in security devices. *Biometric authentication devices* authenticate a person's identity by comparing his or her physical or behavioral characteristics with digital code stored in a computer system.

There are several kinds of devices for verifying physical or behavioral characteristics that can be used to authenticate a person's identity. (● *See Panel 6.18.*)

panel 6.18

Biometric device
A soldier holds a HIIDE scanner during a mission in Afghanistan. The mission was to disrupt Taliban activity and find weapons caches in the southeast tip of Paktika Province, lO miles from the Pakistan Border. HIIDE stands for Handheld Interagency Identity Detection Equipment enrollment and recognition device. It is a biometric security camera, used to identify unknown military people; it incorporates an iris scanner, fingerprint scanner, face scanner, and passport reader.

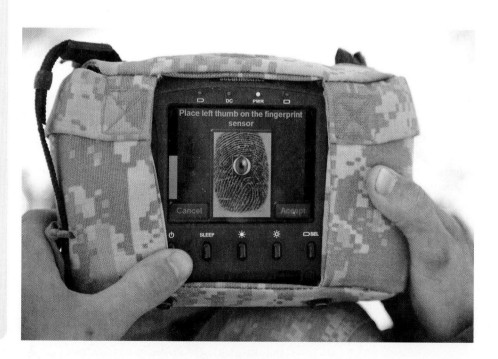

PRACTICAL ACTION
How to Deal with Passwords

ere's how easy it is to get someone's password: In 2005, 35 of 100 Internal Revenue Service employees and managers contacted by Treasury Department inspectors posing as computer technicians provided their computer user name and their password. "With an employee's user account name and password," said the Treasury Department report, "a hacker could gain access to that employee's access privileges. Even more significant, a disgruntled employee could use the same . . . techniques and obtain another employee's username and password."[54] Employees complying with the request, which was in violation of IRS rules, said they were not aware of the hacking technique or they wanted to be as helpful as possible to the computer technicians. Some got approval from their managers to cooperate.

Rules in Creating Passwords

The IRS study suggests the obvious first rule in the following list of rules:

- *Rule 1: Don't tell anyone your user name and password:* Of course you shouldn't tell strangers. You also shouldn't even tell friends or relatives.

- *Rule 2: Don't use passwords that can be easily guessed:* Don't use "12345," the word "password," variations on your name, your nickname, your street address, mother's maiden name, pet's name, college name, or name of your favorite sports team.

- *Rule 3: Avoid any word that appears in a dictionary:* Instead, use weird combinations of letters, numbers, and punctuation. Mix uppercase and lowercase, along with special characters such as !, #, and %.

- *Rule 4: Create long passwords, especially for sensitive sites:* For financial accounts, for instance, 15-character passwords are recommended (which are 33,000 times harder to crack than an 8-character one).[55]

- *Rule 5: Don't use the same password for multiple sites:* Avoid reusing the same password at different sites, since if hackers or scammers obtain one account, they potentially have your entire online life. If you do use the same password for multiple purposes, use it only for low-risk sites, such as newspaper registrations.

- *Rule 6: Change passwords often:* Change passwords often, such as every 4 or 6 weeks or on a set schedule such as the first day of spring, summer, and so on. Change passwords when you use a computer in insecure locations such as libraries, airports, or internet cafés.

Tips for Remembering Passwords

How on earth are you going to remember a dozen or more passwords of at least eight characters, mixing letters, numbers, and special characters—especially if you can't use words? First, Rules 7 and 8 below are things that people do that you *should not do.* Rule 9 offers some suggestions for memorizing your passwords.

- *Rule 7: Don't write passwords on sticky notes, in a notebook, or in a handheld computer or tape them under your keyboard:* Avoid writing out passwords on sticky notes (Post-its) and attaching them to your monitor or putting passwords in a notebook or PDA. And don't hide them under your keyboard—one of the first places a tech-knowledgeable person will look.

- *Rule 8: Don't carry the passwords in your wallet:* Lots of people do this, but of course if you lose your wallet the consequences can be dire.

- *Rule 9: Create a system for remembering passwords without writing them down:* One technique is to think of a phrase from a song, such as, "Oh, say, can you see, by the dawn's early light," from *The Star-Spangled Banner.* Then use the last letter of each word in the phrase to construct the password: *hynueyesyt.* Mix it up by inserting a number or special character (#, ^, +) after each third letter or making every other letter uppercase. Another trick, says one writer, is to "begin with your random-looking string [of characters] and add a constant you memorize, such as '4!5.' End with something related to the website, such as the first four consonants of the domain name."[56]

Technical Tricks for Safeguarding Passwords

There are several technical solutions you can draw on for storing passwords. Two of the most available are the following:

- *Software with encrypted file:* You can save all your passwords in a single, easily accessible encrypted file. (Encryption is discussed below.) Two popular ones are Any Password (free from *www.romanlab.com*) and PasswordSafe (free from *www.ghostware.nl*). PwdHash runs along with your web browsers; when you type a password into a web page, PwdHash encrypts the typed password before sending it on to the website (free test versions at *http://crypto.stanford.edu/PwdHash/*). Norton Confidential and Apple Computer's Keychain also help store keywords in secure encrypted form. Google, IBM, Microsoft, and Yahoo! are backing a system called OpenID, which, in one description, promotes "logging onto one OpenID website with one password, [which] will grant entrance during that session to all websites that accept OpenID credentials."[57]

- **Fingerprint readers for master password:** Microsoft offers fingerprint readers for Windows XP/Vista, and other fingerprint scanners are available such as BioMouse and Ethenticator that are able to encrypt and keep track of all your various user names, passwords, and personal identification numbers (PINs). The fingerprint readers work only with the computer they are connected to, and the security of your various web accounts, bank accounts, frequent-flyer accounts, and so on depends on how unbreakable your passwords are. But at least you no longer have to memorize them.

Besides using encryption to secure email messages or transactions on e-commerce websites, you may also want to protect files on your computer—especially laptops and PDAs, in case you leave them behind on a train or bus. You can use special software to encrypt individual files, but experts recommend deploying whole-disk encryption, cloaking every file on your computer and granting access only to those with the proper password. Windows Vista comes with a free whole-disk encryption system called BitLocker.[58]

- **Hand-geometry systems:** Also known as *full-hand palm scanners,* these are devices to verify a person's identity by scanning the entire hand, which, for each person, is as unique as a fingerprint and changes little over time.

- **Fingerprint scanners:** These range from optical readers, in which you place a finger over a window, to swipe readers, such as those built into laptops and some handhelds, which allow you to run your finger across a barlike sensor. Microsoft offers optical fingerprint readers to go with Windows XP/Vista.

- **Iris-recognition systems:** Because no two people's eyes are alike, iris scans are very reliable identifiers. In Europe, some airports are using iris-scanning systems as a way of speeding up immigration controls. The Nine Zero, an upscale hotel in Boston, has experimented with letting guests enter one of its more expensive suites by staring into a camera that analyzes iris patterns.

- **Face-recognition systems:** Facial-recognition systems may come to play an important role in biometric photos embedded in U.S. passports and those of other industrialized nations during the next few years. The technology, which compares a live face image with a digitized image stored in a computer, is even used now as a security system for some notebook computers.[53]

- **Voice-recognition systems:** These systems compare a person's voice with digitized voice prints stored in a computer, which the individual has previously "trained" to recognize his or her speech patterns.

ENCRYPTION **_Encryption_ is the process of altering readable data into unreadable form to prevent unauthorized access.** Encryption is able to use powerful mathematical concepts to create coded messages that are difficult or even virtually impossible to break.

Suppose you wanted to send a message to a company colleague stating, "Our secret product will be revealed to the world on April 14." If you sent it in this undisguised, readable form, it would be known as *plain text.* To send it in disguised, unreadable form, you would *encrypt* that message into *cyber-text,* and your colleague receiving it would then *decrypt* it, using an *encryption key*—a formula for encrypting and decrypting a coded message.

There are two basic forms of encryption—*private key* and *public key:*

- **Private key:** *Private-key (symmetric) encryption* means that the same secret key is used by both sender and receiver to encrypt and decrypt a

Private-key encryption

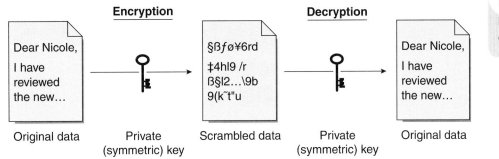

Encryption   Decryption

Dear Nicole, I have reviewed the new…

Original data

Private (symmetric) key

§ßƒø¥6rd ‡4hl9 /r ß§l2…\9b 9(k˜t"u

Scrambled data

Private (symmetric) key

Dear Nicole, I have reviewed the new…

Original data

Public-key encryption

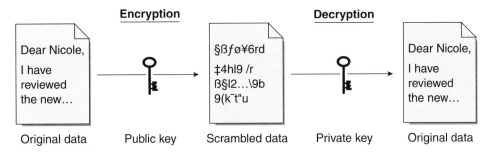

Encryption   Decryption

Dear Nicole, I have reviewed the new…

Original data

Public key

§ßƒø¥6rd ‡4hl9 /r ß§l2…\9b 9(k˜t"u

Scrambled data

Private key

Dear Nicole, I have reviewed the new…

Original data

message. The encryption system *DES* (for "Data Encryption Standard") was adopted as a federal standard for private-key encryption in 1976.

- **Public key:** *Public-key encryption* means that two keys are used—a *public key,* which the receiver has made known beforehand to the sender, who uses it to encrypt the message, and a *private key,* which only the receiver knows and which is required to decrypt the message. Examples of public-key encryption technologies are *PGP* (for "Pretty Good Privacy"), *RSA encryption,* and *Fortezza.*

Examples of the two types are shown above. (● *See Panel 6.19.*)

Encryption Software

Some kinds of encryption software worth investigating:

PGP Personal Desktop (*www. pgp.com*)

WinMagic's SecureDoc (*www. winmagic.com*)

WHAT CAN REPLACE THE PASSWORD? Even if you make every effort to protect your password, there is nothing you can do if, say, hackers break into ATMs in convenience stores and steal customers' PIN codes, including yours. This actually happened in San Jose, California, where hackers got inside Citibank's network of ATMs inside 7-Eleven stores, netting themselves millions of dollars.[59] Thus, experts are suggesting users abandon passwords and use log-on systems that rely on cryptography, accessed with so-called information cards, bringing the concept of an identity card, like a driver's license to the online world.[60]

Wi-Fi connection in Manhattan, New York City

EXPERIENCE BOX
Virtual Meetings: Linking Up Electronically

"I don't usually put on lipstick before making a phone call," wrote Anita Hamilton, "but this time was different. I was placing my first video phone call over the internet."[61]

Although video online chatting has been available for a long time, it has been hampered by the slowness of low-bandwidth dial-up modems, so pictures have not translated well. Now that more people have broadband (DSL, cable-modem, or even TI connections) the online video quality is much better.

The videophone is more than a luxury for personal use, however. In business, organizational ideas about distance are changing, influencing when people meet face-to-face and when they link up electronically. If you're of a generation that's already used to instant-message chats (and multitasking by simultaneously watching TV, talking on the phone, and doing your homework), you may find yourself in a comfortable relationship with virtual meetings at work.[62]

Types of Virtual Meetings: Remote Conferencing

There are several ways in which people can conduct "virtual meetings"—meetings that don't entail physical travel—as follows.[63]

Audioconferencing. *Audioconferencing* (or *teleconferencing*) is simply telephone conferencing. A telephone conference-call operator can arrange this setup among any three or more users. Users don't need any special equipment beyond a standard telephone. Audioconferencing is an inexpensive way to hold a long-distance meeting and is often used in business.

Computer-based audio, involving microphones, headsets or speakers, and internet-based telephony, is also used for audioconferencing.

Videoconferencing Using Closed-Circuit TV. "I was a little nervous about going in front of the camera," said job applicant Mark Dillard, "but I calmed down pretty quickly after we got going, and it went well."[64] Interviewing for a job can be uncomfortable for many people. However, Dillard had just talked to a job recruiter in New York while sitting in front of a video camera in a booth at a local Kinko's store in Atlanta.

Some of the more sophisticated equipment is known as telepresence technology, high-definition videoconference systems that simulate face-to-face meetings between users. Whereas traditional videoconferencing systems can be set up in a conventional conference room, telepresence systems require specially designed rooms with multiple cameras and high-definition video screens, simulating "the sensation of two groups of people at identical tables facing each other through windows," according to one report.[65]

Videoconferencing Using a Webcam. A *webcam* is a tiny, often eyeball-shaped camera that sits atop a computer monitor and displays its output on a web page. Some cameras are able to automatically follow your face as you move. Headsets with built-in speakers and microphones are required. Yahoo! and MSN offer free video chatting through their instant-message programs.

Videoconferencing Using PC Video Cameras. This kind of videoconferencing involves people making a video telephone call over the internet, with both parties being able to see each other as they talk. PC video cameras (which are available for less than $100) are positioned atop computer monitors and are connected to the computer through the USB or FireWire port.

Videoconferencing Using Videophones. Videophones don't involve use of a PC, although the calls take place on the internet. The internet company 8×8 Inc., for example, makes a VoIP (voice over internet protocol) videophone.

Workgroup Computing or Web Conferencing. The use of groupware allows two or more people on a network to share information, collaborating on graphics, slides, and spreadsheets while linked by computer and telephone. WebEx and PlaceWare are two of several web-based services that allow participants to conduct meetings using tools such as "whiteboards," which can display drawings or text, along with group presentations (using PowerPoint, which displays slides on everyone's screen) and online chatting. Usually people do these things while talking to one another on the telephone. Users can collaborate by writing or editing word processing documents, spreadsheets, or presentations.

analog (p. 312) Continuous and varying in strength and/or quality. An analog signal is a continuous electrical signal with such variation. Why it's important: *Sound, light, temperature, and pressure values, for instance, can fall anywhere on a continuum or range. The highs, lows, and in-between states have historically been represented with analog devices rather than in digital form. Examples of analog devices are a speedometer, a thermometer, and a tire-pressure gauge, all of which can measure continuous fluctuations. The electrical signals on a telephone line have traditionally been analog-data representations of the original voices. Telephone, radio, television, and cable-TV technologies have long been based on analog data.*

analog cellphone (p. 336) Mobile telephone designed primarily for communicating by voice through a system of ground-area cells. Calls are directed to cells by a mobile-telephone switching office (MTSO). Moving between cells requires that calls be "handed off" by the MTSO. Why it's important: *Cellphone systems allow callers mobility.*

antivirus software (p. 347) Software that scans a computer's hard disk, floppy disks and CDs, and main memory to detect viruses and, sometimes, to destroy them. Why it's important: *Antivirus software can protect your computer from disaster.*

backbone (p. 322) The main highway—including gateways, routers, and other communications equipment—that connects all computer networks in an organization. Why it's important: *The internet backbone is the central structure that connects all other elements of the internet.*

bandwidth (p. 329) Also called *band;* range of frequencies that a transmission medium can carry in a given period of time and thus a measure of the amount of information that can be delivered. The bandwidth is the difference between the lowest and the highest frequencies transmitted. For analog signals, bandwidth is expressed in hertz (Hz), or cycles per second. For digital signals, bandwidth is expressed in bits per second (bps). In the United States, certain bands are assigned by the Federal Communications Commission (FCC) for certain purposes. Why it's important: *The wider the bandwidth, the faster the data can be transmitted. The narrower the band, the greater the loss of transmission power. This loss of power must be overcome by using relays or repeaters that rebroadcast the original signal.*

biometrics (p. 348) Science of measuring individual body characteristics. Why it's important: *Biometric devices authenticate a person's identity by comparing his or her physical identity with digital code stored in a computer system. Such devices can reduce attempts by unauthorized people to breach a computer system.*

Bluetooth (p. 339) Short-range wireless digital standard aimed at linking cellphones, PDAs, computers, and peripherals. Why it's important: *Bluetooth technology can replace cables between PCs and printers and can connect PCs to PDAs and wireless phones.*

bridge (p. 322) Interface used to connect the same types of networks. Why it's important: *Similar networks (local area networks) can be joined together to create larger area networks.*

broadband (p. 330) Bandwidth characterized by very high speed. Transmission speeds are 1 megabit per second to as high (for super-broadband and ultra-broadband) as 100 megabits per second. Why it's important: *The wider a medium's bandwidth, the more frequencies it can use to transmit data and thus the faster the transmission. Broadband can transmit high-quality audio and video data. Compare with* **narrowband.**

broadcast radio (p. 330) Wireless transmission medium that sends data over long distances—between regions, states, or countries. A transmitter is required to send messages and a receiver to receive them; sometimes both sending and receiving functions are combined in a transceiver. Why it's important: *In the lower frequencies of the radio spectrum, several broadcast radio bands are reserved not only for conventional AM/FM radio but also for broadcast television, CB (citizens band) radio, ham (amateur) radio, cellphones, and private radio-band mobile services (such as police, fire, and taxi dispatch). Some organizations use specific radio frequencies and networks to support wireless communications.*

bus network (p. 322) Type of network in which all nodes are connected to a single wire or cable (the bus) that has two endpoints. Each device transmits electronic messages to other devices. If some of those messages collide, the device waits and then tries to retransmit. Why it's important: *The bus network is relatively inexpensive to install. However, if the bus itself fails, the entire network fails.*

cellular radio (p. 331) Type of radio widely used for cellphones and wireless modems, using high-frequency radio waves to transmit voice and digital messages. Why it's important: *Unlike CB (citizens' band) radio, used by truck drivers, which has a few radio channels that everyone must share, cellular radio channels are reused simultaneously in nearby geographic areas, yet customers do not interfere with one another's calls.*

client/server network (p. 318) Local area network that consists of *clients,* which are microcomputers that request data, and *servers,* which are computers used to supply data. Why it's important: *In small organizations, servers can store files, provide printing stations, and transmit email. In large organizations, servers may also house enormous libraries of financial, sales, and product information. Compare with* **peer-to-peer network.**

coaxial cable (p. 325) Commonly called "co-ax"; insulated copper wire wrapped in a solid or braided metal shield and then in an external plastic cover. Why it's important: *Co-ax is widely used for cable television. Because of the extra insulation, coaxial cable is much better than twisted-pair wiring at resisting noise. Moreover, it can carry voice and data at a faster rate.*

communications media (p. 325) Any medium that carries signals over a communications path, the route between two or more communications media devices. Why it's important: *Media may be wired or wireless. Three types of wired channels are twisted-pair wire (conventional telephone lines), coaxial cable, and fiber-optic cable.*

communications satellite (p. 331) Microwave relay station in orbit around the earth. Why it's important: *Transmitting a signal from a ground station to a satellite is called* uplinking; *the reverse is called* downlinking. *The delivery process will be slowed if, as is often the case, more than one satellite is required to get the message delivered.*

cracker (p. 346) Person who breaks into computers for malicious purposes—to obtain information for financial gain, shut down hardware, pirate software, steal people's credit information, or alter or destroy data. Why it's important: *Crackers can do major damage to computers and networks. Compare with* **hacker.**

denial-of-service (DoS) attack (p. 342) Also called *distributed denial of service (DDoS) attack;* Form of technological assault that consists of making repeated fraudulent requests of a computer system or network, thereby overloading it. The assault may come from a single computer or from hundreds or thousands of computers that have been taken over by those intending harm. Why it's important: *A denial-of-service attack denies legitimate users access to the computer system.*

digital (p. 311) Communications signals or information represented in a two-state (binary) way using electronic or electromagnetic signals. Why it's important: *Digital signals are the basis of computer-based communications.* Digital *is usually synonymous with* computer-based.

digital wireless services (p. 337) Two-way, second-generation (2G) wireless services that support digital cellphones and PDAs. They use a network of cell towers to send voice communications and data over the airwaves in digital form. Why it's important: *This technology is a dramatic improvement over analog cellphones. Voice clarity is better, and more calls can be squeezed into the same bandwidth.*

electromagnetic spectrum of radiation (p. 329) All the fields of electrical energy and magnetic energy, which travel in waves. This includes all radio signals, light rays, X rays, and radioactivity. Why it's important: *The part of the electromagnetic spectrum of particular interest is the area in the middle, which is used for communications purposes. Various frequencies are assigned by the federal government for different purposes.*

encryption (p. 350) The process of using powerful mathematical concepts to create coded messages that are difficult or impossible to read. To send a message in disguised, unreadable form, you would *encrypt* that message into *cybertext,* and your colleague receiving it would then *decrypt* it, using an *encryption key*—a formula for encrypting and decrypting a coded message. Why it's important: *Using encryption to alter readable data into unreadable form can prevent unauthorized access.*

Ethernet (p. 324) LAN technology that can be used with almost any kind of computer and that describes how data can

be sent in packets in between computers and other networked devices usually in close proximity. Why it's important: *Ethernet has become the most popular and most widely deployed network technology in the world.*

extranet (p. 319) Private intranet that connects not only internal personnel but also selected suppliers and other strategic parties. Why it's important: *Extranets have become popular for standard transactions such as purchasing.*

fiber-optic cable (p. 326) Cable that consists of dozens or hundreds of thin strands of glass or plastic that transmit pulsating beams of light rather than electricity. Why it's important: *These strands, each as thin as a human hair, can transmit up to 2 billion pulses per second (2 Gbps); each "on" pulse represents 1 bit. When bundled together, fiber-optic strands in a cable 0.12-inch thick can support a quarter-million to a half-million voice conversations at the same time. Moreover, unlike electrical signals, light pulses are not affected by random electromagnetic interference in the environment. Thus, they have much lower error rates than normal telephone wire and cable. In addition, fiber-optic cable is lighter and more durable than twisted-pair wire and co-ax cable. A final advantage is that it cannot easily be wiretapped, so transmissions are more secure.*

firewall (p. 347) System of hardware and/or software that protects a computer or a network from intruders. Always-on internet connections such as cable modem and DSL, as well as some wireless devices, are particularly susceptible to unauthorized intrusion and so need a firewall. Why it's important: *The firewall monitors all internet and other network activity, looking for suspicious data and preventing unauthorized access.*

gateway (p. 322) Interface permitting communication between dissimilar networks. Why it's important: *Gateways permit communication between a LAN and a WAN or between two LANs based on different network operating systems or different layouts.*

Global Positioning System (GPS) (p. 333) A series of earth-orbiting satellites continuously transmitting timed radio signals that can be used to identify earth locations. Why it's important: *A GPS receiver—handheld or mounted in a vehicle, plane, or boat—can pick up transmissions from any four satellites, interpret the information from each, and calculate to within a few hundred feet or less the receiver's longitude, latitude, and altitude. Some GPS receivers include map software for finding one's way around, as with the Guidestar system available with some rental cars.*

hacker (p. 345) A hacker can be either (1) a computer enthusiast, a person who enjoys learning programming languages and computer systems; or (2) a person who gains unauthorized access to computers or networks, often just for the challenge of it. Why it's important: *Unlike crackers who have malevolent purposes, a hacker may break into computers for more or less positive reasons.*

home area network (HAN) (p. 317) Network using wired, cable, or wireless connections to link a household's digital devices. Why it's important: *A HAN can connect not only* multiple computers, printers, and storage devices but also VCRs, DVDs, televisions, fax machines, video game machines, and home security systems.

home automation network (p. 318) Network that relies on very inexpensive, very short-range, low-power (AA batteries) wireless technology in the under-200-Kbps range, such as Insteon, ZibBee, and Z-Wave. Why it's important: *This network can be used to link switches and sensors around the house and can control lights and switches, thermostats and furnaces, smoke alarms and outdoor floodlights.*

HomePlug (p. 326) Technological standard that allows users to send data over a home's existing electrical (AC) power lines, which can be transmitted at 14 megabits per second. Why it's important: *HomePlug can use a home's existing electric-power wiring to create a computer network.*

HomePNA (HPNA) (p. 326) Alliance of leading technology companies working to ensure the adoption of a single, unified existing wire (telephone and cable) home-networking standard that transmits data at about 320 megabits per second. Why it's important: *This standard allows people to use a home's existing telephone wiring to develop a home network.*

host computer (p. 320) A computer in a client/server network that controls a network and the devices on it, called nodes. Why it's important: *The host computer controls access to the hardware, software, and other resources on the network.*

hub (p. 321) A common connection point for devices in a network—a place of convergence where data arrives from one or more directions and is forwarded out in one or more other directions. Why it's important: *Hubs are commonly used to connect segments of a LAN.*

infrared wireless transmission (p. 330) Transmission of data signals using infrared-light waves. Why it's important: *Infrared ports can be found on some laptop computers and printers, as well as wireless mice. The advantage is that no physical connection is required among devices. The drawbacks are that line-of-sight communication is required—there must be an unobstructed view between transmitter and receiver—and transmission is confined to short range.*

intranet (p. 319) An organization's internal private network that uses the infrastructure and standards of the internet and the web. Why it's important: *When an organization creates an intranet, it enables employees to have quicker access to internal information and to share knowledge so that they can do their jobs better. Information exchanged on intranets may include employee email addresses and telephone numbers, product information, sales data, employee benefit information, and lists of jobs available within the organization.*

local area network (LAN) (p. 317) Communications network that connects computers and devices in a limited geographic area, such as one office, one building, or a group of buildings close together (for instance, a college campus). Why it's important: *LANs have replaced large computers for many functions and are considerably less expensive.*

metropolitan area network (MAN) (p. 317) Communications network covering a city or a suburb. Why it's important: *The purpose of a MAN is often to bypass local telephone companies when accessing long-distance services. Many cellphone systems are MANs.*

microwave radio (p. 331) Transmission of voice and data through the atmosphere as superhigh-frequency radio waves called *microwaves*. These frequencies are used to transmit messages between ground-based stations and satellite communications systems. Why it's important: *Microwaves are line-of-sight; they cannot bend around corners or around the earth's curvature, so there must be an unobstructed view between transmitter and receiver. Thus, microwave stations need to be placed within 25–30 miles of each other, with no obstructions in between. In a string of microwave relay stations, each station receives incoming messages, boosts the signal strength, and relays the signal to the next station. Nowadays dish- or horn-shaped microwave reflective dishes, which contain transceivers and antennas, are nearly everywhere.*

modem (p. 314) Short for "modulate/demodulate"; device that converts digital signals into a representation of analog form (modulation) to send over phone lines. A receiving modem then converts the analog signal back to a digital signal (demodulation). Why it's important: *The modem provides a means for computers to communicate with one another using the standard copper-wire telephone network, an analog system that was built to transmit the human voice but not computer signals.*

narrowband (p. 330) Also known as *voiceband*. Bandwidth used for short distances. Transmission rates are usually 100 kilobits per second or less. Why it's important: *Narrowband is used in telephone modems and for regular telephone communications—for speech, faxes, and data. Compare with* **broadband.**

network (p. 315) Also called *communications network;* system of interconnected computers, telephones, or other communications devices that can communicate with one another and share applications and data. Why it's important: *The tying together of so many communications devices in so many ways is changing the world we live in.*

node (p. 320) Any device that is attached to a network. Why it's important: *A node may be a microcomputer, terminal, storage device, or peripheral device, any of which enhance the usefulness of the network.*

packet (p. 320) Fixed-length block of data for transmission. The packet also contains instructions about the destination of the packet. Why it's important: *By creating blocks, in the form of packets, a transmission system can deliver the data more efficiently and economically.*

pager (p. 335) Commonly known as *beeper;* simple radio receiver that receives data sent from a special radio transmitter. The pager number is dialed from a phone and travels via the transmitter to the pager. Why it's important: *Pagers have become a common way of receiving notification of phone calls so that the user can return the calls immediately; some* *pagers can also display messages of up to 80 characters and send preprogrammed messages.*

peer-to-peer (P2P) network (p. 318) Type of network in which all computers on the network communicate directly with one another rather than relying on a server, as client/server networks do. Why it's important: *Every computer can share files and peripherals with all other computers on the network, given that all are granted access privileges. Peer-to-peer networks are less expensive than client/server networks and work effectively for up to 25 computers, making them appropriate for home networks. Compare with* **client/server network.**

personal area network (PAN) (p. 318) Type of network that uses short-range wireless technology such as Bluetooth, ultra wideband, and wireless USB, to connect a person's personal electronics; also called *wireless personal area network (WPAN)*. Why it's important: *PANs are used to connect personal electronic devices such as cellphones, PDAs, MP3 players, notebook PCs, and printers.*

protocol (p. 320) Also called *communications protocol;* set of conventions governing the exchange of data between hardware and/or software components in a communications network. Why it's important: *Protocols are built into hardware and software. Every device connected to a network must have an internet protocol (IP) address so that other computers on the network can route data to that address.*

radio-frequency (RF) spectrum (p. 329) The part of the electromagnetic spectrum that carries most communications signals. Why it's important: *The radio spectrum ranges from low-frequency waves, such as those used for aeronautical and marine navigation equipment; through the medium frequencies for CB radios, cordless phones, and baby monitors; to ultrahigh-frequency bands for cellphones; and also microwave bands for communications satellites.*

ring network (p. 323) Type of network in which all communications devices are connected in a continuous loop and messages are passed around the ring until they reach the right destination. There is no central server. Why it's important: *The advantage of a ring network is that messages flow in only one direction and so there is no danger of collisions. The disadvantage is that if a connection is broken, the entire network stops working.*

router (p. 322) Special computer that directs communicating messages when several networks are connected together. Why it's important: *High-speed routers can serve as part of the internet backbone, or transmission path, handling the major data traffic.*

star network (p. 323) Type of network in which all microcomputers and other communications devices are connected to a central hub, such as a file server. Electronic messages are routed through the central hub to their destinations. The central hub monitors the flow of traffic. Why it's important: *The advantage of a star network is that the hub prevents collisions between messages. Moreover, if a connection is broken between any communications device and the hub, the rest of the devices on the network will continue operating.*

switch (p. 321) A device that connects computers to a network. Unlike a hub, it sends messages only to a computer that is the intended recipient. Why it's important: *A switch is a full-duplex device, meaning data is transmitted back and forth at the same time, which improves the performance of the network.*

topology (p. 322) The logical layout, or shape, of a network. The three basic topologies are star, ring, and bus. Why it's important: *Different topologies can be used to suit different office and equipment configurations.*

Trojan horse (p. 344) A program that pretends to be a useful program, such as a game or screen saver, but that carries viruses, or destructive instructions. Why it's important: *A Trojan horse can perpetrate mischief without your knowledge, such as allow installation of backdoor programs, illegal programs that allow illegitimate users to take control of your computer without your knowledge.*

twisted-pair wire (p. 325) Two strands of insulated copper wire, twisted around each other. Why it's important: *Twisted-pair wire has been the most common channel or medium used for telephone systems. However, it is relatively slow and does not protect well against electrical interference.*

ultra wideband (UWB) (p. 339) A promising technology operating in the range of 480 megabits per second up to 30 feet that uses a low power source to send out millions of bursts of radio energy every second over many different frequencies, which are then reassembled by a UWB receiver. Why it's important: *UWB operates over low frequencies not used by other technologies, making it a candidate to replace many of the cables that now currently connect household and office devices.*

virtual private network (VPN) (p. 320) Private network that uses a public network, usually the internet, to connect remote sites. Why it's important: *Because wide area networks use leased lines, maintaining them can be expensive, especially as distances between offices increase. To decrease communications costs, some companies have established their own VPNs. Company intranets, extranets, and LANS can all be parts of a VPN.*

virus (p. 343) Deviant program that can cause unexpected and often undesirable effects, such as destroying or corrupting data. Why it's important: *Viruses can cause users to lose data and/or files or can shut down entire computer systems.*

wide area network (WAN) (p. 317) Communications network that covers a wide geographic area, such as a country or the world. Why it's important: *Most long-distance and regional telephone companies are WANs. A WAN may use a combination of satellites, fiber-optic cable, microwave, and copper-wire connections and link a variety of computers, from mainframes to terminals.*

Wireless Application Protocol (WAP) (p. 330) Communications protocol designed to link nearly all mobile devices to your telecommunications carrier's wireless network and content providers. Why it's important: *Wireless devices such as cellphones use the Wireless Application Protocol for connecting wireless users to the World Wide Web.*

wireless personal area network (WPAN) *See* **personal area network (PAN). wireless USB (WUSB)** (p. 340) Wireless standard with a typical range of 32 feet and a maximum data rate of 480 megabits per second. Why it's important: *Because USB is already the most used interface among PC users, a wireless version could combine the speed and security of wired technology with the ease of use of*

wireless. It could be a natural replacement for USB cable links for printers, scanners, MP3 players, hard disks, and the like.

worm (p. 342) Program that repeatedly copies itself into a computer's memory or onto a disk drive until no space is left. Why it's important: *Worms can shut down computers.*

CHAPTER REVIEW

stage 1 LEARNING MEMORIZATION

"I can recognize and recall information."

Self-Test Questions

I. A(n) _____ converts digital signals into analog signals for transmission over phone lines.

2. A(n) _____ network covers a wide geographic area, such as a state or a country.

3. _____ cable transmits data as pulses of light rather than as electricity.

4. _____ refers to waves continuously varying in strength and/or quality; _____ refers to communications signals or information in a binary form.

5. A(n) _____ is a private network that uses a public network (usually the internet) to connect remote sites.

6. A(n) _____ is a computer that acts as a disk drive, storing programs and data files shared by users on a LAN.

7. The _____ is the system software that manages the activities of a network.

8. Modem is short for _____.

9. _____ is a short-range wireless digital standard aimed at linking cellphones, PDAs, computers, and peripherals up to distances of 30 feet.

IO. _____ programs can screen out objectionable material on the internet.

II. Any device that is attached to a network is called a _____.

I2. A set of conventions governing the exchange of data between hardware and software components in a communications network is called a _____.

Multiple-Choice Questions

I. Which of the following best describes the telephone line that is used in most homes today?

   a. coaxial cable

   b. modem cable

   c. twisted-pair wire

   d. fiber-optic cable

   e. LAN

2. Which of the following do local area networks enable?

   a. sharing of peripheral devices

   b. sharing of programs and data

   c. better communications

   d. access to databases

   e. all of these

3. Which of the following is *not* a type of server?

   a. file server

   b. print server

   c. mail server

   d. disk server

   e. database server

4. Which of the following is *not* a short-distance wireless standard?

   a. Bluetooth

   b. PDA

   c. Wi-Fi

   d. WAP

5. Which type of local area network connects all devices through a central hub, such as a file server?

   a. bus network

   b. star network

   c. mesh network

   d. ring network

   e. router

6. Which is the type of local area network in which all microcomputers on the network communicate directly with one another without relying on a server?

   a. client/server

   b. domain

   c. peer to peer

   d. MAN

   e. WAN

Communications, Networks, & Safeguards

7. How do fiber-optic cables transmit data?

   a. via copper wire

   b. via infrared

   c. via AC electric current

   d. via radio waves

   e. via pulsating beams of light

True/False Questions

T F I. In a LAN, a bridge is used to connect the same type of networks, whereas a gateway is used to enable dissimilar networks to communicate.

T F 2. Frequency and amplitude are two characteristics of analog carrier waves.

T F 3. A range of frequencies is called a *spectrum.*

T F 4. Twisted-pair wire commonly connects residences to external telephone systems.

T F 5. Wi-Fi signals can travel up to almost 300 feet.

T F 6. Microwave transmissions are a line-of-sight medium.

T F 7. 2G is the newest cellphone standard.

T F 8. Wi-Fi is formally known as an 802.11 network.

T F 9. A Trojan horse copies itself repeatedly into a computer's memory or onto a hard drive.

stage 2 LEARNING COMPREHENSION

"I can recall information in my own terms and explain it to a friend."

Short-Answer Questions

I. What is the difference between an intranet and an extranet?

2. What is the difference between a LAN and a WAN?

3. Why is bandwidth a factor in data transmission?

4. What is a firewall?

5. What do *2G* and *3G* mean?

6. Explain the differences between ring, bus, and star networks.

7. What is the electromagnetic spectrum?

8. What does a protocol do?

9. What are the three basic rules for creating passwords?

10. What do we need encryption for?

stage 3 LEARNING APPLYING, ANALYZING, SYNTHESIZING, EVALUATING

"I can apply what I've learned, relate these ideas to other concepts, build on other knowledge, and use all these thinking skills to form a judgment."

Knowledge in Action

I. Are the computers at your school connected to a network? If so, what kind of network(s)? What types of computers are connected? What hardware and software allows the network to function? What department(s) did you contact to find the information you needed to answer these questions?

2. Using current articles, publications, and/or the web, research cable modems. Where are they being used? What does a residential user need to hook up to a cable modem system? Do you think you will use a cable modem in the near future?

3. Research the role of the Federal Communications Commission in regulating the communications industry. How are new frequencies opened up for new communications services? How are the frequencies determined? Who gets to use new frequencies?

4. Are you a fan of analog or of digital? Explain.

5. Research the Telecommunications Act of 1996. Do you think it has had a positive or a negative effect? Why?

6. Would you like to have a job for which you telecommute instead of "going in to work"? Why or why not?

7. From your experience with cellphones, do you think it is wise to continue also paying for a "land-line" POTS phone line, or is cellphone service reliable enough to use as your sole means of telephony? As cell service advances, how do you think the POTS infrastructure will be used?

Web Exercises

I. Compare digital cable and satellite TV in your area. Which offers more channels? Which offers more features? How much do the services cost? Do both offer internet connectivity? What are the main differences between the two types of service?

2. Calculate the amount of airborne data transmission that travels through your body. To do this, research the amount of radio and television station broadcast signals in your area, as well as the estimated number of mobile-phone users. Imagine what the world would look like if you could see all the radio-wave signals the way you can see the waves in the ocean.

3. On the web, go to *www.trimble.com* and work through some of the tutorial on "About GPS Technology." Then write a short report on the applications of a GPS system.

4. As mentioned in Chapter 4, microchips are implanted in animals to track them with GPS technology. Humans can now be tracked when they use their cellphones. Visit the following websites for more details:

   www.wired.com/news/business/0,1367,21781,00.html

   www.washingtonpost.com/wp-dyn/content/ article/2007/11/22/AR2007112201444.html

   www.usatoday.com/money/topstories/2008-06-04- 750914861_x.htm

5. What is wardriving? Visit these sites to see what is being done to fix this security hole:

   www.wardriving.com/

   http://havenworks.com/vocabulary/a-z/w/war-driving/

   www.wordspy.com/words/wardriving.asp

   http://en.wikipedia.org/wiki/Wardriving

   www.wardrive.net/

6. Test your ports and shields. Is your internet connection secure, or is it inviting intruders to come in? Use the buttons at the bottom of the page at *https://grc.com/x/ne.dll?bh0bkyd2* to test your port security and your shields and receive a full report on how your computer is communicating with the internet.

7. Learn about the method of triangulation. This method helps when you use your cellphone to locate, for example, the nearest movie theater or restaurant. Visit the sites below to learn more. Run your own search on *triangulation.*

   www.qrg.northwestern.edu/projects/vss/docs/ navigation/1-what-is-triangulation.html

   www.a911.org/wireless/triangulation_location.htm

   www.ehow.com/how_2385973_triangulate-cell-phone. html

   www.securityfocus.com/columnists/376

8. TDMA, GSM, CDMA, and iDEN. What do these terms mean? The following websites do a good job of explaining these technologies and other cellphone-related issues.

   http://reviews.ebay.com/Cell-Phone- technologies-GSM-CDMA-TDMA- iDEN_W0QQugidZ10000000003636609

   www.dslreports.com/faq/5668

9. Security issue—Wi-Fi security issues: As Wi-Fi becomes more widespread, how will users protect their networks? Wi-Fi is hacked almost as a harmless hobby to detect its vulnerabilities. Visit the following websites to learn about some issues of the Wi-Fi future.

   http://wifinetnews.com/archives/008102.html

   http://usatoday.jiwire.com/wi-fi-security-introduction- overview.htm

   www.businessweek.com/the_thread/techbeat/ archives/2007/01/taking_wi-fi_--.html?chan=search

7

PERSONAL TECHNOLOGY The Future Is You

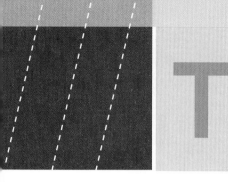

he march of digital technologies through cameras, videos, and a flurry of gadgets is reshaping old standbys and broadening their use," says Gary McWilliams.

"Clock radios are turning into übersteros," continues *The Wall Street Journal* writer, "and cameras into slim wonders that beam images to a TV or printer. Television, which had evolved only gradually since the advent of color in the 1950s, is now a digital jungle of new screen types, shapes, and technologies."[1]

It's all leading to what Jerry Yang and David Filo, the founders of Yahoo!, call the internet's "second act," when broadband extends to every electronic gadget. The internet's first period, they say, involved shifting real-world activities such as shopping and dating into a virtual world, one dominated by the PC. In the net's second act, they believe, "creative power will shift into the hands of individuals, who will be just as likely to generate and share their own content as to consume someone else's."[2]

Indeed, this was readily demonstrated with the cellphone and blog-based outpouring of breaking news and shared information about the December 2004 tsunami in Asia and the July 2005 terrorist subway bombings in London.[3] It's also evident in the phenomenon known as *mash-ups,* in which a person takes a set of data from one website and attaches it to a map file on Google Maps, thus, for example, showing the day's cheapest gas stations anywhere in the United States, the location of potholes in New York, inches of snowfall for skiers, and where trucks that serve tacos are parked in Seattle.[4] (See *www .googlemapsmania.blogspot.com.*) "What we're seeing," says one technology observer, "is nothing less than the future of the World Wide Web. Suddenly, hordes of volunteer programmers are taking it upon themselves to combine and remix the data and services of unrelated, even competing sites. The result: entirely new offerings."[5]

7.1 CONVERGENCE, PORTABILITY, & PERSONALIZATION

What are the pros and cons of the major trends in personal technology?

Is a phone with motion sensing really useful? What happens if you're calling while on a bumpy road? Regardless, the device seems to embody three principal results of the fusion of computers and communications that we mentioned in Chapter 1—*convergence, portability,* and *personalization.* Let's see what these developments, which began to build in strength during the 1990s, are like today.

Convergence

How can I evaluate whether a hybrid convergence device is good or bad?

Ming Ma, 28, a Los Angeles–based systems administrator, bought an Xbox to play videogames. But soon after he brought it home, Ma realized it could be used for multiple purposes. "I initially purchased it to play games," he said, "but now I use it to watch DVD movies, play music CDs, and to chat with friends while we play multiplayer games. I like how I can do everything on one device—I have a small apartment, so this is ideal, for me—plus, I don't have to buy individual devices, so it also saves me money along with space."[6]

As we said in Chapter 1, _**convergence**_**, or** _**digital convergence**_**, describes the combining of several industries—computers, communications, consumer electronics, entertainment, and mass media—through various devices that exchange data in digital form.** Long predicted but not fulfilled, convergence is now a reality, with 62% of all Americans having some experience with mobile access to digital data and tools.[7] More households throughout the world have also been going to broadband, with the faster internet connections changing the computer, cable, telephone, music, and movie businesses. Convergence, as we've pointed out, has led to electronic products that perform multiple functions, such as TVs with internet access, cellphones that are also digital cameras, and a refrigerator that allows you to send email.

Hybrid convergence devices have pros and cons, as follows:

CONVERGENCE: THE UPSIDE Ma's multiple uses of the Xbox are an instance in which convergence makes sense. So, perhaps, is Sony's PlayStation Portable, which you can use not only to play videogames but also to surf the web, watch video, and read e-books. So are cellphones with address books or digital cameras that also shoot video. The new Holy Grail of convergence seems to be a "digital Swiss Army knife," a universal device that will perform several functions. Over the past decade, as computing and communications have migrated from expensive desktop computers, which were mainly used by upper-income Americans, to easier-to-use and more affordable cellphones, users have also changed, with a much greater diversity of people being involved. And they are using their handhelds for many more non-voice data applications, such as taking pictures, accessing the internet for news, playing music, and texting.[8] Indeed, engineers have succeeded in designing the cellphone so you can use it as a universal remote to control your music, your TV, your PowerPoint presentation, or whatever.[9]

CONVERGENCE: THE DOWNSIDE Not all hybrid gadgets are necessarily practical. "Just because companies can converge technologies into one device doesn't [always] mean they should do it," says the research director of Jupiter Research. "Any convergent device where, as a result, a primary feature is compromised is just not a good idea."[10] For example, what about trying to use those tiny keyboards on a cellphone to do texting?

Convergence. Home entertainment centers bring together several electronic functions to access music, video, TV, and the internet, as well as support some computer functions.

Portability

What are the positives and negatives of portability?

Smart cellphones are, of course, an example of portability. Not too many years ago, having a phone in your car was a badge of affluence, affordable mainly by Hollywood movie producers and Manhattan real estate developers. Now, thanks to increasing miniaturization, faster speeds, and declining costs, more and more mobilephone and other electronic components can be crammed into smaller and smaller gadgets. But as today's students are well aware, a host of other devices are also portable: portable media players, digital cameras, BlackBerries, notebook computers, PDAs, tablet PCs, and the like.

Portability also has its upside and downside.

PORTABILITY: THE UPSIDE The advantages of portability seem obvious: being able to do phone calls and emails from anywhere that you can make a connection, keeping up with your social networks, listening to hundreds of songs on a digital music player such as an iPod, taking photos or video anywhere on a whim, watching TV anywhere anytime. One reason that manufacturers have targeted turning cellphones into hybrids, incidentally, is that people carry them wherever they go, unlike laptop computers, portable media players, or digital cameras.

PORTABILITY: THE DOWNSIDE The same portable technology that enables you to access information and entertainment anytime anywhere often means that others can find *you* equally conveniently (for them). Thus, you have to become disciplined about preventing others from wasting your time, as by screening your cellphone calls with **_Caller ID_, a feature that shows the name and/or number of the calling party on the phone's display when you receive an incoming call.** You may also find yourself bombarded throughout the day by unnecessary incoming emails and those web services known as RSS aggregators that automatically update you on new information from various sites.

Nonstop connectivity may rain digital information on you, but it can also have the paradoxical result of removing you from real human contact. Consequently, the professor whose recommendation you may need someday for an employment or graduate school reference may never get to know you, because your interaction will never be face-to-face, as during his or her normal office hours. Businesses, incidentally, have recently had to deal with recurring complaints from employees about their inability to reach coworkers to get critical information they need—because their coworkers don't respond in timely fashion via email—and so some companies have taken measures to increase person-to-person contact, as by banning email use on Fridays.[11]

iPod portability. (*Above*) Apple's iPod Classic, available in 80- and 160-gigabyte models, is a handheld device that allows users to watch TV shows, music videos, and home movies, as well as listen to music and audiobooks. (*Below*) iPod with controls on the headset.

Personalization

What are the pluses and minuses of personalization?

Telecommunications can be organized through two kinds of arrangements: the *tree-and-branch* model and the *switched-network* model. In the **_tree-and-branch telecommunications model_, a centralized information provider sends out messages through many channels to thousands of consumers.** This is the model of most mass media, such as AM radio and network television broadcasting.

In the **_switched-network telecommunications model_, a common carrier provides circuit switching among public users; that is, a temporary connection is established by closing a circuit.** This is the model of the telephone system, of course, and also of the internet. In a telephone network, a connection for voice transmission is made by dialing; in a packet switching network (Chapter 6), a temporary connection is established between points for transmitting data in the form of packets. People on the system are not only consumers of information ("content") but also possible providers of it. During the past several years, mass-media radio and television have been losing listeners and viewers to the more personalized media based on the switched-network model. This has opened the door to more personalized uses of information technology.

PERSONALIZATION: THE UPSIDE As a consumer, you may have downloaded hundreds or thousands of songs, so that you have your own personalized library of music on your computer and portable media player. You may also have created your own list of "favorites" or "bookmarks" on your PC so that you can readily access your own favorite websites. And you may have accessed or contributed to certain blogs, or personalized online diaries. In addition, of course, PC software can be used to create all kinds of personal projects, ranging from artwork to finances to genealogy.

PERSONALIZATION: THE DOWNSIDE The downside of personalization is that people may feel overburdened with *too much choice*. Indeed, Swarthmore College psychology professor Barry Schwartz, author of *The Paradox of Choice: Why More Is Less*, has identified several factors by which choice overload hurts us. As available options increase, he says, the following may happen:[12]

- **Regret:** People are more likely to regret their decisions.

- **Inaction:** People are more likely to anticipate regretting decisions, and the anticipated regret prevents people from actually deciding.

- **Excessive expectations:** Expectations about how good the decision will be go up. Thus, reality has a hard time living up to the expectations.

- **Self-blame:** When decisions have disappointing results, people tend to blame themselves, because they feel the unsatisfying results must be their fault.

One result of having several choices is that many people do ***multitasking*** — **performing several tasks at once, shifting focus from one task to another in rapid succession.** When you read this textbook while listening to music and watching TV, you may think you're simultaneously doing three separate tasks, but you're really not. "It's like playing tennis with three balls," says one psychiatrist.[13] You may think you're one of those people who has no trouble juggling all this, but medical and learning experts say the brain has limits and can do only so much at one time. For instance, it has been found that people who do two demanding tasks simultaneously—drive in heavy traffic and talk on a cellphone, for example—do neither task as well as they do each alone.[14]

Indeed, the result of constantly shifting attention is a sacrifice in quality for any of the tasks with which one is engaged. The phenomenon of half-heartedly talking to someone on the phone while simultaneously surfing the web, reading emails, or trading instant messages has been called "surfer's voice." Experts who study these things call it "absent presence."[15] "Life," says Winifred Gallagher, author of *Rapt*, "is the sum of what you focus on."[16] Another writer says, "You can drive yourself crazy trying to multitask and answer every email message instantly. Or you can recognize your brain's finite capacity for processing information."[17]

Popular Personal Technologies

What personal technologies am I familiar with?

Where are you, technologically speaking, with the personal electronic devices you use every day? Let's explore what's out there (knowing full well that this book won't be able to keep up with all the new devices).

In the coming sections, we consider the following kinds of personal technology:

- Portable media players
- Satellite, HD, and internet radios
- Digital cameras
- Personal digital assistants and tablet PCs
- The new television
- E-books
- Smartphones
- Videogame systems

7.2 PORTABLE MEDIA PLAYERS

What should I know about portable media players?

Exemplified by the Apple iPod, **_portable media players (PMPs)_ are small portable devices that enable you to play digital audio, video, or still-image files.** PMPs are also known as *MP3 players,* portable devices for playing digital audio files. **_MP3_ is a format that allows audio files to be compressed so they are small enough to be sent over the internet or stored as digital files.** (MP3 is short for MPEG Audio Layer 3, an audio compression technology.) MP3 files are about one-tenth the size of uncompressed audio files. For example, a 4-minute song on a CD takes about 40 megabytes of space, but an MP3 version of that song takes only about 4 megabytes.

PMPs differ from MP3 players, however, in that they can handle not only audio but also video and image files. Thus, you may be able to carry several hours of music or video—in the case of an 80-gigabyte Apple iPod as many as 20,000 songs, 120 minutes of video, or 25,000 still images.

How MP3 Players Work

What's useful to know about digital audio players?

The most famous of digital music players is Apple Computer's iPod, although there are many other players as well—with more coming along all the time. These companies have been challenging the iPods on price, looks, and extras such as built-in FM tuners and color LCD screens that can display photo clips and arcade-style videogames, as well as record voice and music.

Basically, however, digital music players can be divided into those that have hard-disk drives for storage (which store more songs but are more expensive) and those that have flash memory (fewer songs but less expensive). Some have both hard-drive and flash memory.

DATA STORAGE—HARD DRIVE Apple dominates the digital music player market with 75%–80% of hard-drive-based players. Apple's full-size iPod models, which all have hard drives, come with up to 160 gigabytes of storage. (Eighty gigabytes holds about 20,000 songs.) The iPod Touch stores 32 gigabytes (good for 7,000 songs). Some hard-drive PMP competitors, all with at least 30 gigabytes of storage, are Creative's Zen Vision and the Archos 505.

DATA STORAGE—FLASH MEMORY If you jog or do other strenuous activity that might make a PMP's hard drive crash, you might want a player with flash memory, which usually takes the form of a card that can be slipped into a player's memory slot and is nonvolatile, holding its contents even after the power is turned off. For example, the iPod nano, which is about the size of

MP3 player

Zen X-Fi, a high-capacity flash-based digital media player that adds Xtreme Fidelity (X-Fi) sound technology, a built-in speaker, a few wireless functions, and a whole lot of extra buttons to the company's original ZEN device.

a playing card and thin enough to slip under a door, has 8 gigabytes of flash memory and holds as much music (as well as album art and photographs) as some hard-drive players. The Apple iPod shuffle is a finger-size, low-priced "mini-mini" music player that holds about 1,000 songs on a 4-gigabyte flash chip. The capacity of flash memory cards ranges up to 8 gigabytes for most portable media players.

SAMPLING RATE How many songs your PMP holds is affected not only by the storage capacity but also by the sound quality selected, which you can determine yourself when you're downloading songs from your computer to your player. Downloading and converting a digital audio track from a music CD to the MP3 format is called *ripping*. If you want high-quality sound when you're ripping (converting), the files will be relatively large, which means your PMP will hold fewer songs. If you're willing to have lower-quality sound, perhaps for the device you use while jogging, you can carry more songs on your player. The quality is determined by the ___sampling rate___, **the number of times, expressed in kilobits per second, that a song is measured (sampled) and converted to a digital value.** For instance, a song sampled at 192 kilobits per second is three times the size of a song sampled at 64 kilobits per second and will be of better sound quality.

TRANSFERRING FILES When you buy a PMP, it comes with software that allows you to transfer MP3 files to it from your personal computer, using a high-speed port such as a FireWire or universal serial bus port (USB 1.0 or 2.0).

BATTERY LIFE Battery life varies. The iPod shuffle will run up to 12 hours before recharging, the iPod nano 14 hours, the iPod mini 18 hours, and the iPod Touch 36 hours.

COLOR SCREENS & PHOTO VIEWING The top-of-the-line 80-gigabyte iPod comes with a crisp 2-square-inch color screen and allows you (with an inexpensive attachment) to download photos directly from your digital camera. If you want, you can even hook up the iPod to a TV and view a slide show. Some flash-based audio players have color screens that can display JPEG and BMP digital images.

OTHER FEATURES Many PMPs, particularly flash-based devices, offer FM radio reception. Many players also are able to make high-quality music recordings, using an extra microphone. Some also have a small internal microphone for voice recording, appropriate for capturing conversation or a lecture but usually unsuitable for music. Some devices come with a pair of earphone jacks so that two people can listen together.

PMP IN YOUR CAR It's dangerous, and in most places illegal, to use earphones while driving. However, there are gadgets that allow you to listen to your MP3 collection while you're behind the wheel. There are two ways to do this—car-stereo adapters and FM transmitters. One way, although an expensive one, is to get a car-stereo adapter, which uses a dock connector on the bottom of dockable iPods and iPod minis. A less expensive way is to get a device that turns your audio player into a miniature radio station that broadcasts an FM signal to your car's radio antenna and thus through your car radio.

Software for soft wear. Instead of wearing your heart on your sleeve, you can wear MP3 and cellphone technology, incorporated into this German-made jacket. The player is controlled through cloth buttons on the left sleeve, and the headphones are built into the collar.

MP3 sunglasses. These sunglasses, called Thump, plug into your computer's USB jack so that you can download MP3s from the computer to the glasses. Then, just put on the glasses, put the earbuds in your ears, and enjoy the music.

The Societal Effects of PMPs

How have audio players changed listening habits?

"I've called the iPod the first cultural icon of the 21st century," says Michael Bull, an instructor in media and cultural studies at the University of Sussex in England. Bull has spent more than a decade researching the societal effects of portable audio devices, starting with Sony's Walkman portable cassette player and extending to Apple's iPod, which was introduced in 2001. The iPod, he says, "permits you to join the rhythm of your mind with the rhythm of the world," causing a cultural shift away from large communal areas—such as a cathedral, "a space we could all inhabit"—to the world of the iPod, "which exists in our heads."[18]

One in five U.S. adults owns an iPod or other MP3 player.[19] Although clearly young people have taken to MP3 players with gusto, so have many older people. Bob Levens, 48, and his wife own three iPods between them, and the device, he says, has helped him to enjoy his music collection more. "Whereas before, I would stick a CD into the hi-fi and sit and listen or maybe read," he reports, "the iPod has allowed me to carry my music around with me and also to listen to some CDs that had been relegated to the back of the shelf. I rarely listen to mainstream commercial radio."[20]

Note: With about 12% of children and teens in the U.S. suffering from noise-induced hearing loss, hearing experts are concerned about the effect of hours of listening to audio players. The threshold for safe, extended listening is 85 decibels for 8 hours, according to the National Institute of Occupational Safety and Health, but the volume of most portable compact-disk players has been found to be 91–121 decibels, with in-the-ear earphones (earbuds) adding another 7–9 decibels.[21]

Using PMPs in College

How could I use an audio player to help me in my college work?

College instructors and students have found ways to expand the uses of the iPod beyond just the enjoyment of music. For instance, some PMPs can also be used to store schedules, phone-number lists, and other personal information management software. At Duke University, instructors have helped their students to employ PMPs as storage drives or as sound devices with the help of microphone attachments. "A journalism professor encourages students to use them to record interviews instead of simply taking notes," says one report. "An economics professor records lectures for her 300-person survey course on her iPod and posts them online as a pre-exam study. An engineering professor has students use their iPods to transfer research data from dormitory computers to laboratory machines."[22] Some other uses are shown below.[23] (● *See Panel 7.1.*)

panel 7.1

College uses for portable media players

- Professors record lectures and post them online for students to download for later review, as when students have dead time (such as riding the bus).
- Interviews with guest speakers and messages from administrators may also be sent straight to students' portable media players.
- Some classes, such as those in music, foreign languages, or radio broadcasting, can especially benefit from use of audio players.
- Students record their own study group sessions and interviews, using their music players with microphones.
- Students record "audio web logs" during off-campus jobs to connect with people on campus.
- Students subscribe to feeds of frequently updated audio content from podcasts; students produce their own audio shows and podcast them. A "PodPage" website can be created that is devoted to such podcasts.

7.3 HIGH-TECH RADIO: Satellite, HD, & Internet

How do the three forms of high-tech radio differ?

"Portable satellite radio receivers . . . offer a real alternative to the iPod in the fight for your pocket space," says one reviewer.[24] He described taking a bike ride around New York City's Central Park listening to comedy legends Eddie Murphy, Billy Crystal, and Richard Pryor—who are not usually available on standard "terrestrial" radio—on a satellite radio clipped to his jersey.

The radio industry, with its 235 million regular listeners, is being transformed by a number of trends, of which satellite radio is only one. Others are *HD radio, internet radio,* and *podcasting.*

Satellite Radio

How would satellite radio be different for me?

<u>*Satellite radio*</u>, **also called** *digital radio,* **is a radio service in which digital signals are sent from satellites in orbit around the Earth to subscribers owning special radios that can decode the encrypted signals.** The CD-quality sound is much better than that of regular radio, and there are many more channels available than there are on regular radio. Unlike standard broadcasters, satellite radio broadcasters are for the most part not regulated by the Federal Communications Commission, although the FCC established the playing field back in the early 1990s when it began selling parts of the radio-wave spectrum for this new class of service.

TWO PROVIDERS MERGE In 2008, the FCC approved the merger of the only two U.S. satellite digital audio radio service (SDARS) providers, market leader XM Satellite Radio, which started delivering content in 2001, and Sirius Satellite Radio, which began in 2002. Most of the content is commercial-free, and the resulting merged provider, called Sirius XM, which offers 300 channels, supports itself by monthly subscription fees starting at $13 a month. There are currently about 18.5 million subscribers.[25] In spring 2009, the company began streaming its service to the iPhone and iPod Touch devices.[26]

The Sirius Starmate Replay, equipped to receive satellite radio

ADVANTAGES OF SATELLITE RADIO A particular attraction with satellite radio is that listeners avoid the endless commercials and limited number of formats of regular AM/FM stations, and the broadcasters serve a diverse group of niche markets, such as reggae, salsa, African folk songs, NASCAR racing, National Football League games, Howard Stern fans, and even 24/7 Elvis Presley songs and other formats not available on existing radio stations.

HD Radio

How does HD radio differ from traditional radio?

Traditional radio broadcasters "were quite nervous back in 1995 when the FCC was considering licensing two satellite digital audio radio service . . . providers," says one account. "This was the potential death knell (or so they thought) of traditional radio. Something had to be done."[27] Enter <u>**HD radio**</u>, **which provides CD-quality sound and allows broadcasters to squeeze one analog and two digital stations on the same frequency.** (● *See Panel 7.2, next page.*) That is, HD Radio combines digital and analog broadcast signals, enabling stations to

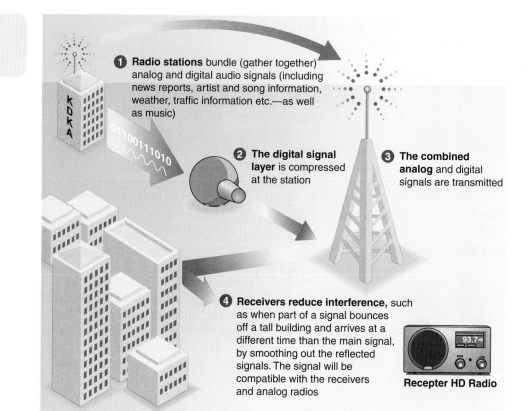

1 **Radio stations** bundle (gather together) analog and digital audio signals (including news reports, artist and song information, weather, traffic information etc.—as well as music)

2 **The digital signal layer** is compressed at the station

3 **The combined analog** and digital signals are transmitted

4 **Receivers reduce interference,** such as when part of a signal bounces off a tall building and arrives at a different time than the main signal, by smoothing out the reflected signals. The signal will be compatible with the receivers and analog radios

Recepter HD Radio

offer an analog main channel and digital "sidebands," so that multiple types of content can be broadcast from the same position on the dial. An additional advantage over satellite radio, at least so far, is that broadcasts are free; there are no subscription charges. (Incidentally, HD does not stand for "high definition"; it is simply the branding language for the technology.)

Traditional broadcasters are hoping HD Radio can introduce more local or innovative programming and blunt the threat from satellite radio. They also say that AM digital will have FM-like audio quality, and both AM and FM digital will be static-free and crystal clear. Wireless data services include on-demand audio, featuring services such as on-demand news, weather, and traffic reports. Specialized HD programming now available across the United States includes classical music, bluegrass, alternative rock, and country music (country musician Gretchen Wilson, for instance, appears on Miami's HD Radio station Gretchen 99.9).

Currently, about 1,800 of the 13,000 AM and FM stations in the United States are broadcasting in HD.[28] HD radios are available ranging from the $50

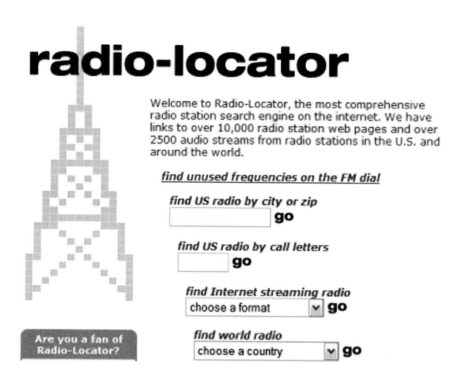

radio-locator

Welcome to Radio-Locator, the most comprehensive radio station search engine on the internet. We have links to over 10,000 radio station web pages and over 2500 audio streams from radio stations in the U.S. and around the world.

find unused frequencies on the FM dial

find US radio by city or zip

[   ] **go**

find US radio by call letters

[   ] **go**

find Internet streaming radio

[choose a format   ▾] **go**

find world radio

[choose a country   ▾] **go**

Are you a fan of Radio-Locator?

Insignia HD Radio Portable Player to $100–$200 models from Sony, Coby, iLuv, and others. Unlike satellite radio, which is available in about half of all new cars, HD radio has been slow to catch on with automakers; however, it is available in cars made by Hundai, Volvo, BMW, and Mercedes-Benz. An HD Radio feature called "iTunes tagging" lets listeners hit a "tag" button on their radio when they hear a song they like, which will be listed on iTunes after syncing with the iPod and purchased.[29]

Internet Radio

How could I benefit from internet radio?

As of mid-2009, there were about 19 million subscribers to satellite radio in the United States.[30] However, a year earlier, internet radio was drawing 33 million American listeners, reaching 13% of the American population over age 12.[31] With ad sales rising at a double-digit pace, traditional radio giants such as Clear Channel Communications have focused more and more on online broadcasting.[32] Shoutcast.com lists thousands of free online stations.

The most popular internet-only radio sites are owned by online companies such as Yahoo!, AOL, and MSN. Yahoo!'s Musicmath service, for instance, allows listeners to pick a category, such as alternative rock, and then play a number of songs in that genre, with fewer ads than are found on traditional radio. However, there are also numerous mom-and-pop web broadcasters, such as Radioparadise.com, described as "a format-busting station that spins a tasteful mix of music ranging from the Beatles to Norah Jones to the Strokes," which is run by a couple from their home in Paradise, California, as a commercial-free operation.[33] Other popular internet music services are Pandora, Last.fm, Slacker, and Rhapsody.[34] Many of these (such as Pandora and Slacker) can be heard on a BlackBerry Storm or an Apple iPhone.

At present, most internet radio listeners tune in at the office. People who listen at home can obtain networking products that enable them to stream music from their computers to their stereo systems. Eventually, as the wireless internet expands, consumers may be able to go online from moving vehicles, with internet radio receivers on their dashboards.

Podcasting

How could I get involved in podcasting?

As we stated in Chapter 2, **_podcasting_ involves the recording of internet radio or similar internet audio programs.** Unlike traditional radio, podcasting requires no studio or broadcast tower, and there's no Federal Communications Commission regulation (so hosts can say whatever they want). Podcasting software now allows amateur deejays and hobbyists to create their own radio shows and offer them free over the internet. Listeners can then download shows onto their portable players. According to eMarketer, the total podcast audience in the United States was 18.5 million in 2007 and will rise to 65 million by 2012.[35]

Some people describe podcasts as "TiVo for radio." Just as TiVo technology allows you to capture a television program while you're away from the set and then watch it at a time of your convenience, podcasting enables people to download their favorite radio shows to an MP3 device and then listen to them later whenever and wherever they please. To subscribe to a podcast, you need not only a computer and PMP but also podcast-receiving software called an *aggregator*.

Free Aggregators

Free podcast-receiving software is available at:

*www.iPodder.orgwww
.dopplerradio.ne*

A tutorial on how to subscribe to a podcast is available at:

*http://radio.about.com/od/
podcastinl/a/aa030805a
.htm*

7.4 DIGITAL CAMERAS: Changing Photography

What are some of the things I can do with digital cameras?

By now both professional and amateur photographers alike have pretty much abandoned film. "The evolution is having profound and unforeseen effects on society," says one analysis, "from changing the way that people record their daily lives to making it harder to trust the images we see."[36]

How Digital Cameras Work

What would motivate me to buy a digital camera?

We described general principles of digital cameras in Chapter 5. Here we consider the subject in more detail.

An Apple Powerbook with a connected digital camera

The most obvious statement to make about digital cameras (or "digicams") is this: They do not use film. Instead, a digital camera uses a light-sensitive processor chip to capture photographic images in digital form and store them on a flash memory card. You can review your just-shot picture on the camera's LCD monitor, the little screen that displays what the camera lens sees, and decide whether to keep it or to try another angle in your next shot.

In general, digital cameras seem to be getting smaller, thinner (the size but not the thickness of a credit card), and less expensive, but they are also capable of performing more tricks. Product releases occur so frequently that it is impossible to present an up-to-date picture of the various models. However, we can outline certain general guidelines.

POINT-AND-SHOOT VERSUS SINGLE-LENS REFLEX (SLR) "Point-and-shoots are fun to tote around," says David Ritz, who runs the 1,200-store Ritz Camera Centers, "but with an SLR, the picture is brighter and crisper."[37]

- **Point-and-shoot: A _point-and-shoot camera_ is a camera, either film or digital, that automatically adjusts settings such as exposure and focus.** Generally such cameras cost under $500. Manufacturers of digital point-and-shoots include Canon, Casio, Fuji, Hewlett-Packard, Kodak, Konika, Nikon, Olympus, Panasonic, Pentax, Samsung, Sony, and Vivitar, whose prices range from $100 up to about $500. (Average: $146.)[38] Point-and-shoots vary in size from subcompacts to compacts to superzooms.[39]

  While a point-and-shoot autofocus will do most of the work for you automatically, you may find it useful to get a camera that also has manual controls, so that you can take it over if you want. (A new example is a brand-new camera format called "micro four thirds," developed by Olympus and Panasonic, which basically "lets compact cameras behave more like expensive SLRs," in one description, so you can use interchangeable lenses and accessory flashes.)[40]

  Of course, there are also disposable point-and-shoot cameras, such as the Kodak Zoom and the Fugifilm QuickSnap True Definition, selling for $12–$16, which are useful if you're afraid you might leave an expensive camera behind on the beach (and if you don't need high-quality images).

- **Single-lens reflex: A _single-lens reflex (SLR) camera_ is a camera, either film or digital, that has a mirror that reflects the incoming light in such a way that the scene viewed by the viewer through the viewfinder is the same as what's framed by the lens.** A digital SLR (DSLR), which may cost anywhere from $450 on up, is the choice of "prosumers" (professional consumers, such as professional photographers and serious amateurs) because it provides more manual options and better image quality and allows the use of interchangeable lenses, from wide angle to telephoto. Some manufacturers in this category include Canon, Nikon, Pentax, and Olympus, whose prices range from $450 to

$1,300 (and $750–$2,700 for advanced SLRs). However, Nikon and Canon now make a less-costly "mini-SLR" that puts sophisticated features into lighter camera bodies.[41]

RESOLUTION: MEGAPIXELS & SENSORS *Resolution* refers to image sharpness. A digital camera's resolution is expressed in **_megapixels_, or millions of picture elements, the electronic dots making up an image.** The more megapixels a digital camera has, the better the resolution and the higher the quality of the image, and so the higher the price of the camera. The millions of pixels are tightly packed together on the camera's image sensor, a half-inch-wide silicon chip. When light strikes a pixel, it generates an electric current that is converted into the digital data that becomes your photograph.

- **How many megapixels are best?** Megapixels measure the maximum resolution of an image taken by the camera at its *top settings*. Megapixels are in the range of 7–12 for subcompact point-and-shoot cameras, 7–12 for compact cameras, and 5–12 for single-lens reflex cameras. "If you shoot mainly 4 × 6s and rarely crop pictures," says *Consumer Reports*, "most cameras that have 7 or 8 megapixels should be fine. But if you print poster-sized shots or do major cropping, an 8-, 10-, or even 12-megapixel model makes more sense."[42]

- **Don't forget sensor size:** But there's another consideration besides megapixels: sensor size. The best overall predictor of image quality is not megapixels but the size of the sensor inside the camera. "Big sensors

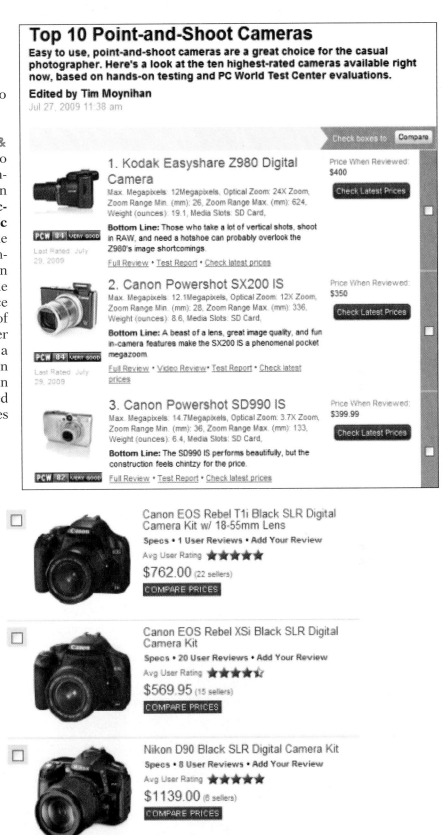

Top 10 Point-and-Shoot Cameras

Easy to use, point-and-shoot cameras are a great choice for the casual photographer. Here's a look at the ten highest-rated cameras available right now, based on hands-on testing and PC World Test Center evaluations.

Edited by Tim Moynihan
Jul 27, 2009 11:38 am

Check boxes to **Compare**

1. Kodak Easyshare Z980 Digital Camera
Max. Megapixels: 12Megapixels, Optical Zoom: 24X Zoom, Zoom Range Min. (mm): 26, Zoom Range Max. (mm): 624, Weight (ounces): 19.1, Media Slots: SD Card,

Bottom Line: Those who take a lot of vertical shots, shoot in RAW, and need a hotshoe can probably overlook the Z980's image shortcomings.

PCW 84 VERY GOOD
Last Rated: July 29, 2009

Full Review • Test Report • Check latest prices

Price When Reviewed: $400
Check Latest Prices

2. Canon Powershot SX200 IS
Max. Megapixels: 12.1Megapixels, Optical Zoom: 12X Zoom, Zoom Range Min. (mm): 28, Zoom Range Max. (mm): 336, Weight (ounces): 8.6, Media Slots: SD Card,

Bottom Line: A beast of a lens, great image quality, and fun in-camera features make the SX200 IS a phenomenal pocket megazoom.

PCW 84 VERY GOOD
Last Rated: July 29, 2009

Full Review • Video Review • Test Report • Check latest prices

Price When Reviewed: $350
Check Latest Prices

3. Canon Powershot SD990 IS
Max. Megapixels: 14.7Megapixels, Optical Zoom: 3.7X Zoom, Zoom Range Min. (mm): 36, Zoom Range Max. (mm): 133, Weight (ounces): 6.4, Media Slots: SD Card,

Bottom Line: The SD990 IS performs beautifully, but the construction feels chintzy for the price.

PCW 82 VERY GOOD

Full Review • Test Report • Check latest prices

Price When Reviewed: $399.99
Check Latest Prices

Canon EOS Rebel T1i Black SLR Digital Camera Kit w/ 18-55mm Lens
Specs • 1 User Reviews • Add Your Review
Avg User Rating ★★★★★
$762.00 (22 sellers)
COMPARE PRICES

Canon EOS Rebel XSi Black SLR Digital Camera Kit
Specs • 20 User Reviews • Add Your Review
Avg User Rating ★★★★½
$569.95 (15 sellers)
COMPARE PRICES

Nikon D90 Black SLR Digital Camera Kit
Specs • 8 User Reviews • Add Your Review
Avg User Rating ★★★★★
$1139.00 (6 sellers)
COMPARE PRICES

Nikon D5000 Black SLR Digital Camera Kit w/ 18-55mm Lens
Specs • 1 User Reviews • Add Your Review
Avg User Rating ★★★★★
$748.99 (17 sellers)
COMPARE PRICES

Point-and-shoot cameras are less expensive than SLR cameras. SLR cameras are more sophisticated than point-and-shoot cameras.

Digicam. HP Photosmart digital camera.

absorb more light, so you get better color and sharper low-light images," points out one technology writer. "Small sensors pack too many light-absorbing pixels into too little space, so heat builds up, creating digital 'noise' (random speckles) on your photos."[43] Thus, in response to a reader who asks whether he should get 7 or 10–12 megapixels for a point-and-shoot, technology expert David Einstein points out that sensors in SLR digital cameras, such as those used by professional photographers, use sensors the size of a 35-mm negative, so they can easily handle more than 12 megapixels. However, he says, "most point-and-shoot sensors . . . are fingernail-size. If you cram too many pixels onto them, they produce interference (noise) that can hurt picture quality."[44] Thus, he suggests looking for a point-and-shoot with 7 or 8 megapixels.

LENSES People talk as though megapixels are the main factor affecting photographic quality, but that's not all. You need to have a lens that ensures that your picture is properly focused and that pulls in enough light to get good exposure.

As for zoom lenses, you should be aware of the difference between digital zoom and optical zoom:

- **Digital zoom:** Manufacturers like to tout *digital zoom*, but, says one description, it's just another way of saying "we'll crop the image for you in the camera."[45] Indeed, it actually lowers the resolution and often can produce a grainier photo.

- **Optical zoom:** Only an *optical zoom* will bring you closer to your subject without your having to move. That is, the lens actually extends to make distant objects seem larger and closer. Optical zooms may be of the telescoping type or internal (untelescoping) type; the latter allows a camera to start up fast.

Most subcompact and compact point-and-shoot cameras come with a 3X to 7X optical zoom, which is good for wide-angle, normal, and telephoto shots. If you're an experienced photographer, you should look for a superzoom camera with 10X to 18X optical zoom.

STORAGE Instead of being stored on film, the camera's digital images are stored on flash memory cards inside the camera. (● *See Panel 7.3.*) Cards come

panel 7.3
Digital camera's flash memory card

in a variety of formats, including Secure Digital (SD), Multimedia, Compact Flash, Memory Stick, and Smart Media. Most cameras come with "starter" cards, usually 16 or 32 megabytes, which hold only a handful of photos. You'll need a card (which is reusable) with at least 128 megabytes of storage space, which will hold about 80 images from a 3-megapixel camera (depending on the resolution you set it at). A 1-gigabyte card will hold 600 still images at top resolution or more than 40 minutes of video from a 5-megapixel camera.

OPTICAL VIEWFINDERS & LCD SCREENS The original digital cameras had tiny screens, which made it difficult to review photos before deciding whether to save or delete them. Now more cameras come with both optical viewfinders and LCD screens.

- **Optical viewfinders:** The *optical viewfinder* is the eye-level optical glass device on the camera that, when you look through it, shows the image to be photographed. Some digital cameras omit the viewfinder, forcing you to use only the LCD, which forces you to hold the camera with arms extended, making you more apt to shake the camera.

- **LCD screens:** The *LCD (liquid crystal display) screens* usually measure 2 inches or more diagonally and allow you to review the photos you take. It's best to get a camera with an LCD that can be seen well in daylight if you do a lot of outdoor shooting.

START-UP TIME, SHUTTER LAG, & CONTINUOUS SHOOTING A digital camera, like a PC, needs time to start up. You should look for one that takes no longer than a second or two, so that you won't miss that one-of-a-kind shot that suddenly appears out of nowhere. Another recommendation: You should look for a digicam with the least shutter lag, that annoying delay between the time you press the shutter-release button and the time the exposure is complete. Many digital cameras have a special setting called "burst" or "continuous" mode, which allows you to squeeze off a limited number of shots without pausing—helpful if you're taking pictures at sports events.

BATTERY LIFE "For digital photographers," says one writer, "film is no longer a worry. But batteries are more important than ever."[46] Some cameras come with rechargeable batteries, although they aren't always replaceable at the nearest drugstore (and replacements can be expensive, perhaps $40–$60). Some require you to recharge the battery inside the camera; others, in a separate charger; others, in both ways. Some cameras also require proprietary batteries, which also aren't as readily available. Regardless, you should be sure you have lots of batteries before setting out on a trip.

"A good rule of thumb," says technology writer Walter Mossberg, "is that a camera should be able to get a day's worth of shooting out of a single battery charge. Depending on how you use your camera, this could mean 20, 50, 100, or 200 shots. Battery life varies depending on the size and quality of the images, how much of the time you use the flash, and whether you keep the LCD screen on all the time or use it sparingly."[47]

Survival Tip

Reformat Your Memory Card to Avoid Losing Your Photos

Some picture takers delete unwanted photos as they go along. But they can lose ("crash") their saved images if they aren't careful. The reason: Using the camera's Delete function to remove unwanted images simply spreads the pictures around the card, causing fragmentation that leads to the same errors that can plague a computer's hard drive. To avoid this problem, you should download all your images to a computer each night and then reformat the memory card. Or if you don't have access to a PC, you should bring extra memory cards.

Reviews of Digital Cameras

For independent reviews of digital cameras, try the following sites:

www.cnet.com *www.dpreview .com*

www.pcmag.com

Digital Camera Battery Help and Tips

Purchasing and getting the most out of digital camera batteries, whether your digital camera uses an alkaline battery, rechargable NiMH battery, or propietary battery.

Free battery tips from *http://malektips.com/digital_camera_battery_help_and_tips.html*

SHOOTING VIDEO CLIPS Although at one time digital cameras could shoot only about 30 seconds of video, today some digicams are available that, with a 1-gigabyte memory card, can shoot as much as 44 minutes at 30 frames per second—the same frame rate as camcorders. However, other cameras shoot at only 15 frames per second, which may store as little as 20 seconds on a clip and present a slightly jerky image. Digicams have begun to become popular for their video features because they are smaller in size than camcorders, which won't fit in a pocket.

Yet despite the advances in video quality, digital cameras still have limitations compared with video camcorders:

- **Zoom:** Most camcorders allow you to zoom in and out while shooting. Most digital cameras don't.

- **Sound:** Camcorders shoot in stereo sound. Digicams record in mono sound from tiny microphones of lower quality.

- **Storage:** A camcorder can store images on a 60-minute MiniDV tape cassette costing about $5. A digital camera storing 44 minutes requires a 1-gigabyte memory card costing about $20.

TRANSFERRING IMAGES Let's assume you've spent a day taking pictures. How do you get them out of your camera? Here are the principal methods:

- **Use a direct connection between your camera and your computer:** You'll need to have used the installation CD included with your digital camera to install the drivers and software on your PC. Then you can connect your camera to the computer using the USB or FireWire cable that came with it. (One end attaches to a slot on the camera, the other end to an open USB or FireWire port on the computer.) Most newer cameras support USB 2.0. After connecting the camera (which must be turned on during the process), you open its software and use it to transfer the photos into the PC, typically placing the pictures into a default folder, such as My Pictures in the My Documents folder.

- **Insert the memory card into your computer or a card reader:** Assuming your PC has a built-in slot for your memory card (USB card) or has a card reader attached to a USB port, you can remove the memory card from the camera and insert it into the slot. External card readers cost $20 or so.

- **Put your camera in a cradle attached to your PC:** Many camera manufacturers include cradles into which you can set your camera and use it to transfer photos to your PC. Some cradles also are able to charge your camera, if it has rechargeable batteries.

- **Use an online photo developer:** After downloading your photo to your computer, you can go online and send your images to an online photo developer, such as Shutterfly, Kodak EasyShare, Flickr, or others mentioned in the Practical Action box on p. 377.

- **Use a photo printer with a built-in card slot:** If you've bought one of the newer photo printers, you can skip using a PC entirely and insert the memory card from your camera into a slot in the printer.

- **Use a portable hard drive, CD burner, or MP3 player:** If you're traveling and don't have access to a PC (not even a laptop), you could pack a portable hard drive. There are portable CD burners available that can record images directly from your camera memory card. Finally, if you have a portable media player, such as an Apple iPod, you can use its several megabytes or even gigabytes of hard drive to store your photos. What's needed is a device (such as Delkin Devices' USB Bridge) that will directly transfer data from the memory card to the PMP.

PRACTICAL ACTION
Online Viewing & Sharing of Digital Photos

You have a great photo of the sunset at Lake Tahoe. How do you share it with others? You could always print it out and mail it via U.S. mail. Or you could try the following alternatives.

- **Send as an email attachment:** You can download your photos to a PC and then send them as attached computer files to an email message. The drawback, however, is that if you have a lot of photos, it can quickly fill up the recipient's email inbox or take a lot of time if you are sending multiple images to multiple people.

- **Use an online photo-sharing service:** Web-based photo-sharing services provide online storage space for your photos and make it easier to share, especially if they are high-resolution files. Examples are Shutterfly, Kodak EasyShare Gallery, Snapfish, Flickr, AOL Pictures, dotPhoto, Webshots, Fotki, MyPhotoAlbum, Funtigo, Smugmug, and PhotoSite. No special software is required for you to upload from your computer, but a broadband connection is strongly recommended. Some charge fees, some do not.

Be sure to find out whether you have to renew membership or make a purchase in order to keep your photos from being deleted after 6 or 12 months.

- **Use an online service that allows direct transfer between computers:** This third approach uses peer-to-peer technology, which avoids your having to upload your photos on the company's server. An example is OurPictures.

- **If you have a camera with Wi-Fi transmitter, transmit your photos wirelessly:** Some kinds of cameras (such as the Nikon P1 and P2 or Kodak EasyShareOne) are built with Wi-Fi transmitters for wireless networking. Thus, if you're within range of a Wi-Fi hotspot in a coffee shop or airport lounge, you can post pictures to your website or to a photo-sharing service such as Flickr.

- **Use a photo-printing kiosk:** Various photo-printing kiosks are available at fast-food restaurants, big retailers, amusement parks, scrapbook-making stores, cruise ships, hospitals, and other high-traffic areas and can produce a standard 4 × 6 print in 4 seconds.

- **Use a photo lab:** Photo stores and labs, as well as Costco, Kinko's, Target, Walgreens, and Walmart, often sell inexpensive services (perhaps $3–$7) in which they will transfer the images on a memory card onto a CD and then clear the card for reuse. They will also print photos for you.

- **Bring along your own card reader and CDs and use others' computers:** If you bring along your own card reader and blank CDs, you can use other people's computers to store your images. These PCs could belong to friends, of course, but also to hotel business centers and internet cafés.

The Societal Effects of Digital Cameras

How have digital cameras changed the way people take pictures?

One result of the evolution in photography is that people are taking their cameras everywhere, either in backpacks or purses or as mobile phones with built-in cameras. (We describe cellphones and smartphones in another few pages.) Another is that people take far more pictures than they used to—perhaps 20 or more of a single scene, instead of three or four—since they don't have to worry about the cost of film and processing, and with digital it's easy to simply delete bad shots. (About 23% of all digital images captured by cameras are deleted.)[48] A third consequence may be that photography is becoming more casual, with more off-the-cuff snapshots being taken instead of subjects being asked to pose stiffly for formal portraits. The digital camera "leads to more openness," says sociologist John Grady of Wheaton College in Massachusetts, whose research specialty involves photography. "People are getting more documentary in style."[49] Yet Grady also thinks that people are taking more care than ever with the photos they keep, shooting a flurry of images but then spending time selecting the best one and touching it up to eliminate small blemishes.

All these developments may be bringing about different sensibilities about the value of photographs. On the one hand, images are now being viewed as less important. People take a quick look at photos emailed to them, for instance, and then immediately trash them. Or, since only a fraction of all digital photos are ever printed out, they park the images on their computer hard drives and then forget about them. (Only about 13% of digital images captured ever end up on paper—compared to 98% of film images.)[50] On the other hand, those photos that do end up being saved and treasured may have been so doctored to improve reality, with the help of photo-altering programs such as Apple's iPhoto or Adobe's Photoshop Elements, that tomorrow's generations may question their authenticity. Muses one writer, will future anthropologists wonder "Why do all those people look so good?"[51]

7.5 PERSONAL DIGITAL ASSISTANTS & TABLET PCS

How could I use a PDA and tablet PC to help me in college?

Downloads for Handhelds

Websites offering software downloads for PDAs and smartphones:

www.download.com

www.handango.com

www.pocketgear.com

There you are in an unfamiliar city, looking for a restaurant. Fortunately, you have your Palm Treo with software, Zagat to Go, that has not only a review of the restaurant but also a map of how to get there and even a formula for calculating tips. Maybe you also have an application called WorldMate, software offering other tools for the sophisticated traveler, such as "weather forecasts, a clock that can display times around the world, a currency converter, a tax and tip calculator, clothing size converters, and international dialing codes," as one report describes it.[52]

Palm and Pocket PC are two of the best-known *handhelds* or *palmtops,* more usually called *personal digital assistants.* As we mentioned in Chapter 1, a ***personal digital assistant (PDA)* is a portable device that stores personal organization tools, such as schedule planner, address book, and to-do list, along with other, more specialized software,** if you want it. In 2007, the top vendors of handheld devices (PDAs) were Palm (36.2% market share) and Hewlett-Packard (25%), followed by Mio, Sharp, and Fujitsu Siemens.[53] However, shipments of handheld devices slipped 53% at the end of that year, as users turned their attention to other devices that could do the same thing, most especially smartphones, the converged devices that combine PDAs and cellphones.

How a PDA Works

What things should I know about PDA operation?

As we've mentioned elsewhere, a PDA is basically a small computer, with specially designed processors and operating system software, the principal ones being Palm OS (found on Palm and Sony PDAs) and Microsoft Windows Mobile (found on Hewlett-Packard and other PDAs). All feature touch-sensitive screens that allow you to enter data with a stylus, by tapping or writing on the screen.

DATA STORAGE Data is stored in RAM (128 megabytes), ordinarily a volatile form of storage that loses all contents when shut off (as in a desktop PC) but which in PDAs is kept functioning with a small amount of power running off the battery even after you've turned the machine off. The built-in RAM can be augmented by storage on flash memory cards (256 megabytes up to 1 gigabyte), which slide into a slot in the PDA. The latest versions contain an actual miniature hard drive, which enables users to view hours of video and play hundreds of songs.

POWER SOURCES Batteries in PDAs are usually lithium ion, which can be recharged. Adapters also enable you to plug your PDA into a standard AC wall electrical outlet.

TRANSFERRING FILES To transfer files from your PDA to your desktop PC or laptop (and the reverse), you can do three things: (1) You can pull out your PDA's flash card and insert it into your computer's card reader, either built in or connected through a USB port. (2) You can put your PDA in a special cradle that is plugged into a USB port. Finally, (3) you can transfer data wirelessly, using (in the latest models) the PDA's built-in Wi-Fi or Bluetooth capability.

The Future of PDAs

In what ways could PDAs evolve?

As smart cellphones continue to usurp many of the personal information management kinds of features that characterized the original PDAs, it seems likely that new PDAs will take on specialized functions. Examples:

DISPLAYING TELEVISION & PHOTOGRAPHS Instead of being personal information organizers, the original purpose of PDAs, handhelds may migrate toward single-purpose uses such as playing TV shows or displaying photographs.

HANDHELD WEATHER METERS A handheld weather meter can range from a simple and inexpensive wind meter, useful for golfers and windsurfers, to a high-tech device that tracks almost all other aspects of weather, including figuring out the wind chill, useful for skiers and snowboarders.

GPS LOCATORS Global Positioning System locators have already become popular with hiking buffs. "With a GPS, rediscovering a swell secret swimming hole year after year can be about as stressful as making your way to your own mailbox," says one writer.[54] Wristwatch models are also available to help runners pace themselves and track performance. Portable GPS navigators, such as those made by Garmin, TomTom, and Magellan, range in price between $149 and $699.[55] However, GPS is yet another feature that is now made available with most smartphones, as we'll discuss.[56]

Tablet PCs

How useful would a tablet PC be to me?

The PDA seems to be evolving into a different kind of appliance, perhaps a smartphone. Could the same be true of the tablet PC?

As we stated earlier, a *tablet PC* is a special notebook computer outfitted with a digitizer tablet and a stylus that allows a user to handwrite text on the unit's screen. The stylus can take the place of a keyboard when users use an on-screen input panel or tap letters and numbers directly on an on-screen keyboard. (● *See Panel 7.4, next page.*)

Tablet PCs have not had the success that was anticipated for them, with only about 3% of laptops sold being tablets in 2007.[57] One problem is that traditionally tablets have cost $200–$400 more than notebook PCs. Even so, these portable devices have found their uses in a handful of schools for student use in classes on such subjects as English, foreign languages, math, science, and social studies.

PDA. (*Top*) LifeDrive mobile managers feature gigabytes of storage and both Wi-Fi and Bluetooth. They allow you to carry files from your desktop computer and access them wherever you go. You can also access the internet and email, record voice messages, and listen to MP3 files. (*Bottom*) Inexpensive Peek mobile email-only PDA.

7.6 THE NEW TELEVISION

What's new about the new television?

"It's a transformation as significant as when we went from black-and-white to color," says *Newsweek* technology writer Steven Levy, "and it's already under way." We are nearing the day when we can watch almost any kind of TV programming anywhere, on a huge high-definition screen or on a smart cellphone.[58]

Interactive, Internet-Ready, & Mobile TV

How do experts distinguish between different technological ways TV can be used?

Today there are many kinds of equipment available for watching TV, some of the more interesting of which are as follows.

INTERACTIVE TV *Interactive TV* **lets you interact with the show you're watching,** so that you can request information about a product or play along with a game show. We see this type of TV used with shows involving viewer voting, such as that for *American Idol* or *Dancing with the Stars.* A system being tested by Backchannel Media offers viewers programs and ads they can respond to by clicking on icons they see on their screens, and the system then sends information to a site on the viewer's computer, where he or she can look it up.[59]

INTERNET TV *Internet TV* **is television distributed via the internet,** allowing users to choose shows from a library of shows. Thus, if you're accustomed to paying $40 or more a month for TV channels, you should know that all the major networks—ABC, CBS, NBC, and Fox—post many of their shows online (see Hulu.com and uStream). About 11% of adults ages 18–34 already watch TV online at least once a week.[60] This means that internet TV can be distributed via broadband, Wi-Fi, cable, or satellite. Thus, for example, you use a Netflix set-top box (made by Roku) to connect your broadband network to your TV and have access to Netflix's library of more than 10,000 movies and TV shows on demand.[61]

INTERNET-READY TV *Internet-ready TV* (which some people also call "internet TV") **consists of television sets that allow viewers to watch TV shows as well as go online to get news, stream movies, view photos,** and the like. The models introduced by LG, Panasonic, Samsung, Sony, and Toshiba feature a built-in Ethernet port, so that you can plug an Ethernet cable into the back of the TV. At present, internet-ready TVs do not have browsers, so you can't just go to any website you want in cyberspace.[62]

If you don't own an internet-ready TV but want to send videos or photos from your PC screen onto your TV set's screen, you can do so by buying a $300 box called SlingCatcher.[63] Some open-source software called Boxee, which you install on your computer, can act as a program guide to a lot of the video available on the internet that you can view on your TV.[64] Finally, Adobe Systems is hoping that its standard for online video known as Adobe Flash will be widely adopted so that Hollywood studios and other content creators can cheaply distribute video to TVs and mobile phones.[65]

MOBILE TV "Tiny TV," television displayed on cellphone screens, has been available in Japan and South Korea for a number of years and more recently in Switzerland and Italy. Now broadcasters across Europe and the United States are investing in the necessary equipment to make mobile TV more widely available.

Three Kinds of Television: DTV, HDTV, SDTV

Why is it important to differentiate among the three types of TV?

When most of us used to tune in our TV sets, we got analog television, a system of varying signal amplitude and frequency that represents picture and sound elements. Since 1996, however, things have become more complicated.

DIGITAL TELEVISION (DTV) In 1996, broadcasters and their government regulator, the Federal Communications Commission (FCC), adopted a standard called *__digital television (DTV)__*, **which uses a digital signal, or series of 0s and 1s.** DTV is much clearer and less prone to interference than the old analog TV, which disappeared on June 12, 2009, requiring viewers to acquire a converter box.

HIGH-DEFINITION TELEVISION (HDTV) A form of digital TV, *__high-definition television (HDTV)__* **works with digital broadcasting signals and has a wider screen and higher resolution than analog television had.** Whereas standard analog TV has a width-to-height ratio, or *aspect ratio*, of 4 to 3, HDTV has an aspect ratio of 16 to 9, which is similar to the wide-screen approach used in movies. In addition, compared to analog display screens, an HDTV display has 10 times more pixels on a screen—1,920 × 1,080 pixels or more. Thus, HDTV could have 1,080 lines on a screen, compared with 525-line resolution for analog TV.

Analog TV

HDTV

Extra image area

STANDARD-DEFINITION TELEVISION (SDTV) HDTV takes a lot of bandwidth that broadcasters could use instead for *__standard-definition television (SDTV)__*, **which has a lower resolution, a minimum of 480 vertical lines, and a picture quality similar to that required to watch DVD movies.** What's important about the SDTV standard is that it enables broadcasters to transmit more information within the HDTV bandwidth. That is, broadcasters can *multicast* their products, transmitting up to five SDTV programs simultaneously—and getting perhaps five times the revenue—instead of just one HDTV program. "Multicast services piggyback on digital signals from local stations," says one report, "including those offering HDTV versions of ABC, CBS, Fox, NBC, and PBS. . . . Stations typically get multicast programming for free and sell five minutes an hour of air time. The networks sell an additional five minutes to national advertisers."[66] With so many extra channels, having enough content becomes a problem. Thus, we will no doubt see tons of reruns of vintage TV shows, from *The Lone Ranger* to *The Addams Family*.

Choosing a TV

For HDTV FAQs, go to

http://hometheater.about.com/ od/televisionbasics/

PRACTICAL ACTION
Buying the Right Flat-Panel TV

Picture-tube, or CRT, televisions are still available, and they are low-priced, but they are bulky and rapidly disappearing. The most popular HDTVs are flat-panels, which are of three basic types.[67]

- **LCD TVs:** Liquid-crystal display (LCD) screens are thin (some about 1 inch thick) and lightweight, so they can be hung on a wall. Smaller sets, those below 40 inches in size, are only available in LCD models. LCDs tend to have a longer life than plasmas, about 50,000 hours, but a narrower viewing angle, so viewers sitting to the sides may see less contrast and color saturation. At one point, LCDs had a reputation for being too slow for fast-paced sports events, but manufacturers have succeeded in fixing this problem.

- **LED TVs:** To increase sales, several manufacturers have introduced what they call LED TVs, but there is really no such thing as an LED TV. As one writer points out, "they are simply LCD TVs that use LEDs [light-emitting diodes], rather than fluorescent lamps, to light the screen."[68] Some LED sets can approach the level of deepest blacks that plasma sets have already achieved, but they could well cost more than twice as much.

- **Plasma TVs:** Although life span is only about 30,000 hours, plasma TVs offer higher image sharpness and better viewing angles than LCD TVs do. They are also often cheaper in price than LCDs.

The Societal Effects of the New TV

How has technology changed the way people experience television?

"The ethos of New TV can be captured in a single sweeping mantra," says Steven Levy, *"anything you want to see, any time, on any device"* (his emphasis).[69]

TIME SHIFTING: CHANGING WHEN YOU WATCH TV Personal video recorders like those marketed by TiVo allow viewers to watch favorite shows at their own convenience rather than following a broadcast schedule. They also enable viewers to freeze-frame action sequences and to skip commercials. (What this could eventually do to advertising as the economic underpinning for free-to-viewers television can only be guessed at.)

Another technology affecting the "when" is **_video on demand_ (VOD or VoD), which consists of a wide set of technologies that enable viewers to select videos or TV programs from a central server to watch when they want,** rather than when TV programmers offer them.

SPACE SHIFTING: CHANGING WHERE YOU WATCH TV New technology is allowing you to download or receive TV programs, either stored or real-time, and watch them on some sort of handheld device. For instance, the SlingCatcher and the SlingPlayer Mobile from Sling Media enable you to watch a program playing on your living room TV on your laptop computer—anywhere in the world.

CONTENT SHIFTING: CHANGING THE NATURE OF TV PROGRAMS Perhaps the most important development is the movement of television to the internet. This is made possible by **_IPTV_, short for _Internet Protocol Television_, in which television and video signals are sent to viewers using internet protocols.** Cable and satellite channels have limited capacity, but the internet "has room for everything," Levy points out. As a consequence, you may be able to cram even *more* programs on your screen simultaneously—and what does that do to the human attention span? (Multiple-channel TV sets are now available with

The SlingPlayer is a companion to the Slingbox. SlingPlayer Mobile lets you watch and control your home TV and DVR, via your Slingbox, on your BlackBerry, iPhone, Windows Mobile, or Palm OS. (*Left*) SlingPlayer Mobile device; (*top*) back of Slingbox; (*bottom*) front of Slingbox.

what are known as "mosaic" screens that allow sports fans, for instance, to watch eight separate games on one screen.)

7.7 E-BOOK READERS: The New Reading Machines

Can electronic books really improve on printed books?

How much content could you comfortably read online? A few paragraphs from a Wikipedia entry? Some gossip about Jennifer Aniston? An entire novel? A textbook?

Many people find it difficult to read at length on a computer screen, which is why printed textbooks, for instance, remain more popular than online versions of the same thing. In recent years, however, e-books and e-book readers have begun to gain some ground over paper-and-print versions of the book.

An **e-book, or *electronic book*, is an electronic text, the digital-media equivalent of a conventional printed book.** You can read an e-book on your personal computer or smartphone (such as the iPhone or BlackBerry), the kind of devices Barnes & Noble is aiming for in offering 700,000 e-books.[70] (Scribd Inc. is one website that allows people to post and read e-books online.)[71] Or you can read it on a specialized piece of hardware known as an ***e-book reader*, a device specifically designed to allow people to read electronic books.** The most well-known examples are Amazon's Kindle (in three versions) and Sony's Reader, but competitors are coming forward with their own devices, such as Barnes & Noble's Plastic Logic eReader.[72] (Other e-book readers: Bookeen's Cybook, Elonex's eBook, Endless ideas's BeBook, Astak's Hanlin eReader and EZ Reader, Interead's COOL-ER, Samsung's Papyrus and SNE-50K, iRex's iLiad and Digital Reader, Foxit's eSlick.)

How an E-Book Reader Works

What is electronic paper?

Different e-book readers use different e-software formats. They include Adobe Acrobat, Microsoft Reader, and an open format called ePub. Amazon's Kindle uses a format called Topaz (which can be read on the iPod Touch and the iPhone as well). The Sony Reader uses ePub, and it can also handle PDF documents.

(*Left*) The Kindle 2; (*right*) Sony Reader PRS 700.

What makes e-book readers supposedly easier to read than e-books viewed on your PC monitor? Both Kindle and Sony use something called Vizplex (made by E Ink), the trade-marked name of a layered substance that makes up the 6-inch-high display area that you read from. Vizplex is an "electronic paper" that was developed to act like real paper, to rely on reflected light, not the backlight used by computers and phone screens, which can be hard on the eyes. Thus, the Kindle 2 supports 16 shades of gray (but no color), to make photos sharp, and there's no glare, no eyestrain—and no battery consumption (you use power only when you actually turn the page; the rest of the time, the ink pattern remains on the screen without power).[73]

Once you've acquired an e-book reader—for what could be $300 (Sony Reader), $299 (Kindle 2), or $489 (Kindle DX), for example—you may then download books by wireless access. In the case of the Kindle 2, this is more than 230,000 titles.[74] The machine features control buttons (next/previous page, menu, and so on). Built-in batteries last about two weeks if the wireless capability is off, about four days if it's on. If you turn the DX on its side, the screen changes from portrait to landscape. The Kindle DX has a 9.7-inch screen (compared to Kindle 2's 6-inch), which is designed to be used with newspapers, magazines, and textbooks.

The Benefits of E-Book Readers

What good would an e-book reader be to me?

There are many benefits to having an e-book reader. One e-book reader can store hundreds or even thousands of books—1,500 books, in the case of the Kindle 2, 3,500 for the Kindle DX.[75] Thus, instead of carrying several books around, you carry just a single gadget, which will be lighter and occupy less space than a conventional book or books. You can download e-books through a wireless connection. Type size and type faces can be adjusted. An e-book can be read in low light. The e-book will automatically open to the page where you left off. Text can be searched automatically and cross-referenced. You can bookmark pages, search within your library, look up definitions, and annotate text. Text-to-speech software can produce an audio version of an e-book.[76] Some machines, such as the Kindle DX, also play MP3s and have a crude web browser.[77]

At present, many e-books are being offered at bargain-basement prices—$9.99 or less, in the case of Kindle, as compared to hardcover prices of (for novels) $25–$27.[78] However, it's doubtful this introductory pricing will last. Although e-books mean publishers save on the cost of paper, binding, and shipping, publishers argue these costs make up only 12.5% of the average hardcover retail list price, while the costs of writing, editing, and marketing remain the same.[79]

The Drawbacks of E-Book Readers

Why might I avoid using an e-book?

The biggest complaint about the 2009 e-book readers has been the high price, although this will no doubt change. Consumers have to weigh the risk of buying a $300 or $400 reading appliance that may be easily lost, damaged, stolen, or hacked compared to buying a regular book at a tenth or less of its price (and that may be resold). One also has to consider that the reader doesn't actually own the e-books that are downloaded to the e-book reader; rather, they are like licensing a piece of software—you can only run them on certain designated devices and they can't be resold or passed on to someone else.[80]

One writer also found fault with the way photographs, charts, diagrams, foreign characters, and tables appeared on the gray screen of the Kindle. The beautiful illustrations and drawings in the print version of one science book turned out to be hard to make out in the electronic version. Tables in a medical book were garbled and the color coding was lost. An elaborate chart in a highly expensive engineering book was totally illegible in its electronic form.[81]

Many students, both high school and college, are reportedly less than enamored with e-books as textbooks. Some complain that the e-texts cost too much at the outset, that they are awkward and inconvenient, that publishers make them difficult to share and print, that they can't be kept for future reference, and that they can't be resold. Indeed, one study of 504 college students found that 75% said they preferred print to digital texts.[82]

Peter Fader, co-director of the Wharton Interactive Media Initiative, believes the e-book reader will probably go the way of other single-use machines. In an age in which cellphones double as cameras, music players, and computers, he suggests, it is only a matter of time before electronic readers will be embedded on some future version of the iPod Touch.[83] Growing numbers of people, however, have already turned to their mobile phones to do their reading.[84] We consider smartphones next.

7.8 SMARTPHONES: More Than Talk

How are smartphones different from basic cellphones?

"There's a digital land rush going on," says *New York Times* technology writer Steve Lohr, "driven by rapid advances in technology that make it possible to put more and more tools of higher and higher quality into phones."[85]

Lohr is referring to **_smartphones_, cellular telephones with microprocessor, memory, display screen, and built-in modem.** A *smartphone* "combines the functionality of a PDA (or Pocket PC) with a phone," in one writer's description.[86] It differs from a standard cellphone, he suggests, in that users can get their email "pushed" directly to their smartphone anywhere in the world as it arrives; they can view the desktop version of web pages; they have more robust applications for keeping track of contacts and appointments; they can read and edit Word, Excel, and PowerPoint documents on the go; and they can tap into third-party applications, from musical instrument tuners to games.[87] Smartphones offer a wealth of gadgetry: email access, text messaging, cameras, music players, videogames, digital-TV viewing, search tools, personal information management, GPS locators, and even phones doubling as credit cards in some locations (as for use with parking meters and vending machines).

Personal Technology

385

The leading worldwide vendors of smartphones midway through 2009—Nokia (38.3% worldwide share of the market), Samsung (19.4%), LG Electronics (11.1%), Motorola (5.5%), and Sony Ericsson (5.1%)—are companies well known for making TVs, camera, and stereos.[88] In the United States, the top-selling smartphones through March 2009 were the RIM BlackBerry Curve (nearly 50% of the market), Apple iPhone 3G, RIM BlackBerry Storm, RIM BlackBerry Pear, and the T-Mobile G1.[89]

Smartphones are rising fast from the status of gadgets to necessities, and they are also edging out other single-function electronic gadgets, such as music players and GPS devices.[90] Let us consider how smartphones work.

Apple iPhone 3Gs with touch-movable application icons

How a Mobile Phone Works

What are the basic elements of a mobile phone?

In Chapter 6, we described how wireless services use their networks of cell towers to send voice and data over the airwaves in digital form to your cellphone, handing off your call from one cell to another as you move through a series of geographically overlapping cells. The cellphone or smartphone contains many of the same attributes as a personal computer: processor, memory, input/output devices, and operating system (such as the Palm OS, Microsoft Windows Mobile OS, or Mac OSx for the iPhone). The OS, which is stored in read-only memory (ROM) and is run by the processor, provides you with the interface that allows you to store data, change settings, and so on.

STORAGE The data you store in your phone, such as telephone numbers, is stored in ROM, which means that when you turn off the phone, the data does not disappear. Phones now come with 8, 16, or even 32 gigabytes of memory in which you can carry your music, photos, videos, and the like.

INPUT At minimum, cellphones have a keypad for entering numbers and text (and doing text messaging) and a microphone for picking up your voice. Some are also mobile speakerphones, giving you a hands-free option and offering voice-activated dialing. Some phones also offer a touch-sensitive screen or a screen with a stylus. Xerox has developed software to turn a phone into a portable document scanner. Of course, there are phones with built-in digital cameras and camcorders, as we'll describe.

OUTPUT A cellphone includes a receiver or speaker, of course, for picking up voice calls. Mobile phones also have displays ranging from LCD to full-color, high-resolution plasma, suitable for watching TV and playing videogames, as we'll describe. Some phones act as MP3 players and offer FM radio and stereo sound. Others are also able to tap into Wi-Fi and Bluetooth networks.

Incidentally, many states are targeting teenagers and other inexperienced or careless motorists to restrict their use of cellphones behind the wheel. Thus, drivers can now be ticketed in many states for talking on a cellphone without a headset or other hands-free device. Many manufacturers make wireless Bluetooth headsets available.[91]

Smartphone Services

What smartphone services would be most useful to me?

Proof that the phone is morphing into an "everything device" is everywhere. The percentages of people who view nonvoice applications on their cellphones as important features, according to one survey, are as follows: text messaging (73%), camera (67%), email capabilities (63%), accessing the internet (61%), music (34%), and video capability (33%).[92] Let's consider these and other services offered for mobile phones.

TEXT MESSAGING *Text messaging,* or *texting,* is the sending of short messages, generally no more than a couple of hundred characters in length, to a pager, PDA, smartphone, or other handheld device, including notebook computer. They can also be sent to desktop computers and land-line phones. Originally text messaging appeared during the days of mainframe computers, when workers sitting at terminals would send short text messages to each other. In the internet world, these evolved into instant messaging and live text chat sessions. Today text messaging combines the portability of cellphones with the convenience of email and instant messaging. Text messaging is particularly appropriate for situations in which making a cellphone call is intrusive, as when you want to tell someone "I'm 15 minutes late."

Sometimes text messages ("texts") are called *SMSes.* **SMS stands for *Short Message Service,* a text message service originally designed for GSM mobile phones but now available on a range of networks,** including 3G networks. As teenagers have become accustomed to texting, there has developed a streamlined language, so-called *text message lingo,* with terms such as *XLnt* ("excellent"), *fbi* ("I'll look into it"), and *PCM* ("please call me"). (● *See Panel 7.5, next page.*) Some people program into their phone such standard reply phrases as "Yes," "No," "Call me," and "Will call you later."

Incidentally, texters need to be aware that it's unwise to assume that when they hit the Delete button, the messages are gone forever. Like email and instant messages, text messages are often saved on servers, at least for a while.

DOWNLOADED RINGTONES When Shannon Dunham's phone rings, it goes "Knick, knack, patty whack, give your dog a bone"—the Reno, Nevada, woman's favorite childhood jingle—and it indicates to her that the person trying to call her is her mother. Dunham also has 17 other distinct ringtone tunes, including "Maple Leaf Rag" to signal it's her boyfriend calling.[93] If your phone's *ringtone,* **the audible sound a phone makes to announce that a call is coming in,** is still an old-fashioned "ring, ring," perhaps you have some catching up to do. Now, as one writer puts it, your phone could be "vibrating, flashing a photo of the caller across the phone's screen, and, above all, playing music—preferably an actual clip from a song like 'Drop It Like It's Hot' by Snoop Dogg."[94]

Some ringtones may be had for free; others, which you may download from your wireless carrier (such as Cingular, Verizon Wireless, Sprint, and T-Mobile), may cost anywhere from about $1.25 to $4 per tune (not per ring). Ringtones may be *monophonic,* sounding more like beeps or the basic sounds that come on your cellphone when you buy it; *polyphonic,* sounding digitized, sort of like elevator music; or *music tones* (also called *master tones* or *true tones*), real audio clips from songs. Ringtones have become so big that at one time *Billboard* magazine, which follows the music industry, even created a chart of popular hits for them.

EMAIL The most well-known handheld device for sending wireless email is the BlackBerry, produced by Canadian company Research In Motion (RIM) Ltd., which practically created the industry. However, RIM has been joined

Voice-to-Text Dictation

The Samsung P207 features built-in "speech-to-text" technology that turns what you dictate into text on the screen. For more information:

www.cingularwireless.com

www.voicesignal.com

Downloading Ringtones

Some are free. Check if your phone is compatible with the site.

*www.3gforfree
.comwww.3gupload.com*

*www.mbuzzy.comwww
.myphonefiles.com*

www.matrix.com

panel 7.5

Text message lingo
(adapted *from http://
medialiteracy.suitel0l.
com/article.cfm/
decoding_text_
messaging_lingo*)

Spell It Like It Sounds!

One way of shortening words is to spell them like they sound. For example:

- any = ne
- are = r
- be = b
- cutie = qt
- see = c
- we = v
- why = y
- you = u

Using Numbers and Symbols as Words or Parts of Words

Many words can be spelled like numbers, or at least a part of them can. Also, don't even think about spelling out numbers! Simply use the actual number.

- anyone = ne1
- and = & or n
- at = @
- ate = 8
- for = 4
- forgot = 4got or 4gt
- great = gr8t
- later = l8r
- no one = no 1
- percent = %
- to/too/two = 2

Other Text Messaging Shortcuts

Common SMS practices for shortening words that can't be condensed with any of the above-mentioned methods:

1. Leaving out vowels,
2. removing the *e* in words ending with *e*,
3. replacing *o* with *u* for correct sound,
4. shortening double consonants to one,
   - at work = @wrk
   - give = giv
   - love = luv
   - please = plz
   - right = ryt
   - sorry = sry
   - thanks = thx
   - through = thru

Making Sense of Text Lingo

To translate regular English into text lingo, go to:

www.transl8it.com

by a host of rivals—most of which also offer telephone and other smartphone capabilities. Examples are those from Apple (the iPhone), Nokia, Palm (the Prē), Samsung, HTC (the Google G1), and Motorola (the Android phone). Dell, Acer, Lenovo, and Asustek have also brought smartphones to market.

As with text messaging, something that most users need to pay attention to before buying is the layout and size of the keys. The BlackBerry 7100 series smartphones, for example, cram all letters and numbers onto just 14 keys. (As you type, built-in software anticipates the correct word, something that takes some getting used to.)

Incidentally, as we mentioned, many of the personal organizing functions formerly found in personal digital assistants—such as address book, schedule planner, and to-do list—have now migrated to smartphones. What happens if you break or lose your cellphone (as people do all the time)? How do you replace your built-in telephone numbers and contacts? Some carriers and technology companies offer services that, for a small monthly fee, back up such data wirelessly.

INTERNET ACCESS Many smartphone owners use their devices to perform web searches of one sort or another, accessing not only Yahoo! and Google but also such things as maps and directions, using the Global Positioning System, if their phones are so equipped. For instance, MapQuest enables you to pull up a map on your mobile phone while you're in transit and then navigate as you go along. Yahoo!, which also provides mapping services, has a local search system for cellphones. If you type in the word *pizza* and an address in Chicago, for example, your phone will display all pizza restaurants in that neighborhood, as well as maps showing their location and driving directions.

An important capability for wireless internet access is the ability to make connections to Wi-Fi networks. For instance, the BlackBerry Curve automatically detects when it's near a pre-set Wi-Fi network and uses that network for voice calling or data instead of T-Mobile's cellphone connections. Phone calls started in the cellular network will switch over to Wi-Fi and vice versa.[95]

Other smartphones, such as the Motorola CN620, allow you to use the VoIP (voice-over IP) technology, which we described in Chapter 2, to make phone calls on the internet. Thus, the device will work where cell service is offered as well as in Wi-Fi-accessible areas.

PHOTOGRAPHY Camera phones are making the spontaneous snapshot an everyday part of life, and, says one observer, "turning ordinary citizens into documentarians, fine-art photographers, and, in cases such as hit-and-run accidents, community watchdogs."[96] Indeed, the devices have even inspired a trend called *mobile blogging*, or "moblogging," in which phones are used to visually record both still photos and videos of all kinds of events, both mundane and highly personal, which are then displayed and transmitted to websites such as Mobog, Textamerica, and Yafro. In one experiment, 52 patients with leg ulcers were examined in person by doctors on-site and remotely by other doctors who had only pictures of the wounds taken by camera phone, and both sets of physicians were in remarkable agreement in their diagnoses and suggested treatment.[97]

Camera phone manufacturers are learning that consumers will take more pictures if the quality is improved and the printing made easier. Thus, there are now available 8-megapixel phones (as from Samsung) and phones that can connect directly to many home printers. Camera phones are also being made with memory card slots, so that images stored on a memory card can then be taken directly to a retailer to have prints made. And the wireless carriers themselves are getting in on the act. Sprint, for instance, charges for using its network to transfer photos from camera phones. Many wireless carriers also make kiosks available for downloading and printing out camera images.

GAMES In the past, cellphones used as game devices left something to be desired, with "flat, cartoonish graphics and simple scenes," in one description.[98] More recent smartphones, however, have powerful graphics chips and better screen quality that allow three-dimensional images, faster computing capabilities, realistic drawings, and fast-moving action.

RADIO & MUSIC Some smartphones allow users to listen to FM radio. Sprint and RealNetworks have introduced an internet radio service for Sprint wireless customers.

Phone games. WildTangent's online video game "24"

In addition, cellphones can now store hundreds, if not thousands, of songs. An 8-gigabyte phone memory card, for instance, can store about 2,000 songs. Some of the biggest music companies and phone companies have been pairing up to make available song downloads—or songs and music videos to watch on mobile display screens—that customers may purchase through their phones.

Short-range wireless Bluetooth technology enables cellphone users to put on headphones so they can connect to their cellphones without cords.

TV & VIDEO One mother confesses she uses her cellphone's TV feature to keep her 3-year-old son occupied while she waits in line at the post office. After tuning in the Cartoon Network, she says, "I just give him the phone and he's quiet."[99] Movie studios have also developed "mobi-toons" that can play as mini-television shows on smartphone displays. Major-league baseball has arranged for TV clips to be posted to phones, offering video coverage of games. With the new generation of phones, viewers should be able to watch TV shows even in moving cars and trains.[100]

TV programs made for a handheld mobile device with a 2-inch or 2¼-inch display screen pose particular challenges. For one thing, although cellphone screen quality has gotten better, there are still limitations in battery life, processing power, and storage capacity. In addition, most viewers don't have the patience to watch a 90-minute feature film on a screen this size. "Cell phone cinema has to hold your attention before your mind jets off to do something else with your phone, such as surf the web, check your email, or, gasp, make a phone call," says one analysis. "No time to develop character. No room for special effects. Not enough screen resolution for moody shadows or shades of meaning."[101] Whether it's a sitcom, news show, or sports highlights, TV programs designed for cellphones have to rely heavily on close-ups, more static shots, and little movement within the frame—the opposite of MTV video. In the end, then, the producers of such fare have to rely more on writing and storytelling.

OTHER FEATURES We have mentioned GPS locators and video cameras, but there seems to be no end of other features existing and forthcoming for smartphones. In the United States, students at the University of California, Santa Barbara, pay for parking stalls by charging the fee to an account through their cellphones. In Japan, customers can pay for purchases not

People are using electronic devices everywhere: digital cameras, computers, cellphones.

with cash or credit cards but by making electronic payments through a smartphone. Also in Japan, mobile phones have been turned into controllers for model racing cars, for use as television remotes, and as devices for fingerprint recognition. In South Korea, cellphones have been modified to allow diabetics to check their blood-sugar levels, and the data can be sent to their physicians.

The Societal Effects of Cellphones

Have mobile phones been a positive or negative force?

The effects of the cellphone and the smartphone are mixed. The positive attributes are many: Parents can more easily monitor the safety of their children, police dispatchers can help people who are lost, information and amusements of all kinds are readily available, you can phone your apologies when you'll be late for an appointment, and so on.

However, people's personal behavior in using phones has not necessarily been improved. One survey found that 78% of those interviewed said that people are less polite, courteous, and respectful in cellphone manners than they were 5 years earlier. (Yet 95% thought their own cellphone manners were just fine.)[103] Cellphones regularly ring—and are answered—in theaters, despite movie screen advisories. Bus and train travelers become enraged by the loud conversations of fellow passengers. The serenity of nature's wonders in national parks is disrupted by people yakking on their phones. Bosses feel obliged to rebuke their employees whose cellphones ring in meetings.

Phone use by car drivers makes even young people drive erratically, moving and reacting more slowly and increasing their risk of accidents.[104] People inadvertently dial numbers in their phone's address book when they've had too much to drink (a phenomenon known as "drunk dialing").[105] Camera-equipped phones have been used to take pictures of people in bathroom stalls, to cheat on school tests, and to allow thieves to capture credit card numbers.[106] Pornography companies see cellphones as a new frontier.[107] Employers can hire companies that can keep track of their employees' out-of-office locations through GPS tracking of their cellphones.[108]

But just as technology can create unforeseen problems, perhaps technology can also provide solutions. Some countries—but not the United States yet—are permitting the use of radio-jamming equipment that keeps nearby cellphones from working whether the phone user likes it or not. This would certainly allow restaurants, theaters, and the like to impose a "cone of silence" that would provide relief to long-suffering members of the public who have been forced to unwillingly share in others' cell conversations.

Big Boss Is Watching?

Read the article at:

http://news.cnet.com/ Big+boss+is+watching/ 2100-1036_3-5379953.html

7.9 VIDEOGAME SYSTEMS: The Ultimate Convergence Machine?

How do the three principal videogame consoles compare?

The "convergence of computing, communications, and entertainment has been promised before," says a *Wall Street Journal* article, "only to evaporate because of consumer indifference and technology that wasn't ready for prime time. But now the pieces are finally coming together. And corporations are scrambling to make sure they aren't left behind."[109]

The principal strategy under which this is happening is the placement of entertainment devices in your living room. Microsoft Corp., for example, is attempting to put its Xbox 360 into people's homes under the guise of providing an online videogame system, but what it is really aiming at is installing a "miniature electronic ecosystem" there, with Microsoft at the center. Someday you may wake up and find that Xbox "entered your house under the humble pretense of being a game machine, a toy for the kids, but it just ate your CD

	Microsoft Xbox 360	Sony PlayStation 3	Nintendo Wii
Optical drive	l2x dual-layer DVD disks	Blu-ray	Proprietary optical drive
CPU	3.2 GHz PowerPC-based three-in-one processing chip	3.2 GHz Cell processor	729 MHz IBM "Broadway" processor from IBM
Storage	20- or l20-gigabyte hard disk; two memory card ports	40- or 80-gigabyte hard drive; memory card slots for SD, MemoryStick,	5l2 megabytes internal flash memory; SD memory cards
Types of online connections	Wi-Fi; built-in Ethernet connection; Xbox Live online service included; USB 2.0 ports; ability to stream from Windows PCs, digital cameras, music portables	Wi-Fi; built-in Ethernet connection; Bluetooth wireless connections; USB 2.0 ports	Wi-Fi; Bluetooth 2.0 for controllers; USB 2.0 ports

panel 7.6

Principal videogame consoles compared

All are supposed to be backward-compatible, so that users can play games developed for earlier gameboxes.

player and your DVD player, and it's looking hungrily at your telephone," suggests a *Time* article. "It's talking to your iPod, your digital camera, your TV, your stereo, your PC, your credit card, and the internet."[110]

Several industries—videogame console makers, consumer-electronics companies, PC companies, cable companies, and telephone companies—are interested in this area. Here let us consider just the first: the makers of gameboxes. The big videogame hardware makers are Microsoft (until now mainly a software rather than a hardware business), Sony, and Nintendo. Let's see how their consoles compare. (● *See Panel 7.6.*)

Microsoft's Xbox 360

Why might I be inclined to buy an Xbox?

Released in fall 2005, the Xbox 360 has double the power of the previous Xbox. As we said, the ostensible principal intended use of the new Xbox is for online videogames; Microsoft has invested heavily in its subscription service, Xbox Live, which allows Xbox players to meet online—and also to talk to people with whom they are playing via voice chat (a possible forerunner to a general internet telephone system). However, Microsoft really is trying to

Multiplayer. Could videogame machines such as the Microsoft Xbox, Sony PlayStation, and the Nintendo Wii become the "miniature electronic ecosystem" that finally represents the convergence of computing, communications, and entertainment that has long been anticipated?

make the device a living-room hub for all kinds of digital media—not only videogames but also movies, music, and online content. The Xbox enables users to connect cameras, digital music players, high-definition televisions, surround-sound stereo systems, and the like, and a 20-gigabyte hard drive is available on which users can copy music CDs, photos, and other digital content. With this gadget, Microsoft is also positioning itself to be a supplier of video on demand in competition with cable operators.

Sony's PlayStation 3

Is the PS3 a better game machine?

Released in 2006, Sony's PlayStation 3, or PS3, is designed to exploit the dominance of the TV-console market that Sony established with the PlayStation 2. The PS3 uses an ultra-powerful multiprocessor, the Cell chip from International Business Machines and Toshiba Corp, which is 35 times more powerful than the one in PS2. It's called a "cell" because software instructions can be divided up in cells and distributed among different processors and devices (TVs, music players, and the like). This means a network can be organized without human intervention, such as, in one demonstration, 48 separate high-definition video feeds to a single display screen. PS3 enables gamers not only to videoconference over the internet but also to have movie-quality graphics, with lifelike textures, colors, and motion. Users are able to stream and download music and movies, handling several streams at once (so that you can play a videogame and watch a movie at the same time).

Showgoers try out games at the PlayStation 3 exhibit, 2009 in Los Angeles, California.

Wii Tech

Nintendo's Wii

What distinguishes the Wii console from the others?

Released in 2006, Nintendo's Wii doesn't emphasize power and graphics so much as innovative, networked game play and simpler, cheaper game development. Thus, the company is positioning itself with new versions of two decades' worth of tried-and-true videogames, such as Mario, Zelda, and Metroid. Its one-handed remote controller, which is fitted with motion sensors, allows players to wave it around frenetically, swish it gently through the air, or kick, punch, jump, or steer their way through on-screen action. Nintendo also introduced the Nintendo DS, an advanced portable game console that enables users to wirelessly connect via Wi-Fi to other users with Wi-Fi capabilities. Unlike Microsoft's and Sony's, however, Nintendo's gamebox won't play movies on DVD unless users buy a separate device.

Experience the joys of gaming or surfing the net with a wireless Wii remote. Attach the compact Wii console to your TV or computer to fit your lifestyle. Game, exercise, and other types of DVDs are inserted in the console slot.

The Results of Personal Technology: The "Always On" Generation

What technological "generation" am I part of?

With all these personal digital devices, it's no wonder that anyone born since 1982 is called a member of the "Always On" generation. They are the generation that has for their entire lives been surrounded by and using the toys and tools of the Digital Age. If you belong to this group, does it make you different from previous generations? We consider this question in the following Experience Box.

Prepared for the Workplace?

Some people believe that Net-Geners are not prepared for today's corporate workplace. Read the article at:

www.zazamedia.de/pages/ Commentary21.html

EXPERIENCE BOX
The "Always On" Generation

Videogames, computers, cellphones, portable music players, email, the internet, instant messaging, the web, video cameras, and similar personal technology. Is this what you grew up with? Then you're a member of the Always On generation, also known as NetGeners (for "Net Generation") and Millennials (for "Millennial Generation").

"Seventy-four percent of teens use instant messaging," says high-tech magazine editor Tony Perkins. "No matter what numbers you look at, the Always On generation is in full swing. They communicate through the computer."[111] A survey by Sprint finds that 76% of teens ages 15–19 and 90% of people in their early 20s regularly use their cellphones for text messaging, ringtones, and games.[112] Indeed, teens with cellphones average 2,272 text messages a month (compared with 203 phone calls).[113] Even low-income teens may regularly owe well over $100 a month in phone charges—and skip lunch so they can pay the bills.[114] Members of this cohort "have never known life without computers and the internet," says one report. "To them the computer is not a technology—it is an assumed part of life."[115] As a result, say observers such as Marc Prensky, "today's students *think and process information fundamentally differently* from their predecessors" (his emphasis).[116]

Not every person in college fits this profile. Indeed, a high proportion of students in higher education, 39%, are over age 25, many going to school part-time, quite often having dependents or being single parents. Those most likely to have the mindset and characteristics of Always On were, as we said, born on or after the year 1982. Unlike older students (members of the "Baby Boomers" and the generation that followed them, "Generation X"), Millennials tend to exhibit distinct learning styles. "Their learning preferences tend toward teamwork, experiential activities, structure, and the use of technology," says Diana Oblinger, executive director of higher education for Microsoft Corporation.[117] With such students, listening to music, sending instant messages, chatting on the phone, and doing homework all at the same time is second nature.

Let's consider some of the characteristics of these students.

Staying Connected Is Essential

After a college class lets out, students step into the hallway and immediately activate their cellphones, PDAs, or notebook computers, talking to or texting friends or checking their email. At rock concerts, when the lights dim, one may see the glow of tiny blue screens, as concert goers text-message friends or have them listen to music via their cellphones—or observe the action through camera phones.

"Connecting is what the current generation of students is all about," says one report. "College students use the internet as much for social reasons as for academic reasons."[118] At the University of North Carolina, for example, sophomore Dax Varkey carries his laptop computer everywhere, using it

not only to take notes in class but also to instant-message or email friends. In his dorm room, he even IMs his roommate a few feet away. He uses his cellphone to call his buddy who lives one floor above him. "I always feel like I have a means of communication—in class, out of class," says Varkey, 19.[119]

Besides maintaining social contacts, students get homework assignments and lecture outlines online and participate in class discussions. They instant-message friends to brainstorm class projects and other assignments. They email professors with questions at any time—a boon for students too shy (or lazy) to visit during an instructor's regular office hours.[120] All in all, the lines between work, social life, and studying are blurring.

Multitasking Is a Way of Life

Multitasking is second nature. "It's perfectly normal for a group of college students to watch TV with their laptops in front of them," said one recent college graduate. "They'll check their campus mailbox once a day but their email every five minutes."[121] Says Prensky, such students "are used to receiving information really fast. They like to parallel process and multitask. They prefer their graphics *before* their text rather than the opposite. They prefer random access (like hypertext)."[122] They are also, having grown up with videogames, accustomed to learning how to take in many sources of information at once and how to incorporate peripheral information. Finally, games have taught them how to use and manage a large database of information.[123]

Students Are Impatient & Results-Oriented

Today's students have grown up on the "twitch speed" of videogames, instant messaging, MTV, and a customer-service kind of culture. Thus, they "have a strong demand for immediacy and little tolerance for delays," says one analysis. "They expect that services will be available 24 × 7 in a variety of modes (web, phone, in person) and that responses will be quick."[124] One result of this is that many students prefer typing to handwriting: It's faster. Another result: Students expect to be engaged, which is why online forums, blogs, and use of RSS aggregators to update subjects are popular.[125] They don't want to be preached to, ignored, or bored. They are also experiential learners—they prefer to learn by doing rather than learn by listening.[126]

They Respect Differences & Gravitate toward Group Activity

NetGeners are racially and ethnically diverse and consequently "accept differences that span culture, ability—or disability—and style," says one report. Indeed, they "are more comfortable with their learning differences than any other generation has been."[127] They also gravitate toward group and team activities, owing to their group-gaming experiences and their constant communication with friends through cellphones, IM, and email.

Caller ID (p. 364) Feature that shows the name and/or number of the calling party on the phone's display when you receive an incoming call, enabling you to screen telephone calls. Why it's important: *Caller ID helps you become disciplined about preventing others from wasting your time.*

convergence (p. 363) Also known as *digital convergence;* the combining of several industries—computers, communications, consumer electronics, entertainment, and mass media—through various devices that exchange data in digital form. Why it's important: *Convergence has led to electronic products that perform multiple functions, such as TVs with internet access, cellphones that are also digital cameras, and a refrigerator that allows you to send email.*

digital television (DTV) (p. 381) Television standard adopted in 1996 that uses a digital signal, or series of 0s and 1s. It uses digital cameras, digital transmission, and digital receivers and is capable of delivering movie-quality pictures and CD-quality sound. The Federal Communications Commission mandated that all TV stations be capable of broadcasting DTV by 2009. Why it's important: *DTV is much clearer and less prone to interference than analog TV. It may allow viewers to receive various kinds of information services, such as announcements from public safety and fire departments.*

e-book (p. 384) Also known as *electronic book;* electronic text, the digital-media equivalent of a conventional printed book. Why it's important: *Allows users to more easily read text, such as books, on personal computer, smartphone, or e-book reader.*

e-book reader (p. 384) A handheld device specifically designed to allow people to read electronic books. Why it's important: *Allows users to download electronic books (text), as by wireless access, and read them as conveniently as printed books.*

HD radio (p. 369) Form of radio that provides CD-quality sound and allows broadcasters to squeeze one analog and two digital stations on the same frequency. Why it's important: *HD radio combines digital and analog broadcast signals, enabling stations to offer an analog main channel and digital "sidebands," so that multiple types of content can be broadcast from the same position on the dial.*

high-definition television (HDTV) (p. 381) A form of television that works with digital broadcasting signals. Why it's important: *HDTV has a wider screen and higher resolution than analog television had. Whereas analog TV has a width-to-height ratio, or aspect ratio, of 4 to 3, HDTV has an aspect ratio of 16 to 9, which is similar to the wide-screen approach used in movies. In addition, compared to analog display screens, an HDTV display has 10 times more pixels on a screen—1,920 × 1,080 pixels or more. Thus, HDTV could have 1,080 lines on a screen, compared with 525-line resolution for analog TV.*

interactive TV (p. 380) Type of television that lets viewers interact with the show they're watching, allowing audience voting, such as that for *American Idol.* Why it's important: *Interactive TV allows viewers to request information about a product or play along with a game show.*

internet TV (p. 380) Type of television service, such as the MSN TV Service (formerly WebTV), that enables users to receive the internet through their television sets, using a set-top box. Why it's important: *Internet TV lets viewers read email, internet text, and web pages on their television sets.*

internet-ready TV (p. 380) (sometimes also called "internet TV") Television set that allows viewers to watch TV shows as well as go online to get news, stream movies, view photos, and the like. Why it's important: Internet-ready TVs allow users to watch TV and do many things on the internet, but, at present, internet-ready TVs do not have browsers, so you can't just go to any website you want in cyberspace

IPTV (Internet Protocol Television) (p. 383) Technology in which television and video signals are sent to viewers using internet protocols. Cable and satellite channels have limited capacity, but the internet has much more room. Why it's important: *Enables the movement of television to the internet.*

megapixels (p. 373) In a digital camera, the millions of picture elements, the electronic dots making up an image; the number of megapixels expresses the camera's resolution, or image sharpness. The millions of pixels are tightly packed together on the camera's image sensor, a half-inch-wide silicon chip. When light strikes a pixel, it generates an electric current that is converted into the digital data that becomes your photograph. Why it's important: *The more megapixels a digital camera has, the better the resolution and the higher the quality of the image.*

MP3 (p. 366) Format that allows audio files to be compressed. MP3 files are about one-tenth the size of uncompressed audio files. For example, a 4-minute song on a CD takes about 40 megabytes of space, but an MP3 version of that song takes only about 4 megabytes. Why it's important: *MP3 allows audio files to be made small enough to be sent over the internet or stored as digital files.*

MP3 digital audio player *See* **portable media player.**

multitasking (p. 365) Performing several tasks at once, such as studying while eating, listening to music, talking on the phone, and handling email. Why it's important: *Medical and learning experts say the brain has limits and can do only so much at one time. For instance, it has been found that people who do two demanding tasks simultaneously, such as driving in heavy traffic and talking on a cellphone, do neither task as well as they do each alone. Indeed, the result of constantly shifting attention is a sacrifice in quality for any of the tasks with which one is engaged.*

personal digital assistant (PDA) (p. 378) Also known as *handheld* or *palmtop;* a portable device that stores personal organization tools, such as schedule planner, address book, and to-do list, along with other, more specialized software. Examples are Palm and Pocket PC. Why it's important: *Because many of the functions of the PDA are also now incorporated in smartphones, sales of general-purpose PDAs have declined, and it's been predicted that the device will die out.*

podcasting (p. 371) The recording of internet radio or similar internet audio programs. Why it's important: *Podcasting software allows amateur deejays and hobbyists to create their own radio shows and offer them free over the internet. Listeners can then download shows onto their MP3 players like the iPod.*

point-and-shoot camera (p. 372) A camera, either film or digital, that automatically adjusts settings such as exposure and focus. Generally such cameras cost under $500. Why it's important: *A point-and-shoot autofocus will do most of the work for you automatically, although you may find it useful to get a camera that also has manual controls, so that you can take over if you want.*

portable media players (PMPs) (p. 366) Small portable devices that enable you to play digital audio, video, and/or still-image files. Why it's important: *Also known as MP3 players, portable devices for playing digital audio files. PMPs differ from MP3 players in that they can handle not only audio but also video and image files. Thus, you may be able to carry several hours of music or video—in the case of an 80-gigabyte Apple iPod as many as 20,000 songs, 120 minutes of video, or 25,000 still images.*

ringtone (p. 387) The audible sound a phone makes to announce that a call is coming in. A ringtone may be an old-fashioned "ring, ring" or a clip from a popular song. Why it's important: *Users can customize the ringtones on their cellphones.*

sampling rate (p. 367) The number of times, expressed in kilobits per second, that a song is measured (sampled) and converted to a digital value when it is being recorded as a digital file. Why it's important: *The sampling rate affects the audio quality. For instance, a song sampled at 192 kilobits per second is three times the size of a song sampled at 64 kilobits per second and will be of better sound quality.*

satellite radio (p. 369) Also called *digital radio;* a radio service in which signals are sent from satellites in orbit around the Earth to subscribers owning special radios that can decode the encrypted signals. Why it's important: *The CD-quality sound is much better than that of regular radio, and because the signals are digital, there are many more channels available than those on traditional radio. Also, unlike standard broadcasters, satellite radio broadcasters are for the most part not regulated by the Federal Communications Commission.*

single-lens reflex (SLR) camera (p. 372) A camera, either film or digital, that has a mirror that reflects the incoming light in such a way that the scene viewed by the viewer through the viewfinder is the same as what's framed by the lens. Why it's important: *A digital SLR, which may cost anywhere from $450 on up, is used by professional photographers and serious amateurs because it provides more manual options and better image quality and allows the use of interchangeable lenses, from wide angle to telephoto.*

smartphone (p. 385) Cellular telephone with microprocessor, memory, display screen, and built-in modem. Why it's important: *Some types of this multimedia phone, which combine some of the capabilities of a PC with a handset, offer a wealth of gadgetry: text messaging, cameras, music players, videogames, email access, digital TV viewing, search tools, personal information management, GPS locators, internet phone service, and even phones doubling as credit cards.*

SMS (Short Message Service) (p. 387) A text message service originally designed for GSM mobile phones but now available on a range of networks, including 3G networks. Why it's important: *Text messaging has long been wildly popular in Europe and Asia but in recent years has become more mainstream in North America.*

standard-definition television (SDTV) (p. 381) A TV standard that has a lower resolution than HDTV, a minimum of 480 vertical lines, and a picture quality similar to that required to watch DVD movies. Why it's important: *The SDTV standard enables broadcasters to transmit more information within the HDTV bandwidth, allowing them to multicast their products, transmitting up to five SDTV programs simultaneously—and getting perhaps five times the revenue—instead of just one HDTV program. (Analog broadcasts only one program at a time.) Thus, instead of beaming high-definition pictures, some broadcasters are splitting their digital streams into several SDTV channels.*

switched-network telecommunications model (p. 364) Model of telecommunications whereby a common carrier provides circuit switching among public users; that is, a temporary connection is established by closing a circuit. Why it's important: *This is the model of the telephone system and also of the internet. In a telephone network, a connection for voice transmission is made by dialing; in a packet-switching network, a temporary connection is established between points for transmitting data in the form of packets. People on the system are not only consumers of information ("content") but also possible providers of it. (Compare **tree-and-branch telecommunications model.**)*

text messaging (p. 387) Also known as *texting;* the sending of short messages, generally no more than a couple of hundred characters in length, to a pager, PDA, smartphone, or other handheld device, including notebook computer, as well as to desktop computers and fixed-line phones. Why it's important: *Text messaging combines the portability of cellphones with the convenience of email and instant messaging. Text messaging is particularly appropriate for situations in which making a cellphone call is intrusive.*

tree-and-branch telecommunications model (p. 364) A model of telecommunications in which a centralized information provider sends out messages through many channels to thousands of consumers. This is the model of most mass media, such as AM radio and network television broadcasting. (*Compare **switched-network telecommunications model.**) Why it's important: *Mass-media radio and television have been losing listeners and viewers to the more personalized media based on the switched-network model.*

video on demand (VOD or **VoD)** (p. 383) Set of technologies that enable viewers to select videos or TV programs from a central server to watch when they want. An example is the device offered by Akimbo, a TiVo-like set-top box with a hard drive that can hold 200 hours of video and offers a library of programs that, for a fee, can be downloaded. *Why it's important: VOD allows viewers to watch programs when they want rather than when TV programmers offer them.*

CHAPTER REVIEW

"I can recognize and recall information."

Self-Test Questions

1. The combining of several industries through various devices that exchange data in digital form is called _____.

2. _____ allows amateur deejays and hobbyists to create their own radio shows and offer them free over the internet.

3. The type of communications model used for the telephone system and the internet is the _____ model.

4. The electronic dots that make up a digital-camera image are called _____.

5. Performing several tasks at once is called _____.

6. A portable, handheld computer that manages personal tasks is called a(n) _____.

7. _____ is a format that allows files to be compressed so they are small enough to be sent over the internet as digital files.

8. Converting a CD audio track to play on an MP3 player is called _____.

9. _____ works with digital broadcasting signals and has a wider screen and higher resolution than standard TV.

10. A _____ camera is one that automatically adjusts settings such as exposure and focus.

Multiple-Choice Questions

1. The number of times that a song is measured and converted to a digital value is called
   a. SLR.
   b. ripping.
   c. sampling rate.
   d. mash-up.

2. The two U.S. satellite radio signal suppliers are
   a. Sirius; Worldscope.
   b. XM; Sirius.
   c. Casio; Konika.
   d. XM; Treo.
   e. Worldscope; Tivo.

3. A digital camera's resolution is expressed in
   a. dpi.
   b. rpm.
   c. pda.
   d. megapixels.
   e. betapixels.

4. Smartphones have
   a. a microprocessor.
   b. a display screen.
   c. memory.
   d. a modem.
   e. all of these

5. Which of the following concerns does *not* apply to smartphone use?
   a. often causes erratic driving
   b. people can track users' movements without their knowledge
   c. users can take photos in inappropriate situations
   d. signals can open locked car doors
   e. loud conversations and ringtones can irritate people in the user's vicinity

True/False Questions

T F   1. The most well-known handheld device for sending wireless email is the Blackberry.

T F   2. The increased availability of broadband connections slowed down the process of digital convergence.

T F   3. MP3 increases the size of digital audio files in order to improve the sound quality.

T F   4. For 8 × 10 photo prints, 2-megapixel digital cameras are best.

T F   5. Memory Stick is a type of flash memory card.

T F   6. Sending photos as email attachments to many people is more efficient than using an online photo-sharing service.

T F   7. One cannot transfer files from a PDA to a desktop computer.

T F   8. HDTV uses analog signals.

"I can recall information in my own terms and explain it to a friend."

Short-Answer Questions

1. Briefly explain how satellite radio works. What are two advantages of satellite radio?

2. What could you use a mash-up for?

3. Why are MP3 files smaller than regular audio files, such as a purchased CD?

4. Why would you use an online photo-sharing service?

5. How does sampling rate relate to the size of MP3 files?

6. What is the difference between satellite radio and high-definition radio?

7. Which digital camera would you choose: point-and-shoot or single-lens reflex? Why?

3 LEARNING ANALYZING, SYNTHESIZING, EVALUATING

"I can apply what I've learned, relate these ideas to other concepts, build on other knowledge, and use all these thinking skills to form a judgment."

Knowledge in Action

1. Does almost everyone you know download and listen to MP3 files? Describe a few ways in which the iPod-types whom you have observed are being distracted from certain activities and some responsibilities. Do you perceive a problem?

2. List five situations in which you often find yourself multitasking. How any things have you done at once? How do you think your manner of multitasking affects the quality of what you achieve?

3. What questions would you ask a friend in order to determine which digital camera, with which characteristics, you would advise her or him to buy?

4. Describe how one can transfer images from a digital camera to a computer.

Web Exercises

1. Current rules of both the FCC and the U.S. Federal Aviation Administration ban in-flight cellular calling. The primary FCC concern has been possible disruption of cellphone communication on the ground. The FAA's worry is how cellphones might interfere with a plane's navigation and electrical systems. However, plans are in the works to assign new bandwidths to allow cellphone use in the air.

2. Do several keyword searches and find three reasons to allow cellphone use during airplane flights, and three reasons *not* to allow it. Provide information to support each reason. What is your opinion on this issue?

3. In 2008, California joined the list of U.S. states that have restricted cellphone use by automobile drivers since New York passed the first such law in 2001. It is now illegal in Connecticut, as well as New York, New Jersey, and major cities such as Washington and Chicago for drivers to use handheld cellphones. Connecticut drivers can be ticketed only if they are pulled over for another moving violation, although in many states, including New York, police can stop drivers using handheld cellphones. However, Connecticut's broad law bans

"any activity not related to the actual operation of a motor vehicle in a manner that interferes with the safe operation of such vehicle." That can include eating, fiddling with the CD player, personal grooming, attending to children, reading, and the like.

In addition, according to the National Conference of State Legislatures, 10 states have enacted legislation restricting use of electronics by teenage drivers.

Do an internet search and find out what the law says about driving and cellphone use in the state where you are going to school and in the state where you come from.

The rules on driving and cellphone use in many other countries are much stricter than they are in the United States; for more information, go to *www.cellular-news .com/car_bans/*.

According to the Automobile Association of America (AAA), hands-free phones are not risk free. The hands-free feature is simply a convenience: it does not increase safety. Studies show that hands-free cellphones distract drivers the same as handheld phones do. Why? Because it's the conversation that distracts the driver, not the device. Search the internet and find some reports that support this view.

Why do you think people don't just turn off their cellphones while they are driving and let voicemail collect messages to be retrieved later?

4. The Convergence Center (*http://dcc.syr.edu/index. htm*) supports research on and experimentation with media convergence. The Center is a joint effort of the Syracuse University School of Information Studies and the Newhouse School of Public Communications. Its mission is to understand the future of digital media and to engage students and faculty in the process of defining and shaping that future. Go to their site and click on What's New, Articles; choose one article to read; then write a couple of paragraphs that summarize the article.

5. Now that cellphones have cameras, camera voyeurism is becoming a problem. The U.S. Video Voyeurism

Prevention Act of 2004 has made this behavior a federal offense. This act prohibits photographing or videocapturing (including with cellphones) a naked person without his or her consent in any place where there can be "a reasonable expectation of privacy." Punishment includes fines of up to $100,000 or up to a year in prison, or both.

Cellphone vendors say this law may be hard to enforce and may even be a deterrent to promising technology and create a false sense of security. Some cellphone manufacturers deny that voyeurs are any more likely to snoop using a cellphone camera than using other technologies such as digital cameras. But other people say the opportunity differs, that most people don't carry digital cameras around with them. With a cellphone camera there is more opportunity to take snapshots of interesting images, and unfortunately this can include images that can threaten privacy. Voyeurs using cellphone cameras could easily pretend to be doing something else, such as dialing or talking.

Some state legislators have proposed legislation requiring camera phones sold to emit an audible noise or flash a light when users press the shutter. But such noise and light would disturb happy occasions such as weddings, where people use cellphone cameras to take pictures and send them instantly to loved ones who couldn't attend.

Research the cameraphone voyeurism problem on the internet. How could you protect your privacy in public situations?

6. Schools are starting to offer online digital photography courses. Check out *www.worldwidelearn.com/online-courses/digital-photography-course.htm.* Are such courses offered at your school? If not, should they be?

7. The Cellular Telecommunications & Internet Association (CTIA) reminds us that text messaging can be a fast, efficient, and reliable way to communicate in the event of an emergency. And if more wireless users rely on text messaging in crisis situations, the people who need to make voice calls the most—emergency responders and 911 callers—can get through more easily.

8. "Everyone should have a plan for communicating in times of emergencies, and text messaging can be an efficient way to reach your friends, family or loved ones. In the time it takes one person to make a 1-minute voice call, hundreds of thousands of text messages can be exchanged," said Tom Wheeler, President and CEO of CTIA. "In these days of increased terrorist threats and heightened awareness, learning all the options on your wireless phone is an important piece of being prepared."

Text messages have also been used around the world to alert citizens in times of danger. In Kuwait, during the 1990 conflict, Kuwaitis were warned about imminent attacks from Iraq via text messaging. And in Hong Kong, some years ago, a wireless carrier set up a system to provide SARS updates via mobile phone. Users punched in a three-digit number and received a text message indicating if they were near any buildings where SARS victims lived or worked. The information was obtained from a daily list released by the Health Department.

In the frantic days leading up to the landfall of Hurricane Rita in September 2005, Houston radio station KRBE offered to deliver hurricane alerts via text messaging across cellphones to listeners, enabling information to be delivered anytime, anywhere, regardless of whether a person was near a radio or a computer. At a time when traditional media networks experienced coverage issues from storm damage, power lines were down, and cars were running out of gas, KRBE was able to provide a continuous two-way stream of information via the cellphone. Many listeners expressed gratitude for information on road closures, fuel availability, evacuation orders, and storm damage during a frightening experience.

Do an internet search on how text messaging has been used to help in various types of emergencies around the world. What types of suppliers have provided the messages? Using what types of systems? How do cellphone users know where/how to retrieve the messages?

Notes

Chapter I

1. Study by Council for Research Excellence, reported in Brian Stelter, "8 Hours a Day Spent on Screens, Study Finds," *The New York Times*, March 27, 2009, **p.** B6.

2. Anthropologist Susan D. Blum, quoted in Christine Rosen, "It's Not Theft, It's Pastiche," *The Wall Street Journal*, April 16, 2009, **p.** A13.

3. "Ground-Breaking Study of Video Viewing Finds Younger Boomers Consume More Video Media than Any Other Group," press release, March 27, 2009, on study conducted on behalf of Council for Research Excellence by Ball State University's Center for Media Design, *www.researchexcellence.com/ news/032609_vcm.php* (accessed May 30, 2009). See also Stelter, "8 Hours a Day Spent on Screens, Study Finds."

4. "A World Transformed: What Are the Top 30 Innovations of the Last 30 Years?" *Knowledge@Wharton*, February 18, 2009, *knowledge.wharton.upenn. edu/article.cfm?articleid=2163* (accessed May 2, 2009). See also "Life Changers," *The New York Times*, March 8, 2009, **p.** BU-2.

5. Kevin Maney, "Net's Next Phase Will Weave through Your Life," *USA Today*, March 2, 2001, pp. 1B, 2B.

6. Sara Rimer, "At M.I.T., Large Lectures Are Going the Way of the Blackboard," *The New York Times*, January 13, 2009, **p.** A12.

7. Katie Hafnet, "In Class, the Audience Weighs In," *The New York Times*, April 29, 2004, pp. E1, E6.

8. Greg Toppo, "Schools Achieving a Dream: Near-Universal Net Access," *USA Today*, June 9, 2004, **p.** 6D.

9. Les Smith, "Technology Can Be Useful in the Classroom," *Reno Gazette-Journal*, March 10, 2009, **p.** 2D. For a brilliant discussion on the use of technology in the classroom in the service of teaching science, see Carl Wieman, "Why Not Try a Scientific Approach to Science Education?" *Scientific Blogging*, March 10, 2009, and his subsequent articles, *www. scientificblogging.com/carl_wieman/why_ not_try_scientific_approach_science_edu- cation* (accessed May 2, 2009).

10. Steve Jones, *Pew Internet & American Life Project: The Internet Goes to College*, September 15, 2002, *www.pewinternet. org/pdfs/PIP_College_Report.pdf* (accessed January 4, 2009).

11. Catherine Yang, "Big Program on Campus," *BusinessWeek*, September 20, 2004, pp. 96, 98.

12. Kim Clark, "E-Learning Clicks with Students," *U.S. News & World Report*, May 2009, pp. 48–50.

13. Greg Toppo, "Profound Shift in Home Schooling," *USA Today*, May 29, 2009, p. 1A.

14. "Federal Student Aid to Undergraduates Shows Slow Growth, While Published Tuition Prices Continue to Increase," The College Board, October 22, 2007, *www.collegeboard.com/press/ releases/189547.html* (accessed July 8, 2009).

15. Dan Carnevale, "Many Online Courses Work Best at No Distance at All," *The Chronicle of Higher Education*, July 30, 2004, **p.** A22.

16. Jeanette Borzo, "Almost Human," *The Wall Street Journal*, May 24, 2004, pp. R4, R10; and K. Platoni, "Seeing Is Believing: Maybe Virtual Reality Isn't Just a Game Anymore; Maybe It's a Way to Build a Better You," *Stanford Maga- zine*, January/February 2008, pp. 48–55.

17. Kim Painter, "Diagnosis by Telemedicine," *USA Today*, February 16, 2009, **p.** 5D. See also Christopher Lawton, "Cough, Cough. Is There a Doctor in the Mouse?" *The Wall Street Journal*, March 5, 2009, pp. D1, D2.

18. Stephanie Nano, "Computers Seen as Aid in X-Ray Reading," *San Francisco Chronicle*, October 2, 2008, **p.** A2.

19. Steve Lohr, "Health Care That Puts a Computer on the Team," *The New York Times*, December 27, 2008, pp. B1, B3.

20. Bernard Wysocki Jr., "Robots in the OR," *The Wall Street Journal*, February 26, 2004, pp. B1, B6; Mike Crissey, "Hospital Robots Aid the Staff," *San Fran- cisco Chronicle*, July 12, 2004, pp. F1, F5; and Robert Davis, "Robo Doc: Medicine by 'Extension,'" *USA Today*, August 4, 2004, **p.** 8D.

21. Jesse Ellison, "A New Grip on Life," *Newsweek*, December 15, 2008, **p.** 64; and Pam Belluck, "In New Procedure, Artificial Arm Listens to Brain," *The New York Times*, February 11, 2001, pp. A1, A17.

22. Associated Press, "Implant Transmits Brain Signals Directly to Computer," *The New York Times*, October 22, 1998, **p.** A22.

23. Cynthia G. Wager, "Money's Digital Future," *The Futurist*, January–February 2003, pp. 14–15.

24. The Nilson Report, cited in "Electronic Transactions on the Rise," *USA Today*, October 6, 2003, **p.** 1B.

25. Jupiter Research, cited in "Online Grocery Sales a Tough Sale," *RedOrbit*, March 17, 2008, *www.redorbit.com/ news/technology/1299393/online_gro- cery_sales_a_tough_sale/index.html* (accessed June 1, 2009).

26. Daniel Nasaw, "A Dollar Here, a Dollar There," *The Wall Street Journal*, May 24, 2004, **p.** R6; and Dan Fost, "Tiny Bills— Big Deal," *San Francisco Chronicle*, September 8, 2004. pp. C1, C4.

27. Heather Green, "Kissing Off Big Labels," *BusinessWeek*, September 6, 2004, pp. 90, 92.

28. Susan Wlosczyna, "When Free Is Profitable," *USA Today*, May 21, 2004, **p.** 1E; Jon Pareles, "No Fears: Laptop D.J.'s Have a Feast," *The New York Times*, September 10, 2004, pp. B1, B8; and Shelly Banjo and Kelly K. Spors, "Musician Finds a Following Online," *The Wall Street Journal*, December 30, 2008, **p.** B2.

29. James Barron, "Best Musical Score (by a Laptop)," *The New York Times*, June 26, 2004, **p.** A13.

30. Bill Werde, "We've Got Algorithm, but How about Soul?" *The New York Times*, March 21, 2004, sec. 4, **p.** 12.

31. Peter Stack, "An Animated Future," *San Francisco Chronicle*, May 19, 1999, **p.** E1.

32. William Keck, "Their World of Tomorrow Revolves around Playtime," *USA Today*, September 6, 2004, **p.** 10D.

33. Laura M. Holson, "Out of Hollywood, Rising Fascination with Video Games," *The New York Times*, April 10, 2004, pp. A1, B2; and Robert A. Guth and Merissa Marr, "Videogames Go Hollywood," *The Wall Street Journal*, May 10, 2004, pp. B1, B4.

34. Ellen S. Miller, "Internet Empowerment," *USA Today*, March 17, 2009, p. 9A.

35. "State Goes YouTube," *U.S. News & World Report*, December 8, 2008, **p.** 23.

36. Tracy Loew, "States Put Spending Details Online," *USA Today*, February 23, 2009, **p.** 3A.

37. Joe Garofoli, "White House Web Site Jolts the Bureaucracy," *San Francisco Chronicle*, January 24, 2009, pp. A1, A6.

38. Justin Berton, "Web Gives Forum for Protest," *San Francisco Chronicle*, October 1, 2008, **p.** A13.

39. David Carr, "Obama's Personal LinkedIn," *The New York Times*, November 10, 2008, pp. B1, B6; Beth Fouhy, "Obama Team Envisions Web List as Potent Tool," *San Francisco Chronicle*, November 23, 2008, **p.** A4; Kenneth T. Walsh, "For Obama, Governing in the Age of YouTube," *U.S. News & World Report*, December 8, 2008, p. 32; Carla Marinucci, "Obama Using Netroots to Lobby

for Stimulus," *San Francisco Chronicle*, February 3, 2009, **p.** A8; Sheryl Gay Stolberg, "Obama Makes History in Live Internet Video Chat," *The New York Times*, March 27, 2009, **p.** A15.

40. See Steve Cerocke, "IT Jobs Are Forecast to Grow by 24 Percent through 2016," *Reno Gazette-Journal*, June 2, 2008, **p.** 7A; Amy Dobson, "Information Technology: The Next Generation," *San Francisco Chronicle*, June 8, 2008, **p.** H1; and Steve Cerocke, "Breaking into Information Technology Sector Requires Some Experience," *Reno Gazette-Journal*, June 17, 2008, **p.** 7A.

41. Susan Stellin, "Getting Your Resume to the Top of the Electronic Pile Can Be a Matter of Paying an Extra Fee; But Does It Translate into Better Results?" *The New York Times*, January 20, 2003, **p.** C3.

42. "Worldwide Mobile Subscriptions to Reach 5.6 Billion by 2013," press release, Strategy Analytics, *www.strategyanalytics.com/default.aspx?mod5PressReleaseViewer&a054018* (accessed June 1, 2009).

43. Bob Tedeschi, "Navigating the New World of Cellphones, as the Options Pile Up," *The New York Times*, June 19, 2008, **p.** C6.

44. ForceNine Consulting/Wirthlin Worldwide and Harris Interactive, in "Cellphones Add Features," *USA Today*, November 29, 2004, **p.** 1D.

45. Michael Specter, "Your Mail Has Vanished," *The New Yorker*, December 6, 1999, **pp.** 96–103.

46. About.com, "How Many Emails Are Sent Every Day?" Heinz Tschabitscher, *http://email.about.com* (accessed July 8, 2009).

47. "Like It or Not, You've Got Mail," *BusinessWeek*, October 4, 1999, **pp.** 178–184.

48. Robert Rossney, "E-Mail's Best Asset—Time to Think," *San Francisco Chronicle*, October 5, 1995, **p.** E7.

49. Adam Gopnik, "The Return of the Word," *The New Yorker*, December 6, 1999, **pp.** 49–50.

50. Deborah Fallows, Pew Internet & American Life Project, "Email at Work," December 8, 2002, *www.pewinternet.org/pdfs/PIP_Work_Email_Report.pdf* (accessed July 1, 2009).

51. Gopnik, "The Return of the Word."

52. Tamar Lewin, "Informal Style of Electronic Messages Is Showing Up in Schoolwork, Study Finds," *The New York Times*, April 25, 2008, **p.** A12.

53. David A. Whittler, quoted in "Living Online," *The Futurist*, July–August 1997, **p.** 54.

54. Pew Internet & American Life Project, "Demographics of Internet Users," February 15, 2008, *www.pewinternet.org/trends/User_Demo_2.15.08.htm* (accessed June 1, 2009).

55. Pew Internet & American Life Project, "Daily Internet Activities," February 15, 2008, *http://www.pewinternet.org/trends/Daily_Internet_Activities_ 2.15.08.htm* (accessed July 1, 2009).

56. Kevin Maney, "The Net Effect: Evolution or Revolution?" *USA Today*, August 9, 1999, **pp.** 1B, 2B.

57. Internet Coaching Library, "World Internet Users and Population Stats," *Internet World Stats*, May 30, 2009, *www.internetworldstats.com/stats.htm* (accessed June 1, 2009).

58. Pew Internet & American Life Project, "Demographic of Internet Users," December 20, 2008, *www.pewinternet.org/Static-Pages/Data-Tools/Download-Data/~ /media/Infographics/Trend%20Data/January%202009%20updates/Demographics%20of%20Internet%20Users%201%206%2009.jpg* (accessed June 1, 2009).

59. Sidney Jones and Susannah Fox, Pew Internet & American Life Project, "Generations Online in 2009," January 28, 2009, *www.pewinternet.org/~/media//Files/Reports/2009/PIP_Generations_2009.pdf* (accessed June 1, 2009).

60. Top500.org, reported in Don Clark, "Los Alamos Computer Keeps Title as the Fastest," *The Wall Street Journal*, November 17, 2008, **p.** B9.

61. David M. Ewalt, "The Next (Not So) Big Thing," *InformationWeek*, May 13, 2002, *www.informationweek.com/story/IWK20020510S0005* (accessed June 1, 2009).

62. Ryan Kim, "Time Is Right Now for Netbooks," *San Francisco Chronicle*, November 29, 2008, **p.** C1, C2; Stephen Williams, "Netbooks Keep It Light," *The New York Times*, December 2, 2008, **p.** F1, F4; "Netbooks Make Big Impact," *Reno Gazette-Journal*, December 8, 2008, **p.** 7A; Kerry E. Grace and Justin Scheck, "Notebook Computers Outpace Desktop PCs," *The Wall Street Journal*, December 24, 2008, **p.** B6; and David Pogue, "When Laptops Go Light," *The New York Times*, March 26, 2009, p. B1, B8.

63. David Einstein, "Custom Computers," *San Francisco Chronicle*, April 15, 1999, **pp.** B1, B3.

64. Ibid.

65. Laurence Hooper, "No Compromises," *The Wall Street Journal*, November 16, 1992, **p.** R8.

66. See John Markoff, "Do You Have That Portable in a Midsize?" *The New York Times*, May 11, 2008, **p.** BU 4; Eric A. Taub, "Smaller Than a Laptop, but Bigger Than a Phone," *The New York Times*, June 5, 2008, **p.** C6; and Roger Yu, "Business Travelers Lighten Up on Tech," *USA Today*, June 19, 2008, **p.** 5B.

67. John Markoff, "By and for the Masses," *The New York Times*, June 29, 2005, **pp.** C1, C5.

68. Robert D. Hof, "The Power of Us," *BusinessWeek*, June 20, 2005, pp. 74–82.

69. Verne Kopytoff, "Citizen Journalism Takes Root Online," *San Francisco Chronicle*, June 6, 2005, pp. E1, E5.

70. For a discussion of meanings of "cloud computing," see Ben Worthen, "Overuse of the Term 'Cloud Computing' Clouds Meaning of the Tech Buzz Phrase," *The Wall Street Journal*, September 23, 2008, **p.** B8; Daniel Lyons, "Today's Forecast: Cloudy," *Newsweek*, November 10, 2008, **p.** 24; Geoffrey A. Fowler and Ben Worthen, "The Internet Industry Is on a Cloud—Whatever That May Mean," *The Wall Street Journal*, March 26, 2009, **pp.** A1, A9; and "No Man Is an Island: The Promise of Cloud Computing," *Knowledge@Wharton*, April 1, 2009, *http://knowledge.wharton.upenn.edu/article.cfm?articleid=2190* (accessed June 1, 2009).

71. David Lagesse, "Taking a Walk in 'the Cloud,'" *U.S. News & World Report*, March 2009, **pp.** 71–73.

72. Tom Forester and Perry Morrison, *Computer Ethics: Cautionary Tales and Ethical Dilemmas in Computing* (Cambridge, MA: MIT Press, 1990), **pp.** 1–2.

73. Psychiatrist Edward M. Hallowell, quoted in Alma Tugend, "Multitasking Can Make You Lose . . . Um . . . Focus," *The New York Times*, October 25, 2008, **p.** B7. Hallowell is the author of *CrazyBusy: Overstretched, Overbooked, and About to Snap!* (New York: Ballantine, 2006).

74. John Tierney, "Ear Plugs to Lasers: The Science of Concentration," *The New York Times*, May 5, 2009, **p.** D2.

75. Winifred Gallagher, cited in Tierney, "Ear Plugs to Lasers." Gallagher is the author of *Rapt* (New York: Penguin Press, 2009).

76. Winifred Gallagher, quoted in book review, David G. Myers, "Please Pay Attention," *The Wall Street Journal*, April 20, 2009, **p.** A13.

77. Francis **P.** Robinson, *Effective Study*, 4th ed. (New York: Harper & Row, 1970).

78. Bruce K. Broumage and Richard E. Mayer, "Quantitative and Qualitative Effects of Repetition on Learning from Technical Text," *Journal of Educational Psychology*, 78, 1982, 271–278.

79. Robin J. Palkovitz and Richard K. Lore, "Note Taking and Note Review: Why Students Fail Questions Based on Lecture Material," *Teaching of Psychology*, 7, 1980, 159–161.

Chapter 2

1. Graham T. T. Molitor, "Five Forces Transforming Communications," *The Futurist*, September–October 2001, **pp.** 32–37.

2. Report by the Pew Internet & American Life Project, reported in Jack Gillum, "A Third of Adults without Internet Don't Want It," *USA Today*, February 3, 2009, **p.** 7D.

3. IDC estimate, reported in David H. Deans, "Digital Landscapes," *Digital Divide Network*, July 7, 2008, *www.digitaldivide.net/blog/dhdeans/view?PostID=27986* (accessed June 4, 2009).

4. John Horrigan, *Home Broadband Adoption 2008*, Pew Internet & American Life Project, July 2, 2008, *www.pewinternet.org/PPF/r/257/report_display.asp* (accessed June 4, 2009).

5. Ibid.

6. Andrew LaVallee, "Postponing Dial-Up's Demise," *The Wall Street Journal*, February 26, 2009, **p.** B8.

7. Azadeh Ensha, "How to Travel at a Million Files a Minute," *The New York Times*, August 21, 2008, **p.** C6.

8. Leslie Cauley, "Rural Americans Long to Be Linked," *USA Today*, June 8, 2008, **pp.** 1B, 2B.

9. John Horrigan, *Mobile Access to Data and Information*, Pew Internet & American Life Project, March 5, 2008, *www.pewinternet.org/PPF/r/244/report_display.asp* (accessed June 7, 2009).

10. For a short history of the development of the Internet and protocols, see Stephen D. Crocker, "How the Internet Got Its Rules," *The New York Times*, April 7, 2009, p. A25.

11. Scarlett Pruitt, "ICANN Works on Going Global," *InfoWorld*, March 26, 2003, *www.infoworld.com* (accessed June 8, 2009).

12. Victoria Shannon, "U.S. Seeks to Keep Role on Internet," *The New York Times*, July 4, 2005, **p.** C6, reprinted from *International Herald Tribune*.

13. Charisse Jones, "New Web Endings Could Be Start of Billion-Dollar Turf Wars," *USA Today*, April 7, 2008, p. 4B; Anick Jesdanun, "Internet Org Paves Way for Hundreds of New Domains," *Wired News*, June 26, 2008, *http://news.wired.com/dynamic/stories/t/tec_new_internet_names?site=wire&section=home&template=default* (accessed June 7, 2009) or *http://thedudedean.newsvine.com_news/2008/06/27/1619091-internet-org-paves-way-for-hundreds-of-new-domains* (accessed July 25, 2009); and Michelle Kessler, "Internet Group Opens Door to Domains Beyond .com," *USA Today*, July 27, 2008, **p.** 1B.

14. Research by Net Applications, reported in John Letzing, "Microsoft Loses Share in Rivalry for Browser," *The Wall Street Journal*, January 5, 2009, **p.** B3.

15. Nick Wingfield and Suzanne Vranica, "Microsoft's 'Bing' to Take on Google," *The Wall Street Journal*, May 29, 2009, **p.** B5; Walt Mossberg, "Is Bing the Thing?" *The Wall Street Journal*, June 2, 2009, **p.** R4; Katherine Boehret, "Microsoft Effort to Best Google Yields Results," *The Wall Street Journal*, June 3, 2009, **pp.** D1, D3; and Stuart Elliott, "Search for Bing? It'll Be Baked in TV and Online Fare," *The New York Times*, June 5, 2009, **p.** B3.

16. "The Size of the World Wide Web," WorldWideWebSize.com, June 8, 2009, *www.worldwidewebsize.com* (accessed June 8, 2009).

17. Kitty Burns Florey, "Around the (Virtual) World in Half a Second" [letter], *The New York Times*, March 2, 2004, **p.** A26.

18. Melanie Hanes-Ramos, "Bare Bones 101: A Basic Tutorial on Searching the Web," University of South Carolina, Beaufort Library, February 5, 2009, *www.sc.edu/beaufort/library/pages/bones/bones.shtml* (accessed June 8, 2009).

19. May 30, 2009, figures from Hitwise, reported in "Top Ten Search Engines," seoconsultants.com, June 1, 2009, *www.seoconsultants.com/search-engines* (accessed June 8, 2009).

20. Linda Bertland, "Searching the Internet: Search Engines and Subject Indexes," May 15, 2009, *www.sldirectory.com/search.html* (accessed June 8, 2009).

21. Hanes-Ramos, "Bare Bones 101."

22. Chris Taylor, "It's a Wiki, Wiki World," *Time*, June 6, 2005, **pp.** 40–42. See also Stacy Schiff, "The Interactive Truth," *The New York Times*, June 15, 2005, **p.** A29.

23. Ellen Chamberlain, "Bare Bones 101: A Basic Tutorial on Searching the Web," University of South Carolina, Beaufort Library, September 7, 2006, *www.sc.edu/beaufort/library/pages/bones/lesson5.shtml* (accessed June 8, 2009).

24. Adam Gregerman, "Online Research Is So Easy, So Unreliable" [letter], *The New York Times*, June 23, 2004, p. A26.

25. Janet Hogan, "The ABCDs of Evaluating Internet Resources," Binghamton University Libraries, November 2, 2004, *http://library.lib.binghamton.edu/search/evaluation.html;* Hope N. Tillman, "Evaluating Quality on the Net," Babson College, March 28, 2003, *www.hopetillman.com/findqual.html;* and Esther Grassian, "Thinking Critically about World Wide Web Resources," UCLA College Library, September 6, 2000, *www.library.ucla.edu/libraries/college/help/critical/index.htm* (all accessed June 8, 2009).

26. E. Schwartz, "Google, Yahoo Video Search Is the Tip of the Iceberg," *InfoWorld*, January 26, 2005, *http://weblog.infoworld.com/techwatch/archives/001024.html* (accessed June 8, 2009).

27. Daniel Terdiman, "A Tool for Scholars Who Like to Dig Deep," *The New York Times*, November 25, 2004, **p.** B6. See also Jeffrey R. Young, "Google Unveils a Search Engine Focused on Scholarly Materials," *The Chronicle of Higher Education*, December 3, 2004, **p.** A34.

28. Jefferson Graham, "Google's Library Plan 'a Huge Help,'" *USA Today*, December 15, 2004, **p.** 3B. See also Kevin DeLaney and Jeffrey A. Trachtenberg, "Google Goes to College," *The Wall Street Journal*, December 14, 2004, **pp.** D1, D4.

29. "Google's Book Scanning Project Runs into Legal Hurdles," *domain-b.com*, June 10, 2009, *www.domain-b.com/companies/companies_g/google/20090610_book_scanning_project.html* (accessed June 10, 2009).

30. Stephen H. Wildstrom, "Search-Boosters for Your PC," *BusinessWeek*, April 26, 2004, **p.** 26.

31. Matt Lake, "Desperately Seeking Susan OR Suzie NOT Sushi," *The New York Times*, September 3, 1998, **p.** D1.

32. Jefferson Graham, "E-Mail Carriers Deliver Gifts of Nifty Features to Lure, Keep Users," *USA Today*, April 16, 2008, **p.** 4B.

33. Michelle Slatalla, "The Office Meeting That Never Ends," *The New York Times*, September 23, 1999, pp. D1, D8.

34. Jeanne Hinds, quoted in Slatalla, 1999.

35. Study by the Pew Internet and American Life Project, reported in Peter Svensson, "Mixed Feelings Found about Jump in E-Mail," *San Francisco Chronicle*, September 29, 2008, **p.** D4.

36. John Schwartz, "Blogs Provide Raw Details from Scene of the Disaster," *The New York Times*, December 28, 2004, **p.** A14. See also John Schwartz, "A Catastrophe Strikes, and the Cyberworld Responds," *The New York Times*, January 2, 2005, sec. 3, **p.** 4; John Schwartz, "Myths Run Wild in Blog Tsunami Debate," *The New York Times*, January 3, 2005, **p.** A9; Scott Shane and Nicholas Confessore, "In Seeking Help and Giving It, Computers Become a Lifeline," *The New York Times*, January 5, 2005, **p.** A8; Kevin Maney, "Cellphones, Net Could Have Saved Thousands from Waves," *USA Today*, January 5, 2005, **p.** 5B; and Rebecca Buckman, "Relief, High-Tech Style," *The Wall Street Journal*, January 5, 2005, **pp.** B1, B6.

37. Lee Gomes, "How the Next Big Thing in Technology Morphed into a Really Big Thing," *The Wall Street Journal*, October 4, 2004, **p.** B1.

38. Antonio Regalado and Jessica Mintz, "Video Blogs Break Out with Tsunami Scenes," *The Wall Street Journal*, January 3, 2005, **pp.** B1, B5.

39. David Pogue, "Video Chats Overcome Clunkiness," *The New York Times*, February 5, 2009, **pp.** B1, B8.

40. Stephen H. Wildstrom, "Google's Magic Carpet Ride," *BusinessWeek*, July 18, 2005, **p.** 22.

41. Steven Levy, "The Earth Is Ready for Its Close-up," *Newsweek*, June 6, 2005, **p.** 13. See also James Fallows, "An Update on Stuff That's Cool (Like Google's Photo Maps)," *The New York Times*, April 17, 2005, sec. 3, **p.** 5; Verne Kopytoff, "Google's Free 3-D Service Brings Views of Earth Down to the PC," *San Francisco Chronicle*, June 29, 2005, **pp.** A1, A16; John Markoff, "Marrying Maps to Data for a New Web Service," *The New York Times*, July 18, 2005, **pp.** C1, C8; and Verne Kopytoff, "Microsoft, Google in Sky Fight," *San Francisco Chronicle*, July 26, 2005, **pp.** D1, D2.

42. Verne Kopytoff, "Google Peeks Beneath the Waves," *San Francisco Chronicle*, February 3, 2009, **pp.** A1, A14.

43. Mike Snider, "Streaming Movies Grows Dramatically," *USA Today*, January 29, 2009, **p.** 1D.

44. Dan Carnevale, "A New Technology Lets Colleges Spread Information to People Who Want It," *The Chronicle of Higher Education*, February 13, 2004, **pp.** A31–A32.

45. Chris Taylor, "Let RSS Go Fetch," *Time*, May 30, 2005, **p.** 82.

46. Janet Kornblum, "Welcome to the Blogosphere," *USA Today,* July 8, 2003, **p.** 7D.

47. Andrew Sullivan, "Why I Blog," *The Atlantic,* November 2008, pp. 106–113.

48. Michael Agger, *Slate.com,* reported in "Blogging for Fun and Profit," *The Week,* October 17, 2008, **p.** 44.

49. Daniel Lyons, "Time to Hang Up the Pajamas," *Newsweek,* February 16, 2009, **p.** 19; and Douglas Quenqua, "Blogs Falling in an Empty Forest," *The New York Times,* June 7, 2009, Sunday Styles, pp. 1, 7.

50. Maggie O'Neil, "Paperless Payments," *Reno Gazette-Journal,* June 19, 2008, pp. 1D, 5D.

51. Virginia Heffernan, "Lost and Found," *The New York Times Magazine,* March 30, 2008, **pp.** 23–24. See also Kristina Dell, "eBay Bids for Revitalization," *Time,* December 22, 2008, **pp.** Global 1–4; Geoffrey A. Fowler, " eBay Retreats as Web Retailer," *The Wall Street Journal,* March 12, 2009, **pp.** A1, A11; Geoffrey A. Fowler, "eBay Sellers Not Sold on Strategy," *The Wall Street Journal,* March 13, 2009, **p.** B3; and Geoffrey A. Fowler, "Auctions Fade in eBay's Bid for Growth," *The Wall Street Journal,* May 26, 2009, **pp.** A1, A16.

52. Alan Krauss, "Piggybacking on Facebook," *The New York Times,* February 20, 2008, **p.** NY 7.

53. Brian K. Williams, Stacey C. Sawyer, and Carl M. Wahlstrom, *Marriages, Families, & Intimate Relationships: A Practical Introduction,* 2nd ed. (Boston: Pearson, 2009), **p.** 160.

54. Daniel Nations, "What Is Web 2.0?" About.com , 2007, *http://webtrends. about.com/od/web20/a/what-is-web20. htm* (accessed June 11, 2009).

55. Michael Arrington, "Social Networking: Will Facebook Overtake MySpace in the U.S. in 2009?" *TechCrunch,* January 13, 2009, *www.techcrunch.com/2009/01/13/ social-networking-will-facebook-overtake- myspace-in-the-us-in-2009* (accessed June 11, 2009).

56. Forrester Research, cited in "'Not a Site, but a Concept': Tapping the Power of Social Networking," *Knowledge@Wharton,* July 9, 2008, *http://knowledge.whar- ton.upenn.edu/article.cfm?articleid=2009* (accessed June 11, 2009).

57. Lee Rainie, *Increased Use of Video- Sharing Sites,* Pew Internet & American Life Project, January 9, 2008, *www. pewinternet.org/PPF/r/232/report_display. asp* (accessed June 11, 2009).

58. Virginia Heffernan, "File-Sharing Fetish," *The New York Times Magazine,* July 6, 2008, **pp.** 17–18.

59. Brad Stone, "Friends May Be the Best Guide through the Noise," *The New York Times,* May 4, 2008, business section, **p.** 4.

60. N'Gai Croal, "Thoughtcasting: U R So Vain," *Newsweek,* June 16, 2008, **p.** 56. See also Walter S. Mossberg, "Birds of a Feather Twitter Together," *The Wall Street Journal,* December 3, 2008, **p.** D8; Don Campbell, "Tweet! (You Won't Believe What I'm Doing Right Now!)" *USA Today,* April 1, 2009, **p.** 11A; and Claire Cain Miller, "Putting Twitter's World to Use," *The New York Times,* April 14, 2009, pp. B1, B4.

61. Nielsen research, reported in Scott Kleinberg, "Facebook, Twitter and Other Social Media Are More Used than Email, Surveys Suggest," *chica- gotribune.com,* March 16, 2009, *www. chicagotribune.com/news/nationworld/ chi-talk--less-emailmar16,0,3686520. story* (accessed June 11, 2009).

62. Timothy L. O'Brien and Saul Hansell, "Barbarians at the Digital Gate," *The New York Times,* September 19, 2004, sec. 3, **pp.** 1, 4.

63. Jared Sandberg, "Monitoring of Work- ers Is Boss's Right but Why Not Include Top Brass?" *The Wall Street Journal,* May 18, 2005, **p.** B1.

64. "Egregious Email," *Smart Computing,* October 2002, **pp.** 95–97.

65. Michael Specter, "Damn Spam," *The New Yorker,* August 6, 2007, **pp.** 36–41. See also Tom Abate, "3 Decades Later, We've Got Spam," *San Francisco Chroni- cle,* May 3, 2008, pp. C1, C2.

66. Sabina Vrhnjak, "Spam Pollutes More than Your Email In-Boxes," *San Fran- cisco Chronicle,* April 16, 2009, **pp.** C1, C2.

67. Tom Spring, "Spam Fighting Tips for the New Year," *PC World,* Janu- ary 24, 2005, *www.pcworld.com/news/ article/0,aid,119358,00.asp* (accessed June 12, 2009); Sean Carroll, "Slam the Spam," *PC Magazine,* February 25, 2003, **pp.** 74–97.

68. Julian Haight, quoted in David Lazarus, "Fan Spam Is Hard to Shake," *San Francisco Chronicle,* February 7, 2000, **pp.** C1, C2.

69. Riva Richmond, "Companies Target E-Mail 'Spoofing,'" *The Wall Street Journal,* June 9, 2004, **p.** D9; and Amey Stone, "How to Avoid the 'Phish' Hook," *BusinessWeek online,* May 24, 2004, *www.businessweek.com/technology/con- tent/may2004/tc20040524_8133_tc024. htm* (accessed June 12, 2009).

70. "Email Spoofing," SearchSecurity. com Definitions, November 20, 2003, *http://searchsecurity.techtarget.com/ sDefinition/0,,sid14_gci840262,00.html* (accessed June 12, 2009).

71. Kim Komando, "Phishing Attacks on the Rise, Getting Personal," *Reno Gazette- Journal,* January 5, 2009, p. 2C. See also Deborah Gage, "Hackers Gain Access to Bank Accounts," *San Francisco Chroni- cle,* September 1, 2008, pp. D1, D2.

72. Brian Grow, "Spear-Phishers Are Sneak- ing In," *BusinessWeek,* July 11, 2005, **p.** 13.

73. David F. Gallagher, "Users Find Too Many Phish in the Internet Sea," *The New York Times,* September 20, 2004, **p.** C4; and Ann Grimes, "No Phishing Allowed,'" *The Wall Street Journal,* Sep- tember 16, 2004, **p.** B4.

74. Kevin J. Delaney, "'Evil Twins' and 'Pharming,'" *The Wall Street Journal,* May 17, 2005, **pp.** B1, B2; and Jon Swartz, "Thieves Hit Internet with Sneakier Software," *USA Today,* May 18, 2005, **p.** 1B.

75. Kim Komando, "5 Tips for Spurn- ing Spyware and Browser Hijackers," *Microsoft Small Business Center,* 2005, *www.microsoft.com/smallbusiness/ issues/marketing/privacy_spam/5_tips_ for_spurning_spyware_and_browser_ hijackers.mspx* (accessed June 12, 2009).

76. David Kesmodel, "Marketers Seek to Make Cookies More Palatable," *The Wall Street Journal,* June 17, 2005, pp. B1, B2.

77. America Online and the National Cyber Security Alliance, *AOL/NCSA Online Safety Study,* October 2004, *www.stay- safeonline.info/news/safety_study_v04.pdf* (accessed June 12, 2009).

78. Lee Gomes, "Spyware Is Easy to Get, Difficult to Remove, Increasingly Mali- cious," *The Wall Street Journal,* July 12, 2004, **p.** B1.

79. Brock Read, "As Security Concerns Rise, New Web Browsers Gain Favor at Colleges," *The Chronicle of Higher Edu- cation,* July 15, 2005, **p.** A37.

80. Joseph Telafici, quoted in Vincent Kier- nan, "The Next Plague," *The Chronicle of Higher Education,* January 28, 2005, **pp.** A36–A38.

81. Ellen Laird, "Internet Plagiarism: We All Pay the Price," *The Chronicle of Higher Education,* June 13, 2001, p. B5. See also Sara Rimer, "A Cam- pus Fad That's Being Copied: Internet Plagiarism," *The New York Times,* September 3, 2008, *www.nytimes. com/2003/09/03/education/03CHEA. html?scp=3&sq=plagiarism&st=cse* (accessed June 12, 2009).

82. Eugene Dwyer, "Virtual Term Papers" [letter], *The New York Times,* June 10, 1997, **p.** A20.

83. William L. Rukyser, "How to Track Down Cyber-Cheaters" [letter], *The New York Times,* June 14, 1997, Sec. 6, **p.** 14.

84. David Rothenberg, "How the Web Destroys the Quality of Students' Research Papers," *The Chronicle of Higher Education,* August 15, 1997.

Chapter 3

1. Alan Robbins, "Why There's Egg on Your Interface," *The New York Times,* December 1, 1996, sec. 3, **p.** 12.

2. Ryan Kim, "OS 3.0 for iPhone in Works," *San Francisco Chronicle,* March 18, 2009, **pp.** C1, C2; Justin Scheck and Nick Wingfield, "A Challenge to Microsoft, PC Makers Test Laptops Run- ning Google Software," *The Wall Street Journal,* April 1, 2009, **p.** B1; and Justin Scheck, "Dell Studies Google's Android for Future Products," *The Wall Street Journal,* May 1, 2009, **p.** B4.

3. Matt Richtel and Ashlee Vance, "In New Age of Impatience, Cutting Com- puter Start Time," *The New York Times,* October 26, 2008, **pp.** A1, A24; Randall Stross, "30 Seconds to Boot Up? That's 29 Too Many," November 2, 2008, Busi- ness section, **p.** 4; Ryan Kim, "Booting Could Get a Kick-Start," *San Francisco*

Chronicle, November 10, 2008, p**p.** D1, D4; and Jefferson Graham, "Imagine Booting Up and Getting Online Before Your Hair Turns Gray," *USA Today,* March 18, 2009, p**.** 4B.

4. Stephen H. Wildstrom, "Tiger Makes Mac's Edge Even Sharper," *Business-Week,* May 9, 2005, p**.** 28.

5. Jonathan Skillings, "Windows 7, Mac OS Make Gains in January," *cnet news,* http://news.cnet.com/8301-10805_3-10154133-75.html, accessed June 20, 2009.

6. Jefferson Graham, "Can Vista Bust Out?" *USA Today,* April 30, 2008, p**p.** 1B, 2B.

7. Randall Stross, "Windows Could Use a Rush of Fresh Air," *The New York Times,* June 29, 2008, Business section, p**.** 4.

8. Walter S. Mossberg, "Free Security Upgrade to Windows XP Has Value but Falls Short," *The Wall Street Journal,* August 19, 2004, p**.** B1.

9. Greg Sullivan, quoted in Edward C. Baig, "Windows Upgrade Makes Strides to Outrun the Bad Guys," *USA Today,* August 12, 2004, p**.** 3B.

10. Irving Wladawsky-Berger, quoted in Deborah Solomon, "Could Linux Outdo Windows?" *USA Today,* March 9, 2000, p**p.** 1B, 2B.

11. Ashlee Vance, "A Software Populist Who Doesn't Do Windows," *The New York Times,* January 11, 2009, Business section, p**p.** 1, 6; Don Clark, "Intel Unveils Software That Rivals Windows," *The Wall Street Journal,* May 20, 2009, p**.** B7; and Nick Wingfield, "Little Laptops with Linux Have Compatibility Issues," *The Wall Street Journal,* May 28, 2009, p**.** D1.

12. Mina Kimes, "Apple's App Store Thinks Small," *Fortune,* May 11, 2009, p**.** 39.

13. Sara Silver, "What's in Store," *The Wall Street Journal,* February 17, 2009, p**p.** R4, R5; and Jeffrey M. O'Brien, "The Wizard of Apps," *Fortune,* May 25, 2009, p**p.** 29–30.

14. "Cloud Computing: The Evolution of Software-as-a-Service," Knowledge @ W. **P.** Carey, June 4, 2008, *http://knowledge.wpcarey.asu.edu/article.cfm?articleid=1614* (accessed July 24, 2009).

15. "Why Software Business Models of the Future Probably Won't Come in a Box," Knowledge@Wharton, February 7, 2007, *http://knowledge.wharton.upenn.edu/article.cfm?articleid=1651* (accessed July 24, 2009).

16. Ryan Kim, "For Apps, Amateurs Finding Success," *San Francisco Chronicle,* April 20, 2009, p**p.** A1, A12; and Ryan Kim, "Stanford iTunes U Class Tops 1 Million Downloads," *San Francisco Chronicle,* May 19, 2009, p**p.** C1, C3.

17. Rhonda Abrams, "Free Applications from Google Make Running an Office Easier," *Reno Gazette-Journal,* October 7, 2008, p**.** 6A.

18. Rhonda Abrams, 2008; and Randall Stross, "The Word Processor Is Looking at Home on the Web," *The New York*

Times, April 5, 2009, Business section, p**.** 4.

19. Walter S. Mossberg, "Quickoffice Brings Editing to iPhones, but Put It on Hold," *The Wall Street Journal,* May 7, 2009, p**.** D1.

20. Study by Kent Norman, Laboratory of Automation Psychology and Decision Processes, University of Maryland, cited in Katherine Seligman, "Computer Crashes Booming Business," *San Francisco Chronicle,* April 17, 2005, p**p.** A1, A21.

21. Survey by Pew Internet and American Life Project, reported in Jack Gillum, "Half of New-Gadget Users Call for Help," *USA Today,* November 18, 2008, p**.** 6D.

22. James Aley, "Software That Doesn't Work; Customers Are in Revolt; Here's the Plan," *Fortune,* November 25, 2002, p**p.** 147–158.

23. Jane Black, "Usability Is Next to Profitability," *BusinessWeek* online, December 4, 2002, www.businessweek.com/technology content/dec2002 (accessed July 24, 2009).

24. Edward C. Baig, "Have You Tried to Get Tech Support Lately? Arrgh!#*!!" *USA Today,* August 27, 2004.

25. Edward C. Baig, "Tech Support: Not Quite at Our Beck and Call," *USA Today,* July 17, 2002, p**.** 3D.

26. Adapted from Jane Spencer, "Computer Glitches? Rent Your Own Tech," *The Wall Street Journal,* August 22, 2002, table, p**.** D3.

27. Stan Sams, quoted in ibid., p**.** D3.

Chapter 4

1. Michael S. Malone, "The Tiniest Transformer," *San Jose Mercury News,* September 10, 1995, p**p.** 1D, 2D; excerpted from *The Microprocessor: A Biography* (New York: Telos/Springer Verlag, 1995).

2. Malone, "The Tiniest Transformer."

3. Laurence Hooper, "No Compromises," *The Wall Street Journal,* November 16, 1992, p**.** R8.

4. "Exabyte," The Sharpened Glossary: Definitions of Computer Terms, *www.sharpened.net/glossary/definition.php?exabyte* (accessed July 29, 2009s).

5. Ernest Scheyder, "Save Some Cash, Get Unplugged," *Reno Gazette-Journal,* April 11, 2009, p**.** 8A.

6. Ibid.

7. Report by 1E and Alliance to Save Energy, 2009 Energy Report, reported in Jon Swartz, "Leaving PCs on Overnight Costs Companies $2.8B a Year," *USA Today,* March 25, 2009, p**.** 4B.

8. Thomas Catan, "Switching Off Standby Mode," *The Wall Street Journal,* November 28, 2008, p**.** B5.

9. Katherine Boehret, "Cool Trays Take the Heat Off Your Lap," *The Wall Street Journal,* April 1, 2009, p**.** D4.

10. Sharon Gaudon, "Intel Squeezes 2 Billion Transistors onto New Itanium Chip," *ComputerWorld,* February 4, 2008, *www.computerworld.com/action/article.do?command=viewArticleBasic*

&articleId=9060900 (accessed July 29, 2009).

11. Peter Svensson, "Tiny Atom Chip Gives Intel Boost," *San Francisco Chronicle,* June 2, 2008, p**.** D3; Don Clark, "Intel Looks to Power Bottom of Market," *The Wall Street Journal,* June 3, 2008, p**.** B3; Laurie J. Flynn, "AMD Set to Introduce a New Chip for Laptops," *The New York Times,* June 4, 2008, p**.** C4; and Joe Nocera, "AMD and Its War with Intel," *The New York Times,* June 21, 2008, p**p.** B1, B8.

12. Nick Wingfield and Don Clark, "With Intel Inside Apple, Macs May Be Faster, Smaller," *The Wall Street Journal,* June 7, 2005, p**p.** B1, B7; Matthew Yi and Benny Evangelista, "Apple Gains Room to Grow," *San Francisco Chronicle,* June 7, 2005, p**p.** A1, A8; Walter S. Mossberg, "What the Apple Plan to Switch to Intel Chips Means for Consumers," *The Wall Street Journal,* June 9, 2005, p**.** B1; John Markoff, "Think Similar," *The New York Times,* June 11, 2005, p**p.** B1, B13; and Peter Burrows, "Tougher Days, Bolder Apple," *BusinessWeek,* June 20, 2005, p**p.** 38, 40.

13. Mossberg, "What the Apple Plan to Switch to Intel Chips Means for Consumers."

14. Stephen H. Wildstrom, "Chips with Two Brains," *BusinessWeek,* August 1, 2005, p**.** 20.

15. Adam Aston, "More Life for Moore's Law," *BusinessWeek,* June 20, 2005, p**p.** 108–109.

16. Wolfgang Gruener, "Intel's 8-Core CPUs Will Have 2.3 Billion transistors," *TG Daily,* February 9, 2009, *www.tgdaily.com/content/view/41371/135/* (accessed July 2, 2009).

17. Michael V. Copeland, "Intel's Secret Plan," *Fortune,* May 25, 2009, p**p.** 52–57.

18. John Markoff, " Do You Have That Portable in a Midsize?" *The New York Times,* May 11, 2008, p**.** BU-4; Tom Abate, "Tiny Via Girds to Defend Turf against Giant Intel," *San Francisco Chronicle,* May 25, 2008, p**p.** D1, D3; Don Clark, "Chip Makers Rush to Fill MID Gadgets," *The Wall Street Journal,* June 2, 2008, p**.** B6; Eric A. Taub, "Smaller Than a Laptop, but Bigger Than a Phone," *The New York Times,* June 5, 2008, p**.** C6; and John Markoff, "Intel's Dominance Is Challenged by a Low-Power Upstart," *The New York Times,* June 30, 2008, p**p.** C1, C5.

19. James Gorbold, "Product Reviews: Intel CPUs," *Custom PC,* June 5, 2005, *www.custompc.co.uk/custompc/processors/reviews/72870/intel-pentium-extreme-edition-840.html.*

20. Don Clark, "Los Alamos Computer Keeps Title as the Fastest," *The Wall Street Journal,* November 11, 2008, p. B9.

21. Frank Bajak, "Peruvian Village Shows Promise of One Laptop Per Child Project," *San Francisco Chronicle,* December 26, 2007, p**p.** D1, D3; John Markoff, "Intel Quits Effort to Get Computers to Children," *The New York Times,* January 5, 2008, p**.** B3; Brian Bergstein, "$100

Laptops to Be Loaded with Windows for an Additional Fee," *San Francisco Chronicle*, May 16, 2008, **p.** C4; and Steve Lohr, "Microsoft Joins Effort for Laptops for Children," *The New York Times*, May 16, 2008, p**p.** C1, C4.

22. Michelle Kessler, "Asus Pins Future on Small but Mighty Laptop," *USA Today*, May 14, 2008, **p.** 3B.

23. Michael Kwan, "Cell Processor Powers the Toshiba Qosmio G55," *Mobile Magazine*, July 15, 2008, www.mobilemag.com/2008/07/15/cell-processor-powers-the-toshiba-qosmio-g55 (accessed July 2, 2009).

24. Don Clark, "Chip Firms Address Energy Drain," *The Wall Street Journal*, June 24, 2008, **p.** B4.

25. Cisco Cheng and Erik Rhey, "Ports," *PC Magazine*, April 26, 2005, **p.** 66.

26. Jefferson Graham, "Power of the Graphics Card," *USA Today*, November 26, 2008, **p.** 4B.

27. Daniel Sorid, "Network Storage Comes Home, Not without Some Difficulty," *The New York Times*, June 19, 2008, **p.** C6; and Walter S. Mossberg, "Network Hard Disk by Western Digital Offers Easy Backup," *The Wall Street Journal*, April 2, 2009, **p.** D1.

28. "Consumers Fail to Properly Back Up Large Digital Libraries, Says CEA," www.reuters.com/article/pressRelease/idUS157293+18-Mar-2008+BW20080318 (accessed August 2, 2009).

29. Edward Baig, "Be Happy, Film Freaks," *BusinessWeek*, May 26, 1997, p**p.** 172–173.

30. Matt Richtel and Brad Stone, "Blu-ray's Fuzzy Future," *The New York Times*, January 5, 2009, p**p.** B1, B4.

31. "Solid Computing, for a Price," *The New York Times*, September 18, 2008, **p.** C8. See also J. Santo Domingo, "Credit-Card Hard Drives," *PC Magazine, Digital Edition*, July 2009, **p.** 17.

32. Peter Wayner, "You Know about Backups; Now, Do It Online," *The New York Times*, October 23, 2008, www.nytimes.com/2008/10/23/technology/personaltech/23basics1.html (accessed July 4, 2009); and Anne Eisenberg, "A Digital Storage Option for Workers on the Go," *The New York Times*, January 18, 2009, Business section, **p.** 4.

33. Ting-I Tsai, "Asustek Adds Online Storage to Low-Cost Eee PC," *The Wall Street Journal*, September 5, 2008, **p.** B3.

34. E. K. Boehret, "Lost Cellphone? Your Carrier Has Your Backup," *The Wall Street Journal*, February 25, 2009, p. D1.

35. Michio Kaku, "What Will Replace Silicon?" *Time*, June 19, 2000, **p.** 99.

36. October 2004 study by America Online and the National Cyber Security Alliance, cited in Rachel Dodes, "Terminating Spyware with Extreme Prejudice," *The New York Times*, December 30, 2004, p**p.** E1, E6.

37. Alan Luber, "Hard Drive Backup & Restore Basics, Part 1," *Smart Computing*, August 2004, **p.** 96; Dodes, "Terminating Spyware with Extreme Prejudice"; Rachel Dodes, "Tools to Make Your Hard Drive Forget Its Past," *The New York Times*, December 30, 2004, **p.** E6; Jeff Dodd, "How to Install Operating Systems," *Smart Computing*, February 2005, p**p.** 60–63; and Nigel Powell, "Archive Your Drive," *Popular Science*, March 2005, p**p.** 73–74.

38. Gordon Moore, quoted in "Gordon Moore Q&A," *Time*, June 19, 2000, p. 99.

39. Gordon Moore, quoted in Matthew Yi, "Faster and Faster, Smaller and Smaller—It's the Law," *San Francisco Chronicle*, April 18, 2005, **p.** E1.

40. Don Clark, "Intel Pushes Ahead with Tiny Circuitry," *The Wall Street Journal*, December 10, 2008, **p.** B4.

41. John Markoff, "IBM Plans to Announce Tiny Transistor," *The New York Times*, December 9, 2002, p. C4; and Don Clark, "IBM, Xilinx Pass a Milestone in Race to Shrink Circuitry," *The Wall Street Journal*, December 16, 2002, **p.** B5.

42. Michael Kanellos, "HP Nanotech Takes Chips beyond Transistors," CNET News.com, February 10, 2005.

43. Aston, "More Life for Moore's Law"; John Markoff, "Chip Maker Develops Denser Storage Method," *The New York Times*, May 9, 2005, **p.** C3.

44. K. Naughton, "Now We're Cooking with Batteries," *Newsweek*, December 1, 2008, p**p.** 42–46.

45. Daniel Lyons, "Hurry Up and Type," *Newsweek*, June 29, 2009, **p.** 27.

46. John Markoff, "Intel Moves to Free Gadgets from Their Recharging Cords," *The New York Times*, August 21, 2008, **p.** C4; and Jordan Robertson, "Intel Lights Up at Idea of Wireless Charging," *San Francisco Chronicle*, August 22, 2008, **p.** C3.

47. Naughton, "Now We're Cooking with Batteries"; and Daniel Lyons, "It Takes Power to Cut the Cord," *Newsweek*, October 13, 2008, p. 24.

48. Dirk Lammers, "Fuel Cell-Powered Devices Coming Soon," *Reno Gazette-Journal*, December 1, 2008, **p.** 7A.

49. Ibid.

50. Don Clark, "Marvell Bets on 'Plug Computers,'" *The Wall Street Journal*, February 23, 2009, **p.** B4.

51. James Canton, quoted in Barnaby J. Feder, "Scientists of Very Small Draw Disciplines Together," *The New York Times*, February 10, 2003, **p.** C4.

52. Barnaby J. Feder, "Nanotechnology Has Arrived; A Serious Opposition Is Forming," *The New York Times*, August 19, 2002, **p.** C3; Barnaby J. Feder, "From Nanotechnology's Sidelines, One More Warning," *The New York Times*, February 1, 2003, p**p.** C1, C3; James M. Pethokoukis, "Devil in the Details?" *U.S. News & World Report*, January 27/February 3, 2003, **p.** 44; Mike Treder, "Molecular Nanotech: Benefits and Risks," *The Futurist*, January–February 2004, p**p.** 42–46; Dan Vergano, "Creating a Monster?" *USA Today*, September 28, 2004, **p.** 6D; Fred Krupp and Chad Holliday, "Let's Get Nanotech Right," *The Wall Street Journal*, June 14, 2005, **p.** B2; and Kevin Maney, "Scared of New Nano-Pants? Hey, You May Be onto Something," *USA Today*, June 22, 2005, **p.** 3B.

53. Paul Glader, "GE Disk Can Store 100 DVDs," *The Wall Street Journal*, April 28, 2009, **p.** B5.

54. Mark Hachman, "The Bottomless DVD," *PC Magazine Digital Edition*, July 2009, **p.** 9.

55. Walter S. Mossberg, "Shopping for a Laptop? Expect Lots of Choices, and a Range of Prices," *The Wall Street Journal*, April 14, 2005, **p.** B1.

56. "Notebooks," *PC Magazine*, November 30, 2004, p**p.** 121–134; Mossberg, "Shopping for a Laptop?"; "Inside Notebooks," *PC Magazine*, April 26, 2005, p**p.** 62–68; Bill Howard, "Multimedia Notebooks," *PC Magazine*, July 2005, p**p.** 89–102; Wilson Rothman, "Laptops and Desktops: Basics, Bells and Whistles," *The New York Times*, August 3, 2005, p. E6; Walter S. Mossberg, "Consider Your Needs, Then Use This Guide to Buying a Laptop," *The Wall Street Journal*, April 10, 2008, http://ptech.allthingsd.com/20080410/consider-your-needs-then-use-this-guide-to-buying-a-laptop/ (accessed August 1, 2008); Aaron Boigon, "Several Things You Should Consider When Buying a Bargain Computer," *Reno Gazette-Journal*, March 14, 2009, **p.** 7A; Randall Stross, "The PC Doesn't Have to Be an Anchor," *The New York Times*, April 19, 2009, Business section, p. 4; Justin Scheck and Loretta Chao, "Leaner Laptops, Lower Prices," *The Wall Street Journal*, April 22, 2009, p**p.** D1, D6; Ting-I. Tsai and Ian Johnson, "As Giants Step In, Asustek Defends a Tiny PC," *The Wall Street Journal*, May 1, 2009, **p.** B1; "Tech Edge: Owner Tested," *Fortune Small Business*, June 2009, **p.** 30; Ashlee Vance, "Acer's Everywhere; How Did That Happen?" *The New York Times*, June 28, 2009, Business section, pp. 1, 6.

57. John Schwartz, "Back to School," *The New York Times*, August 3, 2005, p**p.** E1, E6.

58. Lyons, "Hurry Up and Type"; David Pogue, "Decoding Battery Life for Laptops," *The New York Times*, June 25, 2009, p**p.** B1, B6; and Walter S. Mossberg, "New Mac Laptops Use Batteries Sealed for Power," *The Wall Street Journal*, June 25, 2009, **p.** D1.

Chapter 5

1. David F. Gallagher, "2 Rooms, River View, ATM in Lobby," *The New York Times*, June 6, 2002, **p.** E1.

2. Mary Kathleen Flynn, "Banking with a Big Gulp," *U.S. News & World Report*, April 25, 2005, p**p.** EE10, EE12.

3. "DMV Installs New Kiosks," *The Record-Courier*, August 8, 2008, **p.** 2.

4. Jeffrey Selingo, "Want to Rent a Movie? Help Yourself," *The New York Times*, September 2, 2004, **p.** E3; Linda Stern, "Here Come the Kiosks," *Newsweek*, March 22, 2004, **p.** E4; and Christopher Elliott, "Invasion of the Kiosks," *U.S. News & World Report*, March 5, 2004, **p.** 82.

5. Randall Stross, "When the Price Is Right, the Future Can Wait," *The New York Times*, July 12, 2009, Business section, **p. 3**.

6. Peter Wayner, "A Keyboard That Bends to Your Needs," *The New York Times*, March 12, 2009, **p. B7**.

7. Kevin J. Delaney, "Dumber PCs That Use the Net for Processing, Storage Get Hot—Again," *The Wall Street Journal*, December 27, 2004, **p. B1**.

8. Charles Burress, "A Stunned Crowd Saw the PC Born—Mouse and All," *San Francisco Chronicle*, December 8, 2008, pp**. A1, A15**.

9. Walter S. Mossberg, "A Tiny Touch Screen for Less," *The Wall Street Journal*, March 18, 2009, **p. D2**; Justin Scheck, "H-P Tries to Revive PC Sales with Touch Screens," *The Wall Street Journal*, May 15, 2009, **p. B1**; and Ashlee Vance, "In Novelty of Touching, PC Makers See a Future," *The New York Times*, June 3, 2009, p. B3.

10. Peter Svenson, "Cooked Up for Kitchen Duty," *San Francisco Chronicle*, February 16, 2009, **p. C4**.

11. Jenna Wortham and Matt Richtel, "Makers Hope Touch Screens Will Help Cellphone Sales," *The New York Times*, December 1, 2008, **p. B1, B5**; and Peter Svenson, "Touch Screens, QWERTY to Dominate Newest Cell Phones," *Reno Gazette-Journal*, April 3, 2009, **p. 7A**.

12. Ryan Kim, "Long Nails on Touch Screens Can Be Grating," *San Francisco Chronicle*, December 8, 2008, pp**. D1, D2**.

13. Edward C. Baig, "Start-up Axiotron Converts MacBook into Tablet PC," *USA Today*, May 1, 2008, **p. 1B**; and Edward C. Baig, "Pen May Be Mightier Than MacBook's Keyboard, but Not at This Price," *USA Today*, May 1, 2008, **p. 3B**.

14. David Pogue, "Gadget Fanatics Take Note," *The New York Times*, May 8, 2008, pp**. C1, C9**.

15. Edward C. Baig, "Livescribe Pulse Digital Pen Brings Your Notes to Life," *USA Today*, May 8, 2008, p. 1B; and Edward C. Baig, "Pulse Gets Points for Design, Good Sound," *USA Today*, May 8, 2008, **p. 3B**.

16. Peter Svensson, "A Useful Digital Pen," *Reno Gazette-Journal*, June 9, 2008, **p. 9A**; and David Pogue, "Digital Pens to Write on Any Paper," *The New York Times*, July 3, 2008, pp. C1, C7.

17. John Noble Wilford, "Project Digitizes Works from the Golden Age of Timbuktu," *The New York Times*, May 20 2008, **p. D2**.

18. Marlon Manuel, "Scan-It-Yourself Part, Parcel of Life," *San Francisco Chronicle*, January 30, 2005, **p. E3**.

19. David Pogue, "Grocery Shopping Made Easy," *The New York Times*, June 19, 2008, pp**. C1, C7**.

20. Julie Schmit, "Labels Will Tell Buyers Where Their Berries Grew," *USA Today*, February 2, 2009, **p. 8B**.

21. Thomas Frank, "Paperless Boarding Passes Set to Take Off," *USA Today*, October 22, 2008, **p. 3A**.

22. Byron Acohido, "New '2D Barcodes' Put Info at Your Fingertips," *USA Today*, May 20, 2009, **p. 3B**.

23. Robert Johnson, "The Fax Machine: Technology That Refuses to Die," *The New York Times*, March 27, 2005, sec. 3, **p. 8**.

24. Katie Hafner, "At Your Service (or Wits' End)," *The New York Times*, September 9, 2004, pp**. E1, E7**.

25. David Einstein, "Prepaid Wireless Plan Is an Option," *San Francisco Chronicle*, February 23, 2009, pp. C1, C3.

26. John Markoff, "Google Is Taking Your Questions (Spoken, via the iPhone)," *The New York Times*, November 11, 2008, pp**. B1, B7**; and Edward C. Baig, "Online Voice Searches by Cellphone Can Be Hit or Miss," *USA Today*, February 12, 2009, **p. 6B**.

27. Larry Copeland, "Project Will Help Drivers Go More with Traffic Flow," *USA Today*, June 13, 2008, **p. 1A**; and Larry Copeland, "Test Project Will Gather Highway Traffic Data," *USA Today*, June 13, 2008, **p. 6A**.

28. Alicia Chang, "Sensors to Keep Tabs on Fault," *Reno Gazette-Journal*, March 29, 2009, pp**. 1B, 3B**.

29. William J. Broad, "A Web of Sensors Taking Earth's Pulse," *The New York Times*, May 10, 2005, pp**. D1, D4**.

30. Laura Landro, "The Hospital Is Watching You," *The Wall Street Journal*, November 12, 2008, **p. D4**.

31. John Schwartz, "Graduate Cryptographers Unlock Code of 'Thiefproof' Car Key," *The New York Times*, January 29, 2005, **p. A10**.

32. Peter Sanders, "Casinos Bet on Radio-ID Gambling Chips," *The Wall Street Journal*, May 13, 2005, pp. B1, B7.

33. Jenny Strasburg, "Chase Introduces No-Swipe Plastic," *San Francisco Chronicle*, May 20, 2005, pp**. C1, C6**; and Mindy Fetterman, "Wave-and-Pay Credit Cards May Make Buying Too Easy," *USA Today*, May 24, 2005, **p. 1B**. See also Don Clark, "Enhanced Tracking Technology May Propel Adoption of RFID," *The Wall Street Journal*, April 14, 2008, **p. B4**.

34. James M. Pethokoukis, "Big Box Meets Big Brother," *U.S. News & World Report*, January 24, 2005, pp. 46–47.

35. Mimi Hall, "ID Scan Gives Border Agents Leg Up," *USA Today*, November 24, 2008, **p. 1A**; and Todd Lewan, "Chips in Official ID Cards Raise Privacy Fears," *Reno Gazette-Journal*, July 12, 2009, **p. 4B**.

36. "Theft Deterrence for an Arizona Icon," *The New York Times*, October 12, 2008, news section, **p. 31**.

37. William Falk, "The Two Weeks You Missed," *The New York Times*, September 6, 2008, **p. A23**.

38. Diedtra Henderson, "Implantable Chip Sparks Privacy Concerns," *Reno Gazette-Journal*, October 14, 2004, p. 4A.

39. Benjamin Pimentel, "Biometrics Puts Security at a User's Fingertips," *San Francisco Chronicle*, July 11, 2005, pp. E1, E2; Andrew Morse, "New Biometric Identifier Is at Hand," *The Wall Street Journal*, July 21, 2005, p. B4; and Thomas Frank, "Biometric IDs Could See Massive Growth," *USA Today*, August 15, 2005, **p. 1B, 2B**.

40. Thomas Frank, "Digital IDs Make Clearing Customs Easier," *USA Today*, April 24, 2009, **p. 3A**.

41. Farhad Manjoo, "Boss, I Need a Bigger Screen; For Work Efficiency, of Course," *The New York Times*, January 15, 2009, **p. B9**.

42. Janet Colvin, Nancy Tobler, and James A. Anderson, "Productivity and Multi-Screen Displays," *Rocky Mountain Communication Review*, Summer 2004, pp**. 31–53**.

43. James A. Anderson, University of Utah, quoted in "Multiple Monitor Computing Demonstrates Tangible Benefits for Corporate Workforce," NEC press release, October 6, 2003, *www.necus. com/necus/media/press_releases/template.cfm?DID=1947* (accessed July 20, 2009).

44. Manjoo, "Boss, I Need a Bigger Screen."

45. Walter S. Mossberg, "Printer Makes a New Kind of Polaroid Magic," *The Wall Street Journal*, June 18, 2008, p. D6.

46. "Small Photo Printers Bring Digital Images to Life," *San Francisco Chronicle*, August 18, 2008, **p. D1**.

47. Ryan Kim, "HP Unveils Web-Ready Printer," *San Francisco Chronicle*, June 23, 2009, pp**. C1, C3**.

48. Danielle Weatherbee, quoted in Steve Friess, "Laptop Design Can Be a Pain in the Posture," *USA Today*, April 13, 2005, **p. 8D**.

49. Tom Albin, quoted in Friess, "Laptop Design Can Be a Pain in the Posture."

50. Tamara James, quoted in Friess, "Laptop Design Can Be a Pain in the Posture."

51. Rachel Konrad, "Logitech Spawns New Breed of Mice That Is Twice as Nice," *San Francisco Chronicle*, September 27, 2004, **p. F4**.

52. Albert R. Karr, "An Ergo-Unfriendly Home Office Can Hurt You," *The Wall Street Journal*, September 30, 2003, p. D6.

53. Johan H. Andersen, Jane F. Thomsen, Erik Overgaard, Christina F. Lassen, Lars **P.** A. Brandt, Imogen Vilstrup, Ann I. Kryger, and Sigurd Mikkelsen, "Computer Use and Carpal Tunnel Syndrome: A 1-Year Follow-up Study," *Journal of the American Medical Association* 283 (2003): 2963–2969; and J. Clarke Stevens, John C. Witt, Benn E. Smith, and Amy L. Weaver, "The Frequency of Carpal Tunnel Syndrome in Computer Users at a Medical Facility," *Neurology* 56 (2001): 1568–1570.

54. Cornell University Ergonomics Web, "Carpal Tunnel Syndrome and Computer Use—Is There a Link?" *http://ergo. human.cornell.edu/JAMAMay oCTS.html* (accessed August 8, 2009).

55. *www.ninds.nih.gov/disorders/carpal_tunnel/detail_carpal_tunnel.htm* (accessed August 9, 2009).

56. "Cellular Phone Health," *www.cellular-phonehealth.com* (accessed March 31, 2005).

57. Siegal Sadetzki, Angela Chetrit, Avital Jarus-Hakak, Elisabeth Cardis, Yonit Deutch, Shay Duvdevani, Ahuva Zultan, Ilya Novikov, Laurence Freedman, and Michael Wolf, "Cellular Phone Use and Risk of Benign and Malignant Parotid Gland Tumors—A Nationwide Case-Control Study," *American Journal of Epidemiology* 167 (4) (2008): 457–467.

58. Minouk Schoemaker, Anthony Swerdlow et al., "Mobile Phone Use and Risk of Acoustic Neuroma: Results of the Interphone Case-Control Study in Five North European Countries," *British Journal of Cancer*, August 31, 2005, reported in Matt Moore, "No Link Between Cellphones, Tumors: Study," *GlobeandMail.com*, August 8, 2008, *www.globetechnology.com/servlet/story/RTGAM.20050831.gttumouraug31/BNStory/Technology.*

59. Ronald Herberman, cited in Agam Shah, "Reduce Cell-Phone Cancer Risk," *PC World*, July 31, 2008, *www.pcworld.com/businesscenter/article/149227/reduce_cellphone_cancer_risk.html* (accessed August 8, 2009). See also Tara Parker-Pope, "Experts Revive Debate over Cellphones and Cancer," *The New York Times*, June 3, 2008, **p.** D5.

60. Benjamin Fulford, "Sensors Gone Wild," *Forbes*, October 28, 2002, pp. 306–308.

61. Don Clark, "Low-Cost Device for Monitoring Is Set for Market," *The Wall Street Journal*, September 20, 2004, **p.** B5; and Karen F. Schmidt, "'Smart Dust' Is Way Cool," *U.S. News & World Report*, February 16, 2004, **pp.** 56–57.

62. Cornelia Dean, "Charting Bird Migrations by Using Tiny Backpacks," *The New York Times*, February 13, 2009, **p.** A15.

63. Clark Nguyen, professor of electrical engineering, quoted in Fulford, "Sensors Gone Wild."

64. Mimi Hall, "Sensors to Provide Early Warning for Bioterror Attacks," *USA Today*, January 23, 2003, **p.** 3A.

65. David Perlman, "H-Bomb Sensors Yield New Benefits," *San Francisco Chronicle*, December 9, 2002, **p.** A9.

66. Mimi Hall, "'Virtual Fence' Gets Second Chance on U.S. Border," *USA Today*, March 11, 2009, **p.** 4A.

67. David R. Baker, "Intel's Next Crop of Eco-Devices," *San Francisco Chronicle*, December 4, 2008, **p.** C1; and Michael Totty, "Smart Roads; Smart Bridges; Smart Grids," *The Wall Street Journal*, February 17, 2009, pp. R1, R3.

68. Robert Davis, "Now There's Hope in His Eyes," *USA Today*, June 19, 2008, **p.** 6D.

69. Donna Gordon Blankinship, "Web-Based Program Gives the Blind Internet Access," *Nevada Appeal*, July 20, 2008, **p.** A6.

70. Greg Bluestein, "Tongue May Become a Device Disabled Could Use as a Control," *San Francisco Chronicle*, August 25, 2008, **p.** D2.

71. Justin Berton, "Not Just Sci-Fi: A Growing Urge to Use Tech Objects in Human Bodies," *San Francisco Chronicle*, January 1, 2009, **pp.** A1, A11; and Anne Eisenberg, "Inside These Legends, a Digital Dimension," *The New York Times*, April 26, 2009, business section, **p.** 4.

72. Matthew Philips, "It Makes Teachers Touchy," *Newsweek*, September 22, 2008, **p.** 10.

73. Faith Keenan, "PCs and Speech: A Rocky Marriage," *BusinessWeek*, September 9, 2002, **pp.** 64–66; and Anne Eisenberg, "Teaching Machines to Hear Your Prose and Your Pain," *The New York Times*, August 1, 2002, p. E9.

74. Douglas Heingartner, "Attention, Cows: Please Speak into the Microphone," *The New York Times*, August 1, 2002, **p.** E5.

75. Benny Evangelista, "Microsoft Team Works on Getting Ahead of Its Time," *San Francisco Chronicle*, June 14, 2004, **p.** D4.

76. David Pogue, "Sizing Up a New Species: Camera-Binoculars," *The New York Times*, March 24, 2005, pp. E1, E4.

77. Leslie Berlin, "Kicking Reality Up a Notch," *The New York Times*, July 12, 2009, business section, **p.** 3.

78. Peter Wayner, "Just a Twist (and Tilt) of the Wrist," *The New York Times*, May 29, 2008, **p.** C6.

79. Cliff Edwards, "Soon TVs and PCs May Work Like the Wii," *BusinessWeek*, April 13, 2009, **pp.** 52–53; and Jerry A. DiColo, "'Virtual Touch' within Reach," *The Wall Street Journal*, April 29, 2009, **p.** B5.

80. Verne Kopytoff, "Finding Faces amid Photos," *San Francisco Chronicle*, September 29, 2008, **pp.** D1, D3.

81. Kevin Maney, "Scientists Gingerly Tap into Brain's Power," *USA Today*, October 11, 2004, **pp.** 1B, 2B. See also Andrew Pollack, "With Tiny Brain Implants, Just Thinking May Make It So," *The New York Times*, April 13, 2004, **p.** D5.

82. Alex Nussbaum, "Monkeys Think, and Prosthetic Arms Do," *San Francisco Chronicle*, May 29, 2008, p. A4.

83. Anne Eisenberg, "Moving Mountains with the Brain, Not a Joystick," *The New York Times*, June 8, 2008, business section, **p.** 3.

84. David Ho, "Hearing Voices? It's Not in Your Imagination," *San Francisco Chronicle*, February 19, 2008, pp. E1, E5.

85. Kara Platoni, "iProd," *Stanford*, July/August 2008, **pp.** 65–68.

86. Mike Snider, "3D: Coming at You in a Home Theater Near You," *USA Today*, June 24, 2008, **p.** 6D.

87. Daniel Lyons, "The Paper Chasers," *Newsweek*, December 1, 2008, pp. E6–E9.

88. Jeremy Caplan, "Ink Inc.," *Time*, September 15, 2009, **p.** Global 6.

89. Don Clark, "Videogames Get Real," *The Wall Street Journal*, April 14, 2004, **pp.** B1, B2.

90. Brooks Barnes, "Stereo Vision on the Silver Screen," *The New York Times*, January 12, 2009, **pp.** B1, B6; Brooks Barnes, "A Tiny Studio Enters the Third Dimension," *The New York Times*, February 8, 2009, business section, **pp.** 1, 5; Peter Hartlaub, "3-D Rises from the Dead," *San Francisco Chronicle*, March 20, 2009, **pp.** E1, E2; and Josh Quittner, "The Next Dimension," *Time*, March 30, 2009, **pp.** 53–62.

91. Don Clark, Ben Charny, and Jerry DiColo, "Animators Envision 3-D TV at Home," *The Wall Street Journal*, January 5, 2009, **pp.** B1, B6.

92. Stephen H. Wildstrom, "Coming at You: 3D on Your PC," *BusinessWeek*, January 19, 2009, **p.** 65.

93. Michael V. Copeland, "3-D Gets Down to Business," *Fortune*, March 30, 2009, **pp.** 32–40.

94. Adam Ashton, "If You Can Draw It, They Can Make It," *BusinessWeek*, May 23, 2005, **pp.** MTL7–MTL8.

95. Survey by Ponemon Institute for Dell, reported in "How Workers Damage Laptops," *USA Today*, March 4, 2009, **p.** 1A.

96. Josh Quittner, "The Klutz's Companion," *Time*, October 13, 2008, **p.** 66; and John Biggs, "It Takes a Drop and Doesn't Stop," *The New York Times*, November 13, 2008, **p.** B6.

97. "Computers Causing Injuries in the Home," *Medline Plus*, June 9, 2009, *www.nlm.nih.gov/medlineplus/news/fullstory_85396.html* (accessed July 23, 2009).

98. Melinda Beck, "When Your Laptop Is a Big Pain in the Neck," *The Wall Street Journal*, December 16, 2008, p. D1.

Chapter 6

1. "What Does 'Digital' Mean in Regard to Electronics?" *Popular Science*, August 1997, **pp.** 91–94.

2. Ken Belson, "Dial-Up Internet Starts to Go the Way of Rotary Phones," *The New York Times*, June 21, 2005, pp. C1, C5.

3. Lisa Guernsey, "With Wires in the Walls, the Cyberhome Hums," *The New York Times*, March 27, 2003, pp. D1, D7.

4. S. Zeadally and **P.** Kubher, "Internet Access to Heterogeneous Home Area Network Devices with an OSGi-Based Gateway," *International Journal of Ad Hoc and Ubiquitous Computing*, 3 (1), 48–56.

5. See Michael Fitzgerald, "Finding and Fixing a Home's Power Hogs," *The New York Times*, July 27, 2008, *www.nytimes.com/2008/07/27/technology/27proto.html?ex=1374811200&en=a965d02fc80765e1&ei=5124&partner=permalink&exprod=permalink* (accessed August 12, 2009).

6. Christie Thomas, quoted in Stephanie Armour, "Job Opening? Work-at-Home Moms Fill Bill," *USA Today*, July 20, 2005, **p.** 3B. See also Taylor Lindstrom, "Time to Telecommute?" *San Francisco Chronicle*, June 15, 2008, **p.** H1.

7. Kris Maher, "Corner Office Shift: Telecommuting Rises in Executive Ranks," *The Wall Street Journal*, September 21, 2004, **pp.** B1, B10.

8. David Kline, quoted in W. James Au, "The Lonely Long-Distance Worker," *PC Computing*, February 2000, pp. 42–43.

9. Michelle Conlin, "Home Offices: The New Math," *BusinessWeek*, March 9, 2009, pp. 66–68.

10. WorldatWork, *Telework Trendlines 2009: A Survey Brief by WorldatWork*, February 2009, **p.** 5, *www.worldatwork.org/waw/adimLink?id=31115* (accessed August 7, 2009).

11. Jim Hopkins, "How Solo Workers Keep from Getting Depressed," *USA Today*, May 9, 2001; Stephanie Armour, "Telecommuting Gets Stuck in the Slow Lane," *USA Today*, June 25, 2001, pp. 1A, 2A; Stephanie Armour, "More Bosses Keep Tabs on Telecommuters," *USA Today*, July 24, 2001, **p.** 1B; Katherine Reynolds Lewis, "Working from Home Not Always the Right Fit," *San Francisco Chronicle*, July 14, 2003, **p.** E2; Sue Shellenbarger, "'Shed Boy Is on Line One': Some Tales from the Growing World of Home Offices," *The Wall Street Journal*, June 17, 2004, **p.** D1; Joyce M. Rosenberg, "Letting Staff Telecommute Changes Office," *San Francisco Chronicle*, September 7, 2008, **p.** H3; and Mintel Survey of 812 white-collar workers, reported in "Is Teleworking a Good Idea?" *USA Today*, October 28, 2008, **p.** 1B.

12. Carolyn Said, "Work Is Where You Hang Your Coat," *San Francisco Chronicle*, July 18, 2005, **p.** E5.

13. Robert Smith, quoted in Said, "Work Is Where You Hang Your Coat," **p.** E5. See also Sue Shellenbarger, "Work at Home? Your Employer May Be Watching," *The Wall Street Journal*, July 30, 2008, pp. D1, D2.

14. Pew Internet, "Mobile Internet Use Increases Sharply in 2009 as More than Half of All Americans Have Gotten Online by Some Wireless Means," press release, July 22, 2009, *www.pewinternet.org/Press-Releases/2009/Mobile-internet-use.aspx#* (accessed August 8, 2009).

15. David Pauleen and Brian Harmer, "Away from the Desk . . . Always," *The Wall Street Journal*, December 15, 2009, **p.** R6.

16. 2008 ITIF Broadband Rankings, in Robert D. Atkinson, Daniel K. Correa, and Julie A. Hedlund, Explaining International Broadband Leadership, May 1, 2008, the Information Technology and Innovation Foundation, *www.itif.org/index.php?id=142* (accessed August 12, 2009).

17. Paul Bedell, *Wireless Crash Course* (New York: McGraw-Hill, 2005), **p.** 2.

18. Roger Yu, "GPS Becomes a Vital Tool for Frequent Travelers," *USA Today*, July 8, 2008, **p.** 8B.

19. Berg Insight, reported in Bob Tedeschi, "Exactly Where Are You? New Devices Make the Answer Easier," *The New York Times*, October 19, 2008, p. B10.

20. For other uses, see Marisol Bello, "Holiday Heads Up to Thieves: GPS Devices on Board the Baby Jesus," *USA Today*, December 12, 2008, **p.** 1A; Natalie Angier, "GPS for Forest Creatures on the Move," *The New York Times*, February 3, 2009, pp. D1, D2; David Pogue, "Peekaboo, Zoombak Sees You," *The New York Times*, April 23, 2009, pp. B1, B8; and Marian Bond, "Firm Uses GPS System to Monitor Car Fleets," *Reno Gazette-Journal*, May 5, 2009, pp. 5A, 6A.

21. Christopher Elliott, "Online Maps That Steer You Wrong," *The New York Times*, June 28, 2005, **p.** C8; See also Donna Leinwand, "Caution: Watch Where You're Going," *USA Today*, March 12, 2009, **p.** 3A.

22. Brad Reed, "FCC Details E911 Accuracy Requirements," *PC World*, September 13, 2007, *www.pcworld.com/article/137169/fcc_details_e911_accuracy_requirements.html* (accessed August 14, 2009).

23. Survey by Centers for Disease Control and Prevention, reported in "More Cellphone Users Drop Landlines Entirely," *The Wall Street Journal*, May 7, 2009, **p.** D4. See also Ryan Kim, "Cell-Phone-Only Homes Top Those with Landlines for 1st Time," *San Francisco Chronicle*, May 7, 2009, **p.** C2; and Mike Mokryzycki, "Oklahoma, Utah Lead in Going Cell Phone-Only," *Reno Gazette-Journal*, March 12, 2009, **p.** 3B.

24. United Nations International Telecommunication Union, March 2009, reported in "Cellphones Overtake Land Lines," *USA Today*, May 7, 2009, **p.** 1A.

25. Jason Hidalgo, "iPhone vs. BlackBerry," *Reno Gazette-Journal*, July 23, 2008, pp. 7A, 9A.

26. Kevin Maney, "A Very Different Future Is Calling—on Billions of Cellphones," *USA Today*, July 27, 2005, p. 3B.

27. Data from Ericsson, reported in "Nearly 6.5 Billion Cellphones Will Be in Operation by 2013," *European Telecom*, June 1, 2008, *http://goliath.ecnext.com/coms2/gi_0199-8038098/Nearly-6-5-billion-cellphones.html* (accessed August 15, 2009).

28. Don Clark, "Curtain Rises on WiMax," *The Wall Street Journal*, September 28, 2008, **p.** B8; Leslie Cauley, "Mobile Broadband Hits the Air," *USA Today*, October 2008, pp. 1B, 2B; and Peter Wayner, "With WiMax, Walking on the Wireless Side in Baltimore," *The New York Times*, July 30, 2009, **p.** B5.

29. Darren Murph, "Sprint Unveils WiMax Expansion Cities, Devices for 2009 and 2010," *Engadget*, March 25, 2009, *www.engadget.com/2009/03/25/sprint-unveils-wimax-expansion-cities-devices-for-2009-and-2010/* (accessed August 9, 2009).

30. David Pogue, "Wi-Fi to Go, No Café Needed," *The New York Times*, May 7, 2009, pp. B1, B9; Edward C. Baig, "MiFi Lets You Take Your Own Wi-Fi Hot Spot with You," *USA Today*, May 14, 2009, **p.** 4B; and Katherine Boehret, "Web Surfing in a Wireless Network of Your Very Own," *The Wall Street Journal*, June 10, 2009, **p.** D3.

31. Ryan Kim, "American Airlines Wi-Fi Takes Off," *San Francisco Chronicle*, August 21, 2008, pp. C1, C2; Roger Yu, "In-Flight Net Access Takes Off on Virgin America," *USA Today*, November 24, 2008, **p.** 3B; and David Koenig, "American Airlines to Expand In-Flight Access to the Internet," *San Francisco Chronicle*, March 31, 2009, **p.** C2.

32. Marshall Loeb, "Securing Your Home Wi-Fi Network Saves Money," *Reno Gazette-Journal*, June 30, 2005, **p.** 3D.

33. In-Stat, reported in Rick Merritt, "Ultra-wideband Dies by 2013," *EE Times*, May 4, 2009, *www.eetimes.com/news/latest/showArticle.jhtml?articleID=217201265* (accessed August 10, 2009).

34. Lew Tucker, quoted in Matt Richtel and John Markoff, "Corrupted PC's Discover a Home: The Dumpster," *The New York Times*, July 17, 2005, sec. 1, **p.** 13.

35. "Enhancing Information and Data Security: A Never Ending Quest," *Knowledge@SMU*, June 4, 2008, *http://knowledge.smu.edu.sg/article.cfm?articleid=1144* (accessed August 9, 2009); John Markoff, "Internet Attacks Are Growing More Potent and Complex," *The New York Times*, November 10, 2008, **p.** B8; Deborah Gage, "Rising Threat: Online Crime," *San Francisco Chronicle*, December 9, 2008, pp. D1, D4; John Markoff, "Panel Presses to Bolster Security in Cyberspace," *The New York Times*, December 9, 2008, **p.** B5; Peter Eisler, "Raids on Federal Computer Data Soar," *USA Today*, February 17, 2009, **p.** 1A; and Byron Acohido, "Website-Infecting Attacks Spike to 450,000 a Day," *USA Today*, March 17, 2009, p. 1B.

36. McAfee/NCSA Cyber Security Survey, Newsworthy Analysis, October 2007, *http://download.mcafee.com/products/manuals/en-us/McAfeeNCSA_Analysis09-25-07.pdf?cid=36665* (accessed September 21, 2009).

37. Symantec, *Internet Security Threat Report, Volume XIV: Analysis of Threat Activity, January–December 2008*, April 2009, *www.symantec.com/business/theme.jsp?themeid=threatreport* (accessed August 14, 2009).

38. Munir Kotadia, "One Man Created Most PC Viruses," *San Francisco Chronicle*, July 29, 2004, **p.** C3.

39. Symantec, *Internet Security Threat Report, Volume XIV*, April 2009, *www.symantec.com/business/theme.jsp?themeid=threatreport* (accessed August 9, 2009).

40. Byron Acohido, "Cybercrooks Descend on Twitter with Spam, Attacks," *USA Today*, July 6, 2009, p. 1B; "Sneaky New Attack—Hackers Create Fake YouTube Pages to Spread Virus," *San Francisco Chronicle*, October 13, 2008, **p.** D2; Emily Steel, "Web Ad Sales Open Door to Viruses," *The Wall Street Journal*, June 15, 2009, **p.** B7; and Deborah Gage, "Digital Frames Carry Risk of Infection," *San Francisco Chronicle*, January 2, 2009, pp. C1, C2.

41. Verne Kopytoff, "Koobface Virus Hits Users of Facebook," *San Francisco Chronicle*, December 4, 2008, pp. C1, C2; and Byron Acohido, "Koobface Not Just on Facebook," *USA Today*, March 4, 2009, **p.** 8B.

42. Byron Acohido, "Virus Targets Firms' Financial Accounts," *USA Today*, July 31, 2009, **p.** 1B.

43. Siobhan Gorman, "Virus Was Set to Destroy Fannie Mae Data," *The Wall Street Journal*, February 1, 2009, p. A2.

44. Steve Boggan, "Meet the Hackers," *The Week*, September 26, 2008, pp. 44–45, originally published by *The London Times*; Lolita C. Baldor, "Officials Seek Hackers for Network Defense," *Reno Gazette-Journal*, April 19, 2009, **p.** 7B; and Christopher Drew and John Markoff, "Contractors Vie for Plum Work, Hacking for U.S.," *The New York Times*, May 31, 2009, main news section, pp. 1, 4.

45. Byron Acohido, "Meet A-Z: He's Behind a Cybercrime Wave," *USA Today*, August 5, 2008, pp. 1B, 2B; and Roger Cheng, "Hackers on the Move," *The Wall Street Journal*, August 11, 2008, **p.** R3.

46. Byron Acohido, "Cell Security Seen as Profit Frontier," *USA Today*, June 24, 2008, **p.** 1B; Claire Cain Miller and Brad Stone, "Twitter Hack Raises Flag on Security," *The New York Times*, July 16, 2009, pp. B1, B9; and Jordan Robertson, "Phones Vulnerable to Text Hacks," *Reno Gazette-Journal*, July 31, 2009, **p.** 6C.

47. Federal Bureau of Investigation, quoted in TechTarget Security Media, "Glossary," *http://searchsecurity.techtarget.com/gDefinition/0,294236,sid14_gci771061,00.html* (accessed April 14, 2009s).

48. Peter Eisler, "Raids on Federal Computer Data Soar," *USA Today*, February 17, 2009, **p.** 1A.

49. "The Rise of the Cyberspy," *The Week*, June 5, 2009, **p.** 13; Choe Sang-Hun and John Markoff, "Cyberattacks Jam Government and Commercial Web Sites in U.S. and South Korea," *The New York Times*, July 9, 2009, **p.** A4; Siobhan Gorman and Evan Ramstad, "Cyber Blitz Hits U.S., Korea," *The Wall Street Journal*, July 9, 2009, pp. A1, A4; and John Markoff, "Web's Anonymity Makes Cyberattack Hard to Trace," *The New York Times*, July 17, 2009, **p.** A5. See also Charmaine Noronha, "Group: Hackers' Scope Is Global," *Reno Gazette-Journal*, March 29, 2009, pp. 1B, 4B; and John Markoff and Thom Shanker, "U.S. Weighs Risks on Civilian Harm in Cyberwarfare," *The New York Times*, August 2, 2009, pp. A1, A8.

50. "Teen Is Sentenced to 18 Months in Jail for Computer Worm," *The Wall Street Journal*, January 31, 2005, p. B3.

51. Ashlee Vance, "For Symantec and McAfee, 'Arms Race' for Security," *The New York Times*, July 6, 2009, pp. B1, B6.

52. Duncan J. Watts, "Unraveling the Mysteries of the Connected Age," *The Chronicle of Higher Education*, February 14, 2003, pp. B7–B9.

53. Mary Dalrymple, "Employees Prove Vulnerable to Hackers Posing as IT Employees," *Information Week*, March 17, 2005, *www.informationweek.com/story/showArticle.*

jhtml?articleID=159901703 (accessed August 15, 2009).

54. Anick Jesdanun, "Simple Passwords Don't Suffice Online," *San Francisco Chronicle*, June 1, 2004, pp. C1, C5.

55. Victor Zapana, "Experts Offer Tips to Creating More Secure PINs, Passwords," *San Francisco Chronicle*, July 20, 2009, **p.** D2, reprinted from *Pittsburgh Post-Gazette.*

56. David Einstein, "The Future Is Now for Data Safety," *San Francisco Chronicle*, May 26, 2008, **p.** D1.

57. Randall Stross, "Goodbye, Passwords. You Aren't a Good Defense," *The New York Times*, August 10, 2008, business section, **p.** 4. See also Elaine Mills, "One Key Fits All," *The Wall Street Journal*, September 29, 2009, **p.** R11.

58. Brian Bergstein, "Guarding Computers: Encrypt All Files, Wipe the Drive Clean," *San Francisco Chronicle*, June 1, 2008, **p.** C5.

59. Jordan Robertson, "Citibank ATM Breach Reveals Password Security Problems," *Reno Gazette-Journal*, July 2, 2008, **p.** 6A.

60. Laurie J. Flynn, "Technology Leaders Favor Online ID Card over Passwords," *The New York Times*, June 24, 2008, **p.** C8; and Stross, "Goodbye, Passwords; You Aren't a Good Defense."

61. Anita Hamilton, "Can You See Me Now?" *Time*, March 15, 2004, **p.** 96.

62. David Pogue, "Video Chats Overcome Clunkiness," *The New York Times*, February 5, 2009, pp. B1, B8; Ashlee Vance, "Cisco Says Travel Is Overrated," *The New York Times*, February 9, 2009, **p.** B4; Joe Sharkey, "Embracing a Life without the Roller Bag," *The New York Times*, February 24, 2009, **p.** B6; Jennifer Alsever, "All You Can Meet," *FSB*, March 2009, pp. 39–40; and Walter S. Mossberg, "Easy Way to Log In Face Time," *The Wall Street Journal*, June 17, 2009, **p.** D3.

63. Steve Cerocke, "New Interest in Virtual Communication Solutions Like Video Conferencing," *Reno Gazette-Journal*, July 7, 2008, **p.** 7A; and Steve Lohr, "Face Time That Relies on Screens," *The New York Times*, July 22, 2008, pp. C1, C8. See also Dana Mattioli, "Next on the Agenda: Kisses from the Honey Bunny," *The Wall Street Journal*, June 10, 2008, pp. D1, D4.

64. Mark Dillard, quoted in Marcia Vickers, "Don't Touch That Dial: Why Should I Hire You?" *The New York Times*, April 13, 1997, sec. 3, **p.** 11.

65. Justin Scheck and Bobby White, "'Telepresence' Is Taking Hold," *The Wall Street Journal*, May 6, 2008, **p.** B6. See also Lohr, "Face Time That Relies on Screens."

Chapter 7

1. Gary McWilliams, "It All Connects—and Converges," *The Wall Street Journal*, January 31, 2005, **p.** R3.

2. Jerry Yang and David Filo, cited in Cliff Edwards, "The Web's Future Is You," *BusinessWeek*, April 25, 2005, p. 18.

3. Joyce Cohen, "Armed with Right Cellphone, Anyone Can Be a Journalist," *The New York Times*, July 18, 2005, **p.** C3; and Mark Memmott, "Disaster Photos: Newsworthy or Irresponsible?" *USA Today*, August 5, 2005, p. 4A.

4. Kevin Maney, "Multiple Mash-ups Ensue as Google Maps Mate with Net Info," *USA Today*, August 16, 2005, *www.usatoday.com/tech/columnist/kevinmaney/2005-08-16-maney-google-mashups_x.htm#* (accessed August 29, 2009).

5. Robert D. Hof, "Mix, Match, and Mutate," *BusinessWeek*, July 25, 2005, pp. 72, 75.

6. Ming Ma, quoted in Marc Saltzman, "Convergence Is King with Today's Devices," *USA Today*, May 17, 2004, p. 4E.

7. John Horrigan, ""Mobile Access to Data and Information," Pew Internet & American Life Project, March 2008, *www.pewinternet.org/Reports/2008/Mobile-Access-to-Data-and-Information.aspx* (accessed August 30, 2009).

8. John B. Horrigan, "Seeding the Cloud: What Mobile Access Means for Usage Patterns and Online Content," March 5, 2008, Pew Research Center Publications, *http://pewresearch.org/pubs/754/cloud-computing* (accessed August 20, 2009).

9. John Biggs, "The Universal Remote Dormant in Your Smartphone," *The New York Times*, March 19, 2009, p. B5.

10. Michael Gartenberg, quoted in Saltzman, "Convergence Is King with Today's Devices."

11. Stephanie Armour, "Some Firms Trade Email for Face Time," *USA Today*, December 7, 2004, **p.** 1B.

12. Barry Schwartz, *The Paradox of Choice: Why More Is Less* (New York: HarperCollins, 2005). See also Barry Schwartz, "Choice Overload Burdens Daily Modern Life," *USA Today*, January 5, 2004, **p.** 13A.

13. Edward M. Hallowell, quoted in Alina Tugend, "Multitasking Can Make You Lose . . . Um . . . Focus," *The New York Times*, October 25, 2008, **p.** B7. Hallowell is the author of *CrazyBusy: Overstretched, Overbooked, and About to Snap!* (New York: Ballantine, 2006).

14. Robin Marantz Henig, "Driving? Maybe You Shouldn't Be Reading This," *The New York Times*, July 13, 2004, **p.** D5; Jeremy Peters, "Hi, I'm Your Car. Don't Let Me Distract You," *The New York Times*, November 26, 2004, pp. C1, C3; and "More States Say Phones and Driving Don't Mix," *USA Today*, June 25, 2008, **p.** 3B.

15. Dennis K. Berman, "Technology Has Us So Plugged into Data, We Have Turned Off," *The Wall Street Journal*, November 10, 2003, **p.** B1; and Olivia Barker, "Got That Virtual Glow?" *USA Today*, August 3, 2009, pp. 1D. 1D.

16. Winifred Gallagher, quoted in book review, David G. Myers, "Please Pay Attention," *The Wall Street Journal*,

April 20, 2009, **p.** A13. Gallagher is author of *Rapt* (New York: Penguin Press, 2009).

17. John Tierney, "Ear Plugs to Lasers: The Science of Concentration," *The New York Times,* May 5, 2009, **p.** D2.

18. Michael Bull, quoted in Benny Evangelista, "The iPod Generation," *San Francisco Chronicle,* December 27, 2004, p**p.** E1, E6.

19. John B. Horrigan, "A Typology of Information and Communication Technology Users," May 7, 2007, Pew Internet & American Life Project, *http://ecoustics-cnet.com.com/Wired+but+not+Web+2.0+Thats+normal,+study+says/2100-1041_3-6181884.html* (accessed August 20, 2009).

20. Bob Levins, quoted in Evangelista, "The iPod Generation."

21. Shirley Wang, "Experts: Loud iPods Can Damage Ears," *Reno Gazette-Journal,* August 9, 2005, p**p.** 1E, 5E.

22. Brock Read, "Seriously, iPods Are Educational," *The Chronicle of Higher Education,* March 18, 2005, p**p.** A30–A32.

23. Adapted from ibid.; and Associated Press, "Software Makes Podcasts Mobile," *Reno Gazette-Journal,* August 25, 2005, **p.** 3D.

24. Adam Aston, "Satellite Radio," *BusinessWeek,* May 16, 2005, **p.** 116.

25. Sarah McBride and Amy Schatz, "The Dish on Satellite Radio's Future," *The Wall Street Journal,* June 17, 2008, p**p.** D1, D3; John Dunbar, "Merger of Sirius and XM Satellite Radio Imminent," *Reno Gazette-Journal,* July 25, 2008, **p.** 15A; John Dunbar, "FCC Narrowly Approves XM-Sirius Merger after Long Dispute," *Reno Gazette-Journal,* July 26, 2008, **p.** 10A; Andrew Ross Sorkin, "Sirius Chief Undaunted by Challenge," *The New York Times,* August 6, 2008, p**p.** C1, C4; Jon Birger, "Mel Karmazin Fights to Rescue Sirius," *Fortune,* March 30, 2009, p**p.** 85–88; and Sarah McBride, "Getting Sirius: Satellite Radio Broadens Reach," *The Wall Street Journal,* May 6, 2009, p**p.** D1, D3.

26. Deborah Yao, "Sirius XM Radio Gets Ready to Stream to iPhone, iPod Touch," *San Francisco Chronicle,* March 13, 2009, **p.** C3.

27. Anthony Armstrong, "Satellite Radio vs. High-Definition Radio for the Layperson: The Battle for America's Ears Has Begun," *http://stereos.about.com/od/homestereotechnologies/a/radio.htm* (accessed August 17, 2009).

28. Sarah McBride, "Weak Signals: Can HD Radio Find Listeners?" *The Wall Street Journal,* November 4, 2008, p. D1; and Edward C. Baig, "Two New Riffs on Radio Hit Flat Notes," *USA Today,* July 16, 2009, **p.** 3B.

29. Mike Snider, "HD Radio Sends Strong Signal, but Audience Weak," *USA Today,* July 8, 2008, **p.** 1D; Mike Snider, "HD Tunes In to Everything," *USA Today,* July 8, 2008, **p.** 3D; Chris Woodyard, "More Cars Sing with Digital Radio," *USA Today,* July 8, 2008, **p.** 1B; McBride, "Weak Signals"; Stephanie

Clifford, "Radio's Revenue Falls Even as Audience Grows," *The New York Times,* November 26, 2008, **p.** B2; and David Pogue, "HD Radio Crying Out to Be Heard," *The New York Times,* April 9, 2009, p**p.** B1, B8.

30. McBride, "Getting Sirius."

31. Helen Leggatt, "Internet Radio: 33 Million U.S. Listeners Each Week," *BizReport,* March 19, 2008, *www.bizreport.com/2008/03/internet_radio_33m_us_listeners_each_week.html* (accessed August 30, 2009).

32. Sarah McBride, "As Online-Radio Grows, Rival Ad Sellers Merge," *The Wall Street Journal,* October 16, 2008, **p.** B6.

33. Daren Fonda, "The Revolution in Radio," *Time,* April 19, 2004, pp. 55–56.

34. Bob Tedeschi, "Singing in the Car Along with Your Personal Radio Station," *The New York Times,* June 18, 2009, **p.** B8.

35. eMarketer, reported in Duncan Riley, "Podcasts Taking Off (Again): eMarketer," *TechCrunch,* February 4, 2008, *www.techcrunch.com/2008/02/04/podcasts-taking-off-again-emarketer/* (accessed August 20, 2009).

36. Todd Wallack, "Torrent of Images Is Leaving Film in the Dust," *San Francisco Chronicle,* May 23, 2005, pp. A1, A5.

37. David Ritz, quoted in Jefferson Graham, "Digital Cameras Get Smaller but Do More Tricks," *USA Today,* February 22, 2005, **p.** 6B.

38. Jefferson Graham, "Digital Cameras Are Always Improving, So Here's What to Consider," *USA Today,* December 3, 2008, **p.** 6B.

39. *Consumer Reports Electronics Buying Guide, Spring 2009* (Yonkers, NY: Consumers Union of the United States, 2009), p**p.** 104–111.

40. Jefferson Graham, "New Tech Gives Point-and-Shoot Cameras Fancy New Tricks," *USA Today,* August 20, 2009, **p.** 3B.

41. David Pogue, "The Quest to Shrink the SLR," *The New York Times,* April 16, 2009, p**p.** B1, B8.

42. "Best Digital Cameras," *Consumer Reports,* July 2008, pp. 20–31.

43. David Pogue, "Big Sensor, a Small Step for Cameras," *The New York Times,* July 24, 2008, pp. C1, C8.

44. David Einstein, "For Digital Cameras, More Megapixels May Not Mean Sharper Shots," *San Francisco Chronicle,* August 4, 2008, **p.** D3. See also Russ Juskalian, "Pixels Are Like Cupcakes; Let Me Explain," *The New York Times,* November 13, 2008, **p.** B6; and David Einstein, "Cameras—Sensor Size Does Matter," *San Francisco Chronicle,* June 8, 2009, p**p.** C1, C2.

45. Jefferson Graham, "Tips for Buyers," *USA Today,* May 17, 2004, **p.** 9E.

46. Jefferson Graham, "Get Lots of Batteries before You Go," *USA Today,* July 12, 2004, **p.** 2B.

47. Walter C. Mossberg, "Missed Moments: Pitfalls of Buying a Digital Camera," *The Wall Street Journal,* March 3, 2004, p**p.** D1, D12.

48. International Data Corporation, cited in Maria Puente, "Memories Gone in a Snap," *USA Today,* January 21, 2005, p**p.** 1D, 2D.

49. John Grady, quoted in Wallack, "Torrent of Images Is Leaving Film in the Dust," **p.** A5.

50. Certified Digital Photo Processors, cited in Puente, "Memories Gone in a Snap," **p.** 2D.

51. Puente, "Memories Gone in a Snap," **p.** 1D.

52. Susan Stellin, "Fitting the World's Biggest Travel Guide in a Pocket," *The New York Times,* March 8, 2005, p. C8.

53. "Handheld Devices Sink 53.2% during Fourth Quarter But Protracted Decline Appears to Be Slowing, Says IDC," IDC, February 12, 2008, *http://idc.com/getdoc.jsp;jsessionid=IGVVZD5PNL5OQCQJAFICFFAKBEAUMIWD?containerId=prUS21083408* (accessed August 18, 2009s).

54. Louise Rafkin, "We Are Here," *San Francisco Chronicle Magazine,* May 23, 2004, p**p.** 10–13.

55. Troy Dreier, "Best GPS for Your Budget," *Mobile Gadget Guide,* 2009, pp. 80–83.

56. Christopher Lawton and Sara Silver, "Smart Phones Are Edging Out Other Gadgets," *The Wall Street Journal,* March 24, 2009, p**p.** D1, D3.

57. Statistics from IDC, cited in Edward C. Baig, "Start-up Axiotron Converts MacBook into Tablet PC," *USA Today,* May 1, 2008, **p.** 1B.

58. Steven Levy, "Television Reloaded," *Newsweek,* May 30, 2005, pp. 49–55.

59. Stuart Elliott, "Remote Clicks That Do More Than Just Change Channels," *The New York Times,* June 16, 2008, **p.** C8.

60. Knowledge Networks, reported in Emily Brandon, "Watch TV Free Online," *U.S. News & World Report,* special year-end issue, 2008, **p.** 61. See also Laura M. Holson, "Who Needs a TV? I'm Watching on a Laptop," *The New York Times,* December 4, 2008, **p.** B9; and Brian Stelter, "CBS News to Let a Web Site Pick Up Its Live Coverage," *The New York Times,* June 2, 2009, **p.** B4.

61. Josh Quittner, "The Idiot Box Gets Smart," *Time,* June 2, 2008, **p.** 51.

62. Reed Tucker, "Are You Ready for Internet TVs?" *USA Weekend,* August 21–23, 2009, **p.** 10. See also Nick Wingfield and Don Clark, "Internet-Ready TVs Usher Web into Living Room," *The New York Times,* January 5, 2009, **p.** B3; Saul Hansell, "To Connect to the Internet, Just Turn on Your TV," *The New York Times,* January 12, 2009, **p.** B6; Matt Richtel, "What Convergence? TV's Hesitant March to the Net," *The New York Times,* February 16, 2009, p**p.** B1, B8; and Katherine Boehret, "Yahoo Widgets Lend Brains to Boob Tube," *The Wall Street Journal,* March 25, 2009, **p.** D1.

63. Edward C. Baig, "SlingCatcher Shows Lots of PC-to-TV Potential," *USA Today,* December 4, 2008, **p.** 5B.

64. Stephen H. Wildstrom, "Internet TV Just Got a Lot Closer," *BusinessWeek,*

March 16, 2009, p**p.** 65–66. See also Ryan Kim, "ZillionTV's New Device Aims to Please Viewers, Business," *San Francisco Chronicle,* March 4, 2009, p**p.** C1, C2.

65. Brad Stone, "Adobe in Push to Spread Web Video to TV Sets," *The New York Times,* April 20, 2009, **p.** B4.

66. Kevin J. O'Brien, "Mobile TV Spreading in Europe and to the U.S.," *The New York Times,* May 5, 2008, **p.** C2.

67. *Electronics Buying Guide, Spring 2009,* p**p.** 26–37; and Eric A. Taub, "So Many Flat-Panel TVs. Which Is Right for You?" *The New York Times,* June 18, 2009, **p.** B8.

68. Taub, "So Many Flat-Panel TVs."

69. Levy, "Television Reloaded," **p.** 50.

70. Motoko Rich, "Chain Plans an Extensive E-Bookstore," *The New York Times,* July 21, 2009, p**p.** B1, B5.

71. Jeffrey A. Trachtenberg and Geoffrey A. Fowler, "Simon & Schuster in E-Books Deal," *The Wall Street Journal,* June 12, 2009, **p.** B6.

72. Jeffrey A. Trachtenberg and Geoffrey A. Fowler, "Barnes & Nobel Challenges Amazon's Kindle," *The Wall Street Journal,* July 21, 2009, **p.** B1.

73. David Pogue, "The Kindle: Good Before, Now Better," *The New York Times,* February 24, 2009, p**p.** B1, B2; and Stephen H. Wildstrom, "Kindle 2: The Delight Is in the Details," *Business-Week,* March 9, 2009, pp. 73–74.

74. Walter S. Mossberg, "Amazon's Kindle 2 Improves the Good, Leaves Out the Bad," *The Wall Street Journal,* February 26, 2009, **p.** D1.

75. Pogue, "The Kindle: Good Before, Now Better"; and Edward C. Baig, "Kindle DX Is a Nifty—If Costly—Way to Carry Your Library," *USA Today,* June 11, 2009, **p.** 3B.

76. Geoffrey A. Fowler and Jeffrey A. Trachtenberg, "New Kindle Audio Feature Causes a Stir," *The Wall Street Journal,* February 10, 2009, **p.** B9.

77. Baig, "Kindle DX Is a Nifty—If Costly— Way to Carry Your Library."

78. Jeffrey A. Trachtenberg and Geoffrey A. Fowler, "As Industry Debates E-Book Prices, Small Publisher Withholds a Title," *The Wall Street Journal,* July 13, 2009, p**p.** B1, B2.

79. Motoko Rich, "Steal This Book (for $9.99)," *The New York Times,* May 17, 2009, news section, **p.** 9.

80. Geoffrey A. Fowler, "Buyer's E-Morse: 'Owning' Digital Books," *The Wall Street Journal,* July 22, 2009, **p.** A11.

81. Nicholson Baker, "A New Page," *The New Yorker,* August 3, 2009, pp. 24–30.

82. Study by Student Public Interest Research Group, reported in Ryan Knutson and Geoffrey A. Fowler, "Book Smarts? E-Texts Receive Mixed Reviews from Students," *The Wall Street Journal,* July 16, 2009, pp. D1, D2.

83. "Technological Evolution Stirs a Publishing Revolution," *Knowledge@ Wharton,* August 5, 2009, *http:// knowledge.wharton.upenn.edu/article. cfm?articleid=2307* (accessed August 28, 2009).

84. Olga Kharif, "Shakespeare's on the (Cell) Phone," *BusinessWeek,* January 19, 2009, **p.** 53.

85. Steve Lohr, "How Much Is Too Much?" *The New York Times,* May 4, 2005, p**p.** E1, E9.

86. Dan Hart, "Cell Phones and Smart-phones: What's the Difference?" *Smart-phone & Pocket PC,* August/September 2008, **p.** 18.

87. Ibid., **p.** 19.

88. Statistics from IDC, "Smartphone Growth Encouraging, Yet the Worldwide Mobile Phone Market Still Expected to Shrink in 2009, Notes IDC," press release, July 30, 2009, *www.idc.com/ getdoc.jsp?containerId=prUS21950309* (accessed August 28, 2009).

89. The NPD Group, "RIM Unseats Apple in the NPD Group's Latest Smartphone Ranking," press release, May 4, 2009, *www.npd.com/press/releases/ press_090504.html* (accessed August 28, 2009).

90. Steve Lohr, "Smartphone Rises Fast from Gadget to Necessity," *The New York Times,* June 10, 2009, p**p.** B1, B7; and Christopher Lawton and Sara Silver, "Smart Phones Are Edging Out Other Gadgets," *The Wall Street Journal,* March 24, 2009, **p.** D1.

91. Bob Tedeschi, "A Hands-Free Headset Cool Enough for a Teenager," *The New York Times,* April 23, 2009, **p.** B7; Matt Richtel, "Dismissing the Risks of a Deadly Habit," *The New York Times,* July 19, 2009, news section, p**p.** 1, 18; John Diaz, "Cell Phones in Cars—the Danger and the Denial," *San Francisco Chronicle,* Insight section, July 26, 2009, **p.** E3; "Ban Cellphoning While Driving? Not So Fast" and David Teater, "How Many More Must Die?" editorials, *USA Today,* July 29, 2009, **p.** 8A; and "Driving Must Be Your Only Job When You're Behind the Wheel," editorial, *Reno Gazette-Journal,* July 30, 2009, **p.** 7A.

92. Survey of cellphone users commis-sioned by AccessSystems Americas and conducted by Amplitude Research, reported in "Text Messaging Remains Important Feature for Cell Phone Buy-ers," *Cellular-News,* July 2, 2008, *www. cellular-news.com/story/32172.php* (accessed August 28, 2009).

93. "Who's Calling? Check the Ring," *Reno Gazette-Journal,* October 18, 2004, p**p.** 1B, 3B.

94. Walter S. Mossberg, "Sorting Out the Three-Ring Circus of Ringtones," *The Wall Street Journal,* January 5, 2005, **p.** D8.

95. Katherine Boehret, "A BlackBerry That's Easy on Your Thumbs," *The Wall Street Journal,* January 28, 2009, p**p.** D1, D6.

96. James Sullivan, "Time Waits for Every-one, Now that We've All Got Camera Phones," *San Francisco Chronicle,* May 20, 2004, **p.** E2.

97. "Picture It: A Diagnosis via Cell-phone," *USA Today,* February 22, 2005, **p.** 6D.

98. Anne Eisenberg, "Cellphone Games Take a Big Leap Forward into 3-D," *The New York Times,* June 17, 2004, p. E8.

99. Roger O. Crockett, "Multimedia Phones," *BusinessWeek,* May 16, 2005, p**p.** 100–104.

100. David Lieberman, "Coming Soon to Cellphones: Free, Over-the-Air TV," *USA Today,* January 8, 2009, p. 1B.

101. "Cell Phones: The Next Movie Screens?" *Reno Gazette-Journal,* September 28, 2004, **p.** 3F; reprinted from *Chicago Tribune.*

102. Sara Silver, "You Dropped Your Cell Phone Where? Turn It Off, Dry It Off, Keep Your Cool," *San Fran-cisco Chronicle,* October 265, 2008, **p.** C5; reprinted from *The Wall Street Journal.*

103. 2004 Sprint Wireless Courtesy Report, cited in Steven Winn, "The Cell Phone Warning Has a Familiar Ring. Who's Listening?" *San Fran-cisco Chronicle,* December 16, 2004, p**p.** E1, E4.

104. "Phone Use Slows Driver Reaction," *The Wall Street Journal,* February 3, 2005, **p.** D5.

105. Carol S. Lede, "The New Social Etiquette: Friends Don't Let Friends Dial Drunk," *The New York Times,* January 30, 2005, sec. 4, **p.** 16.

106. "Camera-Equipped Cell Phones Spreading New Types of Mischief," *Reno Gazette-Journal,* July 10, 2003, p**p.** 1A, 4A; Dennis K. Berman, David Pringle, and Phred Dvorak, "You're on Candid Cellphone!" *The Wall Street Journal,* September 30, 2003, p**p.** B1, B6; Carolyn Said, "Are Camera Phones Too Revealing?" *San Francisco Chronicle,* May 16, 2004, p**p.** A1, A10; and Ryan Kim, "School District Bans Taking Photos with Cell Phones," *San Francisco Chroni-cle,* August 23, 2004, pp. B1, B5.

107. Bob Keefe, "Pornography Industry Sees Cell Phones as New Frontier," *San Francisco Chronicle,* January 3, 2005, **p.** F3.

108. Steven Levy, "A Future with Nowhere to Hide?" *Newsweek,* June 7, 2004, **p.** 76.

109. Michael Totty, "Who's Going to Win the Living-Room Wars?" *The Wall Street Journal,* April 25, 2005, pp. R1, R4.

110. Lev Grossman, "Out of the Xbox," *Time,* May 23, 2005, **p.** 51.

111. Tony Perkins, quoted in Bill O'Driscoll, "Expert: Business Needs to Tap the 'Always On'," *Reno Gazette-Journal,* February 12, 2003, p**p.** 1D, 6D.

112. Jyoti Thottam, "How Kids Set the (Ring) Tone," *Time,* April 4, 2005, p**p.** 40–45.

113. Nielsen Co. research, reported in Donna St. George, "6,473 Texts a

Month, but at What Cost?" *The Washington Post*, February 22, 2009, **p.** A1.

114. Heather Knight, "Cell Phones a High Priority, Even among Poor Teens," *San Francisco Chronicle*, February 27, 2005, p**p.** A17, A21.

115. Diana Oblinger, "Boomers, Gen-Xers, and Millennials: Understanding the New Students," *EDUCAUSE Review*, July/August 2003, p**p.** 37–47.

116. Marc Prensky, "Digital Natives, Digital Immigrants," from *On the Horizon*, October 2001, © 2001 Marc Prensky, *www.marcprensky.com/writing/Prensky%20-%20Digital%20Natives,%20Digital%20Immigrants%20-%20Part1.pdf* (accessed May 15, 2009).

117. Oblinger, "Boomers, Gen-Xers, and Millennials," **p.** 38. See also Harry Hurt III, "A Generation with More than Hand-Eye Coordination," *The*

New York Times, December 21, 2008, Business section, **p.** 5.

118. Wendy Ricard and Diana Oblinger, "The Next-Generation Student," Higher Education Leaders Symposium, Redmond, WA, June 17–18, 2003, **p.** 2, *http://download.microsoft.com/download/d/c/7/dc70bbbc-c5a3-48f3-855b-f01d5de42fb1/TheNextGenerationStudent.pdf* (accessed May 15, 2009s).

119. Paul Davidson, "Gadgets Rule on College Campuses," *USA Today*, March 29, 2005, p**p.** 1B, 2B.

120. Ibid.

121. Andrew Payne, quoted in Ricard and Oblinger, "The Next-Generation Student," **p.** 5.

122. Prensky, "Digital Natives, Digital Immigrants," **p.** 2.

123. Marc Prensky, "What Kids Learn That's POSITIVE from Playing Videogames," © 2002 Marc Presnsky,

www.marcprensky.com/writing/Prensky%20-%20What%20Kids%20Learn%20Thats%20POSITIVE%20From%20Playing%20Video%20Games.pdf (accessed June 12, 2009).

124. Oblinger, "Boomers, Gen-Xers, and Millennials," **p.** 40, citing Jason Frand, "The Information Age Mindset: Changes in Students and Implications for Higher Education," *EDUCAUSE Review*, September/October 2000, p**p.** 15–24.

125. Kevin J. Delaney, "Teaching Tools," *The Wall Street Journal*, January 17, 2005, p**p.** R4, R5.

126. Diana G. Oblinger, "The Next Generation of Educational Engagement," *Journal of Interactive Media in Education*, May 21, 2004, pp. 1–18.

127. Ricard and Oblinger, "The Next-Generation Student," **p.** 4.

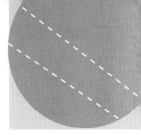

Credits

Chapter 1

Page 1: Coco Marlet/Photo Alto/Getty Images; p. 3 *(bottom)*: CD is Absolute Couples Image 100/Punchstock; p. 3 *(top)*: Ed Bock/Corbis; p. 5: Syracuse Newspapers/Greenlar/The Image Works; p. 7 *(top left)*: Courtesy of IBM; p. 7 *(top right)*: David Silverman/Getty Images; p. 8 *(bottom)*: Shizuo Kambayashi/AP Images; p. 8 *(top left)*: Fujifotos/The Image Works; p. 8 *(top right)*: Fujifotos/The Image Works; p. 10 *(left)*: ©Walt Disney Co./Courtesy Everett Collection; p. 10 *(right)*: Torin Boyd; p. 11 *(bottom)*: Rob Crandall/The Image+ Works; p. 11 *(top)*: Jeff Greenberg/The Image Works; p. 12: Syracuse Newspapers/Jim Commentucci/The Image Works; p. 14 *(left)*: Courtesy of Unisys Archives; p. 14 *(right)*: Mark Richards/PhotoEdit; p. 15 *(left)*: Courtesy of Motorola; p. 15 *(middle)*: Courtesy of Motorola; p. 15 *(right)*: Katsumi Kasahara/AP Images; p. 19: Coco Marlet/Photo Alto/Getty Images; p. 21: Courtesy of IBM; p. 22 *(bottom)*: Courtesy of Hewlett-Packard; p. 22 *(middle)*: Courtesy of Hewlett-Packard; p. 22 *(top)*: Courtesy of Unisys; p. 23 *(bottom left)*: Courtesy of Intel; p. 23 *(bottom right)*: Courtesy of Hewlett-Packard; p. 23 *(middle left)*: MANPREET ROMANA/AFP/Getty Images; p. 23 *(middle right)*: Courtesy of Hewlett-Packard; p. 23 *(top)*: Courtesy of Apple Computer; p. 23 *(top right)*: Courtesy of Gateway Computer; p. 24 *(bottom left)*: Courtesy of Hewlett-Packard; p. 24 *(bottom right)*: Courtesy of Hewlett-Packard; p. 24 *(middle left)*: Courtesy of Intel; p. 24 *(top)*: Courtesy of Motorola Corp. ; p. 28 *(bottom left)*: Courtesy of Intel; p. 28 *(bottom right)*: Don Mason/Corbis; p. 32 *(top)*: Courtesy of Microsoft Corporation; p. 32 *(bottom)*: Courtesy of Microsoft Corporation: p. 33 *(bottom)*: Courtesy of Adobe Systems Inc.; p. 33 *(top)*: Courtesy of Adobe Systems Inc.; p. 34: Shizuo Kambayashi/AP Images; p. 35: Courtesy of PR NewsFoto; p. 36: John Foxx/Getty Images; p. 37: Sean Gallup/Getty Images.

Chapter 2

Page 49: Royalty-Free/Corbis; p. 56: Judy Mason; p. 57: Courtesy of DirectTV; p. 64: Elise Amendola/AP Images; p. 68: Richard Drew/AP Images; p. 82: Courtesy of Research in Motion Ltd.

Chapter 3

Page 129: Courtesy of Symantec; p. 140: Chris Farina/Corbis; p. 141 *(top right)*: Courtesy of Microsoft; p. 142: Dan Lamont/Corbis; p. 143 *(bottom)*: Courtesy of Microsoft Corporation; p. 143 *(middle)*: Courtesy of Microsoft Corporation: p. 143 *(top)*: Courtesy of Microsoft Corporation; p. 148 *(left)*: Courtesy of Palm; p. 149 *(left)*: Courtesy of Hewlett-Packard; p. 149 *(right)*: Courtesy of Socket Mobile; p. 163: Peter Beck/Corbis; p. 175: Tom Wagner.

Chapter 4

Page193: Courtesy of Apple Computer; p. 195: Courtesy of IBM Archives; p. 196: Courtesy of Intel; p. 197 *(bottom right)*: Courtesy of Intel; p. 197 *(left)*: Courtesy of Intel; p. 197 *(top right)*: Courtesy of Intel; p. 204: Courtesy of www.apc.com; p. 206 *(bottom)*: Courtesy of Apple; p. 206 *(top)*: Courtesy of www.apc.com; p. 207 *(bottom)*: Courtesy of AMD; p. 207 *(middle)*: Courtesy of Intel; p. 207 *(top)*: Courtesy of Intel; p. 208 *(bottom)*: Courtesy of Intel; p. 208 *(middle)*: Courtesy of Motorola; p. 208 *(top)*: Courtesy of Dell Computing; p. 214 *(bottom)*: Courtesy of Intel; p. 214 *(top)*: Courtesy of Intel; p. 217 *(bottom)*: Suzie Ross/McGraw-Hill; p. 217 *(top)*: Courtesy of Hewlett-Packard; p. 219 *(bottom)*: Courtesy of Hewlett-Packard; p. 219 *(top)*: Courtesy of Adaptec; p. 220 *(bottom)*: Courtesy of Hewlett-Packard; p. 220 *(top)*: Courtesy of Hewlett-Packard; p. 221: Brian Williams; p. 223: Courtesy of Hewlett-Packard; p. 224: Royalty-Free/Corbis; p. 226 *(bottom)*: Courtesy of IBM; p. 226 *(top)*: Courtesy of Apple Computer; p. 228: Jeffrey Coolidge/PhotoDisc/Getty Images; p. 229: Brian Williams; p. 230 *(bottom)*: Courtesy of Samsung; p. 230 *(top)*: YOSHIKAZU TSUNO/AFP/Getty Images; p. 232 *(bottom)*: Courtesy of Hewlett-Packard; p. 232 *(top)*: Courtesy of Hewlett-Packard; p. 233: Katsumi Kasahara/AP Images; p. 234 *(bottom)*: Fabian Bimmer/AP Images; p. 234 *(middle)*: Tony Cenicola/New York Times/Redux Pictures; p. 235: Courtesy of Corsair; p. 238 *(bottom)*: Frank Franklin II/AP Images; p. 238 *(middle)*: Courtesy of Nokia; p. 238 *(top)*: Kurt Stier/Corbis.

Chapter 5

Page 253: Courtesy of Intermec Technologies; p. 254 *(left)*: Najlah Feanny/Corbis; p. 254 (right): Jon Freilich/AP Images; p. 257 *(bottom)*: Jochen Luebke/AFP/Getty Images; p. 257 *(middle)*: Courtesy of Microsoft; p. 257 *(top left)*: Judy Mason; p. 258 *(bottom right)*: John Slater/Taxi/Getty Images; p. 258 *(left)*: Ryan McVay/Getty Images; p. 258 *(top right)*: Peter Cade/Getty Images; p. 259 *(bottom left)*: Courtesy of Think Outside; p. 259 *(bottom right)*: Courtesy of Ed Loera/FrogPad.com; p. 259 *(top)*: Courtesy of QSI Corporation; p. 261 *(top middle)*: Judy Mason; p. 261 *(top right)*: Courtesy of Logitech; p. 262: Courtesy of Logitech; p. 263 *(bottom left)*: Courtesy of Motion Computing; p. 263 *(bottom right)*: Joe Gill/The Express Times/AP Images; p. 263 *(middle)*: Courtesy of Hewlett Packard; p. 263 *(top)*: Courtesy of IBM; p. 264 *(top left)*: Shell Oil/AP Images; p. 264 *(top right)*: Rich Pedroncelli/AP Images; p. 265 *(left)*: Courtesy of Acer; p. 265 *(right)*: Courtesy of Axiotron; p. 266 *(bottom)*: Courtesy of Livescribe Inc.; p. 266 *(left)*: Courtesy of Wacom Technology; p. 266 *(top)*: Ed Kashi/Corbis; p. 267: Courtesy of Leapfrog Enterprises; p. 268 *(left)*: Christopher Fitzgerald/The Image Works; p. 268 *(right)*: Wenatchee World, Mike Bonnicksen/AP Images; p. 270 *(bottom)*: Courtesy of NCR Corporation; p. 270 *(top)*: Courtesy of Intermec Technologies; p. 271 *(left)*: Courtesy of 3D Scanners Ltd./www.3dscanners.com; p. 271 *(right)*: Courtesy of 3D Scanners Ltd./www.3dscanners.com; p. 272 *(bottom)*: Courtesy of Symbol Technology; p. 273 *(bottom)*: Courtesy of Sony Ericsson; p. 273 *(middle)*: Courtesy of IBM; p. 273 *(top)*: Courtesy of Hewlett-Packard; p. 274 *(left)*: Courtesy of Hewlett-Packard; p. 274 *(right)*: Left Lane Productions/Corbis; p. 276 *(bottom left)*: Courtesy of Sony Ericsson; p. 276 *(bottom right)*: Courtesy of Samsung; p. 276 *(middle)*: Courtesy of Hewlett-Packard; p. 276 *(top)*: Courtesy of Hewlett-Packard; p. 278 *(left)*: William Thomas Cain/Getty Images; p. 278 *(right)*: CP/Aaron Harris/AP Images; p. 279 *(left)*: Gilles Mingasson/Getty Images; p. 279 *(middle)*: Gilles Mingasson/Getty Images; p. 279 *(right)*: Courtesy of Texas Instruments; p. 280 *(left)*: Michael Probst/AP Images; p. 280 *(right)*: Courtesy of Identix; p. 281: Tony Cenicola/New York Times/Redux Pictures; p. 282: Courtesy of Hewlett-Packard; p. 284: Courtesy of Hewlett-Packard; p. 285: Courtesy of Xerox Corp; p. 287: Courtesy of Hewlett-Packard; p. 288 *(bottom)*: Courtesy of JCM American Corporation/PRNewsFoto; p. 288 *(middle)*: Barry Batchelor/PA Wire/AP Images; p. 288 *(top left)*: Peter Thompson/New York Times/ Redux Pictures; p. 288 *(top right)*: Peter Thompson/New York Times/ Redux Pictures; p. 289: Courtesy of Sony Corporation; p. 290 *(bottom)*: Steven Senne/AP Images; p. 290 *(middle)*: Courtesy of Hewlett-Packard; p. 290 *(top)*: Courtesy of Hewlett-Packard; p. 295 *(bottom)*: Richard T.Nowitz/Corbis; p. 295 *(top)*: Owen Franken/Corbis; p. 296: Courtesy of Micron; p. 297 *(bottom)*: Courtesy of Tobii Technology; p. 297 *(middle)*: Rick Friedman/Corbis; p. 297 *(top)*: Dr.Irfan Essa/Georgia Tech; p. 298: Courtesy of E-Ink Corp. and L.G.Phillips.

Chapter 6

Page 309 *(left)*: HO/AP Images; p. 309 *(right)*: Pallava Bagla/Corbis; p. 316: Fievet Laurent/AFP/Getty Images; p. 324: PETER FOLEY/epa/Corbis; p. 325 *(bottom)*: Eric Myer/Getty Images; p. 325 *(middle)*: Ed Degginger/Getty Images; p. 325 *(top)*: Corbis; p. 326: Steve Allen/Brand X Pictures/Corbis; p. 327: Pallava Bagla/Corbis; p. 330 *(left)*: Bob Rowan;Progressive Image/Corbis; p. 330 *(right)*: Brian Williams; p. 331 *(bottom left)*: Pallava Bagla/Corbis; p. 331 *(bottom right)*: HO/AP Images; p. 331 *(middle)*: Olivier Prevosto/Corbis; p. 331 *(top)*: Liu Liqun/Corbis; p. 333 *(bottom left)*: Najtah Feanny/Corbis; p. 333 *(bottom right)*: Courtesy of White Bear Technologies; p. 333 *(bottom middle)*: Courtesy of White Bear Technologies; p. 333 *(top)*: Courtesy of Pulse Data; p. 335 *(bottom)*: Courtesy of Research in Motion Ltd.; p. 335 *(middle)*: Corbis; p. 335 *(top)*: James Leynse/Corbis; p. 336: Judy Mason; p. 338: Courtesy of Kodak; p. 339: Courtesy of IBM; p. 347: Courtesy of Symantec; p. 348: Chad Hunt/Corbis; p. 351: Chris Hondros/Getty Images.

Chapter 7

Page 361: Peter Kramer/Getty Images; p. 362: Lee Jin-man/AP Images; p. 363: Shizuo Kambayashi/AP Images; p. 364 *(bottom)*: Courtesy of Apple Computer; p. 364 *(top)*: Courtesy of Apple Computer; p. 366 *(bottom)*: Courtesy of Creative Technology Ltd.; p. 366 *(top)*: Courtesy of Creative Technology Ltd.; p. 367 *(bottom)*: Reed Saxon/AP Images; p. 367 *(top)*: Martin Meissner/AP Images; p. 369: Courtesy of Sirius/PRNewsFoto/NewsCom; p. 372: Courtesy of Apple Computer; p. 374 *(bottom)*: Eric Risberg/AP Images; p. 374 *(top)*: Courtesy of Hewlett-Packard; p. 379 *(bottom)*: Courtesy of Peek; p. 379 **(top)**: Courtesy of Palm Inc.; p. 380: Courtesy of Panasonic; p. 380: Courtesy of Panasonic; p. 380: Courtesy of Panasonic; p. 383: Courtesy of Sling Media; p. 383: Courtesy of Sling Media; p. 383: Courtesy of Sling Media; p. 384 *(left)*: Courtesy of Amazon.com; p. 384 *(right)*: Courtesy of Sony Corp.; p. 386: Courtesy of Apple Computer; p. 387: PNC/Getty Images; p. 389: Courtesy of PRNewsFoto; p. 390: StockByte/PunchStock; p. 392: Peter Kramer/Getty Images; p. 393 *(top)*: David McNew/Getty Images.

Index

Boldface page numbers indicate pages on which key terms are defined.

Files, **124, 185**
  backing up, 127
  exporting, 154
  graphics, 174–175
  importing, 153–154
  managing, 124–125
  transferring, 367, 376–377, 379
  types of, 153
File servers, 318
File virus, 343
Film making, 9–10
Filo, David, 362
Filters
  email, 85
  spam, 103
Finance, online, 8–9, 97
Financial software, **170–172, 185**
Find command, 156
Fingerprint scanners, 350
Firewalls, **347, 354**
FireWire, **220, 245**
First-generation (1G) technology, 336–337
Fixed disks, 226
Flaming, **91, 109**
Flash memory, 234–235, 366–367
Flash memory cards, **234, 245, 374–375**
Flash memory chips, **215, 245**
Flash memory drive, **235, 245**
Flash memory sticks, **234–235, 245**
Flatbed scanners, **269, 303**
Flat-panel displays, **283, 303**
Flat-panel TVs, 382
Floppy-disk drive, **30**
Floppy disks, 224–225
Flops, 21, **210, 245**
Focusing, 38
Foldable PDA keyboards, 259
Folders, 124, 132
Fonts, 158
Food and Drug Administration (FDA), 280
Footers, 159
Foreign keys, 165
Forester, Tom, 37
Formatting
  documents, 158–160
  hard drives, 236
Formulas, **162, 166, 185**
Fourth-generation (4G) technology, 337
Fragmentation, 128
Frame-grabber video card, 274
Frames, **72, 109**
Freeware, **151–152, 185**
Frequency
  modem technology and, 314
  radio signals and, 329
Frequency modulation, 314
Frontside bus, 222
FTP (File Transfer Protocol), **88, 109**
Full-duplex transmission, 321
Full-hand palm scanners, 350
Full-motion video card, 274
Function keys, **130, 185**
Functions, **162, 185**

G

Games
  online game players, 259
  smartphone, 389
  videogame systems, 391–393
Garden area networks, 318
Gates, Bill, 140
Gateways, **322, 354**
Geocaching, 334–335
Geostationary earth orbit (GEO), 332
Geschke, Charles, 172
Gesture recognition, 296
Gibson, William, 18
GIF animation, 175–176
Gigabit Ethernet, 324
Gigabits per second (Gbps), **52, 109**
Gigabyte (G, GB), 30, **200, 245**

Gigahertz (GHz), 28, **209, 245**
Global Positioning System (GPS), 332, **333**–335, **354,** 379
Gomes, Lee, 92
Google, 79–80, 178, 326
Google Chrome, 64, 147
Google Earth, 94
Google Scholar, 79
Government, information technology and, 10–11
GPS. *See* Global Positioning System
Grady, John, 378
Grammar checker, 158, 159
Graphical user interface (GUI), 131–137, **185**
Graphics
  analytical, 163
  presentation, 168–170
Graphics cards, 221, **223, 246,** 284
Graphics files, 174–175
Graphics processing unit (GPU), **209,** 245–246
Greene, Alan, 7
Groupware, 155

H

Hackers, **346, 354**
Hacktivists, 346
Half-duplex transmission, 321
Hamilton, Anita, 352
Handheld computers, 23
  operating systems for, 148–149
  special keyboards for, 259
  See also Personal digital assistants
Handheld scanners, 268, 269
Handshaking process, 62, 320
Handwriting recognition, **264–265, 303**
Hardcopy output, **281, 303**
Hard-disk cartridges, 227
Hard-disk controller, 227
Hard-disk drive, **30, 42**
Hard disks, 225–227, **246**
  crashing of, 226
  defragmenting, 128
  external, 226–227
  future developments in, 240–241
  large computer system, 227
  nonremovable, 226
  portable media player, 366
  removable, 227
  starting over with, 236
Hard goods, 97
Hardware, **25, 28–32, 42,** 193–251
  buying, 198, 199
  cache, **215**
  communications, 32
  computer case, 202–204
  CPU, **211–213**
  ergonomics and, **294, 300–301**
  expansion cards, **221–223**
  future developments in, 235–241, 294–299
  health issues related to, 291–294, 300–301
  input, 28, **255,** 256–280
  IT timeline and, 196–206, 260–266
  memory, 28–29, 213–215
  microchips, 196, 197
  miniaturization of, 196
  mobility of, 196, 198
  motherboard, 206, 207
  output, 31–32, **255,** 280–291
  ports, **216–220**
  power supply, **204**
  processing, 28–29, 206–209
  protecting, 300
  review questions/exercises on, 249–251, 306–308
  secondary storage, 30–31, **224–235**
  system unit, 202–204
  transistors, **195**

Harmer, Brian, 328
Hawkins, Jeff, 148
Headaches, 293, 300
Head crash, 226
Headers, 159
Health issues
  computer use and, 291–294, 300–301
  medical technology and, 6–7
  online information about, 7
Help command, **137, 185**
Help programs, 183
Hepatic systems, 295
Herberman, Ronald, 293
Hertz (Hz), 282, 329
Hertz, Heinrich Rudolf, 282
High-definition (HD) radio, **369–371, 395**
High-definition television (HDTV), **381, 395**
High-density disks, 240–241
High-speed phone lines, 54–56
HIIDE scanner, 348
Hill, Orion E., 102
History list, 71
Hits, **74, 109**
Hoax virus warnings, 343
Hof, Robert, 36
Home area networks (HANs), **317–318, 354–355**
Home automation networks, **318,** 338, 340–341, **355**
Home entertainment centers, 363
Home page, **65,** 69, **109**
  personalizing, 70
  web portal, 72
HomePlug technology, **326, 355**
HomePNA (HPNA) technology, **326, 355**
Host computer, 60, **320, 355**
Hotspots, **58, 109**
HTML (Hypertext Markup Language), **68, 109,** 160
HTTP (HyperText Transfer Protocol), 66, 68, **109**
Hubs, **321, 355**
Human-biology input devices, 280
Human-centric computing, 296
Human-computer interaction (HCI), 120
Hyperlinks, 68, 71
Hypertext index, 72
Hypertext links, **68, 109**
Hypertext Markup Language (HTML), **68, 109,** 160
HyperText Transfer Protocol (HTTP), 66, 68, **109**
Hyperthreading, 209, 216

I

ICANN (Internet Corporation for Assigned Names and Numbers), 63, **109**
Icons, **132, 185**
Identification systems, 348, 350
Illustration software, 174–175
Image-editing software, 174
Image files
  search tools for, 77–78
  transferring, 376–377
  web-based, 77–78, 94
Imagery, 39
Impact printers, **285, 303**
Importing data, **153–154, 185**
Individual search engines, **74–75, 109**
Information, **25, 42**
  evaluation of, 77, 78
  See also Data
Information technology (IT), **4, 42**
  business and, 9
  contemporary trends in, 34–37
  education and, 5–6
  employment resources and, 12–13
  entertainment industry and, 9–10

ethics and, 37
finances and, 8–9
government and, 10–11
health/medicine and, 6–7
innovations in, 2
jobs/careers and, 11–13
leisure and, 9–10
modern examples of, 5–13
timeline of progress in, 14–22
See also Communications technology; Computer technology
Infrared wireless transmission, **330, 355**
Inkjet printers, **286–288, 303**
Input, **26,** 27, **42,** 255
Input hardware, 28, **255,** 256–280, **303**
  audio-input devices, **273**
  digital cameras, **274**–276
  digital pens, **266**–267
  digitizers, **265**–266
  disabled users and, 295, 297
  ergonomics and, **294, 300–301**
  future of, 295–297
  health issues related to, 291–294, 300–301
  human-biology input devices, 280
  IT timeline and, 260–266
  keyboards, 28, **256–259**
  light pens, **265,** 266
  mouse, 28, **260–263**
  pen-based computer systems, **264–267**
  pointing devices, **260–267**
  radio-frequency identification tags, **279–280**
  remote locations and, 295
  review questions/exercises on, 306–308
  scanning/reading devices, 267–273
  sensors, **278–279**
  source data-entry devices, **267–273**
  speech-recognition systems, **277–278**
  touch screens, **263–264**
  types of, 256
  video-input cards, 274
  webcams, **273**–274
Inserting text, 156
Installation process, 33
Instant messaging (IM), **87–88, 109**
Insteon technology, 341
Instruction manuals, 183
Integrated circuits, 34, **195, 246**
Intelligent sensors, 294
Intelligent terminal, **258, 303**
Intel-type chips, **207–208, 246**
Interactive TV, **380, 395**
Interactivity, **35, 42,** 71
Interfaces, 120
Interleaving, 216
Internal cache, 215
International Telecommunications Union (ITU), 329
Internet, **18, 42,** 49–117
  bandwidth and, **52**
  blogs on, **96**
  business conducted on, 97–98
  cellphone access to, 389
  citing sources from, 78
  college students and, 19–20
  discussion groups, 89–90
  distance learning via, **6**
  domain abbreviations on, 67
  email and, 81–87
  evaluating information on, 74, 77, 78
  examples of uses for, 51
  FTP sites on, 88
  government resources on, 10–11
  historical emergence of, 50–56
  how it works, 60–63
  influence of, 19
  intrusiveness of, 102–106
  ISPs and, 58, 60
  job searching on, 12–13

Index